The German Enigma Cipher Machine

Beginnings, Success, and Ultimate Failure

For quite a long time, computer security was a rather narrow field of study that was populated mainly by theoretical computer scientists, electrical engineers, and applied mathematicians. With the proliferation of open systems in general, and of the Internet and the World Wide Web (WWW) in particular, this situation has changed fundamentally. Today, computer and network practitioners are equally interested in computer security, since they require technologies and solutions that can be used to secure applications related to electronic commerce. Against this background, the field of computer security has become very broad and includes many topics of interest. The aim of this series is to publish state-of-the-art, high standard technical books on topics related to computer security. Further information about the series can be found on the WWW at the following URL:

http://www.esecurity.ch/serieseditor.html

Also, if you'd like to contribute to the series by writing a book about a topic related to computer security, feel free to contact either the Commissioning Editor or the Series Editor at Artech House.

For a listing of recent titles in the *Artech House Computer Security Series* turn to the back of this book

The German Enigma Cipher Machine

Beginnings, Success, and Ultimate Failure

Brian J. Winkel
Cipher A. Deavours
David Kahn
Louis Kruh

ARTECH
HOUSE
BOSTON | LONDON
artechhouse.com

Library of Congress Cataloging-in-Publication Data
A catalog record of this book is available from the Library of Congress.

British Library Cataloguing in Publication Data
A catalog of this book is available from the British Library.

Cover design by Igor Valdman

Cryptologia is a journal devoted to all aspects of cryptology. For further information readers may go to the web site: http://www.dean.usma.edu/math/pubs/cryptologia/ or write directly to *Cryptologia*, Department of Mathematical Sciences, United States Military Academy, West Point NY 10996 USA.

International Standard Book Number: 1-58053-996-3

10 9 8 7 6 5 4 3 2 1

Contents

Introduction
David Kahn vii

The Significance of Codebreaking and Intelligence in Allied Strategy and Tactics
David Kahn 1

The Enigma Part 1: Historical Perspectives
C.A. Deavours and James Reeds 15

The Ultra Conference
David Kahn 25

Why Germany Lost the Code War
David Kahn 37

In Memoriam Marian Rejewski
Christopher Kasparek and Richard A. Woytak 45

A Conversation with Marian Rejewski
Richard A. Woytak 53

Bombe! I Could Hardly Believe It!
Robert I. Atha 67

Who Was the Third Man at Pyry?
Patrick Beesly 71

Some of My Wartime Experiences
William P. Bundy 75

Bletchley Park 1941–1945
William F. Clarke 89

British-American Cryptanalytic Cooperation and an Unprecedented Admission by Winston Churchill
Louis Kruh 97

From the Archives: A Bletchley Park Assessment of German Intelligence on Torch
Ralph Erskine 109

British Intelligence in the Second World War: An Overview
F.H. Hinsley 117

A New Challenge for an Old Enigma-Buster
Wladyslaw Kozaczuk 127

Why Was Safford Pessimistic About Breaking the German Enigma Cipher Machine in 1942?
Louis Kruh 139

Letters to the Editor Regarding Safford Article
Colin Burke and Ralph Erskine 145

Roosevelt, Magic, and Ultra
David Kahn 153

An Enigma Chronology
David Kahn 185

Ultra and Some U.S. Navy Carrier Operations
Ralph Erskine 195

The Counterfactual History of No Ultra
Harry Hinsley 211

The First Naval Enigma Decrypts of World War II
Ralph Erskine 229

Letter to the Editor Regarding Counterfactual History of No Ultra Article
Ralph Erskine 235

An Error in the History of Rotor Encryption Devices
Friedrich L. Bauer 239

The Glow-Lamp Ciphering and Deciphering Machine: Enigma from the Archives (Enigma Sales Brochure) 245

The Commercial Enigma: Beginnings of the Machine Cryptography
Louis Kruh and Cipher Deavours 259

How Statistics Led the Germans to Believe Enigma Secure and Why They Were Wrong: Neglecting the Practical Mathematics of Cipher Machines
R.A. Ratcliff 275

Reviews 289

INTRODUCTION

David Kahn

The story of the Enigma machine begins in embarrassment on the German side, in luck on the British. Among the Germans, it rises from embarrassment through hubris before sinking back into chagrin; among the British from luck to luck to genius before ending in triumph. It is a story of ingenuity defeated by brilliance, of intransigence defeated by flexibility.

The Germans were embarrassed when British memoirs revealed in the 1920s that the Royal Navy had been reading their secret messages through nearly all of World War I. This had enabled it to bottle up the German High Seas Fleet in their North Sea ports and keep it from defeating Britain's Grand Fleet and so winning the war in an afternoon. The memoirs told them that the Russians had seized the main code book of the *Kaiserliche Marine* from the stranded cruiser the *Magdeburg* in 1914 and given it to the British. With this lucky break as their start, the British Admiralty's codebreaking establishment, called Room 40 from its first office, went on to solve other German naval codes and then German diplomatic systems, which culminated in the greatest intelligence feat of all time. This was the solution of the telegram of German Foreign Minister Arthur Zimmermnn to his minister in Mexico urging that country to war on America in return for the "reconquest" of Texas, Arizona, and New Mexico which, when disclosed to President Woodrow Wilson and made public by him, helped push America into World War I, with all that that has entailed. A biography revealed this story in 1925.

This intensified German chagrin. Both the Foreign Ministry and the *Reichsmarine* improved their cryptosystems. The Foreign Ministry does not play a role here, in part because this is a naval story, in part because German diplomacy did not play a determinative role between the wars. And though the main system it put into practice — the one-time pad — could not be solved, logistical problems — mainly the need to distribute sufficient key — made this system impracticable for the armed services. So the navy adopted, with some changes, a cipher machine invented by electrical engineer Dr. Arthur Scherbius, called the Enigma. He claimed — rightly — that, even if the machine were captured by the enemy, it would present so many combinations that its messages could not be solved in time to be of any use. This eliminated the capture problem. The navy adopted its Enigma — improved from the commercial version — in 1926; the army, in 1928.

To Germany's east lay Poland. It had reconstituted itself in 1918 after more than a century of subjugation by three neighboring powers, Germany, Austria-Hungary, and Russia. The post-World War I settlements confirming its existence infuriated Germany, which constantly thundered out demands for border rectification. Poland, needing to inform itself about her neighbor's intentions, assigned three young mathematicians to solve German cryptosystems, in particular the Enigma. Marian Rejewski made considerable progress. But not until information from a German traitor reached him was he able around Christmas 1932 to break through and reconstruct the wiring of the rotors — the heart of the machine. Poland began reading Enigma messages.

Until 15 December 1938. On that date the Germans increased the number of available rotors from three to five. This overwhelmed the Poles' capacity. They then sought the help of Britain and France. At a meeting in July 1939 in the cryptanalysts' offices at Pyry, near Warsaw, they offered their reconstructed Enigma machines and cryptanalytic techniques to their expected co-belligerents. A few weeks later the German blitzkrieg rolled over Poland, whose cryptanalytic strength did not compensate for its military weakness. Codebreaking likewise did not keep France from falling.

Britain fought on. It improved the Polish solutions by two strokes of brilliance. The mathematician Alan Turing invented a mechanism that would see whether the plaintext — such as stereotyped addresses or message beginnings, guessed or assumed on the basis of previous solved or plaintext messages — for a given ciphertext could be produced from any combination of Enigma rotors and starting positions. It employed electrical contacts that would let the mechanism keep running with wrong possibilities and would stop it only at the right possibilities. Thus by eliminating what were called "illegal" keys, it reduced the time needed for reaching the right, or "legal," one. Britain adopted the Polish cryptanalysts' term for their more primitive codebreaking mechanism and called it a "bombe." Next, another Cambridge mathematician, Gordon Welchman, utilized the fact that the Enigma substitutions were reciprocal — if plaintext a became ciphertext Z, then plaintext z would become ciphertext A — to further reduce the number of possibilities. He wired 676 contacts in a square array, which he called a diagonal board, that would do this. These clever ideas helped defeat the fearsome capaciousness of the Enigma machine and reduced the testing of possible keys from the eons the Germans thought it would take to the days or hours the British did it in.

As an island nation, Britain depended upon supplies brought by sea, mainly from North America. Germany's U-boats ravaged these. Since radio messages encrypted in Enigma directed the submarines to the convoys, Britain needed to solve those messages to help win this battle of the Atlantic. But the *Kriegsmarine* Enigma resisted its efforts. Unable to break in cryptanalytically, the British went around the end. Two Royal Navy attacks on German weather trawlers in 1941 captured the books containing the keys for setting the U-boat Enigmas. The cryptanalytic information enabled some convoys to circumvent the wolfpacks and bring more supplies to the United Kingdom. The Germans paid no attention to the losses of the trawlers — they were insignificant in a war in which each day ships, tanks, and airplanes were lost and thousands of men died. But the fears of Admiral Karl Dönitz that his wolfpacks were finding convoys less often than before led him to ask his communications officers whether his secret messages were safe. They assured him that precautions built into the Enigma system guaranteed its security. The addition of a fourth rotor to the Atlantic U-boats' Enigma in February 1942 made this doubly certain. And in fact it did black out the British cryptanalysts. A capture late in 1942 enabled the British to read those messages again — and to the end of the war. The Germans did not believe that such solutions were possible. For their U-boat Enigma system was not only cryptographically excellent, they had taken into account and excluded the human factors that undermine most cryptosystems. But they lacked the life-and-death motivation of the British and perhaps therefore the imagination to conceive the mechanisms that the British invented. They had bright, hard-working men, but they did not have the genius of Turing, the brilliance of other cryptanalysts, the control of the sea, the sheer numbers of men and women — 10,000 at Bletchley Park to perhaps 2,500 in the seven German codebreaking agencies a day — that gave Britain its success. A psychological factor perhaps prevented them from seriously considering the possibility that their messages could be read. For to acknowledge that would mean conceding that they had sent comrades to their deaths and facing the wrath of their superiors and of Hitler. They may not have wanted to deal with that. So Britain won the communications-intelligence struggle. That victory helped Britain survive and, with the aid of the United States and the Soviet Union, go on to win the war.

The papers from *Cryptologia* reprinted here offer a cross-section of the work done at the British codebreaking agency, the Government Code and Cypher

School, generally called Bletchley Park, or B.P., from its headquarters in a stately house 50 miles northwest of London. In its warren of hastily erected huts there labored university dons, clerks, typists, mathematicians, translators, professional cryptanalysts. These articles include technical studies by the best scholar of the Enigma machine, Ralph Erskine, a precious interview with the now deceased chief cryptanalyst of the Enigma, Marian Rejewski, a memoir by an American at Bletchley, William Bundy, a counterfactual study of Ultra by a chief evaluator of it, Harry Hinsley, some historical analyses of the Enigma machine itself, reviews of books on the subject, and some overviews of the British cryptanalytic effort. They do not embrace all of B.P.'s activity. But they offer glints and glimpses of work that, while it cannot be said to have won the war, shortened it.

THE SIGNIFICANCE OF CODEBREAKING AND INTELLIGENCE IN ALLIED STRATEGY AND TACTICS

David Kahn

[Delivered before Session 53 of the American Historical Association annual meeting in Washington, 9:30 A.M. 29 December 1976, in the Regency Ballroom of the Shoreham Hotel, a joint session with the American Committee on the History of the Second World War.]

Let me forestall the awful puns that will certainly be made. I want to assure you at the outset that I'm going to try to talk in the clear and not in code.

The subject is "The Significance of Codebreaking and Intelligence on Allied Strategy and Tactics," in the European Theatre. This is undoubtedly one of the broadest topics ever allowed outside of a 6th-grade composition class, and although I probably won't be able to do it justice, I'm backed up by three high-powered authorities, who certainly can. [This refers to the three commentators on the paper: Dr. Harold Deutsch, Professor Emeritus of History now at the Army War College and author of several books on World War II, General Telford Taylor, an American cryptanalyst with the British in World War II and later chief U.S. prosecutor at Nuremberg, and Dr. Jürgen Rohwer, the leading German naval historian of World War II and director of the Bibliothek für Zeitgeschichte in Stuttgart.]

The subject was given new impetus a couple of years ago with the publication of Frederick W. Winterbotham's The Ultra Secret [1]. It revealed the greatest secret of World War II except for the atom bomb. This was that the Allies had cracked the main high-level German cipher. Winterbotham and others have claimed that the results -- covernamed "Ultra" -- had virtually won the war. Well -- did it? That's what we're going to look into today.

In my talk, I'll be discussing four things: (1) background; (2) some examples of how codebreaking helped the Allies; (3) evaluations of how important this was to the war; (4) whether we historians have to rewrite everything we wrote about World War II in the light of this new information.

One thing I'm not going to talk about is codebreaking in the Pacific theater. The solution of Japanese naval codes played a very important role. I need only mention Midway, the cutting of Japan's lifelines by American submarines who knew where Japanese convoys were heading, and the mid-air assassination of Admiral Yamamoto. But these cases have long been known, and they do not belong to our European theme.

July 1977

What, to begin with, is codebreaking? To keep his plans secret, a general will put his messages to his subordinates into secret form by means of a code or a cipher. His subordinate must naturally know the system, so he can turn it back into plain language. The enemy, on the other hand, now has the time-consuming job of finding out what ZQVBL KKDHR and so forth means. If the enemy can break the code or cipher quickly enough, he can take countermeasures to spoil the general's plans. It's like sticking your head into the other team's huddle.

Up to World War I, codebreaking rarely provided such advantages. The main reason was that messages were hard to intercept. During that war, however, armies used radio extensively for the first time. And radio has a peculiar property. The enemy can hear it just as easily as the legitimate correspondents. This produces an enormous volume of intercepts. And the more messages you have, the easier it is to break a code. Many were broken during that war, bringing victories in battle or in diplomacy.

World War I had two mighty effects on cryptology that are of importance here. The first was this: the value that codebreaking demonstrated during the war led many nations to set up permanent agencies for it even in peace. Three major countries had not had any such agencies before the war but did after it: Germany, Britain, and America. Others had had them before the war and maintained them afterwards. France and Russia, especially, and to a smaller degree, Italy and Austria. The second effect of World War I was that many people sought to mechanize time-consuming and error-prone crypto systems. The first years of peace saw a flood of cipher machines. In these, the code clerk merely had to press letters on a typewriter-like keyboard, and the machine would automatically encipher the message.

The most important principle employed for this encipherment was that of the rotor. The rotor is a wired codewheel. It's a piece of hard rubber or bakelite about the size and shape of a hockey puck. Twenty-six brass electrical contacts stud one face of the rotor and 26 the other. They are connected at random by wires. When several of these rotors are placed side by side in a cipher machine, this wiring forms a maze. When a cipher clerk presses a typewriter key, an electrical current flows through the maze and enciphers the letter. As the rotors turn, the maze changes, and so does the encipherment. The effect was an extremely secure cipher.

This principle was discovered independently and almost simultaneously by four men in four different countries. One of them was Germany. The inventor was an engineer named Arthur Scherbius. He set up a firm in Berlin to make and sell his machine, which he named "Enigma." But there was no business market. In 1926, Scherbius was killed in an accident in his factory [2]. Soon thereafter, the fortunes of his firm changed.

Germany was busy dodging the restrictions of Versailles, and a part of the rebuilding of its armed forces, it wanted modern ciphering equipment. It settled upon the Enigma, modifying the commercial version for greater secrecy. The navy began using it around 1926; the army, on 15 July 1928.

Of all the countries in Europe, the one that then probably feared Germany most was Poland. As part of its general watchfulness, its cipher bureau, a branch of its general staff, analyzed the German cryptograms. When, on 15 July 1928, the characteristics of the German army intercepts suddenly changed, it recognized that the Reichsheer had introduced a new system. Statistical analysis suggested that it was probably the Enigma. But purchase of one of the commercial models showed that the Germans had changed it and that solution would require cryptanalysis.

The cipher gave the job to three young mathematicians whom it had just recruited: Marian Rejewski, Henryk Zygalski, and Jerzy Rozycki. Every day they reverse-commuted from Warsaw to their office in a two-story brick house in the woods near the suburb of Pyry.

They made some progress in analyzing the system, but were not actually able to read any of the German messages. The cipher was simply too strong. Fortunately, at this moment, help came from the French. They had won as a spy a weak and lazy member of the Reichswehr's cipher center. He had access to the operating instructions for the army Enigma and to some of the actual keys used -- the order in which the rotors were to be inserted on certain dates, for example. He sold this to the French, meeting them 19 times over the years and delivering 303 documents, all of them secret or top secret [3]. The French, in turn, who had aid agreements with Poland, gave this information to the Polish cipher bureau [4]. It was just what they needed. The three young cryptanalysts broke through the remaining barriers and cracked the Enigma cryptograms. They built their own Enigma machine to facilitate their work. But each solution still required considerable effort.

Meanwhile, the rumblings from Hitler's Reich were growing louder and more threatening. In July 1939, with the handwriting on the wall, England and France sent their top cryptanalysts to Warsaw. There, at the house in the Pyry woods, Poland presented each of her friends with a reconstructed Enigma. These went by diplomatic pouch to Paris, and one then went to England.

In September, Hitler conquered Poland. The trickle of solutions was too inconsequential, and the Polish army too weak, to prevent this. The cryptanalysts fled to France. Here they worked with the French codebreakers, who, of course, occupied a Renaissance château. They solved mainly Luftwaffe messages. But again tanks and guns and morale overruled cryptanalysis. The Poles worked for a while in unoccupied

France, radioing solved Enigma keys to Britain. When Germany occupied all of France, they slipped away and got to England. The British showed their gratitude by excluding them from any further contact with codebreaking.

In Britain, that activity had moved with the outbreak of war from offices near Victoria station in London to the exurb of Bletchley, 50 miles to the west in Buckinghamshire. The codebreakers installed themselves in an ugly 19th-century country house, Bletchley Park, which soon gave its name to the entire establishment. Its leading light in the Enigma solution and its greatest character was Dilwyn Knox, one of the two who had gone to Warsaw. Knox was a member of a fabulous intellectual family. He had grown up doing crossword puzzles in Latin and puns and anagrams in Greek. One brother was the Roman Catholic convert Father Ronald Knox, famous for his translation of the Bible. Another became the editor of Punch. Dilwyn himself had been a successful cryptanalyst in World War I -- he is credited with having cracked one of the German submarine ciphers in his bath -- and had stayed with the work afterward. He was a tall, thin man who walked obliquely; his head came first, preceded by a large nose with a drip on the end of it. He was the prototype of the absent-minded intellectual. Day after day he would try to leave his office through the closet. Whenever he ruled a line, he ruled his thumb in. But his cryptanalysis was brilliant. He had a remarkable feel for it. One movement of the Enigma machanism had been called a "crab." Knox said, "Where there's a crab, there's a lobster." And he found the corresponding movement.

In part as a result of Knox's work, but mainly because the whole war situation was different, the solutions of Luftwaffe messages that had not helped the French did greatly assist the Royal Air Force during the Battle of Britain. For example, on 14 August 1940, Winterbotham tells us [5], Ultra intercepted Göring's orders for his all-out assault on the R.A.F. for the next day, which he designated Eagle Day. The Luftwaffe's Air Fleets 2, 3, and 5 were to attack, and they were to do so in waves. Perhaps Göring hoped that the R.A.F. would commit too many forces to defend against the first wave and then would be relatively helpless to fight off the later ones. But Ultra disclosed this tactic to the British, who then parceled out their pitifully few fighters to meet the successive waves. Ultra also revealed where the Germans were flying from. This enabled one R.A.F. group to meet them well out at sea and have a longer go at them. This day, 15 August, was one of the climactic days of the Battle of Britain, and Ultra seemed to contribute greatly to the victory of the few.

One case history of this period has stirred a great deal of interest. This is Coventry. According to Winterbotham, seconded by other authors [6], this industrial city - whose destroyed cathedral became a symbol of the blitz - was deliberately sacrificed by Churchill to preserve the secret of Ultra. The story goes that the British had intercepted German messages disclosing their intention to bomb this concentration of British air production. But Churchill and his high advisors feared that to take any precautionary measures would alert the Germans to the fact that the British could read their messages. This would lead them to change their ciphers and so would deprive Britain of vital intelligence for future and more important operations. Consequently, they did nothing, and hundreds of British civilians lost their lives.

Fortunately the story does not stand up. A recent critical analysis of the documents [7], shows the following: The Ultra information was actually misleading as to the target areas. On the other hand, accurate and detailed intelligence about the forthcoming attack came from a prisoner of war. Energetic defense preparations were made on the basis of this information. They failed for a number of operational reasons, and so the German attack succeeded. But there was no deliberate suppression of Ultra intelligence, and no martyring of the population.

Was Ultra the critical factor in the Battle of Britain? In other words, without it, would the R.A.F. have lost air superiority - a superiority that in effect prevented Hitler from invading? No one to whom I have written would make this statement. I did not ask them about radar, but I agree with a comment that Dr. Rohwer made to me that without radar the situation would have been far more serious than without Ultra.

Now during that same first year of the war, German spies began to seep into the British Isles. Many had been dispatched by the Abwehr, the Germany military espionage service, headed by the legendary Admiral Canaris.

The Abwehr organization enciphered its administrative and substantive messages in its own version of the Enigma, a rather simplified version that was easier to solve. This traffic flowed between Abwehr headquarters in Berlin and its outposts. These were in Germany, in the conquered territories, and in neutral countries such as Spain and Sweden. Wire connections were available, but they were often slow and complicated,and it was frequently easier just to raise headquarters by radio [8]. The British intercepted these radio messages, and Bletchley read them. The British soon knew the real names and the cover names of Abwehr officials and spies, the good ones and the lazy ones, and the contents of the spy reports themselves.

There is a funny story that shows how microscopically the British observed the enemy intelligence service. They followed messages dealing with a German police dog named Axel, who was being sent from Berlin to Algeciras, to guard the Abwehr outpost there. On the last stage of his journey, Madrid warned Albert Carbe, alias César, the head of the outpost: "Be careful of Axel. He bites." A few days later, Bletchley read a message from Algeciras to Madrid: "César in hospital. Axel bit him [9]."

Ultra information sometimes enabled the British to capture German agents as they landed. Eventually, it convinced the British that they knew all the German spies in the islands [10]. And these were all controlled.

This knowledge came to fruition in the greatest deception operation of the war. The British used their tame spies to feed false information to the Germans before and during the Normandy invasion. The information helped lead the Germans to believe that there were some 79 Allied divisions in Britain, whereas in fact there were only 45 [11]. The Germans expected that these divisions would be used somewhere, and so they held an entire army, the 15th, to the north in the Pas de Calais while Eisenhower was attacking further south in Normandy. This meant less resistance to the invaders and contributed decisively to the Allied lodgment.

That success would not have been possible without a previous one. This was the battle which, Churchill said, "was the dominating factor throughout the war." [12] This was the Battle of the Atlantic.

The Allies' cryptanalytic victory in this battle was more difficult than in the others, and it came later. The reason was that the German naval Enigma was more complicated than the other versions. It had more rotors than the army's and the air force's.

As a result, Bletchley Park did not crack its first main naval cipher, until, in May of 1941, some naval Enigmas were captured on a weather ship and on the U-110. The following month, Bletchley began reading the most important U-boat cipher. It brought a great rush of new information into the Admiralty's submarine tracking room. It revealed, for instance, the precise number of U-boats in operation, their normal bases, their usual speed of advance when proceeding to or from patrol, the type of signals used for reporting and shadowing convoys. The British used this to steer convoys away from the submarines and, more rarely, to sink them and other enemy warships. In November 1941, Ultra disclosed a proposed rendezvous between a U-boat and the German raider _Atlantis_. The Admiralty sent _HMS Devonshire_ to the spot. It didn't get the submarine, but it sank the pesky _Atlantis_.

But then, after seven months, at the end of January 1942, just as the Battle of the Atlantic was approaching its climax, Ultra went half blind. It lost its ability to read the main U-boat cipher.

Now, a basic point in understanding the operation of Ultra is to recognize that solution does not come permanently in one single blow. Reading a message today does not mean that you can thereafter instantly read every message as soon as you have intercepted it. Rather there are levels of analysis. To read a message, for example, you had to do three things -- and even here I am simplifying. (1) Reconstruct the wiring in all of the rotors. (2) Know which three rotors out of the set of five were used that day. (3) Know the position the rotors were in for the start of that message. You can know one or even two of these factors and still not be able to read a single word of the original message. You must know all three. And this takes time. So you can intercept a message today, but not solve it for three weeks, by which time the message is valueless. On the other hand, sometimes things are going well and solutions are prompt. But in January 1942, this was not the case, and the Allies were "out."

This did not mean that the Allies had lost every form of intelligence concerning the U-boats. In particular, they could locate them by seeing from several points where U-boat radio transmissions were coming from; where these bearings crossed was the position of the submarine. This was high frequency direction-finding, or Huff-Duff. It was extremely useful, but it was not as good as codebreaking. It told only where the U-boats were, while codebreaking often told where they were going to be.

Now another of the vulgar errors commonly made about cryptology is to assume that each country or service has but one cryptosystem. People talk of "the American code" or "the German naval cipher." Nothing could be farther from the truth. Each nation, each service uses dozens of codes at a single time. Different codes serve for different levels of command, for different branches of each service, for different geographic regions within each branch. From time to time, new ones are put into service, old ones removed. And so it was with the Kriegsmarine. It had many cryptosystems. So when Bletchley lost out on the main U-boat cipher, it fell back for information on one of the other naval codes -- that of the German patrol vessels.

The patrol vessels accompanied U-boats on their outward and inward voyages in the Baltic or off Norway or in the Bay of Biscay. They reported these movements to their local naval commands. This enabled the Admiralty to know when a U-boat left for operations and when it returned. It told the Admiralty how many submarines were on patrol at one time. But it was not as good, of course, as the more direct evidence that came from the chief U-boat cipher. And in December 1942, Bletchley got back "in."

Patrick Beesly, who worked in the Submarine Tracking Room, has given a vivid picture of what it was like when Ultra, or "Very Special Intelligence," as they called it, came in [13]: "We usually obtained half and hour or an hour's warning from B.P. [as they called Bletchley Park] that a new flow of Ultra was about to begin. Decks were cleared for action. When the first deciphered signal did arrive it was often a disappointment. It might well be four or five days old and now completely overtaken by events. It might, on its own, be meaningless. 'Group Ritter is to advance its patrol line 150 miles on a line of bearing of 120 degrees.' Not knowing which U-boats constitute Group

Ritter or where their original patrol line had been, one was not much the wiser. Signals might only be weather or fuel reports from a single boat on passage and hundreds of miles from any potential victim or attacker, although in this case one had at least the first bit of the jigsaw, even if it was a very unimportant one.

"However, after a while the signals would begin to pour in and the pace would become fast and furious. Each signal would be quickly scrutinized to decide whether it was sufficiently up to date and informative to justify an alteration in our plot, and if it did, whether it was necessary to call in Dick Hall from next door to discuss a possible convoy diversion. Perhaps it would be necessary to speak to Western Approaches or Coastal Command on the scrambler to enable them to plan escort reinforcements. All the time, [Rodger] Winn, [the head of the submarine tracking room] his deputy or the duty watchkeeper had to decide whether the information was sufficiently up to date and firm to justify action, or whether it would be better to wait a little longer... All this against the background of hundreds of ships at sea relying on our efforts to steer them clear of danger areas."

When Ultra was current, it was passed to flag officers at sea by means of the one-time pad, the only absolutely unbreakable system. They sometimes used this to force patrolling U-boats to dive so deep that they could not see, or in some cases even to sink them, allowing a convoy to pass through a wolf-pack danger zone unmolested.

The same question can be raised about Ultra in the Battle of the Atlantic as in the Battle of Britain. Was it decisive? Ultra played a bigger role on the sea than in the air, but none of the experts whom I have consulted would say that without Ultra the Allies would have lost the Battle of the Atlantic. Basically, various operational factors were more determinative. Just to take one of these: given the number of U-boats, the Germans probably would not have been able to sink ships faster than the Allies could build them once the American shipbuilding program hit its stride. As Mr. Beesly summed it up: Ultra was _a_ war winner, but not _the_ war winner.

World War II was finally won on the continent of Europe. And here, too, codebreaking played a highly contributory role. Perhaps I should point out here that not all solutions for the Allied ground forces emanated from Bletchley Park. There were two other main sources. One was the Allied codebreaking units in the field. They usually solved the messages of German field commands, which were in lower level systems, and therefore easier to crack. The other source was the American solution before the war of the Japanese diplomatic cipher machine, which the Americans called the PURPLE machine. This enabled the Allies to read the messages of the Japanese ambassador in Germany. In September of 1943, for example, he toured the German defenses against the expected Allied invasion. He reported on these in great detail in a long radiogram. A German station pumped it into the ether for the 5,000-mile leap to Japan. But an American intercept station at Asmara, in Ethiopia, plucked it from the airwaves. The Allies read it and learned many valuable details that saved many Allied lives [14].

Nor was the Enigma the only one mechanism cracked by Bletchley. The Germans introduced a new cipher machine in 1943. To solve this on a current basis, Bletchley developed what some characterize as the world's first programmable electronic computer. Called the Colossus, it and the Enigma machines enabled Bletchley to keep up with the flow of top-level communications during the battle on the continent [15]. Dozens of examples attest to Ultra's help.

When General Mark Clark landed at Anzio, he had less than 2 divisions. Suddenly he got intercepts of Hitler messages ordering nine German divisions from the Balkans to Italy. The intercepts were "manna from heaven," he said. He used the intelligence to pull back his forces so that they wouldn't get cut off. "Without it," he said, "we would have had a tough time." [16]

One day Ultra picked up a message from the German Commander in Chief West. He was refusing a request from one of his subordinate army groups that it be allocated all the ammunition from two factories in the northern sector of the Western Front. The exchange of messages disclosed that these two were producing all the medium field howitzer ammunition for the west. Neither factory had ever been attacked by the Allied air forces, who had known of their existence but had not realized their significance. The Ultra representative at the U.S. 9th Air Force brought it to the attention of the director of operations. While some squadrons bombed similar targets nearby as cover, aircraft attacked these factories and destroyed them.

Another time an intercept revealed that the Germans had a strong concentration of motor transport in woods near Marburg. Air reconnaissance confirmed the Ultra report. A squadron of fighter-bombers in the vicinity was redirected to the woods. BOOM! At the end of the day, more than 400 vehicles, including many tanks and armored cars and troop carriers, were claimed destroyed.

Well, what does it all mean? How can the contribution of codebreaking to the Allied victory be summed up?

Early in the war, as I said, radar was more important. Thus in an overall sense, it has to be seen as a more vital form of intelligence, for without it, nothing else might have followed. But later in the war, I believe, codebreaking became more important. Its powers exceeded those of other kinds of intelligence. Prisoners-of-war interrogations provided a great intensity of detail, but at a very low level and a short temporal range. Aerial photography furnished extremely hard and specific intelligence. But it could see only a small portion of the earth's surface, and only at a given instant of time -- which is, of necessity, rather late in the development of an operation. Codebreaking, on the other hand, furnished the orders for an operation from a high-level source beyond the horizon and long before the troops and tanks assembled to have their picture taken. I think, in other words, that it provided the most valuable intelligence of all in the realm of military operations that lies between tactics and strategy - the area that the Germans call operational. This deals with the movement of such large bodies as armies and army groups, and someone has said that all the major decisions of war lie in it. In this area codebreaking outweighed or at least equalled the value of all other forms of intelligence put together.

What about the tactical area? In the air, it was almost certainly less important than radar; at sea, perhaps equal to it and Huff-Duff. On the ground, it may well have remained the single most important source, but it certainly did not equal the others put together. Strategically, I do not believe that codebreaking played a major role. By the time Ultra really took hold, the initiative had passed to the Allies, and there were no longer any major German strategic decisions to learn.

Where it helped, however, it helped enormously. Statement after statement of top commanders testify to this. Here's Eisenhower to the administrative overseer of Bletchley: "The intelligence which has emanated from you before and during this campaign has been of priceless value to me. It has simplified my task as a commander enormously. It has saved thousands of British and American lives and, in no small way, contributed to the speed with which the enemy was routed and eventually forced to surrender." [17] George Marshall said practically the same thing [18]. Marshal of the Royal Air Force Sir John Slessor called it a "gift from the gods." [19] And there are many other similar tributes.

With all this, I wondered whether codebreaking's contribution to the war could be quantified. Would someone in a position to know say how many divisions it was worth, or how many months or years it shortened the war by? The literature showed a few such statements. They all dealt with the Pacific and said that codebreaking had saved a year of war -- one high-level operations officer said two years [20]. The only comment about the European theater that I could get was Mr. Beesly's, who to be nice to me guessed that codebreaking saved nine months in the battle of the Atlantic. Most people declined to make this kind of an estimate. They thought it was impossible and probably meaningless. The most cogent remark came from someone who might have been expected to say quite the opposite. This was General W. Preston Corderman, the wartime head of the Army codebreaking agency. "If you try to do that," he said, "you'd have the quartermaster claiming so many years, the air force so many, and everybody claiming some, and before you know it you'd find that the war should have been over 25 years before it began." [21]

A line like that gives us our perspective back. And a most important factor in that perspective is a realization that codebreaking and intelligence alone do not win wars. The Poles had Ultra in 1939; the French had it in 1940. You can have the best intelligence in the world, but if you don't have a powerful army, it's useless. That's why it's wrong to say that codebreaking won the war, or even that it decided the war. Physical and moral elements did that. I believe that even if we had the worst intelligence and the Germans the best, we would have defeated them. For we conquered through our manpower and our industrial might, through a more efficient form of government and through more realistic leaders. Ultra itself became useful only when we had the power to exploit it.

So. What does all this mean to us as historians? Will we have to rewrite everything? Because it is true that, although Churchill saw everything for his six volumes [22], the official historians were not given access to Ultra material [23].

It's clear that we won't have to rewrite the what of history. Our new knowledge of Ultra does not change the fact that Normandy was successfully invaded on the 6th of June. It does affect the why. Our knowledge of Ultra may explain more distinctly why Eisenhower took some of the decisions he did.

I think that this will require a considerable amount of re-evaluation. Possibly every high-level decision in the European campaign may have to be re-examined to see what Ultra intelligence a commander had. Or, in a climate in which he perhaps had come to depend on Ultra's completeness, what Ultra intelligence he did not have. Operation MARKET-GARDEN, in which Allied paratroops landed in the middle of an SS division, might be a case in point.

But of course we will not know how much work there is until the documents are declassified for us.

And that declassification is proceeding, I regret to say, at a glacial pace. The National Security Agency, which is the declassifying body for these hundreds of thousands of documents, has assigned all of four full-time and six part-time people to do this work [24] out of the 100,000 it controls. There is no doubt that they can make a greater effort. If we press them, and get our Congressmen to press them, we may actually get some of these documents out before our careers are over.

July 1977

To sum up, then:

The secret new science of cryptanalysis, and the self-effacing back-room boys who manipulated it, played a role of high importance in the war against Hitler and all that he stood for. It will require considerable restudy to evaluate this. In my opinion, the subsequent rewriting will not revolutionize our knowledge of how we defeated Nazi Germany. It will deepen it. For it will show, more clearly than ever before, how we expunged from the face of the earth the wickedest regime in the whole history of the world.

Notes (by Kahn) on the Commentators' Remarks

Telford Taylor:

The main U.S. contribution was Japanese codes; the British, German codes.

Knowing the text of an intercept did not mean knowing its meaning: abbreviations, cover names, map grids.

Much work at Bletchley to extract the meaning. Thus afia in a Japanese message actually turned out to represent the German term A-4 (pronounced ah-feer), the covername for what became the V-2 missile.

The contribution of Ultra in the Battle of Britain was negligible, that of radar, critical. During the Blitz, from September 1940 to June 1941, there was a greater contribution by Ultra. Sometimes the British got Ultra messages ordering the Knickebein (radio guidance beams) operators to lay the beams on certain coordinates.

I cannot think of any major strategic decisions made on the basis of Ultra. It was not a determinative factor in Allied offensives. But it protected us in defensive problems. In the Battle of the Atlantic, without Ultra, the pinch on Britain would have been much sharper. It might have had very profound strategic consequences.

Cryptanalytic intelligence is an oil that made things run better than without it.

With Ultra, we can write richer and fuller accounts of World War II.

Jürgen Rohwer:

[A long paper discussing Ultra in the Battle of the Atlantic and not specifically commenting on the Kahn paper.]

Harold Deutsch:

David Kahn leaned too far backwards in assessing the importance of codebreaking. I feel that intelligence was a vital factor in the Allied victory -- I think that without it we might not have won, after all.

In the Battle of the Bulge, the Allies were deprived of Ultra. The Allies won the battle but at tremendous cost.

During the full tide of victory, Ultra made less of an impact than earlier. I regard Ultra as more important in the Battles of the Atlantic and of Britain than Taylor or Kahn. In Normandy I think Ultra may have made a critical difference.

Ultra gave the information to Sir Basil Liddell Hart [the British military historian] about the Ribbentrop-Molotov meeting between the lines in June 1943. [A member of the audience later commented that despite extensive search no evidence for such a meeting has been found outside Liddell Hart's statement and that most historians of World War II believe that no such meeting took place.]

Ultra intelligence was the only kind of intelligence not cluttered by feints -- we knew that this was the actual enemy action.

We'll now have an improvement in the information in memoirs and biographies. The reputations of figures of World War II will have to be re-evaluated.

REFERENCES

1. Frederick W. Winterbotham, The Ultra Secret. (New York: Harper & Row, 1974.)
2. Prof. Dr. Heinz Heimsoeth (Scherbius's cousin), telephone interview, 1969.
3. Gustave Bertrand, Enigma. (Paris: Plon, 1973), 29.
4. Ibid., 37
5. Winterbotham, 47-8.
6. Ibid., 60-61; Anthony Cave Brown, Bodyguard of Lies. (New York: Harper & Row, 1975), 38-44; William Stevenson, A Man Called Intrepid. (New York: Harcourt Brace Jovanovich, 1976), 152-3.
7. N.E. Evans, Air Intelligence and the Coventry Raid, Royal United Service Institution Journal. (September 1976), 66-73.

8. Interviews with former Abwehr communications officers, 1970, 1973.

9. Kim Philby, My Private War. (New York: Grove Press, 1968), 65.

10. J.S. Masterman, The Double-Cross System. (New Haven: Yale University Press, 1972), 3. His citations to "secret sources" at 116 and 122 presumably refer to intercepts.

11. Germany, Bundesarchiv-Militärarchiv, OKH:H22/282, Kräfteverteilung Grossbritannien/Nordirland, 31.5.44; United States, National Archives, Record Group 165, OPD 320.2 TS, Case 15/18 B.P., Deployment of Allied Divisions, 31 May 1944.

12. Winston S. Churchill, The Second World War. (Boston: Houghton Mifflin, 1948-53), 5:6.

13. From articles in a restricted publication.

14. David Kahn, The Codebreakers. (New York: Macmillan, 1967), 508.

15. Brian Randell, Colossus: godfather of the computer, New Scientist. (10 February 1977), 346-8.

16. Telephone interview, 20 November 1974.

17. Dwight D. Eisenhower Library, Eisenhower to Menzies, 12 July 1945.

18. Quoted in Kahn, 606-7.

19. Quoted in Winterbotham, xii.

20. History of the Army Security Agency, ch. XI, p. 289.

21. Interview, 2 November 1976.

22. Sir Frederick William Deakin (Churchill's research assistant), letter.

23. Dr. Maurice Matloff (chief historian, U.S. Army Center for Military History), telephone interview.

24. Norman Boardman, N.S.A. public information officer, telephone interview.

THE ENIGMA – PART I HISTORICAL PERSPECTIVES

C. A. Deavours and James Reeds

Popularization tends to glamorize its subject, generally for the purpose of focusing attention upon it. The price extracted in this process is often the truth. Left behind for future inquisitors to sift through are the half-told tales, distortions, and even outright concoctions which often mark the popularization mode.

This article is an attempt, perhaps only a first one, to unravel and unveil several of the "enigmas" of the Enigma. Many recent best-selling accounts have concerned themselves at length but without substance about the development of the Enigma machine in prewar Germany and its successful cryptanalysis by the British during World War II. In many of these works the ratio of wishful thinking and speculation to truth is large. Part of the problem encountered is continuing and needless governmental secrecy, but, for the most part, the writers themselves are journalists and their information comes not from former cryptanalysts but from those whose first-hand knowledge was peripheral in the first place. Information gleaned from such sources is usually not reliable, often consisting of dimly recalled events long past which were probably not well understood even when they happened.

Official records as always remain silent on cryptanalytic matters of this sort. Recent British release of photos and some accompanying data is exceptional in this regard. The newly revealed British repertory of early computing devices is indeed impressive: the Turing bombes and Colossi which emulated and solved much Enigma enciphered material and the Heath-Robinson series of machines which analyzed the Siemens tele-encipherers of the period. Brian Randell's excellent study of the subject [9] makes clear the fact that some of these devices were of extreme sophistication and embodied design concepts thought impossible of realization at the time. Although most of the major powers involved in the war utilized tabulating machinery to some extent in cryptanalytic work, the U. S. being particularly advanced in this regard, no other nation even attempted to build similar machines during the war. The early history of electronic computers will need to be rewritten in view of the British accomplishments.

When the first information about the British computers was revealed, it was naturally thought that all of these devices were used to attack Enigma encrypted material. We now know that this was not true. It was the early Turing bombes and the Colossi which were used to solve much of the intercepted Enigma text. These cryptographic bombes were constructed and functioned quite differently from the Heath-Robinson machines. From the meager information now available, it may be supposed that the Turing machines worked on the Enigma material by stepping through many of the rotor positions rapidly and partially analyzing each. Exhaustive key search can, however, be ruled out since it was clearly beyond the abilities of even these agile machines. The Heath-Robinson machines appear to have been high speed index of coincidence calculators with additional logic for decision making. The purpose of these devices was to analyze the pinwheel rotor settings of the Siemens tele-encipherers used by the Germans for high level communications. Apparently a number of such machines were in use by the German high command each varying in the number of rotors and pin settings available. As the war progressed, substantially larger portions of decoded intercepts were due to the breaking of these Siemans cryptographs and much of the top level so-called ULTRA material must have been derived through these sources. The British collectively termed the cryptographic systems employed "Fish."

Just what the Turing devices actually did to solve the Enigma text is not yet fully known, although an educated guess can be made. According to the Polish writer Kozaczuk [7], Poland's cryptographers were at the very least instrumental in providing to the British and French authorities the design data concerning Enigma I (the military version of the machine). Kozaczuk further claims that the necessary electronic techniques were also worked out in Poland and these, too, were passed on to the British. Polish excellence in the mathematical and engineering fields renders this assertion believable. The cryptographic bombe was an idea whose time had come. The brief description of the Polish electronic decoder seems to place it in a category whose computational complexity is greatly exceeded by subsequent British machinery but whose structure probably paralleled closely the original Turing device. Both the British and Polish achievements are remarkable and should not be seen as a case of conflicting claims. A tribute is due to both of these nations in their precocious application of electronics to codebreaking. Of course, Polish developments along this line could not continue after the fall of that country in the fall of 1939, but the British went on to grander breakthroughs involving technical accomplishments whose magnitude may be underestimated even today.

What makes the Enigma story so fascinating from the scientific and historical viewpoints are the miscalculations involved. The best German cryptographic thinking of that day viewed the Enigma ciphers as unbreakable in practice. For instance, the well known Dr. Vauk of OKW using group theoretic methods is said to have concluded that about 26,000 medium length messages were needed before one could begin to reconstruct the key settings for a group of messages. The usual methods based on n-gram frequencies and repetitions were thought to be useless. Unless a large quantity of messages all enciphered in the same key were available, the system was believed inpenetrable. Since the 1920's German cryptographers had made one improvement after another to the original commercial models of the Enigma until a point was reached where all concerned felt the machine as secure as could be reasonably done. Exhaustive key search was, therefore, the only remaining technique and this was clearly impossible because of the multitude of settings to be searched.

For reasons not known, the Germans appear to have become more concerned with the security of the Enigma as the war progressed. Keying procedures which were notably lax in the beginning became more secure. Longer messages were sometimes bisected and enciphered in two different keys. New models of the machine introduced in the mid-forties employed four rotors instead of the original three. Keys were changed more and more often – reportedly hourly near the end of the war. Much of the cryptographic burden was shifted to the high speed Siemens machines.

Part of this caution was undoubtedly because a number of the machines were known to be in enemy hands. The rotor wirings were of critical importance to enemy cryptanalysts although it was felt that the machine could withstand any cryptographic assault even if the rotor wirings were known. New rotors were issued. The numbers of sets of rotors from which daily selections were made were expanded. Nor was the mathematical under-pinning neglected. German mathematicians pursued the abstract theory of rotor machines far enough to discover connections with group theory. Since the Germans employed a variety of tabulating machinery in their own cryptanalytic work, they presumably satisfied themselves that no attack along this line could succeed. The machinery available was simply too cumbersome and too slow to be of much real service against the Enigma system.

Curiously, their judgment was substantially correct. None of the usual pencil and paper methods was effective against the machine. Although infrequent keying changes or carelessness could render the Enigma ciphers vulnerable, their security was beyond the ability of most nations to overcome. Enter the bombes! While electronic tabulating machinery could not cope with the Enigmas, computing devices with primitive logic circuitry could do so. In theory, such electronic advances were known to all the major belligerents; in practice, most deemed the complicated circuitry needed too difficult to build and maintain for use. Even the first British machines were highly erratic. At best, large portions of the intercepted material were never solved and individual solutions often took many hours to achieve. The German failure in regard to the Enigmas might be classed as one of vision. There is no reason to believe that the sister machines on the Allied side, the SIGABA of the U. S. and the TYPEX of the British, were any more resistant to analysis than the Enigma, though in the case of the SIGABA the protection accorded it certainly exceeded anything the Germans did to preserve the secrets of the Enigma. Clearly, cryptanalysts on the German side never foresaw the development of high speed computing devices to be used against them.

Whatever method the Turing bombes employed, it seems sure to have been based upon high speed search procedures. The actual cryptanalytic breakthrough was probably not an analytical one based on any new mathematical insight of the cipher generator, but rather, consisted in the design, construction, and reliable operation of the machinery developed. The speed of the bombes appears to have been their chief merit.

To understand more fully just why the Germans placed so much confidence in their Enigma machines, we shall attempt to reconstruct the principal modifications made to the machine during its developmental period, the 1920's and 30's. The invention of an early coding machine which was termed the "Enigma" is attributed to Arthur Scherbius. The early history of the device is well recounted in Kahn's bible of cryptology [13], and needs no retelling here. U. S. patent 1,657,411 filed on 6 February 1923 is generally taken to be the full blown Scherbius Enigma. The patent was filed with Scherbius as assignor for the German firm *Chiffriermaschinen Aktiengesellscaft* of Berlin. Although this patent is ostensibly for a counting device attached to the machine and not the cryptographic element employed, the familiar reflecting rotor arrangement with four rotors is described in some detail. The reciprocal encipherment produced by the reflecting rotor arrangement is characteristic of all later Enigma variations and belongs apparently to Scherbius himself. (Reciprocal encipherment means that if, at a certain key setting, "E" becomes "K", then "K" will become "E".) This widely copied rotor principle did away with the problem of special mechanical constructions for decipherment. If encipherment is reciprocal, one has only to "encipher" the ciphertext, beginning at the same key setting used in the original encipherment process, in order to recover the plaintext. The cost and weight of the cryptographic machine are thus reduced. The "reciprocal encipherment" process, however, permits no letter to represent itself, and this greatly aids the cryptanalyst in placing probable text.

Aside from the reflecting rotor arrangement, the most interesting feature of the Scherbius cryptograph is the arrangement for driving the rotors. All four of the rotors move simultaneously with each encipherment step. Each rotor is normally placed through a constant angular displacement and these displacements varied with each rotor. Some rotors moved in one direction and some in the reverse direction. Such a rotor arrangement makes the machine more cryptographically secure from a probable plaintext attack than later machines using the reciprocal encipherment principle, such as Friedman's M325 [8]. The rotors in the early Scherbius machine were not intended to be removable; and the rotor movement, while ingenious, admitted no variation.

This first Scherbius machine bears little resemblance to later commercial and military models. The 1920's were a decade of feverish development and discovery in cryptology as well as in the arts and sciences generally. Several major principles evolved during this time for strengthening rotor machines. Doubtless all of the cryptographic powers became cognizant of the weaknesses of the early devices and many of the mechanical solutions devised in this first decade of rotor machines remained in use and were further improved upon up until the 1950's when fully electronic devices began to be designed.

A remarkable series of patents by Willi Korn of *Chiffriermaschinen Aktiengesellscaft* can be used to trace Enigma developments during this time. The patents in question are U. S. patents 1,705,641 (filed May 1926), 1,733,886 (filed May 1926), 1,938,028 (filed Nov. 1929), and 1,905,593 (filed Nov. 1929).

In the first of these patents, Korn explicitly sets forth the idea of interchangeable rotors, a conception already present in the earlier Hebern patent, but lacking in the Scherbius patent. More importantly, the characteristic Enigma rotor begins to take shape. Each rotor consists of three main parts:

1. The main coding cylinder consisting of 26 or more randomly connected contacts with a normal numeric or alphabetic marking on the exterior of the cylinder to indicate the position of the rotor with respect to a fixed reference point on the machine;

2. A larger, thin flared, notched wheel which projects over the casing of the machine when closed and is used to set the rotor positions by hand and to engage rollers under the rotor so that the arrangements rest in proper contact position;

3. A smaller, notched rachet wheel used to drive the rotors in an unspecified order.

Glowlamps are suggested as the intended indicating mechanism here. (The Scherbius machine used a papertape perforator as its intended indicating device.)

The earlier variable pitched gear drive of Scherbius has been abandoned in favor of the rachet wheel drive; all rotors move in the same direction. The rachet wheels are, however, attached physically to each rotor separately instead of being separate entities as in the Hebern cryptograph. This rachet wheel arrangement was to have important consequences on later designs.

In patent 1,733,886, rotor development is further complicated by addition of a numbered feed disk whose function is to lock the individual rotors against advancing more than the desired number of steps at each movement.

Patent 1,905,593 eliminates the numbered feed disk but retains the rotor locking mechanism in modified form. This patent describes what was, most likely, the final rotor movement used during the war. The order in which the rotors are fed forward from one another is controlled by notched rings attached to each rotor. The rotor nearest the keyboard steps forward one step at each encipherment. The second rotor is fed from the first, the third is fed from the second. The mechanical construction is a modified form of Hebern's rachet wheel concept. In the Hebern machine, exterior rachet wheels controlled the stepping of all rotors except the first one. These rachet wheels were placed on the sides of the rotor bank and could themselves be fixed as part of the key to determine the point within the encipherment at which the rotor controlled by that rachet wheel moved. (See the previous article on the Hebern device, [4].) The stepping of the rotors was therefore an additional part of the key which was fixed by setting the rachet wheels. In the Hebern cryptograph this rotor movement irregularity was of little consequence to the cryptanalyst, but in Korn's Enigma means are provided for highly irregular movements of the rotors.

The rachet wheels in the Enigma were in the form of notched rings, each attached to a rotor. These notched rings were intended to be in many cases multi-notched. Thus, a complete revolution of the first rotor might cause the second rotor to step forward three steps, if the rachet wheel of the first rotor had three notches in it. Similarly, each revolution of the second rotor could cause the third rotor to step, say, five steps. No shortening of the period of the machine was caused by such a stepping arrangement, provided that the number of notches in each rachet wheel was relatively prime, i.e., having no common factors other than 1, to 26 and the number of notches in the other rachet wheels. For instance, suppose the second rotor moves forward 5 steps for each revolution of the first rotor and the third rotor steps 9 times for each revolution of the second rotor. Since 26 and 5 are relatively prime, the first rotor must make 26 revolutions before the starting position of the first two rotors repeats. In like fashion, the second rotor must make 26 revolutions before the third rotor returns to its beginning position relative to the second rotor, this because the numbers

5 and 9 are relatively prime.

The individual rachet wheels were rotatable with respect to the body of the coding cylinder so that the position within each cycle at which the stepping occurred was variable. In this manner, the movement of the rotors became a significant part of the key itself. Not only would a potential cryptanalyst have to worry about the starting positions of the rotors but also about the initial setting of the rachet wheels. It is difficult to overestimate the importance of Korn's idea in this regard. The same principle remained in use for years after the war, usually appearing in the form of snap-on plastic rings, each having a relatively prime number of settings. The multi-notched rachet arrangement (*Walsen de mobiliatisation*) had made its appearance on the military version of the Enigma by 1938.

Another highly significant modification of the Enigma was carried out about 1928 with the addition of a plugboard to the cryptograph. The plugboard modified the circuit of the machine by introducing a reciprocal monoalphabetic substitution between the keyboard and the first rotor. Twenty-six double plug sockets were provided into which 10 lines each with a double plug at each end were patched. The plugboard was another mechanism to frustrate the potential adversary. The commercial model of the machine was somewhat susceptible to a probable plaintext attack as will be shown later. The plugboard largely removed this weakness. In addition the possibility of exhaustive key search by man or machine could be ruled out provided that the cryptanalyst had to reconstruct the entire plugboard wiring along the way.

The addition of the plugboard and the irregular rotor stepping to the basic Enigma design greatly strengthened the device. Pencil and paper solutions to the cipher were out of the question. With good keying procedures and frequent key changes the British might have had an impossible task on their hands, one that not even the bombes could have overcome. Indications are that keying methods were not all what they should have been. For example, in some sectors even late in the war the plugboard wiring was altered no more frequently than every two weeks. Once the plugboard connections are known, the security of the machine drops greatly. Thus, though a lot of effort was initially necessary to solve the plugboard settings, there was compensating reward in that subsequent messages were much easier to solve during the period in which the plugboard remained unaltered.

A profusion of models of the Enigma appear to have been in use during the war. Allied cryptographic bureaus must have had quite a task keeping track of the models in use. Between 1926 and 1939, French cryptographers became aware of at least four distinct versions of the Enigma:

1. A 29 contact per rotor Naval model employing three rotors chosen from a set of 9;
2. Enigma G, an early plugboard model;
3. Enigma I, the standard *Wehrmacht* model with three rotors chosen from a set of 4 or 5;
4. Enigma II, similar to Enigma I, but with a tape unit attached.

The Naval model of the machine was reputed to be of much higher security than the *Wehrmacht* model, probably because of the additional number of rotors available for use. In the *Wehrmacht* model employing 4 rotors there were $4 \times 3 \times 2 = 24$ ways to insert the rotors as contrasted with $9 \times 8 \times 7 = 504$ ways for the Naval model. The *Abwehr* is known to have used a model of the machine without plugboard during the war. This might be justified on account of the light traffic involved and the real possibility of keeping the rotor wirings secret. In the early forties, a four rotor model of the Enigma came into use. No good reason is yet evident for this change.

The questions of keying methods and rotor movements are critical to any analysis concerning the Enigma. In some versions, the rotor movement used was reputed to be of the straight Hebern variety with the exception that the second rotor occasionally stepped two places at once, making the period of the machine $26 \times 25 \times 26$ characters. Even the distinguished French cryptanalyst Charles Eyraud seems to have been mistaken in his belief that the plugboard insertion destroyed the reciprocity of encipherment in the cryptograph.

Examination of a machine could resolve some of these questions. A number of Enigmas are known to be in private hands, but the authors so far have not succeeded in conducting an examination. Readers with personal knowledge or information concerning the Enigma are invited to communicate with the authors.

Part II of this article, describing methods of cryptanalyzing machines of the Enigma type, will appear in a future issue of *Cryptologia*.

REFERENCES

1. Beesly, Patrick. 1977. *Very Special Intelligence*. London: Hamish Hamilton.

2. Bertrand, Gustave. 1973. *Enigma*. Paris: Plon.

3. Brown, Anthony. 1975. *Bodyguard of Lies*. New York: Harper and Row.

4. Deavours, C. A. 1977. Analysis of the Hebern Cryptograph Using Isomorphs. *Cryptologia*. 1(2): 167-185

5. Eigner, Gustav. 1977. Letter to the author. 16 June 1977

6. Hardie, Bradford. 1977. Letters to the author. 1 February, 15 February 1977.

7. Kozaczuk, W. 1975. The War of Wits. *Poland*. 6, 7.

8. Kruh, Louis. 1977. Cipher Equipment, *Cryptologia*. 1(2): 143-149.

9. Randell, Brian. 1976. *The Colossus, Technical Report Series No. 90*. Newcastle upon Tyne: Computing Laboratory, University of Newcastle upon Tyne.

10. Sacco, L. 1951. *Manuel de Cryptographie*. Paris: Payot.

11. Stevenson, William. 1976. *A Man Called Intrepid*. New York: Harcourt, Brace, Jovanovich.

12. Winterbotham, F. 1974. *The Ultra Secret*. London: Weidenfeld and Nicolson.

13. Kahn, David. 1967. *The Codebreakers: The Story of Secret Writing*. New York: Macmillan.

14. *Gebrauchsanleitung Für die Chiffriermaschine Enigma*. 1940. Berlin: Gedruckt in der Reichsdruckerei. Marked "Secret."

15. *Schlüsselanleitung zur Chiffriermaschine Enigma*. 1937. (Berlin: Gedruckt in der Reichsdruckerei. Marked "Secret."

BIOGRAPHICAL SKETCH

James Reeds is currently at the University of California at Berkeley in the Department of Statistics. This is a recent appointment following an education that included degrees in mathematics, an AB at the University of Michigan, 1969, an MA at Brandeis University, 1972, and a PhD in statistics from Harvard in 1976. He has always been interested in cryptanalysis, and while in college he began using mathematics and computers in this area. His most intense interest is in statistical methods for breaking machine c phers.

Cipher A. Deavours is an Associate Professor of Mathematics at Kean College, Union, NJ, and he is rapidly developing a core of courses in cryptology. Already he has instituted a year sequence in mathematical cryptology and he is now teaching a course on computer aspects of cryptology. He tells us his major research interests lie in partial differential equations and quaternion function theory. But with his steady flow of significant results in cryptology we believe his PDE interests must be losing out, a loss we think is more than compensated for by his work in cryptology. Considering his first name, we believe this is the hand of fate!

THE ULTRA CONFERENCE

David Kahn

ADDRESS: 120 Wooleys Lane, Great Neck NY 11023 USA.

The first international conference of cryptologists took place in Germany in November 1978.

The backroom boys of World War II – Allied communications intelligence experts and Axis communications security specialists – met under scholarly sponsorship to try to determine the effect of codebreaking on the war. They concentrated particularly on the Allied codebreaking of the German Enigma and *Geheimschreiber* machines (these solutions were codenamed ULTRA). The enormous Allied success in cracking these high-level German ciphers and in thereby gaining insight into top German plans and capabilities was the greatest secret of the war after the atom bomb. It also became the longest-held secret of the war: the British did not expose it until 1974, when they allowed F. W. Winterbotham's *The Ultra Secret* to be published. That revelation touched off almost frantic activity among historians of the war. Had it made their work nugatory? Would they have to rewrite the whole history of the war? What was the weight of this intelligence in the conflict as a whole?

It was to answer such questions as these that the conference was organized – and brilliantly run – by Dr. Jürgen Rohwer. Germany's leading naval historian, Rohwer is also director of the *Bibliothek für Zeitgeschichte* (Library for Contemporary History) in Stuttgart, an adjunct professor at the University of Stuttgart, and current head of the *Arbeitskreis für Wehrforschung* (Working Circle for Military Research). The extraordinary warmth of the conference owed as much to his charm and easygoing manner as it did to the camaraderie that sprang up among the participants. The success of the conference – participants agreed that it was one of the most rewarding they had ever attended – owed all to him.

The conference consisted of two parts. On 15 and 16 November, a dozen speakers addressed 250 military and military-industrial leaders in the municipal auditorium of Bonn on the theme "Modern Technology and Its Consequences for the Conduct of War: The Example of Radio Intelligence." This constituted the 45th working session of the *Arbeitskreis für Wehrforschung*; also participating were the *Clausewitz-Gesellschaft* (Clausewitz Society) and the *Deutsche Gesellschaft für Wehrtechnik* (German Society for Military Technology). The speakers used German or English, and simultaneous translation was provided. The program is listed on the next pages. On 17 and 18 November, the *Bibliothek für Zeitgeschichte* and the history department of the University of Stuttgart conducted a colloquium in the Senate room of that university on "What Role Did Radio Intelligence Play in the Course of the Second World War?" Sitting around a U-shaped table, with a score of spectators at one end of the room, about 25 ex-spooks and historians grappled with the subject. The proceedings are scheduled to be published in German by a publisher in Germany and in English by the U. S. Naval Institute Press. The volume will include the texts of the Bonn talks and a summary or, perhaps, a transcript of the Stuttgart meeting. This report will therefore only highlight the major contributions, the most interesting of which emerged in Stuttgart. Though questions were permitted from the floor in Bonn, none yielded any significant new information.

Kahn offered reasons for Allied superiority and German inferiority in cryptanalysis. He listed five general and four technical: (1) the fragmentation of the German effort among several codebreaking agencies compared with the concentration of the Allies; (2) German aggression, which led to a neglect of intelligence, compared with the Allies' defensiveness, which heightened their watchfulness; (3) greater bureaucratic rigidity and greater fear in Hitler's dictatorship, which made it more difficult for German cipher experts to admit that the Enigma was being solved and to take corrective steps; (4) the expulsion of the Jews, which cost the Germans talent; (5) better Allied luck, especially in having a link between cryptanalysts and electronics technicians; and (6) Allied knowledge of the commercial Enigma, which gave their codebreakers a technical and psychological head start, while the corresponding Allied cipher machines were never made public; (7) the employment essentially of only one German machine, which made solution easier and more valuable than the many Allied machines; (8) inept German keying methods, which eased Allied solution; (9) stereotyped reports, which did the same.

Lisicki gave for the first time a clear and – given the nature of the audience – fairly technical description of the Polish solution of the Enigma. He said that the Poles would have solved the Enigma even without a spy's having furnished the Enigma operating instructions and some keys but that it would have taken them about two years longer. He observed that the spy contributed nothing to the fundamental problem of reconstructing the wiring of the Enigma rotors. In the next talk, Calvocoressi, at pains to give a true picture of the operation of the British codebreaking agency at Bletchley Park, remarked, "It is not the case that an eccentric English codebreaker would get an idea in his bath for solving a cipher and then would run back to his office to win the war without putting his clothes on!" Rohwer's talk, illustrated with slides, was a masterly reconstruction of how both sides used cryptanalyzed information to help direct their forces at sea. He warned historians particularly of the danger of thinking that all messages were solved on the day they were sent. Usually there was a delay, sometimes of days, between the interception and the solution, which meant that often these solutions were practically useless to the commands.

The whole first day in Stuttgart, instead of just the morning, as scheduled, was devoted to formal presentations, and another was given on Saturday morning, rather to the disappointment of some participants, who had hoped for a more free-wheeling discussion. Some discussion did creep into the interstices between the presentations, however. For the sake of coherence and space, it seems better to group here all the presentations and then to keep together discussions and comments dealing with a single topic, though they may have been taken up at separate times.

To open the conference, Dr. Eberhard Jäckel, the administrative director of the university's *Historisches Institut*, posed the two questions the colloquium should address: How important was cryptology in World War II? How much must we rewrite World War II history? As a starting point for the discussion, he iterated the reasons proposed by Kahn for Allied superiority. No one ever alluded to them again.

In a paper read for him by Beesly, Vice Admiral (ret.) Sir Norman Denning, who during the war headed the Admiralty's Operational Intelligence Centre, said that Ultra and aerial reconnaissance provided the greater part of his intelligence. The reading of the traffic of the HYDRA key net of the Naval Enigma enabled the Allies to fill in the whole picture of German naval operations, he said.

Dr. Harold Deutsch, professor emeritus at the University of Minnesota, now Johnson professor of military history at the U. S. Army Military History Institute at Carlisle Barracks, Pennsylvania, and author of numerous books on World War II, sought to stimulate controversy in a very lively talk by stating "to the absolute limit" his view on the influence of Ultra. Perhaps Ultra's most important contribution was its educating the higher commanders and their staffs to what was happening on the other side of the hill, he said. Churchill's support of Ultra was his second-greatest contribution to victory, for without this support, "Bletchley Park would have been almost inconceivable." Could the war have been won without Ultra? he asked. His answer: "In virtually all of the important encounters, Ultra played a vital and perhaps decisive role." And, he asked, if

Ultra was so important, why didn't it end the war sooner? His answer was that "It did end sooner."

Sir Herbert Marchant, a former ambassador and Bletchley worker in the same hut of Bletchley Park as Calvocoressi, gave a nuts-and-bolts description of how the papers flowed through the hut. Col. Donald Bussey, U. S. A. (ret.), the Ultra officer for the United States 7th Army, which landed in the south of France, told how the Ultra intelligence came in and was used by that command. "Ultra's greatest contribution on a day-to-day basis," he said, "was the understanding and full knowledge of German order of battle that it provided." He mentioned a remark made by the G-2, Colonel William Quinn, just after he had received an especially valuable piece of Ultra intelligence. "You know," said Quinn, "this just isn't cricket."

Edward Thomas, now a historian in the Cabinet Office helping with the forthcoming official history of British intelligence, told of his experiences in receiving Ultra in his office in a former steward's bathroom aboard the *HMS Duke of York*. It came in by direct wire from Bletchley Park. Because naval intelligence is simpler than army and air, he said, he alone in his office could maintain all his records. "We always had good information on German submarines in the North and Polar Seas," he said.

On Saturday morning, Jones spoke on Ultra's importance to scientific intelligence. He said that Churchill wanted to see the original signals, and as soon as the prime minister learned that the source was Ultra in the case of Peenemünde, where the Germans were making their rocket trials, he accepted it quickly, in part because of Ultra's help in enabling the British to bend the German navigational beams, and in part because of his experiences with cryptology in World War I (when, as first lord of the Admiralty, he received from the Russians a German naval code book that greatly helped Britain in starting its successful cryptanalytic agency, Room 40).

This concluded the set talks. The comments may be grouped under the following headings: (1) specific cases in which Ultra played a role, (2) Ultra's overall importance, (3) the effect of Ultra on the war, (4) the Russians, (5) rewriting history, and (6) miscellaneous.

(1) Specific cases in which Ultra played a role. Dr. Hans-Adolf Jacobsen, professor of history at the University of Bonn and a leading World War II historian, asked for such case histories, saying it was a fundamental point. Bussey told two stories. Ultra-furnished knowledge that no German forces were off to the army's right flank soon after the landing let the invaders concentrate more force on a push to the north. And Ultra revealed an impending German attack near Saverne around 31 December 1944, enabling the American command to better

its dispositions. Beesly said that when Adm. Karl Dönitz, commander in chief of the German navy and commander of U-boats, pulled his U-boats out of the North Atlantic in May, 1943, he left three to emit radio messages to disguise the withdrawal. "But Ultra told us of this so we could move our forces to the new threatened area, west of the Azores," Beesly said. Later, Jäckel asked how Bletchley Park learned that Hitler's planned 1940 invasion of Britain had been postponed. Thomas said that the first decrypts revealing preparations for the invasion dealt with the training of units for the landing. The first indication of the postponement was the abandonment of this training, as well as the release of barges and the maintenance of some element as cover for the preparations for the invasion of Russia. A case in which Ultra did not play a decisive role may be entered under this heading to correct published accounts. Winterbotham and others have written that Ultra ascertained the German tactic during the Battle of Britain of sending their bombers in waves and that this enabled Fighter Command to parcel out its pitifully few fighters most effectively. But Calvocoressi said that Ultra intelligence tended to be late and corrupt and had too few people to interpret it in those days of 1940. When the documents are examined, it would probably be found that Ultra did not play a decisive role in that critical battle for command of the air, he said.

(2) Ultra's overall importance. The German historians persisted on this point. They wanted a single summary assessment of Ultra's global wartime importance. Jacobsen, for example, asked what the value of Ultra was relative to other sources of information. Dr. Michael Salewski, author of a multivolume work on the German navy, asked how Ultra was used in the mass. But the Americans and the Britons who had worked with Ultra denied that answers to such questions were possible. Calvocoressi declared that "The value of Ultra depended on the time and place [in which it was used]. It can't be quantified [over the whole war]." He criticized the "obsession" with individual cases, saying that "By talking about these particulars, one may get a false picture of the source as a whole. The main value was building up a picture from which conclusions could be drawn." Bussey remarked that Ultra was indeed "part of a mixture, but this is to understate the importance of Ultra in that mixture." He said that a useful analogy for Ultra's help was the Allied radar moving target indicator, which pierced through jamming and segregated out the moving target. Both it and Ultra, he said, eliminated the background noise to focus on the meaningful signals. Lewin said that "Any suggestion of a structural flow in which you say Ultra came first [among the sources of information], this came second, and so on, distorts the picture... Sometimes Ultra was the most important, but sometimes it arrived too late." Thomas provided the most lapidary reply to the German question.

"No simple answer, no generalization is possible," he said. But he noted that "Ultra information was most sought when the enemy had the initiative, as in the case of counterattacks."

(3) The effect of Ultra on the war. Dr. Andreas Hillgruber, professor at the University of Cologne and perhaps the leading historian of World War II, asked rhetorically, how would the war have gone without Ultra? He answered that the war was sped up through Ultra and that without it, the invasion of France would have taken place later and the Russians would have gone further west. [Hillgruber seemed to imply that they would have stayed in the areas they conquered. But the Russians – like the western Allies – pulled back from such areas to the territories delimited as final occupation zones: the Russians returned three fourths of Berlin to the Allies, for example.] Dr. Gerhard Weinberg, professor of history at the University of North Carolina and first head of the American project for microfilming the seized German records, retorted with some asperity that "It is ridiculous to argue that if the Atlantic battle had been won more slowly all else would have been unchanged. If things had not gone so well in the Atlantic, the Allies would have put more resources into the Atlantic to keep on their timetable." These resources would have come from supplies intended for the Pacific – "the lesser theater. So if there had been no Ultra in the Atlantic, the United States would perhaps be fighting in the Philippines [in early 1945] instead of on Iwo Jima and Okinawa." Thus the Atlantic Ultra actually helped the Pacific war, he said.

Lewin observed that "The two main decisions of the Casablanca conference do not come in any way from Ultra." These were to give the highest priority to the Battle of the Atlantic and to destroy Germany from the air. The same goes for the invasion of North Africa, he said. "I don't think Ultra fits in the real picture of grand strategy," he concluded. In addition, Gen. Leo Hepp, wartime chief of staff to the German army chief signal officer, said that Allied material superiority was the crucial factor, not Ultra. No one disputed this.

(4) The Russians. Hillgruber commented that everyone forgets the importance of the Russian front, which absorbed two thirds of the German war effort. This importance remains the same with or without the western Allies' Ultra, he affirmed. Dr. Geoffrey Jukes, a former Bletchley worker now at the University of Canberra, who nodded his head vigorously when Hillgruber was making this point, noted that "We don't know whether the Russians could read Enigma and this is as big a gap as Ultra used to be for the West." (Some evidence – nearly all of it German – indicates that the Russians could solve Enigma messages, at least at times. Some discussions at a 1943 conference of German army signal officers centered on this likelihood. In his talk in Bonn, Werther said that the

war diary of Army Group North says 11 Enigma keys have been exposed. A Russian book mentions the recovery of an Enigma from a U-boat in the Baltic in 1944. Tending to corroborate this are the admittedly vaguer observations that the Russians have long been good in cryptanalysis and have also been good in subjects that go along with excellence in cryptanalysis: music, chess, and mathematics. On the other hand, their then relatively impoverished technical background suggests that they were far less likely than the Poles or the British to independently evolve electromechanical devices for automatically solving Enigma messages. Could they have used, instead of such devices, hundreds of men from their vast human reservoirs? A Finnish cryptanalyst, Erkki Pale, who during World War II had solved Russian codes, thought that such an undertaking could not be organized to succeed. Thomas said that, in his delving among the classified archives, he saw no evidence of Russian Enigma solutions. The Russians themselves have said nothing on the topic.)

Jukes raised the possibility that a Russian sympathizer at Bletchley might have told the Soviet Union of the fact of Allied success in this field out of outrage that the western Allies were not sharing this vital intelligence, in the same way as scientists at Los Alamos passed over the secret of the atom bomb. Kahn asked whether the story was true that the British had used the famed LUCY Communist spy ring in Switzerland' headed by Rudolf Rössler, whose sources have never been revealed, as a conduit to feed disguised Ultra information to their Soviet allies. Thomas said that some Ultra intelligence was given to the Russians in concealed form. Calvocoressi said that there was no need for "mysterious people in Switzerland" because "a good deal" was sent through a special mission in Moscow headed by Edward Crankshaw, the writer. Crankshaw was disappointed that more could not be given, he said, and was finally convinced by Sir Stewart Menzies, head of the British secret service, which distributed the Ultra material, that poor Soviet cipher security risked revealing this precious source to the Germans, Calvocoressi said. When Jukes asked whether the Allies should not have told the Russians that their ciphers were weak, Thomas replied: "There's a whole book on this subject. It will not be published." Thomas also said it was very likely that the British attacked and even solved Soviet codes and that this work was mostly done in the Mid East [where the spheres of influence collided, especially in Iran, which was occupied jointly by Russian and British troops in August, 1941].

(5) Rewriting history. Dr. Forrest Pogue, author of the standard biography of Gen. George C. Marshall, U. S. Army chief of staff, said that to suggest that overnight all World War II history must be rewritten is to misunderstand that history is always being rewritten. The Ultra revelations must be seen as part

of this process, he said. He added that 15 to 20 years is the time lag for facts to catch up with fiction. That's how long it will take for the false story that Winston Churchill allowed Coventry to be destroyed and its people martyred to save the secret of Ultra "to stop being used to keep sophomores awake in the classroom." Jacobsen said that only battle history will have to be revised; the overriding political events and global strategy would not be affected. Lewin wondered whether Ultra might become a new form of the stab-in-the-back legend. [Promulgated in Germany after World War I, this held that the German armies did not lose honorably on the field of battle but were betrayed on the home front by Communists and Jews.] Finally, Hepp asked whether, in a one-volume history of World War II, there belongs a chapter on radio intelligence. No, he assured himself. But there might be a chapter on intelligence in general, and radio intelligence would belong in that, he said.

(6) Miscellaneous. (a) An epigram from Werther: "The security of a cipher lies less with the cleverness of the inventor than with the stupidity of the men who are using it." (b) Karl-Otto Hoffmann, author of a three-volume history of the *Luftwaffe* signal corps, said that according to the *Luftwaffe* chief signals officer during the war, Gen. Wolfgang Martini, usually 30% and sometimes up to 50% of *Luftwaffe* intelligence came from radio reconnaissance. He said that one depends more on radio reconnaissance in retreats than in advances, when one has other sources, such as prisoners of war and the population. (c) Charles von Luttichau, a historian with the U. S. Army's Center for Military History, asked whether the Germans ever thought that a single machine might be dangerous. Werther said "yes," but did not elaborate. Hepp said that he had a section to test German cipher systems. That the Enigma was provably unbreakable was never affirmed, he said, only that it could be solved. Consequently the rules for its use were constantly improved, he said. Some in the audience felt that he was placing more emphasis on Enigma solvability in 1978 than was done in 1943, when the emphasis lay rather on the near certainty that the Enigma was not being solved. At a party at the *Bibliothek für Zeitgeschichte* that evening, the present chief of German naval radio intelligence said that to have two machines would have cost more money and more training and would have engendered more errors and failures to get through, thus reducing the trust of the commanders in the machine and in communications. Finally, Calcovoressi noted dryly that the British, too, used but a single machine. (d) Alec Douglas, a Canadian official historian, said that comparisons need to be made between the use of intelligence in World Wars I and II. (e) "I am surprised," Thomas said, "to see so many distinguished minds trying to fit the importance of Ultra into the whole history of the war before we have the evidence, The cart is hurtling before the horse. I

think we have 25 years' work to do in establishing the facts."

The conference ended at 12:10 p. m. Saturday with a graceful tribute by Marchant to the conference organizer. After expressing the thanks of the participants, he said that all present were thankful that Beesly's Operational Intelligence Centre had not caught that German minesweeper in the Baltic on which there was working a young naval officer by the name of Rohwer.

The hard-working historians seemed oblivious during the conference to the human dramas that swirled around them but that did not touch their high purposes. How did the former enemies feel about one another? All said they held no animosities. Capt. (ret.) Heinz Bonatz, who during part of the war had headed the *Kriegsmarine*'s cryptanalytic service, said he did not hate the British. "We fought against one another and now we're comrades – and historians, thank God," he said. But the British seemed a bit more reserved. "They're fine fellows – now," said Beesly. Lewin told of an odd feeling he had during the Bonn meeting. "I was talking about the deception in Normandy, and in front was a row of elderly Germans, one of whom at the end asked a question. Suddenly it shot through my head. 'I was there, and you were there, and here we are.' It was very strange."

A more poignant drama was more suppressed. How did the German cryptographers feel as the British and American intelligence officers cited case after case in which their solutions of a machine which the Germans had said was secure cost Germany battle after battle, U-boat after U-boat, and thousands of German lives and contributed much to the defeat of their nation? Mostly the German cryptographers sat silent, for they had, after all, no comeback to this. And they denied feeling guilt or embarrassment over the proceedings.

Meckel said he feels he did his best. He said he didn't mean he never made mistakes. But he had no certain indication that the Allies had solved the machine – there were always alternative explanations for the apparent Allied foreknowledge of German moves – and so he feels he did not err about the ciphers. Hepp and Bonatz likewise both denied suffering from the situation. "I had a view and I was wrong. Now I have to correct it," said Bonatz.

But others did feel badly. The chief of staff to the U-boat command, Adm. (ret.) Eberhard Godt, not present at the conference, "suffers badly on account of this," Meckel said. And the Finnish codebreaker Pale said, "I felt depressed." Why? "Because I was on the losing side," he explained (Finland fought as a co-belligerent with Germany against Russia). He added, "It must have been very depressing for the Germans with the English firing all those cannonballs from all sides."

Indeed. For what human could not feel at least a twinge of guilt over the fact that his failure, however hard he worked at the time, helped cost his country a war? Yet the answer remains locked in the fastness of the German codebreakers' hearts. And to secrets there, no one, not even the Allies' cryptanalysts, has ever been able to penetrate.

THE PROGRAM IN BONN

Wednesday, 15 November 1978

9:30 Greetings Prof. Dr. Jürgen Rohwer, head of the *Arbeitskreis für Wehrforschung*

10:00 "The Influence of Modern Technology on the Command of Military Forces" Gen. Harald Wust, Generalinspector of the Bundeswehr

11:15 "Communications, Cryptology and Signal Intelligence in the Wars of the 20th Century" Dr. David Kahn, author of *The Codebreakers* Radio Cipher Keys and Their Solution

2:30 "The Development of the German Radio Cipher Machines" Lt. Col. (ret.) Waldemar Werther, wartime worker in the cipher bureau of the *Luftwaffe* High Command and later head of radio cryptanalysis at Air Fleets 1 and 6

3:00 "The Achievement of the Polish Biuro Szyfrów (Cipher Bureau) in Breaking the German Enigma Cipher" Lt. Col. (ret.) Tadeusz Lisicki, participant in the Polish cryptanalytic service The Organization of the Cryptanalytic Services and Their Performance

4:30 "The Organization and Operation of GC&CS (Government Code & Cypher School) at Bletchley Park" Mr. Peter Calvocoressi, wartime watch chief for German air force and army cryptanalyzed intelligence at Bletchley

5:00 "Successes and Failures of the German Cipher Services in the Second World War" Dr. Erich Hüttenhain, wartime head of analytical crypt analysis in the Cipher Branch of the Armed Forces High Command

Thursday, 16 November 1978
Radio Reconnaissance in the Atlantic Battle

9:00 "The Radio Command of the German U-Boats and the Role of the German Naval Cryptanalytic Service" Capt. (ret.) Hans Meckel, wartime officer for radio communications on the staff of the commander of U-boats

9:30 "The British Admiralty's Operation Intelligence Centre and the Battle of the Atlantic" Lt. Cmdr. Patrick Beesly (R. N. V. R. ret.), wartime deputy chief of O. I. C.'s Submarine Tracking Room and author of *Very Special Intelligence*

10:30 "The Effects of German and British Radio Reconnaissance and the Convoy Operations in the North Atlantic" Prof. Dr. Jürgen Rohwer, author of *The Critical Convoy Battles of March 1943*

11:00 "Radio Intelligence and the Turning Point in the Battle of the Atlantic" Vice Admiral (ret.) Brian B. Schofield, R. N., wartime director of the Admiralty's Trade Division (Convoys and Routing)

2:30 "Radio Intelligence and Deception During Operation OVERLORD" Mr. Ronald Lewin, author of *Ultra Goes to War*

3:30 "Electronic Warfare: Its Possibilities, Its Limitations and Its Dangers During the Second World War" Prof. Dr. R. V. Jones, wartime director of scientific intelligence for the Air Ministry

WHY GERMANY LOST THE CODE WAR

David Kahn

ADDRESS: 120 Wooleys Lane, Great Neck NY 11023 USA.

This paper was presented for discussion at the Baltimore-Washington German History Seminar, 8 November 1980, Towson State University, Towson, Maryland. It is a slightly revised form of a portion of "Codebreaking in World Wars I and II: The Major Successes and Failures, Their Causes and Their Effects," *The Historical Journal*, 23 (September, 1980), 617-639, which lists all sources. The technical reasons given below owe a great deal to the kind help of Dr. C. A. Deavours.

A spate of books, articles and reports at historical conferences has made it widely known that the Allies solved the high-level German cipher machine called Enigma during World War II. The Germans, on the other hand, did not solve the equivalent Allied cryptosystems, with the exception of Royal Navy codes up to about 1943. The Allies thus had considerable insight into enemy plans and capabilities that the Germans did not have, and these insights greatly contributed to the Allied victory.

Why were the Allies – meaning the western Allies – so much better than the Germans in this field, which proved so important? In investigating this question, we might begin by clearing away two theories that at first seem plausible but do not in fact apply.

One is that German codebreakers were chosen for their political reliability as good Nazis instead of for their ability. This did not happen with the German cryptanalytic agencies. The civilian technical heads of the agencies of the navy and of the *Oberkommando der Wehrmacht* were not members; indeed, the navy man even ousted an *Alte Kaempfer* in gaining his post. (The military chiefs, who were mainly administrators, were, like all professional soldiers, ineligible to join until 1944.) Of the administrative chief and the three head cryptanalysts of the Foreign Office agency, all of whom held their posts from the 1920s to 1945, none were convinced enough Nazis to have joined before Hitler's accession to power; one never did join and the times of joining of the other three suggest motives other than belief for their doing so; one became a member soon after the *Machtergreifung* and two during the war. The lending officials of the *Forschungsamt*, Goering's wiretapping and codebreaking agency, were, on the other hand, all Nazis. Whether the high-ranking civilians in the army and air force code breaking agencies were party members is not known. Overall, the pattern does not suggest that insistence on party adherence was essential for advancement, but the contrary.

The other false theory is that the Allies were quantum steps ahead of the Germans in cryptology. They were not. Certainly they were more advanced, but the Germans knew the answer to the basic question; how to solve the Enigma. Early in the 1930s, the head cryptanalyst of the *Forschungsamt* said to the head evaluator; "*Seifert, die ganze Enigma ist Mist!*" And he proceeded to demonstrate a solution using alphabet slides that was also known – at least later – to the Allies. Though a modification (the plugboard) vitiated this technique, the German cryptographers always claimed that the machine was not absolutely secure and continually suggested improvements – implying that they could see ways of breaking into the machine. So the theory that the Allies knew how to solve the Enigma and the Germans did not is false and not a factor in the Allied cryptologic superiority.

Separate from these theories lies a hypothesis that appears likely but for which proof is lacking. This is that the Allies' larger population gave them more, and probably also better, people for codebreaking than Germany. But it is not known how many of the approximately 10,000 people at Bletchley, as Britain's codebreaking agency was generally called from its location in that town 50 miles northwest of London, were solving ciphers other than German at any particular time, or how many in the German agencies were solving Soviet, Italian, Japanese, Turkish, Swedish, and other non-U.S. and non-U.K. systems at the same time. Moreover, the contributions of other governments – Canadian, Free French, Dutch, Italian, Japanese, Hungarian – to their respective allies cannot readily be measured in terms of manpower. Finally, the number of persons in field units, both Allied and German, is not known with precision. Still, it seems probable that more people in the most attacked German ciphers than worked in Germany on Allied ciphers and so greater Allied population probably did contribute to greater success. But, without the data that would prove or disprove this conjecture, it cannot legitimately be advanced. A corollary to this theory would be that the Allies' greater industrial capacity enabled them to help both their codebreakers and their codemakers more. But this help would have been so small in relation to either the Allied or the Axis war effort as to be insignificant. So this cannot be adduced as a factor, either.

What, then, are the factors that led to Allied superiority and German inferiority in codebreaking? There are, of course, a variety of causes for so complex a phenomenon. They may be divided into two kinds – general and technical.

There are four of the latter, all of which spring from purely cryptologic roots.

The first chronologically, and probably also the first in order of importance, is that the Allies knew the fundamentals of the German machine. The Enigma, which had been invented shortly after World War I by a private individual, was offered for sale to the public early in the 1920s; the inventor hoped to become rich as businessmen bought his machine to ensure the secrecy of their communications. The Polish, British, French and U.S. codebreaking agencies acquired the advertising brochures, press reports and patents on the Enigma and, at least Poland also obtained a machine. So even though the German navy (the first German government element to use it) modified it for its own use, and even though the army and other agencies of government further varied it for their own use, the Allies had a basic knowledge of the machine. To this must be added the operating instructions of the military version and some actual keys sold to the French by a German working within the German code agencies whom the French recruited as a spy around 1931. Cryptanalytically, all this information gave the Allies a big head start. It also gave them an enormous psychological advantage. The Germans did not enjoy such benefits. The Allied analogues of the Enigma, Britain's Typo-X and the American SIGABA, were developed in secret. Of course, knowledge of a machine is not always essential for its solution. The Americans reconstructed the Japanese PURPLE diplomatic cipher machine without any such assistance. But acquaintance with the machine cannot but help.

The second technical reason is that the Germans mainly used one machine, the Enigma (though they supplemented it with another machine, the *Geheimschreiber*, later in the war), while the Allies, consisting of many nations, used many. The German use of one machine entailed several effects for the Allies. First of all, they could concentrate relatively more manpower on the problem. Secondly, the single system generated a greater proportion of messages enciphered in it, thereby facilitating its solution. Thirdly, a single system increased Allied incentive, because its solution would yield a greater prize than if it were just one system among many. None of those factors operated for the Germans, and it correspondingly depressed their efforts and results.

A third cryptologic reason is that the main high-level cipher machine of the Americans at least, the SIGABA, was far better than the Enigma. Both used the same cryptographic principle, that of the rotor, or wired code-wheel, to create an electrical maze that enciphered the letter. The naval Enigma, the best of the German family, came with a set of eight rotors, of which four were inserted into the machine at one time. Gears controlled their stopping. The SIGABA had 15 rotors, 10 for creating the electrical maze, 5 for moving those 10 in a much more irregular way than gears could, thus making solution more difficult. A cryptologist has said that the SIGABA was "a generation ahead" of the Enigma. It was in fact devised a decade after the Enigma, and because the Americans did not begin equipping their army and navy with cipher machines until the late 1930s, they could utilize this more advanced mechanism without losing capital investment. The Germans, who had mechanized a decade earlier, were stuck with an older, weaker machine.

Fourthly, just as the German hardware was poorer, so was their software. Two of their operating procedures proved fatal to many an Enigma cryptogram. One was the flawed keying method used by the Germans before the war and for its first year or so. It required that a three-letter keying group, such as BOL, be repeated; BOLBOL. The Germans probably did this to enable their clerks to decipher a message even if a garble altered one of the six key letters. But the repetition also created a point of entry for cryptanalysts, which the Poles – who first cracked the machine – and then the British quickly exploited. This keying method was later changed, but by then Enigma had been solved. The Allies, on the other hand, used far more secure keying systems that obviated this sort of attack. The other dangerous operating procedure was the transmission of messages without padding (meaningless words at the beginning and end) and without bisection (dividing messages in half and putting the second part before the first). Both of those techniques protected against the stereotyped beginnings and endings of messages or the routine whole messages that soldiers persisted in sending. The Allies broke into many a new Enigma key because an isolated outpost continued to transmit "*Nichts zu melden*" in the new key just as it had in the old. Allied soldiers likewise often composed, enciphered and transmitted routine messages, especially in the communications to and from convoys. But the Allied use of padding and bisection afforded their plaintexts better protection than German.

Four technical reasons thus played a role in Allied cryptologic success; Allied knowledge of the Enigma compared with German ignorance of Allied machines; the German use of one main machine versus the Allied use of many; a German machine cryptographically poorer than their Allied equivalents; and German operating procedures that were inadequate in contrast to adequate Allied ones. In addition to these, five general reasons contributed to the Allied success. These flowed from external circumstances, or political and social factors.

Perhaps the most important was the fragmentation of German cryptanalysis. The Germans had a great many codebreaking agencies. The *Chiffrierabteilung* of the OKW, Pers Z of the Foreign Office, and Goering's *Forschungsamt* competed on the highest level. For a time, the *Sicherheitsdienst*, the SS's intelligence army, had its own agency. The army, the navy, and the air force each had its own unit, though there was rather more justification for that. But this multiplicity spread the available manpower, which was scarce to begin with, very thin. And it diffused the codebreaking effort. Contrast this with the concentration of effort at Bletchley, Britain's sole codebreaking agency, and with that in America, where the army and navy codebreaking unity worked in the closest cooperation. Of course, there was some cooperation in Germany. But it did not overcome the lethal effects of dispersion, which stemmed from Hitler's assigning duplicate responsibilities to his underlings so that he could retain ultimate control. The charismatic nature of this leadership enabled him to do this in many areas of government. It facilitated his rule – but it devastated his war effort, including codebreaking.

Also fundamental as a reason for Allied cryptologic superiority was Germany's aggression and the Allies' defensive posture. Behind this lies the fact that intelligence is necessary to the defense, but it is only contingent to the offense. Clausewitz defined the characteristic feature of the defense as "awaiting the blow." An army can await a blow only if it believes that a blow is planned, and such a belief can be created only by information about the enemy. That is why intelligence is essential to the defense, and Poland, France, and England, basically in a defensive stance, cultivated it. The offense, on the other hand, is "complete in itself," Clausewitz said. An attacking army does not even have to know where the enemy force is: it can march about, imposing its will, until it runs into its foe. Such an army will put more of its effort into men, tanks, planes and guns and less into intelligence, one form of which is codebreaking. This Germany did. A number of incidents and conditions demonstrate her relative neglect of intelligence and the corresponding greater attention that the Allies paid to it.

France gained the spy who provided the Allies with vital cryptologic information in large measure because she made a great – and generally successful – effort to learn about German rearmament. The Germans, though their spies sometimes delivered useful cryptologic information, never scored a coup like France's – mainly because they never tried as hard.

Before the outbreak of war, Great Britain had established an Operational Intelligence Control in the Admiralty and a Joint Intelligence Committee under the chiefs of staff. Germany never took such steps.

The Allies put better men into cryptology than the Germans. Bletchley Park was an unbelievable galaxy of talent. All American recruits were given an IQ test; those who scored the highest were proposed for cryptologic work. This resulted in extraordinarily high brainpower in codebreaking units. The American army agency could have staffed a first-class university in all departments, one of its leaders boasted, with justice. No such recruiting seems to have taken place for German codebreaking. And their agencies, despite individually bright men, did not dazzle as did the Allied units.

German training for cryptanalysis, too, was poorer than the Allies'. The only textbook the *Kriegsmarine* had was a translation of an elementary French text. Cryptanalysts learned on the job. The United States, on the other hand, had developed its own textbooks and established schools and extension courses to train cryptanalysts. In the same way, the Allied instructions for cipher clerks on how to set up their machines and how to encipher sometimes explained that certain procedures should not be used because they would help the enemy solve the messages. The German instructions never motivated like that.

Furthermore, while the Germans continued using only electromechanical devices for solving ciphers, the Allies added electronic devices. Those in effect multiplied the Allies' manpower and enabled them to do far more in a given amount of time, in particular solving cryptograms enciphered in the new *Geheimschreiber* rapidly enough for them to be of use to the commanders in the field. The cause of this Allied advance seems to have lain in Britain's urgent need for intelligence. In 1940, with invasion still a possibility, wrote one who was there, "Bletchley foresaw that the enemy could introduce new practices which would require the [existing electro-mechanical] breaking machinery to be speeded up by one or two orders of magnitude at least." Such high speeds had been attained in the 1930s by a Cambridge physicist, C. E. Wynn-Williams. He had devised an electronic counter to tally electron-particle events that occurred too rapidly for electromechanical counters. Many of Bletchley's staff had come from Cambridge. They thought of his electronic device when they themselves had to create machinery to count very fast. Their ideas culminated in a remarkable device codenamed COLOSSUS, which many historians of technology regard as the first electronic computer and which significantly contributed to Allied success in cryptanalysis. In Germany, despite a computer pioneers 1940 proposal for an electronic cipher device, which might have suggested the use of electronics in codebreaking to the army's cryptologic authorities, and despite a later naval proposal for an electronic codebreaking mechanism, no agency apparently ever felt the need to build one. And so Germany never took the crucial stop to electronics in cryptanalysis.

All these factors suggested a widespread German disregard for codebreaking relative to the Allies, which may be ascribed to German aggression and Allied emphasis on the defensive.

A third general factor was the expulsion of the Jews. The exodus or extermination of a whole people, many of them highly intelligent, cost German codebreaking – as it cost German mathematics and German physics – many brains.

A fourth general reason was luck. Luck helped the Allies more than the Germans. It certainly played a role in the French recruiting of their important spy, and it was luck that a genius, the mathematician Alan Turing, who had an idea that greatly helped Enigma solutions and that the Germans did not have, was a Briton. But this was not as important a factor as the others.

The fifth and last reason for German inferiority is the broadest: a greater reluctance to face reality. It was this reluctance, combined with the lack of irrefutable evidence for enemy cryptanalysis, which largely kept the naval high command from conceding during several investigations that its cipher might have been broken. The officers found it difficult to admit to themselves, to their chiefs, and to Hitler that everything they had said and done was worthless and would have to be redone. The result was disaster. Of course, the Allies, too, were sometimes reluctant to face reality. Conferences on possible compromises of systems sometimes decided, as the Germans did, that none had occurred, largely because the cryptologists did not want to go through all the work of instituting new systems-devising, manufacturing, and distributing the new machines, training the personnel, and phasing the system into operation with the inevitable blunders that would call down the wrath of admirals and generals. But the conditions under which the Allies worked made it easier for them to confront unpleasant facts. They were less crippled by arrogance than the Germans and so more open to improvement. [For an attempt to trace the historical roots of German arrogance see David Kahn's *Hitler's Spies*, (New York, 1978), pp. 525-27.] SIGABA's greater strength enabled the Americans to restore security in case of a compromise by simply replacing rotors; the Germans would have had to substitute a whole new system for the Enigma. Competition between Americans and Britains in a joint endeavor helped keep failure from being hidden for very long. Civilian draftees or volunteers headed important sections of codebreaking and intelligence agencies more frequently in Allied forces than in German; because they were less concerned about their military careers than the officers and officials who headed the corresponding German sections, these civilians admitted unpleasant facts to their superiors more readily. For all these reasons, the Allies seem to have faced reality more. When an American cipher machine went astray in France in 1944, the American army code agency worked day and night to rewire the rotors of other machines, thus making the missing machine useless to cryptanalysts. And when the Americans got wind of the German solution of their military attaché code, they distributed a new system. So, as one American cryptologist has said, "We never kidded ourselves. The Germans and Japanese did kid themselves."

These, then, are the five external conditions that helped reduce German cryptanalysis to a level inferior to Allied: the fragmentation of the German organization compared to the unity of the Allies; Germany's aggression, which led to a neglect of cryptology, contrasted with the Allied defensive posture, which emphasized intelligence; the expulsion and killing of the Jews; better Allied luck; and greater German reluctance to face reality. When these are joined to the four technical reasons, they help answer why German cryptanalysis was poorer than Allied, and so help explain one of the causes of the defeat of the Third Reich.

BIOGRAPHICAL SKETCH

David Kahn is the Op-Ed page editor for *Newsday*, a large daily newspaper on Long Island, New York. He is a trained historian with his doctorate in modern history from Oxford University in 1974, as well as a professional writer. His work has appeared in a number of scholarly and influential journals and magazines. His discoveries, his solid research and his documentation in addition to his definitive book, *The Codebreakers*, published in 1967, have placed him in a circle with a select few who have placed cryptology in the public arena both academic and commercial.

IN MEMORIAM MARIAN REJEWSKI

Christopher Kasparek[1] and Richard A. Woytak[2]

ADDRESS: (1) 95 Welling Place, Monterey CA 93940 USA and (2) P O Box 221211, Carmel CA 93922 USA.

On February 13, 1980, in Warsaw, Poland, there died, at the age of 74, the man who, more than any other, was entitled to be considered the vanquisher of the German Enigma machine cipher and thus one of the architects of Allied victory in World War II.

Marian Rejewski (MAR-yahn Rey-EFF-ski), foremost of the team of cryptologists who created what became known as the Ultra secret, was born on August 16, 1905, at Bydgoszcz, then called Bromberg as it was in the German-occupied zone of Poland, a country partitioned since the late 18th century between Prussian Germany, Russia, and Austria. He was barely a teenager when his country reappeared on the map in November 1918. At a time when only a tiny proportion of the population attended university, he went to study mathematics at Poznan University.

We hope things are going well for you, that Mary is doing well - still dispensing good eatery to the fitness set, that the kids are doing well. How is my main man, Brian, making out these days? I am glad you went to Francis Marion . . . .helps keep Fox on his toes!!! Keep that up and give him my regards.

In early 1929, while still an undergraduate, Rejewski participated in a cryptology course organized for about twenty selected mathematics students at Poznan University by the Cipher Bureau (*Biuro Szyfrow*) of Section II (military intelligence) of the Polish General Staff. The choice of Poznan for the course had apparently been prompted by an intention to attack German ciphers. This would require knowledge of German which most of the students had: in 1793, in the second of the three progressive partitions of Poland, Poznan had been absorbed into Prussia where it was known as Posen.

After receiving his master's degree in mathematics on March 1, 1929, Rejewski spent a year at Göttingen University in Germany, studying actuarial mathematics. Upon being offered a teaching assistantship in mathematics at his alma mater in the summer of 1930, Rejewski did not return to Göttingen for the second year of the actuarial course but spent the next two years teaching at Poznan, where he also resumed his involvement with cryptology at a temporary Cipher Bureau branch office that had been set up adjacent to the university's Mathematics Institute. Already working there were two students, Henryk Zygalski (HEN-rik Zig-AHLski) and Jerzy Rozycki (YEH-ih Roozh-IT-ski), respectively two and four years his juniors.

Eventually the three young cryptologists received offers of employment at the Cipher Bureau in Warsaw, and as of September 1, 1932, became regular civilian employees at the General Staff. (By extraordinary chance, all that remains since World War II of the General Staff Building where they worked, erected as a private palace in the 18th century and remodeled in the 19th, is the Tomb of the Unknown Soldier that in 1923 had been placed within the colonnade-topped arcade that joined the two wings.) It was here, in the final months of 1932 and the first weeks of 1933, just as Hitler was coming to power, that Rejewski, assisted by his two younger colleagues, broke the German Enigma machine cipher and elaborated means for its regular decryptment. Here, too, from their third-floor office in the north wing, adjacent to the colonnade, they could watch German dignitaries laying wreaths a the Tomb of the Unknown Soldier: the pompous, bemedalled Goering, the demonically grimacing Goebbels, and other notables of the Third Reich who from 1934 on were fairly frequent visitors to Warsaw. The Polish cryptologists drew a sense of intellectual and moral superiority from the awareness that they, anonymous workers in one of the General Staff's backroom units, could penetrate the Germans' most secret and sinister plans.

In 1937, for security, the fourth, or German, section of the Cipher Bureau (*B. S.* 4) was moved to new facilities near Pyry, in the Kobackic Woods south of Warsaw. There, on July 25, 1939, as war loomed, the Poles initiated their French and British allies into the secrets of Enigma decryptment and promised to give them the apparatus and techniques that they had developed. (The transfer took place by mid-August.)

On September 1, 1939, the Second World War broke out, and a week later the Cipher Bureau was evacuated eastwards. On September 10 the special evacuation train reached Brzesc (Brest-Litovsk). The subsequent route led south, and on September 17, the Soviet Army having that day at 4 a.m. entered eastern Poland just 60 miles to the east, the Cipher Bureau joined the long line of Poles who, together with the Polish Government, crossed the Czeremosz River into friendly Rumania at Kuty. Although the three mathematician-cryptologists had departed their homeland–except for Rejewski forever–for them the war was just beginning.

Disobeying Rumanian orders to proceed to an internment camp, Rejewski, Rozycki, and Zygalski took the first train for Bucharest, reported to the Polish military attaché, then went to the British embassy to obtain papers for their transfer to Britain. They remembered that in July the British had shown keen interest in cooperation. Indeed, in December 1939 the British would ask Polish Cipher Bureau chief Lieutenant Colonel Gwido Langer to turn his cryptologists over to them, and at the moment most of their bitterness toward Poland's do-nothing western allies who had contented themselves with merely *declaring* war on Germany was directed at France, with her enormous, well-equipped army and substantial air force. But as chance would have it, just when they had arrived at the British embassy, a bus carrying personnel evacuated from the British embassy in Warsaw rolled into the yard, and the British diplomats gave the Poles what they took to be a brush-off ("Come back in a few days"–or, as Rejewski has commented, "*Manana*"). Constantly in danger of arrest and internment by the Rumanians, the Poles went to the French embassy, where they were given a warm welcome and French visas. The French were eager to get the Polish cryptologists–so much so, that French radio-intelligence chief Lieutenant Colonel Gustave Bertrand, unaware that the trio were already on their way to Paris, went to Rumania to locate them and their Cipher Bureau colleagues.

By October 20, B.S.-4 was back in business at Command Post Bruno–the Chateau de Vignolles in the town of Gretz-Armainvillers, about 20 miles southeast of Paris, where the Poles constituted the heart of the entire operation. Bruno became in that period the mainstay of all Allied radio intelligence. It encompassed monitoring stations, fixed and mobile goniometric posts for direction-finding of enemy radio stations, and other auxiliary facilities. The Poles had the use of three Polish-produced Enigma machines, two secretly taken out of Poland during the evacuation and one presented to the French after the Warsaw conference of July 1939. Contact and collaboration were established with the British at Bletchley Park, northwest of London, who were making their own cryptological bomb, perforated sheets (sometimes called *Zygalski sheets*), and other cryptanalytic devices based on the Polish plans. Bruno was providing German naval and air force signals to the British, who were particularly interested in these, threatened as they were from the sea and the air.

Just before opening their general offensive in the West on May 10, 1940, the Germans changed the procedures for using Enigma in all their armed forces. Nevertheless, within six or eight days the Polish cryptologists were again reading Enigma. In the first days of the German offensive, part of Bruno's personnel were moved from Gretz-Armainvillers to French Intelligence headquarters at 2 bis, avenue de Tourville, Paris, behind Invalides. Here the Polish cryptologists and technicians worked around the clock in three shifts, never leaving the building. As the front disintegrated and other sources of intelligence shrank, Enigma information became increasingly vital. Its authenticity and accuracy soon came to be appreciated, and the *feuillettes jaunes* (yellow pages) printed on thin gold-colored paper in a score of copies were snapped up by generals and colonels of the French High Command, some of whom waited at the entrance to the cryptologists' quarters and even slept in the building in order to get their hands on the hot information. But, as had been the case in Poland, the best intelligence could not by itself stem the tide. On June 10, 1940, Bruno was evacuated. The unit retreated southward by stages, reading German signals along the way. At Toulouse, on June 22, the Poles learned that Marshal Henri-Phillipe Petain had signed an armistice. On June 24, Bertrand managed to fly Bruno's 15 Poles and 7 Spaniards (ex-Republican officers who worked on Italian ciphers) to Algeria.

A little over three months later, on October 1, 1940, the former Bruno, now renamed Cadix, resumed work, at the Chateau des Fouzes near the historic town of Uzes, 50 miles northwest of Marseilles in unoccupied "Vichy" France. Langer's Polish unit, codenamed *Ekspozytura 300* (Field Office 300), reported directly by radio to the Polish commander-in-chief's staff in London. The Polish team's duties included collaboration with Polish intelligence organizations in France and North Africa. But in the meantime the Germans had once again changed their procedures for transmitting message keys, and as a result the Poles' Zygalski sheets had become useless. They now worked on other ciphers. After seven and a half years, their involvement with Enigma decryption had come to an end.

On January 9, 1942, the three Polish mathematician-cryptologists were reduced to two when the youngest, Rozycki, while returning to Cadix from a three-month tour of duty at a Cadix branch in the Chateau Couba on the outskirts of Algiers, went down with the French passenger ship *Lamoriciere*, which had fallen prey to reefs or a mine. Lost with him were two members of Field Office 300's Russian section, Captain Jan Gralinski (chief of the three-man section) and Piotr Smolenski (like Rejewski, Rozycki, and Zygalski, a civilian), and a French officer accompanying the Poles, Captain Francois Lane.

In mid-1942, Rejewski and Zygalski were asked to test the security of the Polish "Lacida" or "LCD" cipher machine that had been constructed before the war and was used for communication with the Polish General Staff in London. Although the cryptologists had never before seen the machine, it took them no more than two hours to break the test cipher.

The designation LCD came from the initial letters of the names *LA*nger-*CI*ezki-*DA*nilewicz. Langer had headed the Cipher Bureau, his deputy, Major Maksymilian Ciezki (*CHEN*-shkee)–*B. S.* -4, and the brothers Ludomir and Leonard Danilewicz (Dah-nee-*LEV*-eech) had worked at the AVA Radio Manufacturing Company that had filled orders for the Cipher Bureau.

The Germans were keeping close watch over southern France, and were always ready to occupy the "Free Zone" (Vichy France) should the need arise. On September 3, 1942, Bertrand, the French chief of Cadix, learned from an official at the German embassy in Paris about definite preparations for Operation Attila, the German occupation of southern France that was to occur automatically in the event of threatening Allied moves. On September 25 Bertrand was informed at the prefecture in nearby Nimes about the arrival, in the vicinity of Montpellier, of a special German radio-location team. The hunt for Cadix was on. Every so often, at all hours of day and night, electric power was cut off to facilitate a precise fix on the Cadix transmitter. At the beginning of November, London notified Cadix that the Allied landings in North Africa were imminent. On November 6, a radiolocation team visited the two neighboring farms, but unaccountably neglected the Chateau des Fouzes. On November 8, 1942, Cadix learned that the Allies had landed in North Africa. Next morning Cadix was evacuated, on November 11 the *Wehrmacht* moved into the "Free Zone," and on the 12th Cadix was occupied by the Germans.

Rejewski and Zygalski, virtually alone of the 15-man Polish team, reached Britain eight and a half months later, on July 30, 1943, via Spain (where they were imprisoned for three months at Belver, Seo de Urgel, and Lerida) and Portugal and Gibraltar. They joined the Polish Army and were put to work breaking double Playfair ciphers of the S. S. Whatever the reason misplaced British distrust, amnesia regarding the Polish origins of the "Ultra Secret," or perhaps more likely, British desire to monopolize the benefits and glory of Enigma decryptment–the Poles were never again allowed to work with Enigma.

On November 15, 1946, according to his military service record, "No. 32145 Lieutenant (Sig[nals]) Marian REJEWSKI [was] discharged on repatriation to Poland." After having (according to Colonel Stefan Mayer of Polish military intelligence) requested and obtained permission from Polish intelligence authorities, he became one of the approximately 10% of the 200,000 Polish soldiers, sailors, and airmen at the wars end in the west, to return to Poland.

In Poland, for a number of reasons, mostly of practical and family nature, it proved difficult for Rejewski to find employment as a mathematician at an institution of higher learning and in the early postwar period he felt it imprudent to apply for a job in cryptology. An obituary published in Poland states, somewhat cryptically, that "on November 21, 1946, he returned to Poland, then for 20 years worked in the administrations of various concerns in Bydoszcz, and in February 1967 retired."

What had Rejewski and his colleagues personally gained from their unique cryptological work?

Not money. To be sure, Mayer has stated that before the war they had received a cash reward, sizable for the time, for having given their country the mastery of Enigma. Rejewski later confirmed that they had indeed received a bonus, but denied that it had been a princely sum.

Certainly their rewards had not included rank. Rejewski and Zygalski were commissioned second lieutenants after two months' military service in uniform, on October 10, 1943, and Rejewski (and probably also Zygalski) was promoted lieutenant on January 1, 1945. In subsequent civilian lives, both ended theirs humbly, Rejewski in an unspecified but apparently not lofty station, and Zygalski, according to Mayer, as a lecturer at the Battersea Technical College in England, where he died (probably near Plymouth) in 1978.

As for distinctions, Rejewski's service record lists only the Gold Cross of Merit, the Silver Cross of Merit with swords, and the Army Medal, all Polish and all relatively lackluster. Considering the uniquely valuable nature of their contributions, all three mathematicians would not have been excessively honored had they been given Poland's Order of Polonia Restituta, France's Legion d'honneur, and Britain's Distingished Service Order.

Rejewski, however, did not seem unduly concerned with the trappings of success. When proposals were advanced around 1978 to bestow on him the degree of doctor *honoris causa* he expressed no interest in attending such a ceremony. He was rather a private person, and moreover he was not feeling in the best of health. In any case, he did not live to take receipt of an honorary degree.

What satisfaction Rejewski derived from his prewar and wartime work doubtless stemmed from the knowledge that he had contributed to the winning of the war, and from the feeling that is enjoyed by those who have made unique discoveries or inventions (he had made both). When public recognition finally came–over 30 years after the war, in the wake of the revelations by Gustave Bertrand (1973) and F. W. Winterbotham (1974)–Rejewski gave unstingily of his time to all who wished to know, through interviews or correspondence, about his achievements. In his last years, he was interviewed by television crews from Poland, West Germany, and Brazil. A master of the German language and also fluent in French and English, he managed to keep abreast of most of the polyglot nonsense being written about Enigma. In 1980 he became one of the heroes of a Polish movie, *Sekret Enigmy*, that used Enigma as what Hitchcock called a "McGuffin"–a more or less plausible business that serves as pretext for a plot–for a Polish-cryptologists-and-German-spies thriller, complete with a spurious love story foisted upon Ciezki, who died in Britain on public relief in 1951. Late 1980 also saw a Polish TV serial based on the Enigma story.

At the time of his death Rejewski was living with his wife on *ulica Gdanska* (Gdansk Street) in northern Warsaw's Zoliborz district, in a spacious, comfortably furnished second-floor apartment in an apparently prewar building that was part of the less than 20% of the city that the Germans had not managed to destroy during World War II.

Rejewski had been suffering for some years from ischemic heart disease. Death came at his home, apparently of a heart attack, just after he had returned from shopping and was removing his shoes. He uttered a cry, fell back in the armchair, and expired. He was given a funeral with military honors at Warsaw's historic Powazki Cemetery, one of the pantheons of Poland's great and valiant.

Historians will, no doubt, long debate exactly what was the influence, upon the course of World War II, of the Allies' ability to read German machine ciphers. However, if but a fraction of what has already been disclosed withstands future scrutiny, verdicts will probably range between significant speeding of the ultimate outcome, with the saving of untold thousands of lives, and what Eisenhower termed a "decisive" influence–one that made possible Britains preservation as a vital base for subsequent operations in Europe, North Africa, and the Atlantic, and vastly facilitated the prosecution of those operations. Of the two great secrets of World War II, the atomic bomb and Enigma decryptment (using what Rozycki had dubbed the cryptological "bomb" and the world's first electronic computers that were at least its spiritual offspring), the second was not only kept secret longer–and much longer than necessary–but "as incomparably the more important to the conduct of the war, since it played a crucial role throughout the duration, whereas the atomic bomb merely put the seal upon the foregone conclusion. It may also be argued that the mirror image of the Enigma secrets positive importance in the Second World War has been the negative effect of its too-long-continued secrecy since the war: a secrecy that has made Allied victory seem *too much* a foregone conclusion and thus has distorted the United States' and western Europe's perceptions of their power to determine more recent world history.

It seems likely that future generations, in studying the history of World War II, will have to give at least as much attention to a handful of cryptologists–most conspicuously Marian Rejewski–as they will to the politicians and generals who have for so long hold the limelight.

BIOGRAPHICAL SKETCHES

Richard Woytak obtained his PhD degree in history from the University of California at Santa Barbara in 1976, and lectures at Monterey Penninsula College, in California. His chief interests are European and U. S. history of the broader period that brackets World War II. It was in the course of researching his book, *On the Border of War and Peace* (Columbia University Press, 1979), that Woytak had the opportunity of meeting, interviewing, and corresponding with numerous top political, military, and intelligence figures of World War II-period Central Europe, many now dead, including key participants in the Enigma cipher epic.

Christopher Kasparek graduated Phi Beta Kappa in Slavic Languages and Literatures from the University of California, Berkeley, where he was a student of Nobel Laureate Czesław Milosz. Later he studied medicine in Warsaw, Poland, and translated works by Prof. Milosz's World War II underground professor of philosophy and aesthetics, Władysław Tatarkiewicz. Dr. (M. D.) Kasparek's translation of Tatarkiewicz' *History of Six Ideas* appeared in 1980 under Nijhoff imprint. While Kasparek was in Poland, he became intrigued by the Polish connection with *The Ultra Secret* and offered to translate a book on Enigma by Dr. Władysław Kozaczuk. The translation, in preparation, is provisionally entitled, *Enigma Solved: How the German Machine Cipher Was Broken and How It Was Read by the Allies in World War II*.

A CONVERSATION WITH MARIAN REJEWSKI

Richard A. Woytak[1]
Transcribed and Translated by Christopher Kasparek[2]

ADDRESS: (1) P O Box 221211, Carmel CA 93922 USA and (2) 95 Welling Place, Monterey CA 93940 USA.

On July 24, 1978, the 39th anniversary of the historic Polish–French-British cryptological conference that opened in Warsaw, Poland, on July 24, 1939, and a year and a half before Marian Rejewski's death, Richard A. Woytak tape-recorded a conversation with the former Polish cryptologist at his home in Warsaw. Below are some highlights of this, possibly the only such extensive interview to have been recorded with the foremost–and last surviving of the Polish cryptologists who broke Enigma.

WOYTAK: [H]ow [did your involvement with Enigma] begin, back in Poznan?

REJEWSKI: Well, it was like this: At the time [in early 1929] I had, actually, stopped being a student [of mathematics at Poznan University]. I was writing my master's dissertation and was no longer attending lectures. But the other, younger mathematics students were still attending lectures. Well, one day or one evening, I don't exactly remember which, one of the younger mathematics students came up to me and said that on such-and-such a day at such-and-such an hour, Professor [Zdzisław] Krygowski [director of Poznan University's Mathematics Institute] wanted me to come to the Institute. This student had some sort of list, and he would go and tell each of the persons on the list about this. Not everybody was invited, only a certain number [of] selected students. What the criteria were, I can only guess. [...] I expect it wasn't Professor Krygowski who selected the students, but rather Section II [the Intelligence Section of the Polish General Staff] that had made the selection. Probably there had been correspondence between Section II and Professor Krygowski, and on the basis of this correspondence Professor Krygowski had given them a list of all the 3rd- and 4th-year students [...] who were close to graduating, and then Section II had by its own methods conducted some kind of selection. In any case, not all the students were selected–so much so, that even Professor Krygowski's *teaching assistant* wasn't informed. That was because she was, actually, of German extraction.

[On the appointed day and hour] we all met at the Institute [in a large] mathematics seminar room. We assembled there, and there were three men. [...] Later we found out [who they were], or maybe Professor Krygowski introduced them [...]. They were [Major Franciszek] Pokorny [...] Captain [Maksymilian] Ciezki [...] and a certain Antoni Palluth. [...] All were dressed in civilian clothes. At the time Major Pokorny headed the Cipher Bureau [of Section II of the Polish General Staff], Captain Ciezki headed the German section of the Cipher Bureau [*B. S.*-4] and Antoni Palluth was a civilian employee at the Cipher Bureau. [...]

[Palluth] was [...] a graduate in engineering of the Warsaw Polytechnic. [He was] a civil engineer, and so he was [...] from a completely different field. But he was also interested in short-wave radio. He was what was called a radio ham. And it was probably on account of his being a ham and also being interested in ciphers that he had found himself at the Cipher Bureau and was one of the oldest workers of the Cipher Bureau.

But to get back to that meeting in Poznan: Major Pokorny explained what it was all about–he said a course was going to be organized in Poznan, and he was inviting all those present to participate. It met once or twice a week for several months, a couple of hours each time. I don't recall exactly where it met, it was somewhere, at some military institution, some fort. It was always that way. Pretty far from downtown [and the University]. [There were] twenty-odd [students enrolled].

The three men lectured in turn. The first was Antoni Palluth, about whom I've told you, who talked about the basics, the elements of ciphers. [I]t was only many years later [in France, during World War II] that I discovered that they [had] quite literally–indeed, even uncritically [...]–repeated what was written in a French book by General [Marcel] Givierge, *Cours de cryptographie* published in 1925. [W]hen [Palluth] had finished, Captain Ciezki lectured. [He] spoke only about a cdrtain period [...] about just one cipher [...] which at the time was not [?] used [...] by the Germans. This was the so-called double transposition. Just how the double transposition was solved, was also spelled out in detail in Givierge's book. [T]his book was the basis of the course. [W]hen Captain Ciezki had finished, the third lecturer was Major Pokorny, but I didn't attend his lectures [...]. I had finished my studies at Poznan [receiving a Master's degree in mathematics from Poznan University on March 1, 1929] but I intended to become an insurance mathematician [...] an actuary. [...] Göttingen, in Germany, had a very good [...] institute of insurance mathematics [which was] Mecca [to persons interested in actuarial mathematics]. So I went there [but] I didn't complete the course [...]. The [actuarial] course at Göttingen [...] basically took two years. But after a year I came home [to Bydgoszcz] for the [summer of 1930] because [...] I didn't want to spend the vacation [in Germany]. [In Bydgoszcz] I found a letter waiting for me, from my [old] professor, Krygowski, offering me a teaching assistantship. A position had opened up, you see, and he was offering me an assistantship. So now I had a choice to make. Either to take over the assistantship and give up finishing [...] the insurance course there, or vice versa. Well, I decided to become a teaching assistant. So I didn't go back to Germany, but was an assistant [at Poznan] for several years. During that time, I began wondering what had ever become of the [cryptology] course. I began asking [around] and I found out that two of the students, [Jerzy] Rozycki and [Henryk] Zygalski, were.... [A]fter the conclusion of the course [...] the Cipher Bureau had set up a branch office in Poznan. Right next to the University, in the vaults of the local military command post [...] on St. Martin's Street [*ulica Swietego Marcina*]. [The office was housed] in one room [...] actually, it was a cellar. [W]hen I found out, I said: "Well, I wouldn't mind doing some work there too." Accordingly [the student] who ran this [operation], Zyglaski [...] contacted, wrote Warsaw, and [some] days later [...] the now [head of the Cipher Bureau, Lieutenant] Colonel [Gwido] Langer [...] came down [...] to see me and agreed that I could work there too. [...]

I don't know [how it was that Rozycki and Zygalski happened to have been chosen to work at the branch office upon completion of the cipher course]. Those who completed [the course] might be able to say. There [...] may have been some kind of final examination. [...] I imagine that there weren't very many persons who *wanted* to go into this. [P]eople had various plans [... Anyway, it was] Zygalski and Rozycki [who] happened to be there. Later I worked with them, too, but only for a very short time. [T]hey were younger than me: [...] I was born in 1905, Zygalski in 1907, Rozycki in 1909. They had started their University studies a little later, and finished later, than me. When they graduated, the Cipher Bureau in Warsaw decided [...] to close this branch office. From the very beginning it had been thought of as a temporary thing, you see [...]

[The Cipher Bureau had apparently not set as a recruiting requirement that the mathematicians be single males, though all three of those finally selected were.] Several female students had also taken part [in the cryptology course] but none of them [...] later [worked] in the branch office [...]. Then [...] in 1931 the Cipher Bureau informed us that the branch office was going to be closed. And

I was once again [...] in [...] the same kind of dilemma as two years earlier; either [I could] stay on [...] as a teaching assistant, or move to Warsaw and break with the University. Well, I decided to break with the University. [...] I took leave of my professor by letter, because this was all [happening] during the vacation [and] the professor was away, he'd gone off somewhere, to–I don't know, to Majorca, or wherever it was he used to go. [By] September 1, 1932, all three of us were in Warsaw [at the General Staff...]

[I]n Warsaw [...] we didn't know [the nature of the work that we would eventually be doing; all we knew was] that we would be solving German codes and ciphers. And we got our first independent job. Because, you see, what we had been doing in Poznan was, as I have said [...] the double transposition. We knew well, thanks to General Givierge's book, how this was solved. We did improve on a few things there [...], especially [...] Zygalski, [and] I also [contributed] a little [...] that was new to [the solution of] that cipher. But when we moved to Warsaw, we got an entirely new, an independent job: to solve a German naval code. That was [our] first independent assignment. [T]he material was a bit old, as it were; that is to say, what we got [...] was complete [...] In German–do you know German?– [...] in philately this is called an *abgeschlossene Sammlungserie* [a closed series]. And there wasn't too much of this material; besides that, we had no experience, we hadn't solved any codes. So it didn't go easily, but somehow we did succeed [in breaking] it. [A] characteristic feature of a code is that it is never really completely solved. You just [...] keep manipulating the material over and over again, you see, and you look [at it] and make guesses – it's a little like [...] crossword puzzles, like riddles, you have to figure out what this [code] group could mean [...]

But when the greater part had been solved [...] it was somewhere around the end of October, maybe the beginning of November... my boss Ciezki called me in [and] asked whether I had some time in the afternoons. I said I did. He said: "In that case, I would like you to come [in] in the afternoons as well. Only don't tell your colleagues anything about this... Two hours a day, in the afternoons." Well, I came in and then I found out what sort of material he had given me, that it was ... That I was now to work with this cipher. My colleagues kept on [with the naval code]... it was just a matter of finishing up... and I got the new cipher. Well, it soon turned out [...] to be [...] a machine cipher–it was Enigma. I can't even say whether I figured that out for myself or whether somebody told me, because there had already been some work one on it. [...] In a staff and particularly in a cipher bureau, it's not customary to ask [questions. I] didn't ask who had worked [on this]. It's only just now, only recently, that I've learned that it had been worked on by Mr. Palluth and by Ciezki[...] the head of the

German section. [B]ut they hadn't come up with anything. In any case, I got this material, and now my own work began. Shall [*laughing*]–shall I go on about this, shall I tell you how things went on from there?

WOYTAK: When did Zygalski and [Rozycki] become involved?

REJEWSKI: A couple of months later. Well, it very soon [...] turned out–and this was no cryptological discovery–that [...] the first six letters of any message held a special meaning. [Y]ou could see that by inspection [...]. As it turned out, this was a doubly enciphered key. Maybe they told me, that I can't say. Anyway, when I began thinking about this, I very quickly got results, and I succeeded in solving [...] these keys [...] these first six letters which constituted the key (every message had its own individual key which was doubly enciphered). [A]nd thanks to my having decrypted these keys, I also had [...] as a bonus some additional material that later served me in solving the whole machine. So if the Germans [...] hadn't enciphered these keys but had given them plain at the head [of the message] they would have come out better in the end. Because I managed to solved the keys anyway, and in addition [I got] this material on which I was able to work and solve the Enigma [machine] itself. [This work] went quickly–it may have [taken me] a couple of weeks [...]

WOYTAK: That quickly?

REJEWSKI: Very quickly. No–that part of it, just the beginning–the beginning. Then, having this... this...

WOYTAK: How many drums were [the Germans] using at the time? [...]

REJEWSKI: [...] There were three.... It depends how you count them... Four. Three rotors and a fourth... a reversing drum [or "reflector"] and you could even say a fifth [drum], if you want to count the so-called entry [ring]. But basically the ones that revolved [...] were three. [...] And the fourth was as in the commercial machine. Oh, something I forgot to say: [...] one day Major Ciezki brought me a commercial machine, when I already had the first results, so that I could get a better feel for the thing. [...]

And now, having [...] all this [...] additional material that [...] I had gotten thanks to the Germans' enciphering the individual keys twice [...] Oh [...] I must tell you one more thing. When I had these results, Major Ciezki made another decision. "You won't work in the afternoons any more; you'll work before noon, but you'll continue working in isolation. As before, don't tell your colleagues anything." Now I didn't come in the afternoons any more [...]. I got a separate little room, and there I [...] now worked [on Enigma] seven hours a day, instead of two hours [as before]. The idea was to speed [things] up.

[T]he subsequent work consisted in manipulating certain equations in order to solve them. Here [...] I ran into problems. [I] hadn't expected [the work] to go quickly, but in any event there was a snag here. This may have been in the first [...] days of December [1932]. And then [...] one fine day, it may have been the 9th or the 10th of December, Major Ciezki brought some intelligence material. I didn't know it came from the French. It might equally well have been furnished by a Polish agent. [...] But anyway this material included [...] tables of keys for two months. September and October 1932, so far as I recall. And this was a great help to me, because thanks to my having these keys [...] the number of unknowns in the equations was reduced, and I was able to solve these equations and one fine day, as I was sitting there writing, the internal connections just came out in the form [...] of letters or numbers, I don't recall [which]...the internal connections ["wiring"] for the first drum [rotor], the one [...] on the far right, which always [...] revolved at every depression of a key.

WOYTAK: Those were the materials from "Asche" [pseudonym of an agent of French intelligence who worked in the German Army's cryptographic service] which [Captain Gustave] Bertrand [chief of French radio intelligence and decryptment] supplied to [Poland's] Cipher Bureau.

REJEWSKI: Yes. [...] I later [...] learned that–I believe it was on December 8 [1932]-Bertrand had gone to Warsaw and delivered this material. I didn't meet him, I didn't know about it. All this took place at a higher level–he describes it in his book [Gustave Bertrand, *Enigma ou la plus grandee enigme de la guerre 1939-1945*, Paris, Plon, 1973]. [T]here is a mistake [in the book] and he gives the year [as] 1931. But later I corresponded with him, and it turned out that it had been [...] 1932. It was the eighth of December, 1932.

Well, once I had that, the work went forward very quickly. I don't know [for sure], I can't swear to it, but I think that by the end of that year, 1932, the machine was solved. Solved, that is, in the sense that the internal connections [wirings] in the three drums [rotors] and the fourth drum were known. Now all that had to be done was to build the machine, in order to be able.... But that took a while longer. So we did it a different way. An ordinary commercial machine was altered...Mr. Palluth simply stepped in here. I doubt whether this was [done] at AVA [the AVA Radio Manufacturing Company, of Warsaw, Poland founded in 1929-30 by persons who in subsequent years would be associated with *B. S.*-4, and which did work for the Cipher Bureau on a cost-plus basis]; it probably took place in one of the rooms [at] the Cipher Bureau. There was a special room where various such technical matters were handled [the "Clock Room," so called on account of the clock over the black-curtained door leading into the employees-only room] so it was probably there that the commercial machine was disassembled [and] the drums removed; [then] they had to be opened, the connections [wiring] removed and reconnected differently. Then there still remained–it was also necessary to make other changes, various small changes. I don't want to talk about all of that, because it's too–fairly complicated. In any case, you could write on it [the machine] just as [...] if it were an original [military Enigma] machine. A little harder: [...] you had to hunt for the ["typing"] keys. The keys would change their order [...]. When a typist gets used to one keyboard, later it's hard for her to type if the keyboard is altered. Well, the keyboard was changed every day, so the typing was rather tedious. But in any event it was possible to read [...] messages to which Bertrand had supplied the keys, for those two months, September and October 1932. Here if this interests you, I would add that it was very important that the months happened to be September and October, in other words, periods that belonged to two different quarters. [This is] because [...] the key consisted of several elements [and] one element of the key was changed only once a quarter. Namely, the order of the drums [rotors]. The drums were numbered: Roman numeral one, Roman numeral two, Roman numeral three. One could insert them [into the machine] in any order that he pleased. Now, at that time they were changed once a quarter. [S]ince September and October belonged to two different quarters, in September and October the orders of the drums [rotors] were different. [With] the method that I had been using to find the connections in a drum [...] I could only solve the [far] right-hand drum, the one that revolved on place every time [a key was depressed]. The point is that, thanks to the keys for September, I could solve the drum that was in the far right-hand position in September. And since I also had the keys for October, using the same method I was later able to find the internal connections in the drum that was at the [far] right in October. [...] So, in this way, I already had two drums [rotors]. [...] And the third drum [rotor] and [...] the reversing drum ["reflector"] now weren't so difficult [...] I managed to find them by other methods. So in this way, thanks to the fact that [we had] the keys for those two months [...] September and October [1932, it proved possible] to reconstruct the whole machine. [T]hen, as I recall, Ciezki said: "[...] We can't have you [...] solving [all] these messages yourself. Now [...] you'll work together with your colleagues again. [They]'ll solve this material for the two months, and I want you to think about how to go on from here." Because [now] we had the machine, but [...] we didn't have the keys [and] we couldn't very well require [...] Bertrand to keep on supplying us with the keys every month. Supposedly he *did* supply [further keys] but I never got any more [...T]he situation had reversed itself: before, we'd had the keys but we hadn't had the machine... we solved the machine; now we had the machine [but] we didn't have the keys. We had to work out methods of find the daily keys. And this, also, we managed to do [...]. Within a short time we had found [...] several methods [particularly] the grill [and] the cyclometer [...]. The cyclometer method especially was very important; [...] it required a lot of preparation, but after that finding the keys would take ten to twenty minutes: it would go very quickly.

WOYTAK: Did you ever have visits from Colonel [Stefan] Mayer [chief of counterintelligence in Section II of the General Staff] or any of the other higher-ups? [...]

REJEWSKI: Basically [...] once a day Ciezki [the head of the Cipher Bureau's German section] would come by. [...] Langer [the overall head of the Cipher Bureau], very seldom. And as for still higher [officers], maybe once, maybe twice during the entire period from 1932 to 1939–once for sure, but [...] at that time I didn't know Mayer well, so I couldn't even say [whether he was one of them]. I don't know who it was; they didn't tell us [...]. They just came in for a moment, then left. [Yes, they were] in uniform [...] I think it was twice.

WOYTAK: Did you explain your methods to them?

REJEWSKI Well, it's pretty hard to explain [these things]. All I could do was tell them [...] superficially. I could say: this is this, that is that. [...]

[The Germans made] changes [of] various kinds [in their ciphering procedures. It's] hard to describe [them] all here. For example, in the first period, only in the first period, that is, at the end of 1932 and the beginning of 1933–how things were before that, I don't know [...] the cipher operators made certain mistakes [...] As you know, for every message they selected an individual key [...] consisting of [three] letters. Well, they would make the mistake [of] favoring [message] keys such as AAA, or BBB, or CCC, and so on. This made things easier [for us]. But after a few months they were forbidden [to do this]. Hm! It's funny that after a few months [they stopped]... But then they started choosing other [cipher] keys [...] Do you have a typewriter? Do you type? [...] On a [Polish] typewriter [...] the keys go in a certain order: Q W E R T Z U I O A S D and so on. After a while, I know by heart how they go. [T]hey would pick three letters [...] three [typing] keys that stand next to each other. Or [...] diagonally [from each other] or like this... excuse me... But by then we already had them [the Germans] in our hands. So... it *availed them nothing [laughing]... that they forbade them ...* to use [combinations like] AAA, or successive letters ABC–phh–now they were using letters [picked] from the keyboard. Six of one to half a dozen of the other. That helped us too. To be sure, they had forbidden [certain combinations], but they hadn't forbidden using those letters... [And] when [eventually] they were forbidden [to use] three letters according to [the lay of] the keyboard, [...] we found another characteristic again. [...] There's no avoiding it... [W]henever there is arbitrariness, there is also a certain regularity. There's no avoiding it. For example, [...] they didn't use letters with the same frequency [...] some letters were used oftener, the Germans didn't like certain letters, I don't know which they were, X or something, and on the basis of that... [*End of tape.*]

WOYTAK: Were you present [at the working meetings of Polish, French and British cryotologists that took place at Pyry, outside Warsaw, on July 25, 1939]?

REJEWSKI: [...] At the working meetings, my colleagues [Jerzy Rozycki and Henryk Zygalski] and I talked with the specialists, the cryptologists. We split things up so that [...] Zygalski and Rozycki talked and explained things in English, as well as they could: they didn't speak English well in fact, hardly at all–but somehow they managed to make themselves understood. They talked with Knox [Alfred Dillwyn Knox, the chief British cryptologist] and I spoke in French with Braquenie [Captain Henri Braquenie of the French Air Force staff]. Since I knew some French, it was only natural [...] that I would take Braquenie. And... [*laughing*] and since my colleagues know neither French nor English, it was absolutely all the same whom *they* took, you see. [...] Just how much Braquenie understood, I don't know; but there is no question that Knox grasped everything very quickly, almost quick as lightning. It was evident that the British] really had been working on [...] Enigma. [...] So they didn't require many explanations. They were specialists of a different kind–of a different class. Knox. Later Denniston [Commander Alastair Denniston, then chief of Britain's "Government Code and Cypher School," during World War II located at Bletchley Park, 50 miles north of London] also came by briefly–but as the chief [of the British cryptological organization]. And Bertrand would also come by.

WOYTAK: Colonel Mayer told me that there was another person present.

REJEWSKI: Yes, there was [...], that's true. [...] But it isn't clear just who he was. There is a suspicion it was Menzies [then-Colonel Stewart Menzies, deputy chief of Britain's Secret Intelligence Service, from the end of 1939 the chief of S. I. S.]. Well, it's possible. [At Pyry] they said [...] his name was Sandwich. [...] But he only came in or a moment... made as if he wasn't even looking, just talked with Denniston [who] happened to be there. No doubt, it had been set up in advance that way, that he would go into that room when Denniston was here, you see; he exchanged a few words with him, I don't know what [about]. That [...] Frenchman Braquenie nudged me with his elbow and said: "Sandwich–his name is Sandwich." [*Laughing.*] And the man left–a moment later he left. It's one of those mysteries. But... Mayer claims it was most certainly Menzies. [...] Mayer met him [again, after the war]. It's hard [to imagine Mayer] making this up. But, then again, Bertrand claims that it wasn't [Menzies], that he knew this Sandwich well, [that] he was a radio expert, or something like that. It's hard to know what to make of this. [...]

SOME LETTERS FROM MARION REJEWSKI TO RICHARD A. WOYTAK

Warsaw, 26 October 1978

Dear and Esteemed Sir,

[...] As for the changes [introduced into] Enigma in 1938, the matter presents itself as follows: In short order, three changes occurred:

1. The first change, of September 15, 1938. There was a change in the system of enciphering message keys. Whereas until then all message keys had been enciphered from the same position (the so-called "*Grundstellung*"), now every message key had its own "*Grundstellung*," given in the heading. Consequently, our earlier methods of reconstructing keys became useless, with one exception. That exception was the S. D. net, which had not introduced the change in encipherment of the message key (the S. D. net introduced it only later, probably in July 1939). Thus we could still read S. D. messages, but for the remaining nets we were forced to create other methods. Those methods were the bomb and the perforated sheets.

2. The second change, of December 15, 1938. Drums [rotors] IV and V were added. This change was introduced also by the S. D. net. But since the S. D. net had not changed its manner of enciphering the message key, we were able to reconstruct drums IV and V, using the old methods. Thus we were still able to solve the S. D. net as before, since in this case drums IV and V constituted only a slight added difficulty. For the remaining nets, however, drums IV and V [entailed] a tenfold increase in the work necessary to overcome the difficulties that had arisen, or, what amounts to the same thing, a tenfold decrease in our output.

3. The third change: As of 1.I.1939 [1 January 1939] there was a sharp increase in [the number of] plug connections [in the commutator], making still more difficult the work, especially the use of the bombs.

[...] In order to present all this more precisely, I would have to expound all of permutation theory and the operation of our methods and devices [...]

1 March 1979

[...] I have in hand the two books that you mention, *The Secret War* [Brian Johnson, *The Secret War*, New York, Methuen, 1978] and *Ultra Goes to War* [Ronald Lewin, *Ultra Goes to War*, London, Hutchinson, 1978]. They show the role of the Poles in the breaking of Enigma to a considerably more faithful degree than did earlier publications, nevertheless the authors have not managed to avoid mistakes. I would point out just one:

The Enigma machine that workers of Section II [Intelligence] of the [Polish] General Staff had the opportunity, in 1928, of examining and analyzing at the Customs Office in Warsaw was not a military but a commercial Enigma. The mistake stemmed from misinterpretation of the words of Col. [Tadeusz] Lisicki, which both authors make reference to [Johnson, on pp. 311-12 (chap. 6: Enigma); Lewin, in the footnote on p. 30].

Whether the British or the Americans passed on to the Russians information obtained from the reading of messages enciphered on Enigma, I do not know. Directly, I would think not; indirectly, perhaps through the "Red Orchestra" or the "Dora" net in Switzerland. But that is nothing definite. [...]

15 April 1979

[...] About [Major Maksymilian] Ciezki, although he was my superior, I can say little [...]. What I write about him below, are largely my conjectures. He came from the Poznan area. When World War I broke out, he was mobilized and mustered into the German army. When the war ended, no doubt he decided, to become a regular army officer. In this character he took part in the Polish-Soviet War of 1920. Later, presumably, he received the directorship of the German section [*B.S.*-4] of the Cipher Bureau [*Biuro Szyfrow*–hence *B.S.*] in Section II of the General Staff.

Since Poland had [in 1918, upon the collapse of Russia, Germany and Austro-Hungary regained] her independence after about 150 years of bondage, there were no people with cryptologic experience. Those who worked in the just created cipher unit, were all completely self-taught, and so therefore was Ciezki. So much the greater was their achievement, for they carried out pioneering work. I imagine that, when Gen. Givierge's book *Cours de cryptographie* appeared in France in 1925, it became a catechism for the workers of the German section. In any case, when a few years later, in 1929, the cryptology course was set up in Poznan, it was entirely and literally based on this very book, as I had occasion to discover when, in France in 1939, this book fell into my hands.

But before that, in 1928, when the first messages enciphered by machine had appeared on the airways, Ciezki and Engineer Palluth had tried to solve the messages, and it may well have been their fruitless efforts that prompted the organization of the Poznan cryptology course.

Ciezki had a family in Warsaw, I believe a wife and two sons. [...]

Since Ciezki was not only the director of the Cipher Bureau's German section but also deputy to the Chief of the entire Cipher Bureau [Langer], he had a great deal of organizing work [on his hands, including supervision of the monitoring stations at Starogard in the Polish Corridor, at Poznan, and at Krzestawice outside of Krakow] and probably by the thirties he was no longer directly working at solving ciphers. As a superior he was very pleasant and very tactful, as indeed was also his chief, Col. Langer.

Were I to characterize Ciezki in a few words, I would say that he was a pioneer in the field of German ciphers and an excellent and tireless organizer of the Bureau's German section. [...]

25 November 1979

[...] About my colleague Jerzy Rozycki, I do not have too much to say. He was the youngest of our trio; he was 4 years younger than me, having been born on 24.VII.1909 [24 July 1909]. He hailed from the Kiev area [in the Ukraine]. His father was a pharmacist. He went to school, so far as I know, in Wyszkow, not far from Warsaw, but he studied in Poznan–simultaneously both mathematics and geography. All three of us began work at the Cipher Bureau on 1.IX.1932 [1 September 1932] and we always worked together, indeed in one room, with the exception of several months in 1932 when I worked completely alone. As a cryptologist he had several nice ideas, [with regard] not only [to] the Enigma cipher but also [to] other ciphers. As a person, he was a very good friend, cheerful, sociable. He died on 9.I.1942 [9 January 1942] when, while returning from Algiers to France, the ship on which he was sailing, the Lamoriciere, sank after hitting submerged reefs or perhaps [a] mine. They had married shortly before the war in Poland, and when he left Poland [in September 1939] he left behind his wife and a child of several months. His son is presently living in England. [...]

To my letter of April 15 of this year I would like to add a few bits of information about Major Maksymilian Ciezki, as in the interim I have met his son, the only one of [his] three [sons] who survives. What did I learn from him? His father was born in 1899 and died on 9.XI.1951. [...] He came from Szamotuty [15 miles northwest of Poznan] in Wielkopolska [western Poland]. [Ciezki's home town–15,200 population in 1975–had, in the second half of the 19th century, been a strong center of Polish nationalism, and later an important center of the Western Polish Uprising of 1918-19 against German Occupation.] He married a woman from Wilno [now Vilnius, capital of Soviet Lithuania]. He took part in the Western Polish Uprising of 1918/19. [...]

With best regards,
M. Rejewski

BIOGRAPHICAL SKETCHES

Richard Woytack obtained his PhD degree in history from the University of California at Santa Barbara in 1976, and lectures at Monterey Peninsula College, in California. His chief interests are European and U. S. history of the broader period that brackets World War II. It was in the course of researching his book, *On the Border of War and Peace* (Columbia University Press, 1979) that Woytak had the opportunity of meeting, interviewing and corresponding with numerous top political, military and intelligence figures of the World War II-period Central Europe, many now dead, including key participants in the Enigma cipher epic.

Christopher Kasparek graduated Phi Beta Kappa in Slavic Languages and Literatures from the University of California, Berkeley, where he was a student of Nobel laureate Czesław Miłosz. Later he studied medicine in Warsaw, Poland, and translated works by Prof. Miłosz's World War II underground professor of philosophy and aesthetics, Władysław Tatarkiewicz. Dr. (M. D.) Kasparek's translation of Tatarkiewicz' *History of Six Ideas* appeared in 1980 under Nijhoff imprint. While Kasparek was in Poland, he became intrigued by the Polish connection with *The Ultra Secret* and offered to translate a book on Enigma by Dr. Władysław Kozaczuk. The translation, in preparation, is provisionally entitled, *Enigma Solved: How the German Machine Cipher Was Broken and How It Was Read by the Allies in World War II*.

BOMBE ! I COULD HARDLY BELIEVE IT![*]

ROBERT I. ATHA

The article on the Enigma and Bombe (NCVA *Cryptolog* Fall 1984) brought back many memories of the time I spent on the program. When I saw the pictures of the equipment, I could hardly believe my eyes. I never believed that pictures of this complex or of the equipment would ever be made. I worked on the equipment from August or September of 1943 until the end of the war with Japan.

My previous assignment had been on a Radio Finger Print (RFP) project under CPOs Detterick and Bill Pick, and I worked at some little RCA radio station taken over by the Navy near Washington, D. C. My change in assignment came about a month after I had married my childhood sweetheart and we moved into a brand new apartment in Congress Heights, a suburb of Washington, not too far from Bellevue. My initial orders were for TDY to Dayton, Ohio, to work at the National Cash Register Company (NCR) for about six weeks. My wife and I sublet our apartment and went to Dayton on a second honeymoon, and I worked at NCR from about 0800 until 2200 or 2300 at night.

The 'Bombe' equipment was being manufactured at the National Cash Register Company. There were already quite a number of Navy personnel there, and the final checkout, assembly and testing was underway when I arrived. Design, fabrication and piece-part assembly was practically finished, and the machines were being made ready.

Upon reporting for work, I was assigned to a civilian employee of NCR. He and I built, assembled and tested machines. I learned how by the process of 'osmosis' or 'on-the-job' training. I was never given an adequate briefing on the purpose, or theory of operation, and I don't think I ever saw a schematic diagram. The 'need-to-know' principle prevailed. Either it was hoped the Navy personnel would absorb what knowledge they needed, or there was such an urgency that the primary objective was to get these things working and into operation as quickly as possible. Nevertheless, we learned and at the end of six weeks I could trouble shoot, fix and maintain just about anything on these monsters except a few little things like relay adjustment and some chassis repair.

The design of the machine was fairly good, probably 'state-of-the-art' as it existed at that time and as modified by the urgency of design and development. The machine was laid out to reduce down time. This worked well for electrical problems and procedures for isolating malfunctions to a specific chassis were developed. Instead of repairing a defective chassis, we replaced it with a spare chassis and put the machine back in operation. The defective chassis was repaired in the maintenance laboratory at a later time. The substitution method was sometimes used to correct problems when we weren't sure because of the intermittent nature of the malfunction.

There were many things of a mechanical nature that would break or need adjustment and this type of maintenance had to be done on the machine – there was no quick mechanical substitution. One of our most annoying little problems was broken carbon commutator brushes. These took time to replace and there were hundreds of brushes on each machine. To replace a brush, it was necessary to remove a brush-holder, and turn it so we could work from the back to put in a new brush, while at the same time being careful not to break any more exposed brushes. Because of the complicated nature of this electro-mechanical marvel, we had more mechanic-type than electronic-type personnel assigned to maintenance crews.

After our training period at NCR, we were sent back to Washington. Our duty station was 3801 Nebraska Avenue N. W. I had never before seen or heard of 3801 Nebraska. What I saw were buildings formerly used by a private girl's school, which had been taken over by the Navy. It was an extremely secure area, with two high chain-link fences enclosing it, and guarded by Marine Corps personnel. Across the street, they were building or just finishing the building of barracks for the WAVE personnel who would be operating the machines we built.

Entry into a building was on a need-to-know basis, and our group had access to only one building. This building was brand new, designed and built for these machines. It had a basement for tools, supplies, lockers and dressing room with showers for the men, D. C. generating equipment, and an air compressor. It also had a receiving and loading platform at the basement level plus two floors above the basement to house the machines. There was also a large elevator suitable to carry one machine up to the operating floors.

Along both side walls of the machine room, large refrigeration air conditioners were installed at about ten foot intervals between windows. Overhead there were exhaust ducts to carry away heat. These 'Bombe' machines generated a great deal of heat and neither the machines nor the operators could have functioned very long, summer or winter, without these air conditioning units. The heat in each machine was generated by over 1500 vacuum tubes (multiple diodes, thyratrons and just plain amplifier tubes) plus relays, drive motor, clutch, brake, back-up motor, electrical losses plus some friction generated by the mechanical drive of the system. And they made a lot of noise.

So, our first job after returning to Washington was to receive these completed units, install and level them and get them working. Once they were in operation, they were never stopped, except for setup time and maintenance. The machines were kept operating on a 24 hour basis until the end of the war. There was never any down time waiting for crypto assignments.

Operationally, two girls were assigned to work together on four machines. It took two girls working together to do a machine check. Machine checks were made before and after each machine 'run'. If a problem was indicated by a machine check or during a machine run, a girl would make out a trouble report and bring it to the maintenance watch chief. I was one of the maintenance watch chiefs. Then we would take over and try to get the machine operating as quickly as possible. The girls got their crypto-assignments from their supervisor. These consisted essentially of instructions as to information on the wheels and type of run (long or short). The short run took about ten or fifteen minutes. The long run obviously took longer. After the 'run', the results, as recorded on a printer, were turned over to the supervisor.

It was mentioned in the *Cryptolog* article that the exact function of the equipment was unknown. Because of the strict need-to-know practice imposed, this total knowledge was probably known to only a few analysts and design engineers. The electronic circuitry certainly wasn't too complicated. I also learned one or two things by reading the article. Of course the basic purpose of the machine was to do the exact opposite of the enciphering machines, without full knowledge of the crypto principles involved and it was done at high speed (for that time). I never monitored wheel speed, so don't know how the trials or samples were made. The *Cryptolog* article mentioned 5000 characters per second and that's possible.

When the machine was in operation, it would run until a function known as a 'hit' occurred. The hit indicated that an electrical pathway had been found. The machine was running too fast to record the hit information, so the electrical signal activated a memory circuit, [which] turned off the power to the drive motor, applied a brake to the drive shaft stopping the forward motion of the wheels. Then a clutch was activated engaging a rewind motor which turned the wheels in the reverse direction until the memory circuit stopped the machine at the correct hit location on the wheels. The wheels might rewind for ten or fifteen seconds before the hit position was located, and the brake [was applied].

(My memory is becoming hazy at this point but I believe the next sequence was approximately as I am going to describe it.) [During the process an] indexing pin [was] engaged, the rewind motor disengaged, [thus] holding the shaft firmly at the proper position and preventing coasting.

When the machine came to rest, a scanning sequence was initiated in the relay chassis and when the 'hit' was located, the printer, located at the end of the machine was activated.

After the printer completed its cycle, the machine started again at forward high speed until another hit was located or it would continue until it stopped automatically at the end of a 'run'.

Today with solid state technology and state-of-the-art computer technology, operations considerably more complex can be done easier and a great deal faster. But these old 'Bombe' machines got the job done with the help of those WAVES living across the street from 3801 Nebraska Avenue, N. W.

The demise of this equipment took place after the war was over. We, the maintenance personnel, were told to destroy them beyond recognition, and we did, with screwdrivers, side-cutters, pliers, wrenches, crowbars and sledge hammers plus a big hot fire for the combustibles. They had served their purpose and were now obsolete.

BIOGRAPHICAL SKETCH

Robert I. Atha has a BS in Electrical Engineering and an MS in Mechanical Engineering from New Mexico State University. He joined the US Navy in 1941 and spent five years in the service. He worked on the "BOMBE" during its lifetime from NCR to when the equipment was smashed in 1945. After his navy discharge he worked in Research and Development in the Armed Forces Security Agency. He then became the Head of the Hawk Missile Program (Test Engineering) at the Army Missile Test and Evaluation Center in White Sands. He retired from that agency in 1971 as Chief, Low Altitude Projects Branch. Currently he lives in New Mexico.

WHO WAS THE THIRD MAN AT PYRY?

Patrick Beesly

ABSTRACT: The third Britisher who, in addition to Alastair Denniston and Dillwyn Knox, met the Poles near Pyry in 1939 to to receive a copy of the Enigma machine has been wrongly identified as Stewart Menzies, head of the British foreign intelligence service. In fact he was Humphrey Sandwith, head of the Admiralty's interception and direction-finding service.

KEYWORDS: Menzies, Sandwich, Sandwith, Pyry, Enigma.

On 24 July 1939 representatives of the French *Service de Renseignements* and of the British Secret Intelligence Service met with some of their opposite numbers of the Polish Intelligence Service in the forest near Pyry, a town some 20 kilometers southeast of Warsaw. Six weeks later such a meeting would have been impossible because Germany had invaded, and was rapidly overrunning, Poland. But as it was, in the very nick of time, this most secret conference resulted in the presentation by the Poles to the French and the British of all the fruits of their successful attack, codenamed Wicher, on the German Enigma cipher system, and a firm agreement for future co-operation between the cryptanalysis teams of the three countries. This was to have a profound, some would say a decisive, influence on the outcome of World War II.

All this is now common knowledge, although there still seems to be some dispute amongst the experts (of whom I am certainly not one) about the exact value of the Polish contribution. Professor F. H. Hinsley has stated that it merely helped the British codebreakers at Bletchley Park by a matter of months [1], but even if one accepts this view (which many do not), months were as vital as years in 1940, when Britain stood alone against the triumphant Nazis. I think that we must all agree that the British, and the free world, owe a great debt to the Poles.

As a footnote to history it may therefore be of interest to try to establish just who were these individuals who reached this remarkable agreement - for nations do not give away their most precious secrets out of mere sentiment and without hard bargaining for a *quid pro quo*. There is no doubt that the French contingent consisted of Captain Gustave Bertrand, head of the cryptographic-espionage section of the *Service de Renseignements*, and a French cryptanalyst, Captain Henri Braquenié. The Polish party was undoubtedly headed by Colonel Gwido Langer, codenamed 'Luc' (appropriately to English speakers), and included Colonel Stefan Mayer, both of the Polish Secret Service, and a number of the cryptanalysts from the 4th, or German, Section of the Biuro Szyfrow, or Cipher Bureau, of the Polish General Staff, one of whom was certainly the mathematician and leading Enigma cryptànalyst, Marion Rejewski. The British sent reserve Commander Alastair Denniston, head of the Government Code and Cypher School, the British codebreaking agency, and his chief cryptanalyst, Dillwyn Knox, both of them old Room 40 hands of World War I fame. But there was also a third member of the British party. Who was this mysterious individual?

Brian Johnson [2] quotes Mayer's story that he was introduced as "Professor Sandwich, a Cambridge mathematician." Ronald Lewin [3], an Oxford man, claimed the doubtful honor for his old university. But both Johnson and Lewin agree that the deception was unsuccessful and that it was obvious to all that the third member of the British team was neither a professor nor a mathematician. Mayer stated that when, some years later, he met Sir Stewart Menzies, who in 1939 was deputy head, but by 1940 head, of the British Secret Intelligence Service, he immediately recognized the fraudulent 'Professor' and that Menzies did not deny it. Johnson accepts this claim with some reservations, Lewin wholeheartedly, and Lewin's great and well-deserved reputation has persuaded a number of other reputable writers, including Peter Calvocoressi and Wladyslaw Kozaczuk [4], to follow suit.

I have always had my doubts about the identification of Menzies as the "third man." I argued unsuccessfully with my friend Ronald Lewin about it. Menzies was a suave Old Etonian, ex-Life Guards' man, a member of White's club, son of a lady-in-waiting to Queen Mary, and typical of a section of the pre-war SIS. He had little technical knowledge and none, so far as I know, of codebreaking. Why should he have been included in a party of experts? Had he been given authority to decide what might or might not be offered to the Poles? If so, he seems to have played a very minor role in the discussions. On the other hand, I remembered [5] a chance postwar remark of Admiral John Godfrey (the brilliant director of naval intelligence from the beginning of 1939 until the end of 1942), who was married to a cousin of mine and whom I knew well.

"I sent Humphrey Sandwith to that meeting in Poland just before the war," he told me, more or less *en passant*. Now <u>there</u> was a likely character. Commander Sandwith was the head of the joint Intelligence/Signals section of the Admiralty's Operational Intelligence Centre, NID/DSD 9. This section was responsible for the development and administration of the Royal Navy's 'Y' interception and direction-finding service. A signalman, a technical expert, a man who could speak with authority to the Poles about one area in which Britain could certainly offer them help: the ability to intercept German radio messages worldwide, the first essential for successful cryptanalysis. Then there was the coincidence of the names – had the Poles just misheard? Polish names were not that easy for Englishmen to get their tongues round; why should English names be any easier for a Pole? All this seemed to me to lend substance to Godfrey's chance remark, but it did not add up to proof. Moreover, when I was writing my biography of Godfrey, I endeavored to get confirmation of my theory from Clive Loehnis [6], Sandwith's deputy at the time, and from Norman Denning [7], the father of the OIC. Both of them told me, truthfully I am sure, that they had no knowledge of any such mission by Sandwith and that they did not even recollect his absence from the Admiralty at any period just before the outbreak of war. I did not find this surprising. After all, the short Pyry meeting could hardly have been more secret and, unless and until positive results in the shape of decrypts of German signals became available, there was no reason why officers even of Loehnis's and Denning's calibre should be informed. However, I still felt it difficult to challenge historians of Lewin's and Calvocoressi's stature, and more or less forgot the matter.

I was therefore delighted to learn in 1984, on the authority of Professor Jean Stengers [8], that Bertrand had written indignantly to him to deny that the 'Professor' was Menzies. He was, affirmed Bertrand, "*Commander Sandwith, le Chef du Service d'Interception de l'Admirauté, qui m'était connu avant de venir a Pyry et n'avait aucune possibilité de ressemblance avec Menzies, que je connaissais encore mieux*" ("...who was known to me before coming to Pyry and had no possibility of resembling Menzies, whom I knew even better").

I think this completely independent confirmation of my identification of the 'Professor' must dispose of the Menzies story once and for all. The third man was Humphrey Sandwith. The episode provides two lessons for historians and researchers. Memory, unless substantiated by other sources, should not be accepted as proof. And the mere repetition of a dubious story by one author after another does not make that story any the more accurate.

NOTES

1. *British Intelligence in the Second World War*, Vol. 1 (HMSO, 1979), p. 494.
2. *The Secret War*, (BBC, 1978), p. 318.
3. *Ultra Goes to War*, (Hutchinson, 1978), p. 43.
4. *Top Secret Ultra*, (Pantheon Books, 1980), p. 36; *Enigma*, (University Publications of America, 1984), p. 59.
5. *Very Special Admiral.* (Hamish Hamilton, 1980) p. 119.
6. Commander Sir Clive Loehnis KCMG, later head of GCHQ.
7. Vice-Admiral Sir Norman Denning KBE.
8. *The Missing Dimension*, eds. Christopher Andrew and David Dilks (Macmillan, 1984), p. 272.

BIOGRAPHICAL SKETCH

Patrick Beesly is the author of *Very Special Intelligence* (1977), a study of the Admiralty's Operational Intelligence Centre, in which he worked, using Ultra intelligence, *Very Special Admiral* (1980), a biography of Admiral John Godfrey, the director of naval intelligence, and *Room 40* (1982), in part a biography of Admiral Sir William Reginald Hall. A Cambridge graduate and a retired businessman, Patrick Beesly died 16 August 1986.

SOME OF MY WARTIME EXPERIENCES

William P. Bundy

ADDRESS: 1087 Great Road, Princeton NJ 08540 USA.

ABSTRACT: The head of the American contingent at Britain's Government Code and Cypher School (GC&CS) at Bletchley during World War II tells how he got into cryptology and about his social and administrative experiences as commanding officer of the 6813th Detachment.

KEYWORDS: Bundy, Bletchley, Government Code and Cypher School, GC&CS, 6813th Detachment.

[This is the edited transcript of a speech give by William P. Bundy at the dinner of the annual convention of the American Cryptogram Association in Union, New Jersey, on August 21, 1982.

None of his biographies — as in *Who's Who in America* — specify what he was doing in the army. His talk cleared up the mystery.]

There really isn't that much mystery about what I was doing during the war. That is what I am going to talk about, if you can take it at this hour. Namely a reminiscence on being the nominal, and I do mean very much the nominal, commander of the American Signal Corps Detachment, the cryptanalytical detachment that worked with the British at Bletchley on the Enigma and some other systems but mostly the Enigma problem. We had what I would still regard as a unique experiment in international living. An experiment in thinking together, as well as a dramatic exposure to the greatest overall achievement in terms of practical effects, certainly in cryptanalytic history. I would think that a safe statement; Mr. Historian [David Kahn], is that a safe statement? So it's what I am going to tell you about.

I hope to do this from just a personal standpoint, not throwing any new technical light on it although I'll be happy to pursue one or two little leads on it as I go along — and I'm perfectly well aware, particularly in this group, that this is a little like a third mechanic in a fleet of C-47s talking to those who have gone onto the supersonic era. In other words, in its time this was an absolutely extraordinary feat of intellect on the British part to have brought this about, but the times have moved on and the techniques have, I would think, now become a part of history and not a part of anything other than some lessons, some very important lessons to be learned. Some or most of which Gordon Welchman, who is at our head table, has pointed out in his recent book *The Hut 6 Story*. It's Hut 6 that I am going to talk about.

But first just a word on how one got to Bletchley in those days and how the United States Army worked in this business. All this background that David was reciting I hope had nothing to do with it. I was sure it didn't in fact. In the beginning was the word, and the word was "greetings." That means your draft notice — personally signed, of course, by President

Franklin D. Roosevelt. In my case, this notice was received rather earlier than some others and that is precisely and exactly the explanation of why I was the commanding officer of this outfit.

William P. Bundy speaking at the American Cryptogram Assocation Convention.

I went into the Army at Fort Devens in Massachusetts and was sorted into the Signal Corps, and so got in the Signal Corps training camp at Fort Monmouth in New Jersey. They took everybody who had no visible talent or aptitude whatsoever for electrical work, or communications in the technological sense, and if they had a certain level of testing score under the Army General Classification Test, bing! Crypt School before you could sneeze.

As a matter of fact, it was not a bad way of deciding who was apt at this business. Later on when I was teaching it, I tried to use those marvelous baker, butcher, candlestick-maker puzzles in the back of *The Complete Lewis Carroll*. And I even exposed a sort of test batch of the students to it to see if this showed up better the qualities that were needed in crypt work, but the Army general test came out a little bit better as a predictor, not of intelligence — although I would dare not say that very loud in this gathering — but of the ability to solve the things we had to solve. In other words, that kind of intelligence. At any rate, there you were, you were sorted in and before you could sneeze, you were in Crypt School and marching up and down the length of Fort Monmouth. I think it's the same today.

We had a perfectly marvelous character, who unfortunately died two or three years ago after working in NSA for years and I'm sure known to some of you at any rate, Lambros D. Callimahos, solo flutist at Carnegie Hall and in Munich before the war. Later on he used to pour out his heart to me about how he couldn't go back after the time he assumed the war was going to last because his lips would never again have the strength. Very, very tough, and indeed he didn't go back, but made an enormous contribution at NSA. Lambros walking back and forth was a mischievous sort of character and he'd throw the beat off. We'd be saying hup, two, three, four and Lambros would be saying hup, huh, three, four. Just throw you off enough so that the whole platoon would be out of step. And this, of course, would enable us to catch hell from every senior officer and generally make life more difficult. Then on December 7, 1941, this particular episode came to an end. I was shipped off along with a whole bunch of others immediately to Washington, not to do fancy, high-level things like cryptanalysis, but to pack boxes in which replacement tapes could be sent to the Pacific to replace the ones that had been lost in the Philippines and other places. The whole distribution system had broken down so it was a question of your becoming shipping clerks. That was my introduction to operational activity.

Then they enormously increased the size of the Officers Candidate School, which enabled some of us to get into the first 1942 class. After graduating from that, I went right back to the Crypt School because they needed more teachers. And so on through the summer and into the fall of 1942, when we moved down to Vint Hill Farms in Virginia. There, the degree of Ph.D. acquired a new significance — posthole digger — and there was another variant of the degree, LL.D. And I'll let you guess what that one was. And we went to school, or I tried to teach school, and go on with that even as we dug in the mud in Virginia. The installation is still there with its great big poles known to everybody - including, I'm sure, the Russian Embassy. And then in due course up to Arlington Hall which was the Army crypt headquarters, in January, 1943, and into a very interesting first test problem, which happened to be a system exactly like the one described in the recent book *Key to Rebecca* [by Ken Follett], where the key was a book. A very brilliant fellow got enough words together to figure out that it must be a certain kind of book and then through some rather devious means, figured out what book it had to be - and lo and behold out she came! It was a very interesting sort-of pilot run.

Then finally the day came in the spring when a group of us were pushed through a door into a briefing room to be told about something called Yellow. The first thing we were told was that after we had listened to this briefing, we would not thereafter go anywhere where you could be captured. End of dreams of glory - if there were any! Yellow was the Enigma machine, which the British had been breaking, as you know of course, well, since roughly early 1940. (I am going to be a little embarrassed talking about what the British have done in the presence of Gordon Welchman, who has just written a superb book about it, and who was the architect of a good deal of it, but that's what I have to do, Gordon, and you can correct me as I go along.) At any rate we were briefed on the machine and briefed on the project and we were told, a bit later, that we were to be early members of a group of Americans who would go over to work with the British on this. This was a high-level deal now described in British terms in the second volume of the British official history of intelligence in World War II by F. G. Hinsley, *et al.*, which if you can slog through it is a goldmine on all this. The idea was that the two nations should not get into a competitive situation either on the Japanese or German ciphers. Basically the United States should stick to the Japanese and the British stick to the German, with a kicker that the Americans wanted the experience, the exposure to this obviously massive and very advanced breaking operation and wanted to contribute to it. So, in the end, 40, 45 of us were just to go over and make ourselves useful, in effect.

And so off we went, the first batch of 20, in the *Aquitania*, about Aug. 4, 1943, out of Fort Hamilton in Brooklyn. On the way over we had to have a cover so we were fated to be pigeon fanciers. Well, pigeon operations were indeed part of the World War I Signal Corps. They occupied, I should think, about a half hour of basic training at Fort Monmouth and so we had to dust off that half hour. The number of canards about the activity and possibilities of pigeons that may still be circulating among the officers with whom we shared 12-to-a-man staterooms in the *Aquitania* must be legion.

But there was another great advantage to our occupation, and why it didn't blow our cover, I don't know. But one of our number — Arthur Levenson — was very good at a simple game that many of you probably know that involves the basic principles of binary mathematics. You have three piles of matches, and you can take any number from any one pile at any one time and the game is to make the other guy take the last match. It is governed by a very simple variant of one of Professor Hardy's theorems. Arthur would take on these Air Corps officers who were going to be pilots and pretty hot stuff and he would say, "I've done this for a while longer than you have so I'll give you 10-1 that you can't beat me." Then he'd say, "You're getting better" because they finally figured that 4-2-1 was a losing position or whatever it was, and so he narrowed the odds to 5-1. But I don't think he had the grace to lose once on that voyage.

Then we arrived in Bletchley — which apart from its euphonic name is about as drab a railway junction as you can find — 50 miles north of London and in those days the junction point between Oxford and Cambridge on a rail line that, as Gordon has just reminded me, no longer runs. Gordon has described in his book the first briefing of the first contingent. I should have said - I guess it was implicit already — that in putting this contingent together we had - and the "we" was U.S. cryptanalyst Frank Rowlett and the personnel people and myself who put it together — we'd been told, "Get the best there is provided it's even remotely available," and fortunately, of course, I'd seen at least all the generations up to that point of the crypt school so we did get an absolutely crack group then and in all categories later. The British — I think it's fair to say, though Gordon glides over this — had a lot of concerns about us. I should think that was an understatement. In those days, we didn't have the kind of contact that we've had in the postwar period. Most of them had never seen an American really to talk to or work with. They didn't know if we had any concept of security. Their general picture of the national culture was that it was apathetic, or even antithetic, to keeping one's mouth shut — and for that there is, I've got to say, some evidence. But anyway, they certainly didn't know whether we'd fit in, whether we'd work out. Moreover, here we were a hierarchical or at least nominally hierarchical military outfit, whereas Bletchley was notorious for the unhierarchical attitudes.

Well, to cut a long story short, they received us in the most extraordinarily open way. I was just saying this to one of your number who asked the question, "Were they condescending?" Not for one minute. We were needed because they were building up for D-Day. But they also were bound and determined to make this thing work. They felt its underlying importance as a sort of symbolic thing, and they were just an extraordinarily receptive group of people all the way up and down the line.

So we went in, fitting where we could, where our talents seemed to fit, fitting without regard to rank which was indeed the situation in the British outfit. It was not at all uncommon to have a senior officer obviously occupying a less important position in a given office than a junior officer. Rank was usually an accident, as indeed was ours, as I've made abundantly clear. And, unfortunately, it could rarely be adjusted to conform to actual responsibilities for which an individual, in our case in the Army, proved himself suited. So you had to fit where you fitted. It was an outfit that was nine-tenths civilian — I think that would be a fair ratio overall at Bletchley, though it was quite different at the intercept stations, and also on the American side in the machine outfits.

Anyway, we lived on the British economy in various inns and digs for three months while they put together a suitable army installation we could occupy. This turned out, as in the case of Arlington Hall, to be a converted girls' school and finally in December of 1943 or so, we moved in there and we built up to our final strength of about 45 professionals, with about 25 drivers, cooks, administrators and so on, the executive officer being the former deputy head of the Georgia State Penitentiary, Louis Dykes. I don't think he ever found a disciplinary problem worthy of his steel. But we were fortunate in having magnificent cooks, who had run a diner in Worcester and a bakery, a very famous bakery, in Philadelphia, respectively.

And we developed over time certain unique attributes. I should think we probably had by all odds the finest library of any American outfit any size anywhere in the world as the collection mounted of the various individuals in the outfit. Two have just retired as full professors at Columbia and at Harvard; others went on to be in senior positions in NSA and it was just an extraordinary and varied outfit.

But its life was interesting because it really had two different sides. As one side, you had the life of work at Bletchley. The British people included mathematicians, the entire British prewar chess team, the linguists, scholars in some cases in apparently very *recherché* disciplines but who were accustomed to putting together a picture puzzle from very, very few pieces. That was a very important skill, particularly for the interpreting of the intelligence and on occasion for the breaking of the ciphers. Some were eminent scholars, but the others were mostly young and particularly young in the breaking business. Gordon, you were what, 33 when you started? Not far off that anyway. Stuart Milner-Barry about the same. And these were the elder statesmen whom we used to think of in somewhat the way that a military officer might think of Douglas MacArthur.

As I say, we came in when they were building up. They emptied the Scottish universities of all their lady graduates (and there were only ladies in those days), and they emptied the squirearchy of England of their pink-cheeked daughters who showed up in Wren uniforms. We were all building up for D-Day. So there was a big burst and it was, as I say, an amazing crew of people. I mention only a few names — there's got to be a little name-dropping — but on the British side working over in the other part of things, which I'll come back to, was Roy Jenkins, then, what, 23 or 24, now a leader of the Social Democratic Party in Britain. In Hut 6 itself, as we were reminded when we had our reunion a year ago May, we had then at the age of 21 or 23 or thereabouts, a future British ambassador to the Soviet Union and we had, in a regimental sergeant major's uniform, again showing the significance of rank, a fellow named Asa Briggs who is now Lord Briggs, provost of Worcester College, Oxford. And those are just a very, very few, because if you took simply the scholarship level they were just extraordinary and they were extraordinarily dedicated.

At that same reunion I had an encounter that's just worth stopping for a second on. I ran into a fellow who'd been in the watch named John Kirby and asked what he had been doing since Hut 6. He said, "Oh, I went right back to the University of — well it was a west of England university of some distinction — and I've been teaching 15th century history. Except for those five years, I've been in the 15th century all my life." Well, there were quite a lot of people at Bletchley who had been in some equivalent of the 15th century all their lives. And there were others who were exceedingly worldly, people who left professions that were not exactly enormous job opportunities in wartime like the stage or modeling or dress designing or various things of that sort. It was a marvelously varied crew. And about 75 percent were women, I suppose.

So there we were, working in that setup, wherever we seemed to fit best and it fit because there was no way it couldn't fit if you came right down to it. You couldn't be transferred to anything else very readily and it would have been exceedingly painful if we had had anybody who didn't measure up. But they did. And without any demeaning jobs or anything of that sort, but not, as I say, always by order of military rank.

Then there was the Army side. And the Army side became the source of quite a little bit of conflict, because our installation was right on the main road, the Old North Road, as it is called, the main road north of London. This meant there was a constant stream of high-level military brass running up and back and forth and lining up this and that for D-Day, and they would see an American installation, with our discrete Signal Corps, 6813th Detachment sign. So they'd come in. Well, this meant that we had to be very, very spit-and-polish if we weren't going to get reported and have our own people down on us.

So we led a kind of a double life. At work we were mostly on first-name terms, informal, mixed-in higgledy-piggledy, behaving in effect like civilians in a very unheroic organization. Then back at the post, we were saluting and we were behaving in the most correct GI fashion for understood defensive purposes.

Then there was a question of leaves because of the intensity of the work — and this has a bearing on what it is like to do this kind of applied cryptanalysis over a long period of time. The British had an absolute rule that nobody on an active shift could refrain from taking a 10-day leave every three months, that you were absolutely away from the place, the further the better for 10 days, and got it off your mind. This was not just simple humanity; it was practical experience that without that people went downhill and maybe cracked up. (Although I didn't happen to know of any cases of that, I'm sure there were.) And so there we were: the men were simply told they were not going to be wanted at the job.

On the other hand, we had certain rules that applied to what was called, in Army terms, the Zone of the Interior, a command held at the time by General John C. H. Lee, otherwise known for his initials as Jesus Christ Himself Lee. And General Lee had laid down a rule (which I can see made a certain amount of sense for other outfits) that nobody but nobody in the Zone of the Interior — where we were obviously simply living on the fat of the land while the others were risking their lives and we were indeed very conscious of that — would take longer than a three-day pass at any time. So what do you do when you're confronted with this situation? Well, we devised an answer that I only revealed sometime later. The men would go off as they usually did to some distance — you could travel cheaply, they wanted to see the British Isles, they'd go off to Edinburgh and they'd have a bad cold along about the middle of the third day and they'd send a wire in, "Have bad cold. Ask extension," and we'd send it back, "Extension granted." And I never really plumbed what a dear friend and exec, Louis Dykes, thought of this practice, but I told him, "Look, if you want to have 'em go nuts around here, and be much less good at the job, fine, let's not do this. Otherwise, I will." It didn't happen all that often because there were men who were entirely happy to go back and forth or to just relax on post, but for some this was important and we tried hard to accommodate.

Then there was the question of food and here again I offer a datum of some interest to those of you who have done it or may do it in the future: cryptanalysts consume calories. That's a slogan. I will demonstrate it by the fact that we — at least, the 45 doing crypt work — had at least one and sometimes two meals within Bletchley Park, on the British civilian economy. They weren't the most extraordinarily nutritious meals — well, they were nutritious, but the man who invented the 40-percent-meat sausage is not reported in the annals of gastronomy. But anyway, you did have a meal and sometimes more on your shift and you had a good solid snack usually to keep you going, too. And you also had three meals available to you at the camp and they were very good meals and all that. Well, the Army in this case was more generous than it meant to be. It provided us with field rations, the same rations that a combat outfit would have had if one had been in a position to have its kitchen set up properly and all that. And finally somebody in the quartermaster corps got wise to this, that this chairborne outfit up country somewhere was getting field rations. So they sent about three people around to see what in fact was happening to all the food that came in on our field rations, and discovered that we were wasting less than the outfits that had been training to get into the first landing craft to Normandy! In other words, cryptanalysts may not be using their feet and their muscles very much, but they burn a great many calories. I offer that as an important datum.

Then there was a fourth problem, and that was getting married, because the Zone of the Interior under General Lee had a rule — called the Barmaid Rule for short — that if you were in the United States Army you could not marry unless you had given your commanding officer 60 days' notice and then waited out the waiting period. You didn't have to have approval, you just had to wait 60 days. I won't even argue the constitutionality of that; I merely say there it was. Well, it so happened that none of our outfit (and this was really very surprising statistically) married any one of the several hundred very attractive and interesting British girls at Bletchley. But one of our officers, and in this case I will leave the name out for his sake, had been engaged before he left to a young lady who was in OSS (the Office of Strategic Services), which was, as you know, into secret intelligence operations. Finally OSS sent her to London in about June, 1944, just after D-Day but before there was any breakout, about the time things might have started to break. So here he was — and they'd effectively been engaged and a barmaid she was not and so what did you do when he came to me as the theoretical commanding officer and said, "We are engaged, as you know, we always were, and we'd like to get married because she may get sent to Paris." This was just about the time that General Bradley and General Patton were breaking out of Normandy. And I said "Well, it's my duty as your commanding officer to tell you that the regulations say you've got to give 60 days' notice and you can't get married without waiting. But my advice to you, man to man, the sooner you do it, the better." And he asked if I would be best man and I said of course I would, if he wanted me. So he found a very cooperative church — the Marylebone Church right across from Madame Tussaud's wax museum — and to this day the official date in their register is the 60-day date although he and I and other witnesses know that the two were married 51 days earlier than that. I don't know which they celebrate as their anniversary but if I were they I would choose the one on which they were married in the eyes of the Deity. That was the kind of problem you ran into with the Army and with our particular situation.

Then there was the problem of promotions. That was less fun because it was very hard to get people commissioned overseas, very hard since you couldn't really talk about what you were doing to anybody but the senior commanding officer. The others weren't even in the picture — that's how closely things were held. You couldn't write out anything in the usual Army way and say, "X has just been instrumental in breaking an army key that had resisted people for the last six months. For heaven's sake, make him a second lieutenant." You just couldn't say that. You couldn't make a convincing case in any way that was compatible with the basic security of an operation that was known only to single individuals up the chain of command. So this produced unrequited cases of extraordinary effort, and I must say the patience of the outfit in that circumstance was extraordinary.

So, it was an intense life. It was also an extraordinarily easy one in many ways, as is obvious. The exposure to all kinds of things was very great. One could go to London, Cambridge or Oxford with special ease. I remember one trip I made to Cambridge that may interest some of you who go back in binary mathematics. There at the high table at Trinity College was Professor G. H. Hardy, the founder of binary arithmetic. (Is that more or less fair, Gordon? At any rate, a leading character in it.) And, of course, I knew who he was at least by reputation. So we talked about what? Golf tournaments in Britain in past years, Bobby Jones, Henry Cotton, and Bernard Darwin! Because one never could so much as hint at what one was doing. It would have been absolutely the wrong thing to say, to get into mathematics. "You must know that your binary discoveries are being exploited in all kinds of ways." Absolutely not. You just didn't do it. But to meet him was a privilege and an interesting occasion and that was typical of a little bit, at any rate, of our lives. For in terms of culture and fun we had a great deal, including our own theatrical productions. The show that was put on one year, I think, could have played the West End or even Off Broadway rather profitably.

Then you also had the sense that you just plain weren't going to make mistakes if you could humanly avoid it. I think the level of performance in that Hut 6 (with the American contingent I hope not letting down the average) was as near to perfect as anything I have ever been or ever expect to be associated with in a somewhat varied experience since then. There just weren't mistakes. You didn't send down programs that didn't fit. They might not have been the wisest ones; that was a question of judgment, of course. Things were not missorted. Mistakes in testing, when the machine "stops" came back from the computers, the bombes could have meant that you'd missed the fact that you had the key solved. I've been using technical terms a little bit but I see that our expert here knows what I'm trying to say. And there was the tension of trying to live up to that felt standard and the tension of knowing that you were sitting on a very big and very important operation.

Now, let me talk for a moment about where we were in professional terms in the breaking at that point. When Gordon Welchman briefed us on our arrival in August '43, by that time Phase I, the initial breaks and the setting up of the machine method of doing this, the bombe and all that, had been done and in a way I think it's fair to say, Gordon, the hut had already gone through a Phase II in the desert campaign in '42, when it had made a large-scale, enormous contribution to all that led up to the Battle of El Alamein and the subsequent rolling up of Rommel all the way to Tunisia and eventually his expulsion from North Africa. And it was now gearing up for what was to be Phase III. The Italian campaign kept it plenty busy, but we were gearing up for the invasion. We were breaking, and these are facts well known to anybody who's read any of the literature, we were breaking a large number of the German air force keys. We were doing much less well with the army keys. We were dealing primarily on the developed knowledge of standardized openings, occasionally closings, occasionally the short message that was an absolute giveaway. The one that comes right to my mind is the 16-letter message that would be *Lage unveraendert* ("situation unchanged"). And spotting those and then putting them onto these bombes that would test what settings in the machine could produce that result, enormously aided of course by the fact that the Enigma machine while it had enormous permutations and combinations, was still finite, that a would never come out A, so that if you wanted to test whether a particular German text could fit at a given point in the coded message, you laid it alongside and if it didn't collide so to speak for x number of letters — anyone of you can do the probabilities of this better than I can — you had a pretty good guess going. So that was its second weakness. Then it had supposedly been strengthened enormously by complicated crosswirings of 10 pairs of the letters of the alphabet but that, too, had succumbed to the ingenuity of one present and so you had a going concern. I can just say the obvious in passing that the Germans never did twig. That was established beyond peradventure after the war by one of the members of Hut 3 as it happened, in careful interrogations of top Germans, but made clear by their actions throughout the war. And obviously they lacked a first-rate analytic capability for reasons that David Kahn has analyzed as far as I know better than anybody [in "Codebreaking in World Wars I and II" in *Kahn on Codes*].

There were two parts of the Hut. There were some standard operations where you sorted the traffic. It came from the interception stations, you sorted it, you analyzed it so that you could say exactly who was communicating with whom, breaking down the call signs and all of that so that you knew that this was from X headquarters to Y headquarters and had the network all together and all the traffic that was in a similar key. By then the Germans must have been using roughly 40 keys, something of that order.

Then you had at the center the watch, which was where the analyzed traffic would be brought to see what cryptanalytic approach you would take. The watch had the job of putting, figuring out what was worth trying on the machines — which cribs you would use, how much priority you would give them, which was a mixture of the likelihood of your having the right answer vs. the importance of breaking that particular key, that particular network on that day, and you would feed that out to the machines which would test it. The machines would then say, this setting would do it or any one of the following eight settings would do it and they'd send them up in series as they came. Those would be tested and, if you got it right, bing, the watch would spring up and this austere British voice would say, "Wallflower is up." We used flowers for the air force, animals for the army, and colors for some of the basic headquarters in the beginning, and then there were odd bits for the scientists and for the railways — I never got it all straight myself because we didn't actually know them except by name. We just knew somebody thinks Wallflower — and that is a real name — Wallflower is important, let's break Wallflower. I can't for the life of me reconstruct now whether Wallflower was in Italy or Germany or whether it was air defense of fighters or bombers or what it may have been. But it was every now and then terribly important and we would go at it with a special priority.

Of the 40 keys we were breaking, and this is very rough from memory, six or eight were our staples, including some of the top-level air force keys. We were breaking another 10 pretty steadily so that we were reading enough traffic to pick up the cribs again and the possibilities. And then another 20 we were breaking only very rarely so that the cryptanalytic operation was divided into two parts — the watch, which was a roster of, I think it was about four of us at a time, but there would be special people during the day usually helping us, five chiefs of watch rotating in a roster of whom I was eventually one. We were doing the current thing, and allocating the bombes generally speaking, but with a lot of advice from the head of the hut, Stuart Milner-Barry, at that time and others. And that was the watch.

And then there was the backwatch, as I think we called it. This took on the really tough ones, the ones where you had to think very hard, where you had very little to go on because continuity was everything. The basis upon which we broke — and this again is no secret, nothing that I'm saying is a secret — the basis on which we were breaking was that the Germans in the air force above all, much less so in the army, broke in wholesale fashion every rule that we had learned as privates in Fort Monmouth in the first two weeks. That is, stereotyped messages, stereotyped addresses, stereotyped encipherment settings, every single rule that you could possibly have operationally, they broke through this overconfidence and I can only assume through some very slipshod training. And of course, that's the most fundamental lesson and it's the lesson on which Gordon Welchman has expanded enormously in his book — you've got to have systems that can be taught and carried out as rigorously as they are designed. And that's only the beginning of the lessons in his book, but it certainly was writ large for us.

This backwatch would come in every now and then and when they did, it was usually very important because the army was, of course, likely to have more direct information. At the same time, because the air force had its liaison officers with the army, that to a very considerable extent filled the gap in the pattern of intelligence. And if you wish to, there are all kinds of books that now tell you what was broken because the decoded messages or at least a very large sample of them have been made available in the Public Record Office in London. So you can see that enormous continuity was achieved and the contributions have been analyzed in various areas. Perhaps the most intense analysis since those became available is a book called *Ultra in the West*, by Ralph Bennett.

But we did have continuity. And during the 18 months or 20 months that we were there, we never lost the thread, or the main threads. The Bulge is a story in itself. As you know the Germans achieved surprise there because they were mostly on landlines and Bennett's book goes into that in great detail, with a very interesting analysis. But we never lost the thread. We never had the experience that our next-door neighbors in Hut 8 had. We were in Hut 6, and Hut 3 [the evaluators of Hut 6's solutions] was in the same low-slung building with the same common entrance — you turned right to Hut 6, left to Hut 3. Next door to us were the naval people. The breakers were known as Hut 8 and the exploiters and translators, senders of messages to the Admiralty in that case, were Hut 4. We never talked to them at all. I don't think I came to know two individuals in either of those huts during the time I was there, not because they or we were unsociable, but just because this was the sense of compartmentation that went through you. Hut 6 never visited in Hut 3. You never talked shop outside. In particular, you never even compared notes, certainly not outside secure space, with anybody about what another office within your particular hut was doing.

But the navy — and this is very vividly recounted now in the second volume of the official history as well as in Patrick Beesly's excellent book [*Very Special Intelligence*] — went through over a year, 15 months roughly, when it was unable to read the main Enigma as used by the U-boats because the Germans had added a fourth wheel position. Ours (air force and army) had three-wheel positions with five wheels that could be put in any one of the three slots. The naval version had four, and it threw them off so that for a year Hut 8 was on very short rations, as they say. The bringing back of Hut 8 and how that was done has now been told in an appendix to the second volume of the official history and is a fascinating story. And it's one in which I and surely tens of thousands of others, hundreds perhaps, had a very direct and personal interest because if you want to look at what the U-boats were doing in the Atlantic during the year when their traffic was not being read, and how that was building up by early '43 — so that and the highest sinking total was in March of '43 — I can only say that those of us who crossed the ocean from then on have much to be thankful for to our unseen and unacquainted friends in Hut 8.

Hut 8 and Hut 4 operated with the same battery of machines, bombes and, as they did so, the competition must at times have been acute because each was under pressure from its consumers, the Admiralty in the case of Hut 8, the various commands in the field in the case of Hut 3 and Hut 6. Yet I was never conscious of this problem being handled — or even that there was a problem. You can see how this would have caused endless trouble if you'd had, say, Mr. Haig and Mr. Weinberger, respectively the then Secretaries of State and of Defense, in those two huts; the explosions would have been heard in London. But in this case you had two men who were both extraordinary, different temperaments, but kindred spirits, Stuart Milner-Barry in Hut 6, Hugh Alexander in Hut 8. And it so happened that they had been respectively — I think I have this right — Nos. 2 and 1 or at any rate very close members of the prewar British chess team, they were intimate friends and as far as I know the issue never came up.

I have said Hut 6 did keep going right through — from the spring of 1940 to the end. But there were tense times. I remember that once the Germans did change a significant feature of the air force key on one circuit and we thought this would spread rapidly and we couldn't resolve it. And that was when I at least had the feeling that we scrubs were there on the sidelines with our uniforms on, ready to go in, but that the first team had better take over. About half a dozen of the special younger people who were Gordon Welchman's recruits in Hut 6 — Nigel Forward and others, some of whom had moved to other huts — came in at 8 o'clock in the evening — the new thing had become visible about 7 o'clock in the evening — and they got the answer at 6 o'clock the following morning. An illustration again that youth and stamina are considerable assets in the field of cryptanalysis. That was the only time we ran into a real check; otherwise, we managed to stay in business all the way through. There was briefly a canard that the Germans put us out of business, but that is totally untrue.

Well, that is enough. The literature on the breaking of Enigma and its companion, the even more difficult and technically more demanding breaking of the *Geheimschreiber*, the long-range big-order teletypewriter system, is now fairly extensive. (That breaking has now been officially acknowledged in volume two of the official history, so again I'm not saying anything that is new.)

The combination of what these did for the war is not something to expand on, I think, at this hour of the evening nor in the time that one should take at an occasion like this. I find it very hard to imagine how the war would have unfolded without what Bletchley did. There are those who say it shortened the war by nine months or by this or by that. I think it would have been just a totally different war in every respect, and the fact that this was done by an operation that maintained security has always made me kind of a bug on security with very strong feelings. These were not diminished, I may say, by having participated in the management of a very tragic war in Vietnam, where it was clear that the other side always knew much more than we did, not through any communications techniques but by a host of human agents. Having your government know what it needs to know is a tremendous asset for peace as well as war and I think that is awfully important.

Bletchley has been a slice of history, history from which there is much to learn. I doubt if any of it is of great technical relevance, or at least significant relevance, to anything going on today. But in its day, it did make the most enormous difference, and I would end this talk as I ended a talk on the literature of intelligence last year at a small lay gathering in Princeton. If you paraphrase what Winston Churchill said in the Battle of Britain, never has so much been owed by so many to so few — 10,000 altogether, but I'm thinking particularly of the core of this group. Ten thousand people who held a secret and did their parts and a handful of very brilliant people, one of whom happens to be here tonight who had the imagination and insights to set it in place and in motion. Never has so much been owed to so few by so many — and that includes all of us.

NOTE

Since William Bundy delivered this speech, the story of the Americans at Bletchley has been well told by Thomas Parrish in the excellent *The Ultra Americans: The US Role in Breaking the Nazi Codes* (New York: Stein and Day, 1986).

BIOGRAPHICAL SKETCH

William P. Bundy headed the American contingent at Bletchley, where Britain's wartime codebreaking establishment was located.

Bundy's father, Harvey H. Bundy, was an aide to Henry L. Stimson when Stimson was Secretary of State under President Herbert Hoover and Secretary of War under President Franklin D. Roosevelt. His mother, Katherine R. Putnam, was a niece of the poetess Amy Lowell and of the astronomer Percival Lowell, the discoverer of Pluto. Bundy was born in Washington on September 24, 1917, and was raised in Boston. He attended Groton and Yale, where he studied history, and then went to Harvard Law School. He enlisted in the army in August of 1941 and got out as a major. In 1943, he married Mary Eleanor Acheson, daughter of Dean Acheson, later Secretary of State under President Harry Truman.

After working as a lawyer in Washington for three years, he joined the Central Intelligence Agency in 1951, concerned with the overall evaluation of international intelligence. In 1961, he became deputy assistant secretary of defense for international security affairs in the administration of President John F. Kennedy; his younger brother, McGeorge Bundy, was Kennedy's national security advisor. In 1964, he became assistant secretary of state for Far Eastern affairs, serving during much of the Vietnam war.

In 1969, when Richard M. Nixon was elected president, Bundy left government to join the Massachusetts Institute of Technology as a visiting professor at the Center for International Studies, but became editor of *Foreign Affairs* magazine in 1972. He retired in 1984. He lives in Princeton, New Jersey.

"Code is usually easier to break if you read it right side up."

BLETCHLEY PARK 1941-1945

William F. Clarke

[William F. Clarke, barrister, received a commission as an Assistant Paymaster RNVR at the beginning of 1915. He was the son of Oscar Wilde's counsel and had been educated at Uppingham and Magdalen College, Oxford, and was fluent in German. In 1916, the Director of Intelligence, William R. " Blinker" Hall, recruited him for Room 40. Clarke was only an average cryptanalyst, but his legal training made him a good Intelligence Officer. After WW I he and Frank Birch, another cryptanalysts, were assigned to compile a secret record of the activities of the German fleet. Clarke was one of the few people who remained with Room 40's successor, the Government Code and Cypher School (GC&CS) from its inception through the end of WW II. He wrote extensively about the history of the organizations in which he served, his experiences, views and co-workers.

This is the third of four sections from Clarke's papers and it was written nine years after he ended a 29 year cryptologic career which began in 1916. Clarke's papers are held by the Churchill Archives Centre, Churchill College Cambridge, with reference identification CLKE 3. The copyright to these papers is held by Clarke's son, Judge Edward Clarke QC, and all excerpts are printed with his permission.]

Forsan et haec olim memisse iuvabit.

[Perhaps someday it will be pleasant to remember this.]

The receipt yesterday of a letter from my oldest and most valued co-worker asking for some information for a very old colleague of mine from whom circumstances have estranged me about a detail relating to our common work in the 1914 - 18 war has led my thoughts back to these years which were certainly the most unhappy of a very happy life so I will try to write my account of them as fairly as I can. I recognise [*sic*] that the events which made them so unhappy for me may have been partly my own fault and partly the result of a sequence of events over which none of us had complete control but compelled as I was to be in the role of an onlooker without any power or responsibility, I may be able to judge fairly.

At the beginning of the year all seemed going well; the Italian section which was under my control was going well despite difficulties; it is true that thanks largely to the stupidity of the detached section in Egypt, which had been established in spite of my protests while I was away for an operation, thanks to an intrigue by Titterton, more care had been taken by the Italians with regard to their codes which were now much more difficult but valuable work by two junior members of my staff Grey and Clarke had shown that a most important part of their communications were ciphered on a Swedish machine, obtainable in the market whose possible use by them had been betrayed by a plain language message. I had handed over to the Head of the German section Bodsworth, my most capable cryptographer and the others were fully employed on other Italian codes. I urged that work on the machine material should be undertaken at once by our general cryptographic section under Tiltman but it was some time before I could get this done.

In the meantime important developments had occurred with relation to the German codes; their machine had come into our hands and great progress was being made. Also the entry of Italy into the war had made the task of Naval section one especially as combined action between the two allies was developing. So in March 1941 I suggested the two sections should be amalgamated under Birch, he was in favour [*sic*] and I was quite willing to work under him as I had in 1919 but at first the proposal did not seem to find favour [*sic*] among the high-ups. At a meeting in April I managed to get my way re the machine and the cryptographic section took on the task which was beyond the powers of my heavily reduced staff whose work was fatally hampered by the retention in Egypt of an Italian captured code book which was in current use by Italian submarines but which in their inexperience they had put aside as useless; it finally reached us after peace with Italy. Early in June the machine secret was solved and a large part of the Italian traffic became legible. This was decisive and on June 15 the merger of the German and Italian sections took place; Birch very properly was to be head and Bodsworth his second, I was to be on the staff in a rather undefined capacity. Bodsworth's position was, I thought and still think was a mistake; he was very bad at managing staff; worse still he took over the management of the Italian section with a Professor Vincent as No 2. Vincent was Professor of Italian at Cambridge, a fine scholar but like many of his class good at his own classics but very poor at the language used by naval officers; when he was working under me my first task on arrival at the office when he had been on night duty was to see how many mistakes in translation he had made and send in the necessary corrections.

Bodsworth was too busy on his own special work to devote much time to the Italian part and was, I think suffering from an inferiority complex as regards Vincent whom as his elder at one time, I think, tutor or at any rate superior at Cambridge, he regarded with some awe. As a result Vincent ran one section with a protegee of his, Crichton, who was useless and idle.

However all went well for a time; the drastic change produced by the solution of the important German and Italian codes necessitated much increase of staff and reorganisation [*sic*]; in this I seemed to be useful. Kinsley, extremely capable had my old 1917 - 18 job of intelligence officer in chief which he kept till the end of the war. A few young R.N.V.R. special branch officers were brought in as I.O.s to maintain constant watch on current traffic; the head of these was Gorley Putt who was excellent in every way. In their early days I used to visit them early in the morning, before Birch arrived and try to train them in their job which after a little experience they carried out most successfully. At first the decode sections worked separately but on August 21st the German and Italian decode sections were merged and all their decodes were passed to Admiralty under one head, Walter Ettinghausen, a very able Oxonian who now I believe is a prominent member of the Israeli government under another name; he was excellent and one pleasant memory of unhappy years is the continued good terms which continued until I left, between him and myself.

The next memorable event which took place was a visit from the Prime Minister on September 6th. This had for me some humourous [*sic*] sides. I had known Winston Churchill for many

The Victorian mansion, Bletchley Park, which was the headquarters of the G.C.&C.S. in WW II.

years, my father was a great admirer and defender of his and I had helped him in the writing of his well known books. The day before his visit I was told by our chief that it was proposed to introduce to him some of the senior staff, including myself and Jimmie Turner. He duly arrived and was shown a sort of composite section, of all kinds, including Vincent who under the guidance of one Wall, a very competent cryptographer of my staff in the pre– amalgamation days, had managed to solve a submarine Italian code which should have been solved a long time before if Vincent had done his work properly. Turner and I were not presented. Winston made us a very nice speech of thanks and went off to lunch at Blenheim. He had arrived in the usual cortege of cars with flags flying and must have been spotted by the local inhabitants; for lunch the B.P. staff crowded out into the town and no doubt talked about the visit to all and sundry; late that afternoon an order came round to say that his visit was to be kept secret, another instance, if more were needed of our wonderful security which had allowed motors bearing the name of a well known tabulating firm to ply to and from our premises.

Late in October our I.O.s were put into watches.

Then came the first big row; it concerned one of my most able helps for many years; she was a Miss White who sent originally to be my secretary, I had found to have the makings of a quite passable cryptographer. She had done remarkably good work helping me; when De Grey came to bring up to date his knowledge in that line, I handed him over to her, so I did Lord Lytton who at one time was anxious to join us but whom I persuaded that he would be better employed elsewhere. On the reorganisation [*sic*] she had been left to work under Vincent and Crichton both of whom were her enemies and who were jealous of her, realising [*sic*] she was better at the job than they; in fact she often had had to teach them their job and point out their mistakes in the past so having attained power they were bent on revenge. In this they were helped by her temperament which was not easy. In spite of my efforts to prevent what I regarded as a calamity, they persuaded Birch to ask for her transfer; Bodsworth collaborated in this in spite of the fact that he had previously told me he could not spare her when I asked she might be lent to me for what I thought was a very important job. Another section was delighted to have her but her work was lost to the section. The full correspondence on this matter will be found in my files labeled The White Conspiracy.

This most unfortunate episode was my first break with Birch who had preferred others advice to mine; I think it shook his previous good opinion of me, certainly his attitude to me in after years showed a great change. All this happened in November and very soon afterwards I was taken ill with a complaint that was to lead to a severe operation a few years later.

Things however apparently settled down and our work went on but during my rather prolonged absence many changes took place. It should be stated here that, acting in accordance with the lessons of the previous war, it had always been my practice to circulate appreciations of messages decoded rather than the text; our experience in the early days of that war had shown that we were not merely a decoding but an intelligence section and that the higher ups made too many mistakes by their incorrect deductions. This was more easy in the days of the old type of codes when some words had to be guessed but when machine codes came in all the words were normally legible, only the language difficulty remaining.

While the two sections were separate I kept to the old method but as it involved a little more work, it was unpopular with my staff and they had while I was away adopted the easier course and the actual text was sent to the O.I.C. whose functions are described in "The War at Sea" Vol. I, p18. I personally think this was a mistake; during the prewar years I had always urged that we should be in close proximity to Operations Division as had been the case at the end of the previous war; the only result had been as I have stated in previous chapters that my German section had been removed to the Admiralty where it was completely useless and I had to build up a new one as the head of which I was lucky to get Birch. This development had taken from me all control over the Italian traffic circulated which I had exercised before my unfortunate illness.

However I found plenty to do, in spite of the fact that relations between me and many of the section were for ever strained. The mass of deciphered intercepts necessitated a largely increased staff and the establishment of a system of indexing and arranging the intercepts to ensure rapid ascertainment of previous information on matters dealt with in a current message. This needed a great deal of supervision as the staff entrusted with these tasks was of necessity inexperienced and many mistakes were made.

Another amusing task I had was to compose differences between Dilly Knox and Birch; Dilly was a genius in cryptography as well as in other matters but he was very temperamental and had to be handled tactfully or else he refused to play; I happened to be one of the few people who understood how to manage him and when these clashes occurred I was called into restore peace and ward off the resignation which he threatened. He died soon after and his death is one of the many for which the high ups at B.P. were responsible, another was Leslie Lambert alias A.J. Alan. Both were sick men and no consideration was shown them. This was characteristic; in the years before the war I had a valuable colleague, Rees, who had had his lungs injured by shrapnel in the First World War; in consequence when there was fog he was grievously distressed and not fit to work but when at these times I sent him away I was reprimanded by Denniston. The same thing happened when I varied the hours of one of my staff who was only temporary and was preparing for an examination; in spite of my protests she was dismissed only to be employed in an important job by the S.I.S.

In the meantime in March 1942 great changes had taken place at B.P. The diplomatic section under Denniston had been moved back to London; if any part were to be moved to this danger area it should have been Naval section or some part of it so as to be nearer Operations Division. This meant that most of my old and experienced colleagues went with it and so I lost most of my friends. Travis was now in supreme command under Quex's successor, a very unworthy heir, named Menzies who disliked me as he was connected by marriage with the Wilson family who had been the subject of bitter comment by my father in the famous Baccarat case. Of my real friends only Strachey was left and he was a sick man. Quex's death early in the war was a real calamity, he was a very brilliant chief who trusted his subordinates and to whom one could go knowing that if your application was wise, and he always investigated fully, you would get what you wanted, be it staff or improvements in organisation [*sic*].

B.P. now consisted of the three service sections and the usual competition started as to which was to be the largest, one had seen this in the former war and its evil results; staff was added to do useless jobs and thanks to the poor material enrolled the work was badly done. Advertisements even appeared in the Times asking for recruits. Naval section was no less to blame in this respect than the other sections.

Quite early on tabulating machines had been brought into use by us and while they were of great use in certain circumstances, they did, in my opinion, a good deal of harm as many idle people thought they relieved them of personal indexing; this, I think, led to the failure to solve many of the hand codes, as contrasted with the machine types.

The increase of staff led to the building of more commodious quarters and a large new block was built for naval section to which we duly removed.

During 1942 the war at sea was chiefly concerned with the submarine menace, apart from the escape of Scharnhorst and Gneisenau from Brest and very important the interception of Italian transports carrying men and supplies to Africa. Thanks to the solving of the Swedish machine this last was very successful. The work of the section had become largely a matter of routine, the Swedish messages were dealt with most successfully by a small section and the German naval traffic outside, the only really active work being in the hands of the circulating party under Ettinghausen and intelligence appreciations by Hinsley and his aides. The larger part of the staff was employed on record keeping. This required constant overseeing and a large part of my time was devoted to this. I was officially shown on so called Naval Section state as part of the Staff but Staff papers were carefully kept from me and most of my activities were sub rosa; however I found most of the subsections glad of my suggestions. I had learnt that my formal submissions were either ignored or turned down so except in more important matters I did not indulge in them. The section was now approaching the 1000 mark as compared with the 24 who had gone down in August 1939.

The Italian section had made no progress with the main codes; the famous submarine code displayed to the P.M. had been changed within a week of his visit, a strange coincidence which might have seemed curious but it had only been solved after being compromised by long use. Work on the German naval traffic had been halted for a while by their employing additional wheels but this had been soon overcome.

So matters went on in the early part of 1943 but the course of events was changing in our favour [*sic*]; things were going badly for our enemies all along the various fronts and our political leaders had started to talk about "Unconditional Surrender". Early in the year a copy of an Italian code "Sigma" came into our possession and helped our anti Italian operations. But Italy was already at its last gasp, the Axis forces had been driven out of Africa by early May and in July Italian territory was invaded. Negotiation for her surrender started and in August the Italian section personnel were dispersed to other duties; on September 9th came the armistice and charge of its remnants was given to me; these consisted of 4 or 5 and their job was to keep a watch on such Italian communications as were permitted and the more interesting task of investigating old traffic which had never been deciphered with the aid of a number of old code books which had come into our hands; these were very incomplete as no condition had been imposed as to their surrender; this was because it was an armistice and not a complete surrender so we had the same situation as we had had in 1918. It was however a quite amusing job and gave me work to do which was really worth doing, a welcome change from the preceding period. The Spanish and French sections were also put under me so again I had plenty to do and as the staff transferred was mostly old staff of mine less the senior members who had got themselves more showy posts, I was happier than I had been for some time. It was nice to be doing cryptographic work again even if it was of very minor importance.

The Spanish section had carried on bravely with its rather monotonous task as the traffic was of no great import but it had been recognised [*sic*] that there was always a possibility of Franco taking sides against us and in this work continuity was of the utmost importance. Once the codes of a nation are put on one side as of no moment it is very difficult to pick up the threads. This had been shown in the case of the French; in 1937 we were reading their traffic with comparative ease but they then had recourse to a system which, though we found the system, was too hard to decipher on the very small amount of traffic intercepted. They found it too complicated and reverted to an easier one but no effort was made to deal with it except as a very part time job of one or two of the diplomatic staff. My staff which the Admiralty kept on reuseing the moment world affairs looked calmer, had their hands too full especially as in 1938, just before the Munich affair I had managed, thanks to Quex's intervention, I having bypassed Denniston, to start a German section. This sounds hardly credible but it is a fact. This section had a narrow escape from extinction, as Quex, impatient of the little information we had been able to get at that time sent a minute to Denniston, asking if he thought our work was going to be of any use in view of the increasing difficulty of foreign codes. Denniston always a pessimist said " No" but I wrote a very strong minute, taking the opposite view; in it I said that machines were in use and this type of ciphering would spread and that in war there was a good chance of their capture. This turned out to be an accurate prediction. When war broke out this work stopped but was resumed shortly after the collapse of France; I was not told of this though I had studied the subject for many years. The staff employed had practically no experience of French methods and made little progress and the section did not last long. Now in 1944 we started again when we had the advantage of dealing with material that was that of a fleet that was allied with us; the traffic was scanty and progress was slow though now the Americans were collaborating but we had seldom found them of great assistance; the staffs they employed were very much larger than ours but our smaller numbers generally produced better results.

But in the meantime we knew of the proposed landing in France and attention was naturally focused on this; it took place in June and success after success followed with only a very occasional setback. The end seemed very near. My mothers death in October upset me and within a fortnight my old trouble returned; it is curious to note that these attacks of mine seemed to have some strange connection with my mental state; an immediate operation was averted; I wanted badly to be in at the death but I had to be away for over two months during which the last desperate German offensive after some initial success was repulsed and Allied progress resumed. My prolonged absence had of course put me out of touch with things and it took me a long time to pick up the threads and Birch's Staff had never liked me and resented my occasional interferences, they treated me with scanty courtesy, and took every opportunity to subject me to minor inconveniences.

V.E. day soon came. We had a thanksgiving service conducted by the local parson; I was deputed to make the arrangements as I had become a sort of office church warden when I arranged every Sunday for the conduct of the very nice little services which the padre, a charming person called Milne who could not do too much for us, always willing to arrange extra services at hours to suite our convenience. Some amusement was caused by Nigel de Grey reading a message to us from Travis whom he described as " Our beloved chief" a description I think Travis himself would have been the first to disclaim; able he was especially in working his way up to get the top job, pushing out Denniston than whom he was a much more efficient organiser [*sic*]; he was always very nice to me.

After this the work of Naval section really came to an end, after almost exactly 21 years of existence during 16 of which I had been its head and its founder; it had started with two or three members, never exceeded 30 before the war and finished up over 1000 strong; I sent a message of my thanks to Hope (N.S.L.), Rees and Miss White who had been with me in the early days, all three were now in London with the diplomatic show. Now two jobs remained, the first the future of the whole organisation and the second the preparation of a history.

The first was considered by a small committee on which there was a lamentable absence of those who had had experience of peace conditions which are so different from those of war; I gave evidence before it but my views carried little weight, I fear, though I never learnt what recommendations were made though I did last long enough to see some of the first steps in reorganisation with which I profoundly disagreed.

The second, as to which I can only speak of the Naval Section side, was complicated by the masses of captured documents which had fallen into hands. These were in the first place entrusted to a section which was quite unsuited for the task and my efforts to have the material divided into historical and cryptographical sections was only considered by of the junior Staff with no real knowledge either of history or cryptography and so remained without success. The task of writing the history of Naval section during the war was entrusted to the various existing subsections who apparently on the assumption that all had started from scratch in 1939 or even later; thus the identification of call signs, a very important job was stated to have begun with a Miss Linahan who had not had anything to do with it until very late in the war it had actually been very important from the very start of Naval Section in 1924. The Roman historian Livy says somewhere *Semper enim quod postremum adjectum est, id rem totam videtur traxisse,* a translation of which sage remark is "For the last stroke to a business seems to get the credit for the whole performance". Of course the question of a history on the lines of that in which I had assisted Birch in 1919 was under discussion and now (October 1954) nine years afterwards seems from the query to which I have referred in the opening lines of this chapter of events to be still in course of preparation was another matter for consideration and Birch at any rate hinted that I might be of use to him in this; he was given the job but I never heard any more about it; as it has turned out this is fortunate for me at least as I have enjoyed nearly nine years of peace in retirement. Travis informed me of the fact that I was to be retired on September 26th 1945, I received the formal notice from the F.O. on October 8th, a couple of days after I had made the acquaintance of Mr. Ernest Bevin, then Foreign Minister, at my London club of which somewhat surprisingly he had recently become a very popular member.

My days in G.C. & C.S., our official description, were numbered and on October 17th my old complaint flared up again and this time an operation was necessary; I left B.P. in a hurry that day and never went back; some of my papers were sent to me as they happened to be locked up in a box of which I had the key but most of them were taken by Birch and I shall never see them again; I expect most of them have either been destroyed or placed with the records of Room 40 O.B. which Birch and I among others so carefully put in order in 1919. Anyway they have gone and these reminiscences have had to be compiled without them which must be my excuse for such misstatements as have been made. I have tried to be fair even to my most bitter enemies to all of whom I must be grateful for nine years of peace.

Commenced October 24th 1954.
Finished October 28th 1954.

BRITISH-AMERICAN CRYPTANALYTIC COOPERATION AND AN UNPRECEDENTED ADMISSION BY WINSTON CHURCHILL

Louis Kruh

ADDRESS: 17 Alfred Road West, Merrick NY 11566 USA.

ABSTRACT: Great Britain and the United States seek a closer relationship between their cipher experts and Churchill admits decrypting America's diplomatic codes.

KEYWORDS: Prime Minister Winston S. Churchill, President Franklin D. Roosevelt, cryptanalytic cooperation, World War II, General George C. Marshall.

[All letters used in this article except two are from the Franklin D. Roosevelt Library. The letter from Gen. Marshall came from the George C. Marshall Foundation and the letter from George V. Strong came from an intelligence agency.]

Winston Churchill (l) and Franklin D. Roosevelt (r).

In early 1942, the issue of cryptanalytic cooperation with Great Britain was reviewed by President Roosevelt based on a letter he had received from Winston Churchill on February 25.

Harry L. Hopkins
Photograph: United States Army Signal Corps

The letter from the Prime Minister was extraordinary in what it admitted. After suggesting the importance of a closer working relationship between their army cipher experts, Churchill acknowledged that British cryptanalysts had been intercepting and decrypting America's diplomatic communications. That was astonishing because governments rarely, if ever, admit they engage in codebreaking and even more rarely disclose any attempts to break the codes and ciphers of their allies. Even in the United States, the most open society in the world, every WW II declassified document dealing with communications intelligence will refer only to codes and ciphers of enemy countries: when neutral or friendly governments are involved their names are deleted. Much to the chagrin of historians, this is even the case with WW I documents despite the information being 70 years old.

Obviously, Churchill's intent was to alert Roosevelt to the insecurity of United States diplomatic systems, but it is still most surprising that he did not choose another way to inform him. Less cynical readers may not smirk at his promise that, "From the moment when we became allies, I gave instructions that this work should cease."

Churchill's letter follows as does various memoranda generated by its receipt.

On March 17, Roosevelt sent the letter with a note to Harry Hopkins, his special adviser, asking him to prepare a reply.

Almost five months later, on July 6, 1942, Lois Berney, Hopkins' secretary, wrote to Dorothy Brady, Roosevelt's secretary, asking if the correspondence could be filed.

The following week, on July 9, Roosevelt, apparently made aware that nothing had been done, sent memos to the Army Chief of Staff General George C. Marshall and Secretary of State Cordell Hull and Harry Hopkins.

In response to Roosevelt's note, a memorandum dated that same day, July 9, an example of excellent staff work by Major General George V. Strong, Assistant Chief of Staff, G-2, assured Marshall that cryptanalytic cooperation was satisfactorily in progress. This note, above, is being made public for the first time. I had been engaged in an intensive search for the memo before I finally located it in the archives of an intelligence agency where it had to be declassified before release.

Two days later, on July 11, Marshall's reply assured Roosevelt that cryptanalytic cooperation was satisfactory.

Perhaps as a result of the above correspondence, in addition to exchanges of cryptanalytic information already underway, a regular posing of American liaison officers to Bletchley Park and British cryptologists at Arlington Hall was initiated.

10, Downing Street,
Whitehall.

February 25, 1942.

My dear Mr. President,

One night when we talked late, you spoke of the importance of our cipher people getting into close contact with yours. I shall be very ready to put any expert you care to nominate in touch with my technicians. Ciphers for our two Navies have been and are continually a matter for frank discussion between our two Services. But diplomatic and military ciphers are of equal importance, and we appear to know nothing officially of your versions of these. Some time ago, however, our experts claimed to have discovered the system and constructed some tables used by your Diplomatic Corps. From the moment when we became allies, I gave instructions that this work should cease. However, danger of our enemies having achieved a measure of success cannot, I am advised, be dismissed.

I shall be grateful if you will handle this

Page 1 of Churchill Letter to President Roosevelt

-2-

matter entirely yourself, and if possible burn this letter when you have read it. The whole subject is secret in a degree which affects the safety of both our countries. The fewest possible people should know.

I take advantage of the Ambassador's homeward journey to send you this by his hand, to be delivered into yours personally.

With every good wish & my kindest regards Believe me,

Yours sincere friend,

Winston S. Churchill

The President of
The United States of America.

Page 2 of Churchill Letter to President Roosevelt

THE WHITE HOUSE
WASHINGTON

March 17, 1942.

MEMORANDUM FOR

HARRY HOPKINS:

FOR PREPARATION OF REPLY.

F.D.R.

Roosevelt Memo to Hopkins

THE WHITE HOUSE
WASHINGTON

July 6, 1942

Dorothy: Brady

Mr. Hopkins has been holding this all this time. I assume that the question has been discussed since the letter was written and that this can be filed.

Lois

Memo from Lois Berney, Harry Hopkins' secretary, to Dorothy Brady, President Roosevelt's secretary

General George C. Marshall
Photograph: United States Army Archive

Secretary of State Cordell Hull

THE WHITE HOUSE

WASHINGTON

July 9, 1942.
MEMORANDUM FOR

GENERAL MARSHALL:

Some time ago the Prime Minister stated that our cipher experts of the United States and British Navies were in close touch but that he was under the impression that there was not a similar intimate interchange between our two Armies. I wonder if you could take this up with General [John] Dill [Senior British military representative in Washington] and let me know.

F.D.R.

THE WHITE HOUSE

WASHINGTON

July 9, 1942.

MEMORANDUM FOR THE

SECRETARY OF STATE:

Some time ago the Prime Minister stated that our cipher experts of the United States and British Navies were in close touch but that he was under the impression that there was not a similar intimate interchange between our State Department and the Foreign Office. I wonder if you could take this up with the British Ambassador [Lord E. W. Halifax] and let me know.

F.D.R

Major General George V. Strong, Assistant Chief of Staff, G- 2
Photograph: National Archives

COPY

July 9, 1942

MEMORANDUM For: Chief of Staff

1. Reference is made to attached memorandum for General Marshall, dated July 9, 1942.

2. Intimate interchange of technical cryptanalytic information between the British and the American Armies has been in progress for over a year, and appears to be quite satisfactory to both sides. Studies and conferences pertaining to a similar exchange of technical cryptographic information to facilitate communication among the American Army on the one side and the RAF and the British Army on the other side in all echelons have been in progress for about three   , and will be completed very soon. If interchange of similar material appears to be more advanced between the British Navy and the American Navy, it is because actual intercommunication between these two services has been necessary for a much longer period of time.

George V. Strong,
Major General.
Assistant Chief of Staff, G-2

Attached:
Memo. 7-9-42

COPY

July 11, 1942.

MEMORANDUM FOR THE PRESIDENT:

I have taken up the question of interchange of information between cipher experts in the British and American Armies with Sir John Dill.

We find that an interchange of cryptanalytic information has been in progress for over a year and appears to be satisfactory to both services. A similar exchange of technical cryptographic information to facilitate communications between the American Army, the RAF, and the British Army in all echelons is now being studied and will be put into effect in the near future.

(Sgd) G. C. Marshall
Chief of Staff.

mej

Copy for Chief of Staff

RESEARCH NOTES

A number of documents could not be located in official files. A review of the chronology highlights the absent items.

February 25, 1942	Churchill to Roosevelt (response not located)
March 17, 1942	Roosevelt to Hopkins
July 6, 1942	Lois (Hopkins' secretary) to Dorothy (Roosevelt's secretary)
July 9, 1942	Roosevelt to Marshall
	Roosevelt to Hull (response not located)
	Roosevelt to Hopkins (response not located)
July 9, 1942	Strong to Marshall
July 11, 1942	Marshall to Roosevelt

There are three documents which seem to be missing; a response from Hull to Roosevelt, Hopkins to Roosevelt, and a reply from Roosevelt to Churchill.

There is also a fourth missing document. On Roosevelt's memo to Hull there is a notation that Hull sent Roosevelt's note to his Assistant Secretary of State, Gardiner H. Shaw, on July 13 for his attention. Thus, Shaw's response to Hull also must be considered absent.

It can be speculated that due to the extreme sensitivity of the subject – note Churchill's suggestion that Roosevelt "burn this letter when you have read it" – that Roosevelt's reply was conveyed to Churchill orally. It seems odd, however, that neither Shaw's response to Hull nor Hull's reply to Roosevelt could be found. Possibly they were also given orally.

Finally, information could not be located on the reaction of Roosevelt or the State Department to Churchill's revelation of England's decrypting of United States' diplomatic correspondence. The following actions, however, first by the Secretary of State and then a warning about cryptographic security distributed by the Joint Chiefs of Staff may have resulted from Churchill's disclosure. The latter step which specifically refers to State Department codes and ciphers is surely related to it.

On June 22, 1942, Hull wrote to Secretary of War Henry L. Stimson asking for the transfer of an expert cryptographer from the Office of the Chief Signal Officer to serve with the State Department.[1, p. 108]

In November 1942, the Joint Chiefs of Staff sent the following letter to the heads of all non-military agencies using codes and ciphers. It was signed by Brigadier General John R. Deans, Secretary, Joint Chiefs of Staff.

> The ease with which codes and ciphers of the non-military agencies of our enemies are being broken by our experts has raised the question in the minds of the Joint Chiefs of Staffs as to the security of codes and ciphers used by similar agencies of our Government. The ability of our cryptanalysis experts to decode enemy messages has been our most valuable source of information. The Chiefs of Staff wish that you be informed of this, *as a matter of great secrecy*, in order to emphasize the importance of security in these matters. They feel that we must credit the enemy with having its experts who are just as capable as ours in cryptanalysis work. They are deeply concerned over the hazards to which our ships and troops may be exposed through the use of ineffective codes by various Governmental agencies.
>
> The Joint Communications Board, an agency of the Joint Chiefs of Staff, has at its disposal the best cryptographic experts in the United States. The services of these experts can be made available to the State Department to analyze its codes and ciphers from the standpoint of security and to suggest methods for their improvement. It is hoped that you will make use of the services of these experts. This can be accomplished by communicating with the Secretary of the Joint Chiefs of Staff who will make the necessary arrangements. [1, p.109]

REFERENCES

1. U. S. Army Security Agency. 1948. *History of the Signal Security Agency, Volume One.* Washington DC: Army Security Agency.

ACKNOWLEDGMENTS

A note of thanks to the institutions and archivists who graciously assisted my research efforts in a most professional manner: Library of Congress, Manuscript Division (Cordell Hull papers); John N. Jacob, Archivist, George C. Marshall Foundation; Milton D. Gustafson, Chief, Diplomatic Branch, National Archives; Robert Parks, Archivist, Franklin D. Roosevelt Library; and an intelligence agency archivist.

BIOGRAPHICAL SKETCH

Louis Kruh is an indefatigable researcher and collector of cryptologic memorabilia, particularly cipher devices. He is co-author with Dr. C. A. Deavours of *Machine Cryptography and Modern Cryptanalysis*, published by Artech House, Inc. in 1985. He has his MBA and JD degrees and is Director – Sales Advertising for New York Telephone.

FROM THE ARCHIVES: A BLETCHLEY PARK ASSESSMENT OF GERMAN INTELLIGENCE ON TORCH

Ralph Erskine

ADDRESS: 25 Hawthornden Rd., Belfast BT4 3JU NORTHERN IRELAND

ABSTRACT: A Bletchley Park assessment of German intelligence about Allied intentions before the landings in North Africa in November 1942 is reproduced, with annotations.

KEYWORDS: Bletchley Park, German, intelligence, landings, North Africa, Torch.

British and American grand strategy for the prosecution of the Second World War was settled at the Washington Conference of December 1941 (*Arcadia*) when, among other things, it was agreed that the ring around Germany - from Archangel, the Black Sea, and the Northern seaboard of the Mediterranean to the western seaboard of Europe - should be tightened.[1] After much debate, American plans to invade France in April 1943 (*Roundup*, with which was associated a project for an emergency attack in France in 1942 (*Sledgehammer*)), were eventually dropped in favour of more realistic proposals to move against French North Africa (*Torch* - formerly *Gymnast* and *Super-Gymnast*).[2]

As cover for *Torch*, various deception plans were prepared under the aegis of the London Controlling Section [3] (responsible to the Chiefs of Staff for coordinating all strategic deception), including [4] -

(a) *Overthrow* - a fictitious operation against Northern France (based on *Roundup* and *Sledgehammer*, which by that time had been abandoned);

(b) *Solo One*, which was intended to make the Germans believe that Norway was the target;

(c) *Solo Two*, under which the troops were to be given the impression that they were bound for the Middle East via the Cape of Good Hope;

(d) *Kennecott* - a cover story for preparations being made at Gibraltar, which was intended to suggest that they were part of a Malta convoy;[5]

(e) *Quickfire* - cover for the United States forces going to North Africa;[6]

(f) *Pender I* and *II* - to disguise the movements of General Eisenhower (Allied Commander in Chief for *Torch*) and Admiral Cunningham (Naval Commander in Chief, Mediterranean).[7]

In addition to these cover plans, Casablance, Oran and Algiers (where the landings were to be made) were, at Churchill's suggestion, and to Eisenhower's discomfiture, [8] called *Dunkirk*, *Calais* and *Boulogne*, respectively.[9]

Some indications of Allied intentions came to the notice of German and Italian intelligence, whose political and military leaders also had their own views on where (and when) an attack might be made. Hitler believed that a landing might be attempted in Norway [10], which was indeed favored by Churchill.[11] The German navy, for reasons of its own, thought that Dakar, the Azores, the Canaries or the Cape Verde Islands (the last three of which were at one time the subject of various Allied pre-emptive plans [12]) would be the target.[13] With so much "noise" present, the Germans found it difficult to work out where the *Torch* landings would take place.[14] In contrast, largely as a result of better political judgement, the Italians made a sound assessment of developments at a relatively early stage. On 9 October, after a long conference with General Cesare Amè, head of SIM (Italian military intelligence), Count Galeazzo Ciano, the foreign minister, recorded that "All information and conversations lead one to conclude that the Anglo-Saxons are preparing to land in North Africa."[15]

The document set out here shows, at least in part, what the intelligence analysts at the British Government Code and Cypher School at Bletchley Park (BP) knew about German and Italian knowledge of the Allied plans by 20 September 1942 - seven weeks before the landings took place on 8 November.[16] Surprisingly, it does not mention any other BP paper on the subject, which suggests that no earlier Sigint-based analysis of German intelligence had been carried out. By 14 October, when the Joint Intelligence Sub-Committee (JISC) recorded that most of the German and Vichy French intelligence reports suggested that the operation would be against Morocco and Algeria or Dakar, there had been little change, but the JISC thought that German air reconnaissance of Gibraltar must have resulted in their drawing "some correct deductions from activity observed."[17] However, even when the Luftwaffe found a battleship, two aircraft carriers, five cruisers, 20 destroyers, and many steamships and aircraft in Gibraltar on 4 November [18], the German Naval Staff (Seekriegsleitung) advised that the concentration of shipping pointed to a convoy to Malta, and that a landing on the northwest coast of Africa did not appear likely.[19] As late as 6 November, Hitler told Kesselring in Italy that any Allied operation, if it came at all, would be directed against Tripoli or Corsica, Sardinia or Derna (about 200 kms east of Benghazi).[20]

Although the huge *Torch* convoys escaped detection until those from Great Britain reached Gibraltar, 190 ships (out of 340 eventually eastbound) were observed by the Germans by 6 November as they passed through the Straits of Gibraltar.[21] Even so, until late on the 7th, General Alfred Jodl, chief of the Wehrmacht operations staff, thought that an Allied invasion of French North Africa was very unlikely, largely because he believed that it would drive the French into the arms of the Germans – a striking example, like many of the other German assessments of *Torch*, of how a misreading of political and strategic factors can distort intelligence appreciations.[22]

NOTES

1. Michael Howard, *Grand Strategy*, Vol. IV (London, 1972), 599.

2. On the background to *Torch*, see *ibid*, xv-xxv, 111-140; on the intelligence aspects of *Torch*, see F. H. Hinsley, with E. E. Thomas, C. F. G. Ransom and R. C. Knight, *British Intelligence in the Second World War: Its Influence on Strategy and Operations*, Vol. 2 (London/New York, 1981), 463-490; for an insider's view of American opposition to *Torch*, see Albert C. Wedemeyer, *Wedemeyer Reports!* (New York, 1958), 147-168.

3. *Torch* was the London Controlling Section's (LCS) first opportunity to plan and implement deception on a major scale: COS (42) 416 (O), 26 November 1942 (AIR 20/2508 - files cited are at the Public Record Office, Kew, London (PRO)). For the membership of LCS, see COS (42) 453 (O), 15 December 1942 (AIR 20/4504) and, for a memoir by one of its members, Dennis Wheatley, *The Deception Planners: My Secret War* (London, 1980).

4. Charles Cruickshank, *Deception in World War II* (London, 1979), 36-47; also Winston S. Churchill, *The Second World War*, Vol. IV (*The Hinge of Fate*) (London, 1951), 405; Martin Gilbert, *Winston S. Churchill*, Vol. VII (*The Road to Victory*) (London, 1986), 155, 156; Harry C. Butcher, *Three Years with Eisenhower* (Kingswood, 1946), 44, 52; J. C. Masterman, *The Double-Cross System in the War of 1939 to 1945* (New Haven/London, 1972), 109, 110. Dakar was vetoed as a cover target, on the ground that it was French: Wheatley, 93; Ewen Montagu, *Beyond Top Secret U* (London, 1977), 134 (who does the Foreign Office an injustice).

5. A well-meaning attempt by one senior officer to further this strategem led to his being described as a "half-witted general": Montagu, 136!

6. *Quickfire* even had its own deception plan, *Sweater*.

7. On Axis agents among the Spanish workforce in Gibraltar, see Masterman, 175.

8. Butcher, 102.
9. Gilbert, 228.
10. *The Fuehrer Conferences on Naval Affairs* (hereafter *FCNA*), *Brassey's Naval Annual 1948* (London), 289.
11. Churchill, 290.
12. J. M. A. Gwyer and J. R. M. Butler, *Grand Strategy*, Vol. III (London, 1964), 8, 515. On British plans to occupy the Canaries, see ADM 205/11, 363-394.
13. *FCNA*, 141-143, 145, 147-9, 152, 153, 166, 198, 221, 292.
14. Walter Warlimont, "The decision in the Mediterranean 1942," in Hans-Adolf Jacobsen and Jürgen Rohwer (eds.), *Decisive Battles of World War II: The German View* (London, 1965), 206; Howard, 65.
15. Malcolm Muggeridge (ed.), *Ciano's Diary: 1939-1943* (London, 1947), 508.
16. On additional intelligence available to the Germans, see David Kahn, *Hitler's Spies* (London, 1978), 468-476.
17. JIC (42) 405 (O), 14 October 1942 (PREM 3/349/19).
18. *Kriegstagebuch des Oberkommandos der Wehrmacht* (hererafter KTB/OKW) (Percy E. Schramm, ed.) (München, 1982), Vol. II, 901, 902, 906.
19. *Ibid*, 902. The Seekriegsleitung advice is set out in Kahn, 476- 7.
20. Notes, KTB/OKW, 917.
21. Warlimont, 207. The German Gibraltar organisation mentioned in "Use of German reporting centres at Lisbon and Gibraltar for U-boat operations" of 30 September 1942 (ZG 184 on ADM 223/3) could not give the destination of ships sailing from Gibraltar in advance: Ost. 1671 of 3 September 1942.
22. Warlimont, 209; Churchill, 558; cf *Ciano's Diary*, 519, 520; Howard, 171; I. S. O. Playfair and C. J. C. Moloney, *The Mediterranean and the Middle East*, Vol. IV (London, 1966), 135.

[ZG 181 (on ADM 223/3), which is in the custody of the PRO, is reproduced with the permission of the Controller of Her Majesty's Stationery Office.]

MOST SECRET
NAVAL SECTION[1]

20.9.42 ZIP/ZG/181[2]

INCREASED GERMAN INVESTIGATION OF ACTIVITY AT GIBRALTAR VIA AGENTS AND RECONNAISSANCE

1) Rumours reaching the enemy.

Since about 20/8 several different reports have been received by the enemy, from Madrid, Lisbon, Bilbao, Vichy, Oporto, Toulon, Lobito, Pernambuco[3] and other centres, to the effect that

(a) an allied committee is investigating plans for the reconquest of the Mediterranean (See D.S. 108349[4] from Japanese Minister, Madrid to Tokyo, repeated by German and Italian sources to Berlin and Rome)

or (b) action is intended against the Canaries and the Azores preparatory to a landing in Dakar (Ost. 1599[5] from Bilbao, BJ 108837 from Pernambuco, DS 108810 from Vichy, BJ 108892 from Madrid, BJ 108791)

or (c) the taking of Dakar and preliminaries at Gibraltar are in preparation for the occupation of French North Africa. (BJ 108384; rumours reaching Vichy reported in 1550/25/8 from Tangier to D.N.I.; Ost. 1610; CX/22440/27[6] reporting rumours received by the Germans; and BJ 108791).

[1]The naval section at BP, whose head was Frank Birch (a Room 40 veteran), was based in Hut 4.

[2]ZG 181 is mainly derived from at least five different series of decrypts, most of them of high- grade ciphers (hence "Z"). The 350 odd ZG papers appear to be the only BP intelligence appreciations (naval or other) to have been transferred to the PRO - such of the earlier Z series as have survived (Hinsley, *cum al.*, Vol. 1 (London/New York, 1979), 564 reproduces Z 320), are yet at the PRO.

[3]Lobito is in Angola, and Pernambuco (Recife) in Brazil.

[4]DS 108349 was probably enciphered on the Japanese Purple cipher machine. It is not clear whether "DS" represents a separate series to the BJ (Black Jumbo) diplomatic decrypts (compare the numbering).

[5]"Ost" appears to be a series of decrypts taken from Abwehr material: for a few verbatim Ost signals, see ZG 184 (ADM 223/3). It may be derived from [O]liver [St]rachey despite - or possibly as cover for - the existence of the "ISOS" decrypts (Intelligence Services Oliver Strachey - which dealt with Abwehr hand ciphers).

[6]"CX" refers to material from agents, and is not a decrypt series (despite its similarity to "CX/MSS" - see note 11 below).

2) Enemy Reaction to these Reports.

An immediate reaction was to request additional information from agents in the Gibraltar area:

(i) On 24/8 Madrid ordered Algeciras[7] to report at once what was known of English intentions to land in Marseilles from Gibraltar and to quote the number of English and American troops at present in Gibraltar (Isk. 16361).

(ii) On 25/8 Berlin asked Madrid whether military activity was specially noticeable at Gibraltar, so as to suggest intentions of making a landing (Isk. 16510).[8]

(iii) Madrid replied that there was no evidence yet (Isk.16533) and the Italian Minister at Tangier, apparently in reply to a similar query, expressed the same opinion. (BJ 108544).

(iv) In spite of this, Italian agents "have intensified their watch on arrivals from the Atlantic" (BJ 108544) and on 7/9 Madrid informed Algeciras that "all facts ascertained regarding landing operations, such as an increase in tugs, barges and light vessels in Gibraltar, are particularly urgent." (Isk.17276). Apart from this increased vigilance there has been no sign of any enemy activity which is directly the effect of the above rumors.

3) Extension of G.A.F. reconnaissance to Gibraltar.

(a) But since the beginning of September, G.A.F. reconnaissance patrols in the Western Mediterranean have been extended to Gibraltar and there has been an increase in G.A.F. reconnaissance activity in this area:

---

[7] The Abwehr had observation stations at Algeciras, across the bay and only a few miles from Gibraltar, and at Ceuta on the African side of the Straits. Algeciras used heat sensing equipment which could detect ships at night: see F. H. Hinsley *cum al.*, Vol. 2, 720; R. V. Jones, *Most Secret War* (London/New York, 1978 - American title, *The Wizard War*), 255. For details of this equipment, see Helmuth Giessler, *Der Marine-Nachrichten-und-Ortungsdienst* (München, 1971), 95, 148-9.

[8] "Intelligence Services Knox" (the BP section headed by Dillwyn Knox - later Peter Twinn) broke the Abwehr version of Enigma (Hinsley *cum al.*, Vol. 2, 668; Kim Philby, *My Secret War* (London, 1968), 38), which lacked a plugboard and could therefore be cracked without the aid of the Turing/Welchman bombes. For extracts from ISK 18825, a report of 3 October to Berlin by agents in Lisbon on an impending operation "of considerable size" (that is, *Torch*), see minute of 8 October 1942 by Flt. Lt. John Pope-Hennessy (AI 3(a)2) (later a director of the British Museum): AIR 20/4504; for the text of this report (from German records), which is a masterly collection of convincing, but uninformative, detail, see Kahn, 472-3: the intelligence probably therefore came from British-controlled agents (the Double Cross operation).

(i) up to the end of August German reconnaissance in the Western Mediterranean was not instituted until reports of British movements east of Gibraltar were received from other sources, and was rarely carried out farther west than 02° W. (See ex/Salu 9).[9]

(ii) during the first half of September reconnaissance in the Western Mediterranean was flown on 10 occasions.

(iii) On 2/9 visual reconnaissance of Gibraltar was noticed when a German aircraft reported 2 B/S and 1 cruiser "more" in harbour.[10]

(iv) Other position reports in air to ground traffic show that German aircraft were in the vicinity of the Rock on 10/9, 11/9, 14/9 and 15/9.

(v) German aircraft were seen over the Rock on 2/9, 10/9 and 14/9. (See for example A.H.Q. Gibraltar's 1905Z/14 to Air Ministry).

(vi) CX/MSS 1411/T14[11] of 15/9 stated that "reconnaissance as far as Gibraltar, at present at the turning point, has produced no sightings up to now", thus confirming other evidence that reconnaissance patrols have been extended to include Gibraltar itself.

(b) The extension of reconnaissance to Gibraltar followed immediately upon the Germans appreciating, on 30/8, that "the enemy will shortly attempt a new break through to Malta with supplies". (CX/MSS 1346/T13), and reconnaissance reports from the aircraft over Gibraltar on 15/9 were anxiously awaited because the possibility was entertained of the approach of a Malta convoy. (CX/MSS 1406/T21).

(c) On this evidence, increased G.A.F. effort in the Western Mediterranean and the extension of reconnaissance patrols to Gibraltar since the beginning of September are most probably due to a desire to be completely informed of any further operations to supply Malta, especially since the period of a fortnight before the beginning of September saw two false alarms on the subject of Gibraltar-to-Malta convoys. (See CX/MSS 1309/T5; 1386/T28; 1346/T13).

4) Conclusions.

(a) During the past month the enemy has received several reports which, though conflicting on points of detail, all indicate the existence of British intentions in the Western Mediterranean and N.W. Africa.

[9] A subsection of BP's air section which integrated high and low-grade sigint: Hinsley *cum al.*, Vol. 2, xv.

[10] On air reconnaissance over Gibraltar, see Hinsley *cum al.*, Vol. 2, 476; Cruickshank, 48.

[11] "C" (Head of MI6), "MSS" (Most Secret Source: Enigma decrypts.)

(b) On this account agents in the Gibraltar area have been put on the alert, with particular reference to evidence of preparations for landing operations from Gibraltar.

(c) At present, the enemy is apparently experiencing some difficulty in dissociating these rumours from the (what has now become) perennial question of supplies to Malta.

(d) It is probably to counter the latter eventuality, frequently and falsely rumoured, that since 1/9/42 G.A.F. reconnaissance in the Western Mediterranean has been increased, and at the same time extended to cover Gibraltar regularly.

Distribution
The Director.[12] D.D.C.[13] (2 copies) I.D.8.G.[14] Wing Cdr.Jones.[15] I.E.

BIOGRAPHICAL SKETCH

Ralph Erskine is a lawyer in Northern Ireland. He has temporarily transferred his PRO research from naval Enigma to naval HFDF (ship and shore), on which he welcomes information.

[12]Either the director of naval intelligence (Rear-Admiral John Godfrey) of the director of BP (Commander Edward Travis.)

[13]Deputy director of naval intelligence, [Operational] Intelligence Centre (OIC) - Commander Norman Denning.

[14]Naval Intelligence Division 8, General, at the OIC: ADM 223/257 (which contains organisation lists of all personnel at the OIC.)

[15]Wing Commander Eric Jones, then head of BP's Hut 3 (army and Luftwaffe Enigma), who was later the director of GCHQ from 1952 to 1960.

BRITISH INTELLIGENCE IN THE SECOND WORLD WAR: AN OVERVIEW

F. H. Hinsley

ADDRESS: St. John's College, Cambridge CB2 1TN ENGLAND.

ABSTRACT: During World War II, signals intelligence was always and increasingly the most valuable of Great Britain's intelligence sources. The Poles first solved the German Enigma cipher machine. Britain, which first solved the general Luftwaffe key in May 1940 and a naval Enigma key in June 1941, exploited these and other keys, though with interruptions, to the end of the war. Other sources – espionage, aerial photography, captured documents, the underground in occupied countries – also provided valuable information. The operational influence of intelligence varied. After the summer of 1941, most battles were influenced by Allied superiority in intelligence. But its impact was not always decisive. Intelligence alone did not win the war. Still, massive, continuous, and frequently current information enabled the Allies to speed their victory by setting the time, scale, and place of their operations so as to economize their lives and resources and to cost the enemy more of his. Intelligence shortened the war by perhaps 4 years.

KEYWORDS: Second World War, intelligence, signals intelligence, Ultra, Enigma, Poles, U-boats.

In the Second World War, if we leave aside the information they obtained by overt means from embassies, the press, the radio and other such channels - information which they did not call intelligence - governments got their intelligence - defined as information which other governments were at pains to keep secret - from four sources. They were:

1. physical contact in the form of captured documents, the censorship of mail and the interrogation of prisoners;
2. espionage;
3. aerial reconnaissance, particularly aerial photographic reconnaissance; and
4. signals intelligence, sigint for short.

About these four sources we should note two preliminary points. Essentially, each of them had always existed. There never was a time when governments did not avail themselves of censorship, captures, prisoners and spies; aerial reconnaissance was old-fashioned reconnaissance greatly extended by the development of flying since the beginning of this century; sigint, in the same way, was the product of the marriage of one of the most ancient of crafts - cryptanalysis - with the advent of wireless communication from the same date. In the second place, and by the same token, all governments exploited all these sources in World War II or did their best to do so.

Until the autumn of 1941 - for the first two years of the war - the intelligence bodies on both sides achieved roughly equal success. To illustrate this further point by reference only to sigint, which was always and increasingly the most valuable of the sources, British success in breaking the cypher used by the Germans in the invasion of Norway in April 1940 and in reading the communications of the German Air Force from May 1940 was balanced by the fact that Germany read between 30 and 50 per cent of British naval traffic in the North Sea during 1940, and a considerable amount of that of the French army from the outbreak of war to the fall of France. The fact, again, that the British were reading the high-grade cyphers of the Italian army, navy, and air force from September 1940 to the end of 1941 was offset by Axis successes during most of that period against equivalent British cyphers in the Mediterranean and the Middle East.

Axis successes against British cyphers did not cease at the end of 1941. With few exceptions, however, of which the most notable was Germany's ability to read for much of the time from January 1942 to June 1943 the codes and cyphers associated with the Atlantic convoys, the previous rough equivalence of advantage in sigint gave way from the autumn of 1941 to massive Allied superiority. It did so in a process by which, while Axis openings were successively blocked, the Allied penetration of Axis communications, and especially of German communications, was progressively expanded. It was expanded to a degree that had never previously been achieved, even in wartime. Leaving aside the decryption of tactical codes and cyphers - confining ourselves to the highest-grade decrypts for which London used the codename Ultra and Washington used the codenames Ultra and Magic - the Allies were reading from early 1943 some 4,000 German signals a day and a large, if somewhat smaller, volume of Italian and Japanese traffic, whereas to Germany, Italy and Japan virtually all the Allied cyphers had by then been made invulnerable.

How was this transformation brought about? In the answer to this question nothing is more striking than the extent to which both fortune and foresight, both good luck and good judgment, played their part. This point is best illustrated by the long and tangled history of that achievement which was most central to the transformation - the conquest of the German Enigma machine.

The Enigma was Germany's answer to the problems raised by the wish to harness radio to efficiency in military operations: the need for impregnable cyphers if large volumes of signals were to be put on the air and the need for speed in cyphering and decyphering large volumes of signals. In order to achieve the further advantages of mass production, she chose to rely almost exclusively on the single resulting electromechanical typing machine, distributing it widely throughout each of the three services and within such other organisations as the Abwehr, the railways and the police. By each of its user organisations, however, the machine was adapted to different arrangements and procedures, and each of them operated it with different keys for different functions and in different theatres. Some 250 keys, each constituting virtually a different cypher, were identified during the war, and at no time after 1941 were fewer than 50 in force concurrently. As each key was reset daily once war had begun, and as the finding of any setting involved the selection of one out of many millions of possible solutions even by those who might have captured the machine and its wired wheels, the Germans felt confident that even in war conditions the Enigma would remain safe against all but local and temporary compromises of settings. And yet the machine was radically, if not yet irretrievably, compromised as early as 1932, and beginning in May 1940 after an interlude since September 1938, the British went on to recover 180 of the wartime keys.

The prewar compromise owed almost everything to chance or, as the Germans might think, to misfortune. The Poles broke into the machine by methods which involved great mathematical ingenuity, though not profound mathematics, but the methods were possible only because in 1931 a German cryptologic official had supplied its operating instructions and settings for two months to the French Secret Service, which passed them to Warsaw. Fortune played no part, on the other hand, in the wartime conquest of the Enigma.

The Polish success had been brought to an end in 1938 by the last in a sequence of prewar German security improvements. Despite the invaluable assistance obtained from the Poles, and despite the fact that from September 1939 the Germans were using the machine more heavily in operational conditions, whereas they had previously used it sparsely and mainly for practice traffic, the British did not fully solve any wartime keys - bring them to the point at which the settings were found daily without great delay - until the spring of 1940, when they mastered the key used in Norway from 10 April and the general purpose key of the German air force from 20 May. Many regional and specialised keys of the air force were thereafter solved, often as soon as they were brought into force, but it is further testimony to the formidable problems presented by the Enigma that no naval keys were solved regularly before June 1941, no Abwehr keys before December 1941 and no army keys (with the exception of one of the Russian front from June 1941) till the spring of 1942. Nor need we doubt that but for careful preparations over a long period of time the British authorities would not, even then, have overcome these problems.

Without their foresight in centralising cryptanalysis on an interdepartment basis after World War I, in recruiting the best available talents to it from 1938 and not least in recognising that those talents should be interdisciplinary, the conquest of the Enigma would have been impossible. For while it would have been impossible without brilliant mathematicians, and particularly without their development of machinery of a sophistication which the Germans had not allowed for, it would equally have been impossible without the input of a whole array of nonmathematical ingenuity. Mathematicians provided the means by which the 24-hourly solutions could alone be found, but the ability to apply the means rested on continuous and sometimes inspired analysis of German operations, German signals procedure, and even the habits and methods and vocabulary of German wireless operators.

These successes once achieved, they could not be counted on to continue. They were subject to two threats. The Germans, who had made successive improvements to the security of the Enigma before the war, might continue to do so as a matter of ordinary precaution. Or they might refashion it from suspicion or conviction that it had been radically compromised. In the event, under the pressures of war and in view of the unexpectedly wide dispersal of their armed forces, the German authorities, with one notable exception, deferred precautionary overhaul until after the middle of 1944, and not until early in 1945, when the Enigma settings were in any case wide open to physical compromise, did they take measures in the belief that it was no longer secure. The exception was the U-boat Command. In February 1942, motivated initially by suspicion - which was, however, set aside after an enquiry - it took the precaution of bringing into force a new Enigma key, one that used an additional wheel and was 26 times more difficult to solve.

The effects of this setback, as of those which came from the burden of solving the ever increasing proliferation of ordinary keys, were offset, though not without some delay, by another of the novel developments for which World War II is remarkable in the history of intelligence. From the spring of 1942, the British and U.S. intelligence bodies created for sigint, as for intelligence as a whole, a single organisation in which the amalgamation of resources and the division of labour were virtually complete. But as the Allies wrestled after the autumn of 1944 with Germany's adoption of wider security measures they had to fear that not even their combined resources would suffice to maintain their critical advantage over her. In the event, as a result of Germany's delay in introducing these measures, they kept their advantage, and even extended it, down to the end of the war.

It is tempting to attribute this delay to the fact that, to undue confidence in the invulnerability of the Enigma before the outbreak of war, the German signals and security authorities subsequently added incompetence and complacency. But there are good grounds for holding that their original confidence was not unreasonable, and that to think otherwise is to belittle the ingenuity and the versatility of the Allied sigint effort. These were displayed against Japanese and Italian cyphers as well as against Germany's and against other German cyphers besides the Enigma - most notably against the system which Germany introduced for communication between her high-level headquarters in signals based on teleprinter impulses that were automatically cyphered on transmission and decyphered at the point of reception. From the end of 1942 the British solved the product of this further technological advance, and did so before it was fully operational, by developing an approximation to the modern computer. In the last two years of the war its decrypts made a contribution to the stock of intelligence that was even greater in value, though not in volume, than that made by the Enigma. And in the same way the argument for wartime German incompetence overlooks some important considerations.

In continuing to make no allowance for the extent to which machine methods might be developed against the Enigma, the Germans were undoubtedly swayed by their own inability to make any progress against Allied machine cyphers, but this inability was chiefly due to the fact that the Allies applied their knowledge of Enigma to strengthen their own cyphers. The danger that, even so, the enemy would come to believe that, if only as a consequence of captures, the Enigma had become insecure - this was contained until almost the end of the war by, on the one hand, the existence of the other intelligence sources and, on the other, exceptionally careful Allied security precautions.

The other sources produced valuable intelligence. Espionage and photographic reconnaissance threw as much light as sigint on the early development of the V-weapons. The first news of the development of revolutionary new types of U-boats and aircraft came from prisoners. Eighty percent of the information about the fixed anti-invasion defences on the French coast was provided by photographic reconnaissance, and over 50 percent of the intelligence about the German army's order of battle in the west before the Normandy landings was obtained from captured documents and from the French, Belgian, Dutch and Polish underground organisations. But it was not only the case that the intelligence value of these sources was greatly enhanced because they could be guided by and mated with sigint; they were less useful for their intelligence than for the security they provided for sigint. Because the enemy was oblivious of the existence of sigint but knew that the Allies possessed the other sources, he attributed to prisoners, deserters, spies and traitors the setbacks he encountered as a result of Allied sigint - and this was especially so in the case of Germany, who fought alongside unreliable allies in occupied countries with hostile populations.

The British authorities themselves utilised the other sources to preserve the secrecy of sigint in relation to their own forces, citing them as the basis for orders or evidence which were in fact inspired by sigint and severely restricting knowledge of the existence of sigint to the highest echelons of command. Security in relation to their own forces, however, was only one part of the meticulous system of precautions the Allies evolved to avert the enemy's attention from the use they were making of Ultra intelligence in the course of their operations. At some stages in the war - as it happens, with the assistance of Italian machine decrypts as well as of Enigma decrypts - the British were sinking 60 percent of the Axis shipping that plied between the European Mediterranean ports and North Africa, but no Axis ship was attacked before the enemy had learned that it had been sighted by an aircraft or warship which, unknown to itself, had been put in a position to do the sighting. There were occasions on which, to the alarm of the Allied authorities, the regulations broke down - when orders were issued which referred to the intelligence or when cover was not provided for the action that might result. There were situations to which the regulations could not be applied. In the Atlantic, in particular, there was a long period in which the decrypts of the instructions to U-boats, though used to great effect, were used only passively or negatively, to route convoys out of the path of U-boats rather than to steer the escorts to where the U-boats were waiting or refuelling; and in such a situation, in which more and more U-boats made fewer and fewer sightings, the mere absence of sightings of convoys was bound to create enemy suspicions unless cover was found. Immense trouble had to be taken to lull these suspicions by exaggerating the extension of Allied air reconnaissance to the mid-Atlantic and by propagating the rumour that the Allies had invented a miraculous radar which detected submerged U-boats over great distances.

As against these considerations, it may still be felt that the Allied precautions were effective only because the Germans were extraordinarily overconfident or extraordinarily careless. The moral is, rather, that while it is unwise to be confident about anything, ever, that is a counsel of perfection in human affairs. This is illustrated by an example of fallibility on the part of British authorities. With all the benefit they were deriving from sigint, and despite their preoccupation with keeping it secret, they did not suspect that Germany was reading their convoy cyphers until, from the end of 1942, the truth was revealed in decrypts of the signals of the U-boat Command. But this conclusion prompts another question. If, whether on account of German stupidity or as a result of British security or from a combination of the two, the British superiority in intelligence could remain undetected for so long, what was its value? Can its influence have been decisive, as is so widely believed?

In addressing this question it is important to distinguish between the impact of intelligence in the course of operations and, on the other hand, its strategic value.

As every commander and any intelligence officer knows, intelligence is only one among many elements affecting the course of battles. It is necessary to consider much else when reaching decisions, and many other factors besides the decisions affect the outcome. In the Second World War for these reasons the operational influence of intelligence was always variable, not to say haphazard.

It was especially so up to the summer of 1941 when, as well as giving roughly equal advantage to both sides, intelligence was limited in volume and usually obtained with some delay if obtained at all, which was only sporadically. Although claims to the contrary have been made, few British operations before that date benefited from intelligence, least of all from sigint. Although the German air force Enigma was read from May 1940, the decrypts were practically useless during the invasions of Norway and France and in the Battle of Britain because Whitehall had not yet solved the enormous problems that had to be overcome before they could be safely distributed. With photographic reconnaissance, but with assistance from no other source, the authorities were able in the autumn of 1940 to time their bombing of the concentrations of invasion barges in the Channel so as to obtain maximum effect. In the winter of 1940-1941 they were able somewhat to mitigate the ferocity of the Blitz with the help of sigint, prisoners of war and equipment recovered from crashed enemy aircraft. In the spring of 1941, thanks to advance warnings from sigint, the *Bismarck* was sunk at the beginning of her cruise, whereas the *Graf Spee* had been caught at the end of a long sortie without benefit of intelligence; the navy was able to intercept the Italian fleet and defeat it at the battle of Matapan, and the defending force was able to extricate itself from Greece without great losses and inflict a severe mauling on the German airborne troops in the invasion of Crete.

After the summer of 1941, in contrast, most battles or sizeable encounters in the European and Mediterranean theatres were influenced by the Allied superiority in intelligence. But the contribution made by intelligence was by no means always important, let alone decisive. Random factors like luck or misjudgment were sometimes uppermost. A great deal was known about the enemy's intentions when the convoy PQ17 sailed for Murmansk in June 1942, but the convoy still ran into disaster because he was constantly changing his plans. On the other hand, the sinking of the *Scharnhorst* in the Arctic at Christmas 1943 was almost wholly brought about because intelligence, though small, became crucial when the enemy made mistakes. Sometimes relative strength settled the question. In the first battle of Alamein in June-July 1942, intelligence about the Africa Korps was not yet plentiful, but it was decisive in enabling the British commander to prevent Rommel's greatly superior armour from breaking through to Cairo - and this despite the fact that Rommel was also better supplied with field intelligence. Before and during the second battle of Alamein in October 1942, the amount of intelligence about Rommel's forces was massive, but those forces were by then so inferior to Montgomery's that it played little part in the British victory.

The upshot was that when intelligence was operationally decisive, its decisiveness was masked from outward gaze. It would be wrong, moreover, to assess the significance of intelligence for the outcome of the Alamein battles by measuring only its direct impact on them. What limited Rommel's superiority before the summer of 1942, and helped to eliminate it by the autumn, was the British use of sigint to destroy his supply shipping. Axis losses, rising to a peak of more than 60 percent of southbound Mediterranean shipping in November 1941 and to another peak of nearly 50 percent in October 1942, were almost entirely attributable to decrypts of cypher keys which had been solved regularly since June 1941. Nor was this the only direction in which the transformation of the intelligence situation to the advantage of the Allies now laid the basis for the indirect, long-term, strategic effects that intelligence was to exercise till the end of the war. Also from June 1941, for the first time, the British read the U-boat traffic regularly and currently, an advance which almost wholly explains why they prevented the U-boats from dominating the Atlantic during the autumn of 1941 and the winter of 1941-1942.

What, then, was the overall influence of intelligence on the war? It is not easy to give a precise assessment. If its impact on individual operations was not always decisive, and was sometimes nil, its strategic impact was indirect and cumulative, and it is thus difficult to measure it now, as it was difficult for the enemy to discern it at the time. But two conclusions may be advanced without qualification. In the first place, the claim that intelligence by itself won the war - a claim that is self-evidently absurd - may be dismissed. The British survived with little benefit from it before Germany invaded Russia in June 1941, and as Russia's survival was followed by the entry of the United States in December 1941, the Axis would have been defeated even if the Allies had not acquired at about the same time the superiority in intelligence which they retained till the end of the war. Till the end of the war? Nearly four more years is such a length of time that it might be thought that, far from not producing on its own the Axis defeat, intelligence made little contribution to it. That this was not the case, however, is the second point that may be made without qualification.

The war effort of the Western Allies on every front after the end of 1941 was guided by massive, continuous and frequently current information about the enemy's dispositions, intentions, resources and difficulties. The information was so comprehensive, though never complete, that, though they occasionally misinterpreted it, the expectations they based on it, whether positive or negative, were generally correct. This enabled them not only to strike some decisive operational blows and avoid some operational setbacks, but also to shorten the war by setting the time, the scale and the place of their own operations in such a way as to achieve enormous economies for themselves in lives and resources and to add enormously to the burdens the enemy had to bear.

By how much then did the Allied superiority in intelligence shorten the war? Even if the question is limited to the war in Europe, the answer can only be approximate, but some elements in the calculation are firm enough. By keeping the Axis out of Egypt it probably brought forward the conquest of North Africa and the reopening of the Mediterranean to Allied shipping, which were completed in the middle of 1943, by at least a year. By preventing the U-boats from dominating the Atlantic in the winter of 1941-1942, and by contributing heavily to their defeat there in the winter of 1942-1943, it probably saved the Allies another two years. Had delays of this order been imposed by shortages of shipping and specialised landing craft on the Allied invasions of the Continent, those undertakings would have been further delayed by other considerations. As it was, the invasion of Normandy was carried out on such very tight margins in 1944 that it would have been impracticable without precise intelligence about German strengths and order of battle and the fact that the Allied commands could be confident that the intelligence was accurate. If the invasion had had to be deferred, it might well have been delayed beyond 1946 or 1947 by Germany's

V-weapon offensive against the United Kingdom and her ability to finish the Atlantic Wall, not to speak of her deployment of revolutionary new U-boats and jet and rocket aircraft which, as intelligence revealed, became imminent in the early months of 1945. At the best, the return to the Continent might have been delayed till 1948 and the defeat of Germany till 1949, and that is probably a conservative estimate.

Neither the Western Allies nor the Russians would have been idle in these circumstances. What different strategies would they have pursued? Would the Russians have defeated Germany, or Germany the Russians? What would have been decided about the atom bomb, which, as was known from intelligence, Germany had not got? Historians cannot answer these questions, but fortunately they are concerned only with the war as it was. And it was not least because of the actual contribution made by intelligence to the course of the war that such questions do not arise.

BIOGRAPHICAL SKETCH

Sir Harry Hinsley, Emeritus Professor of History of International Relations in the University of Cambridge, and until recently Master of St. John's College there, worked at the British Code and Cypher School throughout World War II and is the leading author of the official *British Intelligence in the Second World War* (London and Cambridge, 1979-1988), 3 volumes in 4 parts.

CRYPTOLOGIA July 1990 Volume XIV 3 Number

A NEW CHALLENGE FOR AN OLD ENIGMA-BUSTER

WŁADYSŁAW KOZACZUK

ADDRESS: ul. Bobrowskiego, 3/M15, Warsaw POLAND.

ABSTRACT: In the summer of 1976, Marian Rejewski, Polish mathematician-cryptologist, the solver of the German Enigma cipher, was sent, by a former signals office from England, a letter including a photocopy of an enciphered message, dated 26 April 1904. This was the period of the Russo- Japanese War. The piece was a correspondence between the Polish Socialist Party (of which Józef Piłsudski was a leader) and its emissaries in London. Despite his advanced age and prolonged ailment, and contrary to his initial objections, Rejewski solved the cipher, which turned out to reveal an interesting historical document.

KEYWORDS: Enciphered message, cryptanalysis, codebreaking, Marian Rejewski, Piłsudski, Poland, Japan, Russia.

[Ed. note: Appreciation is expressed to Christopher Kasparek for suggestions on this manuscript and his assistance in translating some of Marian Rejeski's reemarks.]

The story I wish now to recount, poring over old but only recently acquired documents about Enigma, happened in the mid-1970's, when heated discussions in newspapers and learned debates of historians over two sensational books[1] were at their peak.

By 1976, in Poland's capital, a kind of "hotline" existed between the 71-year-old Marian Rejewski, the mathematician-cryptologist who had just become world famous as the solver of the German Enigma machine cipher, and myself, a historian who strove to keep pace with the burgeoning mass of publications on Enigma, some enlightening but many inaccurate.

So it was not unusual that on that sunny summer afternoon of August 17, 1976, having been summoned by a call from the other end of the line, I jumped into my old German Wartburg to speed through the crowded streets of central

[1]Gustave Bertrand *Enigma, ou la plus grande énigme de la guerre 1939-1945* (Paris, 1973); F. W. Winterbotham, *The Ultra Secret* (London, 1974).

Warsaw to the northern district of Żoliborz ("Joli Bord," or "Beautiful Shore") where Rejewski and his family lived.

Just as we were about to immerse ourselves in the reading of newly received correspondence from West and East Germany, Sweden, Belgium, France, or Brazil, the doorbell rang and Rejewski's 7-year-old grandson Wojtek brought in a small, inconspicuous letter; he was a keen collector of postage stamps and was always the first to greet the postman with a polite "Good morning." This time Wojtek was disappointed: the envelope bore only a small olive-gray stamp with an image of Her Britannic Majesty, with her familiar refined profile.

The letter, dated 10 August 1976, was from one of Rejewski's permanent correspondents, Tadeusz Lisicki, a Polish World War II signals officer and former commander of a radio-communications center located at Boxmoor in Greater London, where Rejewski and other Polish cryptologists, who had escaped in 1943 from German-occupied southern France, had resumed work on cracking Nazi ciphers almost to the end of the war. In fact it was only after he and fellow codebreaker, Henryk Zygalski (nearly as brilliant as he) had in August 1943 reached the British Isles and been installed at Boxmoor that mass reading of German SS, Gestapo and Himmler's other secret radio traffic had started.

Since the start of the war, the British had enormously enlarged their decryption center at Bletchley, some 50 miles northwest of London, where more than 9,000 cryptologists, technicians and intelligence officers were busy solving, translating, analyzing, and passing to Allied field commands hundreds of thousands of German, Italian, and other Axis military and political radio messages. But Rejewski and Zygalski never saw Bletchley: they only learned of its existence 30 years later, when in 1973 and 1974, respectively, Bertrand's and Winterbotham's books about the Allies' "most secret source," as Winston Churchill called it, revealed it and opened the subject of Allied cryptanalysis to more comprehensive study.

As of this date, two dozen books and innumerable scholarly papers have been published on various aspects on Enigma and Ultra in Britain, Poland, the U.S., France, Germany, Italy, Yugoslavia, Belgium and other countries.

The letter from Lisicki included three sheets of paper, darkened and streaked in poor photocopying. It took close scrutiny to discern the numerals and letters of a handwritten cryptogram. The date of its composition was the easiest thing to establish: at the top of the first page, in plain text, was the date "24.IV.1904." There were also several unenciphered words, including some Polish first and last names. It was one of 80 enciphered messages between the Polish Socialist Party and its emissaries in London, now held in the Piłsudski Institute in New York.

This letter had been written in the period of the Russo-Japanese War, which had begun on February 8, 1904, and the name – actually a pseudonym – "Mieczysław" stood for none other than the Polish Socialist and future head of independent Poland, Józef Piłsudski, who in 1904 was staying in Austrian-governed Kraków. Another pseudonym, "Karski," stood for Piłsudski's closest aide and emissary to London, Tytus Filipowicz. In the spring of 1904, Piłsudski and several colleagues were trying to reach an agreement with the Japanese diplomatic representatives in Britain, and through them with the Japanese government in Tokyo.

Why negotiations between the Poles, then partly under Russian and partly under German rule, and the land of the Rising Sun?

The Poles hoped to receive Japanese support on the international scene for the restoration of an independent Poland. Piłsudski's Polish Socialist Party also sought to obtain from the Japanese modern rifles, together with substantial stocks of ammunition. In return, the Poles would divert the Czarist armies with a rising of underground forces and would provide intelligence on the Russian order of battle and troop movements. The prospects for this seemed more realistic since the spring, when reports from Manchuria suggested the eventual defeat of the Czarist armies. A more practical near objective of the Poles was to obtain better treatment for the Poles drafted into the Russian army who had been captured by the Japanese and were being held in atrocious conditions in Japan's Manchurian prisoner-of-war camps.

It seemed doubtful, however, whether these historical facts would be helpful in attempting to decrypt the ciphers. Rejewski was not at all pleased to have received them.

> "The enclosures to your letter," wrote Rejewski in his reply, "are truly a gift of the Danae. I feel a very strong temptation to start work on them but, at the same time, I do not want to do so since this is not my field, nor is it for my age and condition of health. I have, nevertheless, taken a closer look at them. That this in an encipherment procedure in which three different keys are used is no real discovery, as this can easily be guessed from the several words given in plain language, and not only from the different frequencies of cipher groups. To be sure, there are many repetitions, but they are too short for a simple cipher [as a rule, they comprise only two groups each]. The brevity of the repetitions could be explained, for instance, by the fact that, as substitutes for certain common letters, several different symbols were used, or that the symbols represent certain bigrams, such as <u>ch</u>, <u>cz</u>, <u>sz</u>, certain short words such as <u>nie</u> ["no" or "not"], or numerals or punctuation marks.

> "But one may also attempt to explain the brevity of the repetitions by other hypotheses, for instance, that the cipher has been peppered with meaningless 'null' groups of numerals, etc. But if one wished to study all this, he would have to prepare operational sheets on which he could freely mark with zigzags, flourishes, etc., using variously colored pencils. All that would be rather difficult to manage, however, since some of the cipher groups are illegible, and the middle page has been photocopied so badly that part of the cipher text has been cut off.
>
> "The essence of the matter, however, is that I am reluctant to undertake this job, particularly in this season of the year: it is the end of August, and soon it will be my favorite month, September; we will have our golden Polish autumn and under the circumstances I have no desire to pore over ciphers in a closed room. Maybe in the winter I'll set to work on it, but I wouldn't like to make any promises."

Rejewski's reluctance to attack the cipher was no doubt caused mainly by his declining health and by his plans to vacation, as usual, during the "golden Polish autumn." He had not yet completely recovered from the emotional aftereffects of a sudden loss of consciousness, during the night of 5-6 March 1976, after which he had been hospitalized for several weeks in the Neuropsychiatric Clinic in southern Warsaw. After Rejewski had returned home, his wife Irena used to phone me, unbeknownst to her husband, when she became alarmed at the strenuous demands that he placed on himself or at the exhausting visits of swarms of press, radio and TV reporters and interviewers, of second- and third-rate writers and of other sensation-mongers. To keep them at bay was not easy even with the joint efforts of Mrs. Rejewska and myself.

In mid-August 1976, a few days after her husband had received the letter in question, a phone call from Irena dealt for a change not with such intruders. She was concerned about her husband's "suspicious" behavior. Did I have any idea as to the cause of his restlessness and excitement? Could it have some connection with the letter that he had received from Britain?

During my last meeting with Rejewski, he had shown a noticeable lack of interest in the letter with the cipher. Why should he now be agitated or excited, pacing, as his wife told me, back and forth in his room, muttering to himself something that she could not understand? And why should he have mentioned to her on two or three occasions that he would rather stay home while she and Wojtek took a vacation out of town?

But it would be a difficult task to try to convince Rejewski to take better care of his health and to go along with his wife's wish to detach him from strenuous, if voluntary, mental labors, at least during that year's golden September. His evident gentleness, his refined manners and self-possession in speech and behavior, with glimpses of subtle irony and dry humor that tended to self-deprecation, but without any tendency to hurt others or to diminish the achievements of his two mathematician-colleagues who had been involved in cracking Enigma – all these traits only camouflaged his quiet yet adamant will. Hence, I hesitated to invade his world of thoughts and decisions. Perhaps it really would be better for him to spend his beloved September, not in a noisy spa on the Baltic coast, but in his quiet district of Warsaw, after his family had left, and having plenty of time for quiet walks in the nearby Bielany Park, decked out in its autumnal colors. It was in the same Bielany Park that he had used to walk almost every weekend up to September of 1939, when he went to war, continuing his own war of wits with the Nazis which had begun seven years earlier, when he had begun work on Germany's Enigma ciphers.

Neither was I, for that matter, planning to leave Warsaw for a September vacation that year. Hence, I was far from taken aback when I got a phone call asking me urgently to come and "discuss a number of matters that have just cropped up." I gave in immediately, as it has become my custom since 1973, when Enigma began to play havoc with my life and with the established history of the Second World War, revealing many new angles and hitherto unknown aspects. In a word, I called the same afternoon at Rejewski's apartment.

This time Rejewski was not his usual controlled self. He had dropped his manner of carefully guarding his state of mind and emotions and he was evidently elated.

Since 1973, it had become Rejewski's custom to pass me carbon or cyclostyled copies of practically all the papers he wrote as well as the comments and remarks he made on books and other publications concerning Enigma or cryptology. This was also true of copies of those documents that he thought might be used by researchers dealing with the history of Enigma and of cryptology. That was why I had been called in that day.

My appearance in his apartment resulted in his brusquely waving a single sheet of paper at me, which, he said shortly, was the fruit of a month of efforts to break and convert into intelligible language an arcane handwritten cipher dating back to the 1904 Russo-Japanese War. Though his voice was calm and impassive when he handed the text to me, I could see his delight on his face. I refrained from pushing him into replying to the questions I wanted to ask, leaving him to venture his comments when he thought fit. After all, he had clearly done the job despite his own earlier and forcefully expressed objections.

So I got down to scrutinizing the contents of that sheet of paper and as I did I became increasingly absorbed by what I encountered. For this was a fascinating display of a brilliant mind at work, sensible words and whole sentences extracted by the codebreaker's alchemy from the seemingly meaningless raw material of the indistinct rows of figures on the three pages presented to me one month earlier.

Rejewski had cryptanalyzed the text and the translation appears below:

> Grzegorz [Gregory]
>
> 26th April 1904
>
> Dear Friend,
>
> Part I enciphered with our usual key.
>
> Part II: Bystrzycki, Part III with the Bolek and Mieczysław key. Karski told me it exists only in our yard (the Intelligence Bureau). It was then proposed 90 to 93 (i.e. for 3 points).
>
> The requirements set for what is in parentheses above are as follows: Kharkov Moscow Siberia, one special agent for each AN. EO of the Army Corps mobilization, the number of transferred troops, their time of departure.
>
> Kharkov, it is known that the first four Army C[orps] are in Manchuria. It is confidentially known that the 17th will be or has been mobilized [and] will depart in early May. The next to go will be the 10th Army Corps, stationed in Kursk and [Kharkov?] in July. Obtain information concerning strength and composition and check whether and where it is to go.
>
> II. Moscow: Information required on each regiment passing through, where it is going and by what route. Siberia: how many trains go every day, the number of men and the quantities of ammunition and food; also when the circular road around Lake Baikal will be opened, the same [...] to it.
>
> III. Exact description of the Baltic Fleet and when it is to go East. The number of men and artillery dispatched to the war in Manchuria in the second half of last year and in the first and second halves of the present year.

> Dear Friends,
>
> What was promised has been done. The friend [...] reports that his friend + who lives near his wife [?] is ready to do all that is required but in return for this affair he is asking for almost double the amount envisioned in today's conversation.
>
> + Colonel
>
> It has been late. Greetings SK (the last key!)

I do not think that Rejewski really cared about the meaning hidden in those deciphered rows of digits. He was very far from being any kind of a *homo historicus* or *homo politicus*. To the historian interested in that specific period, however, this text was no minor find.

On June 2, 1904, two and a half months after the message had been written, Piłsudski turned up in London, where he met the Japanese ambassador, Hayashi, several times. The result was an invitation to visit Tokyo. On 11 June, Piłsudski arrived by ship in New York accompanied by Tytus Filipowicz (Karski) (later Polish ambassador to the United States) and on 21 June, he arrived by train in San Francisco. The next day he embarked on the S. S. Coptic for Japan, arriving there on 10 July.

In the end, Piłsudski's political negotiations in Tokyo had little practical consequence. But he did gain one thing: the Japanese military command agreed to substantially facilitate the purchase of weapons and ammunition and issued appropriate instructions to that effect to Japanese military attachés in several European countries.

I am more than convinced that Rejewski's solution did not come like a bolt of genius out of the blue – unlike a significant portion of his solution of the Enigma. That is clear from the number of auxiliary cryptological tables that reveal some of the secrets of his intellectual workshop. And if a moment of illumination did arrive, it had to be supported and developed with his patient perseverance, the endless, painstaking toil which is the classical cryptologist's lot. With this in mind, someone not acquainted with the manner in which Rejewski expressed his thoughts and feelings, the way in which he played down his efforts and the results they bring, would surely be misled by taking literally the wording of the letter he sent the same day, 17 September 1976, to Lisicki:

> "Thanks for your letters of the 29th August and 8th September 1976. They arrived almost simultaneously. I shall deal with them in a moment, but before I do a couple of words on the 1904 cipher. At the end I did tackle it for it was giving me no rest and, additionally, seemed to offer no real problems. In effect I had no great trouble in cracking it (if it had been more difficult and time-consuming I would not have touched it). The contents of the message as I read it are presented on the enclosed separate sheet, together with the keys I used and the method applied. There should be little trouble with solving the remaining material [in the Piłsudski Mstifute] even if the keys used differ. I must admit that I feel some satisfaction with solving that cipher, which I might compare with the successful tackling of a difficult crossword, but I would prefer not to try to solve any more ciphers ever again: I cannot or do not want to tackle more difficult ones. As far as these specific ones are concerned, they ceased to fascinate me once I had broken them. Now I would like to get back to your letters."

He then delved into the intricacies and personalities of the Enigma solution in four densely typed pages – four of the more than 1,000 in Polish, English, French and German addressed to persons the whole world over: in France, Britain, Sweden, Germany, Yugoslavia in Europe, to the USA and Brazil in the Western Hemisphere. The most frequently mentioned topics were the technical intricacies of the cipher machine, the wartime friendly and efficient cooperation among British, French and Polish code-breakers and the officers who commanded the various outfits in which they served. But also there was much about the rivalries and infighting among the wartime allies, as well as lots of political and social gossip and, even tidbits bordering on libel. Truly, a treasure-house of facts and opinions for present and future historians. A common feature can be discerned in all his letters: they are miracles of precision though marked by his own, unmistakable understatements and refined humor.

One last remark on that cipher from the 1904-1905 Russo-Japanese War. Rejewski cracked it in August 1976 when he was 71 and had been ailing for several months; the thing I possibly best remember of what he told me when I arrived that day to see and appreciate the results of his efforts was a reflective remark he uttered, looking rather absent- mindedly out of an open window towards some imaginary horizon which he alone could see.

"You know," he said "something durable can surely be expected from anyone who claims to be a cryptologist, a codebreaker. Do you agree?"

APPENDIX

The alphabet used comprises 25 letters (six fewer than the complete Polish alphabet)

a ą b c d e ę f g h i k l ł m n o p r s t u w y z

which are written into a 10×10 grid in accordance with the key selected.

I. PASTERNAK ("parsnip");

II. BYSTRZYCKI (adjective formed from "Bystrzyca," a river and town in southwestern Poland);

III. LITERA ("letter" of the alphabet),

as shown below in I, II, and III.

The empty squares serve as null groups which are written into the ciphertext every few letters in order to mislead the cryptanalyst.

I

	1	2	3	4	5	6	7	8	9	0
1	P									
2	A	ą	b	c	d					
3	S									
4	T	u	w	y	z					
5	E	ę	f	g	h	i				
6	R									
7	N	o								
8	A									
9	K	l	ł	m						
0										

II

	1	2	3	4	5	6	7	8	9	0
1	B									
2	Y									
3	S									
4	T	u	w							
5	R									
6	Z	a	ą							
7	Y									
8	C	d	e	ę	f	g	h			
9	K	l	ł	m	n	o	p			
0	I									

III

	1	2	3	4	5	6	7	8	9	0
1	L	ł	m	n	o	p				
2	I	k								
3	T	u	w	y	z					
4	E	ę	f	g	h					
5	R	s								
6	A	ą	b	c	d					
7										
8										
9										
0										

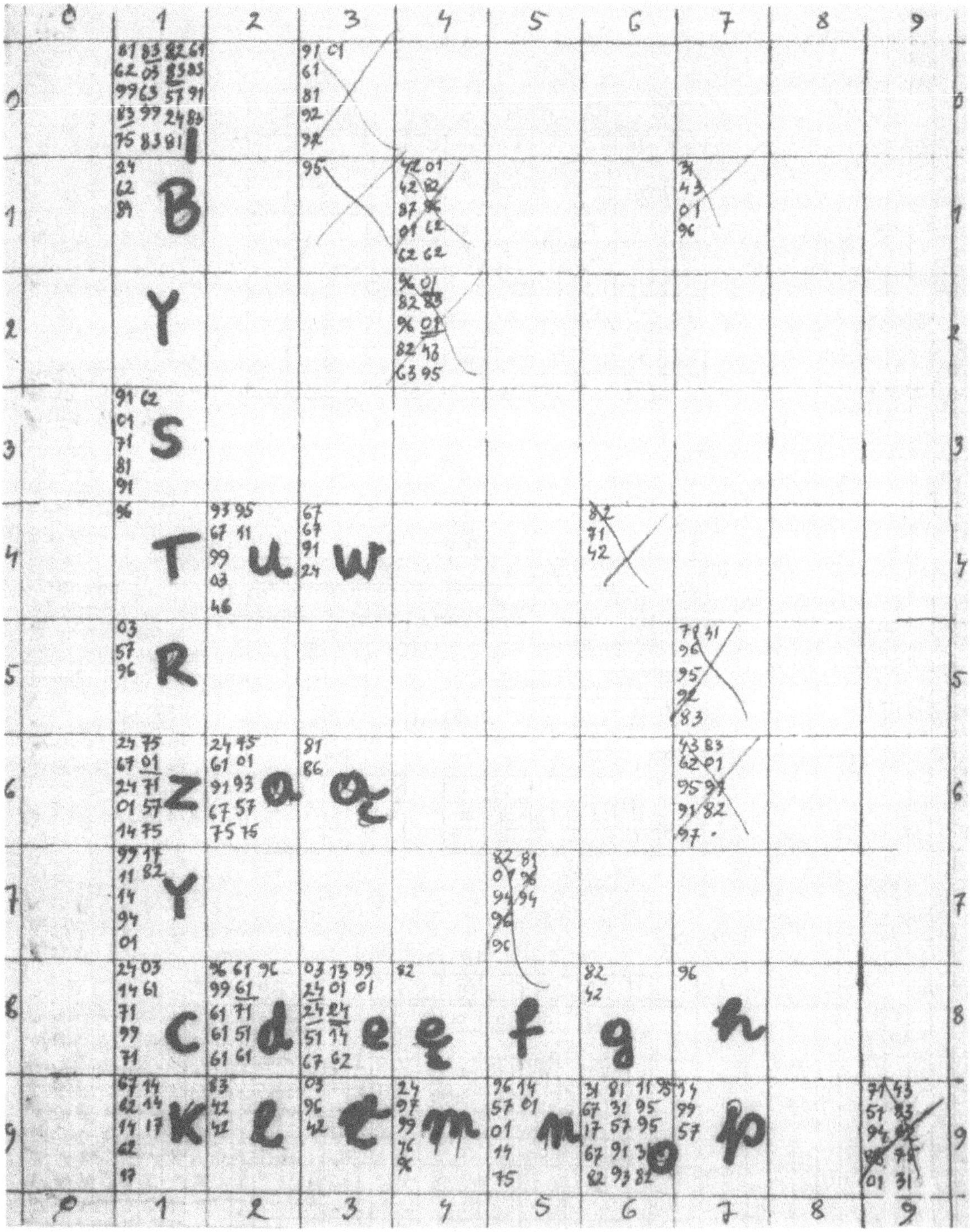

Rejewski's summary worksheet for Part II.

Rejewski's trial worksheet for Part II.

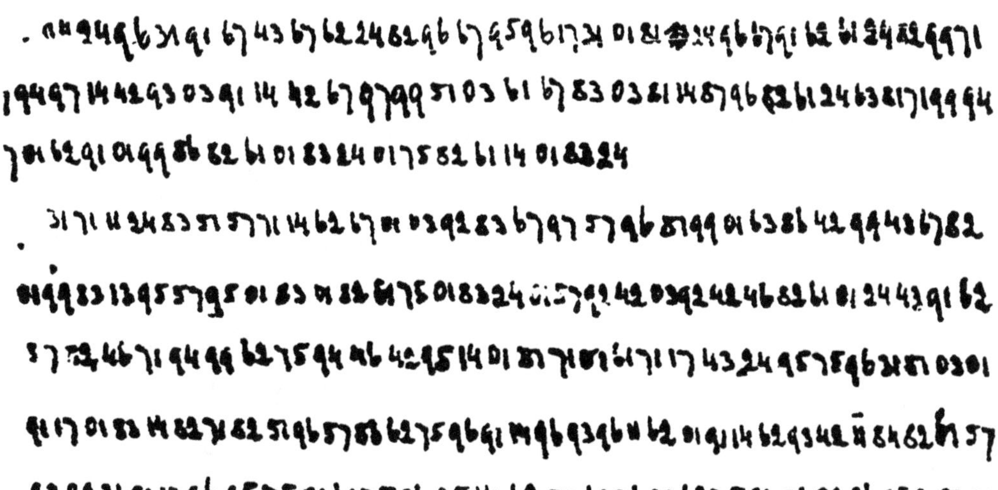

The original copy of Part II of the message.

BIOGRAPHICAL SKETCH

Dr. phil.Władysław Kozaczuk, a Polish historian, is the author of a number of books, including, *Wehrmacht 1933-39* (a standard Polish work on German rearmament and war preparations), *Secret Battle: The Intelligence Services of Poland and the German Reich, 1922-39*, *Enigma*, *The Peripheries of the Hell* (concerning Switzerland's armed neutrality in World War Two, published recently.)

WHY WAS SAFFORD PESSIMISTIC ABOUT BREAKING THE GERMAN ENIGMA CIPHER MACHINE IN 1942?

Louis Kruh

ADDRESS: 17 Alfred Road W., Merrick NY 11566 USA.

ABSTRACT: In 1942, Captain Lawrence F. Safford doubted that the German Enigma would be broken. This implied that he was unaware that the British had already broken the Enigma Cipher. Various authorities and colleagues of Safford speculate on his assertion.

KEYWORDS: Safford, Enigma, Weeks, Currier, Rosen, Sinkov, Rowlett, Kahn.

This article is reprinted, with permission, from the Winter 1988 (Volume 9, Number 2, pp. 3, 11), issue of *Cryptolog*. *Cryptolog* is a publication of the Naval Cryptologic Veterans Association, 3421 Stack St., Eugene OR 97404 USA.

In a memorandum dated March 18, 1942, Captain Lawrence F. Safford wrote, "Our prospects of ever breaking the German 'Enigma' cipher machine are rather poor." (See section 2 in the complete memo which follows.)

Safford's assertion implies that he was not aware that the British had solved German Enigma ciphers. But, he wrote this memo a year after Navy Lieutenant Robert H. Weeks and Ensign Prescott Currier along with Captain Abraham Sinkov and Lieutenant Leo Rosen of the Signal Intelligence Service had visited Britain's Government Code and Cipher School at Bletchley Park.

Some authors have speculated that the British may not have informed the American mission of the extent of their success with the Enigma.[1, p.312] Also, the April 11, 1941 report prepared by Sinkov and Rosen on their trip did not mention the Enigma. (Information is unavailable on any Weeks-Currier report.) The Signal Security Agency official history, however, points out that for security reasons the omission of Enigma was deliberate. The British had obtained a special pledge of secrecy from the American officers who agreed to reveal what they learned to just three persons: the Assistant Chief of Staff, G-2; the Chief, SIS; and Mr. William F. Friedman. Only then did the British disclose "the existence of their 'E' operations (a successful attack upon traffic enciphered by

Op-20-Q MEMORANDUM FOR OP-20. March 18, 1942

Subject: Security of information obtained from enemy communications.

1. During World War I (1914-18), the British Admiralty was very successful in reading German naval messages and tracking German submarines by D/F. This was a well-guarded secret during the war. After the war, the British let down the bars of secrecy and told the world what they had done and how good they were. Apparently, it never occurred to the British that the Germans would profit by these revelations.

2. In World War II, the German ciphers and communication procedure are such that the information obtainable by radio is substantially zero. With the exception of "weather codes" and certain other "minor systems" the only German naval messages which have been read have been the result of captures. Our prospects of ever breaking the German "Enigma" cipher machine are rather poor.

3. We are much more fortunately situated with regard to the Japanese Navy. Our solution of Japanese naval systems began back in 1925. We are able to read most of the messages in the most important Japanese naval ciphering system and have completely solved one of the secondary systems. This is the result of sixteen years of unremitting effort along these lines. We are also getting considerable information by direction finding. We are faced with constant danger that news of our success will leak out, whereupon the Japanese will adopt steps which will nullify our efforts.

4. In 1938 and 1939, the Japanese Navy used a system which we have never succeeded in solving. They abandoned this system in 1940 and adopted a system which we can solve. The reason for abandoning the secure system is not known, but we surmise it was due to its slowness and complexity. There is nothing that will stop their return to it if they find out that we are reading their messages.

5. What is even worse, they may adopt the German Navy cipher machine if news of our success leaks out. If this happens, our source of information will be reduced to direction finding and traffic analysis.

6. This memorandum is submitted for the purpose of impressing upon all concerned that we must not compromise our one sure source of enemy information by a too wide dissemination of information.

Respectfully,
L. F. Safford,
Captain, U. S. Navy, Op-20-Q.

the German high- security cryptographic machine known as the Enigma ...)."[2, pp.12-13]

Presumably, Weeks and Currier made similar pledges – the Signal Security Agency history does not discuss Navy details – but surely Safford, head of the Navy's cryptographic unit, OP-20-G, would be among the Navy people permitted to receive the information. However, if Safford knew about British success with Enigma ciphers, what is the explanation for his seemingly uninformed comment.

Frank B. Rowlett, a key member of SIS who knew Safford, was asked for his opinion on the apparent discrepancy. He wrote,

> I do not consider it possible that Safford was not aware of the British success with the Enigma at the time he wrote the memorandom in 1942. As you know, an American team of cryptologists visited England in 1941 and were told of the UK work on the Enigma intercepts. I do not see how the information on the German Enigma brought back by Weeks and Currier could have been kept from Safford, considering the position he held in the Navy cryptologic organization.

One possible reason for Safford implying that the Enigma had not been broken is perhaps best described by the word "disinformation." The subject of Safford's memo was "Secrecy of information obtained from enemy communications" and what better way to protect Enigma derived intelligence then to highlight dismal prospects of ever breaking Enigma ciphers. Or as Winston Churchill said in 1943, "In war-time, truth is so precious that she should always be attended by a bodyguard of lies."[3, p.338]

Another view comes from David Kahn, author of *The Codebreakers* and the leading historian on cryptologic matters. He says that Safford was referring only to the Naval Enigma, which had been decrypted with the assistance of clues gathered from captured U-boats and other German ships. Kahn also suggests that Safford may have been alluding specifically to the then current inability to crack the new 4-rotor Enigma Shark cipher which was introduced 1 February 1942. (It was not solved until early December 1942 with the help of a codebook taken from the captured U-559.)[4, pp.749-750]

The opinions of naval officers who had worked with Safford were also solicited. None of the replies had a definitive answer but two of them had some pertinent information.

A retired Lieutenant Commander wrote:

> Prior to the Pearl Harbor incident, Captain Safford, though chiefly concerned with the Japanese problem, did devote considerable time

with the embryonic German Naval section, discussing at length with Mrs. Driscoll matters associated with the German Naval problem.

Around July or August 1940, the section was comprised of four persons. Since Mrs. Driscoll was severely handicapped in walking because of an earlier auto accident, it was my job to relay the various requests and questions directly to Captain Safford - this occurred frequently and I spent much time in his office.

Such was the climate of our operations until either late 1940 or early 1941, when Commander Wenger became our boss and we no longer had contact with Safford. I must stress that I am not certain of these dates - it could have been later, but I do clearly recall that this shift did take place.

By March 1942 (the date of the memorandom in question) the German Naval section had expanded considerably.

It may have been around June 1941 when the first of the English visited us - and by the fall of 1941, plans had already started for the development of the U.S. Navy version of "Bombe". Again, I'm pretty vague as to exact months.

I have no knowledge as to why Captain Safford made the statement you quoted from the memorandom - but one may draw some conclusions:

1. Since he had been out of touch with the German section since either late 1940 or early 1941, he may not have been up to date in the progression of things since the development of Bombe plans in mid 1941, though he was aware of the information that Weeks and Currier brought back from England.

2. The memorandom was written in March 1942, 3 months after Pearl Harbor. Things were in a great state of flux, and the matter of the Winds message must have placed a great stress and inner turmoil on his over-worried mind, so that he may have overlooked or forgotten the actual facts.

Another retired officer explained that "My personal knowledge of the naval Enigma was in February and March 1941. At the time the British had several copies of the machine and sets of rotors and umkehrwalz, some of which, at least, had been taken in the Lofoten raid. They had only the key/starting setting material for a few days, and their big problem was trying to solve the coding of each message's starting settings. As you are aware from the extensive literature on the Enigma, they apparently did solve this, but I do not know when."

In regard to the Currier-Weeks trip to Bletchley Park, he said they returned with,

> ...several days' settings and a "paper" Enigma, with all the rotor and umkehrwalz laid out. With this material we were able to decipher messages taken from our intercept logs of the days covered. Captain Safford's "except by capture" seems to bear this out. What the exact situation was by March of 1942, I do not know. I feel sure he would have known of any recent successes in the matter.

One final conjecture is that Safford's pessimism was based on the apparently remote possibility of a purely cryptanalytical solution of the Naval Enigma cipher in contrast to one assisted by capture of rotors, key lists, etc., which had been the situation up to that time.

Supporting or contrary views are welcome.

REFERENCES

1. Bamford, J. 1982. *The Puzzle Palace*. Boston: Houghton Mifflin Co.

2. U.S. Army Security Agency, History of the Signal Security Agency, Vol. Two. 1947. *The General Cryptanalytic Problems*. Washington, D.C.: Army Security Agency.

3. Churchill, W. 1949. *The Second World War*, Vol. V. Boston: Houghton Mifflin Co.

4. Hinsley, F. H., et al. 1981. *British Intelligence in the Second World War*, Vol. II. London: HMSO.

BIOGRAPHICAL SKETCH

Louis Kruh is an indefatigable researcher and collector of cryptologic memorabilia, particularly cipher devices. His interest in cryptology spans more than 40 years and he responds knowledgeably and promptly to all queries regarding literature and equipment. He is co-author with Dr. C. A. Deavours, of *Machine Cryptography and Modern Cryptanalysis*, (Artech House, Inc. 1985). He retired as Director of Advertising for New York Telephone in June 1990 and he is setting about practicing the law he studied.

LETTERS TO THE EDITOR

The following two letters relate to the article, "Why Was Safford Pessimistic About Breaking the German Enigma Cipher Machine in 1942," by Louis Kruh which appeared in *Cryptologia*, (1990) 14(3): 253-257.

From Colin Burke, 6319 Red Haven Rd, Columbia MD 21045 USA.

October 1990

Dear Editors

I enclose some general comments re the Safford memo, p. 254, and my conclusions.

a) The political setting: When Safford wrote this memo he was well on the way to being permanently shoved out of any significant role in OP20 but was not yet put totally aside. And, he may have been continuing his attempt to return to a role in "G". The Redman group was on its way in and was beginning to forge its new policies.

   I think Safford was giving policy advice to the new group. The memo has to be placed in a political as well as a technical context to appreciate it:

   1) he is advising the new group to stand against political pressures and to keep Magic to as few people as possible—that might have been one of his responsibilities as 'Q'
   2) he is warning the new group, which included Wenger, who had always been an advocate for the use high speed equipment, not to count on a quick way into Enigma, a system he had been tackling since early 1941
   3) he is perhaps warning the new men not to give Britain too much about or from Magic

b) Conclusions: I agree with your final conjecture, p. 257. Placed in the appropriate contexts, Safford's assertions that only "captures" had allowed the previous entries into Naval Enigma and that prospects for re-entry were rather poor, seem reasonable. Given what England had probably told us about methods by early 1941, his history was well grounded. The importance of the later capture to the re-entry into submarine Enigma at the end of 1942 validated his prediction. If we add the helpful but not critical assumption that OP20G had not been informed of the "bombe" and its allied methods by early 1942, then Safford's memo is explained.[1] And, even if the assumption about the bombe is dropped, Safford's statements were those of a well informed man. Note that the British bombes were in operation long before the mid-1941 break into the 3 wheel Naval Enigma which suggests that some captures might have been needed to initiate bombe usage, even for the simplest 3 wheel systems.

Finally, the materials in this article reinforce my beliefs about how much and how soon Britain shared the Ultra secrets with us. Again, why were there no references to the bombes, even guarded ones, by Safford or the two Navy men you quote?

Comments on Particular Points

I) p. 253: "Our prospects of ever breaking the German "Enigma" cipher machine are rather poor." There are several ways to interpret this. Let me cite some that are not emphasized in your article.

1) "our" could well refer to OP20G, not to both Britain and America—thus he could have known of the earlier 3 wheel break by Britain and yet made his assertion. The following support this.

   a) Safford did not trust England nor did he approve of sharing American secrets with it
   b) Safford thought ("Rhapsody in Purple") that Britain had not kept its promises concerning the February-March 1941 exchange
   c) he wanted an independent American capability for all systems for all nations

2) "ever breaking"

   a) the Weeks-Currier trip came before England had cracked even the three wheel Naval Enigma so that it could not have told the Americans how to enter it via any general method (also see your article, p. 257)

[1] Joe Eachus' surprise when he discovered the use of the diagonal board in the Turing bombe when he went to England in late summer, 1942, is only one among many small indications that Britain had not told OP20G all about its Enigma capability.

- b) I have seen no hard evidence that Britain told OP20G the necessary details to allow it to enter the 3 wheel system by itself after England's entry in mid-1941 when more 'pure' techniques were available (also see you article, p. 257)
- c) I have not seen any evidence that Britain gave OP20G knowledge of more general techniques (pure cryptanalytic) for Naval Enigma systems before 1942
- d) Safford's reference seems to be to "naval" Enigma — he could have known of the more pure or general British approaches to air force or other Enigma but was correct that Naval systems awaited captures
- e) certainly, in March 1942, the prospects of either England or America cracking the 4 wheel system were low and, I believe, Safford wanted an independent American capability
    - i) I have some reason to believe that when the Americans started their bombe project (Feb-March) 1942, the design was very different from Turing's and the logical approach to a solution was also very different
    - ii) the U. S. surely knew that Britain had been locked out of the 4 wheel system and that it could not promise a speedy re-entry

II) p. 255: "A Retired Lieutenant Commander wrote...." This man seems to have his dates wrong, he is consistently one year too early

1) the official history or OP20G states that no Enigma work was begun until early 1941 (NOT 1940)
2) Wenger did not return from "sea duty" until late 1941 and probably did not begin any OP20G operational work until early 1942
3) Safford did not leave (get kicked out) as head of G until 1942
4) although the Americans decided to build some sort of bombe on their own in early 1942 it was not until the fall of 1942 that anything like a firm commitment to a design was made
5) because of the above we should conclude that Safford was well aware of what was going on in March, 1942

III) p. 256: "Another retired officer...." This man also seems to be somewhat confused about dates, but is perhaps a few months rather than a year off the mark. Despite that possible 'slip' he says much that seems acceptable and much that is very important to the questions of how much and when Britain shared it methods, and the Safford memo, as well.

1) Didn't the Lofoten raid come after the conclusion of the Weeks-Currier visit (and if this isn't one of those men someone else who I should know of was at GC&CS in 1941)? [Editor's note: The Lofoten raid occurred on March 4, 1941, and it is known that the two Army members of the U. S. intelligence mission to England remained there through the end of March; presumably so did Weeks and Currier.]
2) if this man was either Weeks or Currier and if England sent over the techniques which allowed them into the three wheel Enigma in mid-1941, he should have known more about all this

IV) Your comment, p. 257: "One final conjecture...." Much of my wandering depends upon a meaning for the elusive concept, "a purely cryptanalytic solution" and this section is directed more to the general question of how much Britain told us than to the Safford memo in your article.

1) In conjunction with the "several days' settings" quote Safford's "captures" assertion strongly suggests that England did not tell us about their "bombe" and its use of 'cribs' in 1941
   a) why wasn't the bombe mentioned along with the mention, p. 257, of the paper Enigma given the Americans?
   b) why didn't Safford include something about the Turing bombe approach in the memo, at least to directly discount the possibilities of such an approach?

From Ralph Erskine who can be reached c/o *Cryptologia*, Rose-Hulman Institute of Technology, Terre Haute IN 47803 USA.

10 October 1990 - Belfast NORTHERN IRELAND

Sir

In a recent article, Louis Kruh asked for views on Captain Lawrence Safford's knowledge of the British breaking of Enigma.

Safford's memorandum was expressly intended to emphasise to others the paramount need to ensure that the US Navy breaking of, in particular, the JN 25 series of codes was not revealed to the Japanese. He was anxious that this might occur due to the resulting intelligence being disseminated too widely. His passing reference to Enigma, occupying only about one line, is clearly not an exhaustive statement of the Allied capability to break any form of Enigma.

Safford was right to be concerned. His memorandum is dated 18 March 1942. On 30 August 1942, 3 Skl II Staffel in the Seekriegsleitung (the German Navy's war staff) is apparently recorded as stating –

> When the Japanese were presented with some captured documents from the prize ship "Nankin", the [Japanese] Navy suspected that its signal methods were no longer unknown to the enemy and it requested German assistance in revising its coding systems.[2]

The Australian ss *Nankin*, bound from Freemantle, had been captured by the German raider *Thor* on 5 May. Documents seized from the *Nankin* were transferred to a German supply ship, *Regenberg*, and reached the German naval attache in Japan, Rear-Admiral Paul Wenneker, only on 18 July. It would seem that the papers seized included intelligence summaries which could only have been derived from the Allied breaking of Japanese naval codes. On 29 August, after being authorised by Berlin to do so, Wenneker showed some of the reports to the Japanese — hence the remarks by 3 Skl quoted above.[3]

The further event that Safford feared — the supply of Enigma by the Germans to the Japanese also took place, although perhaps not until around 1943. Fortunately, it would appear that the Germans did not hand over the plugboard version of Enigma. If they had done so and Enigma's rotors had been rewired (as elementary security would have required), the US Navy would have had the utmost difficulty in penetrating "Japanese" naval Enigma — if the Japanese could have produced it quickly and distributed it in sufficient numbers.

Safford was writing purely in a naval context and not referring to Luftwaffe or Army ciphers, machine or otherwise. Moreover, since naval Enigma ("Enigma M") presented special problems to the cryptanalysts, it was almost irrelevant whether Luftwaffe or Army Enigma ciphers were being broken by the British or not. In the last sentence of paragraph 2 and the first of paragraph 3, Safford is clearly referring to US Navy cryptanalytical work. It is therefore reasonable to read the penultimate sentence of paragraph 2 (stating, in effect, that Enigma M — "German naval messages" which were not "weather codes [or] other minor systems" — had been read only as a result of captures), as also referring to American naval work on Enigma, and therefore only to Enigma M.

The first effective breaking of naval Enigma ("Enigma M") by Bletchley Park ("BP") started on 12 March, after the capture of Heimisch (the main Kriegsmarine Enigma cipher at that time) keylists for at least part of February on 4

[2]Report on documents from 3 Skl II Staffel (NID 24/T50/45): PRO ADM 223/255.

[3]See James Rusbridger, "The Sinking of the "Automedon", the Capture of the "Nankin," *Encounter* 64(5) (May 1985), 8.

March 1941 during a commando raid in the Lofotens.[4] However, the British had not then recovered the bigram tables used to encode the message key on Enigma M, which held BP back badly, despite the fact that the keylists gave the main settings — another indication just how difficult it was to penetrate Enigma M.[5] BP read or broke 26 Heimisch daily keys for dates between 1 February and 9 May, which led to the decipherment of about 340 signals — probably less than 10 per cent of the naval traffic intercepted during that period. The British captured further important Enigma M material in late April and mid-May, including keylists and a weather short signal book, the Wetterkurzschlüssel, which was immediately to prove a crucially important source of cribs.

According to Safford, and the second retired US Navy officer quoted in the article, the US Navy also read some Enigma M traffic, probably around May 1941 (after Lieutenant Weeks and Ensign Currier returned to the States).[6] The British must, at the minimum, have supplied the US Navy with —

> a "paper" copy of Enigma M (the wiring of its 8 rotors and its reflector);
> some keylists (probably those for part of February 1941).[7]

BP's possession of this material was one of the United Kingdom's most closely kept secrets. Only a select few on each side of the Atlantic knew about the captures, but Safford was clearly one. And since the US Navy in Washington would have realised, from at least September 1941 on, that the British were breaking naval Enigma, it would be most surprising if Safford, in view of his position in Op 20 G, was not aware of that fact.[8]

Because the US Navy was primarily concerned with escorting the Atlantic convoys, it was really only interested in the radio traffic to and from the Atlantic U-boats, and not in the signals to surface vessels. On 1 February 1942 the Atlantic U-boats had begun to use four-rotor Enigma (M4) on Triton (known to the Allies as "Shark") — a cipher introduced specially for the Atlantic U-boats on 5 October 1941. Worse still, a second edition of the Wetterkurzschlüssel had been introduced on 20 January 1942. Lacking that edition, BP was therefore without its only source of Triton cribs for the bombes (fast key-finding aids) and, for the first time, blinded by the Triton traffic. In the result, BP broke Triton on only three days between 1 February and 11 December 1942.

---

[4] Ralph Erskine, "Breaking Heimisch and Triton," *Intelligence and National Security*, (1988) 3: 162.

[5] *Cf.* the retired officer quoted in Kruh, 256.

[6] Kruh, 254 (paragraph 3).

[7] Kruh, 257.

[8] See e.g. Ultra signal 1334A/8 September 1941 to CNO Washington, giving U-boat positions: PRO ADM 223/102.

Since there was no prospect of BP reconstructing the new Wetterkurzschlüssel cryptanalytically in 1942, the Allies were dependent on capturing it, probably from a U-boat, without the Germans realising that the code had been compromised. The codebook was printed using water soluble ink, so that recovering it intact from a sunk U-boat would have been virtually impossible.

The capture of the Wetterkurzschlüssel (and another short signal book, the Kurzsignalheft) required something approaching a minor miracle, and the supreme sacrifice by Lieutenant Tony Fasson and AB Colin Grazier (both from *HMS Petard*) on 30 October 1942. They had boarded the sinking U 559 in the Eastern Mediterranean, but were unable to escape from the submarine when it suddenly went down. For their bravery, which undoubtedly helped significantly to shorten the war, so saving many thousands of lives, they were awarded the George Cross (the second highest British medal). Tommy Brown, a 16 year old canteen assistant who helped them, received the George Medal for his part in the capture. But it was not until 2 December that BP became convinced that it could break into Triton again.[9] And that happened because, by great good fortune, the U-boats sent weather short signals on Triton using M4 in three-rotor mode, so that the absence of four-rotor bombes was not too much of a handicap; the three-rotor bombes sufficed — just about. Given the run of luck required by the Allies before M4 could be broken, it is little wonder that Safford was pessimistic in early 1942.

A further factor in Safford's thinking may have been that the knowledge then available to the Allies possibly suggested that four-rotor bombes would also be required to break Triton on M4. And he would have probably have known that there was little prospect of those bombes entering service before July 1943. In March 1942 who, then, would have rated the chances of breaking Triton as higher than, in Safford's words "rather poor"?

So far as is known, the US Navy did not break Enigma M cryptanalytically in 1941 — or indeed in 1942. All of Safford's statements are entirely consistent with his referring in March 1942 only to Enigma M4. Read in that light, they are extremely accurate, showing Safford to have been very well-informed indeed, since breaking M4 was truly a problem of horrifying proportions.

Safford refers to the breaking of the German naval meteorological cipher by the US Navy. This once again highlights the lack of liaison between the US Navy and the US Army on cryptanalytical matters. The German navy met cipher was in fact a code which was super-enciphered using trigram tables. It was broadcast by Norddeich (call sign DAN) on 125 and 150 kHz, and included reports from numerous met stations in occupied Europe, Portugal and other

[9] See Erskine "Breaking Heimisch and Triton", 170.

countries. Apparently, although the US Navy had broken the met cipher before March 1942, the US Army meteorological cryptanalytical section (under Captain Edmund J. Wrigley) was unaware of that fact in mid-1942, notwithstanding that the Army was interested in breaking it. It would be interesting to know whether the US Navy was still breaking the met cipher at that time.

Perhaps the most significant part of the memorandum is Safford's statement that "German [non-minor — that is Enigma M] naval messages ...have been read". As we have seen, it means that the British must have given the US Navy Enigma M's wiring, and some captured keylists. It is confirmed by the remarks to the same effect (by the second retired US Navy officer) quoted in the article.[10] This directly controverts Safford's post-war claim that the British reneged on a bargain to supply Enigma material in exchange for the Purple machine handed over to BP by the Sinkov/Weeks/Currier mission in January 1941.[11] Since the memorandum was written less than a year after the events and is supported by other evidence, it is to be preferred to Safford's post-war account. Further evidence on the issue would be welcome, in view of the seriousness of Safford's charges of bad faith.

---

[10] Kruh, 257.

[11] Dundas P. Tucker "Rhapsody in Purple: A New History of Pearl Harbor — Part I," *Cryptologia* (1982) 6: 214-7.

ROOSEVELT, MAGIC, AND ULTRA*

David Kahn

ADDRESS: 120 Wooleys Lane, Great Neck NY 11023 USA.

ABSTRACT: Exhaustive research finds little about what solved German and Japanese intercepts went to President Franklin D. Roosevelt during World War II and nothing about how he used them. However, a picture is given of Military Intelligence's Special Branch, which selected and edited the intercepts for presentation to the president and other high officials, and of the intercepts' presentation to and reception by the president.

KEYWORDS: Roosevelt, MAGIC, ULTRA, PURPLE, Special Branch, McCormack, Clarke, and Corderman.

I

What MAGIC and ULTRA information went to President Franklin D. Roosevelt during World War II, and how did he use it?

It may as well be said at once that exhaustive research provides only a sketchy answer to the first question and merely unproved hypotheses for the second.

Extant records specify only a few of the solved German and Japanese messages that went to the president. Moreover, no documents or recollections have come to light suggesting any action that he took based on, or even influenced by, these intercepts.

Despite these disappointing results, it may be worthwhile to set out what has been learned about the production of MAGIC (Japanese solutions) and ULTRA (German) and their selection for and presentation to Roosevelt. Doing so will at least outline how one intelligence organization operated in preparing information for the highest authority in the land. And it will provide a framework in case any papers are discovered that answer, or at least shed more light on, the fundamental questions about Roosevelt, MAGIC, and ULTRA.

Foreign intercepts began going to the White House for the first time in 1937.[1]

*Reprinted with slight changes from *Historians and Archivists*, ed. George O. Kent (Fairfax, Va.: George Mason University Press, 1991).

[1] Rowlett. I know of no evidence that earlier American signals intelligence results—during the Civil War, World War I, or the Washington Disarmament Conference of 1922, to name the three cryptanalytically most likely events—went to the White House.

They came from the Army's Signal Intelligence Service, the Signal Corps' codemaking and codebreaking agency. Founded in 1929[2] under the great cryptanalyst William F. Friedman, SIS directed its first nontraining codebreaking at Japan, starting in 1932.[3] At first it solved Japanese diplomatic codes.[4] But these turned out to encrypt only insignificant messages. High-level, important traffic was apparently protected by a machine cipher.[5] In 1935, when SIS realized this and had obtained more experience and greater knowledge of Japanese communication habits from its code solutions, it attacked the machine.[6] By 1936, cryptanalysts Frank B. Rowlett and Solomon Kullback,[7] perhaps helped by information about a simpler Japanese Navy machine cipher that the U. S. Navy had solved,[8] cracked what the Japanese Foreign Office called its "A" machine and what the Americans called RED. With this, the United States gained access to more and better intelligence than ever before.[9]

This included advance information starting in March 1937 about Italy's possible adherence to the German-Japanese anti-comintern pact of the previous November. The intercepts revealed the early indications that Italy might join, the start of negotiations, the discussion over whether Italy should accede to the existing treaty or sign a separate agreement with Japan, a statement that Hitler

[2] *The Origin and Development of the Army Security Agency 1917–1929* (Laguna Hills, Calif.: Aegean Park Press, 1978), 8–9.

[3] Hannah, 11–14.

[4] Rowlett; SRH-001, 303- 04.

[5] *Ibid* ., 305.

[6] *Ibid.*, 301; Hannah, 14–15.

[7] Hannah, 14.

[8] Lewis, ed., 12; SRH-305, 020; SRH-149, 8; SRH-355, 161- 62; Layton, 79. Rowlett disputes this (Hannah, 15), but the several naval officers' statements suggest that the Navy contributed something, though perhaps more in a general than a specific way.

[9] Hannah, 15; Rowlett. On RED and PURPLE, see Cipher A. Deavours and Louis Kruh, *Machine Cryptography and Modern Cryptanalysis* (Dedham, Mass.: Artech House, 1985), 211–245. Rowlett says, on p. 2 of a memorandum of 1 March 1980 prepared for author John Toland, that "G2 showed no more than a passing interest in the S. I. S. output [of Japanese diplomatic solutions] until a partially decoded circular message from Tokyo indicated that a secret codicil was being formulated to the tripartite treaty which Japan was negotiating with Germany and Italy." Actually, this intercept could only have concerned not the "tripartite treaty," which was not signed until 17 September 1940, but negotiations for the Anti-Comintern Pact between Germany and Japan. This was signed 25 November 1936, the year in which the A machine was solved; negotiations for Italy's adherence did not begin until 1937. The intercepts reflect this. Italy adhered to the pact on 6 November 1937 but was never told of its secret codicil between Germany and Japan. Parrish, 43, likewise errs in ascribing the army interest to negotiations on a "tripartite treaty." Ironically, the Japanese message of 14 November 1936 that provided a synopsis of the secret codicil was not solved until 13 November 1937 (from solved Japanese diplomatic messages dealing with the Anti-Comintern Pact kindly declassified for me by the National Security Agency). No "partially decoded circular message" was included in the messages supplied to me. (The agreement between Germany and Italy that in effect created the Axis, the so-called Pact of Steel, was signed 25 October 1936.)

wanted Italy to participate in the existing agreement, Italy's apparent acceptance, the emperor's approval, and part of the text of the treaty, which was signed 6 November 1937.[10]

U. S. diplomats did not start reporting until October on this rapprochement between three aggressive nations, to the east and to the west of the United States—and even then their information was far less specific than the intercepts.[11] So these seized the attention of officials in Army and Navy intelligence, in the State Department, and in the White House. Information from solved foreign cryptosystems, which had never before been of sufficient value to reach the topmost level of government, began going to the White House,[12] probably to the president.

On 20 February 1939, the Japanese introduced a new and more complicated cipher machine to supersede RED, whose mechanisms were wearing out. The Japanese called it their "B" machine; the Americans, PURPLE.[13] There followed nineteen months of concentrated cryptanalytic attack by a team under the general supervision of Friedman and the immediate direction of Rowlett, with some help from the Navy (which resumed diplomatic cryptanalysis to assist with PURPLE after having abandoned that field around 1938 or 1939 to concentrate on Japanese naval solutions). Their efforts were crowned with success in September 1940.[14] Thus, even after Japan discontinued use of the RED machine on 21 August 1941,[15] the PURPLE solution assured American officials of being able to read Japan's most secret diplomatic messages.

---

[10] Solved Japanese diplomatic messages declassified by N. S. A. In the following citations, the date of the telegram is given first, followed, in parentheses, by the date the codebreakers submitted the translation to the Army G-2. Note the increasing speed of solution. All dates are 1937. Berlin-Tokyo 19 January (8 March) and Berlin-Tokyo 9 March (5 April) for early indications; Tokyo-Rome 15 September (1 October) for start of negotiations; Rome-Tokyo 2 August (23 August) for existing treaty or separate; Berlin-Tokyo 7 October (15 October) for Hitler; Tokyo-Rome 26 October (3 November) for acceptance; Tokyo-Rome 4 November (8 November) for emperor's approval; Tokyo-Rome 31 October, 31 October and 1 November (all 5 November) for part of text. Some of the memoranda to G-2 bear the handwritten initials of Friedman, Rowlett, and John B. Hurt, a translator.

[11] *FRUS, 1937*, 1:608. British cryptanalysts likewise seemed to have obtained information about these negotiations only in September-October 1937 (John D. Ferris, "From Broadway House to Bletchley Park: The Diary of Captain Malcolm D. Kennedy, 1934–1946," *Intelligence and National Security*, 4 [July 1989], 421–450 at 447–448).

[12] Rowlett.

[13] SRH-145, 001, 008–09.

[14] Hannah, 5, 15–19; Kahn, 20–22. Lewis, ed., 14–15 for Navy diplomatic solutions.

[15] SRH-001, 308.

II

Growing cryptanalytic production—from an average of about one diplomatic solution a day in the first half of 1937[16] to fifty a day in the last half of 1941[17]—compelled the Army and the Navy to share the burden. In August 1940, SIS and the Navy's OP-20-G arranged that diplomatic messages originating in Tokyo on odd-numbered days would be handled by the Navy, those on even-numbered days, by the Army.[18] The two agencies exchanged the solutions.

Then, on 23 January 1941, the Army and the Navy agreed that their code-breaking results, which had been given the covername MAGIC, would be delivered to the White House by the Army in odd months, by the Navy in even.[19] But after a few months the Army stopped taking MAGIC to the White House.[20] In part this was because it felt that diplomatic intelligence should go to the president through the State Department, in part because the president's military aide, Brigadier General Edwin M. (Pa) Watson, had breached security by forgetfully throwing a MAGIC summary into his wastebasket some time after the Army's turn either in May or in July.[21] The final delivery in one or the other of those months seems to have been the last time an Army officer brought intercepts to Roosevelt. Henceforth, the naval aide was the person by whose hand MAGIC went to him.[22] This apparently came about because of the following events.

Near the end of September, an Army month, during which no intercepts were delivered to the White House, the president said he wanted to see them. In October, the Navy continued to send him memoranda based on MAGIC. Early in November, an Army month, during which again nothing was delivered to him, Roosevelt again told his naval aide, Captain John R. Beardall, that he wanted to see MAGIC. The aide told him it was an Army month. The president replied that he knew that and that he was either seeing MAGIC or being told what it said by Secretary of State Cordell Hull but that he still wanted to see the original intercepts. Beardall thought the reason was that the president grasped things more quickly by eye than by ear. On Monday, 10 November 1941, a

[16] S. I. S. serial 320 was solved on 12 February, serial 461 on 26 June—141 messages in 135 days.

[17] Kahn, 29.

[18] *PHA*, 8:3923, 18:3313-14; Lewis, ed., 15; SRH-270, 024.

[19] *PHA*, 2:288, 4:1734.

[20] Kahn, 30.

[21] *Ibid* ., 26. *PHA*, 11:5475, implies May. But Watson was receiving occasional deliveries of MAGIC in July.

[22] Clarke, in reply to my question of 2 December 1985 as to who brought solutions to Roosevelt, wrote: "Navy—always. They never let their poor relations near the old con man." *PHA*, 2:789, which states that from 1 November 1941 intercepts to the president were delivered through the naval aide, may refer only to the time up to Pearl Harbor.

conference changed the distribution setup. Henceforth, the Army would bring MAGIC to the State Department and the Navy to the White House. At 4:15 p. m. Wednesday, 12 November, the first intercepts were delivered to the White House under this system.[23]

Neither war nor changes in the production of MAGIC affected this arrangement. On 25 January 1942, a month and a half after hostilities began, the cryptological officers of the Army and the Navy agreed orally that the Army would intercept and cryptanalyze all diplomatic traffic as well as enemy army and air force messages. This was formalized in a written agreement of 30 June 1942, which specified that the Navy would solve enemy naval messages and that the Army would continue to give the Navy the diplomatic solutions. The Joint Chiefs of Staff approved this on 6 July.[24] Another agreement, on distribution matters, made 25 May 1942 between representatives of the Army, the Navy, and the Federal Bureau of Investigation, likewise did not alter Navy responsibility for White House delivery. It merely stated that, while the president should see diplomatic intelligence, he should not be given enemy naval, enemy military, western hemisphere clandestine (spy messages), or international clandestine intercepts.[25] (The reason was certainly not to conceal information from him but rather not to burden him with that which he could barely use.) Thus, although the Navy no longer generated the cryptanalytic intelligence that went to the White House, the naval aide continued to take it in to Roosevelt, who had been an assistant secretary of the Navy in World War I. By then, it was coming from a new Army agency.

III

After recovering from the shock of Pearl Harbor, the secretary of war, Henry L. Stimson, decided that a centralized analysis of the intercepted Japanese messages might have prevented the surprise.[26] He felt that an organization should be set up to study the intelligence from cryptanalysis more fully and carefully than before. Stimson, a lawyer, consulted with his assistant secretary, John McCloy, a lawyer, and they decided that the job should be handled by a lawyer, particularly one having experience in large cases involving many and complicated facts. They settled upon a former partner of McCloy in one of New York's most

[23] *PHA*, 11:5475-76.

[24] SRH-200, 184, 198, 042.

[25] Howe, 6; SRH-200, 038.

[26] SRH-116, 006-07; Henry L. Stimson and McGeorge Bundy, *On Active Service in Peace and War* (New York: Harper & Row, 1947), 454–55.

prestigious Wall Street firms who had represented Edwin Armstrong in his suits to protect his invention of the regenerative circuit. This was Alfred McCormack, a big, brilliant, demanding Brooklyn-born graduate of Princeton University and Columbia Law School.[27] He was appointed special assistant to Stimson on 19 January 1942, six days after his 41st birthday.[28]

Because the Signal Corps had for years produced the raw material—the intercepted and solved messages—that went to Army intelligence, one of the two slots allotted to the Signal Corps in the General Staff was in G-2, or intelligence. It was filled, at that time, by Colonel Carter W. Clarke, a tall, slim, energetic career officer with strong likes and dislikes, salty modes of expression, and very good common sense.[29] Clarke had no signal intelligence background—he had replaced an officer who had signal intelligence experience but had been shifted to prepare for censorship as war approached[30]—but was extremely capable. On 15 May 1942, he was placed in charge of the new organization; McCormack, who was commissioned in June, became his deputy.[31] They worked very well together, each recognizing that the other had strengths that he lacked. McCormack was ideally qualified to run an intelligence unit while Clarke was just right to fit it into the Army.

The new unit, named Special Branch, was a highly secret element of the Military Intelligence Division;[32] the coordinate branches were administration, intelligence, counterintelligence, operations, and plans. All depended directly from the Army's assistant chief of staff for intelligence, the G-2.[33] A reorganization of the Military Intelligence Division in June 1944 changed some titles—McCormack became director of intelligence within the Military Intelligence Service, of which Clarke was deputy director[34]—but had little effect on the work and output of Special Branch.

The intercepts being distributed early in 1942 still consisted merely of the

---

[27] Kai Bird, *The Chairman: John J. McCloy: The Making of the American Establishment* (New York: Simon & Schuster, 1992), 142; SRH-185, 77–83; *Who Was Who in America*, 3:572, s. v. McCormack, Alfred; "Alfred McCormack, Lawyer, Dies; Former Director of Intelligence," *The New York Times* (12 July 1956), 23:4–5; Shute; Nelson, Fontana.

[28] SRH-116, 007.

[29] Shute; Ervin; Nelson; Clarke (1963), "Carter W. Clarke Dies at 90, An Army Intelligence Officer," *The New York Times* (7 September 1987), A24:5.

[30] Corderman.

[31] Howe, 6; SRH-185, 002.

[32] SRH-146, 001.

[33] SRH-185, 015.

[34] SRH-062, 001, 080; SRH-146, 002. For the 1944 reorganization, see Otto L. Nelson, *National Security and the General Staff* (Washington: Infantry Journal Press, 1946), 526–535.

translations of Japanese messages with some footnotes. These gave the dates and intercept numbers of earlier messages referred to in those texts or said that those earlier messages were "not available."[35] This was raw intelligence. McCormack felt that the persons who got this exceptionally valuable information were entitled to have each detail in it illuminated by other information and the intercept itself placed into a larger context.[36] This would provide the recipients with finished—and therefore much more useful—intelligence. It would be presented to them in the form of a daily report. Moreover, surveying the intercepts over days or weeks would develop data that could be processed into long-range and specialized intelligence.[37]

For these jobs, McCormack sought men whose training "teaches them to deal with evidence, to be inquisitive and skeptical, to pursue an investigation through to a conclusion, to meet unfamiliar situations of fact and, most important, to do very detailed work without losing their sense of values."[38] He found these abilities not among historians, not among journalists, not among scientists nor detectives nor even parents of quarreling siblings, but exclusively among lawyers, and he began recruiting among members and former members of his law firm, Cravath, de Gersdorff, Swaine and Wood.

Clarke, meanwhile, handled administrative, security, and external matters. He prevailed upon the Signal Corps to expand its intercept facilities—the radio posts that monitored the foreign transmissions and so supplied the codebreakers with cryptograms to solve. He instructed the Signal Corps on assignment priorities—which cryptosystems intelligence wanted broken, which enemy circuits should be monitored. Perhaps most important of all, he alleviated the residual friction between SIS, a Signal Corps unit, and Special Branch, the glamorous organ of intelligence.[39]

IV

When Special Branch started, its offices were on the second floor of the front wing of Washington's Munitions Building, an ugly World War I temporary structure on Constitution Avenue between the Washington Monument and the Lincoln Memorial. In the rear wing of the same floor was SIS. Both moved in the fall of 1942: Special Branch to the newly built Pentagon, SIS to Arlington Hall, a former

[35] See intercepts in *PHA*, 12:1-248.

[36] SHR-116, 008-9.

[37] *Ibid.*, 009.

[38] SRH-185, 004.

[39] SRH-185, 00203; SRH-116, 010.

girls' school in Arlington, Virginia, half a dozen miles from the Pentagon.[40] As Special Branch grew, it expanded from its original single room into neighboring offices. The walls were temporary partitions that were constantly being shifted for new people. From time to time the branch moved;[41] for a while, at least, it was located in Rooms 2D715, 719, and 732.[42]

Though Clarke, McCormack, and some of the specialists had individual offices or offices shared with one or two people, the men preparing the daily intelligence reports—the heart of the operation— worked in a largish open area with desks facing each other in two rows. This enabled them to talk easily back and forth, to pass papers to one another, to go quickly and informally to another's desk to look at something to discuss it.[43]

The branch grew rapidly. From the dozen officers and civilians at the start, it swelled to 400 officers, enlisted men, and civilians in Washington and 80 abroad.[44]

Officers of Special Branch could not at first enter the supersensitive codebreaking agency,[45] even though the two organizations adjoined one another. But many questions arose in their work:[46] Was a message translated correctly? Did the codebreakers have other messages on the same subject? Could the intercept facilities pick up wanted traffic? In the first months, these matters were resolved by Clarke's consulting personally with the head of the Signal Intelligence Service, a fellow Signal Corps officer, at first Lieutenant Colonel Rex Minckler, and after April 1942, Lieutenant Colonel Frank W. Bullock.[47] Clarke carried written questions from his staff members to the codebreakers. Later a single officer of each agency handled liaison. But it was still a bottleneck.

Then, in February of 1943, Lieutenant Colonel W. Preston (Red) Corderman, who had studied in the SIS School in the 1930s, took charge of the codebreaking agency, now called the Signal Security Agency (SSA). It was Corderman who had been moved to handle censorship and whom Clarke had replaced in intelligence in the General Staff; they had known each other since 1927, when Corderman reported at Fort Monmouth, New Jersey, to the 51st Signal Battalion's B Com-

---

[40] SRH-117, 007, 008.

[41] Ervin; Shute; Fontana.

[42] SRH-062, 084-85.

[43] *Ibid.*

[44] SRH-145, 009.

[45] SRH-117, 008.

[46] SRH-132, 6.

[47] Kahn, 575.

pany, whose commander was Lieutenant Clarke.[48]

At once the liaison situation eased. Special Branch added several officers to handle the work. Secret teletype and secure telephone communications were established between Arlington Hall and the Pentagon.[49] The chief liaison officer with the codebreakers, Captain Thomas Ervin, a lawyer who had a flair for telling stories, would spend half his day with Special Branch and half with the codebreakers. He brought them questions Special Branch's analysts wanted answered and got from them both question and requests for information that would help in their solving, such as which one of five possible solutions of a name was the right one.[50] Finally, toward the end of the war, the ultimate step was taken and many Special Branch evaluators began working in the same room as the codebreakers,[51] greatly facilitating the work of both sides.

Once a day, and perhaps later in the war several times a day, a courier driven in a staff car brought the hundreds of daily translated intercepts to Special Branch from Arlington Hall.[52] Urgent ones were teletyped.[53] Most were Japanese army or diplomatic—the Japanese army material comprised 150 intercepts a day in the middle of the war, 700 at the end—a few were low-level German diplomatic, the higher-level German diplomatic codes not having been solved.[54] Italian messages did not figure prominently. It seems likely that every message solved and translated was sent to Special Branch: if Arlington Hall thought it worth translating, it was sent over.[55] In addition, an American unit under Colonel Telford Taylor at the British codebreaking agency at Bletchley Park, the Government Code and Cypher School, selected and then cabled to Special Branch, as it did to high military commands in the European theater, German military, air, and naval solutions, called ULTRA.[56] This began 27 August 1943.[57]

All messages, when they arrived at Special Branch, went to McCormack. He skimmed them to keep track of what was going on,[58] then, from 1943, divided

[48] *Ibid.*; Corderman.

[49] SRH-117, 009.

[50] Ervin.

[51] SRH-113, 010.

[52] SRH-132, 6; Ervin.

[53] SRH-062, 43.

[54] Ervin.

[55] *Ibid.*

[56] Shute. For the origins of this unit: Howe, 10–12, 90, 125– 131.

[57] Parrish, 181–2.

[58] Fontana.

Brigadier General Carter Clarke, head of the Special Branch, which processed German and Japanese intercepts for delivery to President Franklin D. Roosevelt and other high officials, congratulates his deputy, Alfred McCormack, a lawyer in civilian life, whom he has just awarded the Distinguished Service Medal for his work during World War II.

All photographs are from the National Archives.

They carried MAGIC and ULTRA to Roosevelt.

Captain John R. Beardall, naval aide

Captain John McCrea, naval aide

Rear Admiral Ross T. McIntire,
physician and acting naval aide

Lieutenant Commander William C. Mott,
assistant naval aide

Command John A. Tyree,
assistant naval aide

Brigadier General W. Preston Corderman,
head of the Signal Security Agency

Marine Corps Colonel Ronald A. Boone, deliverer of MAGIC and ULTRA to the president, arrives on assignment in Alaska.

Roosevelt smiles as he pins a Distinguished Service Medal on his departing naval aide, Vice Admiral Wilson Brown, 28 April 1942.

them into diplomatic and military and distributed them respectively to Henry Rigby and Benjamin Shute. These two lawyers, both in their early thirties (Rigby formerly of Cravath, and Shute on leave from it),[59] read the intercepts more closely. They kept those that dealt with immediate matters and gave those that dealt with longer-range or background matters to the specialists.[60]

Many of the specialists were academics with backgrounds in particular areas. They related the intercepts to other sources of information that flowed to Special Branch,[61] such as newscast transcripts and prisoner-of-war interrogations, to produce a full-fledged report on a particular aspect of an enemy nation's economy, military organization, internal unrest, new technology, and the like.[62] These were published as completed or as needed.

The messages that were kept by Rigby, Shute, and later another lawyer, William R. Perdue, were edited by them and by the two other lawyers under each to produce the daily intercept reports.[63] These were the MAGIC Summary (later called the MAGIC Diplomatic Summary), edited by Rigby; the Military and Diplomatic Supplement to the MAGIC Summary (which began in the summer of 1943 and which from 1 July 1944 was called the MAGIC European Summary), edited by Shute; and the Far Eastern Summary (which began 10 February 1944 and dealt with Japanese military matters), edited by Perdue.[64] For these, the teams studied the day's file of translated decodes from the Signal Security Agency. They passed some to the specialists for information or comment.[65] They scanned other material for background. The editors working on the Far Eastern Summary, for example, looked at the 300 daily Japanese Navy intercepts; at cables from the field; outgoing cables on MAGIC intelligence; diplomatic and commercial intercepts; other MAGIC intelligence such as Japanese order of battle; the codebreaking agency's Weekly Report, giving the status of cryptanalysis of Japanese army systems; at the Boston Series of plaintext German diplomatic messages obtained by the Office of Strategic Services; and at noncodebreaking intelligence material, such as field command intelligence reports, photo interpre-

---

[59] SRH-185, 003, 013; Shute.

[60] Bell, 52.

[61] SRH-141, 220–23.

[62] SRH-116, 015–19; Bell, 55, 58.

[63] SRH-146, 1.

[64] SRH-062, 087–88; SRH-035, 18; Bell, 50, 52, 56; SRH-062, 049; Perdue, who was in charge from 1942 of what was then called the Japanese Army Supplement; Rigby. Though SRH-062, 038, says that F. A. O'Connell Jr. prepared the Far Eastern Summary, this may refer to a later time.

[65] Fontana; SRH-146, 5.

tations, and Allied operational cables.[66]

From the translated decodes the editors selected the most important messages. That was their basic job. Most of their effort went into deciding what to leave out.[67] In addition, they spoke with the cryptanalysts and translators, often over the secure telephone, to rectify errors or fill in lacunae caused by garbles in the ciphertext and to clarify ambiguities in the Japanese and in the English. Even after this, many messages were, by themselves, scarcely intelligible.[68] To squeeze the maximum out of them, the editors called for files on items mentioned in the intercepts and sought elucidation.[69] They asked research personnel at the Military Intelligence Service to provide information about lesser known people, places, or things, about obscure events or allusions to forthcoming operations. They visited the who's who section, in which each mention of a name or operation was card-indexed, and determined who the person or what the event was.[70] This would be inserted as a footnote to the intercept. The editors conferred with one another on the meaning of a word. Some important intercepts were run verbatim in the summaries, but most were summarized. Rarely, if ever, were comments made beyond identifications; the editors did not evaluate the significance of the information.[71] The editors assembled the several summaries or texts and the identifications into a single writing, which went to Rigby and then to McCormack for final editing. McCormack was an extremely meticulous editor, who often spent a great deal of time making sure that the reports would be quickly and fully intelligible to their readers.[72]

The manuscript then went for typing to one of the two chief secretaries, both male legal stenographers who had worked at Cravath. One of them, at least, Vincent Fontana, followed the Cravath form book in typing the summaries: indent text 15 spaces from the left, indent 25 spaces for a paragraph start, indent 20 fewer for a quotation set apart in the text.[73] Reports averaged ten to twelve pages. The typescripts then were reproduced in bluish-purple ink by the Ditto process in about ten copies—later apparently more. Each was bound in a spiral

[66] SRH-062, 043-44. Anthony Cave Brown, *The Last Hero: Wild Bill Donovan* (New York: Times Books, 1982), 278–286, for Boston Series.

[67] SRH-116, 12.

[68] SRH-062, 044.

[69] Fontana.

[70] SRH-146, 5; Ervin; Shute; Nelson; Fontana.

[71] The summaries themselves.

[72] Fontana; Ervin.

[73] Fontana.

binder, using a device that Special Branch had for this.[74] Then each was put in a locked leather briefcase,[75] called a pouch, and distributed by officer couriers in regularly scheduled staff cars. The diplomatic summary went out early in the afternoon; the military ones were reproduced and bound in the evening and distributed the next morning.[76]

The Army delivered its copies of the MAGIC Summary to the secretary of war (Stimson), the chief of staff (General George C. Marshall), the assistant chief of staff for war plans, the assistant chief of staff for intelligence, the Navy for further distribution, the secretary of state (Cordell Hull) and the assistant secretary of state who followed signal intelligence (probably Adolf A. Berle).[77] The Navy passed the 10 copies it got to the White House, the secretary of the navy (Frank Knox), the commander-in-chief of the U. S. Fleet and chief of naval operations (Admiral Ernest J. King), the chief of war plans, the director of naval intelligence, the vice chief of naval operations, the director of naval communications, the radio intelligence center, the domestic intelligence section and a file.[78] The Far Eastern Summary also went to the president. It was at first distributed in 23 copies; by the end of the war the number of copies rose to 75.[79]

V

Delivery to the president was made by the naval aide. This had been the practice since before Pearl Harbor. For a few months in 1941, Roosevelt's physician, Admiral Ross T. McIntire, acted as naval aide and so brought the intercepts to the chief executive.[80] Once, in the summer, when McIntire was not available, a naval intelligence specialist, who did not want to entrust the pouch to the president's private secretary and who felt that the intercept he had could not wait, brought a message to the president. He was Lieutenant Commander Alwin D. Kramer, a Japanese language expert who headed the translation section of OP-20-G and who, because of his expertise on Japan and MAGIC, carried the intercepts to the high-level naval recipients so that he could answer their questions on MAGIC.[81]

[74] *Ibid.*

[75] Mott; SRH-123, 3.

[76] SRH-132, 3.

[77] SRH-035, 18.

[78] SRH-145, 049.

[79] SRH-062, 049.

[80] *PHA*, 9:3985.

[81] Kahn, 11.

The intercept perhaps concerned Japanese-American negotiations the next day.[82]

When, a little later, Rear Admiral John Beardall became naval aide, Kramer—a methodical and dedicated man whom some called "The Shadow"[83]—took the intercepts to him for delivery to the president.[84] Kramer explained to Beardall points in the summaries about which the president was asking. Beardall, whose office, like Kramer's, was in the Navy Building, would ask Kramer late in the afternoon whether any MAGIC would be coming over for the president. Kramer would say, "There is no MAGIC ready for the president now" or "There might be something later" or "Nothing until tomorrow morning."[85] When there was something, Beardall would receive the intercepts in his office from Kramer and would carry them to the White House, a few blocks away, arriving around 5:30 or 6:00.[86]

About the first week in December 1941, a junior naval officer was assigned to bring MAGIC to the president when Beardall was off duty or at dinner or otherwise unavailable. This was a communications intelligence specialist, Lieutenant Lester R. Schulz.[87] He was assisted, beginning 6 December, by an Ensign Carson.[88] This was the system in effect at the time of Pearl Harbor.

Beardall had a key to the MAGIC pouch and sometimes opened it for the president, sometimes not. Normally, the president returned the sheaf of papers to Beardall when he had finished with it, though on 2 or 3 December 1941 he said he wanted to keep a copy of a Tokyo-Berlin intercept warning that "War may suddenly break out between the Anglo-Saxon nations and Japan . . . quicker than anyone dreams." Kramer prepared the copy and gave it to Beardall; he never got it back.[89] Though Beardall never discussed the intercepts with the president, he sometimes called attention to what he considered were important ones. On 4 or 5 December, for example, he said to Roosevelt of an intercept revealing that the Japanese were burning their codes: "Mr. President, this is a very significant dispatch." Roosevelt read it carefully, and then said to Beardall, "When do you think it will happen?" Beardall, thinking that Roosevelt meant

---

[82] *Ibid.*, 30.

[83] Mott.

[84] *PHA*, 11:5475.

[85] *Ibid.*, 5269, 5277.

[86] *Ibid.*, 11:5277, 5278.

[87] *Ibid.*, 10:4660, 11:5278. He was technically on temporary duty at the White House as communications assistant to the naval aide.

[88] *Ibid.*, 10:4660, 11:5280.

[89] *Ibid.*, 9:4072.

the start of war, said, "Most any time."[90]

The most dramatic case of Roosevelt's receiving intercepts took place on the evening of Saturday, 6 December 1941. Schulz had been ordered by Beardall to stand by and bring some MAGIC expected that evening to the president. It was the first time that MAGIC was delivered after the close of the ordinary working day.[91] Schulz was waiting in Beardall's small office in the corner of the White House's basement mail room when Kramer arrived about 9:15. He was bringing the first thirteen parts of a fourteen-part PURPLE message; the Japanese had deliberately delayed transmitting the fourteenth part, which would break off negotiations with the United States. Schulz obtained permission to bring the MAGIC to the president and an usher accompanied him to the oval study on the second floor and announced him.

Roosevelt, who had excused himself from a dinner party, was seated at his desk. Only his confidante, Harry Hopkins, was with him in the quiet lamplit room. Schulz unlocked the briefcase in which the MAGIC was distributed with the key Beardall had given him, removed the sheaf of intercepts, and handed it to the president. Roosevelt read the thirteen parts in about ten minutes, while Hopkins paced slowly up and down. Then Hopkins read them. The thirteenth part rejected the final American offer and, when Hopkins passed the papers back to the president, Roosevelt said, in effect, "This means war." Hopkins agreed, and for about five minutes they discussed the situation, the deployment of Japanese forces, the movement towards Indochina, and similar matters. The president mentioned a message for peace he had sent the emperor of Japan. Hopkins replied that it was too bad that the United States could not strike the first blow and prevent any kind of surprise in the inevitable war.

"No," the president said in effect, "we can't do that. We are a democracy and a peaceful people." He raised his voice. "But we have a good record." He tried unsuccessfully to get the chief of naval operations on the telephone, deciding against having him paged at the National Theater for fear of causing undue alarm.

The president then returned the papers to Schulz, and, about half an hour after he had entered the study, Schulz left. He returned the papers to Kramer, who was waiting on a bench in the mail room, and soon thereafter went home.[92]

The next morning, Beardall brought the president the fourteenth part, which had been intercepted and solved during the night. It expressed the Japanese government's regret that "it is impossible to reach an agreement through further

[90] *Ibid.*, 11:5284.

[91] *Ibid.*, 11:5278.

[92] *Ibid.*, 10:4659-665.

negotiations." It was about 10 a. m., and the president was in his bedroom. He said "Good morning" to Beardall, read the contents of the pouch, and then commented, in substance, "It looks like the Japanese are going to break off negotiations." There was no further discussion; Beardall took the pouch back to the Navy Department, and was as surprised as everybody else when news came of the attack on Pearl Harbor.[93]

Beardall was replaced as naval aide in January 1942 by Captain John McCrea. He saw or telephoned the president almost every day. To him went the MAGIC intercepts, brought over by an army courier. He also received copies of important naval dispatches that high naval officers thought should be shown to the president. Much of this arrived at his office in the Navy Building. Twice a day, McCrea picked out the naval dispatches he thought would be of interest to the president, added to these all the MAGIC intercepts, stuck them in his pocket or his briefcase, and headed for the White House, where he was expected.

When McCrea arrived in the morning, Roosevelt would usually be either in bed, in which case McCrea would hand him the papers, or in the bathroom, shaving. If the latter, the naval officer would go in, close the toilet cover, sit down on it, and in that inglorious setting would read the leader of the most powerful nation in the world some of the most secret documents of the greatest war in history. In the afternoon, the president, if he were not in the Map Room, a chart-lined office in the basement of the White House, would be seated in a neighboring room in a chair like a dentist's, having his sinuses packed by McIntire or his polio-deformed legs rubbed down by a masseur. Here again, McCrea would read the documents aloud to him.[94]

When the president was at his home in Hyde Park or at his Maryland mountain retreat, Shangri-La, McCrea would tell him about the documents by telephone.[95]

In 1942, the MAGIC documents were reaching McCrea's office in the Navy Department about 2:30 p. m.[96] OP-20-G had, since before Pearl Harbor, flagged the important items by sliding paper clips on them.[97] McCrea commented that although the selection was in general "accurate as to the possibility of their interest to the president," he often spotted other items that only he knew would

[93] *Ibid.*, 5283.

[94] McCrea. As an interesting confirmation, Franklin D. Roosevelt Library, Map Room File, Box 195, Folder Chart Room Log and Standing Orders, p. 67, notes that McCrea saw the president in the doctor's office on 14 and 16 May 1942.

[95] McCrea.

[96] SRH-200, 052.

[97] Kahn, 30.

also interest Roosevelt. After showing the documents to the president, he returned them to the courier for destruction by OP-20-G. In the summer of 1942, when Admiral William D. Leahy became Roosevelt's chief of staff, MAGIC documents may have been addressed to him,[98] though he himself rarely took them in to Roosevelt.[99] That function was still mainly exercised by McCrea, his 1943 successor Rear Admiral Wilson Brown, Brown's assistant, Commander John A. Tyree, and a young naval officer working in the Map Room under Leahy, Lieutenant Commander William C. Mott. All briefed the president orally in the morning and in the afternoon, often when he was getting his sinuses packed and was, Mott said, "a captive audience." They reported the intercept intelligence with the other information that they thought he would want to know and that they had boiled down for his consumption. If Roosevelt wanted to read some papers, they would give them to him; the intercept material was on separate sheets. Mott often underlined on these pages what he thought the president ought to know. The president struck the aides as extremely well informed.[100]

During Roosevelt's trip to the Casablanca conference with British Prime Minister Winston Churchill in January 1943, he was sent messages from Washington that were based on MAGIC Diplomatic Summaries. They were "from Colonel Boone"—almost certainly Marine Corps Colonel Ronald Aubry Boone, an Annapolis graduate who had been in naval intelligence in Washington since February 1939 and had spent eight years in Peking and Shanghai on language, intelligence, diplomatic, and public-relations missions.[101] One such "Colonel Boone" message, of 17 January 1943, identical with MAGIC Diplomatic Summary 296 of the day before, states that "Yamaguchi in Berlin reports to Tokyo that Nazis are upset about American military supplies reaching Vladivostok in Russian bottoms X. They reach Moscow quickly by rail X Germans say until this supply route is cut off, any advance in Russia quite impossible X ..."[102] On 27 January, "Colonel

[98] Adams, 237. Smedberg said that "probably Leahy brought it [MAGIC] around to him [Roosevelt]." Tending to support this is that Leahy knew of MAGIC since, in the late 1930s, he was chief of naval operations, when a cryptanalyst said of his attitudes to signal intelligence that "We couldn't ask for better. He is thoroughly sold" (SRH-355, 259). On the other hand, Elsey doubted that any MAGIC or ULTRA documents went through Leahy, and Mott said that Leahy did not have access to the intercepts he was bringing to Roosevelt.

[99] Mott; inferred from Elsey.

[100] Mott; Tyree.

[101] Service record, Serial No. 093, National Personnel Records Center, St. Louis, Missouri. Clarke said that the colonel delivering to the White House was not in the Army but was a Marine. This would keep delivery in the Navy Department and eliminates a Colonel Boone who was in Army intelligence at the time—Colonel Joseph W. Boone, O15341 (U. S. War Department, Adjutant General's Office, *Army Directory*, April 20, 1943 [Washington], 174). The only Marine Corps Colonel Boone at the time was Ronald Aubry Boone. Department of the Navy, Marine Corps, Headquarters, History and Museums Branch, Reference Section.

[102] Franklin D. Roosevelt Library, Map Room File, Box 15, Folder Casablanca Conference Trip File, Item QMU 171938Z (UTAH 53), and SRS 839, "Magic" Summary No. 490, 19 July 1943.

Boone has indicated for last three days that a Jap movement in strength toward southern Solomons is shaping up X ..."[103] There are about half a dozen such messages to Roosevelt during the conference.

Churchill sometimes sent Roosevelt ULTRA—which the prime minister referred to by his own codename for it, BONIFACE. While they were at the Quebec conference in September, 1944, for example, Churchill passed some to him, which he later said "appeared to me to be of profound significance." More often Churchill gave him documents based on intercepts or referred to information based on them. In a note to the president of 13 August 1943, while both were at the president's home in Hyde Park, New York, Churchill provided an analysis of the situation in Yugoslavia of which he said, "Much of it is taken from BONIFACE sources." In October, he wrote about movements in Italy that "We know from BONIFACE that the enemy is withdrawing to the north.[104]

Likewise, during Roosevelt's visit to Canada for the QUADRANT conference of July and August 1943 and his subsequent fishing trip, he was sent two Colonel Boone messages: One was on 21 August: "Colonel Boone indications that Jap barge traffic from Shortland to Kolombangara and Vella area (in the Solomon Islands) may be proceeding along south Choiseul coast to vicinity Sami Head (7 22 S 156 08 E) then across the channel to destination."[105] The other, four days later, dealt with a report of the Japanese ambassador in Hanoi.[106]

In November of 1943, a Marshall aide and Churchill sent Roosevelt intercepts that they wanted him to see. But he was away at the conferences at Cairo and Teheran when they arrived. He first saw them when he returned on 16 December 1943. After transferring from the battleship *Iowa* to the presidential yacht *Potomac* for the trip up to Washington, he was handed a brown manila envelope in a briefcase that a Map Room watch officer, naval reserve Lieutenant (j. g.) R. H. Myers, had brought with him on the yacht. The intercepts dealt with German forces and forts that would be defending against the Allied invasion

---

[103] *Ibid.*, Item WHITE 21. Cochran, "The Influence of 'Magic' Intelligence," 348, errs in stating that item WHITE 8 in the above folder is identical to MAGIC Diplomatic Summary of 7/29/43; they are different.

[104] Winston S. Churchill and Franklin D. Roosevelt, *The Complete Correspondence*, ed. Warren F. Kimball (Princeton: Princeton University Press, 1984), 3:321 for "appeared to me," 2:389 for "Much of it," 2:502-503 for "We know." Other references to intercepts at 2:4, 389, 502-503, 666-667, 672-673, 677, 3:229, 256, 321, 341, 388. Kimball says that all the intelligence files have not been declassified and suggests that intercepts sent by Churchill to Roosevelt but not yet published might be found therein. This is reinforced by Martin GIlbert's footnote in Randolph Churchill, then Martin Gilbert, *Winston Churchill* (Boston: Houghton Mifflin, 1966-1988), 6 (1983): *Finest Hour, 1939-1941*, at 1260, based on a personal communication, that Churchill sent Roosevelt intercepts via "C," the chief of the Secret Intelligent Service, Sir Stewart Menzies, minuting on them "Make sure the President knows this" or "Make sure the President sees this."

[105] Franklin D. Roosevelt Library, Map Room File, Box 16, Folder Canadian Fishing Trip and Quadrant Conference, WHITE 112.

[106] *Ibid.*, WHITE 128.

of Europe. The Japanese ambassador, General Hiroshi Oshime, and his aides had inspected the Atlantic Wall and reported to Tokyo in great detail on the German measures: "...All the German fortifications on the French coast are very close to the shore and it is quite clear that the Germans plan to smash any enemy attempt to land as close to the water edge as possible.... The coastal defence divisions are distributed as follows: Netherlands Defence Army (covering the Netherlands down to the mouth of the Rhine), 4 divisions; Fifteenth Army (covering the area extending from the mouth of the Rhine to west of Le Havre), 9 divisions; Seventh Army (extending thence to the southern bank of the Loire), 8 divisions...." These messages, all probably decrypted from PURPLE radiograms intercepted at Asmara, Ethiopia, where SSA monitored Berlin-Tokyo traffic in the dun-colored block building of a former Italian radio station, have been called the greatest military intelligence coup of all time—and it certainly gave an insight into enemy plans unprecedented in history in both detail and scope. In July of 1944, Churchill asked that Roosevelt be shown another message. But, Clarke noted in a memo, that one had already been reported in Special Branch's Far Eastern Summary of 20 July 1944 and had been delivered to the White House that day. It was a Japanese message saying that the enemy must not be given any pretext to use chemical warfare.[107]

VI

Roosevelt's confidence in the MAGIC decrypts had been settled well before Pearl Harbor. When he was given the solution of the Japanese ambassador's report of a private audience with himself, he appeared much impressed and commented, as he read the translation, "Yes, I said that" and "That is correct; he said that."[108]

But did ULTRA and MAGIC, which had to compete with so many other messages and problems, capture his interest? The evidence is contradictory.[109]

[107]SRH-111; Carl Boyd, "Significance of MAGIC and the Japanese Ambassador to Berlin: (V) News of Hitler's Defense Preparations for Allied Invasion of Western Europe," *Intelligence and National Security*, 4 (July 1989), 461–481 at 472–474; Hinsley, 3:2:32–33, 771–775.

[108]SRH-305, 24.

[109]Gerhard L. Weinberg, *Reflections on Running a War: Hitler, Churchill, Stalin, Roosevelt, Tojo*, Transcription of the 6th annual Phi Alpha Theta distinguished lecture on history at the State University of Albany on March 20, 1986 (n. p., n. d.), 11, is no doubt correct in observing that Roosevelt got through an enormous amount of paperwork each day and that he "kept track of the 'ultra' materials." Likewise, Cochran, "The Influence of 'Magic' Intelligence," 346, concludes that Roosevelt had "more than a passing interest in intelligence." On the other hand, Adams says, 237, that while Leahy continued to bring ULTRA to the president as it seemed pertinent, "Roosevelt was not much interested in details." None of these comments answers the significant question of whether he much used the intercepts in running the war. On January 1944, Roosevelt, in a message to Churchill, cited an intercept as a possible answer to a puzzling international incident (Kimball, ed., 2:672-673, 677). This might indicate that he was reading the intercepts voluminously and carefully. On

In February 1944, Marshall wrote the president, "I have learned that you seldom see the Army summaries of 'Magic' material." Marshall's remedies—improving the presentation, separating the wheat from the chaff and correlating the items with other information, binding the summaries in a Black Book for convenience of reading—suggest that the president was not particularly interested in the information.[110]

On the other hand, McCormack said of his MAGIC summaries that the president and his advisers "read them avidly."[111] He commented that "the fight for personnel was made easier by high praise which the [Special] Branch received from time to time by General Marshall and other high officials, and occasionally from the President."[112] General Corderman said that although none of the Signal Service Agency's many commendations were ever known to have come from the president, he had the impression that Roosevelt was a great user of the intercepts and a great supporter of those who produced them.[113] Frank Rowlett, the cryptanalyst whose solution of the RED machine had started it all, said that the usefulness of the intercepts to the top leadership was made clear to the cryptanalysts in the most valuable way possible: the cryptanalysts were asked, "Do you have anything more on this? Give it priority!" That request for more of their results was, said Rowlett, "better than any pat on the back."[114]

No doubt the president was glad for the information he got—hence the appreciation sensed by the codebreakers and the evaluators. Nevertheless, the impression remains that the intercepts had only a secondary interest for Roosevelt. The reason may be that—unlike the military and naval men—he could not much use the information they gave him.

During hostilities, intercepts on diplomatic affairs—either of the Axis or of neutral nations—dealt at best with nonbelligerents. But geography and the war situation influenced them far more than Allied pressure. Roosevelt understood this, and so perhaps interested himself but little in the intercepts dealing with these matters. For instance, the Allied invasion of North Africa had given rise to fears that Spain might admit German troops who could close the Strait of Gibraltar and trap Allied forces in the Mediterranean.[115] McCormack later

the other hand, his staff might have provided this information to him–an impression reinforced by Kimball's putting a bracketed "WDL?" at the end of the message to suggest that Leahy might have drafted it for him.

110 National Archives, Record Group 218, Leahy Papers, Folder 126, p. 189.

111 SRH-185, 013.

112 *Ibid.*, 004.

113 Corderman.

114 Rowlett.

115 Dallek, 362, 370.

claimed that Special Branch had provided the best intelligence about Spain's postinvasion intentions.[116] But however valuable the information Roosevelt may have gleaned from MAGIC, he seems not to have acted upon it: he sent no instructions to his ambassador in Madrid and did not mention guarding against the German threat in any of his postinvasion messages to Churchill.[117] In August of 1942, however, a MAGIC solution seemed of unusual importance. Marshall pointed out to Roosevelt intercepts showing that Japan had decided not to attack the Soviet Union and urged that Roosevelt tell Soviet leader Joseph Stalin about this. Roosevelt did—without, however, specifying the source of his information, which he affirmed was "definitely authentic."[118]

The MAGIC and ULTRA dealing with military matters was, of course, of extraordinary value to the generals and admirals, and Roosevelt urged it upon them. "Be sure Ernie King sees that!" he would sometimes tell McCrea when shown an intercept. But neither McCrea nor Mott nor Tyree saw cases in which an intercept impelled the president to take a particular action.[119] In part this was because he delegated the detailed running of the war to his military chiefs and seldom interfered.

In this Roosevelt contrasted sharply with Churchill. Soon after messages were solved at the codebreaking center at Bletchley Park, they were sent, together with their interpretations, to MI6 headquarters at Broadway Buildings in London, where a selection was made, put in a special buff-colored box, and taken by messenger to 10 Downing Street, five minutes away. The prime minister, who carried the key to the box on his key ring, sometimes read up to 200 ULTRA intercepts a day, discussed them at his daily meetings with his chiefs of staff, drew the attention of his field commanders to individual items, was told of such technical successes as the solution of a U-boat key, and in general utilized the intercepts in directing the war. But Churchill was much closer to the fighting and bombing than Roosevelt and, as minister of defense, much more intimately involved in the details. The intercepts were therefore of far greater value to him. Not to know what he saw would distort the picture of how he worked during

[116] SRH-035, 18–19; SRH-116, 014.

[117] Nothing in Kimball, ed., 2, checking especially 20, 41–42, 75, 76; *FRUS, 1942*, 2:303–315; *FRUS, 1943*, 2:595–97; Willard L. Beaulac (an American diplomat in Spain at the time), *Franco: Silent Ally in World War II* (Carbondale: Southern Illinois University Press, 1986); James W. Cortada, *Two Nations Over Time: Spain and the United States, 1776–1977* (Westport, Conn.: Greenwood Press, 1978); or in Carlton J. H. Hayes (the ambassador), *Wartime Mission to Spain* (New York: Macmillan, 1945).

[118] Franklin D. Roosevelt Library, Map Room Files, Box 167, Naval Aide's File: A/16-Japan and Japanese Islands, 1942–1945, Memo for the President from Marshall, 5 Aug 1942; *FRUS, 1942*, 3:616. I am obliged to Dr. Carl Boyd for this information.

[119] McCrea; Mott; Tyree.

World War II.[120]

Can the same be said of Roosevelt? Not with our present knowledge. Perhaps he used MAGIC and ULTRA extensively in his running of the war, and perhaps he did not. All known sources do not provide enough facts to permit a conclusion one way or the other. He and his advisors cannot be asked, and the chances seem slight that papers yielding direct evidence on the matter will come to light. Possibly comparisons of MAGIC and ULTRA with actions taken in the war will develop a pattern convincing enough to let historians say that the one affected the other. But here, too, the uncertainty even about what intercepts Roosevelt saw and the tenuousness of such influence even with solid data reduce the likelihood of success. Of the two efforts made so far, one fails to convince—even its proposer offers it diffidently—and the other, more plausible, awaits a documentary basis.[121] The almost complete lack of traces of Roosevelt's use of MAGIC and ULTRA despite the great volume of material may indeed suggest that Roosevelt did not much use them. But this is at best a negative argument, and in no way conclusive. In the end, we historians can only say that we do not now know how Roosevelt used MAGIC and ULTRA. And probably we never will.

NOTES

A name alone refers to an interview. Numbers for SRH items beginning with 0 or 00 when under 10 or 100 are the page numbers stamped on the document by archivists; they differ from the document's original typewritten page numbers.

---

[120] Gilbert, 6:611, 613, and the numerous references under "Enigma decrypts" in 7 (*Road to Victory*); Martin Gilbert, memorandum, 17 March 1987; Hinsley, 2:4 and entries under "Churchill" in the index.

[121] The effort that fails to convince is that of Cochran. He says, at 346, that the decision to get Italy out of the war "could well have been based upon Magic information" about "major strategic differences between the Axis powers, desperate economic and social conditions in Italy, and growing political instability among the fascist elite," citing 17 reports from April to June 1943. But not only did many nonintelligence factors contribute to this decision, not only had the idea been considered even before the North African invasion, but, as Cochran admits, no evidence links the intelligence to the decision, and without evidence his hypothesis remains unproved. The more plausible effort is that of Rohwer. He argues that Churchill knew via ULTRA of Hitler's 21 June 1941 order to U-boats that they not attack large warships whose nationality they did not know, that Churchill passed this information to Roosevelt, and that it encouraged the president to support Britain in the Atlantic more energetically than if he feared German retaliation. Rohwer says that U. S. Navy situation maps show the U-boats dispositions and that this is "clear evidence of the re-transmission of 'Ultra' intelligence from London to Washington." But National Archives, Record Group 457, SRMN-033, Part I, "Cominch File of Messages on U-Boat, Estimates and Situation Reports October 1941-September 1942," which gives individual submarine positions and estimated positions, does not reach back to June, the Navy's Operational Archives does not have any earlier files, and none of the messages in Kimball, ed., 1:210-281 (21 June to 7 December 1941) deal with any such instructions to U-boats. Thus, plausible as Rohwer's suggestion is, it must await further documentation before winning at least my acceptance.

Note

Though this article concludes that cryptologic information was little used by Roosevelt, such material was of enormous value in military operations, including at the highest level. Special Branch prepared the material for use by these high officials. But because this article focuses on Roosevelt, it excludes many details of the workings of the Special Branch. Almost every sentence dealing with that operation could—and some day should—be expanded into an article. The sources offer clues to this.

My claim of exhaustive research requires that I list the sources that I checked for information about Roosevelt and MAGIC and ULTRA. They are:

- Franklin D. Roosevelt Library, Hyde Park, New York. The only records of MAGIC for the president are those for some of his trips away from Washington. These are cited below. The Map Room files have no logs of ULTRA or MAGIC documents or the summaries based on them that went to the president, nor any mention of the couriers who brought him ULTRA or MAGIC documents, nor any record of what the naval aides (as Captain McCrea) brought him in its noting of their visits to him.

- William Emerson, at the time of my inquiry director of the Roosevelt Library. He knew of no unpublished documentary material concerning Roosevelt's receipt of or use of ULTRA or MAGIC.

- Robert Dallek, *Franklin D. Roosevelt and American Foreign Policy, 1932–1945* (New York: Oxford University Press, 1979). The work does not mention ULTRA, and Dallek, who went through all or nearly all the papers dealing with Roosevelt and foreign policy, said on the telephone 14 April 1986 he does not remember seeing anything about it in the documents. He believes that such material would have jumped out at him and that he would have used it in his book as a good story.

- Robert Myers of the White House Map Room staff said that both he and George Elsey of that staff picked up intercepts from the commander in chief, U. S. Fleet (Admiral Ernest King), and Admiral John Tyree, assistant to the naval aide, said that Myers picked up intercepts from the Navy. On the other hand, Elsey said that, although he dealt with messages of Winston Churchill and Joseph Stalin to Roosevelt, he knew nothing about MAGIC or ULTRA documents or summaries going to the president. I have not been able to clear up the contradiction. Asked for any intercepts sent by the Navy to the White House during World War II, the Navy Security Group Command headquarters replied in a letter of 18 April 1988 (Ser GH/4057) that it had only duplicates of Army-originated diplomatic intercepts.

- All of the interviewees were asked about how the Special Branch summaries went to Roosevelt and what use he made of that information; they knew little about the distribution and none knew anything about the president's use of the material.

- Archive of Contemporary History, University of Wyoming. I was told 16 April 1986 by Professor Emmet Chisum that he has never seen anything about distribution of MAGIC to Roosevelt in the papers of Laurance Safford, Dundas Tucker, and C. C. Hiles, all naval officers who worked in or knew about communications intelligence.

- Dundas P. Tucker, "Rhapsody in Purple: A New History of Pearl Harbor," ed. Greg Mellen, *Cryptologia*, 6 (July 1982), 193–228, (October 1982), 346–367, has nothing on MAGIC or ULTRA to Roosevelt.
- Library of Congress, Manuscript Division, Papers of William D. Leahy, Diary. A skim showed nothing dealing with ULTRA or MAGIC. Moreover, these papers became available to the public before ULTRA material was declassified.
- National Archives, Record Group 218, Joint Chiefs of Staff, Leahy Papers. None of the following folders have anything about MAGIC or ULTRA to Roosevelt:
  - Folder 54, Value of OSS
  - Folder 82, Miscellaneous Messages 1945–46
  - Folder 83, Dispatches 1944 Miscellaneous
  - Folder 84, Miscellaneous 1944
  - Folder 89, Conference Teheran 1943
  - Folder 100, Prime-President 1944
  - Folder 101, Prime-President 1943
  - Folder 102, Hurley—"Special"—and Harriman
  - Folder 104, High-Level (not Prime), 1945
  - Folder 105, High-Level Message 1943 1944 not Prime
  - Folder 125, Memoranda to and from President 1945
  - Folder 127, Memos to and from President July 1, 1943 to Nov. 1943
  - Folder 128, Correspondence signed by the President
  - Folder 138, Messages between President and Admiral Leahy
- U. S. Naval Institute, Annapolis, Maryland, "Reminiscences of Vice Admiral William R. Smedberg III, U. S. Navy, Retired," an oral history, July 1979, has nothing on Roosevelt on pages 281–313, which deal with Smedberg's service from September 1944 to March 1946 as combat intelligence officer on the staff of the commander in chief, U. S. Fleet.

I have not credited or used the statements in William Stevenson's *A Man Called Intrepid: The Secret War* (New York: Harcourt Brace Jovanovich, 1976) ascribed to Sir William Stephenson, head of British Security Coordination during World War II, that he brought ULTRA information to Roosevelt. These statements are unsupported by other evidence and my confidence in the book's unsubstantiated statements has been undermined by its basic and numerous errors.

SOURCES

Published Documents

United States. Congress. Joint Committee on the Investigation of the Pearl Harbor Attack. *Pearl Harbor Attack*. Hearings. 79th Congress: 1st and 2nd Sessions. Washington: Government Printing Office, 1946. 39 vols. Cited as *PHA* followed by volume and page number.

———. Department of State. *Foreign Relations of the United States: Diplomatic Papers*. Washington: Government Printing Office. Cited as *FRUS* with year followed by volume and page.

1937, 1: *General*; 2: *British Commonwealth, Europe, Near East, Africa*; 3 and 4: *The Far East* (all 1954).

Japan, 1931–1941, 2 (1943).

1942, 2: *Europe* (1961); 3: *Europe* (1961).

1943, 2: *Europe* (1964).

Unpublished Documents

National Archives. Record Group 457. Records of the National Security Agency.

SRH-061. "Allocation of Special Security Offices to Special Branch, Military Intelligence Service, War Department, 1943–45." 33 pp.

SRH-111. "MAGIC Reports for the Attention of the President 1943–1944." 32 pp.

SRH-116. "Origin, Functions and Problems of the Special Branch, M. I. S." [A memorandum by McCormack to Clarke, 15 April 1943.] 55 pp.

SRH-118. "Incidental Exhibits re Pearl Harbor Investigation" [Collection of Japanese Diplomatic Messages 12 July 1938–21 January 1942. Department of the Army Intelligence Files.] 481 pp.

SRH-141. "Papers from the Personal Files of Alfred McCormack." Parts 1 and 2. 570 pp.

SRH-145. "Collection of Memoranda on Operations of S. I. S. [Signal Intelligence Service] Intercept Activities and Dissemination 1942–45." 293 pp.

SRH-153. "M. I. S., War Department, Liaison Activities in the U. K. 1943– 1945." 20 pp.

SRH-185. "War Experience of Alfred McCormack." 83 pp.

SRH-270. "Army-Navy-F. B. I. Comint [Communications Intelligence] Agreements of 1942." 5 pp.

SRDJ-113,785–114,000. Japanese Diplomatic Translations. Station "C" Intercept Message File. [10 September 1940–7 April 1941.]

SRS. Diplomatic "MAGIC" Summaries 1943. September, October, December.

———. Record Group 218. Joint Chiefs of Staff. Leahy Papers. Folder 126, Memos to the President from General Marshall.

Franklin D. Roosevelt Library, Hyde Park, New York. Map Room File.

Box 15. Presidential Trips 27 September 1942–28 April 1943. Folders Casa- blanca Conference Trip, Presidential Trips Hyde Park 6 February–5 April 1943.

Box 16. Presidential Trips 14 May–7 November 1943. Folder Canadian Fishing Trip and Quadrant Conference 31 July–29 August 1943.

Box 192. Map Room Logs—Incoming Dispatches. 1941–July 1943. Folder Log of Incoming Dispatches April May 1942. Folder Log of Incoming Dispatches December 1941 January February March 1942. Folder Log Sheets September 1942.

Box 195. Map Room Logs: 1942–1945. Folder White House Chart Room—Special Log President-Churchill Dispatches. Folder Chart Room Log and Standing Orders [a log of calls and visitors]. Folder 1-A [log of Map Room].

National Security Agency.
Translated solutions of intercepted Japanese diplomatic messages dealing with the accession of Italy to the Anti-Comintern Pact.

Interviews

In Person

Carter W. Clarke. Head of Special Branch. 6 December 1963.
Thomas Ervin. Liaison officer in Special Branch. 11 March 1986.
Vincent Fontana. Typist and production manager in Special Branch. 12 March 1986.
C. Roger Nelson. Assistant editor of MAGIC Diplomatic Summary. 12 December 1985.
Benjamin R. Shute. Editor of German military summary. 8 March 1986.

By Telephone

Cletus Beard. Head of Asmara intercept post in 1950s. 20 April 1986.
Carter W. Clarke. 10 January and 19 October 1986.
Arthur Compton. Liaison officer in Special Branch. 27 October 1986.
W. Preston Corderman. Head of Signal Security Agency. 20 April 1986.
George Elsey. Deputy to Leahy in Map Room. 12 February 1986.
Forrest McCluney. Head of Special Branch couriers. 9 March 1986.
John McCrea. Naval aide to Roosevelt. 4 and 12 March 1986.
William Mott. Assistant to Leahy. 13 January and 23 March 1987.
Robert Myers. Assistant in Map Room. 26 April 1987.
William R. Perdue. Editor of Far Eastern Summary. 16 February 1987.
William McKinley Rigdon. Assistant to Leahy. 9 March 1986.
Frank Rowlett. Head of cryptanalytical teams that solved RED and PURPLE. 22 April 1986.
W. R. Smedberg. Head of naval combat intelligence. 12 May 1980.
John A. Tyree. Assistant to naval aide. 19 May 1987.

Letters

Carter W. Clarke. December 1985.
W. Preston Corderman. Commander of Signal Service Agency, 1943–1945. 5 December 1983.
John J. McCloy. Assistant secretary of war. 18 July 1984.
Henry W. Rigby. Editor of MAGIC Summary. 10 February 1987.
Lester R. Schultz. Delivered MAGIC to Roosevelt. 3 and 24 January 1986.
J. C. Sharp. Deputy chief, information policy, National Security Agency. 4 November 1986 (Serial J9420A).
Telford Taylor. Head of Special Branch unit at Bletchley Park. 6 January 1985.

Secondary Sources
(Includes only items cited more than once in the notes or of basic importance)

Adams, Henry H. *Witness to Power: The Life of Fleet Admiral William D. Leahy*. Annapolis, Maryland: Naval Institute Press, 1985.

Bell, Ernest L. *An Initial View of ULTRA as an American Weapon.* Keene, New Hampshire: TSU Press, 1977. (A reprint of SRH-005, "Use of [CX/MSS ULTRA] by the United States War Department, 1943–1945," 82 pp., and of SRH-006, "Synthesis of Experiences in the Use of ULTRA Intelligence by the U. S. Army Field Commands in the European Theatre of Operations," 29 pp.)

Cochran, Alexander S., Jr. "The Influence of 'Magic' Intelligence on Allied Strategy in the Mediterranean." In Craig L. Symonds, ed., *New Aspects of Naval History: Selected Papers Presented at the Fourth Naval History Symposium, United States Naval Academy, 25–26 October 1979* (Annapolis, Maryland: Naval Institute Press, 1981), at 340–348.

———. *The MAGIC Diplomatic Summaries: A Chronological Finding Aid.* New York: Garland Publishing, 1982.

Hannah, Theodore M. "Frank B. Rowlett—A Personal Profile." *Cryptologic Spectrum* (National Security Agency), 11 (April 1981), 4–22.

Hinsley, F. H., et al., *British Intelligence in the Second World War* Cambridge and New York: Cambridge University Press, 1979–1988.

Howe, George F. *American Signal Intelligence in Northwest Africa and Western Europe.* [Unclassified]. United States Cryptologic History, Series IV: World War II, Vol. 1. [Fort Meade, Maryland]: National Security Agency/Central Security Service, 1980.

Jones, F. C. *Japan's New Order in Asia: Its Rise and Fall, 1937–1945.* London: Oxford University Press, 1954.

Kahn, David. *The Codebreakers: The Story of Secret Writing.* New York: Macmillan, 1967.

Kesaris, Paul, ed. *The MAGIC Documents: Summaries and Transcripts of the Top-Secret Diplomatic Communications of Japan, 1938–1945.* Index compiled by David Wallace. Frederick, Maryland: University Publications of America, 1982.

Lewis, Graydon A., ed. *A History of Communications Intelligence in the United States with Emphasis on the United States Navy.* Denver: Naval Cryptologic Veterans Association, 1982.

Parrish, Thomas. *The Ultra Americans: The U. S. Role in Breaking the Nazi Codes* New York: Stein and Day, 1986.

Rohwer, Jürgen. "Ultra, the United States and the Battle of the Atlantic 1941." Paper delivered at the 2nd U. S. Army War College International Conference on Intelligence and Military Operations, Carlisle Barracks, Pennsylvania, 12–14 May 1987.

National Archives. Record Group 457. Records of the National Security Agency.

SRH-001. "Historical Background of the Signal Security Agency." Vol. 3. "The Peace." Preface signed by Historian, Army Security Agency. [Assistant Chief of Staff, G-2, 12 April 1946.] 416 pp. Reprinted as *The Origin and Development of the Army Security Agency 1917–1947* (Laguna Hills, Calif.: Aegean Park Press, 1978).

SRH-029. "A Brief History of the Signal Intelligence Service." By William F. Friedman, June 19, 1942. 18 pp. Reprinted in Kesaris, ed., 17–31.

SRH-035. "History of the Special Branch, MIS [Military Intelligence Service], War Department, 1943–1944." 63 pp.

SRH-041. "M. I. S. Contributions to the War Effort." December 1945. 22 pp.

SRH-061. "Allocation of Special Security Officers to Special Branch, Military Intelligence Service, War Department, 1943–45." 33 pp.

SRH-062. "History of Military Intelligence Service. Reports Unit." September 1945. 116 pp.

SRH-117. "History of Special Branch, M. I. S." June 1944–September 1945. Unsigned. 11 pp. Reprinted in Kesaris, ed., 55–67.

SRH-132. "History of the Special Distribution Branch." 7 pp.

SRH-146. "Handling of Ultra Within the Military Intelligence Service (M. I. S.) 1941–1945." [A memorandum by Lieutenant Colonel Thomas E. Ervin, 29 January 1946.] 7 pp.

SRH-149. "A Brief History of Communications Intelligence in the United States." By Laurance F. Safford, Captain, U. S. N., Ret. 22 pp. Reprinted in Kesaris, ed., 1–16.

SRH-152. "Historical Review of OP-20-G." 17 February 1944. [Unsigned]. 13 pp.

SRH-154. "Signal Intelligence Disclosures in the Pearl Harbor Investigations." 47 pp.

SRH-159. "Preliminary Historical Report on the Solution of the 'B' Machine." By William F. Friedman. 14 October 1940. 10 pp.

SRH-305. "The Undeclared War: 'History of R. I.' [radio intelligence]." By L. F. Safford. 15 November 1943. 29 pp.

SRH-349. "The Achievements of the Signal Security Agency in World War II." February 1946. 115 pp.

SRH-355. "Naval Security Group History to World War II." Prepared and compiled by Captain J. S. Holtwick, Jr., U. S. N., Ret. June 1971. Part I, 464 pp.

AN ENIGMA CHRONOLOGY

David Kahn

ADDRESS: 120 Wooleys Lane, Great Neck NY 11023 USA.

ABSTRACT: A list of important events in the making and breaking of the German Enigma cipher machine of World War II is given in the order of their occurrences.

KEYWORDS: Enigma, chronology.

In view of the importance of ULTRA to the history of intelligence, and in view of the errors in dating that appear in so many accounts, I thought it would be worthwhile to establish a list of important dates in the story of the Enigma cipher machine and its solution. Most deal with the naval machine.

This chronology comes mainly from my book, *Seizing the Enigma* (New York: Houghton Mifflin, 1991), which is based as much as possible on primary or on solid secondary sources, chiefly F. H. Hinsley et al's magisterial *History of British Intelligence in the Second World War* (Cambridge: Cambridge University Press, 1979-1988). For my book, the Naval Historical Branch in London made available to me a key primary source for much naval dating, but I promised not to cite it by name, a promise that I am honoring. Information about the times of naval solution comes from analyses of intercepts in the Public Record Office, London, and in the National Archives, Washington. To avoid burdening this list with a heavy biographical apparatus, I have given as sources the page numbers in Hinsley or in *Seizing the Enigma* that specify these dates or detail those incidents. Notes in the form 2:659 refer to Hinsley; those in the form 140 refer to Kahn, in which the notes to the text cite the source. "GC&CS" is the Government Code and Cypher School, the British codebreaking agency at Bletchley Park. Names in capital letters of colors, insects, and birds are GC&CS's covernames for Enigma keys.

An important element in the history of the solution of Enigma is that the Luftwaffe Enigma was solved more easily by GC&CS than the naval Enigma, though until 1 February 1942 both used the identical machine with identically wired rotors. One reason is that the air force (like the army) chose the three rotors inserted into its machines from a set of five rotors while the navy chose its three from a set of eight. In addition, air force key settings could often be recovered in the first few months of the war from the key indicators at the head of the cryptograms and later from blunders by the ciphering clerks in making up their part of the key. This gave GC&CS insight into Luftwaffe messages, providing enough cribs for a daily recovery of keys. The naval settings, on the other hand, were taken from books and permitted neither the indicators nor the blunders approach; without some early solutions, GC&CS could not at first get enough messages to yield future guesses of plaintext for cribs. Captures of the books were thus the necessary first step for solution of the naval Enigma. The Enigma keys used by the army were seldom solved because the army cipher clerks, more experienced than those of the Luftwaffe, seldom made blunders.

Solution of the Enigma consisted of guessing an intercepted cryptogram's plaintext (either from knowledge of the traffic previously passed between posts or from solutions of the same messages in other cryptosystems) and then seeing whether the bombes (which were in effect multiple Enigmas) found a setting of the Enigma rotors that would produce such a ciphertext from the assumed plaintext. If they did, that setting was the key for the day on that cipher net and permitted the reading of other messages on the net. The process had to be repeated for each net each day.

Not included here are minor matters, such as the dates of early improvements in Enigma construction or keying, of techniques the Poles used to overcome these changes, or of the solution of secondary keys, such as the Luftwaffe's practice key. (I consider keys minor if they did not contribute significantly to the fighting. Some people may of course differ with my judgment.) A full list of solution dates is given in Hinsley, 2:658-668, 3:1:483-487, 3:2:855-857. In some cases, Hinsley does not state for how long the solutions continued. The date of 24 May 1943 at 2:667 is a misprint for 24 May 1945, Hinsley told me.

Date		Enigma	The World
1918	Feb 23	Arthur Scherbius files for a patent for the Enigma cipher machine (Patentschrift Nr. 416291)	
	Apr 15	Arthur Scherbius offers the Enigma to the German navy (31)	
1918	Nov 11		World War I ends
1921	Feb 19		France and Poland sign accord for "concerted measures for the defense of their territory"
1926		German navy begins using Enigma (40-41)	
1928	Jul 15	German army begins using Enigma (51)	
1931	Nov 8	Hans-Thilo Schmidt betrays army Enigma instruction manual and keying methods to the French, who give them to the Poles (59)	
1932	Dec	With the help of keys betrayed by Schmidt and given by the French to the Poles, cryptanalyst Marian Rejewski reconstructs the wiring of the three Enigma rotors, enabling the Poles to begin solving German army Enigma messages (65-66)	
1933	Jan 30		Führer of the Nazi party, Adolf Hitler, named chancelor of Germany
1938	Dec 15	Two new rotors (making a toitl of five) go into service on army Enigma; Rejewski recovers wiring, but tenfold increase in number of keys overwhelms Poles, requiring them to ask aid from their allies (77)	
1939	Mar 30		Britain and France guarantee to help Poland if she is invaded by Germany as Czechoslovakia was
	Jul 24	Poles reveal success to British and French (79)	
	Sep 1		Germany invades Poland
	Sep 3		Britain and France declare war on Germany

Date		Enigma	The World
1940	Jan 6	British break into Luftwaffe Enigma using hand methods (1:108, 2:659)	
	Feb 12	British seize two of the three unknown rotors used in the naval Enigma from a crew member of the U-33 captured after the submarine was sunk (114; 3:2:957)	
	Apr 9		Germany invades Denmark and Norway
	May	First bombe installed at GC&CS (1:494, more likely than August installation date given at 1:184 because regular solution of RED began May 22)	
	May	First break into naval Enigma: using documents salvaged 26 April from the trawler *Polares* (303, 3:2:957), GC&CS solves April messages (117)	
	May 10		Germany opens massive offensive against France; Winston Churchill, a long-time supporter of communications intelligence, named prime minister
	May 22	GC&CS begins solution of Luftwaffe general purpose key (RED) continuing virtually uninterrupted to end of war (1:109, 144)	
	Jun 10		Last Norwegian troops surrender
	Jun 22		France surrenders
	Aug	The last unknown naval rotor obtained from a naval capture (3:2:957)	
	Aug 12		Adlertag (Eagle Day): Germany attempts to win air superiority over England as invasion preparation
	Sep 15		Battle of Britain D Day: it becomes clear that Germany's attempt has failed
	Oct 12		Hitler postpones invasion of Britain until spring
	Dec 10	SS (Schutzstaffel) general-purpose key (ORANGE I) first broken by GC&CS (2:668)	

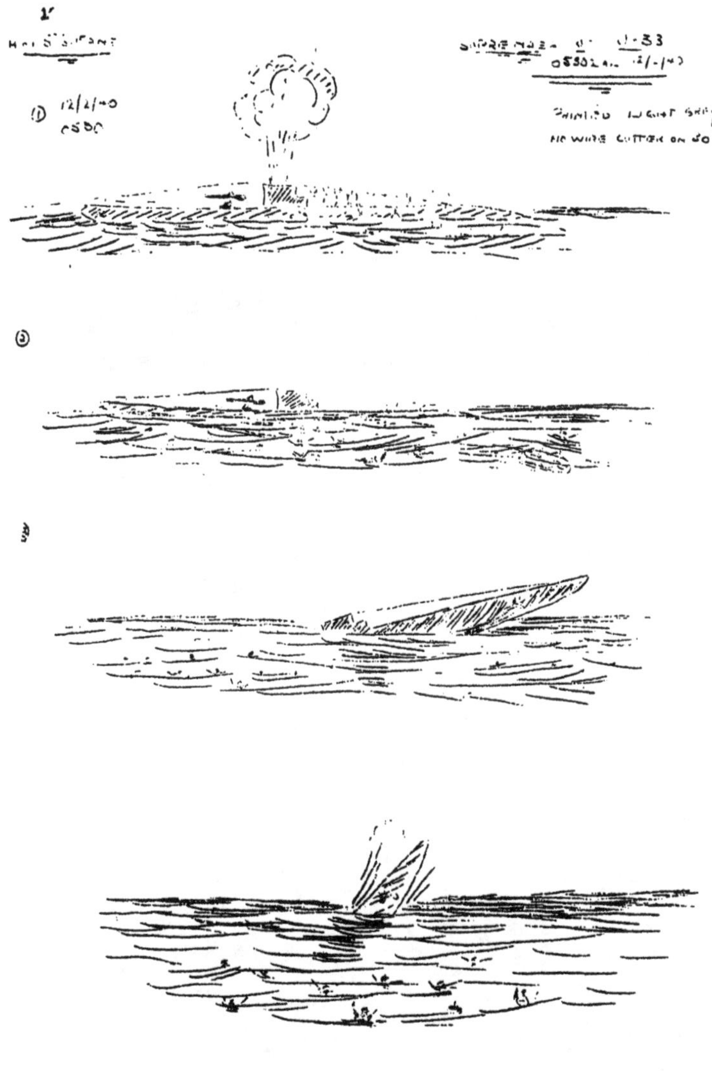

12 Feb 1940

A series of sketches – artist not indicated – showing the end of the U-33 after it surfaced in a vain attempt to escape the minesweeper *H. M. S. Gleaner* in Scotland's Firth of Clyde 12 February 1940. The sketches show (1) a shower of sparks from the coning tower; (2) crew members in the water as they abandon ship; (3) more in the water as the submarine starts to sink; (4) the U-boat in her final dive with survivors swimming away from her. Three rotors were recovered from a crew member who forgot to take them from his pocket and drop them in the ocean.

(Public Record Office, ADM 199/123, p. 54)

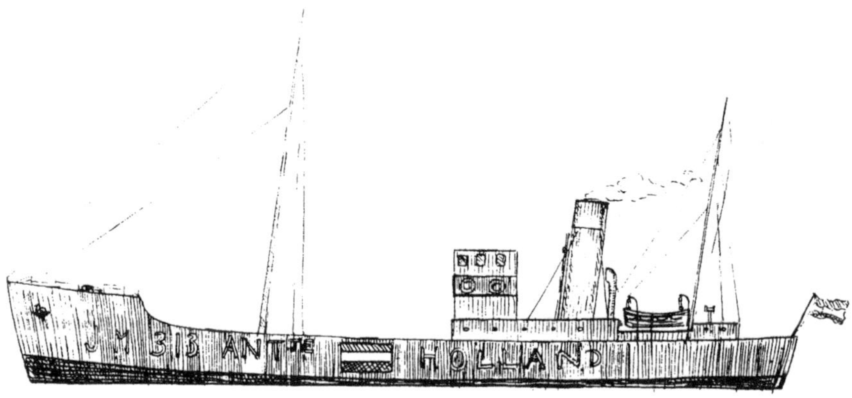

May 1940

The former trawler *Julius Pickenpack*, now a German attack vessel disguised as the Dutch ship *Polares*. From one of its canvas bags, thrown overboard on the approach of British warships but saved by a British sailor, the British obtained cryptographic documents useful in solving German naval Enigma traffic.

(Public Record Office, ADM 199/476, p. 243)

1 June 1941

The officers and crew of the U-110, in port, await an approaching inspecting officer while the skipper, Lieutenant Fritz-Julius Lemp, 28, approaches the gangplank to greet him. On patrol, the submarine was seized by the British and, before it sank, yielded an Enigma machine and keying documents. These enabled the British to read U-boat messages for June 1941. Lemp was lost during the action.

(David Kahn collection)

2 July 1941

Hinrich Gewald, 58, skipper of the *Lauenburg*, whose capture by the British led to the seizure of Enigma keying documents that enabled the British to read U-boat messages for July 1941.

(David Kahn collection)

2 July 1941

The *Lauenburg*, just before being boarded on 28 June 1941.

(David Kahn collection)

Date		Enigma	The World
1941	Jan 28	Luftwaffe operational key for Africa first solved by GC&CS; solutions end 31.12.42 with introduction the next day of separate Fliegerkorps keys (2:660)	
	Feb-Mar	2 U. S. Army and 2 U. S. Navy cryptanalysts visit GC&CS and learn Enigma cryptanalysis (235-237)	
	Feb 15		General Erwin Rommel named commander of German forces in North Africa
	Mar 12	Documents seized from patrol ship *Krebs* permit reading of some March and all April and May naval messages in the Home Waters key net, also used for U-boat messages (137)	
	Jun 1	GC&CS reads Home Waters (and U-boat) messages for a month with keys seized from weather ship *München* and U-110 (169)	
	Jun 27	GC&CS breaks German army Russian front key (VULTURE I); solutions last until spring 1944 (2:662)	
	Jun 22		Germany invades the Soviet Union
	Jul 2	GC&CS reads Home Waters (and U-boat) messages for a month with keys seized from weather ship *Lauenburg* (182)	
	mid-Aug	Home Waters key (DOLPHIN), then also used by U-boats, begins to be solved daily in 36 hours without seized keys on bases of knowledge gained in two preceding months; solutions continue to 7 May 1945 (1:338, 2:663-664)	
	Sep 6	Churchill visits GC&CS at Bletchley Park (184-85)	
	Oct 5	TRITON key net for U-boats separates U-boat keys from Home Waters key (205); solutions continue on both nets in times ranging (in January) from 12 to 120 hours	

Date		Enigma	The World
	Dec	GC&CS first solves Enigma of the Abwehr, the armed forces espionage service; solutions, called ISK (Intelligence Service [Dillwyn] Knox), continue to end of 1944 (2:668)	
	Dec 12		Germany declares war on the United States
1942	Jan 1	Keys for Luftwaffe's Fliegerkorps IX (WASP) and Fliegerkorps X (GADFLY) broken on day of first appearance and continuing to end of war; key for Fliegerkorps IV (HORNET) broken to December 1943 (2:660)	
	early	New Short Weather Key goes into service (2:750), ending GC&CS's ability to use meteorological messages as cribs to read naval Enigma (189-190)	
	Feb 1	4-rotor Enigma goes into service on TRITON; U-boat solution blackout begins (2:179)	
	Apr 3		Rommel begins offensive against British
	Apr 22	GC&CS breaks the Luftwaffe key for ground-air cooperation in Africa (Fliegerführer Afrika, or SCORPION); this ends February 1943	
	Jun 30		Rommel halts offensive at El Alamein
	fall	U. S. Navy liaison officer starts at GC&CS	
	Oct 23		British attack at El Alamein begins German rout
	Oct 30	New Short Weather Key captured from U-559 (220, 226)	
	Nov 8		Americans and British invade North Africa
	Dec 13	GC&CS, using new Short Weather Key to get cribs, breaks 4-rotor Enigma keys (SHARK); blackout ends (226, 2:667) but solutions irregular and at first slow (sometimes 8 days), by end of month much faster (around 12 hours)	

Date		Enigma	The World
1943	Jan and Feb	SHARK solutions stutter, but when working some are fast enough to be of operational value (229)	
	Mar 10- Jun 30	90 SHARK keys solved in 112 days (230)	
	Mar 14-20		Greatest convoy battle of the war, in which 21 ships are sunk, leading Allies to fear that the Atlantic lifeline to Britain could be cut
	May 24		Commander of U-boats Admiral Karl Dönitz withdraws his submarines from the North Atlantic, signifying a major Allied victory in the Battle of the Atlantic
	Aug	SHARK being read almost solid and fast (242)	
1944	Jun 6		Allies invade Normandy
	Nov	Individual U-boat keys end SHARK solutions, but so great is Allies' strength in ships and airpower that this no longer matters much (262)	
1945	May 8		Germany surrenders

ULTRA AND SOME U. S. NAVY CARRIER OPERATIONS*

Ralph Erskine

ADDRESS: c/o *Cryptologia*, Rose-Hulman Institute of Technology, Terre Haute IN 47803 USA.

ABSTRACT: The Ultra background is given to some operations by U. S. Navy escort carriers against U-boats in 1943 and 1944.

KEYWORDS: Enigma, Ultra, Kriegsmarine, U-boats, refueling, U-tanker, escort carriers, F-211, Op-20-G, Bletchley Park, OIC, Winn, Knowles.

This article describes the complex intelligence background to some operations in World War II against the U-boats by the United States Navy escort carrier (CVE) task groups, and the catastrophic results for the U-boat fleet, especially the U-boat tankers. The operations show a significant difference of approach in the way in which the United States and British naval authorities employed Ultra (or special intelligence) from naval Enigma - and escort carriers.[1]

By the end of May 1943, the tide had turned in the Battle of the Atlantic. A devastating combination of centimetric radar, shipborne high frequency direction finding (HF/DF), very long range aircraft, new weaponry and, above all, the efforts of Allied seamen and airmen had inflicted catastrophic losses on the U-boats. Intelligence from Enigma probably did not affect the losses much, since it was still being employed only to guide convoys past the U-boats, and not

*In the footnotes ZPTG and ZTPGU references are to decrypts in DEFE 3, but the dates given are those of the original signals, and not of the decrypts. Files are at the Public Records Office, Kew, London, unless otherwise stated.

[1] A wartime member of British naval intelligence has repeatedly stated that "information from decrypts is now erroneously if conveniently referred as Ultra. The correct designation is Special Intelligence. Ultra was merely a security classification" (Patrick Beesly, "British Naval Intelligence in Two World Wars", in Christopher Andrews and Jeremy Nokes (eds.), *Intelligence and International Relations 1900-1945* (Exeter, 1987), 269; see also Patrick Beesly, *Very Special Intelligence* (London, 1979), 100). However, this statement is itself incorrect. A signal of 20 August 1944 (cited in full in G. E. Colpoys, "Admiralty Use of Special Intelligence in Naval Operations" (ADM 223/88), 43, and replacing signals of 28 January 1943 and 1 November 1943), makes it clear that for all three British services Ultra was "a short title" for "special intelligence", with both terms meaning "intelligence resulting from the solution of high-grade codes and ciphers". See also signal 0956/16 March 1941, conveying intelligence from decrypts to a Royal Navy Mediterranean command, citing "indications from Ultra" (ADM 223/76).

offensively. No fewer than 39 U-boats had been sunk in May out of a total operational fleet (that is, excluding boats undergoing trials and training) of about 235. Admiral Karl Dönitz, the Kriegsmarine's Admiral Commanding U-boats (Befehlshaber der U-boote, or BdU) ruefully noted in his war diary that the exchange rate had plummeted from one U-boat lost for ever 100,000 tons of Allied shipping sunk to one boat for 10,000 tons.[2] Even the iron-willed Dönitz, who was nicknamed "Der Löwe" (the Lion) by his men, felt compelled to conclude that the U-boat losses had reached "unbearable heights."

In a long signal to U-boat commanders of 23 May, attempting to explain the recent losses and promising remedies, BdU included the sentence "I shall be drawing my own further conclusions about the choice of attack areas".[3] He followed this by a signal on 24 May redeploying 16 boats.[4] In addition, in a rare example of group radio deception in the Atlantic, he ordered a few other U-boats in a large area southeast of Greenland and southwest of Iceland to transmit signals in an attempt to mislead Allied traffic analysts into thinking that packs were available to attack North Atlantic convoys.[5] Although the 24 May signal was in Offizier (a doubly enciphered form of the German cipher machine, Enigma) and even the general (Allgemein) *Triton* cipher used by the Atlantic and Mediterranean U-boats on four-rotor Enigma was then proving extremely difficult to break, BP (as the British codebreaking establishment at Bletchley Park, a country house on the outskirts of Bletchley, northwest of London, was called) read the signal within five hours of its transmission. However, BP's hold on naval Enigma was then so tenuous that, had the signal been sent a few days earlier, it would not have been read for many weeks, with potentially deadly consequences for the seamen in three Allied convoys.[6]

In his 24 May message, Dönitz had sent his 16 submarines to "naval grid square 87 of the large square west of [disguised square] TT". But "TT" disguised the true letter pair of the grid reference. This presented the Allies with a major

---

[2]KTB (Kriegstagebuch) BdU, 24 May 1943 (microfilm T1022, reel 4064 (National Archives (NA), Washington)).

[3]ZTPGU 14191 (TOO (time of [German] origin] 1753/1842/2032/23 May 1943); also KTB BdU, 24 May 1943.

[4]ZTPGU 14208 (24 May 1943).

[5]KTB BdU, 24 May 1943; cf OIC SI 614 of 14 June 1943 (ADM 223/98).

[6]ZTPGU 15488 to 15490 of 16 May were not broken until 23 July 1943, although they were not even Offizier; ZTPGU 14967 (26 May 1943) succumbed only on 22 June. On Offizier, see Germany, Kriegsmarine, *Der Schlüssel M-Verfahren M Offizier und Stab* (M. Dv. Nr. 32/2) (Bundesarchiv-Militärchiv, Freiburg); Ralph Erskine, "Naval Enigma: The Breaking of Heimisch and *Triton*", *Intelligence and National Security*, 3(1) (1988), 162. On breaking Offizier, see Joan Murray, "Hut 8 and Naval Enigma, Part I" in *Codebreakers: The Inside Story of Bletchley Park*, F. H. Hinsley and Alan Stripp (eds.) (Oxford, 1993), 117 and Rolf Noskwith, "Hut 8 and Naval Enigma, Part II", ibid, 120, 121.

problem.[7] The decrypt was sent as usual by teleprinter to the Royal Navy's Operational Intelligence Centre (OIC), where Commander Rodger Winn, head of the Submarine Tracking Room, was an acknowledged expert on BdU's psychology who had often successfully anticipated Dönitz's plans. It was also received by Winn's opposite number in the U. S. Navy's equivalent of the Tracking Room, F-211, the much less experienced Commander Kenneth Knowles. Winn had been reading BdU's signals for 14 months, Knowles for a bare five months. Knowles wore two hats: one as head of the Atlantic Section, Combat Intelligence, on the staff of the Commander-in-Chief U. S. Fleet, who was Admiral Ernest King, and the other as chief, Intelligence Staff, Tenth Fleet, whose commander in chief was also King.[8] King, who was chief of naval operations and thus the head of the U. S. Navy, had established the Tenth Fleet on 20 may 1943 to fight the Battle of the Atlantic. Specifically, he charged it with responsibility for convoys and routing and for issuing orders to U. S. Navy task groups in the Atlantic, though it had no ships.

Winn thought that the effect of the "TT" signal was that the U-boats had been assigned to an area "south of Sable Island (about 200 miles east of Nova Scotia)" while Knowles and his team considered that they had been ordered to a position about "600 miles south-west of the Azores" - a difference of about 1,000 miles.[9] On 4 June it appears that the British still held to their original estimate. By 5 June, the codebreakers in the Kriegsmachines B-Dienst had solved a U-boat situation report of 4 June (nominally American, but almost certainly based on the standard British report) which disclosed that the Allies estimated that about 20 U-boats lay between Newfoundland and Greenland.[10] In reality, only about three boats, the residue of the deception team, were then still in that part of the North Atlantic, north of 47° north and west of 35° west.[11]

But for Knowles and his tiny staff, BdU's plan would have succeeded, and many men and ships would probably have been lost. We do not know how Knowles saw through BdU's plan. Knowles may have reasoned that, although the area south-west of the Azores was off the main convoy routes (and so offered

[7] On the Kriegsmarine naval grid and disguised squares, see Ralph Erskine, "The German Naval Grid in the Second World War", *Cryptologia*, XVI (1992), 39. Disguised squares used an Addressbuch (see Erskine). The convoluted method used in the "TT" signal of referring to what was in fact square CD 87 was necessary because CD did not have an Addressbuch equivalent, unlike CE, to its east.

[8] Kenneth A. Knowles, "Ultra and the Battle of the Atlantic: The American View", in Robert W. Lowe (ed.), *Changing Interpretations in Naval History* (New York, 1980), 444; Ladislas Farago, *The Tenth Fleet* (New York, 1962), passim; Samuel Eliot Morison, *History of the United States Naval Operations in the Second World War* (Boston, 1947-1962) X, *The Atlantic Battle Won* (1956), 21-25.

[9] OIC SI 603 of 31 May 1943 (ADM 223/98).

[10] KTB BdU, 5 June 1943 (NA, T1022: 4064); cf OIC SI 610 of 7 June 1943 (ADM 223/98).

[11] KTB BdU, 5 June 1943; cf OIC SI 614.

fewer targets), BdU would have wanted to station his U-boats as far away as possible from airfields with anti-submarine aircraft. Be that as it may, Knowles was able to back his views by actions, and proceeded to do so. This was doubly fortunate, because the basis of BdU's redeployment of the 16 U-boats had been a B-Dienst report that UGS 9, an eastbound convoy to Gibraltar, would be in the area of Kriegsmarine grid square CD 87 (an area of 54 sea miles by 54 in the middle of the North Atlantic, centered on 35° north, 42° west) at around 2000 on 31 May, the time by which he had ordered his boats to be at that point.[12] In fact, GUS 7A, a westbound convoy from Gibraltar to the States, was due to reach CD 87 before UGS 9. Knowles had GUS 7A diverted southwards, and it by-passed the 16 boats, which Dönitz had formed into the *Trutz* group. Knowles also ensured that the U. S. Navy Task Group 21.12, comprising the escort carrier *Bogue* and the destroyers *Clemson*, *Greene*, *Osmond Ingram*, and *George F. Badger*, was ordered to 35° north, 45° west (in the general region of group *Trutz*), in order to support GUS 7A and UGS 9 and another eastbound convoy, Flight 10 (consisting of about 20 infantry landing craft and an accompanying tanker).[13]

On the evening of 4 June, Flight 10 was approaching the southern end of the *Trutz* patrol line (see Figure 1). Fortunately, with the help of a HF/DF bearing taken from *Bogue* herself, Avenger aircraft from *Bogue* had found and attacked *U 228*, *603* and *641* at that end of the line in the late afternoon. Although the attack did not sink any U-boats, at least two were damaged. All three were forced to submerge, leaving a gap through which Flight 10 could slip safely, albeit with the narrowest of margins - at one time *U 603* was only 10 miles away from the lumbering convoy. At around 0700 on 5 June, a Wildcat piloted by Lieutenant R. S. Rogers and an Avenger flown by Lieutenant (jg) Alexander McAuslan (both from *Bogue*) sank *U 217*, the most southerly boat in the line).[14]

Although *Bogue* finished escorting UGS 9 to the east on 9 June, she was not able to prevent *U 488* a Type XIV supply boat capable of holding more than 400 tons of fuel, from refueling all 14 or so surviving members of *Trutz* without

---

[12] KTB BdU, 24 May 1943.

[13] "Allied Communication Intelligence and the Battle of the Atlantic" (NA, Record Group 457/SRH 008), volume II: 105 (henceforth "Allied Communication Intelligence"). This internal history was written by Knowles. For BdU's intelligence on Flight 10, see KTB BdU, 27, 29 May 1943.

[14] "US Escort Carrier Operations" (containing duplicates of U. S. Navy reports for May-August 1943) (ADM 199/1408); William T. Y'Blood, *Hunter-Killer* (Annapolis, 1983), 52-53; Morison, X: 111-112. *Bogue* had been fitted with a HF/DF set (probably the excellent British FH4 model) in Belfast, Northern Ireland, between 2 and 19 May 1943 (Y'Blood, 39). Although technical factors made escort carriers relatively poor platforms for taking accurate HF/DF bearings, the combination of Ultra, HF/DF and seaborne airpower was to prove devastating to the U-boats (cf minute, 12 February 1944, ADM 199/1408).

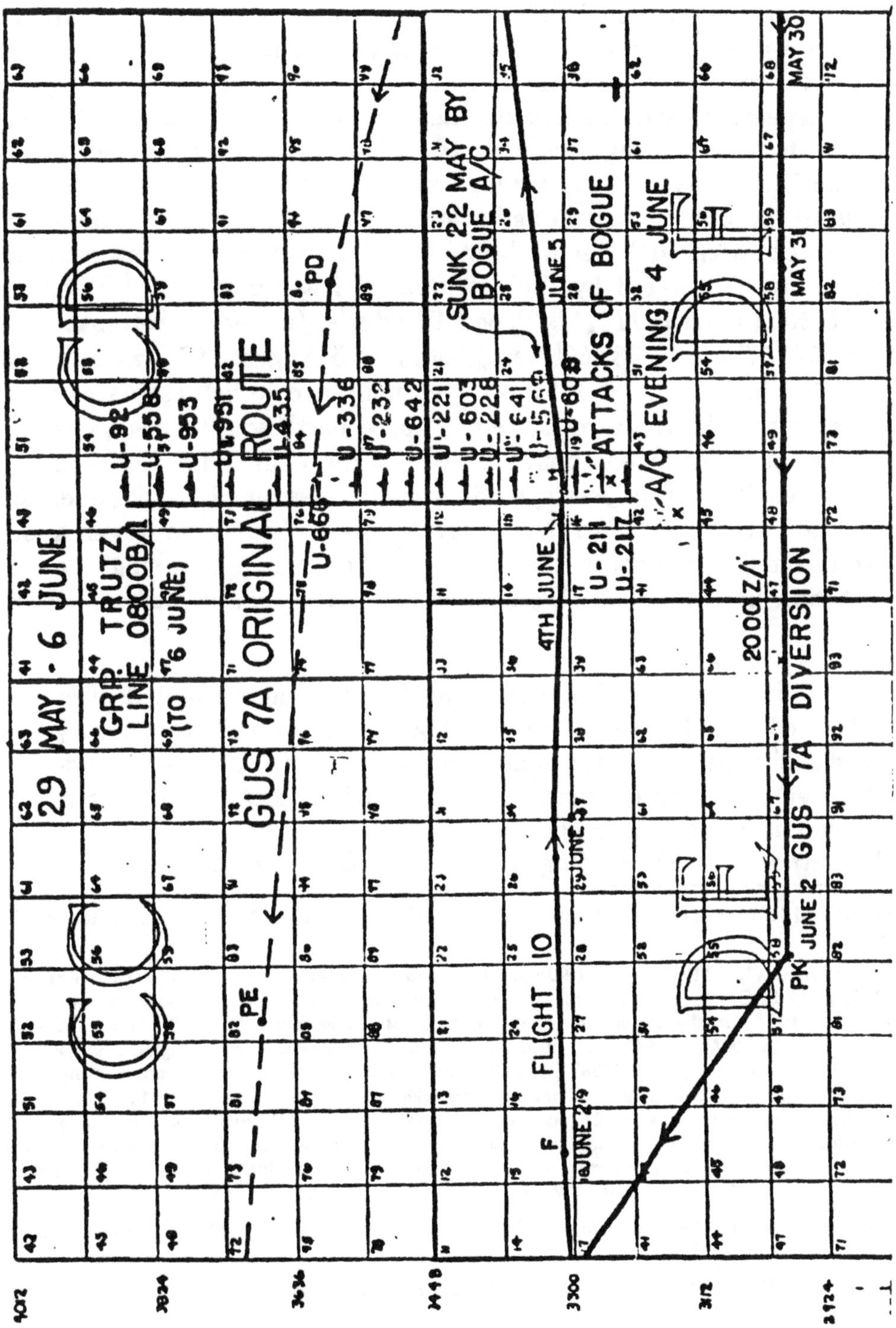

Figure 1. Group *Trutz* and convoys GUS 7A and Flight 10 plotted on the German naval grid.

incident by 13 June.[15]As a ruse, Dönitz required two boats to transmit dummy short signals in a different area. He also ordered extra precautions to protect the supply rendezvous. Normally, the boat being refueled used homing signals (the letter V repeatedly transmitted on medium wave for three minutes, on which other boats took bearings) in order to facilitate contact with the tanker. But on 5 June Dönitz banned the transmission of homing signals at refueling rendezvous until the boats involved had searched for each other for two days.[16] The difficulties experienced by some boats in attempting rendezvous without homing signals are illustrated by the attempts of Kapitänleutenant Friedrich Markworth (*U 66*) to find *U 117*, his Type XIV refueler (under Korvettenkapitän Neumann) at 37° 57′ north, 38° 30′ west, from 3 to 5 August 1953, when a new rendezvous in 38° 51′ north, 38° 14′ west, eventually had to be designated.[17]

After being refueled, *Trutz* re-formed in three north-south lines along 50° west on 16 June, to await an eastbound convoy on the 17th and a westbound on the 20th. But despite further re-dispositions of its lines on 27 to 29 June, and changing its name to *Geier 1* to *3* in early July, by which time it was about 500 miles from the Spanish coast, the *Trutz* group did not fight a single convoy actions, and sank no ships.[18] BdU's assessment of the group's lack of success states:

> We assume in each case that the patrol line was circumvented after being located ahead of the convoy by high-flying aircraft (this theory has been substantiated by the commanding officer of *U 558*, an experienced officer) ... As we are unable at present to intercept enemy aircraft radar, there is no point in sending any more U-boats into Mid-Atlantic for the purposes of intercepting UG and GU [Gibraltar] convoys.[19]

[15] KTB BdU, 11 and 13 June 1943 (T1022: 4064); ZTPGU 14724 (11 June), 15483 (5 June), the latter being broken on 23 July.

[16] "dummy short signals": ZTPGU 14588 (9 June 1943); "homing signals": ZTPGU 15482 (5 June 1943, broken on 23 July). ZTPGU 10343 (14 March 1943) had urged boats at an earlier rendezvous not to use homing signals, if possible. On the use of such signals by boats at rendezvous, see ZTPGU 10331 (14 March 1943), 10688 10705 (both 12 April 1943). See also Ralph Erskine, "U-boats, Homing Signals, and HFDF", *Intelligence and National Security*, 2(2) (1987), 324. The possible interception of rendezvous homing signals was discussed by the British U-boat Warfare Committee on 4 February 1943, but discounted (ADM 205/30). The Kriegsmarine was surprised that some 27 refueling operations between 21 February and 5 March 1943, 400 to 600 miles north of the Azores, by the U-tankers *U 460* and *U 462* were not discovered and attacked in view of the extensive radio traffic that they generated on medium and short waves [Günter Hessler - a former senior member of Dönitz's staff], *The U-boat War in the Atlantic* (London, 1989), para. 288.

[17] ZPTGU 15948 (6 August 1943); on the abortive rendezvous, see ZTPGU 15695 (1 August), 15941 (5 August).

[18] KTB BdU, 11 July 1943 (T1022: 4064); Morison, X: 116, 131. For an order reforming *Trutz*, see ZTPGU 15011 (21 June 1943).

[19] KTB BdU, 11 July 1943; on the report from *U 558*, see KTB BdU, 2 July 1943.

BdU apparently thought that the carrier aircraft were using radar extensively, although there was no scientific evidence whatsoever to support this very flawed hypothesis. As so often, BdU was floundering in the wizard war.

For the *Geier* boats, there was no hiding place on either side of the Atlantic. Although following the activation of rotor gamma (and its associated reflector, thin C) for four-rotor Enigma on 1 July 1943, BP read no July signals on *Triton* until after midday on 19 July, the OIC had learned about the deployment of the *Geier* (ex-*Trutz*) boats from *Triton* signals at the end of June.[20] Planes from the RAF's Squadron 179 at Gibraltar and the U. S. Army Air Force's Anti-Submarine Squadrons 1 and 2 (based in Morocco) were then quickly assigned to swamp *Geier*'s operational area. They sank three of the group's boats (*U 951*, *232* and *435*) on 7, 8, and 9 July, respectively, compelling BdU to order others to return to base prematurely.[21]

The fate of *Trutz* represents the beginning of the end for the Atlantic U-boats, which never again posed a serious threat to any Atlantic convoy. BdU had formed *Trutz* "in the hope of encountering less air activity,[22]" but he had completely underestimated the flexibility of the escort carriers, and the U. S. Navy's readiness to use them in free-ranging search and destroy operations, and not merely to defend convoys. No pack attack was mounted by any of the Atlantic U-boats in June, July, or August, although individual boats made 24 sinkings, which rose from 38,00 tons (seven ships) in June to 126,000 tons in July in the Atlantic and Arctic.

We now turn to an incident during the early days of the *Trutz* Group and to some operations against the U-tankers, which supplied the combat submarines with fuel, torpedoes, medical services, food and other necessities. On 11 June, BP had read a signal of 8 June giving a position at which *U 118* (under Korvettenkapitän Czygan), a Type XIV refueler, was to look for the damaged *U 758* in the vicinity of *Trutz*, as well as an acknowledgement by BdU of a short signal from *U 118*, giving its position.[23] Notwithstanding the protection afforded by disguised grid references, the insight afforded by these signals, together with shore HF/DF fixes, enabled Knowles to guide *Bogue* to *U 118*'s area, after

[20] On gamma and M4, see Ralph Erskine and Frode Weierud, "Naval Enigma: M4 and its Rotors", *Cryptologia*, XI (1987), 235. As to *Triton* before 19 July, OIC SI 641 of 19 July 1943 (ADM 223/98); as to the deployment of *Geier*, ZPTGU 15128 (26 June), 15200 (28 June), Ultra signals 1543/4 and 1846/5 July 19843 (ADM 223/182).

[21] Morison, X: 130-131; ZTPGU 15735 (13 July 1943 - broken 1 August) ordered the return of three boats.

[22] "Fuehrer Conferences on Naval Affairs", 5 June 1943, in *Brasseys Navy Annual 1948* (London, 1948), 331.

[23] Allied Communication Intelligence, II: 136. Acknowledgements of short signals by the shore control set out their contents in full. The acknowledgement may not have used disguised references, since short signals had to give positions using the standard naval grid: ZTPGU 3881 (18 January 1942), citing the Kartenschlüssel (the instructions for grid enciphering).

Bogue transferred UGS 9 into the protection of Africa-based aircraft on 10 June. Around noon on 12 June, at least eight Avengers and Wildcats from *Bogue* swarmed round *U 118*, and sank it.[24]

Ultra later revealed that the sinking of *U 118* had led to at least one boat, *U 530*, being recalled prematurely and had deprived many boats of fuel. The sinking had a severe knock-on effect on U-boat operations, since some boats which were to have been refueled by *U 118* had instead to be supplied by *U 488*. BdU was forced to draw on future fuel supplies to keep other boats going, but could not make up the deficit. The sinking of the tanker *U 117* by aircraft from the *USS Card* on 7 August had even more dramatic results. Declaring the supply situation to be "extremely grave", BdU ordered boat upon boat to curtail its cruise and begin its return passage.[25] The importance of refueling is revealed by the statistics: no fewer than 54 of the 121 U-boats on operations in May 1943 had been refueled at sea.[26] Without refueling, most of the combat boats would have had much shorter cruises. Only about 67 boats would have been on patrol at any one time. The U-tankers therefore substantially increased the effective size of the operational U-boat fleet.

To protect refueling operations, wireless silence was generally ordered within a radius of 250 to 400 miles from the rendezvous. However, there were sometimes significant exceptions, such as signals of "tactical importance": BdU's need for intelligence in order to mount pack operations outweighed even the risk to his precious U-tankers.[27] Other precautions ordered included a ban on attacks on independent ships (except large troop transports) within 300 miles of a supply point, lest they might bring Allied anti-submarine forces to the area.[28] But as supply boat after supply boat was lost in the summer, BdU became increasingly desperate in his efforts to protect his fast-dwindling tanker fleet, as the following signals revealingly disclosed:

1. During supply operations the most important object is the protection of the tanker. On her depends the full exploitation of many operational U-boats, and accordingly the continuation of convoy operations with as many units as possible.

---

[24] "US Escort Carrier Operations"; see also Y'Blood, 55-59; Morison, X: 114.

[25] "extremely grave": ZTPGU 16215 (17 August 1943); "return passage": ZTPGU 16200 (19 August), 16210 (17 August). See also KTB BdU, 14 August 1943; Allied Communication Intelligence, II: 139, 140; David Kahn, *Seizing the Enigma: The Race to Break the German U-Boat Codes, 1939-1945* (New York, 1991), 274.

[26] Allied Communication Intelligence, II: 79. For a brief summary of the U-tankers' operations, see Eberhard Rössler, *The U-Boat* (London, 1981), 166-167.

[27] ZTPGU 15084 (19 June), 15271 (25 June), 16240 (7 August), 18030 (17 October - all 1943).

[28] ZTPGU 15152 (20 June 1943).

2. ...

3. The following orders are therefore issued:

   a) Boats not engaged in the supply operation will form a protective screen round the tanker for flak protection, distance 500 metres.

   a) During air attacks the tanker will dive at the first favorable moment, the remaining boats, using everything and going completely into action, will cover her diving by defensive fire and by closing the scene of diving. Only when the tanker is at a safe depth may the other boats dive.[29]

This signal was prompted by the sinking of yet another U-tanker, *U 460*, at a rendezvous on 4 October 1943, following confusion over which boat should dive first during a half-hour fire-fight against four or more aircraft from the *USS Card*. Kapitänleutenant Hartung Looks, the commanding officer of *U 264*, one of three surviving U-boats, later dramatically recounted the sinking:

> 1230 Four more aircraft approach. The commanding officer of the tanker [*U 460*] shrugs his shoulders and gesticulates as though not knowing what to do... *U 264* dives. Underwater bomb detonations heard and noises as if a U-boat were endeavoring to blow tanks.

U 460 had been lost to a "Mark 24 mine" (a code name for an acoustic homing torpedo that was more often known as "Fido" or "Wandering Annie") dropped by Lieutenant (jg) Robert Stearns, who was later awarded his second Navy Cross for the sinking. The huge, slow diving U-tankers had little chance against aircraft armed with the devastatingly effective Fidos even if they did not manage to dive.[30] A few days after this incident, BdU increased the precautions still further, by ordering boats to remain submerged on the day of the rendezvous, to make contact only two hours before sunset and generally to refuel only at night.

Knowles had realized that the supply U-boats were BdU's Achilles heel and had been determined to exploit the weakness, although he fully appreciated that doing so involved some risk to naval Ultra. The OIC was distinctly unhappy about this: its rule, like that of BP, was that the Enigma source must never be hazarded.[31] In contrast, Knowles was prepared to risk using Ultra to position

[29] ZTPGU 17663 (7 October 1943).

[30] KTB *U 264*, as cited in Hessler, para. 424; on the sinking, see Y'Blood, 102-104; Morison, X: 160. Mark 24 mines were a significant factor in the high success rate of the U. S. Navy escort carrier pilots: ADM 199/1408. On their use, see "Analysis of Attacks with Mark 24 Mines," ADM 219/66, and reports on ADM 205/30.

[31] Allied Communication Intelligence, II: 127; Beesly, *Very Special Intelligence*, 203. For an early example of a reprimand of a Royal Navy commander for compromising Ultra, see 1105/29 July 1941 (ADM 223/78) to CinC Mediterranean.

the escort carrier groups near the refueling rendezvous: he believed that destroying the supply U-boats could shorten the war, by greatly restricting pack and independent operations. And so it proved. At the end of August 1943, only 30 operational boats were at sea - mostly homeward bound, their cruises cut short - compared with 71 at the end of July. A mere three boats were on independent cruises in distant areas, out of 24 at the beginning of August.[32] Ultra eventually helped the carrier groups to destroy eight of the 14 supply U-boats sunk after 1 June 1943. It is a measure of the skill of F-211 (as to which, see below) and Knowles that this was achieved notwithstanding the use of disguised grid references and other security measure which, by masking the rendezvous, at times baffled the more experienced OIC. All the same, 30 years later, Knowles still remembered the quiet rebuke sent to him by Winn after the sinking of several U-boats at a rendezvous (perhaps in early August): "Your 1157/9. Too true to be good."[33]

The role of the "Secret Room" (whose correct title was "F-211") of Combat Intelligence of the Commander-in-Chief, U. S. Fleet, was crucial to Knowles's work, and to the U. S. Navy's anti-U-boat operations as a whole. The room was established on 27 December 1942, a bare 14 days after BP first effectively broke into *Triton* on four-rotor Enigma.[34] F-211 was at first across the hall from the main U-boat tracking room. Later, after the section moved, it was given a room opening only to the main tracking room. Its function was to receive and analyze all Ultra intelligence sent to it by the U. S. Navy codebreaking center at 3801 Nebraska Avenue, Washington DC, which held the Navy's four-rotor bombes. It also received HF/DF plots, as well as other forms of radio intelligence, such as TINA information (derived from oscillograph recordings of the U-boat radio operators' fists.)[35]

F-211 had remarkably few staff. Lieutenant John E. Parsons was in charge, with Lieutenant (jg) John V. Boland as an assistant, and Yeoman Samuel P. Livecchi and Ensign R.B. Chevalier as the principal other members. Knowles was the main user of the room. Indeed, he was the only member of Atlantic section who had access to F-211, although Admirals King and Edwards (F-01) visited it on occasion. Naval Ultra from Enigma was therefore controlled much more tightly by the U. S. Navy, with far fewer people knowing of its existence,

[32] KTB BdU, 31 July, 31 August 1943 (T1022: 4064-5); Allied Communications Intelligence, II: 158; inevitably, the figures differ slightly.

[33] Knowles, 446; Beesly, Very Special Intelligence, 170.

[34] "Functions of Secret Room of Cominch Combat Intelligence, Atlantic Section" (NA, RG, 457: SRMN-038); memorandum by F-2111 (NA, SRMN-051), para. 1. I am indebted to David Kahn for referring me to these documents. On the Secret Room, see also *Seizing the Enigma*, 242-243.

[35] "Functions of 'Secret Room' of Cominch Combat Intelligence, Atlantic Section."

than by the Royal Navy. In a post-war account, Knowles stated that this was largely because of the "wide separation of [the U. S. Navy's] commands" and the consequent difficulty of keeping the Ultra operation secret.[36]

By 1 March, BdU had a mere two U-tankers left. On 11 March, British naval forces sank *UIT 22* (formerly the Italian submarine *Bagnolini*), a freight U-boat en route to Japan with a miscellaneous cargo including mercury, at a rendezvous several hundred miles south of the Cape of Good Hope. The German tanker, *Brake*, was then sunk in the Indian Ocean on 12 March by a destroyer attached to HMS *Battler* (an escort carrier), after an incomplete refueling rendezvous with *U 168*, *U 188*, and *U 532* on 11 March.[37] Later on 12 March, Korvettenkapitän Junker (*U 532*) signalled BdU: "Presume the refuelings have been basically compromised." The Seekriegsleitung (the German naval war staff) resolved that "Extended checking must be made on the question of cipher security and the possibility of treason."[38]

In the ensuing enquiry, the head of the Kriegsmarine's Marinenachrichtendienst (Naval Communication Service) found that *UIT 24* (a boat scheduled for a later refueling) had sent several signals between 28 February and 8 March. Although the signals were not received in Germany, decrypts of reports from the efficient British HF/DF net apparently led the Kriegsmarine to think that HF/DF had enabled the British to work out that a U-boat was on an eastward course, possibly to a refueling rendezvous.[39] But as a German historian of the Battle of the Atlantic (who was writing at a time when the the Ultra secret had not been revealed) observed:

> This, however, could hardly be the full explanation, for the most that could be obtained from bearings was information about the course of the boat and not theexact time of supplying, while the enemy had

[36] Knowles, 445. Knowles's explanation in his hastily prepared paper is somewhat unclear. He may have had in mind the danger that, if even one operational command was informed about the Ultra secret, too many people might have heard about it. Cf. Commander L. F. Safford's memorandum of 18 March 1942, warning against a "too widespread dissemination of information [from cryptanalysis]," as set out in "Why Was Safford Pessimistic about Breaking the German Enigma Cipher in 1942", Louis Kruh (ed.), *Cryptologia*, XIV (1990), 253. Wartime Washington was notoriously leaky - it was common knowledge on the cocktail circuits that Japanese codes were being broken.

[37] BdU KTB, 12 March 1944 (T1022: 4064); on the sinking of *Brake*, see Colpoys, "Admiralty Use of Special Intelligence in Naval Operations," 33, 34; also *The U-Boat War in the Atlantic*, para. 424; Morison X: 278. ZTPGU 22800 (3 March) had ordered a rendezvous with "*Brake* at 1200/11 in naval grid square 1631 of third large square east of disguised square Blau AO."

[38] "Basically compromised": ZTPGU 23001 (12 March 1944); "extended checking": Seekriegsleitung KTB, 12 March 1944 (T1022: 4065).

[39] For a German assessment of British shore HF/DF, see Seekriegsleitung KTB, Part C, IV (PG 32176) "Peilorganisation, England," 26 June 1944 (Naval Historical Branch (NHB), Ministry of Defence, London, microfilm).

> started up his air reconnaissance only one day before the replenishment operation was sure to begin... Treason, compromise of the U-boat codes or interception of radio traffic to Japan may have been contributory causes, but nothing definite could be established.[40]

There is a remarkable parallel here with an incident in World War I, when the British submarine *E 35* sank *U 154* at a rendezvous point about 150 miles west of Cape St. Vincent on 11 May 1918. *U 153*'s commanding officer, who had seen the attack, advised his superiors of his belief that the cipher used to arrange the meeting had been compromised. As in 1944, his suggestion was dismissed, on the basis that the cipher could not have been broken, and that direction-finding must have been responsible - precisely the same erroneous ground as was advanced 25 years later.[41]

In 1944 the Kriegsmarine at least changed the *Triton* U-boat Enigma settings on 13 March by issuing an emergency cue word ("Stichwort"). This required U-boat commanders holding *Triton* to open a sealed envelope, inside which was a keyword ("Kennwort"), such as "baden", which modified all general *Triton* Enigma setting until new tables, or a further keyword, came into force. The letters of the keyword were converted to their numeric equivalents (2, 1, 4, 5, 14 for "baden"), which were then added to components of the daily settings (see Figure 2 for an example).[42] Although the British official history states that this emergency procedure was new in March 1944, an earlier form was in force as early as August 1941, and the version to which the history refers probably took effect in April 1943.[43]

Ever suspicious about cipher security, despite the reassurance of his experts, BdU took even more stringent precautions to protect the safety of his two remaining U-tankers. On 14 March, he informed the commanding officers of four U-boats that an Offizier signal would shortly be issued to them under the coverword "Maske" and that the substantive text of the later signal, after the word "Maske" would first be enciphered with special Offizier settings, known only to the four boats involved. For *U 123*, these required the standard Offizier settings to be modified - by forming the Offizier message key from the initial of the Christian names of the surgeon, second officer and chief quartermaster, and

[40] Hessler, para. 442.

[41] Robert M. Grant, *U-Boats Destroyed* (London, 1965), 119.

[42] Germany, Kriegsmarine, *Der Schlüssel M-Allgemeine Bestimmungen* (M. Dv. Nr. 32/3), paras. 100-128. as amended by deckblat 7 of 25 April 1943 (NHB).

[43] F. H. Hinsley, with E. E. Thomas, C. F. G. Ransom and R. C. Knight, *British Intelligence in the Second World War: Its Influence on Strategy and Operations* (London and Cambridge, 1979-1988), 3: 1 (1984), 321; cf a receipt of 26 August 1941 for "Stichwortbefehl 'Jupiter' fur Ausserheimische Gewässer zur Änderung der Schlüssel M" (PG 34522 (T1022: 2325)), 1 and ZTPG 16906 (15 November 1941).

than of the surname of the surgeon (giving, for example, GYCS), and by adding (modulo 26) the house number of the home address of Seaman Lelanz to each of the Offizier plugboard settings.

Keylist for 28 January

Rotor Order	VI	I	VIII	
Ring Settings	Z	S	Y	
Plugboard connections	26/9	3/17	7/15	etc.

Keyword "Tasche"
t=20; a=1; s=19; c=3; h=8
Using the original keylist -

(a) add (modulo 8) the number representing the first letter of the keyword to the rotor numbers.

(b) add (modulo 26) the numbers representing the second, third and fourth letters to the numbers of the letters (treating the German alphabet as containing 26 letters) of the ring settings of the left, middle, and right rotors, respectively, and

(c) add (modulo 26) the number representing the fifth letter to each of the plugboard connections.

Modified settings, 28 January, after using keyword "Tasche"

Rotor order	II	V	IV	
Ring settings	A	L	B	
Plugboard connections	8/17	11/25	15/23	etc.

Figure 2. Modification of Naval Enigma settings, using keyword.

The complete text of the signal plus the addresses and the word "Maske" were then to be re-enciphered, as usual with *Offizier*, but with the key word modifired general settings. Only the few words enciphered with those setting could be read by each boat's radioman, who had to give the remainder of the message to an officer for deciphering. Similar instructions, using the names and addresses of their own crew members, were issued to *U 488*, *U 801*, and *U 843*.[44]

After finding the general settings (as altered by the 13 March keyword), the Allied codebreakers then had to solve the internal Offizier settings, which were often extremely difficult to break. Offizier signals of 13 and 28 September 1941 were read only on 3 and 13 November 1941, and one signal in 1943 was not broken for six months.[45] But the Maske signal of 14 March 1944 succumbed

[44]ZTPGU 23085 (14 March 1944).

[45]ZTPGU 15050, 16849; ZTPGU (3 March 1943, broken on 18 September).

the following day, revealing that BdU had signaled four named U-boat captains, including Oberleutenant zur See Studt (commander of *U 488*), ordering Studt to fuel:

(a) Kapitänleutenant Herwartz (*U 843*) on 19 March in "1489 of the square to the east of disguised square blue BQ" (hereafter rendezvous 1); and

(b) Kapitänleutenant Hans Joachim Brans (*U 801*) on 23 March in "disguised square blue HF 9558" (hereafter Rendezvous 2).[46]

The decrypt was clear, but the OIC and F-211 once again took very different views of the true position of the disguised references.

F-211 gave Rendezvous 1 as 16° 51′ north, 35° 33′ west (Kriegsmarine grid square EH 1489) and Rendezvous 2 as 14° 27′ north, 37° 27′ west (Kriegsmarine grid square EG 6558) (respectively 600 miles west, and 700 miles west-southwest, of the Cape Verde Islands, off Dakar, in Senegal), while the OIC thought that Rendezvous 1 was 08° 45′ north, 27° 27′ west (Kriegsmarine grid square ES 1489) and Rendezvous 2, 06° 21′ north, 29° 21′ west (Kriegsmarine grid square ER 6558) (both estimates being about 700 nautical miles apart).[47] The U. S. Navy ordered a task group, which included the escort carrier *Block Island* to operate "within 600 miles west of the Cape Verde Islands" (that is, to F-211's estimate of Rendezvous 1).[48] An analysis of German and British records shows that F-211 was again correct in its assessment, as with the withdrawal order of 24 May 1943, for both rendezvous which were indeed Kriegsmarine grid squares EH 1489 and EG 6558 respectively, and that the OIC was badly out.[49] Knowles and his tiny team in F-211 had on a second important occasion proved better at divining German intentions than Winn and the OIC.

After being attacked by planes from *Block Island* in 16° 45′ north, 29° 45′ west, on 16 March *U 801* was ordered to Rendezvous 1. The destroyers *Corry* and *Bronstein*, in the *Block Island* group, sank *U 801* on 17 March in 16° 42′ north, 30° 28′ west. On 18 March, *U 1059*, a Type VIIF torpedo supply boat with 25 torpedoes and cipher material for Penang, the German U-boat base in the Far East, was ordered to fuel from *U 488* at Rendezvous 2 in 23 March. *U 1059* was attacked and sunk on 19 March by aircraft from *Block Island* in 13° 03′ north, 33° 28′ west.

---

[46] ZTPGU 23089 (14 March 1944).

[47] Minute, Winn, 25 March 1944 (ADM 223/262).

[48] Ibid.

[49] See ibid, ZTPGU 23089 (15 March 1944) and KTB *U 123*, 14 March 1944 (NHB, microfilm, also T1022: 2073).

When sunk, *U 801* and *U 1059* were approximately 300 miles from F-211's estimates of their respective rendezvous.[50] But that distance should not lead us to conclude that F-211 was wrong in its assessments. *U 801* was sunk two days before its supply rendezvous, with the corresponding period for *U 1059* being less than four days. Had they not been sunk, both U-boats could therefore easily have reached their rendezvous on time at their cruising speed of around 10 knots. Contemporary German records and subsequent calculations show conclusively that F-211's appreciation of the rendezvous points was accurate down to the last minute of latitude and longitude.[51] However, in order to result in sinkings, F-211's assessments had to be complemented by superb teamwork by the men of the *Block Island* group. Having regard to the vast swaths of ocean in the search areas, the two sinkings so many days ahead of the rendezvous represented a magnificent achievement by the highly-honed crews of *Block Island*.

The sinkings of *U 801* and *U 1059* led an alarmed Admiral Sir Andrew Cunningham, the British First Sea Lord, to express his concern to Admiral King that the *Block Island*'s operations might have imperilled Ultra. The British were anxious lest BdU introduce further procedural changes that would outwit the Allied naval cryptanalysts - and lest the change also be applied to Germany army and air force Enigma, with devastating consequences for the Allied invasion of Europe.[52] After the British sinking of *Brake*, Royal Navy commanders in West Africa had been ordered on 16 March 1944 to keep their forces clear of the area of Rendezvous 1 and 2. Unprecedently, on 17 March the Admiralty therefore ordered all naval Ultra recipients to take positive action to ensure that their forces did not make contact with U-boats in any rendezvous area during March and April.[53] King, however, kept to his philosophy of taking calculated risks. On 26 April 1944, destroyers attached to the escort carrier *Croatan* group sank *U 488* with the help of signals intelligence - almost certainly Ultra-based, and not merely HF/DF. Following the sinking of supply submarines *U 220* and *U 490* on 12 June and 5 July 1944, again as a result of Ultra, BdU was left with but one supply boat out of a total of 17 boats that had been built or adapted as tankers.

---

[50] Winn, minute, 25 March 1944; on the sinkings, see Y'Blood, 146-149; Morison, X: 279, 280.

[51] The northwest corner of square EG was at 18° 35′ north, 44° 10′ west; that of EH was at 18° 35′ north, 36° 05′ west. Applying the formula for converting grid references to latitude and longitude in Reinhart Reche, Die Quadratur der Meere-zur Umrechnung der Marine-Quadratkarte 1939-1945", *Marine-Rundschau*, 81 (1984), 120, with "M" being 10, puts EH 1489 (Rendezvous 1) at 16° 51′ north, 35° 33′ west and EG 6558 (Rendezvous 2) at 14° 27′ north, 37° 27′ west. For EH 1489 and EG 6558 as the rendezvous, see KTB BdU, 14 March 1944.

[52] Although not connected with these incidents, the Kriegsmarine introduced new keying procedures for its Baltic cipher net on 1 April 1945 which for all practical purposes defeated BP; Hinsley, 3: 2 (1988), 853. Those measures were to have been applied to all its nets on 1 May 1945 and could probably have been implemented much earlier.

[53] Ultra signal H4260/17 March 1944 (ADM 223/ 191); cf. minute, Colpoys, 21 July 1944 (ADM 223/261).

Eight of the supply U-boats had been suck by U. S. forces with the assistance of Ultra.

Knowles later generously summed up the difference between the British and American approaches to naval Ultra intelligence by suggesting that "The British were more clever in its use, we, more daring ... but then they had so much more to lose." He also considered, rightly, that the U. S. Navy escort carriers were used more aggressively than those of the Royal Navy in search and destroy missions.[54] And indeed a British study shows that the U. S. Navy escort carriers were seven times more effective than their British counterparts, which was only partly attributable to the British carriers sometimes operating in very difficult Arctic waters.[55]

Unfortunately, Knowles's very considerable contribution to victory in the Atlantic has received little recognition in print, although the late Patrick Beesly (Winn's former deputy) accorded him the high accolade of being Winn's equal.[56] The lack of more widespread knowledge of Knowles's work is regrettable, since there can be little doubt that without his hand at the helm of American operational naval intelligence in 1943, the Battle of the Atlantic, and with it the war as a whole, would have been even more prolonged and bloody than it was. And since Admiral King has come under severe criticism for his reluctance to introduce convoy in early 1942 and a failure to take adequate steps to prepare for the U-boat onslaught on American coastal shipping,[57] it is only fair to award him full credit for giving Knowles his complete backing at all times.

ACKNOWLEDGEMENTS

I am indebted to R. M. Coppock, Naval Historical Branch, for assistance with documents and for information about some of the grid squares mentioned.

BIOGRAPHICAL SKETCH

Ralph Erskine is a lawyer in Northern Ireland, who has now mostly - retired. His main area of research is naval intelligence in World War II.

[54] Knowles, minute of 24 December 1943 (in Y'Blood, 286).

[55] Report, 12 February 1944, in "U. S. Escort Carrier Operations" (ADM 199/ 1048).

[56] Beesly, "Special Intelligence and the Battle of the Atlantic: The British View", in *Changing Interpretations of Naval History*, 416.

[57] See, in particular, Michael Gannon, *Operation Drumbeat* (New York, 1990), 390-393, 412-414.

CRYPTOLOGIA October 1996 Volume XX Number 4

THE COUNTERFACTUAL HISTORY OF NO ULTRA

Harry Hinsley

ADDRESS: c/o St. John's College, Cambridge CB2 1SB ENGLAND.

KEYWORDS: Ultra, Enigma, Soviet Union, counterfactual, World War II.

Following is the text of a talk by Sir Harry Hinsley, a key member of the staff of the British cryptologic unit at Bletchley Park during World War II and the chief author of the official history of British intelligence during that conflict. He spoke to the University of Cambridge Computing Laboratory Security Seminar on 19 October 1993. His answers to questions are included in this transcript which has been slightly edited for publication.

As you have heard I've been asked to talk about Ultra and I shall say something about both sides of it, namely about the cryptanalysis and then on the other hand about the use of the product – of course Ultra was the name given to the product.

And I ought to begin by warning you, therefore, that I am not myself a mathematical or technical expert. I was privileged to be an assistant to the mathematicians led by Max Newman and Alan Turing, but I have never myself learned to master or even to approach mastering their art.

Ultra, of course, was the product of ciphers. It was used only for the product of the solution of the more important ciphers, and from the spring of 1941 at Bletchley we broke most ciphers to an unprecedented extent and with an unprecedented lack of delay. There were two reasons for that success.

First of all, alone among the governments of those years, the British Government as early as the 1920s concentrated all its cryptanalytical effort in one place which it called the Government Code and Cypher School. And, secondly at Bletchley, the staff rose from about 120 in 1939 to about 7,000 at the beginning of 1944.

Of course that staff was not entirely cryptanalytical; it consisted also of an immense amount of staff used, for example, for signalling the products to commands in the rest of England or abroad. And so it wasn't entirely cryptanalytical staff – it was a very mixed staff compared with prewar.

In addition, those men and women, recruited mainly from universities, developed methods and machinery of a sophistication hitherto undreamt of, including as you all know the first operational electronic computer which was called Colossus.

Without those advances, at least the most difficult of the ciphers, which were (although I will make some qualifying remark about this in a minute) those based on the German Enigma and those still more complex systems which Germany introduced for ciphering nonmorse transmissions, would have been for all practical purposes invulnerable.

Now the value of the resulting Ultra was all the greater because the enemy states – Germany, Italy, and Japan – remained unaware of the British successes.

The main reason for that was that they didn't allow for that sophistication of method and machinery which the British brought to the attack on their ciphers. They didn't allow for that when they constructed their ciphers.

Nothing very surprising in that. As I have said, the methods and machinery developed were of a sophistication hitherto unthought of.

But it still remains necessary to say that, despite that sophistication, the German belief that the ciphers would remain invulnerable was almost right, almost correct.

The ciphers nearly escaped effective exploitation.

In the case of the Enigma (which was an electromechanical machine) the first solutions were made by hand by mathematicians relying on German operators' errors. The German air force was always more untidy in its signalling than the other users of the Enigma.

And for that purpose (although you will understand it better than I do) the mathematicians used perforated sheets and exploited these mistakes made by German operators.

For keys other than the air force, especially those of the army and the navy, and especially for the regular and speedy solution of those keys, it was necessary to develop an effective answering cryptanalytical machine.

That was the key in the end to the prompt decrypting of the machine ciphers.

It was a machine called the bombe – a name originally given to it by the Poles who invented an early prototype in the 1930s. The bombe developed in Bletchley by Turing and Welchman – all luminaries of the Cambridge scene – was helped a little by the Polish machine, but it was about fifteen times more powerful than the Polish machine. And it was because of the greater difficulties of dealing with the Enigma that it had to be that powerful.

But it wasn't enough to have that machinery developed. Except in the case of the air force, we had to capture some keys before the machinery – even this Bombe machinery – could break into them.

And that is where people like myself who were nonmathematical came into the story. It was because I was in close touch with Turing, for example, that I was fully aware of what he had to have before the machine which he had developed could exercise its powers.

And I was able to arrange – with other people of course, including the navy – how to capture them. I stress that because, both in the case of the navy and of the army, and at dates which are later than we realise (I will give you the dates later), we needed in addition to this superb mathematics, which was assisted of course by superb Post Office engineering, we needed also these side assets – essentially captured material.

That was the Enigma. Now with the nonmorse machine which we called Fish, the first successes were again obtained by hand methods. And those hand methods by mathematicians again exploited German operators' errors. In fact, the actual understanding of the machine theoretically (in other words as opposed to breaking it every day), the actual understanding of how it worked was obtained because the Germans went through a long series of experiments with it on the air before they brought in into operational use.

And it was these experimental transmissions which primarily were the errors which gave the entrée.

But it was obvious that any regular or at all reasonably speedy decryption would be impossible if again machine methods were not developed. In particular that they would be impossible without machines because the different Fish ciphers proliferated, just like the different Enigma keys proliferated, and you were dealing with a lot of ciphers concurrently.

And so in this case, as you know, the machine was developed which came to be called Colossus.

It was of course much more complex. It wasn't a mere electronic electromechanical thing – it was the first computer. It had to be like that in proportion to the fact that the Fish was for more complex than the Enigma.

Now it will be clear from what I have said that the problem wasn't merely to master the machines. The Germans recognised when they were constructing (in their view) an invulnerable set of machines, that of course in wartime they would be open to capture and therefore locally and temporarily they would be read.

But they also felt that the mere local (by which I mean reading one key instead of another key) and temporary reading (in other words that would complete your fundamental knowledge of the machine) wouldn't help you to read it regularly and daily. And they were right; without this machinery that would have been impossible.

And in particular it would be impossible because of the Enigma and the Fish were used by the Germans as the basis not merely for one cipher each, not merely one Enigma and one Fish, but as the basis for a wide range of different ciphers, each cipher having its different key.

At one time the Germans were operating concurrently about 50 Enigma keys, some in the army, some in the air force, some in the navy, some in the railways, some in the secret service. And so you were faced not merely with understanding the machine and with breaking a key regularly, but with breaking 50 sometime regularly at once, or as many of them as you could without delay.

And Fish similarly rose from just one link, one cipher, one key to about 22 cipher links, all quite separate except they were using the same machine. And remember that each of them – the Enigma daily and the Fish at varying interludes, usually every few days – changed the keys.

So you are on constant alert – every day you had to start again at midnight, and you had to start on perhaps 30 Enigmas or five Fishes and so you could see the mere load put it beyond any manual solution.

That was one reason – that in spite of their confidence which was not far from being fully justified – that was one reason why the German confidence was proved to be unfounded. The other was (perhaps it is no less important) the fact that steps were taken to avoid arousing enemy suspicion.

The British imposed strict secrecy of course on the Ultra production process. Strict regulations about its distribution – who should be indoctrinated – strict regulations against carelessness by users when using it.

Those regulations were pretty effective. There were from time to time cases in the war where the Germans did sufficiently suspect to have an enquiry. There were cases when the Italians suspected and advised the Germans to have an enquiry.

I ought to say that everything I have been saying about the complex nature of the attack on the ciphers hardly applied to the Italian ciphers – and this is where I am going to bring my ironical remark in about ciphers which will interest you people as machinery experts.

The Italians ran only one machine and it was a baby really compared with the Enigma. It was a machine built by a firm called Hagelin (we called it C-38). The American armed forces used it occasionally, but it was easily broken. We broke it. It didn't come into use until the beginning of '41 and we broke it by June '41.

It was a very valuable cipher for shipping in relation to North African operations but it wasn't a cryptanalytical problem of the kind I have been describing in the case of the German ciphers.

Ironically the Italians, except for that one cipher and also for one they used for their diplomats, didn't use machines. They used book ciphers, and ironically we couldn't read the Italian book ciphers for the army, the navy, and the air force after they brought new ones in between June and November 1940 preparatory to or as a consequence of their own entry into the war.

Book ciphers proved to be invulnerable when the machinery proved not to be invulnerable!

And as I say the Italians occasionally, who rather looked down on machine ciphers, warned the Germans that they thought that there was evidence that the way the Allies behaved suggested that maybe they were reading the German ciphers. And the Germans said 'Pooh, pooh, we are all right!' Apart from occasional suspicions, precautions used by the Allies worked.

They were wholly justifiable ones. Any confirmation reaching the Germans that this system that they had constructed wasn't safe would have led to not easy but not impossible steps to render it safe.

But of course the precautions complicated the task of establishing the value that Ultra had in the war.

Contemporary reports and the memoirs and histories that have been published before the records about Ultra became available, allow for, incorporate, the contribution Ultra made to decisions and the course of events, but they don't acknowledge it. Because either the writers of the reports and the memoirs didn't know about it, or they were not able to mention it.

So historians now have to identify that contribution from the written records about the war and it is a straighforward job to do that now that Ultra is available. We know what Ultra went to what commands, we know what time it arrived, we know what other intelligence they had at the time the Ultra arrived, we know what decisions and orders followed from its arrival, and frequently we have discussions on record about what they thought about what they ought to do about it before they reached their decisions.

It is not enough to establish accurately the availability of the Ultra and to reach reasonable conclusions about its influence on British and American assessments and decisions. You have also got to consider the consequences of those assessments and decisions on the war.

Let me give an example of the distinction. Once you have identified the Ultra (which you now can from the decrypts in the Public Record Office) you can see pretty clearly (if you have also got the record of the war) that Ultra was the main reason the British were able to reduce the depredations of the U-boats in the Atlantic in the second half of 1941.

But what was the value of that effect in the North Atlantic in that second half of 1941 on the course of the war? What was the consequence of that use of Ultra on the course of the war? And those effects too are already incorporated into the record, which shows that the U-boats were defeated in the North Atlantic in the second half of 1941.

Of course in order to assess the true significance of Ultra we have got to assume that it didn't exist in the North Atlantic at that time. We have got to strip it out of the record in order to get its true significance into focus.

This is what historians call counterfactual history. To calculate something assuming that some factors in it didn't exist. And I am sure it is a process well known to mathematicians and other people like yourselves.

But it is still the case that there is a great deal of danger in using counterfactual history unless you use it very carefully. For example, it is very common among historians to use counterfactual history either from a desire to shock or because its user hasn't got any judgement. And you have therefore got to use it in relation to the possibilities that were practically available in the circumstances that you are considering.

There is no danger whatever in reconstructing the course of the war on the assumption that Ultra hadn't existed.

As I have said the story of its acquisition is of near legendary, even science-fiction proportions, because it might so easily not have taken place. You are not making a huge assumption when you start playing with the record of the war on the basis that Enigma hadn't been solved, Ultra hadn't been obtained.

Ultra was by no means fortuitous or miraculous. It was the consequence of forces deliberately brought together. But it was far from being inevitable that the forces would succeed. The proposition that we might have had to fight the war without Ultra is a reasonable and necessary element in the assessment of its true significance.

On the other hand if you apply counterfactual history and use this proposition that Ultra might not have existed, you are undertaking a pretty bold enterprise in hypothesis and speculation and you must control that exercise by a constant reference to the straightforward facts about what Ultra actually did do.

If you apply that check, then I think we can draw two pretty sound conclusions. First of all, though we did obtain Ultra in such amounts, amounts rising to 2,000 of those Italian Hagelin decrypts a day at the peak of the Mediterranean war and to 30,000 a month rising to 90,000 a month of Enigma and Fish decrypts combined – that is a very big number of decrypts. It is still the case that those volumes and the speed with which they were got out were not fully established until the second half of 1941.

Up until June '41 the successes were confined to decrypts of the German air force Enigma and some of the Italian book ciphers which were quite readable before Italy came into the war and for a month or two afterwards.

Those helped to produce isolated Allied successes like the Battle of Matapan when we defeated the Italian fleet, and wouldn't have done so but for a few Enigma and Italian signals which gave enough warning to the British Alexandria fleet.

The distances in the Mediterranean are such that unless you have got some notice you can't cover the thousand miles or the 750 miles.

So Matapan was one success. The sinking of the *Bismarck* was another. Again I am speaking of the period before June '41. She was sunk in May '41 just before the turn. The defeat of the Italians in East Africa and in North Africa – those were Allied successes, but they were slightly isolated successes.

Again in the same period Ultra did something to mitigate British disasters. It greatly assisted the British forces that were sent to Greece to retreat without serious loss when it became obvious that they couldn't hold a line against the scale of the German invasion.

It gave us – here was another disaster – all the information required to destroy the German attack on Crete. We didn't destroy the attack but we made it an extremely damaging exercise for the Germans, which was done because the Ultra signals were so complete.

Some people think we should have prevented or destroyed the invasion – an air-landing invasion. In fact Bletchley Park felt very strongly for the first time in the war that its product had not been used properly in the case of the Crete invasion. I think possibly that we were wrong, now that we can see the evidence in more detail, but at least it helped to make it a disastrous operation for the Germans even though they got Crete.

And so in all that story you can see that the British survived the war with little benefit from intelligence until the Germans invaded Soviet Russia. And since Soviet Russia survived the German invasion, and that invasion was followed by the entry of the United States in December '41, we can safely conclude that Germany was going to be defeated in the long run, even if the enormous expansion of Ultra from the summer of 1941 had not from that date given the Allies this massive superiority in intelligence they retained until the end of the war.

They were hardly ever rivalled by Axis success in reading our ciphers. There were two major exceptions to the lack of success by the Axis against Allied ciphers. One was that they did have some success in reading a British naval cipher which was for a longish time also shared with the American navy in relation to convoy escorting.

They were successful in reading that for a long period from 1940 to the end of '42. And the other was that they didn't exactly capture but they managed to extract a copy of the cipher that was being used by the American military attaché in Cairo for a period when Rommel was at his most dangerous. And from that too the Germans obtained some great advantage.

But generally speaking, except possibly in relation to the convoy cipher, there was never any great cryptanalytical rivalry. The Germans were completely outclassed in terms of Ultra. The Italians also made very little progress against any important allied cipher.

In June 1941, however, (we survived until then with very little value from the Ultra), the end of the war was still four years away. And that is such a length of time that we might be tempted to jump to the other conclusion and say that far from producing by itself on its own the defeat of the Axis, it made only a marginal contribution to it.

Here we are, we start getting this Ultra coming on stream in June '41 as opposed to the slight trickle before that date, and yet you have still got four years of war. How can it have made much difference?

But that second conclusion can, I think, be as firmly dismissed as the one I have been discussing about how Ultra didn't really win the war.

The second real conclusion that stands out is that Ultra was decisive in shortening the war from the time, beginning in the summer of 1941, the cryptanalytical successes were extended from the German air force Enigma keys to the Enigmas used by the navy and the army and the secret service, to the nonmorse ciphers of the German High Command which came on stream in mid 1941, and to a new Italian machine cipher, the one I have mentioned which also was brought into force beginning of '41 and broken in the summer of '41. And to the ciphers of the Italian and German and especially Japanese embassies.

The Japanese embassies in Europe were in the second half of the war to prove of immense intelligence value because they were repeating back to Tokyo their versions of German assessments and their knowledge of German intentions. They were almost as valuable on some subjects (like for example the Normandy landings) as were the direct Ultra from the German horse's mouth.

From the moment we began that expansion you can see that the influence is continuous. I have spoken of the amount of Ultra. The lack of delay, the fact that it was obtained with very little delay was equally important. After all, one of the crucial characteristics of intelligence is that to be useful it must be quick.

In the case of the Enigmas we didn't exactly reach a position in which the new keys, having come into force at midnight, were broken by breakfast, but of, shall we say, 20, 25 Enigmas running concurrently (the number varied according to different stages of the war), we should be reading 20 to 25 at most times. Of that 20 to 25 the ones to which highest priority was given on the limited number of bombes available would be out by breakfast. Which meant that the whole of the rest of that 24 hours' signals from the moment you broke the key for the day, the setting for the day, would be read instantaneously, as soon as the message was intercepted it would be decrypted.

Fish was a bit slower. It didn't change daily like the Enigma. It varied, on different links; it changed with different frequency. The average was that the setting of the keys changed every five or six days.

Again the number we read varied from time to time but from the end of '42 when Fish on the German side got going strongly, we were generally reading four or five Fish links at any one time.

Generally we were reading them about seven, six, five days late – after their transmission. That didn't matter with Fish (at least it didn't matter so much as it would have done with Enigma) because, whereas the Enigma like that Italian machine was used for what you might call operational purposes, below army level, for something that was happening tomorrow or happening today, Fish was reserved for communications between the highest commands of the German armed forces. Between Berlin and the army groups or the armies. And then never lower than armies. It was a system that increasingly replaced the landline transmissions between Berlin and Kesselring in Rome and von Rundstedt who was commander in the west in Paris by 1943.

They were on landlines normally but gradually with Fish being perfected as they thought and with landlines being damaged by bombing they put more onto the air.

So Fish was carrying intelligence of a character that didn't really depend for its value on immediacy. It would carry long-term estimates, or it would carry prolonged discussions between German headquarters on the Russian Front or in Italy and Berlin about what was the best thing to do next. So you didn't have the immediacy requirement there as you did with the Enigma.

Speaking on the whole then we can see the fact that we were getting Ultra in the amounts I spoke of and with the speed that I emphasised as being a very important characteristic of valuable intelligence. It was no use having Enigma a week late, and it wouldn't be much use having Fish more than a month late.

If you had that amount of decrypts with that small amount of delay, it would, I think, on the face of it, be surprising if Ultra hadn't contributed to the very considerable shortening of the war, given the fact that on the other side the enemy is blind and his intelligence is increasingly deteriorating because of the Allied possession of the superiority in intelligence.

I will give you an example of that. We read all the Enigma signals of the German Abwehr which meant that we captured every spy that arrived in the United Kingdom by having advance knowledge of his arrival. Which meant that we could turn such as we needed and use them to send messages we wanted the Abwehr to receive and monitor the reception and the reaction of the Abwehr. All that signal intelligence underlay the effective use of what was called the Doublecross Operation for the purposes both of stopping German reception of intelligence (other than false intelligence) and also of creating deception by sending them false intelligence.

So given that they were so blind and we were getting this increasing amount with less and less delay, it would be surprising if it hadn't, from the middle of '41, contributed pretty appreciably to the difficulties of the enemy and to the accurate appreciations of the Allies.

Now the question remains how much did it shorten the war, leaving aside the contribution made to the campaigns in the Far East on which the necessary work hasn't been done yet. My own conclusion is that it shortened the war by not less than two years and probably by four years – that is the war in the Atlantic, the Mediterranean and Europe.

The detailed answer for those theatres begins in the Mediterranean. There, in the autumn of 1941 against Rommel it turned almost certain Allied defeat into a stalemate. If not then, then certainly in the summer of 1941 after Rommel had returned to the Egyptian frontier it made a decisive contribution to keeping him out of Egypt between his victory at the Battle of Gazala in 1942 and the British getting ready for their own victory at El Alamein.

It did this chiefly by killing off his seaborne supplies. Both the Italian machine cipher and the air force Enigma and a bit of naval Enigma contributed decisively to starving Rommel of fuel and replacement hardware and ammunition.

Without that, the commander of our forces at the time, General Auchinleck, concluded that Rommel would have got through to Egypt.

As you know at that time the Allies themselves were landing in North West Africa. If we had lost Egypt we might have abandoned the operation against Northwest Africa, especially as we would also have lost Malta if Egypt went, and decided to alter our strategy (we have to allow for this possibility) and go back and concentrate on the North Sea and the direct Second Front.

Now if we had stayed in the Mediterranean it would have taken us at least a year longer than it actually took us from Tunis and from the Western Desert to complete the conquest of North Africa and open the Mediterranean. That was successfully achieved in May '43.

It wouldn't have been achieved in less than a year beyond that, if we had gone on in spite of the loss of Egypt trying to do it. It wouldn't have been achieved in time to do the Normandy landings in 1944.

If the Allies had abandoned the idea reconquering North Africa, the most probable course would have been in fact what the Americans had always wanted to do, to do the cross-Channel invasion more quickly then in fact occurred. It in fact occurred in June '44. We would have turned back and done that straight away; that was our obvious alternative.

What would have been the prospect for that undertaking if Ultra hadn't become available against the U-boats in June 1941 and radically reduced their successes against the convoys.

We know that in that second half of 1941 U-boat successes were cut back to 120,000 tons a month average. That has to be compared not with the monthly average of 280,000 tons a month in the four months before June 1941 but with the sinkings they would have achieved with their greater number of U-boats.

It has been calculated that the Ultra saved about 1.5 million tons in September, October, November and December '41.

And even if Britain's essential imports had not without that saving been reduced to a dangerously low level, the intermission that was provided was invaluable in enabling the British to build up reserves in merchant shipping and develop antisubmarine defences.

So that when the U-boats returned to the Atlantic after their first defeat (they did that in the autumn of 1942), they had been delayed in making a decisive thrust for more than a year. Now when they returned they had been supplied with an advanced Enigma, one that instead of using three wheels concurrently used four wheels, which noticeably increased the mathematical difficulties of solving the key.

In fact Bletchley couldn't solve it from February to December 1942. Mercifully for us (though not for the Americans) most of the U-boats were on the Atlantic American coast at that time, but as they came back to the North Atlantic convoys they were still using this cipher and they brought about another crisis in the Atlantic.

It again was the Ultra which brought them under control. The figures of sinkings of Allied shipping reached the highest in the war in March '43. They had been brought down by May '43 to lower proportions than ever before in the war as a result of this return of Ultra to the scene.

And so you can see that the problem of undertaking the Normandy landings if those two defeats and controls of the U-boats hadn't occurred would have been very pronounced.

Then there was the contribution of Enigma to the Normandy landings themselves (I can't go into detail and will answer questions if you need). I think it is no exaggeration to say that even if the U-boats had prevented it from being attempted only until '45, we would have found it an infinitely more difficult operation to do than in 1944. The Germans would have completed the Atlantic defences, they would be bombarding Britain with V weapons on a massive scale, all of which was in the event cut off by the '44 landings. And they would have had a much bigger panzer army to deal with the problems.

My own calculation is we wouldn't in fact have been able to do the Normandy landings, even if we had left the Mediterranean aside, until at the earliest 1946, probably a bit later. It would have then taken much longer to break through in France and Germany than it did in fact take, which was a year from '44. And altogether therefore the war would have been something like two years longer, perhaps three years longer, possibly four years longer than it was.

I am sorry I have exceeded my length of time but I hope you will forgive me, and I will do what I can to answer questions.

Q. Would we have won the war without Ultra?

A. My own view is that given that the Soviets survived the German attack and the Americans came in as they did, the combined forces of Russia, America and the British would eventually have won the war. The long-term relative strengths of Germany and those three countries were such that Germany was bound to lose in the end. But how lengthily and with what damage and destruction we should have succeeded I don't know. I think we would have won but it would have been a long and much more brutal and destructive war.

Q. Was Bletchley involved at all in cryptanalysis of the Russian theatre?

A. We read a large amount of German signals from the Russian front, but no work was done against Soviet signals after Germany invaded Russia, on account of the high priority given to Axis signals. On the other hand, co-operation with the Soviets was never as close as it was with the U. S. A.

Of course when the Americans came into the war in December '41 we had already begun some development of a cryptanalytical partnership with them, and when they came into the war that partnership became almost so complete as to constitute a single joint cryptanalytical effort. Of course that effort involved division of labour and the division of labour is much directed by the interception facilities. For example, except for the Atlantic traffic the American coast couldn't intercept European, German and Italian signals. That was all being intercepted in the U. K. Obvious solution – U. K. concentrates on decrypting, on cryptanalysis against German and Italian. America which can intercept the Pacific from the Pacific and also has headquarters in Brisbane and various places in the Pacific – America concentrates on working on the Japanese.

But there are overlaps. For example we have a cryptanalytical annex at Bletchley, we have it in Singapore, it moved to Hong Kong, it moved to Ceylon, and from there it pitches in its bit by serving the decrypts direct to the American headquarters. Similarly because the U-boat traffic can be heard both in America and in Britain, the two sides – Bletchley and the American navy – swapped keys. They have got a direct line. They say 'We will take 4th June, you take tomorrow 5th June,' and so they split the keys and swapped solutions. So there was an almost total amalgamation of resources and a logical division of labour.

Q. Is it not the case that the arrival of the atom bomb in 1945 would have bought a quicker solution?

A. This is a problem because strict, sensible, proper counterfactual history can't really take into account something like that. It is speculation. But of course if my scenario is right and the war was still struggling on and we had the bomb which presumably we would still have had, the problem of whether to drop it on Germany would have arisen. And in some respects the dropping of it on Germany would be more justified than the dropping of it on Japan because Japan was visibly on her knees when we dropped it on her, but in my scenario Germany would have been far from on her knees. So yes the prospects of it being dropped as the solution are quite high. I would mention it in a speculative scenario.

Q. How closely did Bletchley work with the Russians on decryption?

A. It couldn't be as close as the collaboration I have described with the Americans for a variety of reasons. One is of course that there just hadn't been the close relationship between the two countries as existed historically between the British and the Americans. The other was that when we actually broke the ciphers – Enigma in the first instance, but Fish later – that were relevant to the Eastern Front, they were coming in to us at a time when it was uncertain whether Russia would survive. And then later on when Russia had survived and we were reading more ciphers both Fish and Enigma from the Eastern Front, there was the problem that we knew from the Enigma that the Germans were reading Russian ciphers, so that if they had too much Enigma intelligence in their ciphers the security risk was extremely high. Then fourthly the Russians were not collaborative. They wanted any intelligence we supplied but they wouldn't give any in return. Not that they had much sigint, but they had a lot of other intelligence.

The answer to your question is with all those difficulties we couldn't have so close a collaboration with the Russians as we had with Washington, but we started sending them a summary of signal intelligence a week after they were attacked by the Germans in '41. We sent it via the British Military Mission in Moscow where there were people to hand it over to the Russian General Staff.

We had to have a cover for it, had to explain to them that this is the horse's mouth but it is coming to us (this is the kind of cover we used) from very high ranking German officers who are slipping in the news to us through Berne or somewhere like that, and we are getting it quickly because we have got pretty direct connections with Switzerland.

A steady stream of information about German intentions and dispositions – air force and army on the Eastern Front – were sent to them. They were interrupted from time to time when the Russians were being particularly beastly. For example at the top of Russia, Murmansk at the Kola Inlet where all the convoys taking arms and supplies to Russia were going, we had to keep seamen, sailors, both to man the Allied facilities, unloading facilities – of course the Russians were there too but we had to keep some British sailors there. And then we persuaded the Russians to let us have an intercept station there because half of the traffic around the top of the North Cape was difficult to intercept even in northern Scotland.

And of course we covered the risk that they would suspect that we were reading Enigma or that they would do more than suspect that, by saying that the value of the traffic to us was that it enabled us, by traffic analysis, to judge the German reactions to the movements of the convoys. So we had this little intercept station and then the Russians locked up its personnel because they thought we were spying on them, so you had all sorts of little rows with them like that. From time to time when it wasn't vital we did say if you don't behave better than this we won't send you your daily summary. And we stopped it for a short time, then we started again. But it had to be of that character – the collaboration.

Q. Is there scope for counterfactual historians studying the siege of Leningrad – if they had had access to the Ultra information – that you could have given them.

A. Again you have to bear in mind that there were problems. For example, one of the areas in which we found it extremely difficult to intercept German signals because of radio conditions or atmosphere conditions or whatever it is, was the North Cape; and the other was the Leningrad area. It was very difficult to intercept from the Leningrad area because whatever frequency they were using relative to the distances and the ionosphere we never could cover the Leningrad are properly. Caucacus on the other hand, Central Front, we could hear them as clear as a bell.

Q. If the collaboration had been as close as with the Americans...?

A. It would have been an advantage if it had been as close as with the Americans, it is quite true. But on the other hand the risks which I briefly portrayed were quite considerable. And we did our best to make sure that they knew about all the important forthcoming developments. Don't forget the Russians had very good intelligence of their own, not primarily sigint but they had very good air reconnaissance and air superiority after a certain time, and they had an enormous espionage system behind the German lines. So they weren't without information. But we did do our best to make sure that they got crucial early notice whenever we got it ourselves.

It was a big dilemma and one that was fought about. Churchill wanted to risk it and let them have more. Naturally the Ultra authorities didn't want to risk it because everything hangs on it, you see, so there was a tussle all the time about how much to send.

Q. There was a programme recently on Kursk – one might say that a Russian counterfactual historian would say that if we didn't have the Ultra which we got in various ways, then we wouldn't have been able to win the battle of Kursk and Hitler would have been able to carve up Russia. This is perhaps another case.

A. Another case. Stalingrad of course is another one. Those two battles were crucial, especially Stalingrad. Again it wasn't only through us they were getting ... we did give them the central facts in advance of Kursk. But as we now know, we didn't know at the time, the one single Russian agent in

Bletchley was at that time (just that short period of time before and after Kursk in '43) actually giving them decrypts through the Russian embassy in London. So all sorts of complications about the story. He didn't know that they were getting the supply from London officially, and we didn't know that he was sending the decrypts unofficially. Quite a complex problem!

Q. Did they never figure out that this was coming from decrypts?

A. We are never quite clear. Certainly when this man at Bletchley who only surfaced after the war – the secret about him only surfaced after the war – they knew that what they were getting from him was decrypts. They must then have known that our summaries were decrypts. But that didn't alter our practice because we didn't know that he was sending them the decrypts.

Q. How was the Ultra information disguised so that the Germans couldn't work out that you were decrypting them?

A. How did we disguise what we had got, you mean?

Q. How did you disguise, for example, that a particular submarine was going through a particular area? How could you disguise it so that it wasn't obvious that you'd intercepted it?

A. Let me give you an example of how we took the precautions, using it without on the other hand giving grounds for suspicion to the other side. The most dramatic example comes from the Mediterranean where we sank at two or three stages in the war something from 40% to 60% of all ships that left the north shore of the Mediterranean for North Africa. Sixty percent of the shipping was sunk, for example, just before the Battle of Alamein and again just before Gazala when Rommel was stopped.

Every one of those ships before it was attacked and sunk had to be sighted by a British aeroplane or submarine which had been put in a position in which it would sight it without it knowing that it had been put in that position, and made a sighting signal which the Germans and the Italians intercepted. That was the standard procedure. As a consequence of that the Germans and the Italians assumed that we had 400 submarines whereas we had 25. And they assumed that we had a huge reconnaissance air force on Malta, whereas we had three aeroplanes!

But solemnly that procedure had to be followed by the commanders. When they in their little centre in Cairo or, as it was later on Algiers, said we can't sink all those 17 ships today, which five are we going to take first and which five will we take second, when they were doing this they had to arrange that procedure before they hit a single ship.

Similar precautions were taken in the Atlantic, but there the problem was different. That is why the Germans got most suspicious about the Atlantic. The great feature there was that the Enigma was used in the first instance not to fight the U-boats but to evade them. And the problem was how could you evade them without their noticing. You have a situation on the graph in which the number of U-boats at sea in the Atlantic is going up, and the number of convoys they see is going down!

How do you cover that? We did cover it but it was done by a different system from what I have just described in the Mediterranean. We let captured Germans, people we had captured from U-boats write home from prison camp and we instructed our people when interrogated by Germans – our pilots for example – to propagate the view that we had absolutely miraculous radar which could detect a U-boat even if it was submerged from hundreds of miles. And the Germans believed it.

They had an enquiry, saying 'Surely it must be possible that it is the Enigma that isn't safe.' And the cipher men come back and say, 'It can't be the Enigma.' So somebody gets up and says, 'Well, it must be this bloody radar that we have heard about.' And so they decided. But you see different solutions had to be adopted for each particular situation. But these were the kind of precautions that were taken I think with great success. I mean they never really did tumble to the idea that it was unsafe, which is pretty marvellous really.

BIOGRAPHICAL SKETCH

Sir Harry Hinsley analyzed naval Enigma intercepts in Bletchley Park during World War II. He later was the chief author of the official, multivolume history, *British Intelligence in the Second World War*. Author as well of several works of history and international relations, he served as master of St. John's College, Cambridge. As a lecturer, he is particularly dramatic.

CRYPTOLOGIA January 1997 Volume XXI Number 1

THE FIRST NAVAL ENIGMA DECRYPTS OF WORLD WAR II

Ralph Erskine

ADDRESS: c/o *Cryptologia*, Department of Mathematical Sciences, United States Military Academy, West Point NY 10996 USA.

ABSTRACT: Comments on, and text of, the first naval Enigma decrypts of World War II.

KEYWORDS: Naval Enigma, decrypts, Bletchley Park, *Schiff 26*, *V 2623*.

The document set out in the Appendix sets out the first text derived from naval Enigma signals by the British codebreakers at Bletchley Park (BP) in World War II. Strictly speaking, the texts are not decrypts but reports, expressed in the past tense, of the contents of the signals, as distinct from the text of the signals themselves. However, since virtually the only difference consists of the insertion of "informed", "asked", "told" or some similar word in the text of the original signal, for all practical purposes they are decrypts and are so referred to here.

Although these decrypts contained virtually nothing of real intelligence value, BP gleaned a considerable amount of information from the six days' traffic of which they form part. In 1940, BP read naval Enigma for only those days (22 to 27 April 1940) and for a few more days in November. The decrypts of the April signals were a critically important part of the process which eventually led to BP breaking Heimisch (codenamed Dolphin by BP), the main cipher used by the Kriegsmarine, on an almost continual basis from the beginning of August 1941 until the end of the war.

The decrypts were made with the help of cipher forms (*Schlüsselzettel*), containing matching plain and cipher text, recovered from the German armed trawler *Schiff 26* (the former *Julius Pickenpack* and possibly also known by the Germans as *V 2623*) on 26 April 1940.[1] HMS *Griffin* had encountered and stopped *Schiff 26*, which was flying the Dutch colors and bore the name *Polares*, about 60 miles

[1]For reports on the effect of the loss of *Schiff 26* on cipher security, see "Verlust *Schiff 26* und 37 und Schlüsselsicherheit," 3 May 1940 and "*Schiff 26* und Schlüsselsicherheit," 21 May 1940: both KTB 2/SKL - Naval Historical Branch (NHB), Ministry of Defence, London. I am indebted to R. M. Coppock, NHB, for these references.

west of the Norwegian port of Ålesund. When a boarding party from *Griffin* noticed a canvas bag floating in the sea, Master Gunner F. H. W. T. Foord went into the water on a line to recover the bag. Although Foord almost drowned when the line broke and he went under three times, he managed to retrieve the bag, which apparently contained cipher-related papers. Unfortunately, *Schiff 26* was looted, either by *Griffin*'s crew or a shore party in Scapa Flow, to which she was towed, and few other cipher papers were recovered from her.[2] The looting was so bad that some cipher forms were found "strewn all over the ship", with one being discovered underneath a mine on her deck.[3] It may even be that the papers received by BP to break the April signals were among those documents, and not in the canvas bag retrieved by Foord. *Schiff 26*'s radio log, which would have given BP plain text to match with previously intercepted cipher text, was also recovered, but there is nothing to suggest that BP broke traffic for other days with its help.

The British official history states that "cypher settings" were captured from *V 2623* and that six days' traffic was solved in April, but cites no evidence for its statement.[4] In fact, no such settings were recovered, but merely the cipher forms mentioned above.[5] BP took a few days to break the traffic for 23 to 25 April, first solving signals for 23 April only on 11 May.[6] The signals for 22, 27 and 26 April were not broken until 18, 22 and 26 June, respectively, which is completely incompatible with cipher keys having been captured.[7] Hinsley's errors suggest that he once again relied on the mid-1945 history of Hut 8, which was largely written by Hugh Alexander, who had been in Hut 6 when the April signals were being solved.

The signals for 22, 26 and 27 April were broken by Joan Clarke (now Joan Murray), a young mathematician recruited by Gordon Welchman, who had arrived at BP only on 17 June. Despite the importance of her work, she was paid only £2 (then about $8) a week. She used the first British bombe (a fast key-finding aid), which had been installed at BP on 18 March 1940, to help to produce the decrypts, although that bombe lacked the refinement of the "diagonal board"

[2] HMS *Griffin*, report of proceedings, 26-28 April 1940; minute, port minesweeping officer, Lyness, 20 May 1940: both ADM 199/476. Files are at the Public Record Office, Kew, London, unless otherwise stated.

[3] "Report on *Griffin* by Pennell," 4 May 1940 in "Security I": ADM 223/297. Although not clear from that report, it would seem that the scattered forms may have contained text.

[4] F. H. Hinsley, with E. E. Thomas, C. F. G. Ransom and R. C. Knight, *British Intelligence in the Second World War: Its Influence on Strategy and Operations*, 1 (London, 1979), 163, 336; also David Kahn, *Seizing the Enigma: The Race to Obtain the German U-Boat Codes* (Boston, 1991), 117.

[5] Information from R. M. Coppock. For an example of a cipher form, see Kahn, *Seizing the Enigma*, 287.

[6] Z 1 in the Appendix: ADM 223/620.

[7] For 24 April, see Z 1(b); 25 April, Z 6; 22 April, Z 81; 26 April, Z 116: all ADM 223/620.

invented by Welchman.[8]

Naval Enigma had three special rotors (VI to VIII) available, which were not issued to the German Army and Air Force.[9] Hinsley states that the British recovered rotors VI and VII from U-33 in February 1940 and that rotor VIII was not captured until August 1940, but does not say where it came from.[10] Rotors I to V were, of course, given to BP by the Poles in August 1939, together with a reconstructed Enigma machine.[11] It would therefore appear that rotor VIII was not used in any of the keys for 22 to 27 April, since otherwise BP would have been unable to read the traffic for the day in question, unless of course it had reconstructed the rotor's wiring - which Hinsley does not suggest happened. But that, in turn, leads to the slightly surprising conclusion that the Kriegsmarine did not exploit rotors VI to VIII to the full by using each of them in turn, without repetition in the next pair of days.[12]

A considerable number of signals were eventually read for 22 to 27 April - some being solved as late as the end of July.[13] BP's naval section in Hut 4 exploited them to the full to build up information about the Kriegsmarine, although they were broken much too late for them to be used by the Admiralty's Operational Intelligence Centre. The signals seem to have led BP to conclude that captures of Kriegsmarine indicator books and keylists were essential if BP was to be able to break naval Enigma quickly, given that few bombes were likely to be available to test naval Enigma's possible 336 ($8\times7\times6$) rotor permutations.[14] The indicator books were needed in order that BP might employ a complicated method called Banburismus to reduce the number of permutations to be tried. BP's thoughts about "pinches" were not to bear fruit until the spring of 1941. In the meantime, the lack of hard intelligence from Enigma and other sources was so acute that the Director of Naval Intelligence, Rear-Admiral John Godfrey, was driven to obtain Hitler's horoscope and to suggest that some reliance should be put on it,

[8] Joan Murray, "Hut 8 and Naval Enigma - Part I," in Alan Stripp and F. H. Hinsley (eds.), *Codebreakers: The Inside Story of Bletchley Park*, (Oxford, 1993), 113. However, note that Mrs. Murray implies that all the signals were broken in June, whereas those for 23 to 25 April were solved in May, before she arrived.

[9] On naval Enigma machines, see Ralph Erskine and Frode Weierud, "Naval Enigma: M4 and its Rotors", *Cryptologia*, 9 (1987), 235.

[10] The British do not seem to have made any significant capture of a German warship in August 1940. Rotor VIII may possibly have been recovered by a diver from a U-boat which had been sunk earlier near the British coast. It would seem that the wiring was not recovered cryptanalytically.

[11] Hinsley *et al.*, *British Intelligence in the Second World War*, 3(2) (1988), 950, 957.

[12] The internal settings of a naval Enigma key, including the order in which the rotors were inserted in the machine, remained in force for two days at a time.

[13] "E bar" short signals (known to the Germans as alpha signals) for 22, 23 and 25 April were not solved until 29 July: Z 169 ADM 223/620.

[14] Z 191 of 10 September 1940, p. 3: ADM 223/620.

because Hitler apparently attached importance to advice from astrologers.[15]

ACKNOWLEDGEMENT

Z 1 is reproduced with the permission of the Controller of Her Majesty's Stationery Office.

APPENDIX: REPRODUCED Z 1 MESSAGES

German Naval Section, G. C. & C. S. Z No. 1.
11.5.40

23.4.40

1231/8330	ADM. WESTKUESTE informed GRUPPE WEST and ADM. NORWEGEN that there were no salvage tugs available at HAUKESUND or STAVANGER. He requested that two powerful salvage-tugs should be sent to Bergen.
1723/8330	GRUPPE (? WEST) asked ADM. WESTKUESTE and HAFENKOMMANDANT STAVANGER whether certain steamers in BERGEN were ready to sail and what was the speed of THERESIA RUSS and of the two Finnish steamers which had been brought to STAVANGER.
1725/4225	M 1 informed ADM. WESTKUESTE that she had been delayed owing to fuelling and taking troops on board. She would arrive about 2200.
x 1942/390	KIEL passed the continuation of a signal (the first part of which is not known) to the effect that ships proceeding out must wait at Lightship K for [the R BOOTE sent to meet them. The R BOOTE] [the arrival of the boats, which] with their gear out were then to proceed ahead of the ships. For a ship to proceed unaccompanied was dangerous and forbidden.
1943/4225	STAVANGER told M 1 that according to aircraft report there was a submerged submarine in 60° 9' 18" N., 5° 9' 30" E.
1955/390	T155 warned all ships urgently of a submarine in square 4185.
2050/8330	The HAFEN-KOMMANDANT, NARVIK, was given leave to return home.
2130/8330	The CHEF 2. Z Flottille reported that the HAFEN- KOMMANDANT and ADMIRAL NORWEGEN had that day discussed the situation thoroughly.

[In manuscript]

x 1st Part (1942/390)
(1934/4090) Broadcast: Until notice given to the contrary, all outgoing ships from Lightship K to Lightship H will be escorted by boats of the 4th H. S. Flotilla. The boats proceeding out etc-

[15] J. H. Godfrey, minute, 30 September 1940: ADM 223/463.

BIOGRAPHICAL SKETCH

Ralph Erskine is a semi-retired lawyer in Northern Ireland. His main research interest is naval intelligence in World War II.

LETTER TO THE EDITOR

Dear Editor

Sir Harry Hinsley's interesting "The Counterfactual History of No ULTRA" (*Cryptologia*, 20(4): 308-324) provides considerable food for thought. However, I was puzzled about a few items in it, probably because it was a talk, given to an unspecialised audience. I therefore wrote to Sir Harry, enclosing a draft of this letter, and later spoke to him.

In fairness to Sir Harry, readers should be aware that, when he gave the talk in October 1993, he did not know that it would be submitted to *Cryptologia* for publication. He was not even aware that it had been published until I contacted him.

I turn now to some detailed points for the record.

Page 317: "We read all the Enigma signals of the German *Abwehr* which meant that we captured every spy that arrived in the United Kingdom by having advance knowledge of his arrival". However, while the *Abwehr* attempted to infiltrate agents into the United Kingdom from September 1940 onwards, the Government Code and Cypher School ("GCCS") did not start to read *Abwehr* Enigma until over a year later, on 25 December 1941, when it issued ISK 1 (Intelligence Series Knox, 1), the first decrypt derived from one of several versions of the Enigma machine used by the *Abwehr*, which had been broken by Dillwyn Knox: Ralph Erskine, "Eavesdropping on Bodden: ISOS v. The *Abwehr* in the Straits" *Intelligence and National Security* (forthcoming); cf. F. H. Hinsley and C. A. G. Simkins, *British Intelligence in the Second World War*, Vol. 4 *Security and Counter-Intelligence* (1990) 108. The Intelligence Series Oliver Strachey (ISOS) decrypts of *Abwehr* signals using manual ciphers began around March 1940, when GCCS first read some simple *Abwehr* single transposition ciphers. It did not start to break the more complicated *Abwehr* double transposition ciphers until around December 1940: Hinsley and Simkins, *British Intelligence* 4: 89.

While the ISOS and ISK decrypts were undoubtedly invaluable in countering the *Abwehr*, they were far from being the sole, or even the main, means of rounding up its agents in Britain. Out of 26 agents sent to the United Kingdom in 1940 and caught, only one was captured as a direct result of special intelligence ("Ultra" - which was only ISOS, and not ISK, in this context in 1940): "The Counter-Intelligence and Counter-Sabotage Value of Special Intelligence During the European War," 30 May 1945 (PRO ADM 223/298).

Page 315 refers to the Germans reading "to the end of '42" a British naval cipher "which was ... shared with the American navy" for convoy escort purposes: Naval Cypher No. 3 - the so-called "convoy code" (codenamed Frankfurt by the B-Dienst). The B-Dienst (the German naval codebreaking agency) broke Naval Cypher No. 3, which was a code, and not a cipher, until 1 June 1943, when a new codebook, Naval Cypher No. 5, was introduced: F. H. Hinsley, *et al.*, *British Intelligence in the Second World War: Its Influence on Strategy and Operations*, Vol. 2. (London: 1981) 636.

Sir Harry mentions various forms of Hagelin, adding that "The American armed forces used it occasionally, but it was easily broken" (page 311). In fact, more than 140,000 M-209 Converters (the American version of Hagelin) were made for the U. S. Army during the war. Although the *Luftwaffe*'s Sigint service (the *Funkaufklärungsdienst*) did not give priority to the interception of M-209 traffic, it apparently intercepted around 100 U. S. Army Air Force messages enciphered on M-209 daily in Western Europe and 40 daily in the Mediterranean. The German Army is said to have often intercepted 10 times as many signals.

In referring to Hagelin being easily broken, Sir Harry had in mind mainly the Italian version, C-38M. Italian Hagelin was badly used: for example, too many signals had a standard opening (see Luigi Donini, "The Cryptographic Services of the Royal British and Italian Navies," *Cryptologia*, 14(2): 97-127, for other procedural weaknesses when using C-38M). However, not all Hagelin succumbed so easily. Except during October 1944, when the keys for a U. S. Army Air Force net in the West were captured, the *Funkaufklärungsdienst* probably read M-209 traffic in the West only on six to 12 days each month, and between two and five days each month in the Mediterranean. Neither GCCS nor the U. S. Army's Signal Security Agency could break Norwegian diplomatic Hagelin, probably because it was used in accordance with sound instructions which, in particular, limited the length of signals enciphered with a given key.

Finally, Sir Harry referred to the GCCS outpost known as H. M. S. Anderson (although he does not mention it by name) in Colombo, Ceylon. Anderson worked on Japanese naval codes, such as JN-25. In response to a question, Sir Harry said (page 320) that Anderson sent "decrypts *direct* to the American headquarters" (emphasis added). The published wording implies that a direct radio or cable link was used. As Sir Harry is aware, there was a running battle between Anderson and GCCS on this issue. Anderson wanted to liaise directly with the U. S. Navy in Washington, but GCCS insisted on being the link between them, which caused delays. GCCS acted as a relay for all messages between Washington and Colombo, even after a special communications service was established between Washington, GCCS, Pearl Harbor, Melbourne and H. M. S. Anderson in early 1944: N. I. D. History, Vol. 42 "Far East and Pacific", III "H. M. S. Anderson and Special Intelligence in the Far East" (PRO ADM 223/297).

Sincerely
Ralph Erskine
c/o *Cryptologia*, Department of Mathematical Sciences,
United States Military Academy, West Point NY 10996 USA.

AN ERROR IN THE HISTORY OF ROTOR ENCRYPTION DEVICES

Friedrich L. Bauer

ADDRESS: 19 Noerdliche Villenstrasse, D-82288 Kottgeisering GERMANY

ABSTRACT: Many historians have erred in giving credit for the Enigma cipher machine of World War II famed to Hugo Koch and not to the rightful inventor, Arthur Scherbius. This is corrected here.

KEYWORDS: Enigma, rotor, NSA, Hugo Koch, Arthur Scherbius, David Kahn, Arvid Gerhard Damm, Siegfried Türkel, Edward Hugh Hebern, patents, Securitas.

In a recent publication of the National Security Agency, a leaflet with the attractive title *The Bombe: Prelude to Modern Cryptanalysis*, an historical error on the Enigma is repeated that has been copied for decades. It states that "Hugo Koch, a Dutchman, conceived the machine in 1919. Arthur Scherbius first produced it commercially in 1923." It is time to return to historical correctness.

The error is concerned with two inventors of the rotor principle: Arthur Scherbius and Hugo Alexander Koch. In 1967, David Kahn, in his famous book *The Codebreakers*, correctly stated that on October 7, 1919, Hugo Koch, a Dutchman, filed for a Netherlands patent (No. 10,700) for a *Geheimschrijfmachine*. Kahn neglected to mention the German patent filed by Arthur Scherbius; and gave only a facsimile of the U. S. patent (No. 1,657,411) that Scherbius was granted in 1926. In his 1991 book *Seizing the Enigma*, Kahn gave more information, in particular that Scherbius on April 15, 1918, had approached the German Imperial Navy about his cipher machine patent for which he had applied on February 23, 1918 under file number Sch 52638 IX/42n. Kahn reported that "the naval staff examined Scherbius's machine and found that it afforded 'good security, even if compromised.' But it decided not to buy it 'because with the present kind of naval cipher traffic, the use of machines is not worthwhile.' Instead, it recommended that the Foreign Office examine the machine to see if it were suitable for diplomatic correspondence. But the Foreign Office was not interested either."

The German patent that Kahn did not specify was issued July 8, 1925, as No. 416,219 with priority of February 23, 1918 (Figure 1). Thus, Scherbius

DEUTSCHES REICH

AUSGEGEBEN AM 8. JULI 1925

REICHSPATENTAMT

PATENTSCHRIFT

— № 416219 —

KLASSE 42n GRUPPE 14

(Sch 52638 IX/42n)

Gewerkschaft Securitas in Berlin.

Chiffrierapparat.

Patentiert im Deutschen Reiche vom 23. Februar 1918 ab.

Es gibt bereits elektrische Chiffriermaschinen, bei denen Zeichensender und Zeichenempfänger in beliebiger Weise durch elektrische Leitungen miteinander verbunden sind. Die Veränderung der Anschlüsse (des Chiffrierschlüssels) erfolgt bei dieser entweder durch Auswechseln fester Platten, welche entsprechende Leitungen tragen, oder durch Drehen eines nach dem Grundschlüssel angeschlossenen biegsamen Kabels oder durch Drehen eines Leitungsmagazins.

Die Erfindung verfolgt den Zweck, Maschinen dieser Art einfacher und leistungsfähiger zu gestalten. Sie ist auf der Zeichnung beispielsweise veranschaulicht.

In Abb. 1 ist 1 der Zeichensender, 2 der Zwischenleitungsträger und 3 der Zeichenempfänger. Auf dem Zeichensender 1 sind Kontakte *a* bis *k* angeordnet. Auf dem Zeichensender 1 sind Kontakte *A* bis *K* (Glühlampen, Typen usw.) vorgesehen. Der Leitungszwischenträger 2 verbindet in beliebiger Weise die Kontakte *a* bis *k* mit den Anzeigern *A* bis *K*. Wird z. B. *c* auf Sender 1 gedrückt, so wird *A* auf 3 angezeigt. Nun ist der Leitungszwischenträger 2 beliebig weit und oft drehbar. Wird derselbe z. B. um eine Teilung im Uhrzeigersinn weiter gedreht, wie Abb. 2 zeigt, so wird aus dem Buchstaben *c* der Buchstabe *E*. Die Verdrehung des Leitungszwischenträgers 2 kann selbsttätig und zwangläufig mit den zu chiffrierenden Buchstaben erfolgen.

Wie ersichtlich, liegen immer sämtliche Leitungen des Leitungszwischenträgers 2 in Bereitschaft. Derselbe ist, im Gegensatz zu einem Leitungsmagazin stets voll ausgenutzt. Es sind also nicht mehr Leitungen, Kontakte usw. vorhanden, als unbedingt gebraucht werden. Für diese Anordnung ist es kennzeichnend, daß die Verschiebung des Leitungszwischenträgers 2 in Richtung der Verbindungslinie der Kontakte 4 erfolgt.

Der Leitungszwischenträger kann auch eine andere Gestalt haben. In Abb. 3 hat er z. B. die Form eines Zylinders (Walze), auf dessen Mantel die Leitungen liegen.

In Abb. 4 ist er als gerader Schieber ausgebildet. Die Leitungsanschlüsse auf 1 und 3 müssen hier verdoppelt werden, um stets eine Leitungsverbindung von 1 nach 3 zu erhalten. Die drehende Bewegung des Leitungszwischenträgers 2 aus Abb. 1 bis 3 wird hier zu einer hin und her gehenden.

Um die Zahl der Schlüssel zu vermehren, werden zweckmäßig mehrere Leitungszwischenträger hintereinandergeschaltet. In Abb. 5 ist dieses für drei Leitungszwischenträger 2^a, 2^b und 2^c in Form von Walzen gezeichnet. Bei 25 Kontakten entsprechend den 25 Buchstaben des Alphabetes, d. h. bei 25 möglichen Stellungen der einzelnen Walzen, ergeben sich $25 \times 25 \times 25 = 15625$ Schlüsselstellungen. Allgemein werden es bei n Walzen 25^n Schlüssel. Bei 10 Walzen erhält man über 95 Billionen Schlüssel.

Zum Dechiffrieren muß der Strom die Chiffriereinrichtung in umgekehrter Richtung durchlaufen. In Abb. 1 wären also die Druckknöpfe an Stelle der Anzeiger *A* bis *K* und die Anzeiger an Stelle der Druckknöpfe *a* bis *k* zu setzen. Beim Chiffrieren wird z. B. aus dem Buchstaben *c* der Buchstabe *A*. Wird jetzt nach der Vertauschung der Zeichensender und Zeichenanzeiger der Buchstabe *A* gedrückt, so erscheint

Figure 1. First page of the Scherbius patent of 1918

patented a rotor invention more than a year earlier than Koch (and also earlier than another rotor inventor, the Swede Arvid Gerhard Damm with his Swedish patent application of October 11, 1919). Scherbius, in 1918, described 10-contact rotors (Figure 2) and 25-contact rotors as well as combinations of 3 (Figure 3) or more, up to 10, such rotors, using electric or pneumatic switching. He also described means for irregular movement of the rotors.

The patent numbers may be found in the highly interesting book on cipher machines by the Austrian criminologist Dr. Siegfried Türkel, *Chiffrieren mit Geräten und Maschinen* (Graz, 1927). However, Türkel gave details only of the Koch patents and thus invited confusion. A second patent by Scherbius, No. 416,833, issued July 27, 1925, with priority of June 2, 1918, completed Scherbius' rotor invention.

There is no question that Edward Hugh Hebern (1869–1952) was the first inventor of a rotor encryption machine, for which he made drawings as early as 1917 and on which he started construction in 1918 — due to unhappy circumstances, however, he filed for a U. S. patent only in 1921, later than Scherbius, Koch, and Damm, and finally received it (No. 1,510,441) in 1924.

Somehow, writers mangled this chronology into the following form: Koch invented the Enigma, and Scherbius, in 1923, bought the patents. It would go too far to list all the occurrences of this error in the popular literature; it is found in the book by Antony Cave Brown, *Bodyguard of Lies* (New York, 1975), p. 15: "Scherbius did build a machine from Koch's plans" and in the book by Brian Johnson, *The Secret War* (London, 1978), p. 309: "Koch does not appear to have constructed his invention; at all events a German engineer, Arthur Scherbius, bought the patent rights and made the machine, renaming it 'Enigma'." The error even crept into Władisław Kozaczuk's fine book *Enigma* (Frederick MD, 1984), p. xiii: "Later, the German engineer would develop the 'Enigma' machine that had been patented in Holland in the fall of 1919 by the inventor Hugo Koch, who subsequently sold the patent to Scherbius."

The error may have been spread by the book of Cipher A. Deavours and Louis Kruh, *Machine Cryptography and Modern Cryptanalysis* (Dedham, 1985). There, the Koch patent, filed on October 7, 1919, is explicitly mentioned, but listed only are a U. S. patent, No. 1,584,660 by Scherbius, received May 11, 1926, for a 10-contact rotor, and the aforementioned No. 1,657,411, received in 1928, "for a machine he named 'Enigma', but which was not similar to the commercial model sold afterwards." The erroneous wording in the book reads (p. 7) "... and Arthur Scherbius, a German engineer acquainted with Koch who held patent rights to a *later* [my emphasis] design." In fact, Scherbius much later (Kahn, in *The*

Abb. 1.

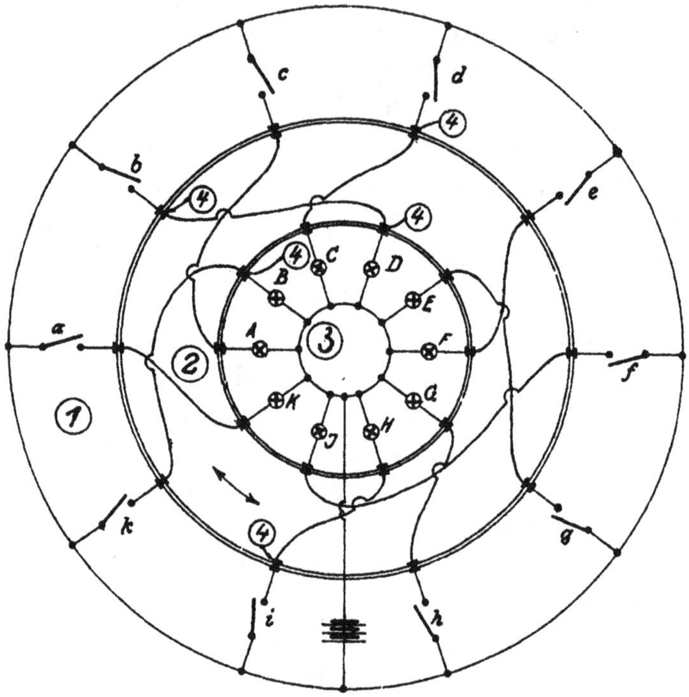

Figure 2. Details from the Scherbius patent of 1918.

Abb. 5.

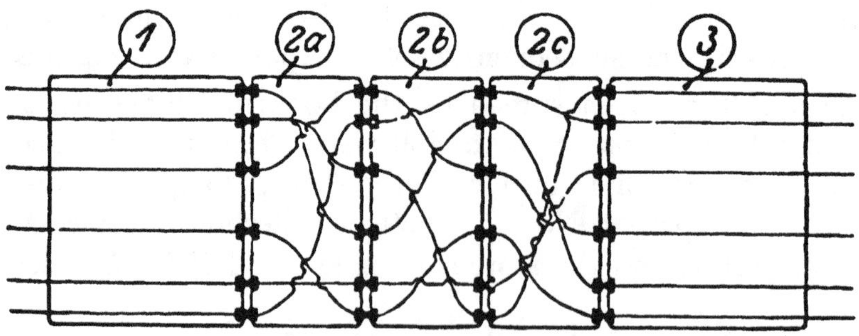

Figure 3. Details from the Scherbius patent of 1918.

Codebreakers, gives 1927), did indeed buy the Koch patents, but obviously not because he did not own patents before; presumably he wanted to protect his patents. (It should also be noted that Scherbius's company, *Gewerkschaft Securita* founded in Berlin in July 1923 the *Chiffriermaschinen Aktiengesellschaft*. Koch's patents were held by *Naamlooze Vennotschap Ingenieursbureau Securitas* in Amsterdam.)

The error can now be found in the Internet and thus is propagated worldwide. It is time that historians give Scherbius recognition for his work — on which Poland, Great Britain and the United States achieved one of their greatest cryptanalytic successes. The correct order in which the two inventors should be listed, is Scherbius–Koch.

REFERENCES

1. Bauer, Friedrich L. 1997. *Decrypted Secrets, Methods and Maxims of Cryptology.* Berlin: Springer-Verlag.

2. *Deutsches Reich, Reichspatentamt.* Patentschrift Nr. 416219 Klasse 42n Gruppe 14 (Sch 52638 IX/42n).

BIOGRAPHICAL SKETCH

Friedrich L. Bauer, born in 1924, a German computer pioneer, has won the Computer Pioneer Award of the IEEE Computer Society for his invention of the computer stack. Professor emeritus at the Technical University Munich, Bauer is the author of *Entzifferte Geheimnisse*, published in English in 1997 as *Decrypted Secrets* (Springer, Berlin–Heidelberg–New York). A second English edition is under way.

THE GLOW-LAMP CIPHERING AND DECIPHERING MACHINE: ENIGMA FROM THE ARCHIVES

[Editor's Note: We reprint what may be the first Enigma sales brochure produced around the mid-1920s to encourage all businesses to "keep their correspondence absolutely secret" by using Enigma. The cover reads, *Chiffriermaschinen, Aktiengeseelschaft, Berlin W 35, Steglitzer Str. 2. Fernspr.: Nollendorf 2899, Tel. Adr.: Chiffrier Berlin.* Measuring 20.8 cm wide by 14.5 cm high with elegantly framed text on 16 pages, this pamphlet promoted the Enigma while "educating" the reader into a need for such a device in commerce. The original brochure is from the collection of Louis Kruh, one of *Cryptologia*'s founding editors. Slight grammatical corrections have been made.]

WHAT PERSONS IT IS CALCULATED TO SERVE AND HOW?

It is a well-known fact that, now and forever, for purposes of both war and peace, politicians and military men, industrial producers and commercial houses are compelled to keep their correspondence secret. This is a point increasing in importance from day to day. Decisive battles have been lost, by land and by water, in the air and in debating with each other, because the adversary had a better method of keeping his correspondence secret, or a good apparatus being capable of considerably quickening the speed, and multiplying the number of information sent and received. Hand-writing systems will prove insufficient in times of great excitement and hurried proceedings.

If you have no good coding system, you are always running a considerable risk. Transmitted by cable or without wire, your correspondence will always be exposed to every spy, your letters, to being opened and copied, your intended or settled contracts, your offers and important news to every inquisitive eye. Considering this state of things, it is almost inconceivable that persons interested in those circumstances should delay securing themselves better against such things.

Yet, ciphering and deciphering has been a troublesome art hitherto. Much time and expenses and experience were required to give a man that qualification. Nevertheless, the result obtained couldn't be but very imperfect, for the secret code you made use of, was always accessible to many persons, or the ciphering clerk was ill or absent for any other purpose. Thus, expenses and efforts were always of little avail only. All kinds of losses and prejudices, perhaps irreparable, always threatened everybody's and the States business and existence.

Now, we can offer you our machine "Enigma", being a universal remedy for all those inconveniences. The machine has been tried and improved in the course of many years. At the present time this machine is a perfect instrument capable of any effect desired. It is of so simple a construction that every non-expert can learn and remember the few manipulations within a few minutes. Henceforth, no especial clerk is required for ciphering and deciphering. The managers may do the work themselves or with the aid of some reliable assistants. Spending once only a trifle, you will have a whole coding office, always ready for service, entirely reliable, free of charge when out of service, and costing but a few farthings a day when working. Moreover, the life of this machine being nearly endless, the time required for amortizing the funds invested is, theoretically, likewise nearly endless.

It is generally agreed upon that not only armies, navies, air-navigation, diplomatic representations, police-departments, in a word, the whole administration of a State, but also all commercial houses, especially those engaged in exportation, all industrial undertakings, banking establishments (for instance in order to prevent every kind of fraud in bank assignments), shipping-companies, stockbrokers, inquiry offices, press people, large political and economical associations, Chambers of Commerce, and many others must keep their correspondence absolutely secret. The correspondence of a commercial house with their representatives and branch establishments is under the same necessity. This applies not only to information, sent to distant places, in which case the trouble and the expenses for journeys, conferences and couriers are saved, but is also true in such cases when documents, production-methods, explanations of drawings and the like are to be kept secret The natural inquisitiveness of competitors is at once checkmated by a machine which enables you to keep all your documents, or al least their important parts, entirely secret without occasioning any expenses worth mentioning. One secret, well protected, may pay the whole cost of the machine. Of course, the machine cannot make a code altogether superfluous. But you need not any longer make use of expensive private and secret codes. You may safely avail yourself of any public code, simple or voluminous, in order to obtain a ciphered document resisting to every attempt of deciphering after having passed our machine. It is, moreover, superfluous to say that in sending written news, brevity is always much less important than security against inquisitiveness. An information, ciphered by our machine, may be safely sent by an open post-card without any danger of being deciphered.

Working with our machine is much less intricate than that with a writing-machine. Every beginner can learn the few manipulations required within a few minutes. The rapidity of writing is, practically, unlimited and only depends on the degree of rapidity with which the eye can perceive the flashing-up letters. There is no searching for ciphered letters in lists, on rules or discs, the bugbear of every specialist. There is no getting fatigued, not even with long work. You only need press down a certain key of the keyboard to make appear the corresponding ciphered letter, or, in deciphering the original text. In case of clerical errors, only put back the machine, the mistake will be corrected within two seconds. Moreover, there is no preventing you from deciphering the text, even if it should have been falsified or mutilated by the telegraph,

For this triumph we are, again, indebted to electricity. Before flashing up, each letter is eight times permuted by electrical power. No purely mechanical apparatus possesses such a degree of capacity. Besides, each time each letter is taken from a different permutation alphabet. And all this may be done several millions of times without a pause.

You know that, in each language, the different letters occur with a different frequency. Our machine makes away with this difference, which offers so many possibilities to every attempt of deciphering a text. Amongst a thousand letters the letter "e" occurs quite as many times as the letter "z". The safety of working admits of no objection. There are many machines of ours that have been worked every day for many years without requiring any repair. The working is secured for 3 - 6 months, without any pause, by a regular little dry battery of 4 volts tension, lodged within the machine. In case of need one pocket-lamp battery is quite sufficient. The machine works almost without any noise. There is no clock mechanism making superfluous noise, needing permanent winding, and destroying the whole machine, whenever the spring is broken. Our machine "Enigma" is always ready for working.

DIMENSIONS AND WEIGHTS

The outer dimensions of the portable machine, lodged in an oakwood-box, are:

Machine without box:			Box:
Breadth	...	25.5 cm	28.0 cm
Length	...	27.0 cm	29.0 cm
Height	...	11,5 cm	15.0 cm
Weight	...	6.77 kg	2.04 kg

Our machine is provided with a regular dry battery of 4 volts tension, which lasts about 3–4 months, if used freely every day. In case of need a common pocket-lamp battery is quite sufficient.

There are also connecting terminals for an accumulator of 4 volts tension.

Only use glow-lamps of 12.5 mm diameter and of hemispherical shape, such as are usually employed in the ordinary electric torch-lamps (3.5 volts, 0.2 amp.).

There are two spare-lamps R (II) on the right and left hand of the middle row of glow-lamps, between two white points, and ten at the inside of the lid of the box within a particular band,

WHAT CAPACITIES MUST A CIPHERING MACHINE POSSESS?

A ciphering machine must give a greater security than any handwriting system, be this ever so complicated. This is the principal condition to be fulfilled. But it must equally enable you to work more rapidly than with the list system, be this ever so simple. From these two principal conditions we may derive the following secondary ones and the following facts:

a) From a merely practical point of view the rapidity of ciphering and deciphering may be called unlimited. Pressing down a key immediately makes appear the corresponding ciphered letter. The rapidity only depends on the degree of rapidity with which the eye can perceive the flashing-up letters. If not relieving a man from the necessity of seeking after the corresponding cipher in permutation alphabets, a machine is a failure being by no means superior to handwriting systems. This necessity of searching for things produces countless mistakes, wearies you rapidly and takes too much time, especially in case of long texts to be ciphered (for instance 500 letters).

b) When discussing the rapidity of a machine, it would be a fault only to consider the time it takes you to transform the original text into ciphers, and vice versa. It is nearly quite as important that a machine should enable both the sender and the receiver to adjust the whole key within a minimum of time. If the very adjusting of the key for a telegram containing 10 words takes you 10 minutes, your machine is of no avail, for the hand works more rapidly with pen and list. Adjusting the whole key—(11 parts) of our machine (inside and outside) will not take you more than 70 lo 80 seconds. The outside adjustment (including 450,000 possibilities), taking 10 seconds only, doesn't make you lose any time, then.

c) In case of clerical mistakes, a machine must admit of repeating the last ten written letters, for instance. With our machine this can be done within five seconds.

d) Errors and omissions occasioned by the telegraph must not delay the deciphering or render it impossible. With our machine, the omission of two groups of five letters will occasion a delay of 10 seconds only.

e) Even if hidden in the text of a communication, the key must be easy to transmit. If a key be composed of 50 or 60 parts, a machine is not simple enough and liable to failure. The key of our machine consists, therefore, of eight letters and three figures only (of one digit each). Yet four letters are sufficient to give you about 450,000 possibilities, and this number will rise to 2,700,000 possibilities by employing 4 letters and 3 figures. Seven characters are easy to hide even in short communications. The other 4 letters will, moreover, offer you another series of 450,000 possibilities. There is, however, no need of them, because changing a single letter of the key, whatsoever it may be, will always change the whole system.

f) It is a well-known fact that, in combining a number of objects in whatever manner you like, you will always obtain, besides numerous combinations being very different from each other, a great deal showing but very slight differences and, therefore, being very similar to each other and liable to confusion. This circumstance must compel you to select your key with utmost carefulness, will make you lose considerable time and expose you to countless mistakes, not only when establishing your first key, but also in changing it in the course of your work. This annoying inconvenience is now, entirely, removed by our machine. Ii is so calculated that changing a single letter of a key it whatever manner you like, will always give a new system showing not the least likeness to that employed before. If, for instance, some text, for the first time, be ciphered with the aid of the outside key "ajkl", you will obtain quite a different text by employing, for the second time, the key "ajil" (the inside adjustment remaining the same). This secures you all the more from every attempt of unauthorized deciphering.

g) Every exchangeable part of a machine that has to be transported independently from its body is liable to particular loss and damage. Every machine must be a coherent system. This ideal condition is entirely fulfilled by our machine. The exchangeable rollers (cylinders) are solidly joined with its body, and every exchange is exclusively effectuated by changing the path of the electric current.

h) There are many ciphering apparatus employing the so called "letter of influence" as a particular means of increasing the "security" against deciphering. The nature of this method consists of changing the regular course of the working machine, whenever a certain letter, "n" for instance may occur in the original text, by hand, automatically, or by mental transformation of the key. This mode of producing is generally known and, from a theoretical point of view, not altogether useless. Yet, in practice, ii is of no value at all. For every error of the telegraph, every omission, and ever clerical mistake will render a ciphered document almost entirely undecipherable. Our machine doesn't exclude this method, but renders it superfluous, because of being, even without it, entirely protected from every inquisitiveness.

SECURITY AGAINST UNAUTHORIZED DECIPHERING

1. When discussing the security of a machine against unauthorized deciphering, you can never hope to succeed, for any length of time, in keeping secret the construction of the machine with all its accessories. It is, moreover, quite evident that you cannot change your key at every moment if it consists of 26 or 52 letters of one or two alphabets, and if a particular correspondence with

your friends, and, thus, a considerable while be needed, whenever another key is to be introduced. Our machine makes away with all that, it will take you some seconds only to change one letter of your key and, thus, to obtain an entirely different ciphered document. And it will take you no more than 30 or 40 seconds to change the whole key consisting of seven letters and figures. Even if the whole key of seven characters should become known, the remaining four letters secure the document from every attempt of deciphering. There is no difficulty whatever to change the whole key at any time.

2. To increase the security, keys can be divided, and each part entrusted to various persons. In case of the key list being lost, another key can immediately be established while writing, of you make a general stipulation. For instance, it can be agreed upon that, whenever the letter "z" occurs three times consecutively in a document to be deciphered, the next letter is to mean the outside key - letter with regard to a certain roller, or that every sixth, ninth, tenth and fourteenth letter of the text is to mean the outside position of the key. Such agreements, countless in theory, will protect you from treason as well as from the consequences o a key lost. We can never sufficiently emphasize the importance of the fact that, with our machine changing a single letter always changes the whole key without lengthening the text.

3. You are not always and everywhere in a position to put a machine in a locked-up iron-safe, when leaving a room for a moment. Nor are you able to prevent the machine being in service from being photographed inside and outside. Our machine need not be protected from photographers, even if they should take photos of the several parts. Without taking the whole machine to pieces nothing can be ascertained, and, with all that, it would still take an unauthorized person several hour to make out all connections established But, moreover, whenever you are compelled to leave you' working-room, be it for ever so short a while, you only need pass your hand slightly over the notched wheels of the ciphering rollers, thus destroying the key-adjustment in so radical a manner that nobody would be able to reconstruct it even by long years' labor and although he might possess a machine of the same kind and the same connections. With our machine, even a key discovered by treason given no fixed point to attempt of deciphering a document written with a changing key.

4. Every machine contains a certain number of fixed elements such as cog-wheels, notched wheels connection-joints etc. After having worked for a

certain time, each of these parts must return to the position it had when starting, and thus the whole machine, after having ciphered a certain number of letters, must return to its original position, the position it had before beginning to work. The time required for this return is called a "period". Now, if a machine have only a short period of about 300 letters, the original position will already reappear after every fifth line, and a clever man would be able to decipher the document on this basis, if it have any considerable length. Our machine has a "period" of about 8 or 10 typewritten pages so that even a long document will never exceed the period.

5. The security of a machine against deciphering depends by no means on gigantic figures. The "simple Caesar" (substitution of a letter for another) gives no less than 26 possibilities or a figure of 27 digits. By making use of this method four times consecutively we shall obtain fantastic figures (of more than 100 digits), which, however, are of no avail in practice, since no new combination can be secure unless giving a system that differs sufficiently from that employed before. v Our machine allows every possibility, a number which exceeds by far 100 digits. But we only speak of 2,700,000 possibilities, because these alone will give sufficiently different results. To find them out, you only need a perfect knowledge of all parts and connections of our machine.

6. Although gigantic figures cannot prove anything in favor of a machine, let us see which possibilities are offered by our machine!

   Each one of the four ciphering cylinders can be connected in 26 ways. Thus we obtain a figure of 27 digits, or of more than 100 digits, when taking all the four cylinders together. Consequently it would be possible to provide each person in the world with several machines having the same adjustment. A key discovered by treason would be entirely useless, then. Well, but now the three cylinders on the right side can be exchanged as you like. Suppose you have only seven spare-cylinders, you would obtain about two million different keys, and would be able to cipher each text in two milliards of ways. That is to say: if a man were able to adjust, night and day, a new key at every minute, it would take him 4000 years to try all those possibilities through on after another. Do you see now that our machine can hold its ground against every attempt of this kind?

7. Yet, we must never forget that not every possible combination is at the same time a useful one. By combining the 26 keys of a typewriter, we obtain a gigantic number of possible keys, but every mathematician will tell you that no more than 60% are different enough to serve for practical purposes. It

I

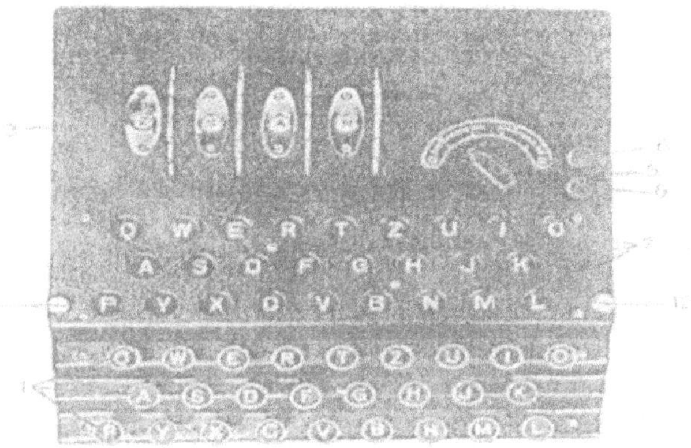

II

Illustration	I, 11:	1. Key-board.
"	I, II:	2. Glow lamp board.
"	I:	3. Windows.
"	I, II:	4. Ciphering cylinders (rollers).
"	I, II:	5. Switch-handle.
"	I, II:	6. Connecting terminals for accumulator working.
"	II:	7. Spring for adjusting the 1etter-ring.
"	II:	8. Letter-ring.
"	II:	9. Lever.
"	II:	11. Reversing cylinder.
"	II:	12. Lid screws.
"	II:	14. Dry battery.
"	II:	15. Guide pin.
"	II:	R. Spare-lamps.

Explanation of the Illustrations I & II

is the greatest advantage of our machine that it excludes, from the very beginning, every useless combination, without any loss of time or labor. Changing one single letter of a key employed will always change the whole system in a radical manner.

INSTRUCTIONS FOR USE

I. KEY ADJUSTMENT

a) Opening the lid and taking out the cylinders.

Put the switch-handle 5 (I & II) parallel to the right edge. Unscrew both lid-screws 12 (I) open the lid. Put the lever 9 (II) in a vertical position, push the reversing cylinder 11 (II) to the left, to stop, press together the three right ciphering cylinders (rollers) by the notched wheels, move them upwards, and pull them from the shaft. in order to be able to adjust the machine to the key agreed upon, the following manipulations are necessary:

b) Selection of the cylinders and order of same.

From the existing ciphering cylinders take out those three which are required by the key agreed upon. Slide them on to the shaft in the stipulated order (collar of shaft to the left, letter-ring on left side of cylinder). Then put the cylinders in and shift the lever 9 (II) to the rear as far as stop,

c) Adjustment of the rings upon the cylinders.

Removing the spring 7 (II) turn the letter-ring of each cylinder so far that the join of the rings upon the spring catches the hole beyond the letter which has been agreed upon. the cylinders.

d) Outside adjustment of the letters in the windows.

the lid and turn the notched wheels till the letters agreed upon become visible in the windows.

e) Combinations of the key

Let us take, for instance, the key (always start from left hand): II, III, I; G, X, M, Z; I, S, A, N.

1. The group II, III, I is to design the order of the cylinder, and means to say that the ciphering cylinders'4 (I & II) which bear these marks on the frontal side of the movable contacts have been put on the shaft in this order (counting from collar of shaft). If there are more than

three ciphering cylinders, the roman figures mean at the same time the cylinders to be selected.

2. The group G, X, M, Z means to say that the pin of the spring 7 (II) catches beneath the holes below these letters of the letter-rings.
3. The group Z, S, A, N means to say that these letters become visible in the windows 3 (I).

f) In round numbers 2.7 million of different and useful keys possible.

If possible, change the key so often that no more than 30 typewritten pages may be written with the same key. As nearly 3 millions of keys are given, this can easily be done and only depends on organization. Adding the possible change of letter-rings, possible you will obtain about 1OOO milliards of possible keys.

g) Transmitting the key and keeping it secret.

If need be, the keys may be divided, and each part entrusted to another person.

In order to hide the key, various stipulations can be made between the correspondents. You may thus stipulate that the tenth, eleventh and twelfth letter of every communication is to mean the order of the cylinders mark them with letters) and that the eighteenth, twentieth and twenty-first letter is to mean the visible letters. If is, however, sufficient to change a single letter of the key in order to obtain a completely different text.

You may also stipulate that the number of the current month has to be added to the number of the place the transmitted key-letter occupies in the alphabet. For instance, if "B", the second letter of the alphabet, is transmilted in the fourth month (April), you are to understand the sixth letter "F"

It is thus possible to find out many hundreds of protective measures against unauthorized use of keys which have become known. As a rule, it suffices to change every day the letters appearing in the windows, whereas the inside adjustment only need be changed every week or month.

II. CIPHERING

The switch-handle 5 (II & III) has to be set to "maximum" (hell). When the letters flash up too dimly, set it to "minimum" (dkl.). It is advisable to employ square paper for writing, The text is ciphered, letter by letter, by pressing down the keys 1 (I & II) as it is done when type-writers are being used. Each key must be sufficiently pressed down to make a lamp 2 (I & II) flash up. If intervals between the words are desired, for instance, the key "X" may be pressed down after each word.

Examples:

Original Text:

``Bieten Sie bei Zwangsversteigerung bis vierzigtausend."

Ciphered Text:

afmuz pglae rillz lfiep mgrsa basti vwbac mxgyi noffe pbluo arl.

If figures are to be written, the first ten letters may, for instance, be employed instead of same in pressing down, in the same time, the key "Y". When passing from figures to letters, press the key "Y" down once more. In short: insert "X" before letters, "Y" before figures and other signs.

III. DECIPHERING

Every machine is available for deciphering as well as ciphering. Adjust the machine to the stipulated key, connect the current by turning the switch-handle 5 (I & III), and copy the ciphered document letter by letter, by pressing down the corresponding keys. Then the flashing-up letter will show the original text.

Examples:

Ciphered Text:

afmuz pglae rillz lfiep mgrsa basti vwbac mxgyi noffe pbluo arl.

Deciphered Text:

bieten x sie x bei x zwangsversteigerung x bis x vierzigtausend.

IV. CLERICAL ERRORS

Having pressed down, by mistake, a wrong key, put back, by two steps, the ciphering cylinder on the right side. Try the last correct letter once again, then, in order to see whether one of the other cylinders has moved together with the right one.

Having written but a few letters, you may, in order to repeat the twenty-third letter, for instance, press down any key you please twenty-two times, and then repeat the desired letter.

V. THE MACHINE TESTED IN PRACTICE

Being the result of many years' labor, our machine has been the object of countless trials and experiments under most unfavorable circumstances. If you treat the machine carefully, interruptions can scarcely take place, and, when occurring, easy to remove (see particular directions to be delivered with each machine.)

THE COMMERCIAL ENIGMA: BEGINNINGS OF MACHINE CRYPTOGRAPHY

Louis Kruh[1] and Cipher Deavours[2]

ADDRESS: (1) 17 Alfred Road West, Merrick NY 11566 USA (2) Department of Mathematics, Kean University of New Jersey, Union NJ 07083 USA.

ABSTRACT: A brief history and description of the first four models of the Enigma cipher machine, designed for the commercial market, taken in part from the authors' book [1].

KEYWORDS: Arthur Scherbius, ciphering typewriter, wired codewheel, rotors, *Umkehrwalze*, reflecting principle, Hugo Koch, Model A, Model B, Model C, Model D, ratchet wheel notch, wiring, *Chiffrienmaschinen AG*.

Within a three-year period, four inventors in four different countries came up with the idea of using a rotor or wired codewheel to scramble letters in a cipher machine. They were Edward H. Hebern, United States, 1917; Arthur Scherbius, Germany, 1918, Hugo Alexander Koch, Netherlands, 1919; Arvid Gerhard Damm, Sweden, 1919. None was financially successful but Scherbius, who called his machine Enigma, was responsible for introducing several models of what eventually became the best known cipher machine in the world.

In 1918, Scherbius, an electrical engineer, and E. Richard Ritter, a certified engineer, founded the firm of Scherbius and Ritter and tried to interest the Imperial German Navy in its cipher machine. The naval staff found the machine provided good security but felt that current traffic did not make it worthwhile. Following a suggestion from the naval staff, Scherbius approached the Foreign Office to consider it for diplomatic correspondence but there was no interest. Subsequently Scherbius and Ritter transferred the cipher patent rights to the Gewerkschaft Securitas. On July 9, 1923, Securitas founded the Chiffriermaschinen Aktien-Gesellschaft (Cipher Machines Stock Corporation). Scherbius and Ritter were on its board of directors.

The corporation promoted an early model of its cipher machine with a two-page flier. (Figure 1A and Figure 1B) It also exhibited the Enigma at the 1923 Congress of the International Postal Union in Bern, Switzerland. This was Model A of what was to be a long line of Enigma variations. The machine was heavy and

Die schreibende Enigma - Chiffriermaschine

Typenhebel – Elektrischer Antrieb

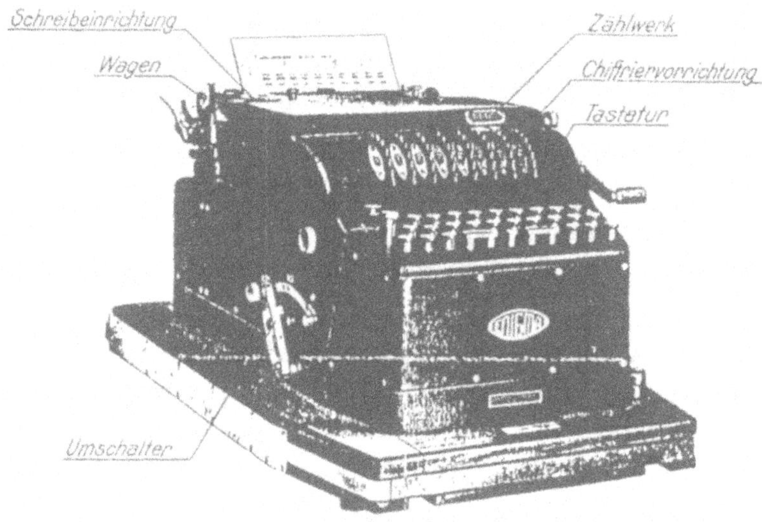

Unangreifbar in ihrer Chiffriersicherheit

Jeder Entzifferungsversuch Zeitverschwendung

Volle Geheimhaltung auch bei Uebermittlung
von Schlüsselwechseln in Klarschrift

17 576 Perioden / Jede Periode 15 777 450 Zeichen

In einer halben Minute
ist jeder der 277 304 461 200 Schlüssel eingestellt

Kein Teil wird zur Schlüsseländerung ausgetauscht

Figure 1A. First page of two page flier promoting Enigma.

bulky, bearing a standard typewriter keyboard for input. In fact, the machine could be used as a regular typewriter, even in the middle of ciphering text, if desired. Enigma A (Figure 3 and Figure 4) followed closely the original Scherbius patent in construction, and consisted of four rotors which were driven by four geared wheels. These four drive wheels each drove one rotor and were gapped in their number of teeth. They revolved in regular fashion with periods of 11, 15, 17, and 19. The 11th wheel had only five teeth with the other six positions being gaps. The 15th wheel had nine teeth and six gaps, while the 17th and 19th wheels each had 11 teeth with six and eight gaps, respectively.

English Translation of Figure 1A

The printing
Enigma Cipher Machine
Type Bar — Electrical Drive

[Captions on picture, left side]
Printing mechanism
Carriage
Switch
[Right side]
Counting register
Cipher mechanism
Keyboard

Unassailable in its cipher security
Every attempt at solution wastes times
Full secrecy even during cleartext transmission of key changes
17,576 periods / Each period 15,777,450 symbols
Any one of the 227,304,461,200 can be input in half a minute
No part will be exchanged during a key shift [language unclear]

Figure 2A. Translation of two page flier promoting Enigma. (Opposite) Figure 1A. Translator: David Kahn.

The rotor movement was quite irregular looking because rotors paused whenever they encountered a gapped sector of their wheels. For the sequence of rotor movements to repeat required $11 \cdot 15 \cdot 17 \cdot 19 = 53,295$ steps. However, the rotors will not have returned to their starting positions when the drive wheels have returned to their starting positions and so the period is generally much longer and depends on the exact placement of the gaps in the wheels. The number of initial settings for a given rotor was, clearly, $11 \cdot 15 \cdot 17 \cdot 19 \cdot 28^4$, because each rotor had 28 contacts. (The Enigma A had a 28-letter alphabet, which included three accented letters for the German language, but omitting one letter of the alphabet

Die schreibende Enigma

chiffriert **dechiffriert**	300 Zeichen in der Minute.
schreibt	auch Klarschrift.
teilt	das Chiffrat in Reihen von 50 und in Gruppen von 5 Buchstaben ein.
liefert	das Dechiffrat in **Ursprungsform** mit Buchstaben, Ziffern, Interpunktionszeichen, Wortabständen.
zählt	die Zeichen.
dechiffriert	alles richtig übermittelte, auch bei Lücken im Chiffrat.
verweigert	ihren Dienst, solange falsche Bedienung.
bedient man	nach einer Lehrzeit von 30 Minuten.

Abmessungen:			
	Länge	etwa	65 cm
	Breite	etwa	45 cm
	Höhe	etwa	38 cm
	Gewicht	etwa	50 kg

Chiffriermaschinen Aktiengesellschaft

Berlin W 35, Steglitzer Straße 2

Fernsprecher: B 3, Nollendorf 28 99

Figure 1B. Second page of two page flier promoting Enigma.

not often used in German.) The following year, Enigma A was exhibited at the 1924 International Postal Congress held in Stockholm, Sweden.

English Translation of Figure 1B

The Printing Enigma

Ciphers
300 symbols per minute
Deciphers

Prints cleartext as well

Divides the ciphertext into rows of 50 and groups of 5 letters

Delivers the plaintext in original form with letters, numbers, punctuation, word divisions

Counts all symbols

Deciphers everything if it is correctly transmitted, even if there are gaps in the ciphertext

Cannot be operated if improperly used

Can be used after 30 minutes instruction

Dimensions:
Length about 65 cm
Width about 45 cm
Height about 35 cm
Weight about 50 kg

Cipher Machine Inc.
Berlin W35, Steglitzer Strasse 2
Telephone: B 3, Nollendorf 2899

Figure 2B. Translation of two page flier promoting Enigma.
(Opposite) Figure 1B. Translator: David Kahn.

While Enigma A was not a great financial success despite the publicity it attracted, the company soon had three other models: B, C, and D. Model B (Figure 5) was of similar construction to Model A, but had the usual 26-contact rotors. Models C and D were portable and cryptographically unlike the A and B versions of the machine. Both machines had four 26-contact rotors but the fourth rotor, or *Umkehrwalze*, was, in effect, a "half" rotor. This "reflecting" rotor caused current entering it to be turned back through the three previous rotors along a different path from that taken upon entry. As one faced the machine, the reflecting rotor was on the left with the entrance rotor on the right. If we denote the rotors R, I, II, III, then the enciphering current traversed the rotors in the order III, II, I, R, I, II, III. The reflecting principle was invented by Hugo Koch, and meant that, at any rotor setting, if a given letter, let us say A is enciphered into W, then W must also encipher into A. This means that each cipher alphabet generated by the machine is reciprocal. Additionally, no letter could represent itself because the reflected rotor path could never intersect the direct path. Because of the reflection process, no deciphering switch was necessary on the machine. One had only to arrange the rotors in the same order and starting position as used in encipherment and then type the ciphertext letters to recover the plaintext as glow-lamps indicated the results.

Figure 3. Model A.

The enciphering equation of this commercial Enigma is:

$$pKC(i)WC(-i)C(j)VC(-j)C(k)UC(-k)RC(k)U^{-1}C(-k)C(j)V^{-1}C(-j)C(i)W^{-1}C(-i)K^{-1} = c$$

where R denotes the reflecting rotor, and U, V, W are the other three rotors viewed facing the machine. K was the standard A-Z sequence, or identity transformation in Model C, while on Model D it was the keyboard permutation which was based on the standard German typewriter keyboard of that day, namely:

```
INPUT:   Q W E R T Z U I O A S D F G H J K P Y X C V B N M L
OUTPUT:  A B C D E F G H I J K L M N O P Q R S T U V W X Y Z
```

Figure 4. Model A with face plate removed.

Although Model C (Figure 6) and Model D (Figures 8 and 9) resembled one another, there were some minor differences. The reflecting rotor in Enigma C (Figure 7) could not be set and was confined to one of two possible positions in the machine. Additionally, the keyboard and glow-lamps were set up in the traditional A-Z sequence. The reflecting rotor of Model D (Figure 8) could be set, but did not move during encipherment. In both models, the fast rotor was the right-most one, the medium rotor to the left of the fast one, and the slow rotor to the left of the medium one. The ratchet wheels on the Enigma were built into the rotors instead of being separate, which gave rise to some anomalies in rotor movement.

Figure 5. Model B (Top view).

When the ratchet wheel notch on the fast rotor reached a certain point in its revolution, a pawl drove the medium rotor one step forward. When the ratchet wheel notch on the medium rotor reached a certain point, the slow rotor was moved similarly. However, whenever the slow rotor stepped, the medium rotor also stepped because of the mechanical construction. Thus, at certain positions, the medium rotor could take two steps in succession. Therefore, the potentially maximum cycle length of $26^3 = 17,576$ was not obtained. The basic cycle was of length $26 \cdot 25 \cdot 26 = 16,900$. Because one could obviously set the three right rotors in any one of 26^3 positions, then there must be some rotor starting positions that had no predecessors as well as some, which had more than one possible predecessor. It should be noted that the patent for this machine made provision for multi-notched rotors.

To facilitate the initial setting of the rotors, each had an "alphabet ring" bearing either the standard A-Z alphabet or the numbers 1-26. The alphabet rings could be rotated with respect to the body of the coding cylinder; thus, the ring setting was a part of the machine's key. The ratchet notch on each rotor was rigidly attached to the body of the coding cylinder in this version of the Enigma. The rotors were removable and interchangeable (except for the reversing rotor, which was always placed on the left).

Figure 6. Model C.

After a short time, Enigma C became extinct with the D model becoming the widely sold commercial version of the device. Chiffrienmaschinen AG produced well-written documentation for their machines. The lengthy sales pamphlet, which accompanied the machine, described the need for cryptography, the extreme ease of use of the machine, and the amount of text, about 30 typewritten pages, which could be safely enciphered at one key setting. Additionally, methods of forming keys and secretly transmitting them in the ciphertext were illustrated. Strangely enough, the one short example of plain/cipher text given was bogus. The company had its "ciphering typewriter" examined by foreign experts in the field and salesmen were provided with favorable reviews to use in sales promotion. For example, after a two month test of the Enigma, a Captain Henri Koot, Dutch Army cryptologic expert, wrote,"I dare say that it satisfies all requirements, be they ever so high even the possession of an equal machine with the same electrical connections both in the ciphering cylinders and in the other parts of the machine will not enable an unauthorized person to find out its solution."

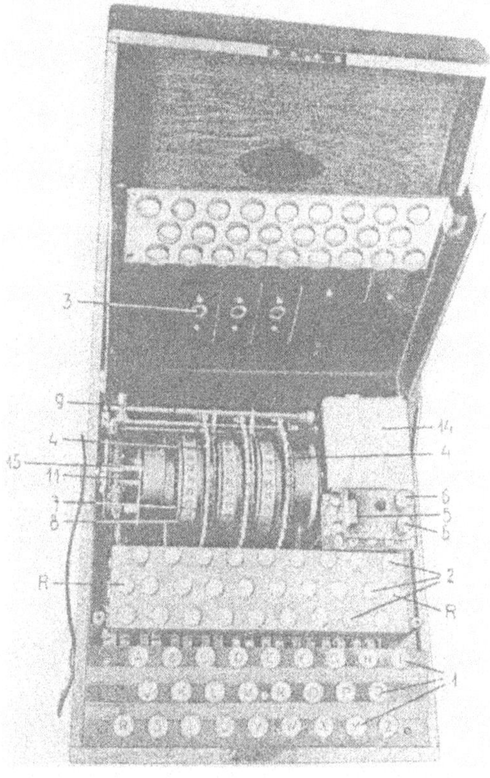

Figure 7. Model C with inner lid open.

The wiring used in the commercial Enigma D was as follows:

	0	2	2	2	2	2	2	2	1	1	1	1	1	1	1	1	1	1	0	0	0	0	0	0	0	0
CONTACT:	1	6	5	4	3	2	1	0	9	8	7	6	5	4	3	2	1	0	9	8	7	6	5	4	3	2
INPUT:	A	B	C	D	E	F	G	H	I	J	K	L	M	N	O	P	Q	R	S	T	U	V	W	X	Y	Z
STATOR:	J	W	U	L	C	M	N	O	H	P	Q	Z	Y	X	I	R	A	D	K	E	G	V	B	T	S	F
ROTOR 1:	L	P	G	S	Z	M	H	A	E	O	Q	K	V	X	R	F	Y	B	U	T	N	I	C	J	D	W
ROTOR 2:	S	L	V	G	B	T	F	X	J	Q	O	H	E	W	I	R	Z	Y	A	M	K	P	C	N	D	U
ROTOR 3:	C	J	G	D	P	S	H	K	T	U	R	A	W	Z	X	F	M	Y	N	Q	O	B	V	L	I	E
REVERSE:	I	M	E	T	C	F	G	R	A	Y	S	Q	B	Z	X	W	L	H	K	P	V	U	P	O	J	N

The contact numbers are printed on the coding cylinder bodies. The wiring given here is read when the alphabet ring on each rotor is placed so that the letter A corresponds to contact point 1. Each coding cylinder body had its ratchet notch at contact position 21 (G) and caused movement when contact 2 (Z) appeared in the setting window. Thus, with the alphabet rings set as above, successive rotor positions would be:

```
W Z Y X
W Z Y Z
W Z Z A
W A A B
W A A C
W A A D
```

A number of governments bought Enigmas for study. Among the interested parties was the German Navy, which in 1925 decided to put an Enigma machine into use the following year. The first Naval Enigmas had 29-contact rotors (included ä ö ü in German, x was left unchanged) and used three rotors chosen from a set of nine. Possibly, certain other modifications may have been made to the Navy machine.

The Italian Navy adopted the commercial Enigma as Naval Cipher D. Studies based on matching cipher and plain text indicate that the Naval machine was rewired as might be expected. The British solution of this Enigma variation largely led to the Italian defeat at the battle of Matapan.

The German army, which previously had been considering adoption of the Enigma, now undertook to redesign and strengthen the machine's ciphers. By 1928, early models of the redesigned *Wehrmacht* machine, denoted model G, were in use, and in June 1930, the final "revised standard" version of the device, Enigma I came into use by the Army.

Enigma I was distinguished from the commercial Enigma by the following changes:

1. The reflecting rotor was made static and greatly reduced in size to save money.
2. The rotatable alphabet rings were retained, but the stepping ratchet notch was rigidly affixed to this ring instead of the coding cylinder body.
3. A plug-board was inserted into the front of the machine whose 26 plug-holes could be connected in pairs by plugs. The earliest such plugs, (*Stöpselstellung*) were later replaced by double-ended banana style ones (*Steckerverbindung*). The plugs functioned the same way, however, in both constructions. The plug-board introduced a variable reciprocal permutation

Figure 8. I (above) Model D and II (below) Model D with lid removed.

Illustration	I, 11:	1. Key-board.
"	I, II:	2. Glow lamp board.
"	I:	3. Windows.
"	I, II:	4. Ciphering cylinders (rollers).
"	I, II:	5. Switch-handle.
"	I, II:	6. Connecting terminals for accumulator working.
"	II:	7. Spring for adjusting the letter-ring.
"	II:	8. Letter-ring.
"	II:	9. Lever.
"	II:	11. Reversing cylinder.
"	II:	12. Lid screws.
"	II:	14. Dry battery.
"	II:	15. Guide pin.
"	II:	R. Spare-lamps.

(Opposite) Explanation of the Figures 8 I & II

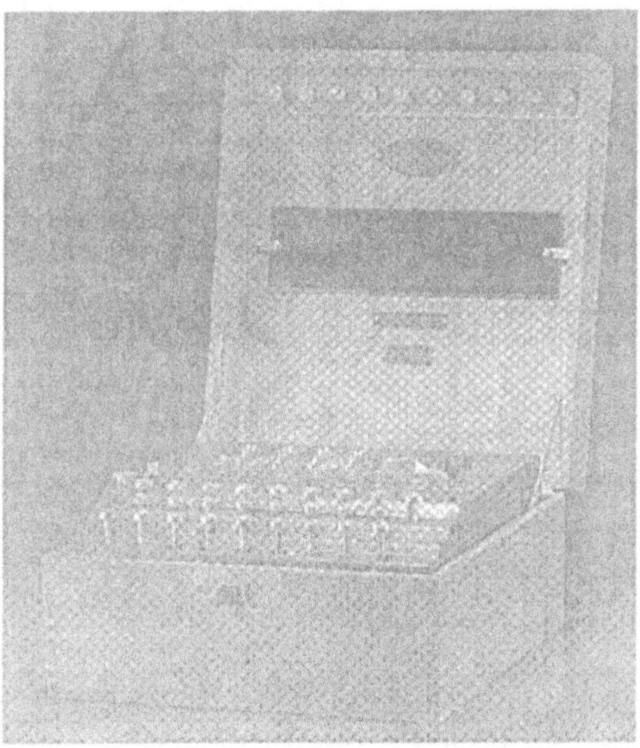

Figure 9. Model D "Enigma enciphering machine" was sold at auction in London, 12 April 2001, for $15,220. Illustration downloaded from Christies' (auctioneer) web site.

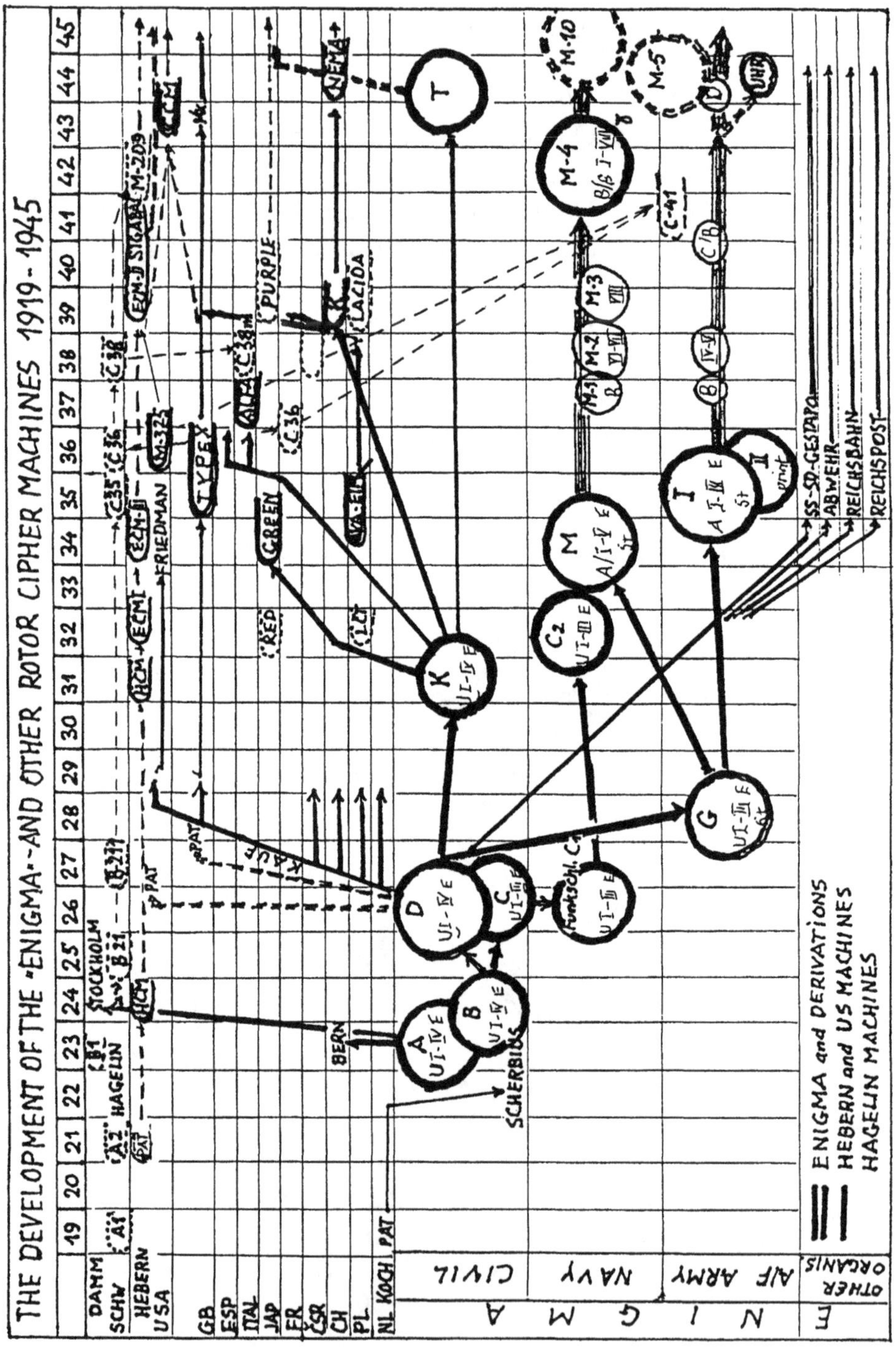

Figure 10. Evolution of the Enigma Cipher Machine.
Diagram created by Jürgen Rohwer.

between the keyboard and the fast rotor, and the inverse permutation between the fast rotor exit point and the lamp-board. (The reciprocal encipherment was retained in this manner.)

4. The keyboard entrance permutation was changed from that of the standard typewriter to the identity permutation, A=A, B=B, et cetera. (The arrangement of letters in the keyboard was unaltered, however.)

This model of the Enigma became the most widespread of the ensuing Enigma variations, used by the German Navy beginning in October 1934 and the Air Force beginning in August 1935.

In 1974, when the British revealed *The Ultra Secret*, the world became aware of the German Enigma Cipher Machine and the vital role it played in World War II. It also learned how breaking Germany's most important cipher system helped in its defeat and shortened the War by at least one and possibly two years, according to some authorities. Since then, hundreds of books, newspaper and magazine articles, television programs, major motion pictures and even a Broadway play have made the Enigma the most widely known cipher machine in the world. On April 12, 2001, a Model D Enigma was sold at auction in London for $15,220. Few people, however, are aware that the machine was initially rejected by Germany and Arthur Scherbius, after developing four different Enigma models, was still a failure in his efforts to convince business people that: "One secret, well protected, may pay the entire cost of the machine."[1]

ACKNOWLEDGMENTS

A special note of thanks to David Kahn for his suggestions for improving the text.

Our deep appreciation to Jürgen Rohwer who graciously allowed us to use a new version of his chart, which illustrates the evolution of the German Enigma and some other rotor cipher machines.

REFERENCES

1. Deavours, Cipher A., and Louis Kruh. 1985. *Machine Cryptography and Modern Cryptanalysis*. Dedham MA: Artech House.

2. Garlinski, Józef. *The Enigma War*. New York: Charles Scribner's Sons, 1979.

[1]The Glow-Lamp Ciphering and Deciphering Machine: Enigma. *Cryptologia*, 25(3): 163–174. This article is a reprint of the original , mid-1920's, sales brochure for the Enigma.

3. Kahn, David . 1991. *Seizing the Enigma: The Race to Break the German U-Boat Codes, 1939-1943*. Boston: Houghton Mifflin.

4. Kahn, David. 1996. *The Codebreakers: The Story of Secret Writing. Revised ed.* New York: Scribner.

5. Kozaczuk, Wladyslaw. 1984. *Enigma: How the German Machine Cipher Was Broken and How it Was Read by the Allies in World War Two*. Frederick MD: University Publications of America.

6. Rohwer, Jürgen and Eberhard Jäckel. 1979. *Die Funkaufklarung und ihre Rolle im Zweiten Weltkrieg*. Stuttgart: Motorbuch Verlag.

7. Singh, Simon. 1999. *The Code Book: The Evolution of Secrecy from Mary Queen of Scots to Quantum Cryptography*. New York: Doubleday.

8. Türkel, Siegfried. 1927. *Chiffrieren Mit Geráten und Maschinen*. Graz: Ulr. Mosers Buchhandlung.

BIOGRAPHICAL SKETCHES

Louis Kruh, a founding co-editor of *Cryptologia* and co-author of *Machine Cryptography and modern Cryptanalysis*, has an enormous collection of cryptologic items amassed over 40 plus years. This collection supplied most of the illustrations for this article and, between writing reviews and articles for *Cryptologia*, he is trying to compile a computerized list of his holdings.

C. A. Deavours, a founding co-editor of *Cryptologia* and co-author of *Machine Cryptography and modern Cryptanalysis*, is a faculty member teaching mathematics and computer science at Kean University of New Jersy in Union NJ. Professor Deavours has a distinguished career of consulting, cipher busting, crypto teaching, and computer connecting. His most recent interest is web-based learning and keeping the university's web radio station, WKNJ Internet Radio, on air.

HOW STATISTICS LED THE GERMANS TO BELIEVE ENIGMA SECURE AND WHY THEY WERE WRONG: NEGLECTING THE PRACTICAL MATHEMATICS OF CIPHER MACHINES

R. A. Ratcliff

ADDRESS: 1046 Eden Bower Lane, Redwood City CA 94061 USA. cliffrat@hotmail.com.

ABSTRACT: Only in 1974 did German intelligence and cryptologists admit that the Enigma cipher machine was not, and had not been, a secure system. Throughout World War II, German experts relied on a theoretical statistical security that took neither wartime operational reality nor their opponents' years of attention and attack into account. They ignored the far more important operational weaknesses and human errors that actually provided enemy cryptanalysts with their most valuable entries into the cipher system.

KEYWORDS: World War II, Enigma, Ultra, signal intelligence, signal security, operational security, stastistics, German military intelligence, *Wehrmacht*, machine ciphers, cryptanalysis, cribs, key repeats, re-encodements.

> "[W]e believe that the enigma cannot be solved... Enigma when used according to instructions is unbreakable. It might be broken if a vast Hollerith [punch card machine] complex is used but this is only slightly possible."
>
> Dr. Erich Hüttenhain, cryptologist, Cipher Bureau of the German High Command (Chi/OKW), in post-war interrogations.[1]

German intelligence officers ended World War II certain of one thing: Enigma machine ciphers had kept their communications secure. After the war, Allied officers interrogated German cipher machine operators, cipher experts and military officers in countless conversations and written homework. Over and over German intelligence officers and cryptologic experts repeated their confidence in

[1]National Archives and Record Agency: Record Group 457 Historic Cryptographic Collection Box 1006 NR 3142 - Statements by POWs re: Work on American and British Systems, p. 5.

the Enigma machine's security. They had, after all, conducted numerous investigations of their cipher systems' security. A quarter century later, Heinz Bonatz, wartime head of the *Kreigsmarine* [German navy] intelligence division, wrote

> ...the Enigma Cipher Machine M was secure against break-in and the German naval radio signals could not be read.[2]

Then in 1974, F. W. Winterbotham's book, *The Ultra Secret*, revealed that the Allies had read Enigma ciphers throughout the war. Bonatz and other intelligence officers had to admit, finally, that Enigma was not, and had not been, a secure system. In the rush of works that followed, the Germans learned that Enigma had been compromised almost from its adoption by the *Heer* [Army] in 1928 - the Polish mathematician Marian Rejewski had made the first break into the machine in 1932.

Gradually a remarkable - and now familiar - story emerged, revealing the Allied development and use of intelligence based on decrypts of Enigma material. The success of this Allied decryption effort raises questions about German intelligence and security. Why did the Germans believe Enigma secure? Why did they not realize - through the course of the war and in the following decades - that their entire system had been compromised and inadequate?

In fact, the Enigma machine itself was neither inadequate nor insecure. Used correctly and judiciously, an Enigma will challenge even today's computers. Allied cryptanalysts themselves said during the war "that the Enigma machine, if properly handled, is unbreakable by any known methods."[3] The Germans were right - in theory.

The theoretical mathematical possibilities[4] made the cryptologic system formidable indeed, although the physical development of Enigma created many restrictive mechanical elements that reduced the actual number of possible permutations. Even this mechanical hardwiring did not prove the undoing of the Enigma machine's security. In the end, Enigma succumbed because of the humans who operated the machine.

Enigma's Theoretical Strength

Enigma's strength comes in part from the "astounding number" of possible encipherments for each letter. The three-rotor Enigma used by the *Heer* [Army] and

[2]Captain Heinz Bonatz, *Die Deutsche Marine Funkaufklärung* (Darmstadt: Wehr & Wissen, 1970), 86-87.

[3]NARA: RG 457 HCC Box 880 NR 2612 - Captain Walter J. Fried Reports, Hut 6 weekly report 14 October 44, p. 2, quoting British cryptanalyst Stuart Milner-Barry.

[4]For the following mathematical formulae, I, a nonmathematician, am indebted to Ray Miller of the NSA and his pamphlet, "The Cryptographic Mathematics of Enigma" (Fort Meade, MD: NSA, n.d.).

Luftwaffe [Air Force] theoretically had approximately 3×10^{114} possible configurations for each day's setting. Mathematicians derived this number for possible settings from the Enigma's five primary variables. The variables include the rotors' internal wiring, their *Ringstellungen* (ring settings), their initial positions, the *Stecker*board (or plugboard) and the reflector rotor. The equations for each of these variables can be found in the National Security Agency pamphlet on Enigma.[5] Even today 3×10^{114} is an unbelievable number, a number beyond comprehension. For comparison, some scientists estimate that there are only about 10^{80} atoms in the entire observable universe. Such a truly astronomical number lends credence to the confidence that German cryptographers had in their machine.[6]

THE ENIGMA REALITY

Theory, however, rarely translates directly to practice. As with other cipher machines (notably the Japanese "Purple"), or indeed any crypto-system, practical use limited the theoretical security of the original design.

Enigma's physical manifestation lowered the theoretical numbers primarily in two ways: by the hardwiring of some possibilities into the machine and by operational limits.

The Hardwiring Limitations

The three-rotor Enigma originally had only three rotors, but by the time the war began it had five to choose from. This hardwiring of the rotors and limiting of the number of rotors available dramatically reduced the number of possible wirings.

In fact the Poles had reconstructed the wiring of the original three rotors shortly after their first break into the machine, and eventually the Allies learned the wiring of all the later rotors. Since they knew the wirings of all five existing rotors for the basic machine, the Allies and their equipment did not have to search for each one of the 26! possible wirings for each rotor. They had only to consider five possible rotors.

Moreover, since each Enigma came with a single set of five rotors (numbered I through V), the operator could use only one of each rotor at a time (eliminating settings such as "II II II"). So the Allies had only to check which three of the five possible rotors were being used, and in which order. ($5 \times 4 \times 3 = 60$). (Note that when the Polish team tackled Enigma between 1930 and 1932, the machine

[5]See Miller, passim, and also the description of and the calculations for such substitution alphabets in David Kahn's *The Codebreakers* (New York: Scribner, 1996), 136ff, 145.

[6]Miller, 11.

had only 3 rotors, which meant only ($3 \times 2 \times 1 = 6$) possible positions for the three rotors.) Nor could either the rotors or their notches be reversed. They fit into the machine in one direction only.

In addition to these five interchangeable rotors, all Enigmas had the *Umkehrwalze* [reflector rotor]. Although the *Umkehrwalze* could be removed from the machine and replaced as the other rotors were, in practice most machines held the same rotor all the time. The number of these rotors remained very small through the war. Only the pluggable *Umkehrwalze*, nicknamed *Umkehrwalze* Dora or Uncle D, began to exploit the full potential of reflector rotors. Uncle D could literally be re-plugged on the spot. It could have had the effect of creating multiple reflector rotors and so increased the machine's possible combinations well over 100 million-fold.[7]

The "pluggable" reflector rotor terrified the Allied cryptanalysts working against Enigma at Bletchley Park. It appeared in *Heer* and *Luftwaffe* Enigma nets late in the war. However, the military commands did not introduce the new rotor uniformly. Several units did not receive the rotor on time, so virtually identical messages went out in both the Uncle D and the regular settings, allowing Bletchley Park to figure out methods for reconstructing Uncle D's changing wiring. Eventually enough Enigma operators had difficulty with the pluggable rotors that the military virtually halted its adoption of the new versatile reflector.

Enigma had one more flaw in the design of its rotors, which does not play a role in these statistical figures, but nonetheless made the machine easier to break: the regular stepping of all the rotors. Enigma's rotors all had a metric or quasi-metric stepping - i.e. they stepped in one direction, one step at a time, the way an automobile odometer does. Enigma rotors only moved forward, they did not move backward. This regularity assisted the Allies when they turned to regular reading of German messages. Once in possession of the setting for one section, a cryptanalyst had only to count the letters and he knew the rotors had moved that same number of steps. This highly regular progression meant that a break into any one part of a message almost inevitably led the cryptanalyst to a successful reading of the entire message.

Multiple notches in a rotor, however, did change the pattern of the next rotor to the left. With the extra notches, the slower rotors moved more frequently than every 26 clicks of the fast rotor. However, these extra notches would not turn out to be much of an advantage because of another idiosyncrasy of the physical implementation. The actual Enigma turns out to have had a limitation that cryptologists would not have calculated. After 26 rotations of the second or medium rotor, all the rotors were lined up to rotate over on the next letter - the

[7]Miller, 10-11, 15.

notch on the first rotor to turn the second, the notch on the second (middle) rotor to turn the third. On the next letter all three rotors rotated together, a movement nicknamed "lobster" by the British.[8] With this triple rollover, however, the fast rotor did a two-step, moving two positions instead of one. Cryptanalysts nicknamed this two-step the "Click process".

This double progression of the fast rotor reduces the rotors' period by one rotation, from the theoretical number of 17,576 to 16,900. When the *Heer* and *Luftwaffe* introduced double notched rotors, the click process occurred more frequently. In the worst-case scenario - both fast and medium rotors having two notches - the period for the rotors to return to their initial setting dropped to 16,224.

Finally, Enigma included an anomaly that completely undermined the goal of randomness in encipherment: no letter could ever be enciphered as itself. Originally the Germans had included this impossibility of self-encipherment to simplify the machine's reciprocity; that is, its ability to turn enciphered messages back into plain text. However, this restriction opened the door to standard codebreaking techniques. Once the Allies learned that self-encipherment could be ruled out, they realized that wherever 'e' appeared in a signal, the plain text would *not* contain an 'e'.[9] This detail allowed the Allies to use letter frequency rules in reverse and exploit mechanical means of eliminating possible rotor settings that produced self-encipherment for any one letter. Once again the restrictions of the physical Enigma had produced unintended openings for its compromise.

These hardwiring and mechanical limitations of the physical machine reduced the theoretical security of Enigma somewhat. Yet these realities did not prove the ultimate downfall of the machine. The numbers of possible combinations remained daunting in the precomputer age and the Germans were content with numbers far smaller than the 3×10^{114} theory. Although the limitations of the physical Enigma - particularly the earliest machines - did assist the Poles and the British in their successful attack, they did not ensure Enigma's compromise. Far more limiting than the physical factors was the way in which the Germans operated Enigma. In the end, the weakness of Enigma came not from the machine's limitations, but from its operation.

[8]See David Kahn's description of the 'crab' and the 'lobster', *Seizing the Enigma* (Boston: Houghton Mifflin, 1991), 112.

[9]See one story of how this characteristic led to a complete reconstruction of an Italian Enigma key. Kahn, *Seizing the Enigma*, 139.

The Operational Limitations[10]

The types of limitation that German operating procedures created varied. Several of the restrictions simply made the lives of Bletchley Park's cryptanalysts slightly easier, whereas others doomed the security of the machine completely. For example, the restrictions placed on the *Stecker*board diminished its complication. First, as the calculations show, the *Stecker*s substituted letters only in pairs. Secondly, the Enigma variations did not use *Stecker* pairs randomly, but according to precise rules. In the *Heer*, the cryptologic staff's theoretical examination of the Enigma determined that 10 pairings of *Stecker*s produced the optimal number of variations.[11] So 10 and only 10, neither more nor fewer, were used every day. (Here, in fact, the Germans made an additional mistake. The number of *Stecker* pairings that created the greatest number of variations was not 10, but 11. With 11 pairs of *Stecker*s, the number of combinations rose to 205,552,193,096,250, whereas 10 pairs created 150,738,274,937,250.[12])

Many nets took the additional step of eliminating any *Stecker* combinations that connected sequential letters, such as a *Stecker* linking a to b or x to y. The Allies took advantage of this rule and created the CSKO - Consecutive *Stecker* Knock Out jack - which ruled out any Enigma setting that included *Stecker*s in consecutive letters.[13] Thus the formidable *Stecker*board lost some of its complexity and the number of *Stecker* combinations fell to one-third of the possible theoretical combinations.

In its operational form, the reflector rotor completely lost its potential. German nets, with few exceptions, used only one reflector rotor, so it became a constant, rather than an additional daily variable, for Allied cryptanalysts. Since the Allies knew the wiring of the reflector rotor by 1940, its contribution to Enigma's overall equation reduces to 1.

With these operational restrictions, the number of possible configurations for the three-rotor Enigma machine decreased significantly. By restricting the *Stecker* pairings, not changing reflector rotors, and creating only a very limited number of rotors, the Germans eased the enemy cryptanalyst's task. In particular, once the Allies reconstructed the rotor wirings, the number of possible combinations became far less formidable.

---

[10]For many of the following points I am indebted to conversations with Steve Kelly and Steve Budiansky. See Stephen J. Kelly, *Big Machines* (Laguna Hills, CA: Aegean Park Press, 2001).

[11]NARA: RG 457 HCC Box 1407 NR 4541 - Codes and Ciphers: Germany German Cryptanalytic Documents - "*Aktennotiz 6 zum Chiffrierverfahren mit der Enigmamaschine.*" 30 July 1940, p. 4; and Ibid., "*Aktennotiz 5 ...*" passim.

[12]See the calculations in Miller, 9.

[13]NARA: RG 457 HCC Box 1283 NR 3814 - Decoding German Enigma Machine Messages, p. 34.

Possible wiring of the rotors (known to the Allies, so simply the choice and position of 3 of 5 rotors) (when naval operators could choose from 8 rotors, this number grew to 366)	60
Possible settings for the *Ringstellungen* (again, with a possible 3 of 8 rotors, the number rose to 476,976)	676
Possible initial positions for the rotors	17,576
*Stecker*board possibilities	150,738,274,937,250
Reflector wiring possibility (known and generally unchanging)	1
The product of these numbers is:	1×10^{23}

Enigma 3-Rotor Reality

Although by no means the astronomical number of the theoretical version, this number meant the Allies were still faced with a daunting prospect.[14] Indeed, the Germans would still have considered 1×10^{23} a formidable wall against cryptanalytic attack.

Before the war, cryptanalysis had little in the way of mechanization and most of the German mechanization consisted of punch card cataloguing and sorting. Under these circumstances, even the reduced number of Enigma permutations seemed close enough to infinity in those pre-digital computer days. Even with IBM or Hollerith machine sorting capabilities, sifting through raw messages looking for repeats among these numbers of possibilities would have taken an enormous amount of time. Had the Allies been forced to try all of these possible combinations every day, they would have rarely, if ever, read any Enigma messages in time to influence the war. The Germans were correct in their belief that the hardwired version of the Enigma could stymie a cryptanalyst using the latest in punch card and similar mechanical sorting assistance.

They failed, however, to consider electromechanical capabilities. Although their own Enigma encryption system used electromechanics, they did not apply the same level of technology to cryptanalysis. They did not actively investigate how machines could be used in cryptanalysis beyond statistical counting and sorting. In particular, they apparently never considered using Enigma against itself. Yet the Polish mathematicians did so, successfully, in the early 1930s. German experts found mechanized solving only a remote possibility, "even though the fancy of some analysts had been occupied with this idea."[15] In a formerly

[14] Miller, 13.

[15] NSA Museum collection: DF 187A (*Wehrmacht* cryptanalyst chief Wilhelm Fenner), 27.

top secret, post war list comparing Allied and German rapid analytic machinery in cryptanalysis, numerous Allied machines have no German equivalent. German cryptologists imbued their mechanical ciphers with great prowess, yet they did not much consider the potential of mechanical decipherment. They did not expect Enigma to face machines of its own caliber.

The Human Factor

Most important of all, the Germans did not fully reckon with that most vital factor of cryptology: human error. The greatest damage to Enigma's security came from the humans operating the machines, particularly those in the *Heer* and *Luftwaffe*. Lazy cipher clerks and tired, bored or homesick Enigma operators kept producing vulnerabilities for the Allies to break into the daily keys. These entry points arose from three major types of errors: key repeats, re-encipherments (called re-encodements at Bletchley Park), and stereotyped phrases.

Code clerks created key repeats by reusing part or all of a daily key. The basic daily key had four elements: 1) the choice and order of the rotors, 2) the *Ringstellung* or position of the rotor notches, 3) the placement of the *Stecker*s, and 4) the discriminants, that is, the letters telling the cipher clerk which net or type of Enigma traffic the message was.[16] Clerks creating a net's monthly books of daily settings often reused one or two of the pieces from another net's codebook. The Allies soon found that patterns in the Enigma key's daily setup traveled from net to net predictably. The month's worth of discriminants and rotor orders from one net would appear the next month in a different net, while the *Ringstellungen* and *Stecker* settings surfaced on a third net. The next month the same pieces of the daily key would be shuffled again and redistributed through the same signal nets, giving the cryptanalysts at Bletchley Park an easier entry into all of the connected nets.

One example (see Figure 1) had pieces traveling through four nets in what the British nicknamed a "quadrilateral."[17]

Portions of the Primrose net's monthly setting would appear the next month in each of the other three nets. The third month each piece would move to yet

[16]Each cipher key connected a specific group of planes, U-boats, or units in a network. Each network had two names, one German and one British; thus the U-boat key in the North Atlantic was known as 'Triton' to the Germans and 'Shark' to Bletchley Park. [see NARA: Microcopy T-1022 (German Navy records 1850-1945) Roll 2310.]

[17]NARA: RG 457 HCC Box 1126 NR 3620 - E Operations of the GC&CS at Bletchley Park, p. 40. BP grouped code names in categories: main *Luftwaffe* codes were colors (Red, Blue, etc); Weather codes were vegetables, such as Leek, Garlic; *Heer* codes were birds (Sparrow, Falcon), the S. S. fruit (Orange, Quince), and the Baudot ciphers were "Fish" (Tunney and Sturgeon). See one list of names in Box 1009 NR 3175 - Cryptanalytic Report on Yellow Machine, p. 10.

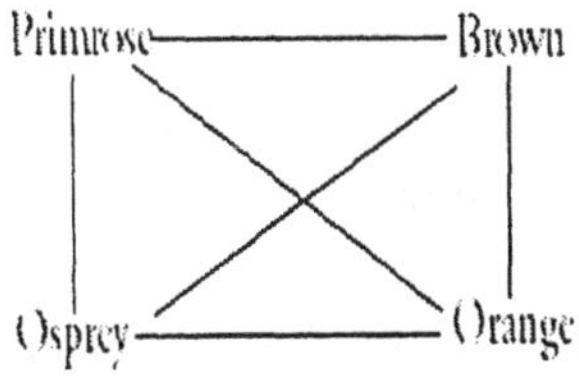

Figure 1. The "quadrilateral" of four nets.

another net in the square. This constant shifting meant that each piece of the daily key would be used four times over four months, so the clerk charged with creating months of daily settings could save himself considerable mental effort.

This quadrilateral of shared key pieces was not unique. In an unrelated *Luftwaffe* arena, Bletchley's cryptanalysts found that a clerk had fallen into a similar habit of repeating pieces of the daily setting among a set of four signal groups (Bletchley had named them Mosquito, Leek, Cockroach and Cabbage). As such repeats rotated, Bletchley cryptanalysts could break into all four networks. Once they recognized a pattern, the cryptanalysts would know at least a portion of the daily key by the time the day's messages began to arrive.

Such key repeats proved blatantly disastrous to Enigma because they reduced or even eliminated the cryptanalytic work that the Allies and their machines did to read a day's messages. If the cryptanalysts at Bletchley Park knew the day's setting, they simply set up their own Enigma machines,[18] and began typing in the cipher text; the machines produced plain text just as they would have for the German cipher clerk intended as the recipient.

Two other major errors - re-encipherments and stereotyped phrases - gave the Allies another way to break into the day's signals: cribs. Cribs occur when a cryptanalyst either knows or can guess the wording of the message's plaintext. With that wording, the cryptanalyst can work backwards to uncover the daily key and - daily key in hand - can begin reading all the other messages sent that day on that same net.

The Allies generally discovered such cribs by following the habits of cipher clerks and their superiors. The re-encipherments occurred when clerks made the serious mistake of repeating the same message virtually verbatim in more than one cipher. As in any military, the Germans needed to send the same information to different sections of its forces. Many clerks found the routine messages tedious and the cryptographic regulations unimportant, so they enciphered them without

[18]The first Enigmas the Allies had were reconstructions built by the Polish team before the war. Later the British modified their own cipher machine, the Typex, to mimic the Enigma. See Wladyslaw Kozaczuk, *Enigma* (Frederick, MD: University Publications of America, Inc., 1984) and Peter Calvocoressi, *Top Secret ULTRA* (New York: Pantheon Books, 1980).

changing the wording significantly. Sometimes they did not paraphrase at all and the message was repeated from one net to the next without a single change except the address. These repeated messages opened a door from the more easily broken net to a more difficult one.

At times the re-encipherment came from unexpected sources. For example, the Germany military espionage division, the Abwehr, produced some useful re-encipherments. A certain Oberinspektor Menzer served as the Abwehr expert in charge of vetting ciphers and security procedures. Concerned about security lapses, he sent word of a procedural upgrade to all the Abwehr stations throughout Europe. From Bletchley's point of view, his message provided the perfect re-encipherment, and as each Enigma operator dutifully repeated Menzer's warning and upgrade from one site to the next, the cryptanalysts pried their way into "several links hitherto unbroken."[19]

Because the Allies recognized operators and stations that frequently practiced these sloppy re-encipherments, they would often break one message, see that it mirrored another message of similar length, assume the plaintext to be the same, and discover a crib. With such a clear series of re-encipherments as those of Oberinspektor Menzer, they could uncover the day's setting for one or more new ciphers and thus break into another net for the day, which might in turn lead to more breaks in the future. Although the Germans periodically issued warnings against reciphering without significant paraphrasing, their threats usually did not leave a lasting impression and the re-encipherments quickly reappeared.

These two errors - key repeats and re-encipherments - often linked different sections of the *Wehrmacht* together in regular patterns. Allied cryptanalysts soon found the many *Heer* keys of the Mediterranean intertwined so tightly that they essentially formed a single cryptologic problem. Once one key succumbed to the day's attack, the rest of the *Heer*'s Mediterranean nets usually followed quickly.[20]

The third major operational error that gave Bletchley Park's cryptanalysts considerable assistance arose from phrases that frequently appeared with precisely the same or very similar wording. These stereotyped phrases would reappear in signals traveling between the same stations on a regular, often a daily, basis. Of course, all military dispatches tend to follow a predictable pattern and the German military proved no exception. Message openings often gave cryptanalysts an excellent starting point, e. g. *An Fliegerfuehrer Afrika Korps*. Many German addresses provided cribs of so many letters that enemy cryptanalysts could break some nets simply on them.

[19]NARA: RG 457 HCC Box 880 NR 2612 - Capt. Walter J. Fried Reports/SSA Liaison with GCCS, p. 4

[20]Public Record Office (Kew, England): HW 14/62 - "Appreciation of the "E" Situation" Dec 42, p. 10.

Other breaks came from daily reports signaled by far flung stations. Reports from some operators became very predictable - to the point where British cryptanalysts wanted certain stations left intact by the advancing Allies as long as possible. The predictable patterns emerged when operators followed standard reporting formats, such as the operator in Czechoslovakia who regularly reported the number of "wine barrels on hand." Sometimes the conditions being reported simply did not vary much and the operators became accustomed to using exactly the same wording every day. An obliging operator in France, for example, always signaled the presence of enemy aircraft, telling his superiors "RAF plane over airport." A polite signaler in Norway began his daily messages with "Good morning," whereas one lone operator in the North African theatre signaled the same situation report every morning, saying "Quiet night."[21] These regular, mundane operational habits provided the British with an end run around Enigma's complex calculations. The familiar patterns of German clerks and signalers did more damage to the cipher system's security than any flaw produced by the hardwiring of the machine.

The Illusion of Statistical Security

One last limitation on the part of the German military made Enigma's vulnerability enduring: the Germans did not take a creative, nonlinear view of attacking security. When reporting on the security of Enigma or even of other ciphers, including enemy systems, they focused on the statistics of cryptology. Their security investigations and cryptanalytic reports examined either the problems of physical compromise or of possible statistical methods for breaking a system. Among the surviving wartime documents, no reports deal with the more subtle ways around and into a cryptologic problem.

The various branches of the German military had cryptanalysts attack their own Enigmas and investigate several Allied cipher machines as well. In these attacks Germany's experts seem to have stuck to statistical and straightforward approaches. They conducted statistical attacks on Enigma-enciphered traffic, both with and without the help of 'captured' documentation. They did recognize many of the statistical limitations in Enigma's design. At least two German cryptologic bureaus found methods to crack the original unsteckered versions of Enigma.[22] However, they apparently never tackled live traffic and instead

[21]NARA: RG 457 HCC Box 1283 NR 3814 - Decoding German Enigma Machine Messages, p. 3.

[22]NARA: RG 457 HCC Box 1405 through Box 1409 NR 4541 - Codes and Ciphers: German Cryptanalytic Documents Folder 3, October, November 1943 on In 7's work; Adolf Paschke. *Das Chiffrier- und Fernmeldewesen im Auswärtigen Amt: Seine Entwicklung und Organisation*. Bonn 1957. Signatur at Auswärtiges Amt: Aktengruppe VS Band 6025 (2 volumes) discusses the Pers Z work pp. 54ff.

stuck to straightforward attacks conducted under artificial conditions. Needless to say, all of these examinations concluded that the machine would defeat enemy cryptanalysts.[23] Throughout these investigations, German cryptologists seem to have never realized the true reduction of Enigma's statistical possibilities under real conditions, particularly those reductions arising from operational procedures and human error.

German cryptanalysts had no luck breaking British and American high-grade cipher machines and this lack of success only reinforced their belief in Enigma's strength and vice versa. The British high-grade cipher machine Typex had a stepped rotor design reminiscent of Enigma's inner workings; but where Enigma had three rotors, the Typex had seven. Since Enigma had proved unbreakable, top German cryptanalysts concluded the more complex seven-rotor Typex would prove even more impervious to attack and hence they did not expend much effort on the assault.[24] Indeed, after a mere six weeks of work on Typex, the *Kreigsmarine*'s cryptanalytic experts abandoned their assault.[25] Faced with a system that they calculated as statistically unbreakable in a reasonable period of time, they simply gave up.

Relying too heavily on theoretical statistics made the Germans vulnerable. Even their cryptologic experts did not believe Enigma compromised until faced with the British government's admission of Ultra in 1974.[26] They knew the British had captured Enigma machines and material, at least by the middle of the war.[27] They knew the British had a history of successful cryptanalysis and they appreciated the ability of British intelligence. Yet they relied on a statistical security that took neither operational reality nor their opponents' years of attention and attack into account. They ignored simple factors which could have hindered, if not completely defeated, their enemies. Had the *Wehrmacht*, for example, completely replaced Enigma's rotors even once, rather than just adding to the existing set, they might have ended the Allies' success.

Both then and now, the problem for the cryptanalyst remains that numbers don't tell the whole story. A cryptologic system's theoretical complexity by

---

[23] *Bundesarchiv/Militärarchiv*: RM 7/108, pp. 19-21, for example.

[24] Dr. Erich Hüttenhain, chief cryptanalyst at OKW/Chi. NARA: RG 457 HCC Box 1006 NR 3142 - Statements by POWS, p. 5.

[25] *Bundesarchiv/Militärarchiv*: RM7/104 3./Skl, 29 Feb 1941, p. 40.

[26] See for example the presentations given at the conference on Ultra intelligence in Stuttgart and Bad Godesberg in 1978. E. Jäckel and J. Rohwer, *Die Funkaufklärung im Zweiten Weltkreig* (Stuttgart: Motorbuch Verlag, 1978).

[27] They did not know that a German, Hans-Thilo Schmidt, had passed documents on Enigma to the French a decade before the war began. See Gustave Bertrand's account of handling Schmidt in the 1930s in *Enigma ou la plus grande énigme de la guerre 1939-1945* (Paris: Plon, 1973).

no means assures operational security. In the end, cryptologic theory suffers the greatest reduction in security from a single element - humans. Humans gravitate towards regularity, towards habits and patterns that help us make sense of the world. This regularity undermines the randomness that cryptology tries to create. In this case Enigma's security suffered most from officers who did not replace rotors, from code clerks who tired of coming up with something new every month, and from worn out Enigma operators who used easy, repetitive openings and message phrasings.

The Germans did recognize many of these procedural problems and they frequently reprimanded Enigma operators for such insecure habits. In addition, several of the signal intelligence agencies conducted investigations into Enigma security that hinted at the system's general compromise. These theoretical and compartmentalized investigations of Enigma's security did not suffice. Throughout the nearly two decades of Enigma's operation, none of these investigations ever fully examined the machine's operational limitations or even examined live traffic. Only the examination of live traffic under real conditions could have suggested the true level of security for Enigma - or any other system.

In short, the only real security lies in realizing that nothing is truly secure in practice. Whatever the statistical security of a cryptologic system, the practical security will rely on human operations. The most complex computer cryptography collapses when humans fail to practice such basic safeguards as avoiding repetitive phrasing, changing settings frequently and randomly, and, above all, guarding their keys and passwords appropriately. Knowing one's enemy thoroughly - and never underestimating him - offers a cryptanalyst the most valuable information of all. No theoretical element plays as large a role in security as the human.

BIOGRAPHICAL SKETCH

R. A. Ratcliff, a graduate of Bryn Mawr College, has a PhD from UC Berkeley's Rhetoric Department, taught history at the University of San Francisco in San Francisco, California, worked in the high tech industry, and currently freelances in history and communications in Silicon Valley.

Reviews

REVIEWS OF ENIGMA-RELATED MATERIAL PUBLISHED IN CRYPTOLOGIA

Over the years *Cryptologia* has published many reviews related to Enigma material. We include a full set of these reviews. The running heading of the section under which the review ran is offered and the author of the review is identified in this heading. The specific volume, issue, and page information of the review is in the details of the title, author, and publisher information.

ULTRA GOES TO WAR
Bradford Hardie

Lewin, Ronald. *Ultra Goes to War*. 1978. New York: McGraw-Hill. 398 pp. $12.95. 3(2): 122-126.

Here is an outstanding book for the followers of World War II, historians, and cipher buffs. In 1974 Group Captain F. W. Winterbotham broke the ice of *The Ultra Secret*, based on his memories of the use of the German cryptograms enciphered on the Enigma cipher machine and solved by the British and Americans. Now in writing his more detailed book, Ronald Lewin has used official copies of these messages, has interviewed many users and distributors of these decrypts and appears to have interviewed a good cryptanalyst, whom he does not name. He has produced a marvelous book for cipher enthusiasts and a great many others.

In outline his book is a history of the solutions of the Enigma and of their translation, interpretation distribution, and effects. Because the method of solution is still under wraps, he has to talk mostly of a few well names. He believes that the Poles made the original break, that the French may have furnished a German instruction manual, and that the British brought the bombes – the devices for automatically running through Enigma key settings – to a perfection for that time. He calls the bombe the Bomba, possibly a Polish term, while bombe is French. Lewin tells us that the small French Unit using Polish knowledge, equipment and nationals solved some Enigma messages before the loss of France. He gives the names of the same three Polish workers who have previously been listed as the discoverers of the basic weakness in the military Enigma. He thinks the Poles were more motivated than were the British, Americans or Germans to make the discovery.

The three Polish discoverers are described as mathematicians and Lewin mentions group theory and the theory of cycles. We wonder how much mathematical theory may have helped in this solution. The same quality of mind that helps in mathematics may help in cryptanalysis. After the scheme of cryptanalysis is discovered, it may be fitted into a more general mathematical framework. Cryptanalysis seems to be based on a fairly exact knowledge of the working of the cipher and then on trying to discover the secondary consistencies present. C. A. Deavours, one of the editors of this magazine who has done magnificent original work on the solution of the commercial Enigma, can probably give us a good essay on the relation of cryptanalysis to mathematics.

The Poles furnished commercial Enigmas modified to military form as well as bombes to the British and French. Lewin stresses that the bombe was an electro-mechanical machine and not electronic as some loosely-writing authors have said. The Colossus, another British cryptanalysis machine, was electronic and possibly the first mass employment of vacuum tubes, having 1500 in its circuit.

Perhaps the best chapter is "Ultramarine," the story of the effects of Ultra on the *Kriegsmarine* (German navy) and on the Italian navy. This is largely the story of the solution of Cipher M, the German name for the naval Enigma. Lewin tells us this was finally a four-rotor Enigma with eight regular rotors, and I'm told two narrow rotors and two narrow *Umkehrwalzen* (reflectors), and used three regular rotors, one narrow rotor, and one *Umkehrwalze* at a time, while the army and German air force used a three-rotor machine with the three chosen from a set of five. These were duplicates of five in the set of eight Cipher M rotors. Lewin says the British began to solve army and air force Enigma ciphers in 1940 but not the naval ciphers until 1941, when they broke into Hydra, the general-purpose key net for ships in the North and Baltic Seas, for mine-sweepers, coastal convoys, and patrol craft off the Norwegian and French coasts, and in 1941 still for all U-boats. Later they broke into the "big ship" key net Neptun and the Key nets used in the Mediterranean, Süd and Medusa. The big start into Cipher M was given by the seizure of U 110's cryptographic material by Sub-Lieutenant Balme, R.N., who received the Distinguished Service Cross from the king.

Lewin for this book used a taped interview of David Balme, which had been make earlier by Peter Hennessy of *The Times*. On 1 February 1942 the Atlantic U-boats ceased using Hydra and began Triton, which connected them directly with U-boat Command. It was first solved in December 1942 but became unsolvable again on 8 March 1943 when the four-rotor Enigma came into use. This change caused a gap only until the end of March when good coverage began again. The Tetis key net, which was used in the Baltic training program, was solved too. Lewin describes the Battle of the Atlantic, the sinking of the *Bismarck*, the escape of the *Scharnhorst* and *Gneisenau* up the English Channel, and the sinking of the *Scharnhorst* in the Artic on Boxing Day. Such dramatic events as sinkings and crawlings over abandoned submarines enliven this chapter. The men of the German navy believed their Enigma to be much more secure than the army Enigma, and here we have its story.

Lewin tells how users questioned some translations and asked to see the original German in order to satisfy their doubts. Unobtrusively he may be using some language taken from British translations of German cryptograms. On page 203 he writes of the ability to process German naval ciphers at speed. This expression "process ciphers at speed" is a splendid translation of the German verb "mitlesen," which is not listed in German dictionaries. In context German people will understand it in analogy to "mitessen," "mitarbeiten," and "mitgehen;" it means that two people read the same material at the same time, the people being the authorized recipient and the unauthorized cryptanalyst. Perhaps some German cryptograms about Allied convoys used "mitlesen" in their texts.

We are surprised at the emphasis put into the distribution of the processed decrypts. This matter was stressed in Winterbotham's book possibly because it was his field of experience. It is again stressed in this book. The necessity of denying the enemy any firm basis of suspecting his cipher to be at fault is unquestioned by any cryptanalyst. A government rarely changes from a strong cipher to a weaker one. Practically always a cipher already solved is better to contend with than a new cipher. So we get TOP SECRET ULTRA. Experience has apparently convinced governments that being able to read a foreign cipher is one of the matters which if revealed will break up their country, so cryptanalysis is classified TOP SECRET In a note on page 365 Lewin says that Ultra essentially indicated highest security classification. He is probably more right when he quotes from Roskill that Ultra meant their contents were derived from signal intelligence or other very secret sources. It seems that Ultra to most people meant the material came from enemy cryptograms. On 7 May 1945 in his affidavit to Colonel Clausen as part of the Pearl Harbor attack investigations, General MacArthur said, "I believe I saw every Ultra message that was delivered to the HQ USAFFE." In the context this implies that Ultra referred to matter derived from cryptanalysis. Could there have been CONFIDENTIAL ULTRA on a document derived from traffic analysis?

Another outstanding chapter tells about the use of the solutions of the *Abwehr* cipher in making D-Day in Europe a success. The *Abwehr* was the military espionage section of the German armed forces high command; Lewin explains that its cipher was an Enigma without the pluggable connections used by other versions. We can imagine that the double agents in England could furnish some plaintexts which had been enciphered on the Enigma in an earlier portion of their travels, and when enough of these accumulated under the right circumstances, Bletchley broke into the highest grade *Abwehr* traffic, which was carried on this Enigma. I had not previously appreciated how important deception was to the D-Day and later operations and how reading the *Abwehr* traffic had helped.

"The Glow-lamp Machine" is the title of the chapter which tells about the Enigma machine, which was early described in English as 'The Glow-lamp Ciphering and Deciphering Machine "Enigma."' It appears the Enigma was described in this manner because the illumination of the letter to be written down for the cryptogram was by *eine Gluh-lampe*, which means an incandescent light. Glowlamp is more glamorous.

Another matter from the naval chapter is a footnote about the "short signal" which the German navy adopted for better communication security: less time on the air and another step in the encipherment. But it was possibly more stereotyped. It was a code system for brevity followed by encipherment on Cipher M. This too was conquered and is illustrated in an example supplied by Lewin. Without doubt the German navy was concerned throughout the war as to how their enemy found so many of their submarines. They considered radar, direction finding, and aircraft, but they appear to have always felt that the cipher was not at fault. In the German army it was said that early in the war the cryptologic personnel had expressed to the generals some doubt about German cryptographic security, but the generals said, "No chance. We're winning, aren't we?" The German navy seems to have felt after 8 May 1943, when the four-rotor Enigma came into use as Cipher M, that if the army Enigma was reasonably secure, this new Cipher M was absolutely secure. We might wonder today whether, if a civil service employee found a defect in our ciphers, he would have the courage to report it, especially if the cipher was his own creation. It seems to take the enemy to properly grade our cryptographic security. The Poles graded the Germans.

The only defect I found in this wonderful book was Lewin's use of the word "professionalism" a few times. In America today this is a meaningless word and consequently is widely used in advertising and political speeches. I seemed to have found an error on page 34 where Major P. W. Evans, then Assistant Military Attaché in Berlin, reports twice that the Enigma in 1931 had enciphering wheels with 25 contact points on each face. Although Hagelin built a cipher machine which handled an alphabet of only 25 letters, it seems unlikely that the Enigma ever handled only 25 letters.

This book includes several moving statements like the account of Sub-Lieutenant Balme and the visits of the top naval commanders to Bletchley to thank the workers. Working with ciphers during the war sounds like exciting and absorbing work, but in England close to the actual fighting many men thought jobs in combat which could not be done by women might be what they should be doing. Some of the work was rather monotonous too, so these visits by high sea officers were appreciated.

General George Marshall in the United States set a fine example of an appreciation of the value of Ultra or Magic. Lewin says it was considered in his daily staff meetings in the Pentagon. Lewin thinks Marshall may have been a little too close with Magic as contrasted with the British, of course especially before Pearl Harbor. This difference is sometimes explained by saying that in England and in combat areas handlers of Ultra could appreciate the danger from the enemy and could be trusted not to help him in any manner, but in the United States this danger was not so apparent, so more precautions had to be taken. Lewin quotes from a letter by General Marshall to General Eisenhower on 15 March 1944 outlining the duties of the distributors of Ultra. Marshall also wrote General Eisenhower in February 1945 a strong letter about the disappearance of the SIGABA in Colmar. He also composed the famous letter to Governor Dewey, one of the best essays on the value of cryptanalysis in existence.

Ultra Goes to War is a first-class book with a glossary, interesting illustrations, useful notes, an appendix of typical productions from Bletchley Park, bibliography, index and 398 pages. In the field of the Enigma it may not be equaled in our times.

FROM THE ULTRA CONFERENCE
Louis Kruh

Rohwer, Jürgen and E. Jäckel. *Die Funkaufklarung und ihre Rolle im Zweiten Weltkreig.* Motorbuch Verlag, Postfach 1370, 7000 Stuttgart 1, WEST GERMANY 19/9. 406 pp. D. M. 54, about $31.00. 5(1): 58.

In November 1978, an international conference of cryptologists was organized by Dr. Jürgen Rohwer, Germany's leading naval historian and Director of the *Biblothek fur Zeitgeschichte*, to examine the role of radio intelligence in World

War II with emphasis on Ultra and the breaking of the German Enigma cipher machine [1].

Noted historians and cryptologists from all countries involved in the war were present and gave talks and participated in discussions over a two day period After Rohwer opened the conference and David Kahn delivered the keynote address the program included talks on, "The Development of the German Radio Cipher Machines" by a member of the German cipher bureau; "The Achievement of the Polish Cipher Bureau in Breaking the German Enigma Cipher" by a member of the cryptanalytic service; British speakers provided insight to the uses they made of the Ultra decrypts and procedures at Bletchely Park; plus much, much more.

This magnificently printed book is an almost verbatim account of the proceedings and the "give and take" among the participants, which provides the kind of information that could only come from the people who actually took part in the "war of the cryptologists." The book is illustrated with many photographs of the various German Enigma machines and other cipher devices which were on display, numerous candid shots of the participants, and the fascinating illustrations used by the speakers.

A most informative volume worth owning even if you do not read German.

REFERENCES

1. Kahn, D. 1979. The Ultra Conference. *Cryptologia*. 3: 1-8.

UNRAVELING THE ENIGMA STORY
Bradford Hardie

The Enigma War. Josef Garlinski. New York: Charles Scribner's Sons. 1980. 219 pp. $14.95. 6(1): 61-63.

This book is of great importance to all interested in the Enigma cipher machine and its history. Even people who had wartime knowledge of some of this material will learn more.

Josef Garlinski, who was born in Poland in 1913, wanted, in writing this book, to do justice to his homeland and to Great Britain, his adopted country. He is a historian with a command of Polish, German, French, and English; this is his eighth book. He was aided in cryptological matters by retired Colonel Tadeusz Lisicki, who helped in aspects of the Enigma solution in Poland and who now lives in England.

The book gives us the most complete picture yet of the Polish cryptanalysis and how it spread to the French and British and what effects followed. In the appendix, Lisicki details the Polish methods for attacking the Enigma indicators, which consisted of three letters and the same three letters repeated, all enciphered in sequence. He also describes making use of stereotyped beginnings, saying the most frequent one was anx, an being German for *to* and x being the word separator. He describes the use of the punched sheets, one of which is shown in the main portion of the book. It's interesting to see the pattern repeated four times. Just as sliding strips need to have one strip with a repeated alphabet, so a two-dimensional slide needs two-squared repetitions. Prof. R. V. Jones in his foreword expresses the opinion that the British were held up initially by assuming that the wiring from the keyboard of the military Enigma to its right-hand rotor was in the order Q W E R T..., as in the commercial Enigma, while the Poles already knew it was A B C D E....

Garlinski believes the Japanese machine called PURPLE by American cryptanalysts was based in some way on the Enigma. Another writer feels that it was related to the Kryha machine, a sliding strip arrangement rather than rotors. Some day perhaps Japanese writers will supply some real details on their machine. *The Pearl Harbor Attack* volumes show that it had a plugboard, which makes it sound like the military Enigma, otherwise we were in the dark.

According to Garlinski, the American and British crytanalysts were reading each other's cryptograms during World War II. This seems only natural to him. He feels that the Americans could solve the British TYPEX and the British, the American SIGABA – both rotor machines. Because the Poles could solve the military Enigma, everything seems possible, except solving the one-time pad. We will probably never know about this feeling of Garlinski's, but most cryptanalysts in wartime are so busy working on and solving enemy ciphers that they don't have time to work on their allied ciphers. It seems there must be grades of security in cipher machine – Donitz, the German *B-Dienst* commander, in his book *Die Deutsche Marine Funkaufklarung 1914-1945*, differentiates the M-209 and the Enigma. Because of his experience with removing mutatives (additives or subtractors) from codetexts he calls the M-209 a plaintext mutative system and says the Enigma was better because it was not a plaintext mutative system. But we can imagine further classes of cipher machines.

Garlinski points out that a system was developed during World War II so that a SIGABA machine could talk to a TYPEX machine. They were each modified in some way to make a common machine.

This book discusses the *Geheimschreiber* as if it were the title for one kind of machine only. Documents in the U. S. National Archives and else where indicate that the Germans called two different machines by this name. Both were used in teletype or teleprinter systems. One was a sizeable attachment to be used with a standard German teletype machine manufactured by Standard Elektrik Lorenz. The other was a single unit composed of a teleprinter mechanism and a ciphering system. So this book does not make clear which of these machines is being described. The first sizeable electronic computer was used in England against the German teletype or teleprinter systems.

The book has many interesting details. It makes clearer the arrangement of the German Enigma M machine, which was the naval cipher machine. Enigma M had initially five rotors in its set, using three at a time in the machine. As the war progressed three more rotors were added to the set. Then space was made for a fourth rotor to be used in the same machine, and in time three different rotors which could be used in the fourth position were added to the set. The regular rotors were designated by the Germans I to VIII, in Roman numerals, and the fourth position rotors were called α, β, γ, in Greek letters.

The book has a few minor errors. On page 7 it says transposition where it should say substitution. This is possible because in mathematics a trans position is a cyclic permutation of two objects. Garlinski says of Alberti's cipher, "The machine was used for transposition and for deciphering and was operated manually." Now Alberti's cipher was two disks to be rotated with respect to one another. If the alphabets had been alike but proceeding in opposite directions, the substitutions would have been transpositions in the mathematical sense. But the only illustration of Alberti's disks I have seen does not show reciprocal alphabets. The outer alphabet is of 20 letters in standard order followed by the digits 1, 2, 3, 4. The letters on the inner disk appear in a scrambled order. It seems best in writing on cryptography to eliminate use of transposition in the mathematical sense and call such a cyclic permutation of two letters a reciprocal substitution.

A picture of the Enigma rotor on page 24 calls the axle the spring knob and calls the *Ringstellung* the button. The index of the book is faulty in listing only names and locations and cipher systems nor cryptanalytic methods.

The Polish bombe, according to Garlinski, had six Enigma mechanisms incorporated into it. We know how one Enigma can be used. If the complete setting for the machine that enciphered the cryptogram in known, one machine can be put to the same setting and used to decipher or solve the cryptogram. Now if nothing is known of the setting, the cryptogram can still be deciphered when every possible setting for the machine is tried on one machine and the cryptogram deciphered at each of these settings.

Each Enigma at a given setting furnishes one complete alphabet. Each letter in a cryptogram also represents one complete alphabet, so six Enigmas could represent six letters in a cryptogram. Because this bombe gave solutions, it implies that six letters in a cryptogram properly related to one another can furnish a solution.

It would seem that this solution would be obtained in one-sixth of the time required to use one machine and to decipher the cryptogram beginning at every setting. Perhaps this is an example to illustrate how time and space are both included in a single basic aspect of our universe. Perhaps number of machines (space) multiplied by time is a constant. William F. Friedman in his and his wife's *Shakespearean Ciphers Examined* describes Claude Shannon as believing that 25 letters are sufficient and necessary to determine that a cryptogram in English has been solved. Because of the nature of the Enigma and the manner in which it was used the Poles needed only six letters if properly related to one another.

This practice of giving space to gain time has an old history in cryptanalysis. The solution of the Caesar cipher makes use of it. Instead of trying two sliding strips at every possible different juxtaposition to each other, we write out whole alphabets and see at a glance the correct line and key. Or we use a whole set of sliding strips rather than two only.

The exchange of space and time is characteristic of written language and thought. Perhaps these lines of poetry strengthen our feeling for this conception.

> Yet we, who are borne on one dark g-rain of dust
> Around one indistinguishable spark
> Of star dust, lost in one lost feather of light
> Can by the strength of our own thought, ascend
> Through universe after universe.
>
> ALFRED NOYES

The Polish bombe was the application of an ancient idea to current material. This book is the best summary presently available of all the information on the Enigma. It forms a superior foundation for more detailed studies.

FROM THE DEPTHS TO THE HEIGHTS STORY
William P. Bundy

British Intelligence in the Second World War: Its Influence on Strategy and Operations.F. H. Hinsley, E. E. Thomas, C. P. G. Ransom, and R. C. Knight. New York: Cambridge University Press. 1979. Volume 1. 601 pp. $24.95. 6(1): 65-74.

Ultra in the West: The Normandy Campaign 1944-45. Ralph Bennett. London: Hutchinson and Co. 1980. 305 pp. £9.95 pounds. 6(1): 65-74.

Top Secret Ultra. Peter Calvocoressi. New York: Pantheon Books. 1981. 131 pp. $10.95. 6(1): 65-74.

Since the initial English-language revelations in 1974 that the British had broken and read most of the top-level German ciphers during World War II, the "Ultra" story has produced a spate of personal and historical accounts ranging from the tight and superb (R. V. Jones on the scientific side, Patrick Beesly on the naval, Ronald Lewin on the relationship to strategy) to the voluminous but mediocre (Anthony Cave-Brown on deception operations) all the way to overblown popularization and downright bad history (Intrepid) [1].

Each of these was written without the full benefit of official documents on the activities of the Bletchley codebreakers or on the material sent from there to commands. And, while British official histories of the strategic conduct of war skirted the question of broken ciphers, using the material only on a disguised background basis, the British sensibly refrained from doing any official study of the role of intelligence until they could, as it were, bring Hamlet onto the stage.

Now at last, published in Britain in the spring of 1979, we have the first volume of what will become a three-volume official series covering the contribution of British intelligence during the war. Volume 1 covers from before the war to the German invasion of Russia. Appropriately, its lead author, Barry Finsley, professor of international relations and master of St. John's College at Cambridge, served at Bletchley as a senior civilian. (He was then in his 20's, in a shop where few of the top people were over 40, and where experience and accomplishment alone gave true seniority.) And his three colleagues come respectively from strong backgrounds in naval intelligence, the Foreign Office, and scientific R and D. They have had the run of the complete files at all levels, and have been permitted to refer specifically to all except for those that might disclose "the methods by which this material was obtained." And on one or two critical points the authors use even this 1Atter material at least to the extent of saying that it does not change the conclusion reached from other sources.

The result is, as might be expected, a monumental contribution, the most thorough history we are ever likely to get on the work of an overall organization that produced in the end the most effective and sustained intelligence in the history of warfare. Monumental, but also in a few respects maddening – is it truly against the law to write official history in a vivid and compelling way, with adequate mention of key personalities, good signposting and cross-referencing to enable the reader to follow themes, and even a single comprehensive bibliography from which the reader can readily pick up the full sourcing of otherwise hard-to-trace footnotes – I gather that British reviewers have noted many of these points, and one may hope that the authors will be a bit less buttoned up in the second and third volumes, without sacrificing the extraordinarily high standard they have set for care and objectivity. Perhaps the delay in the appearance of the second volume, which was to have appeared by the summer of 1980, reflects this kind of revision.

Or perhaps the dryness of tone was imposed, at first, by the melancholy nature of the early story. At the outbreak of the war, British intelligence was – on this account – in very sorry shape indeed: its chiefs met principally to administer and to adjudicate petty jurisdictional problems, it had been starved or funds over the years, the Foreign Office claimed rights of supervision even as it instinctively downplayed the importance of "intelligence" of any sort, and within the military services intelligence was, in almost all cases, a stepchild. Any resemblance to American intelligence as of 1941 (or from 1946 to 1950) is, of course, entirely coincidental,

So the record was one of failure, in Norway, in France, finally in the Dakar debacle of September 1940. Even the intelligence that helped to save the British Expeditionary Force at Dunkirk came chiefly from a single chance capture of a document in the field, and to some extent from tactical interception of plaintext messages. Of strategic or operational intelligence there was almost none, and what little there was had no one to assess it properly either in the field or at home.

But in fact the tide had begun to turn, and cryptologists will be pleased to have it confirmed that it was the breakthrough on the German Air Force, Enigma cipher machine, more than any single factor, that transformed not only the supply of intelligence information but, in due course, the machinery for handling and using it. A key theme of this volume, indeed, is that "reliable intelligence, the sovereign remedy for false assumption, is also a pre-condition of profitable collaboration" (p. 170). Much as one might argue that the fullest possible sharing and analysis are all the more needed when raw information is at a minimum (as it has so often been vis-á-vis the Soviet Union since the war), it seems to be true of intelligence, as of economics, that sharing is easier when the pie is bigger.

As to how the Enigma came to be broken on a regular basis, the book – on its face at least – adds little. But the careful reader of the first of many useful appendices at the rear will find there what may well be the best appraisal yet of just what the Poles and the French contributed, and how much the British did on their own. It seems unquestionable that the British had been slower than the other two, and were greatly indebted to the Poles for working out the wiring of the wheels, assisted in the early stages by a spy for the French. But it was indeed the British who, starting with the wiring diagrams delivered by the Poles in July 1939, developed (largely through Alan Turing) an essentially new design for a machine to reproduce at high speed the action of the Enigma. Although this machine had the same name as the earlier Polish one ("Bombe"), it was in fact very little, if any, indebted to the earlier Polish work. The appendix concludes rather dryly that, since the British did not capture Enigma wheels till February 1940 (from a naval vessel), the Poles made a difference of seven months in the development of the British bombe, without which the main German air force system in particular ("Red" as it was called) would not have been broken regularly until January 1941 instead of late May 1940.

Technically, I believe this is a correct appraisal; from a standing start, the British bounded ahead once they had the wheel wiring, and achieved a breakthrough probably far beyond the capabilities of the French or even of the gifted Polish mathematicians. But even if the Polish contribution was "only" these seven months, what an enormous difference it made as one returns to the main text and follows the impact of daily breaking of the main *Luftwaffe* key from late May 1940 onward (The account skirts completely the methods of breaking the special keys of the German scientists, which legend has it were often solved by hand as a result of security breaches even more atrocious than those perpetrated regularly by *Luftwaffe* encoders and operators.) The accurate reading of German bombing strategy in the Battle of Britain, the gradual correction of initial substantial overestimates of German air strength, the evidence from mid-September that the invasion of Britain had been called off for the winter (affecting reinforcement of the Middle East), the timely warning achieved by November 1940 of the Blitz attack on Britain – these are only examples of what Ultra meant to the very survival of Britain in these critical months. And if one tries to imagine the British breaking Red with their new bombe in January 1941 rather than in May 1940, one must ask whether they would have learned the tricks of interpretation rapidly enough to deduce from the take the kind of clear and persuasive conclusions that were in fact produced in the spring of 1941 concerning Greece, Crete and (eventually) the German invasion of Russia? How much later would it have been before, in North Africa, they became aware of the German superiority in Sigint signal intelligence itself and gradually set things right-

So, in the end, even if their working out of the wiring was of a lesser order of cryptanalytic accomplishment than the British bombe, the Poles are owed an immense debt in terms of history. The same appendix concludes that since the German Navy and Army Enigma keys were not broken until late summer and fall of 1941, respectively, these successes would probably have been achieved in roughly the same time frame even without the head start provided by the Poles. This volume does provide fascinating detail o the carefully planned program of ship seizures that produced a series of captured monthly naval keys in the spring and early summer of 1941; with the information gleaned from these, and with an expanded array of bombes just available, most of the German Navy Enigma keys were thence forward broken regularly and currently to the end of the war (the chief exception was of the main U-boat key, which was not broken during most of the critical year 1942). But again, if there had been no bombes at all till January 1941, would there have been enough to handle both the Navy and Air Force in the late 1941 time frame? Perhaps it is an "iffy" question, the answer to which must await a cryptanalytic history drawing on official sources [2]. But if I were a Pole, I would find the suggestion a little too pat.

Equally fascinating is the definitive account of the warning provided of the devastating German bombing of Coventry in November 1940, giving the flesh of verbatim messages to a spine of conclusion already laid out by Michael Roward and others in reviews and articles published in Britain. In essence, although the information available should have pointed clearly to Coventry as the target at least two days in advance, the correct conclusion was not drawn until the evidence of navigational beams became conclusive on the afternoon of the raid – and even then its size was underestimated. Although there were indeed cases where Ultra was not used – and people died – because of the need to protect a vital intelligence source, Coventry was not such a case.

Ending as it does in the summer of 1941, this volume touches only lightly, and in tantalizing fashion, on intelligence relations between Britain and the United States. But even the four pages (pp. 311-314) devoted expressly to the subject do a lot to set the record straight, especially some of the allegations in *A Man Called Intrepid*. Sir William Stephenson, as the SIS representative in the United States, did indeed play a critical role in getting cooperation started, and above all in educating William Donovan so that the latter moved to set up the first U.S. civilian foreign intelligence agencies. But his connection with Ultra was nothing like what *Intrepid* claims – far from his personally supplying Ultra material to Roosevelt, the fact is that what the British sent to the White Rouse from August 1940 onward, via the British Embassy, was what was called the Dominions Wire, based on the daily summary of the British Joint Intelligence Committee (JIC), but undoubtedly with the Ultra material carefully sanitized. There was indeed, by June 1941, a lot of exchange of intelligence, chiefly through the military and naval missions exchanged in early 1941, and the foundation had been laid for the future. But, pending the fuller account still to appear in the second volume, one would have to conclude tentatively that no American was in the Enigma picture up to June 1941, although there was a fairly full exchange on Japanese and Italian ciphers [3].

Indeed, it is hardly surprising that the British were not more forthcoming. One of the special values of the book is the light it throws on the tightness of British security respecting the Enigma. Although some of the early Red material was shared with the French high command through a liaison mission in May 1940, it was apparently so sanitized that the Germans, having captured the whole of the high command files, found nothing that shook their faith in the security of Enigma. (That the Polish and French cryptanalytic organizations, which were aware of the British success, dispersed without ever betraying the secret redounds everlastingly to their credit.) Then, later, when the first systematic naval breaks might have been used to great effect against individual ships, the Admiralty refused to allow this – an attitude which Patrick Beesly's book suggests changed gradually at the height of the U-boat menace. In any case, the secret held.

I have noted already that only with the first real Enigma breaks did the British seriously reform their procedures for processing and evaluating intelligence from all sources. Even so it was not until May 1941 that the Joint Intelligence Committee finally had its own drafting staff charged with both making estimates on agreed issues and looking ahead to the unexpected. All through the winter of 1940-41 the army in particular had simply refused to credit the growing volume of intelligence pointing to the invasion of Russia, and even with a proper coordinating structure the JIC lagged well behind Churchill himself in grasping what was up.

Indeed, the extraordinary personal role of Churchill – with his weight of experience and passion for primary materials – makes much of the history of wartime British analysis and interpretation so unique as to be almost valueless to other nations in other circumstances. One may sympathize with the prime minister's complaints about "this mass of stuff which reaches me in a single morning, most of it having already appeared in the . . . telegrams," and about "this vast congregation" with access to Ultra. But one suspects that though his own voracious appetite for the Enigma material – he received a daily box of decrypts and analysis from Bletchley, from all keys (p. 295) – made him a useful gadfly to service commanders and their intelligence officers, it also stultified more in-depth analysis and interpretation. So long as Enigma results were plentiful the damage was minimal, but one can see emerging even by the spring of 1941 an extraordinary degree of dependence on this intelligence source, taken raw.

By the spring of 1944, of course, that dependence had been reinforced by an almost unbroken string of intelligence successes, largely based on Enigma, in North Africa, Sicily and Italy, and by the crucial role of Ultra in the massive exception campaign to persuade the Germans that the planned landing in Normandy was only a sideshow and that the main thrust would come in the Pas de Calais making use of (largely mythical) divisions under the command of the General George S. Patton. From the fall of 1943 onward, Bletchley had been expanded greatly and the whole orchestra of British intelligence and covert operation brought to concert pitch.

Ronald Lewin's excellent *Ultra Goes to War* has already recounted much of the story of Ultra and the Normandy Campaign. But Ralph Bennett's new *Ultra in the West* is the first case study to draw on the store of 25,000 messages from Bletchley to the field commands that was finally declassified and made available in the British Public Records Office in 1977. Like Hinsley a historian, now at Cambridge college Magdalene, Ralph Bennett had also been at Bletchley – in the section for the translation, interpretation and evaluation of the German army and air force intercepts (known as Hut 3), eventually as one of five duty officers who rotated shifts with the responsibility of sorting the take and sending out the very series of messages he now analyses. As he notes at the outset:

> It is unusual to have the opportunity, when young, of sharing in the creation of an archive and then to be able to use it in later life for the purpose of historical research.

It is an opportunity Bennett has used to the fullest, in a book that should be of consuming interest to students of military history as well as those concerned with the story of Enigma. Never letting his personal role intrude, the author imparts to his reader how it really feels to be in the middle of intelligence production and evaluation in a constantly critical situation. This is a Bletchley memoir as well as a first-rate work of scholarship [4].

> Ref. CX/MSS/T271/132 XL 5461 IN TWO PARTS PART ONE
>
> ORDERS TO SEVENTH ARMY AND GENERL DER PANZER TRUPPEN EBERBACH EVERBACH ONE EIGHT HOURS NINTH. ATTACK ON SOUTHERN WING OF SEVENTH ARMY WILL BE CONDUCTED BY PANZER GRUPPE EBERBACH EBERBACH AFTER REGROUPING AND BRINGING UP OP DECISIVE OFFENSIVE ARMS. ON ITS SUCCESS DEPENDS THE FATE OF BATTLE OF FRANCE FRANCE. QUOTE I ORDER UNQUOTE COLON (ONE) COMMAND OF ATTACK COLON GENERAL EBERBACH EBERBACH TO WHOM A NEWLY FORMED FUEHRUNGSTAB IS BEING BROUGHT UP WITH OBERSTLEUTENANT VON KLUGE VON KLUGE AS CHIEF OF STAFF.

FOR REASONS OF UNIFIED COMMAND (LATER PARTICIPATION OF SEVENTH ARMY) AND SUPPLY, EBERBACH EBERBACH IS BEING SUBORDINATED TO GOC GOC SEVENTH ARMY. (TWO) OBJECTIVE OF ATTACK COLON THE SEA AST AVERANCHES AVRANCHES.

APGP/RFB/DC 100349Z/8/44

AN ULTRA INTERCEPT
An intercepted and solved German message as it was distributed to various commands. This intercept disclosed German intenentions to attack at Avranches in August, 1944, to try to cut off the American forces that had broken out there. It permitted the Allies to take countermeasures that stopped the German attack and cost the Germans heavy casualties. The story is told in Ralph Bennet's *Ultra in the West: The Normandy Campaign of 1944-45*, from whose jacket this illustration is reproduced. The "ZZZZZ" means top priority. The "RFB" at lower left may be Bennett's initials.

While the account necessarily scants the pre-invasion deception operations (neither Bennett nor Hinsley get into the double agent operations recounted by Sir John Masterman in *The Double-Cross System In the War of 1939 to 1945*, the full detail it gives on the Ultra picture of German perceptions prior to and during the invasion fleshes out that story in important ways. Then came the grinding period of Cherbourg and Caen, and after that the triumph both of military force and advance intelligence at Mortain. Here again the detail is fascinating, on a general story now well known and well told by Lewin.

But Bennett's main focus is on the two later cases when – at least so it has been alleged – Ultra failed and the commanders in the field were taken by surprise. On the first of these, the Arnhem debacle (Market Garden), made famous by the book and motion picture *A Bridge Too Far*, I find Bennett totally convincing that the location of the decisive German armored divisions, as well as the possibility that their equipment had been significantly refurbished, was reported in ample time. That the information was not acted on to abort the operation or at least modify the plan can only be ascribed, as the author does, to the sense of euphoria and near-invincibility that pervaded the top command at the time, especially in the airborne commanders who had not yet been in action. It was most definitely not the fault of intelligence or Ultra that the operation failed so tragically.

The other great "failure" was, of course, the Ardennes offensive in December. Here Bennett, conceding at once the lack of explicit warning, presents a careful and detailed picture of the bits and pieces from Ultra that might (in his view probably should) have been put together to form a picture of the main two German armored armies that attacked. From October on there were indeed a number of indications, especially from the Enigma used by the railway units, that pointed to large new concentrations west of the Rhine and north of the Moselle. But the theory in the various intelligence shops was that this must be to provide a counterattacking force; as in the case of Market Garden, German recuperative and organizing powers were underrated – perhaps partly because so much was known from Enigma about low equipment levels, but partly also because of unchallenged assumptions. Beneath it all, there was an element of intelligence overconfidence similar to the military overconfidence that led to Arnhem – by this time both commanders and their key intelligence officers counted so heavily on clear warning from Ultra that they had perhaps let up just a fatal little bit in putting together every scrap, Ultra included.

One wonders, too – though Bennett only faintly suggests the point – whether there was a slight defect of organization here. Hut 3 by this time seems to have been largely a service unit not seeking, at least in the case of intelligence concerning military operations, to work out its own hypotheses or to inject its own views (as it had done, on the Hinsley volume's account, in some earlier cases, notably the evidence in May 1941 concerning the German invasion of Russia). This was surely sound at least 90 percent of the time. But one has the feeling that the army group commands, and even the Supreme Headquarters, Allied Expeditionary Forces, may have lacked the accumulated experience of Bletchley in making little pieces form plausible pictures, and that in the kind of period of uncertainty and sharply limited intelligence that prevailed from early November 1944 on, it might have been wise to bring the various levels together or invite the producers and their analysts to speculate.

This is, of course, rank hindsight. In later years I was involved in intelligence task forces that threw light, and others that probably added to the fog. It would probably have taken extraordinary imagination to come up with the right prediction even if all the indicators had been properly interpreted. But, for those who seek contemporary lessons, it is worth reminding ourselves that the pre-Ardennes state of Allied intelligence was much nearer the whole post-war experience, and indeed that of commanders throughout history, than the miraculous service that Ultra provided for most of the war from May 1940 on, and especially throughout the crucial months of the Normandy Campaign itself.

Peter Calvocoressi's book is more truly a Bletchley memoir. He too was in Hut 3, in the end as head of the air section, but his account goes beyond the work of that hut to cover in summary form the whole of the process from intercept to outgoing signal. And his selection of highlights of the importance of Ultra to the war effort, as well as his succinct summary on this subject at the end, is absolutely first-class – he being already a distinguished military historian of the war.

For cryptologists the book is also of special significance in its excellent short chapter on the Polish contribution. Essentially, this confirms the judgments of the Hinsley official history, but with considerably more detail. His presentation of how Enigma was broken by the Bletchley cryptanalysts throws useful light on the German errors that permitted the initial breakthroughs, and how "cribs" were used to supply the "bombes" with the necessary input, in effect a computer program. This is not the account of a professional cryptanalyst and might be corrected in one or two trivial respects (such as the reference to Enigma as a "transposition cypher"), but it is the best account I know of in the public prints.

All in all, Calvocoressi has compressed an enormous amount of information and "feel" into a short volume.

In the end, none of these three complementary volumes seeks to answer the question whether what we now know about Ultra means that the whole military history of World War II should be rewritten, or at least key judgments reassessed. Each is permeated by a professionalism that needs no extravagant claim to supplement the sense of a job extraordinarily well done; the most that any of them claims is that individual situations do have to be looked at anew. Rash Americans can be left to rack up, from the Hinsley volume, the bases of disaster avoided or mitigated in the part of the war when no intelligence could have provided victories, and, from the Bennett study, how much longer and tougher the European battle after Normandy would have been, as well as whether Allied Forces would have been nearly as far to the east as they were when the surrender came.

From any standpoint, neither the Hinsley telescope nor the Bennett and Calvocoressi microscope does anything but fortify one's admiration for what the British did in the Ultra operation. Those of us who had the enormous privilege of being close to that effort will always know that we saw a peak of human achievement under pressure. These books tell us how far there was to go in the beginning and what the smell of reality was in the last phase. They should be on the shelf of any connoisseur of intelligence and especially of the history of cryptology.

REFERENCES AND NOTES

1. The most widely known English-language revelation was, of course, F. W. Winterbotham, *The Ultra Secret*, (New York: Harper and Row, 1974), which remains a useful overview and is especially useful on the methods of sending Ultra to the field and protecting it – but also contains a number of the errors natural in a book based almost entirely on personal recollection. Actually, the breaking of the *Abwehr* Enigma, and also of strategic Enigma messages, was disclosed in 1973 in an unlikely source, the second volume of the memoirs of the distinguished journalist Malcolm Muggeridge. *Chronicles of Wasted Time: Chronicle 2: The Infernal Grove*, (New York: William Morrow, 1974, and London: Collins, 1973, pp. 127, 129, 150-151, 187-189, 201, 204). And the footnotes to the present Hinsley volume (p. 489) now disclose at least to me, that a Polish author had written briefly in Polish of the success against Enigma as early as 1967.

The five later works mentioned are: R. V. Jones, *The Wizard War: British Scientific Intelligence. 1939-45*, (New York: Coward, McCann and Geoghegan, 1978); Patrick Beesly, *Very Special Intelligence*, (Garden City, New York: Doubleday, 1978); Ronald Lewin, *Ultra Goes to War*, (New York: McGraw-Bill, 1978); Anthony Cave-Brown, *Bodyguard of Lies*, (New York: Harper and Row, 1975); William Stevenson, *A Man Called Intrepid: The Secret War*, (New York: Harcourt, Brace and Jovanovich, 1976). The hero of the last of these, Sir William Stephenson, was indeed a distinguished intelligence officer whose genuine contributions had already been covered in B. Montgomery Hyde's *Room 3603: The Story of the British Intelligence Center in New York During World War II*, (New York: Farrar, Straus, 1963). The great bulk of what is true and important in *Intrepid* will be found in Byde's work, without the distortions and exaggerations that plague *Intrepid*. It is, in my judgment, the worst put-on in recent intelligence literature and has been rightly torn apart by competent British reviewers.

2. The British official papers on the technical side of the breaking of Enigma remain closed (even to their authors), although there has been at least one unpublished manuscript based on personal recollection.

One of my private readers of the draft of this review has suggested that senior American cryptanalysts may have been advised of the British success against Enigma as early as the spring of 1941. [According to Abraham Sinkov, a U. S. Army cryptanalyst who was one of four American cryptanalysts bringing a reconstructed Japanese PURPLE cipher machine to Britain in January 1941, the Americans were told in a general way at that time of the British success as a kind of *quid pro quo*. Ed.]

Of the earlier contributors to the Ultra story, Group Captain Winterbotham was based at Bletchley only briefly at the start of the war, while Jones and Beesly were always based in London and Lewin was serving in the Field Artillery. At Bletchley the work of translation and evaluation (Hut 3) was carried on after 1941 in the same building as the main cryptanalytic, sorting and intercept control operations (Hut 6). It was a nondescript one-story structure stretching into wings in all directions, through which one passed to, and only to, one's place of duty. For 18 months I was at the other end of a vacuum tube from Bennett, and perhaps 30 yards away across a court; although we were in a sense opposite numbers, we never met or visited each other's room except for one fleeting glimpse on my part of the main watch desk in Hut 3.

REMARKS ON APPENDIX 1 TO *BRITISH INTELLIGENCE IN THE SECOND WORLD WAR* BY F. H. HINSLEY – Marian Rejewski

Translated by Christopher Kasparek with Prefatory Note by Richard A. Woytak. 6(1): 75-83.

While researching my book *On the Border of War and Peace* (Boulder, CO. 1979), I had the pleasure of meeting Marian Rejewski, the last of the trio of Polish mathematician-cryptologists who in 1932/33 vanquished Enigma and read it until November 1942. Since the publication in 1974 of *The Ultra Secret* by F. W. Winterbotham, Rejewski had become increasingly disturbed by the distortions, propaganda and simple nonsense being published about the Enigma story.

Winterbotham's best-seller spoke of "a Polish mechanic... employed in [an Enigma] factory in Eastern Germany" who "was sacked and sent back to Poland" and "got in touch with our man in Warsaw." By 1975, perhaps due to the outcry from Poles living in England who knew better, Anthony Cave Brown in his aptly titled best-seller *Bodyguard of Lies* had promoted the nameless Polish mechanic to a "Richard Lewinski (not his real name)" who "had worked as a mathematician and engineer at the [Enigma] factory in Berlin," a "dark man in his early forties, thin and bent; [British] Commander [Wilfred] Dunderdale later said that he reminded him of a 'raven plucking an abacus." Just to be on the safe side, though, Brown took the precaution of mentioning "Polish cryptanalysts, led by two leading Polish mathematicians, M. Rejewski and H. Zygalski" as well as a German "officer of the *Forschungsamt*, the Reich's main cryptographic bureau" – apparently meaning the "Asche" who only after selling Enigma documents to the French was transferred to Goering's *Forschungsamt*, which was mainly a wire-tapping outfit where he had no more access to Enigma documents.

In 1976, another British best-seller, *A Man Called Intrepid* by the Canadian

William Stevenson, put up further candidates for Enigma laurels. Stevenson went one better than Cave Brown by adding another Polish mathematician. Stevenson came up with "Jerzy Różycki, Henryk Zygalski, and Mademoiselle Marian Rejewski" – thereby managing, with masterful economy of expression, to get wrong both Rejewski's sex and marital status. Then, apparently still having sex very much on his mind, Stevenson went on to an exciting story about a spy codenamed CYNTHIA, the "Minneapolis-born daughter of a U. S. Marine Corps major and Cora Wells, whose father was a Minnesota state senator." CYNTHIA, who was " married to a British diplomat, Arthur Pack, who had been transferred to Warsaw... formed a series of liaisons with top-ranking members of Poland's Foreign Service." Polish Foreign Minister Jozef Beck "was on good terms with Nazis in Berlin. [So were several thousand other people – which generates tremendous storytelling potential – R. A. W.] Beck's confidential aide was one of CYNTHIA's lovers."

In conversations with me, Rejewski, in Warsaw, and Colonel Stefan Mayer, the prewar chief of Polish military counter-intelligence, in London, have denied that there is any truth in any of these British best-sellers' accounts. Yet, such is the magic of best-sellers that I have been solemnly assured by a ranking U. S. intelligence official that Cave Brown's book is an important source of new information on World War II intelligence operations.

The official history of *British Intelligence in the Second World War*, by F. B. Hinsley *et al.* (see review elsewhere in this issue), vol. 1, (London: Her Majesty's Stationery Office, 1979) repeats, in Appendix 1, the story about "a Pole who was working in an Enigma factory in Germany," but prudently avoids stating the Pole's level of professional qualifications.

I sent Rejewski a copy of Hinsley's appendix. What he returned on December 2, 1979, has been kindly rendered into English by Dr. Christopher Kasparek.

P. 487, lines 5 ff.: The description [of "modifications" to the Enigma machine made by the Germans up to World War II] is rather unclear and imprecise. On June 1, 1930, the *final* model of the military Enigma was introduced, complete with "plugboard". What was later changed pertained only to changes in accessories such as change of the reflector, (November 2, 1937), addition of rotors IV and V (December 15, 1938), a gradual increase in number of plug connections to as many as 13, ever more frequent changes of daily keys (during the war, every 8 hours), a gradual increase in the number of nets, each using different keys, but above all several changes in the *manner of enciphering the message key*.

P. 487, line 16 [Hinsley states that "anyone not knowing the setting" of the rotors "was faced with the problem of choosing from one hundred and fifty million, million, million solutions – 1.5×10^{20}.] The author, to be sure, says how many possibilities there are of setting the machine, but he does not say how many possibilities there are for the internal connections ["wiring"] within the rotors. Given three rotors, those possibilities come to 500 million million million... million [the word "million being written a total of 15 times – and the whole number thus being 5×10^{92}], and that after all is the most important matter, because it is synonymous with reconstruction of the machine. More generally, I have noticed that all the British publications avoid this very question, as though taking it for granted that the connections within the rotors could have been obtained only by the theft, capture, or otherwise illicit acquisition of the machine.

P. 488, line 8 [Hinsley: "From Asche, according to Bertrand, the French obtained no less than 303 documents... about the Enigma," including "instructions for one of the Enigma machines, Army Enigma keys for 1932, 1933 and the first half of 1934, and a long text encyphered on the machine together with its clear text..."]. Only a small part of those documents pertained directly to Enigma (see Bertrand, p. 29). Anyway, what mattered was not what Bertrand had obtained but what he gave us. [Colonel Stefan] Mayer [of Polish military intelligence] in a letter to Bertrand confirms that we Poles received only several documents. For my part, I state that these documents were four: a *Gebrauchsanweisung* [operating instructions], a *Schlusselanleitung* [keying instructions], a table of daily keys for the month of September 1932, and a table of daily keys for the month of October 1932. I received no other documents, including any text given both in plain and in cipher, which would have been of no use to me anyway.

P. 488, line 20 [Hinsley: "the Poles... had been working on the Enigma since 1928 with a strong team of mathematicians..."]. True, the Poles had been working since 1928 at solving Enigma, but these had not been mathematicians, only one regular Army officer and one engineer. It was not until October 1932 that one mathematician began working [on it, i.e., Rejewski], and from the beginning of 1933, three mathematicians.

P. 488, line 3 from bottom [Hinsley: "following French contact with Warsaw in 1933 several experimental models of the Enigma machine were put together between 1934 and 1938..."]. These were no experimental models. As soon as I had gotten the connections in the drums, the AVA factory [an electrical equipment factory] received an order to make a dozen or so copies of the military machine, based on the commercial-model machine bought considerably earlier, on photographs of the military machine to be found in the *Gebrauchsanweisung* document supplied by Bertrand, and on the connections in the drums given by me on a scrap of paper. [Bertrand's first visit to Warsaw was not in 1933, but on December 7-11, 1932, and the first, already definitive Polish Enigma copies were produced in 1933-Translator.]

P. 489, line 5 [Hinsley: "A memorandum by... Mayer... written in response to Bertrand's book... makes no mention... of the Asche material."]. On the contrary. Mayer's letter to Bertrand does mention Asche's materials. I have had this letter in my hand, I have read it.

P. 489, line 24 [Hinsley: "Recruited in September 1932," the Polish mathematicians "took barely four and a half months to 'crack the system of the early version of the Enigma'. From 1934, greatly helped by a Pole who was working in an Enigma factory in Germany, they began to make their own Enigma machines."]. That was no early version of Enigma, it was the same military Enigma that was [later to be] used throughout the war; and what he [Hinsley] writes further on about a Polish worker employed at a German factory in Berlin is of course a fable. [The three mathematicians' involvement with the Polish General Staff's Cipher Bureau had begun in January 1929 when they were still students at Poznan University; they became regular Cipher Bureau employees in Warsaw on September 1, 1932. It took them about four months to fully master Enigma, beginning in late September or early October 1932. – Translator.]

P. 489, line 2 from bottom [Hinsley: "The first break-through, a mathematical one... at the beginning of 1933, and the construction of Polish copies of the Enigma machine from 1934 were followed from 1937 by... the 'cryptographic Bombe'...]. The Polish "bombs" were constructed later, after October 1938, in connection with a change in key encipherment procedure of September 15, 1938. [The theoretical reconstruction of the Enigma had come in late December 1932, construction of the first Enigma copies was commissioned in early February 1933. – Translator.]

P. 490, line 1, [Hinsley: "Improved versions of the Bombe were constructed up to 1939."] There were no improved versions of "bombs" in Poland. All six were produced at the same time in mid-November 1938.

P. 490, under the line [asterisk footnote]. True. The bombs were electromechanical devices.

P. 490, line 3: The reading of messages enciphered on Enigma proceeded currently from the beginning of 1933. It depended only on the number of intercepted messages. To break a given net's key for a given day, one needed about 60 messages [*sic*: Elsewhere Rejewski gives a figure of 80 messages – Translator]. Thus is also depended on the number of nets being formed and the number of messages broadcast by each of the units. That is why initially only messages in the *Wehrmacht* net were read; there were too few Navy messages and Air Force messages; but in the final years before the war there appeared a new net of the S.D. [*Sicherhuitsdunst* - the intelligence branch of the SS] with an adequate number of messages, and for that reason this net was then regularly read. The Navy likewise in the final period before the war began broadcasting more messages, and that is why messages in the Navy net were also sporadically read at this time.

P. 490, line 8 [Hinsley: "A German report on the Polish work states that on ... account" of "the German armed forces... continuously improving the Enigma machine" during the 1930s, the Polish work "suffered from long interruptions from January 1935 and again from October 1938."] Until September 15, 1938, there were no interruptions in reading, after September 15, 1938, there was a partial interruption (of which more later). In particular, there were no interruptions in January 1935, especially as at this time there were no changes in the manner of using Enigma.

P. 490, line 10 [Hinsley: "the Germans at first changed the Enigma keys only once every three months, but later began to change them monthly and eventually changed them daily."] Daily keys, from the very outset to the beginning of the war, were changed once daily; during the war (I do not know the exact date) the Germans proceeded to change the key every eight hours. It was only one part of the key, the sequence of drums, that was changed at first once every three months, then beginning February 1, 1936, once a month, and from October 1, 1936, daily.

P. 490, lines 14-16 [Hinsley: A Polish account "claims ... that 'Nazi messages' were read regularly from the first break-through until 1938."] The statement is true. In general, during this period, the recovery of a key was a matter of 10-20 minutes.

P. 490, lines 16-18 [Hinsley: Another Polish account "says only that after the introduction of the Bombe in 1937 an Enigma key could be broken in 'no more than 110 minutes'."] The bombes were ready only in November 1938, since they had been invented in September 1938 to recover keys after, on September 15, 1938, the Germans had changed completely the procedure for transmitting message keys. Then the key should have been recovered after at most 110 minutes, that is, after the execution of a complete cycle by the bomb.

P. 490, lines 18-26 [Hinsley: "the Mayer memorandum ... claims that 'by the end of 1937 our cryptologists had completely mastered the reading of intercepted German radiograms' and adds that in January 1938, in a two weeks' test, 'circa 75 percent of the material was then decyphered'. But it does not specify which Enigma keys were mastered or how extensive the material was. Nor does it say whether the material was read currently, and the reference to a two weeks' test may mean that current messages were not being decyphered."] As I have mentioned, the complete mastery of keysolving dated from the beginning of 1933, and Mayer did not have to wait until January 1938 in order to conduct a dress rehearsal. Nevertheless, it is true that in the meantime we had built certain additional devices (card files, cyclometer) that speeded up and facilitated the recovery of daily keys. However, from the premise that the "test" covered a two-week period the author [Hinsley] has drawn the entirely erroneous conclusion that the messages were not read currently. Mayer needed a two-week period only in order to make the results independent of chance and to obtain a good average.

P. 490, line 27 ff.: What a confusion of everything The "pre-1931 model" [that Hinsley says the Poles had "made their initial break into"] was the same final, single model all the time, but it was not the Navy model [as Hinsley says]. Keys for two, not three [as Hinsley says], months were supplied by Bertrand, therefore we did not steal them; if anyone did steal them, it was that traitor Asche. We did not find the Navy keys "currently" – if that be construed to mean continually, constantly – but only sporadically. I have no idea what to make of the statement that we read the Navy from 30 April to 8 May 1937. Where precisely do these exact dates come from?

P. 491, line 8 [Hinsley: The Poles had read "military Enigma ... until 15 September 1938, when the Germans introduced two additional wheels" – rotors – "thus increasing the number for selection from three to five"; the Poles "had subsequently worked out the wiring of the new wheels; but... by mid-December 1938 they had ceased to be able to read the traffic."] On September 15, 1938, the Germans did not introduce the additional rotors IV and V, but changed the system for transmitting message keys. Rotors IV and V were introduced on December 15, 1938. We quickly found their [internal wiring] connections.

P. 491, line 15: The Enigmas used in Italy, Spain and Switzerland were machines of the commercial type, i.e. they had no 'plugboard,' and moreover all the signals on a given day were enciphered from the same starting position, which tremendously facilitated the reading of messages. The German Navy used the same type of Enigma as the Army and Air Force, except that [the Navy] earlier [than the Army and Air Force] had five drums instead of three. We were unable to read the Navy at first due to lack of [cipher] material.

P. 491, line 26 [Hinsley: In January 1939 Bertrand organized a Polish French-British conference in Paris "because the Poles had not reported any success to him, and he was becoming desperate."] [Colonel Gwido] Langer [head of Poland's Cipher Bureau] had not been authorized to disclose that we had long since broken Enigma.

P. 491, line 2 from bottom [Hinsley: "when suggesting the July" 1939 "meeting the Poles announced that something new had happened..."] "*Il y a du nouveau*"

["There is something new"] was an agreed-upon code phrase. The only thing new was that the chief of [the Polish General] Staff had given permission to reveal the secret of Enigma's solution.

P. 492, line 3 [Hinsley: "As it happens, the Germans did not add extra wheels to the army and air Enigmas in the summer of 1939, though they made other changes..."] They did not introduce new rotors. Correct. However, on January 1, 1939, they increased the number of plug connections, which the author does not mention at all; and the change of July 1, 1939, [a date mentioned by Hinsley in an admittedly incorrect context] consisted in this: that the SD net, which up to then had been using the old procedure for transmitting message keys, now switched to the system used by the other nets.

P. 492, line 8 [Hinsley: In July 1939 the Poles "had not yet overcome the difficulties caused by the much greater change of September 1938."] We overcame very quickly the difficulties caused by the changes of September 15, 1938, by building 6 bombs and beginning production of perforated sheets. More serious difficulties arose on December 15 with the introduction of rotors IV and V. To be sure, we quickly found the connections within the rotors, but the introduction of the new rotors raised the number of possible sequences of drums from 6 to 60, that is, ten-fold, and hence also raised ten-fold the work of finding the keys. Thus the change was not qualitative but quantitative. We would have had to markedly increase the personnel to operate the bombs, to produce the perforated sheets (60 series of 26 sheets each were now needed, whereas up to the meeting on July 25, 1939, we had only two such series ready) and to manipulate the sheets.

P. 492, line 13: No, it was not [as Hinsley suggests, cryptological] difficulties of ours that prompted us to work with the British and French, but only the deteriorating political situation. If we had had no difficulties at all we would still, or even the more so, have shared our achievements with our allies as our contribution to the struggle against Germany.

P. 492, line 17 [Hinsley: Although the Poles "had recovered the wiring of the September 1938 wheels..."] December 1938 rotors.

P. 492, line 19 [Hinsley:... they "had not been able to read the military Enigma since the end of 1938... "] We continued reading the SD net on a current basis until July 1, 1939. After December 15, 1938, we had read only 10 percent of the military net, after July 1, 1939 [we read] only 10 percent of the SD net.

P. 492, line 26 [Hinsley: At the Polish-French-British conference at Warsaw in the last week of July 1939, "it was settled that the British would concentrate on finding a method of breaking the daily keys while the Poles retained responsibility for more theoretical work."] This was only Mayer's wishful thinking. The closeness of war made it impossible even to think of theoretical work. All our effort during these few weeks up to the moment of our evacuation was directed exclusively at recovering the greatest possible number of keys with the aid of the six bombs and two series of perforated sheets that we had. We had absolutely no time to even begin perforating a third series of sheets, much less to think theoretical work.

P. 492, line 33 [Hinsley: "It is clear... that the Polish cryptanalysts, who were transferred to Bertrand's Paris organisation at the beginning of October," 1939, "were not themselves reading the Enigma at the time" - as the British were unable to, even after having received "the various papers from the Poles... in particular the wheel wirings": the Poles "believed that the Germans had again made wholesale changes to the Enigma on the outbreak of war, whereas the Enigma then underwent no change."] No, here again that's not how it was. Naturally, at first in France we could not solve Enigma messages, but not because we assumed that the Germans had again changed something, but because we had destroyed all our work tools-the perforated sheets and bombs – before leaving Poland, and without them any work was entirely out of the question.

P. 492, line 2 from bottom [Hinsley: "In the event the first war-time break into the Enigma was made with help from GC&CS" – Britain's "Government Code and Cypher School" – "by the Poles at Bertrand's organization in Paris at the end of 1939."] What was the nature of this "help from GC&CS"? They [the British] copied our perforated sheets and in mid-December 1939 sent one set of 60 series of 26 sheets each to France for us Poles.

P. 493, Line 28 ff. [Hinsley: "Bertrand claims that up to 14 June," 1940, 'in the period from 28 October 1939, 121 Enigma keys were solved; he also implies that the results were all produced by his organization. But Mayer states that as well as investing in the development of the Bombe, which the French left to the British, GC&CS broke 83 percent of the keys that were read at this time; he adds that in all 126 keys were broken in this period, for 100 days from 6 July 1939 to 16 June 1940."] I have the impression that the difference in counts of solved days comes from a misunderstanding. Of course Mayer was right in stating that 83 percent of the keys in this period were sent over [to us in France] by the British. And Bertrand no doubt gave the days that we read, and after all we read both the messages of days in which we had found the keys and those of days for which the British sent us the keys.

P. 493, line 4 from bottom [Hinsley: Mayer "explains that GC and Cuss's preponderance was due to the agreed division of labor, by which Paris concentrated on research while GC&CS gave priority to technical development aimed at the quicker breaking of daily keys, and of the fact that GC&CS was better organised and equipped than Paris to intercept and decypher the German traffic."] The situation is perfectly obvious: How could it be otherwise, when there were three of us Poles, later two [after Jerzy Rózycki on January 9, 1942, went down with a French ship while returning from a Algerian stint to the secret codebreaking center near Uzes, not far from Marseilles, in Vichy France – Translator], and [there were] at least several hundred British cryptologists, since about 10,000 people worked in Bletchley and the environs. Besides, recovery of keys also depended on the amount of intercepted cipher material, and that amount was far greater on the British than on the French side. Finally, in France (in contrast to the work in Poland) we ourselves not only sought for the daily keys, but after finding the key also read the messages. In such circumstances, conceptual work really was out of the question. One can only be surprised that the Poles had as may as 17 percent of the keys to their credit.

P. 494, line 1 [Hinsley: "It should be added that GC&CS's punched-hole sheets turned out to be much less laborious than the non-Bombe methods developed by the Poles... "] I hope that what the author writes about the British "punched-hole sheets" and the Polish "non-Bombe methods" is not written from a motive of ascribing authorship to the British, but from ignorance. After all, they adopted this [the perforated sheets] from us; the only difference was that we used millimeter-ruled paper and they used paper divided into inches, that our paper was white and theirs was cream-colored, that we cut the holes out toilsomely with razor blades and they used a perforator. But the way the author presents it, he creates the impression that they came up with something new and better.

P. 494, line 16 [Hinsley: "It is virtually certain that the GC&CS Enigma team would... have realized the need to develop analogue machinery for recovering the daily keys as soon as it had discovered the wirings of the Enigma wheels..."] "As soon as it (GC&CS) had discovered the wirings of the Enigma wheels." Exactly. With that one brief phrase they [the British] have disposed of the most important matter. They got the connections of the first five drums from the Poles, and subsequent ones (in the Navy) when they managed to capture a submarine with intact drums. They did not discover any connection in the drums on their own by cryptological means. Their effort, to be sure an enormous one, concentrated mainly on recovering keys on the basis of a machine that they already had.

P. 494, line 21 [*sic* – Rejewski probably means Hinsley's lines 29 ff.: "The first British capture of Enigma wheels was made from U-33 in February 1940. As this was seven months after GC&CS's receipt of details of the wheels from the Poles, the first [British] Bombe would in the absence of Polish assistance have been delivered to GC&CS in January 1941 instead of in May 1940."] Erroneous calculation: According to what Winterbotham states and according to our other sources, it was only in May of 1941 that the British obtained from a sunken submarine (I believe, the U-110) the set of five rotors that we had supplied them in July 1939. [Editor's Note: Hinsley states, p. 337, that the U-11O, captured by chance on 9 May 1941, included that "special settings used in the Navy for 'officer-only' signals..."]

Is it not truer, what Ronald Lewin says in his book *Ultra Goes to War*: "They (the Poles) made Ultra possible" (p. 50)?

BRITISH INTELLIGENCE - VOLUME II
Ralph Erskine

British Intelligence in the Second World War: Its Influence on Strategy and Operations, by F. H. Hinsley, E. E. Thomas, C. F. G. Ransom and R. C. Knight. London: Her Majesty's Stationery Office, 1981. £ 15.95. New York: Cambridge University Press. \$39.50. Volume Two. 850 pp.
8(2): 173-180.

This volume starts in mid-1941, where Volume I, reviewed in *Cryptologia* (January, 1982),[1] left off. It continues the story until mid-1943, covering all areas except the Far East, which was excluded because it was so much within the United States' sphere of influence and inadequately included in British records. The war at sea and in the air are dealt with comprehensively. On land, the North African campaign naturally falls for the most attention.

For those who were disappointed by the style or even by some of the content of Volume I, this volume comes as a pleasant surprise. That volume made rather heavy reading. Overall, Volume II ranks among the better written of the British series, even if it still cannot be said to be lively or anecdotal. Official histories, being works of record, have to set out a multitude of facts, which does not lend itself to a light style.

When reviewing Volume I, William P. Bundy complained of the lack of references to individuals and of the fact that there was no bibliography[1]. The latter will, we are assured, be remedied in Volume III. The former is typical of most of the British official histories, many of which had the same general editor as this volume. And this reviewer has much sympathy with the view of the authors that such a work should follow Flaubert's precept: *pas de monstres, et pas de heros*. Given the subject matter, how could any general history distinguish between the contributions made by the many individuals at the Government Code and Cypher School ("GC&CS" or "Bletchley") to the breaking of Enigma? A further reason for the emphasis on organizations is that the work has been based mainly on written records. We can hardly complain since, given the size of the task, it could scarcely have been otherwise. Other writers can fill in the interstices by tracking down and interviewing those of the participants who are still alive.

Although the authors had virtually unrestricted access to official files, the constraints included a bar on publication of "details of the methods by which [intelligence] was obtained" [2]. There is therefore no description of the cryptanalysis of Enigma or *Geheimschreiber* (Fish) by GC&CS. So we will have to content ourselves with accounts elsewhere[3].

Readers of *Cryptologia* will probably search first for the treatment of cryptographic topics. There is material in plenty. The index is a good guide to the work's coverage. The entry for GC&CS covers almost 5 columns, that for Enigma, 7. Some items are short, and poignant, histories in themselves ("Italian Navy – GC&CS breaks cyphers of...; GC&CS loses cyphers of...;"). There are several columns on Sigint and a few inches on C38m (modified Hagelin).

However, the book is about much more than cryptology. Essentially, it deals with the organization of intelligence and its integration into the command structure. No single element of intelligence, no matter how important, could sensibly be considered and used on its own. Enigma-based intelligence ("Ultra" in British terms) was supplemented by lower grade intelligence collected by the Y Services (nets of listening posts established by the Army and Air Force[4]), electronic intelligence[5], traffic analysis and other measures: all played their part. And then the results had to be analyzed, distributed and used. Perhaps that is why there is, and had to be, so much discussion of committees and structure in these volumes. It was in the efficient organization and use made of all intelligence that the Allies excelled.

The introductory four chapters (which start with chapter 15) consider developments in the organization of intelligence. Chapter 16 describes arrangements with the United States and relations with the Soviet Union. While there were some initial differences with the United States Navy Department, by June 1943 there was very full collaboration. A visit to the United States by GC&CS in October 1942 ensured that the Navy Department would receive Enigma decrypts and technical assistance from the British The Navy Department agreed to supply GC&CS with Japanese Naval decrypts and other intelligence and allowed GC&CS to coordinate work done by American bombes. It also agreed to construct only 100 of its own three-wheel bombes, as they had merely half the capacity of the British model. But later on, British four-wheel bombes (needed to break the four-wheel version of Enigma used by the U-boats) had a low serviceability rate and were wholly supplanted, by end-1943, by American bombes.

The concordat with the Navy Department had its price. It led to friction with the War Department[6], which had not been consulted, so that it was not until

May 1943, after various missions and high-level interventions, that there was a similar, but even more far-reaching, agreement on the Army side. This left all German and Italian military ciphers to GC&CS and the Japanese ciphers to the War Department.

As one would expect, there was little progress towards exchanging intelligence with the USSR. Information on how to solve German police ciphers and *Abwehr* hand ciphers was given to the Russians. Since Ultra revealed that various Soviet ciphers were being read by the Germans, the British intelligence authorities were reluctant to release Ultra to the Soviets even when the source was not disclosed. When they did so, they were yielding to pressure from the prime minister. The history states categorically that there is no truth in the suggestion that the Lucy ring[7] was used by the British to pass intelligence to the USSR A lot of operational intelligence was sent through the British military mission in Moscow. The Soviets were very reluctant to give anything in exchange, even information about captured German equipment.

One feels that the authors are most at home when writing about naval affairs, including the U-boat war. Indeed two of them (Hinsley and Thomas) worked on naval intelligence at Bletchley. They survey fully the events surrounding the introduction, in February 1942, of the additional wheel into the U-boats' Enigma machines. Even though the development had been foreshadowed in Enigma decrypts as early as the spring of 1941, it was not until December 1942 that GC&CS managed to break the four-wheel version (codenamed Shark by the Allies). This notwithstanding that, due to the classic error of an operator using four-wheels prematurely and then repeating the message on three, the wiring of the fourth wheel was recovered in December 1941. Appendix 19 discusses the breaking of Shark and the reasons for the delay, which was to contribute to heavy Allied shipping losses. Those losses were made worse due to the fact that in February 1942 the *Beobachtung-Dienst* ("*B-Dienst*", the German Navy's radio intelligence section) finished its solution of Britain's Naval Cypher No. 3, so that they could read most Allied signals about the North Atlantic convoys.

Solving Shark was obviously of considerable importance. The authors do not, however, describe it as the decisive factor in defeating the second U-boat campaign which began against the convoys in December 1942. They do not therefore wholly agree with the German naval historian Jürgen Rohwer, in his assessment that the turning point would otherwise have come "months, maybe many months" after May 1943[8]. The book also brings out the use of Ultra, in the war at sea, in other ways as well as against U-boats. An auxiliary raider (*Komet*, or Raider B) was attacked and sunk because its movements were known, largely due to Ultra. Blockade runners were intercepted. Linelaying operations by Bomber Command were stepped up considerably because Ultra showed them to be especially useful against German coastal shipping. Many other examples are given.

The air war presented a very different picture from the war at sea. U-boat operations, being based on the pack, were controlled by the German submarine commander in chief, Admiral Karl Donitz, through two-way wireless communications. The German Air Force in the West largely used land lines and transmitted little of consequence in Enigma. So there were few nuggets of strategic importance to be gleaned from *Luftwaffe* Enigma. Sigint and, in particular, the RAF Y service therefore provided much useful intelligence about *Luftwaffe* operations, including night defenses.

There is full coverage of the war in the Mediterranean and North Africa. The book demonstrates just how important Ultra was in contributing to the defeat of the Axis in North Africa. Important, but the battle of Gazala in May and June, 1942, showed that Army Y intelligence could be more helpful than Ultra during a battle (not least because, being provided locally, it was generally available more quickly) and that it was vital to integrate "Y" fully into the headquarters' structure.

The appendices, totaling about 140 pages, contain some of the most interesting material in Volume II for the general reader, mainly because they are more analytic in tone. Appendix 1 considers British cipher security during the war and gives the reasons for the Admiralty's reluctance to adopt the Typex machine[9], hitherto inexplicable to this reader. Instead it depended on codes (confusingly, a 4-figure code used by officers was called a cypher), which were recoded by a subtractor system. GC&CS did not dissent from this decision because it believed that messages would be secure if the recycling tables were replaced at frequent intervals. The volume of traffic prevented that. The real culprit was divided responsibility for the Navy's cipher arrangements, which was split between three different sections.

Appendix 1 also gives an account of the results of German cryptanalytic work on British codes and ciphers. The well-known *B-Dienst* success against naval codes was considerable. This was especially so for Naval Cypher No. 3, which was used from 1941 to at least the end of 1943 by the United States, British and Canadian navies in the Atlantic. Although there were signs from other decrypts in the second half of 1942 that it had been cracked, it was not until Shark was broken that GC&CS realized the full extent of the penetration. There is a short summary of work done against Allied merchant marine and merchant ship codes.

A separate part of Appendix 1 considers the security of Ultra[10]. The reader is left with the impression, from that appendix and the book as a whole, that there may have been too many risks taken, even though Ultra itself showed that the Germans were having doubts about their own cipher security, albeit that the messages did not show their concern, on occasion, about Enigma. More is to appear on this subject in Volume III. How was the arrival of British submarines at Cape Verde during a U-boat rendezvous in September 1941 to have been explained by the Germans? Or the sighting by Allied destroyers of a refueling between submarines on January 13, 1943? The cover stories must have been very thin. Interestingly, the fourth wheel added to the U-boats' Enigma was a step taken against only "internal insecurity" (the risk of Enigma being read by persons on other Enigma nets[11]).

Appendix 3 is the only place where the names of individual cryptanalysts feature. It sets out in full a letter from Alan Turing, Gordon Welchman, Hugh Alexander and Stuart Milner Barry[12], all of whom worked in Ruts 6 and 8. Following a visit from Winston Churchill to Bletchley, they appealed to him over the heads of officialdom for about 60 to 100 extra staff. Churchill treasured Ultra, which he knew as Boniface. On the same day that he received the letter, he wrote an "Action this Day" minute asking for Bletchley to "have all they want on extreme priority." Their needs were very soon met.

Appendix 4 is the fullest list yet published of various Enigma keys[13]. The naming system adopted by GC&CS is given (insects for *Fliegerkorps* keys, birds for the Army's, fish for the Navy's and so on). By the war's end, about 220 keys had been attacked, of which only 20 or so were naval. The German Army home administration key, used throughout the war, was broken only 13 times and some of those breaks required prisoner-of-war help. A key used by the Gestapo, also for the entire war, was never solved. Although this is described as a classic mystery of Hut 6, both keys illustrate just how secure Enigma could be when used sensibly. Welchman states that it would then have been impregnable[14]. The examples of these keys, taken with the length of time required to crack Shark, may serve as indirect testimonials to the pioneering achievement of the Poles, working as they did with exiguous resources of men, money and machines.

Another appendix covers German police and hand ciphers. A considerable effort was mounted against them, because they provided an entry into Enigma, and much the same system was used by the German Army and Air Force. It also confirms, as first revealed by Peter Calvocoressi[15], that GC&CS knew, from spring, 1942, until February, 1943, the precise numbers of deaths in 10 German concentration camps, including Auschwitz and Dachau.

No mistake should be made about the importance of this volume. Quite simply, it is the key to a full understanding of the history of the period. Virtually every other book published so far on the history of World War II in the areas covered by it has to be interpreted in its light. There are no startling revelations, because the general story, including that of Enigma, is now well known. Since most, but not all, of the papers seen by the authors are now in the Public Record Office, there will be other books which may on occasion take a different view to that of the authors or expand the treatment of specific topics. None is ever likely to replace it.

This work will remain a classic and be consulted for very many years to come. For the historian, it is essential reading. The average reader is more likely to want to dip into it from time to time; he will almost certainly profit from doing so. For each, Welchman's book complements this volume on the technical aspects of work on Enigma at Bletchley, as well as filling in some of the human background.

The book is excellently produced and reasonably priced for a specialist work. The proofreading and the index are superb. One looks forward to the next volume (which is to appear in two parts) with a sense of real anticipation, which could not be said after reading Volume I.

No assessment is made in this volume of the ultimate effect of the Allies' ability to read Enigma. Hinsley takes the view that is shortened the war by about three years[16]. Whatever the period, many thousands of lives must have been saved as a result. Ultra could have no better epitaph.

REFERENCES AND NOTES

1. William P. Bundy, "From the Depths to the Heights," *Cryptologia*, 6 (January 1982), 64-73.

2. *House of Commons Debates*, 941 (January 12, 1978), cols. 829 830.

3. On the cryptanalysis of Enigma, see Marian Rejewski, "Mathematical Solution of the Enigma Cipher," *Cryptologia*, 6 (1982): 1-18; the appendix by Tadeusz Lisicki in Jozef Garlinski, Intercept: The Enigma War (London, 1979); Gordon Welchman, *The Hut Six Story: Breaking the Enigma Codes* (New York, 1982).

On the breaking of *Geheimschreiber* by GC&CS, see Welchman, 176-179; Brian Johnson, *The Secret War* (London, 1978), 338-347.

4. For a fascinating and well written autobiographical account of the RAF's Y Service, see Aileen Clayton, *The Enemy is Listening* (London, 1980).

S. See Alfred J. Price, *Instruments of Darkness*. (London, 1977).

6. Welchman states that, even as late as 1944, similar difficulties made it impossible for the United States Army and Navy cryptanalytic divisions to discuss Enigma topics with each other directly although they wanted to do so. The British acted as a go-between: Welchman, 74, 75.

7. A Soviet intelligence net in Switzerland that is alleged to have provided quantities of valuable intelligence. Its sources have never been discovered. See further, Garlinski, 107-118; Pierre Accoce and Pierre 'Acquet, *The Lucy Ring* (London, 1967).

8. Jürgen Rohwer, "Ultra and the Battle of the Atlantic. The German View," Presentation in 1977 to the U. S. Naval Academy, 12. [Cited in Volume II.]

9. On this machine, see Louis Kruh and C. A. Deavours, "The Typex Cryptograph," *Cryptologia*, 7 (1983), 145.

10. What was perhaps the greatest danger to Ultra's security has received too little attention in this work (only the barest of references in a footnote on page 145 of Volume I). Following the invasion of Poland, the team of Poles who first broke Enigma, including the now famous trio of Rejewski, Zygalski and Rózycki, worked in France under Colonel Gustave Bertrand of the French Army, from October 1939 until November 1942. They were first based near Paris and, after France's defeat in June 1940, in unoccupied France at Uzes (near Avignon). Known as Unit 300, they had to escape when the Germans occupied all of France in early November 1942. Some, including Bertrand and Colonel Gwido Langer of the Polish Army, were captured. At least one, Antoni Palluth, the chief engineer of Unit 300, died in a German concentration camp. It is to the eternal credit of all those taken prisoner that none revealed anything about their work, although some were questioned by the Gestapo: Johnson, 321-323; Christopher Kasparek and Richard Woytak, "In Memoriam Marian Rejewski," *Cryptologia*, 6 (1982), at 22,23; Garlinski, 132,133.

11. Welchman, 39 and the signal of April 22, M41, from the commander in chief of the German Navy, prohibiting unauthorized tuning in to the U-boat net, in Andrew Hodges, *Alan Turing: The Enigma* (London, 1983), 199.

12. On each of these, see Welchman, and Ronald Lewin, *Ultra Goes to War: The Secret Story*. (London, 1978.) 179.

13. On the components of a key, see Welchman, 43, 44.

14. Welchman, 168.

15. Peter Calvocoressi, *Top Secret Ultra* (London, 1980),

16. The Times [of London], (September 9, 1981), 5.

ALAN TURING: THE ENIGMA
Ralph Erskine

Alan Turing: The Enigma, by Andrew Hodges. London: Burnett Books, 1983. £18.00. New York: Simon and Schuster. $22.50. 587 pp. 8(4): 332-336.

The title, of course, holds the key - and not only for readers of this journal. Alan Turing worked at the United Kingdom's Government Code and Cypher School ("GC&CS") at Bletchley Park in World War II, mainly on cracking Enigma. He was also a fascinating, and complex, person. He played a major part in designing the British electro-mechanical bombes, which were used to ascertain the key settings of Enigma machines by the probable word method, a task for which his talents and prewar research made him almost uniquely qualified[1]. It was a massive stroke of good fortune for GC&CS and his country that, while at Princeton in 1938, he declined the offer of a post as assistant to John von Neumann unless, as seems unlikely, he had been approached by GC&CS before his departure for America in 1936. However, Bletchley was only a small part of Turing's life, notwithstanding that it was vital to the Allied cause. He was, first and foremost, an applied mathematician of genius and a profoundly original thinker in the fields of computers and machine intelligence.

This review concentrates on the author's treatment of Turing's work at GC& CS (pages 160 to 314). One reviewer has commented that "Andrew Hodges' account of the mathematical, logical and engineering work in the whole Enigma story is, perhaps, the most revealing yet published."[2] It is difficult to agree; anyone who buys this book with a view to learning much more about the work of GC&CS on Enigma than has already appeared in print will probably be disappointed. For the general background of Bletchley, Hodges relies heavily on Gordon Welchman's and Professor Henry Hinsley's books[3]. And Welchman's comes alive in a way that Hodges' does not. There is no significant new material, although the author contacted Barry Golombek, Jack Good, Sir Stuart Milner-Barry and many other old Bletchley hands. The constraints imposed by the United Kingdom's Official Secrets Acts are almost certainly responsible: people who worked at Bletchley are still barred from revealing any technical details of the methods used to break ciphers[4]. Hodges' book scarcely touches on the mathematics of the cryptanalysis of Enigma. There is nothing to compare with the papers by Colonel Tadeusz Lisicki (of the Polish Army)[5] or Marian Rejewski (the Polish cryptanalyst who first cracked Enigma in 1932) himself[6]. however, he does describe the general design of the Polish bombes, which used "a brute force method" and of the British versions which, having internal logic and menus, were much more sophisticated[7].

There are various tantalizing references to special machines designed by Turing to deal with the main naval Enigma and to assist Golombek in analyzing key used by German motor torpedo boats, a key, incidentally, which is not mentioned in Hinsley's list of those tackled by GC&CS[8]. A method (called "Turingismus") for dealing with *Geheimschreiber*, a teleprinter-type 10 wheel cipher machine, is described as "important and general." No details of the Turing machines or of Turingismus are given. It is not clear whether it was based on an earlier method (called "Banburismus") which employed probability theory and sequential analysis[9] against Enigma. It is typical of Turing in part of Banburismus, he independently rediscovered and developed Peirce's concept of the weight of evidence (or logarithm of the Bayes Factor). Jack Good has commented on the interesting relationship between the weight of the evidence and aspects of Claude Shannon's mathematical theory of communication[10] and, with Toulmin, suggested the advantages of replacing entropy by anticipated weight of evidence in the proof of some of Shannon's coding theorems[11].

These lacunae are compounded by the fact that Hodges, a mathematician, is not fully at home with cryptological topics. Abraham Sinkov is referred to as a naval cryptanalyst. And he writes of *Geheimschreiber* (codenamed "Fish" by GC&CS) that his "understanding is that there was more than one machine covered this generic term"[12] but does not cite *Cryptologia*[13], Lewin[14] or other authority. Indeed, he seems to be unaware of *Cryptologia*. as it is never mentioned, although articles on Enigma. in particular, give information which is not available elsewhere.

Colossus, which was "arguably the world's first electronic computer"[15] was built for GC&CS in 1943 to help in cracking Fish. Turing applied his statistical theories to fish analysis but did not work on Colossus despite his theoretical studies on universal machines. One forms the impression that he unsuited for team work on such a large project. In addition, he was in the United States on a liaison mission between November 1942 and March 1943, meeting William Friedman and Claude Shannon, among others. Around late 1943, he moved "sideways and downwards" from Bletchley to Hanslope Park an out station. With only a few assistants and little by way of material resources (they had to make their own frequency analyzer), he designed a rotor based V8F speech scrambler, codenamed Delilah. Completed in the spring of 1945, it never went into service, even in peacetime. Hodges describes it as being 15 years ahead of its time.

After the war Turing worked at the National Physics Laboratory on a plan for an advanced system of computers. Because of various frustrations, he resigned in 1948 and moved to Manchester University to work on its early computers. He also acted as an occasional consultant to the Government Communications Headquarters, which GC&CS became in the postwar years. He was elected a fellow of the Royal Society in 1951, in no small measure due to his paper on "Computable numbers"[1]. which he had written at the age of 23.

Turing's tragedy, especially in the England of the 1950s, was that he was both homosexual and socially extremely naive. In 1952, following a complaint to the police that his house had been burglarized, he was convicted of an offense and required to undergo hormone treatment. In June 1954. he committed suicide. He was only 41. Hodges thinks that he was virtually hounded to his death by an unjust and hypocritical establishment, a theme which overdominates the somewhat florid last chapter of his book. However, Donald Michie (now professor of machine intelligence at Edinburgh University), who as a very young man worked with Turing in Bletchley, believes that he may have thought that he had burnt himself out and that, for a lonely and unstable genius, suicide seemed to be the only solution[16].

It is unfortunate that the Bletchley side of the book does not add greatly to the sum total of our knowledge because. in general. Andrew Hodges has carried out his research splendidly, hampered though he was by secrecy and a lack of documents in many areas - not only those relating to GC&CS. Inspired (there is no other apt word, since it took him two penurious years to research and write this book) by his membership of the gay liberation movement, his interest in and commitment to his hero are complete and help him to convey the full flavour of his subject. All the old stories about Turing are apparently true (wearing a gas mask to ward off attacks of hay fever, losing silver ingots by burying them during the war and so on). Some are new. While his book contains only small items of additional information about Bletchley, it collects other material (much of it from out-of-the-way publications) in convenient form for the first time. Its real strength is that it is virtually indispensable, albeit far from light, reading for anyone interested in Turing or who wants to learn about him. That should be tribute enough.

REFERENCES

1. Turing. A. M. 1937. On computable numbers, with an application to the *Entscheidungs* problem. *Proc. London Math. Soc.*, (2) 42: 230 (in which he discusses the use of machines to solve mathematical problems).

2. Steiner, G. 1983. Machines and the man, *The Sunday Times* [of London], October 23: 42.

3. Welchman, G. *The Hut Six Story: Breaking the Enigma Codes* (New York. 1982); F. H. Hinsley, E. E. Thomas, C. F. G. Ransom and R. C. Knight, British Intelligence in the Second World War, Volumes 1 and 2 (London. 1979 and 1981).

4. See *House of Commons Debates*, 941 (January 12, 1978), cols. 829-830.

5. The appendix to Josef Garlinski. *Intercept: the Enigma War* (London, 1979).

6. Rejewsk, M. 1982. Mathematical Solution of the Enigma Cipher, *Cryptologia*. 6: 1.

7. Hinsley merely states that the British Bombe was of quite different design from the Polish, volume 1, 494.

8. Hinsley, volume 2, appendix 4.

9. Good, I. J. Studies in the History of Probability and Statistics XXXVII A. M. Turing's Statistical Work in World War II, *Biometrika*, 66 (1979) 393; *Probability and the Weighing of Evidence* (London. 1950); and *The Estimation of Probabilities*. (Cambridge MA. 1965) 18, 31, 32, 68.

10. Good, I. J. 1979. *Biometrika* 66: 393.

11. Good, I. J. and G. H. Toulmin. 1968. Coding theorems and weight of evidence. *J. Inst. Maths. Applics*. 4: 94.

12. Note 4.45.

13. Davies, D. W. The Siemens and Halske T52e Cipher Machine, *Cryptologia* 6(1982): 289. The early models of the Siemens and Halske T52 Cipher Machine, *Cryptologia* 7(1983): 235.

14. Lewin, R. 1978. *Ultra Goes to War*. London: Hutchison and Co. 132.

15. Laver, M. 1983. A century of catching up with Babbage. *New Scientist*. September 15: 780, 781. On Colossus, see B. Randell, " The COLOSSUS" in N. Metropolis. J. Bowlett and G. C. Rota (eds.) *A History of Computing the Twentieth Century*. (New York. 1980).

16. Michie, D. 1984. A loner, a misfit, a genius, *New Scientist*. February 9: 36.

POLISH ENIGMA ATTACK DOCUMENTED
Louis Kruh

Kozaczuk, W. (C. Kasparek, ed. and trans.) *Enigma: How the German Machine Cipher Was Broken and How it was Read was the Allies in World War II*. University Publications of America, Inc., 44 Market Street, Frederick MD 21701 USA. 1984. 348 pp. $24. 8(4): 366-367.

Although there have been several excellent books on the cryptanalysis of the German Enigma cipher machine such as R. Lewin's *Ultra Goes To War* and G. Welchman's *The Hut Six Story*, this is the first English work which tells the story in a detailed and authoritative fashion from the Polish perspective.

Published originally in Warsaw and now competently translated and edited with additional appendices, the book starts in 1929 at Poznan University's Mathematics Institute where top mathematics students who knew German were asked to participate in a cryptology course. Three students who managed to complete the course, which was based on M. Givierge's *Cours de cryptographie*, were Marion Rejewski, Henryk Zygalski and Jerzy Różycki. Based on interviews, letters, personal papers and documents written by this brilliant trio and other key Polish General Staff Intelligence and Cipher Bureau officers, the author relates the dramatic events which led to one of the most important cryptanalytic feats in history. He follows the adventures of the trio after the invasion of Poland as they continue their work on Enigma ciphers in Paris and, when it is overrun by the Germans, in southern France and North Africa, before having to flee for their lives to Spain, Portugal, Gibraltar, and finally reaching the British Isles in mid-1943. Oddly, after their arrival in England, Rejewski and Zygalski – Różycki had died in a boat sinking in 1942 – who had made the British Enigma-breaking operation possible by their solution of the Enigma ciphers which was turned over to the British, were never invited to Bletchley Park and were not able to continue their work on the decryptment of Enigma messages. (The author's wry comment is that, "Everything connected with the German machine cipher had become a British monopoly.") Instead they devoted their efforts to breaking German S. S. and S. D. ciphers.

The importance of the Enigma solution is highlighted by the many instances told of how Ultra decrypts were successfully used in the land and sea war. The author, justifiably proud of the Polish accomplishments, demonstrates their significant contribution to the winning of the war. Because this book was written after the Lewin and Welchman books, Kozaczuk is able to point to errors and discrepancies despite their otherwise fair treatment of the Polish role in the breaking of the Enigma.

In a series of fascinating appendices, there are these important papers by Rejewski: The Mathematical Solution of the Enigma Cipher; How the Polish Mathematicians Broke Enigma; and Summary of Our Methods for Reconstructing ENIGMA and Reconstructing Daily Keys, and of German Efforts to Frustrate Those Methods. Other appendices include a transcript of an interview with Rejewski by Richard Woytak and several letters from him, all dealing with his crypto work; a brief note on his post war life; and, using Welchman's book for technical input, Kasparek and Woytak outline Polish and British Methods of Solving Enigma.

The book contains dozens of photographs and drawings, many of them not previously published in this country, plus extensive footnotes, often containing additional important information.

This book is vital for a complete understanding of how the German Enigma cipher machine was broken.

BRITISH INTELLIGENCE
Louis Kruh

F. Hinsley, *et al.* *British Intelligence in the Second World War, Vol. 3. Part I*. RMSO Books/Bernan Assoc., 9730 E. George Palmer Highway, Larham MD 20706 USA. 1984. 693 pp. $36.00. 9(2): 181-182.

The third and final volume of this exceptional history is being published in two parts with Part I devoted to events from the summer of 1943 to the summer of 1944. The thrust of this volume is on the influence of intelligence on strategy and decision making on these events which include: the capture of Sicily, the Italian surrender, fighting on the Russian fronts, operations in Yugoslavia and British involvement with their resistance movements, U-boat warfare, the war in the air covering both German and Allied air offensives, and the V-weapons during this period.

The overwhelming role of cryptanalysis is revealed by references on virtually every page to the use of Enigma decrypts, often citing specific Army, Navy or Air Force Keys (an appendix lists over 45 Enigma keys attacked by the Government Code and Cypher School). An increasing source almost rivaling Enigma in importance was the *Geheimschrieber* (Fish), an on-line cipher machine (another appendix is devoted to various versions of this high grade machine and the use of Colossus to speed the solution of its ciphers). Still other sources were Japanese diplomatic decrypts, and in Italy, British cryptanalysts were reading The book has 27 appendices which include information on various aspects of cryptologic operations plus many other intelligence areas.

While the writing is sedate, as might be expected from an official history, the work is an outstanding contribution to an understanding of the part played by British intelligence in Allied strategy and operations in WW II.

BRITISH INTELLIGENCE – VOLUME 3, PART 1
Ralph Erskine

British Intelligence in the Second World War: Its Influence on Strategy and Operations. F. H. Hinsley, with E. E. Thomas, C. F. G. Ransom and R. C. Knight. London: Her Majesty's Stationery Office, 1984. £17.95. New York: Cambridge University Press. $39.50. Volume 3, Part 1. xvi and 694 pp. 9(3): 262-272.

This volume carries the story forward from June 1943 (when volume 2 finished[1]) to summer 1944: the concluding date for individual sections varies slightly. During that period the staff employed by the United Kingdom's Government Code and Cypher School ("GC&CS"), whose headquarters were at Bletchley Park, England, expanded from 5,052 to 7,723.

As before, the European theater is the main area covered in the air and land war. Separate sections, comprising two or more chapters each, deal with strategic intelligence assessments, the Mediterranean, the war at sea and in the air and the V weapons (V 1 pulse jet and V 2 rocket). The organization of intelligence does not feature as large as in volumes 1 and 2, being relegated to an appendix.

The author's style is substantially similar to that in volume 2: Professor Hinsley is really in his stride. Sometimes the main text is still hard pounding for the reader – mainly when fact is relentlessly piled upon fact, unrelieved by comment, analysis or the name of anyone with a rank lower than that of general. Obviously a lot depends on one's own main areas of interest; as it is, almost every page repays close study. Again, the appendices, some 27 in all, totaling 101 pages, constitute the most readable section, being more discursive in tone, and not crammed with the same mass of detailed events as the main text.

The most interesting single cryptological section is Appendix 2, which devotes six pages to *Geheimschreiber*, the German radio teleprinter cipher traffic known to GC&CS as Fish. Fish was enciphered on three different machines, the Lorenz *Sclüsselzusatz* SZ 40 and 42, and the various models of the *Siemens und Halske T 52* (respectively codenamed "Tunny" ["Tuna," for Americans] and "Sturgeon" by GC&CS), and "Thrasher," about which nothing is known [2]. Tunny was used by the army, Sturgeon by the air force and navy.

Fish was first detected in 1940, but traffic was spasmodic until mid-1941. By summer 1942, GC&CS had worked out the design and operation of both main machines. Tunny had two principal exchanges by 1944, with 26 links, which are charted. Messages could be very long: one had 60,000 characters. The interception and recording of the signals proved extremely difficult; a special station for the purpose was set up at Knockholt, which eventually employed 600 people.

Unprecedently for this work, the cryptanalyst who made the first break into Fish is named as the late Brigadier (as he became) John Tiltman. Andrew Hodges suggests that this was achieved because a German operator made the I catastrophic mistake of enciphering two identical messages with a key which also was identical, except that it advanced by only one character throughout[3]. Hinsley backs up that account. W. T. Tutte then saw that there was a pattern in the keying system for the Fish wheels [4].

Even when the wheel settings were known, the manual deciphering of Fish was too slow; a deciphering machine, which is not described, was therefore installed in June 1942 to help. Improvements to German operating procedures led to the construction of a high speed, if primitive looking, machine, Heath Robinson (after the British equivalent of Rube Goldberg) as an aid to breaking the more difficult settings [5]. Only three Robinsons became operational. Instead, a faster and much more complex machine, Colossus, was developed [6].

Colossus I used no fewer than 1500 vacuum tubes and Colossus II, 2400 – unheard of numbers for those times. They were the world's first electronic computers, although they were very specialized and could not store programs. Colossus I was operational in February 1944. A massive effort by the design and building team led to Colossus II being installed on June 1, 1944. It made an invaluable contribution to the success of the D-day landings (Operation *Overlord*). No details are included, but may appear in the final part.

Fish was used at the highest level – between armies and army groups. It therefore included important messages of a strategic nature and was the perfect counterpart to Enigma. Solution delays tended not to be so critical as with Enigma. The Germans added a further security device for all Fish transmissions in February 1944, that led initially to a 50 percent drop in the number of decrypts by GC&CS. Ironically, it also caused problems for the Germans, so that they stopped using it in September.

In part, special attention was given to Fish because the Germans were tightening up on Enigma and radio procedures as the war went into its fifth year. GC&CS was very worried that it might lose access to most of the traffic. False information was given in Enigma messages with a view to deceiving the Italians, which also caused alarm at GC&CS. The German precautions before June 1944, included an end to discriminants in Enigma messages and periodical changes of radio frequencies [7]. As usual, Hinsley is the essence of discretion in such security matters, giving few details beyond saying that the value of Red, GC&CS's name for the *Luftwaffe*'s general key and GC&CS's favorite, was reduced after a "new wheel" was introduced for *Luftwaffe* keys. The index refers to this as a fourth wheel, which scarcely fits an extra rotor (unless, which is unlikely, it was for a machine akin to the four rotor navy Enigma). It may have been the fourth reflecting rotor ("D") mentioned by Welchman [8].

More frequent references appear to decrypts of reports from the Japanese ambassador in Berlin [9], whose messages contained a great deal of valuable intelligence, of both a strategic and a technical nature [10]. The machine cipher of the Japanese naval attaché in Berlin was initially broken by GC&CS in early 1944. His signals yielded extremely useful technical intelligence, including a specification of the HS 293 (a new guided missile) and details of the advanced Type XXI U-boats: the latter had been causing the Admiralty great anxiety lest they were powered by the Walter closed-cycle engine, which used hydrogen peroxide as fuel. Appendix 11, an eight-page Admiralty intelligence appreciation of those boats, is entirely based on reports from the Japanese naval mission in Berlin.

Nothing is revealed about the machine used by the Japanese naval attaché. But presumably either the attaché's reports, or those of the ambassador, were encrypted using Purple (or its predecessor, Red) and deciphered by GC&CS with the aid of the copies of the Purple or Red machine sent by the United States to England in 1941 [11]. No reference has been made in any of the Hinsley volumes to those copies.

In the year ending June 1944, 50 new Enigma keys were broken: these are listed in Appendix 3. The *Luftwaffe* Red key continued to yield information about the army, as did other air force keys, which were on the whole used more carelessly than those for army nets. Porpoise, a naval key, also provided intelligence about fighting on the ground, for instance in Sicily.

Sigint proved valuable in the planning of the invasion of Sicily, indicating that the Germans considered it to be the prime target, with Crete, Sardinia and Corsica next on the list. This led to the mounting of a deception plan (Operation Mincemeat), in which the body of a man wearing a British uniform was cast up by the sea on the Spanish coast [12]. It carried a letter to General Alexander, the Allied deputy commander-in-chief, purporting to give Sicily as a deception target only. Sigint revealed that the Germans largely took the bait, issuing warnings that the attack would come in the Peloponnese!

"One of the most valuable decrypts of the whole war" gave very full details of Field Marshal Kesselring's counterattack on the Anzio beachhead. With intelligence of this quality manifesting itself, one can fully understand the reason for Kesselring's complaint, on a different occasion, that "the enemy always comes on the boundaries" between military units and the exasperated reply, from General Lemelsen, acting commander of the German 10th army – "the devil knows how he always finds out where they are" [13].

At sea, Enigma was employed to devastating effect against U-boats refueling in mid-Atlantic, which were the subject of a special operation by the United States Navy. Before June 1943, the Allies had been reluctant to mount such an exercise because they did not want to take ships away from escort duties and were anxious about the risk to Ultra's security. After Enigma disclosed the dramatic effects that the sinking of a supply U-boat had on U-boat operations, they changed their policy. Disguised grid positions, special officer-only Enigma settings and radio silence availed the Germans little. Numerous U-boats were sunk, including the vital fuel-carrying "milk-cows." The loss of the latter led to boats being recalled; others had their missions shortened. By the end of August 1943, only 40 operational U-boats were still at sea (there had been 70 in July), most of which were returning home or on curtailed patrols.

The story is much the same with the blockade runners to and from the Far East. In August 1943, GC&CS had broken their special key, Sunfish. Combined with other intelligence, including Japanese diplomatic decrypts, the result was almost total success for the Allies. Four out of five of the westward-bound ships were sunk, as were several of their escorts. No ship managed to sail for the East from the Biscay ports between November 1943 and January 1944, after which no further attempts were made.

In the air war, the RAF's Bomber Command was still largely incapable of precision attacks on targets such as aircraft factories, notwithstanding that navigation and bombing aids such as Oboe and H2S were in service [14]. It therefore continued the area bombing of German cities in the vain hope that it would destroy civilian morale and wreak havoc with the economy. Enigma and similar intelligence, including diplomatic decrypts, gave some support for that hope. The British air ministry had severe reservations about some of the wilder proposals of Air Chief Marshal Harris, the commander of Bomber Command, such as his plan to "wreck Berlin from end to end – thereby winning the war, in his view. However, there just was not enough clear evidence to prevail against the RAF's belief in the efficacy of its tactics. Eventually, it was probably the horrendous scale of the RAF's losses due to German night-fighter operations, as much as evidence about the continuing strength of the German economy, that led to the abandonment of the air battle of Berlin.

Technical details relating to aircraft, rocket, and submarine development feature prominently, as does electronic warfare. 10-cm radar, used in the search for U-boats, was countered by the *Naxos* and *Fliege* radar receivers, which in turn were defeated by 3-cm radar, against which the Germans then fitted the *Mücke* receiver: all of those German countermeasures, and others, were revealed by Enigma [15]. Various forms of radar used by the RAF, such as H2S (centimetric radar, incorporating the revolutionary magnetron) and IFF (identification friend or foe), were turned against it by the Germans, who employed them to track the planes operating those systems [16]. "Smart" weapons appear with the BS 293 radio-controlled, rocket-propelled, air-to-surface missile and FX free-fall, radio-guided bombs [17]. Although RS 293 was described in the Oslo report [18] and referred to in at least one Enigma message, ships at sea were not warned before it was first used against them, so that initially no countermeasures, which were comparatively simple [19], were available. The Admiralty was distinctly disturbed about the lack of advance notice, so accustomed had it become to

Enigma disclosing this kind of development. The highly volatile T-stoff (an 80 percent concentration of hydrogen peroxide) showed up in various projects, including the Me 163 rocket-propelled fighter, which was a frightening machine for anyone unlucky enough to have to work with it [20].

ADI(Sc) (the assistant director of scientific intelligence at the air ministry, the prescient Dr. Reginald Jones, until recently professor of natural philosophy at Aberdeen University) is referred to frequently. It is illuminating to compare this part with the relevant sections in his *The Wizard War*, as well as those in related books [21]: it also helps to enliven these sometimes arid pages. Jones' book, in particular, shows very clearly just how intelligence was gleaned from the raw Enigma decrypts and other material.

It is, of course, a fundamental mistake to focus too much attention on Enigma or any single source of intelligence. Everything had to be pieced together with other material, interpreted and disseminated: only then could it be acted upon. This book shows how important the integration of intelligence was; it does not highlight interpretation. And, trite though it may be, even the best of intelligence was not enough on its own. Enigma played an important role in the war against the U-boats. But so did long-range Liberators (B-24's) and escort carriers, centimetric radar and other technological developments. Intelligence also had to be implemented at the sharp end of the fighting. Sigint gave some, if not perfect, warning of the evacuation of Sicily by the German and Italian forces. Due to very poor planning and coordination, the Allies did not mount an effective operation against the evacuation, which was greatly assisted by the geography of the heavily defended short crossing to the mainland.

At times it is easy to fall into the trap of thinking that Enigma was all-revealing, so that it is salutary to be reminded that it left some significant lacunae, which were not necessarily filled by Fish, Y [22] or other sigint sources. Perhaps the biggest single gap arose because there was little direct Enigma coverage of the overall German economy. While there were indirect indicators of war production in the form of statistics for aircraft and tanks coming into service, these were by no means a true guide to the numbers coming off the production lines. One method of assessing aircraft production was by reference to the numbers stenciled on German aircraft. Surprisingly, this worked until spring 1943. It failed then because spaces were deliberately introduced in those numbers, presumably for counter-intelligence reasons.

Enigma gave no hint for nine months of a new 85-megacycle airborne radar, *Lichtenstein* SN2, which came into service on German night fighters. It operated to considerable effect before its wavelength was discovered, yet it had always been vulnerable to a long *Window* ("chaff" – aluminium strips which, when dropped from the air, confuse radar operators by producing false echoes) [23]. The fallibility of the human factor is illustrated by the fact that a rough sketch from an agent had misled many people (but not Jones, although he accepted that he could be wrong) into believing that SN2 operated at about 165 megacycles. The first reliable evidence to the contrary came from a remarkably clear camera-gun photograph [24]. In the meantime, SN2, when coupled with other radar developments and improved night-fighter tactics [25], led to Bomber Command's suffering very heavy losses: in its worst night of the war, 94 aircraft were lost out of 795 during the March 30, 1944, raid on Nuremburg.

Nothing appeared for 15 months to reveal that the Germans were using H2S radar emissions to track RAF aircraft at the then vast range of 250-300 miles with *Naxburg*. In part, the reason for *Naxburg*'s success was that the British scientists involved did not want to believe that their latest invention also assisted the enemy so soon after its introduction, despite repeated evidence that all radar transmissions were inherently vulnerable in this way. Time and time again this volume illustrates the truth of Rowley Scott-Farnie's aphorism - "Intelligence is rarely dramatic – the best results are obtained from the continuous study of details, which although singly are of little value are collectively of great importance ... it is incorrect to draw conclusions through wishful thinking, sincere but faulty observations, ambiguous or inaccurate recording" [26].

The scant references to agents in enemy territory in this volume illustrates the vital nature of sigint, in particular, to the Allies; thus no information, was obtained from agents directly from Sicily to assist in the planning of its invasion – apparently the British secret service had no agents on the island However, agents and members of the various underground movements performed much valuable intelligence work. To give but two examples, members of the Polish Home Army captured substantial portions of wreckage from a crashed V-2: 50 kilograms of important components were airlifted out from Poland [27]. Agents among the foreign workers at Peenemünde sent information about the development works there [28]. Many lost their lives among the 600 of those workers killed in the Peenemünde raid on the night of August 17-18, 1943. We must never forget those who "in lone obscurity and of their own free will risked torture and death" [29] on our behalf.

My few criticisms mostly concern detail. The lack of the promised bibliography is still a nuisance. Until it arrives, there are tantalizing references to such items as *The Handling of Naval Special Intelligence* (p. 217), *History of Sigint in the Field* and *The History of the Special Liaison Units* (both p. 111): they are probably internal histories and may go to the Public Record Office. Jargon is refreshingly absent, but what was a "Concrete" telegram (pp. 105, 203) or a "Siebel ferry" (pp. 96-98)[30]? There is no definition of "*B-Dienst*" (quite frequently used in all volumes).

Hinsley's predilection for anonymity is overdone: pages 363 and 364 refer to the controller of projectile development (CPD) (who gave cabinet committees technical advice on rockets in connection with investigations by Duncan Sandys into the V1 and V2 threat); a parenthetical reference to explain that this was the then Dr. A. D. Crow, as on page 396 (which gives no initials), would have been welcome. That is not an isolated example – the Japanese ambassador to Germany [9] is never named. The index sometimes helps – if you know the right name in the first place.

Cryptologically minded readers may be able to work out what "a depth' resulting from the re-use of key" is (p. 481) in relation to the cryptanalysis of Fish – but will others? It is mystifying, and more, to be told that, in North Africa, No. 30 Commando captured "a new high-grade *Abwehr* machine cypher, hitherto unbroken" leading to six weeks' traffic on the link being read, without any further hint as to what the machine was. If Enigma, the key is not clearly mentioned in the list of keys in Appendix 3. It was scarcely Fish, so what was it?

I have only one major reservation. This is history from the files – and depersonalized history at that – with the limitations that such an approach inevitably entails. Hinsley almost certainly recognizes this drawback but, if he had used different methods, volume 2 might still not be finished – or worse [31]. So this history is by no means the full story; at times the real explanation of some complex of events will lie outside these pages [32]. Thus you will hunt high and low here and still not find the reason underlying the hostility of Lord Cherwell (Churchill's personal scientific advisor) to Sandys' appreciation of the V2s. Typically, it is given by Jones, but in a work not referred to by Hinsley – "Cherwell did not like Duncan Sandys, and once Duncan Sandys had begun to believe the evidence and say that it was a serious danger, Cherwell reacted the other way" [33].

Overall, the book is well produced, with few typographical errors (e.g. "Medit-terranean", p. 155, the alignment of a rule on p. 420 and "Collosos", p. 479). The admirably lengthy index, which looks like Hinsley's own work, is a delight to use, being well cross-referenced. There are ten useful maps, eight of which are fold-outs.

Professor Hinsley's erudition, industry and unrivalled mastery of his subject have given us one of the best works in the series of excellent British official histories. We will be forever in his debt. Roll on, the last part.

NOTES

1. For a review of volume 1, see William P. Bundy, "From the Depths to the Heights," *Cryptologia*, 6 (1982), 64; for volume 2, Ralph Erskine, "British Intelligence – Volume II – Book Review," *Cryptologia*, 8 (1984), 173.

2. Bradford Hardie was one of the very few people to foreshadow both the Lorenz and the Siemens machine, "Unravelling the Enigma Story," *Cryptologia*, 6 (1982), 62.

3. Andrew Hodges, *Alan Turing: The Enigma* (London, 1983), 230.

4. Hodges, 230; see also Brian Johnson, *The Secret War* (London, 1978), 342.

5. On Heath Robinson, see Jack Good, "A Report on T. H. Flowers's Lecture on Colossus," *Annals of the History of Computing*, 4 (1982), 56.

6. On Colossus, see Brian Randell, "The Colossus" in N. Metropolis, J. Howlett and G. C. Rota (eds) *History of Computing in the Twentieth Century* (New York, 1980); T. B. Flowers and others in "Colossus at Bletchley Park," *Annals of the History of Computing*, 5 (1983), 239-262.

7. Gordon Welchman, *The Hut Six Story: Breaking the Enigma Codes* (New York, 1982), 125.

8. Welchman, 137.

9. General Uiroshi Ōshima, Japanese ambassador to Germany from February 1941 to 1945.

10. There is no mention as yet of his November 1943 report on the Atlantic wall (see David Kahn, *The Codebreakers* (New York, 1967), 508).

11. Kahn, 23.

12. See Ewen Montagu, *The Man Who Never Was* (London, 1953). For the story behind that book, see R. V. Jones, *Most Secret War* (London, 1978), 217 (published in New York as *The Wizard War*).

13. C. J. C. Molony, with F. C. Flynn, H. L. Davies and T. P. Gleave, *The Mediterranean and Middle East* (London, 1973), Vol. V, 494.

14. On Oboe and H2S, see Alfred J. Price, *Instruments of Darkness* (London revised ed., 1977).

15. Before these became operational, an elegant spoof carried out by an Allied prisoner of war, probably on his own initiative, had played successfully on German fears that an earlier receiver, Metox, emitted radiations on which Allied planes were able to home. This caused them to waste considerable energy on unnecessary countermeasures. On this episode and the other radar devices, see Alfred J. Price, *Aircraft Against Submarine* (London, revised ed., 1980).

16. Instruments of Darkness deals with both *Naxbur* and *Flammen*) see Jones, ch. 41 for *Flammen*. As Price points out, the use of radar emissions in this way is

further confirmation of the German adage "*Alle Funkverkehr ist Landesverrat*" ("All radio traffic is treason"): Instruments of Darkness, 176.

17. On the RS 293, see Johnson, 298-300.

18. A remarkably accurate report of November 1939 on German weapons research that was sent anonymously by a German scientist to the British naval attaché in Oslo. Its full text is given in Appendix 5 to Vol. 1 of this work. For the surprising background to the report, which was regarded as a plant by most of the British defence scientific establishment, see Jones, cL 8. Jones has said that "during the few quiet moments of the war, I used to turn up the Oslo report to see what was coming next": Johnson, 9.

19. Johnson, 301.

20. On the Me 163, see Johnson, 276-282.

21. E.g. Price (both books), Johnson. On the post of ADI(Sc) – "assistant" was something of a misnomer – see Jones, 182, 183.

22. The interception, analysis and decryption of low grade cipher and other radio traffic in the field.

23. Codenamed "Rope"; Price, Instruments of Darkness, contains a photograph.

24. This photograph is reproduced as plate 18c in Jones; it also appears in Price, Instruments of Darkness.

25. *Zahme Sau (Tame Boar)* in which fighters attacked the bombers on their way to targets. Ground controllers first inserted twin-engined planes equipped with SN2 into the bomber stream; a homing device on, or messages from, the "twins" allowed the controllers to direct single seater fighters to the stream.

26. Public Record Office file AIR 40/2243. Cited in Aileen Clayton, *The Enemy is Listening* (London, 1980), 51.

27. Josef Garlinski, *Hitler's Last Weapons* (London, 1978), 151-165.

28. Jones, 337-339.

29. Jones, dedication.

30. Righly maneuverable craft, with a broad beam and a formidable battery of anti-aircraft weapons, that could carry 450 men or 10 vehicles: S. W. Roskill, *The War at Sea.* (London, 1960), Vol. III, Part 1, 145.

31. In 1981, Professor Michael Howard completed his official history of British counterintelligence operations in WW II, on which he had worked for ten years. He then submitted it for governmental evaluation so that publication would not prejudice current security work. No decision on publication has yet been taken: *House of Commons Debates*, 53 (February 6, 1984), col. 427.

32. This shows up glaringly in Appendix 1 of Vol. 1 – probably the weakest section of this history, despite the importance of its subject matter – in which

Hinsley considers the Polish contribution to the breaking of Enigma by GC&CS. At p. 494, he concludes that the Poles gained GC&CS seven months as respects the delivery of the first British bombe and its reading of *Luftwaffe* Enigma. As well as being in error in other respects (see Marian Rejewski, "Remarks on Appendix 1 to *British Intelligence in the Second World War* by F. H. Hinsley," *Cryptologia*, 6 (1982), 74), this takes no account of the important factors subsequently stressed by Welchman (Welchman 164, 165). Those factors led Welchman to the view that, without the Poles Hut 6 Ultra [cryptanalysis of *Luftwaffe* and army Enigma] would never have gotten off the ground" (p. 289), but it is unlikely that they appeared on the files.

33. Johnson, 130.

WASN'T THAT COLOSSUS?
Ralph Erskine

B. Randell, The Colossus. pp. 47-92 in N. Metropolis, J. Howlett and G.-C. Rota (eds.) *History of Computing in the Twentieth Century*. Academic Press, 111 Fifth Avenue, New York NY 10003 USA. 1980. pp. 659. $32.50. 9(4): 296.

Brian Randell's paper describes Colossus I and II, which were, in effect 2,400 vacuum tube (or valve) computers, but without stored programming, and their non-electronic predecessor, Heath Robinson: all three were used at Bletchley Park in World War II to crack various versions of *Geheimschreiber* (the Siemens and Halske 10 wheel teleprinter-type machine known to Bletchley as Fish). He also gives a substantial amount of general background about Bletchley. Because of the restrictions which applied when he wrote, his paper includes very little about the detailed design of Colossus and nothing whatsoever about cryptanalysis. It is recommended non-technical reading anyone interested in Bletchley or the world's first, very special purpose electronic computer.

WHAT IS AN ULTRA IMPORTANT COLLECTION DOING ON A FILM LIKE THIS?
Louis Kruh

Ultra. A microfilm collection of intercepted German military signals. Clearwater Pub. Co., Inc., 1995 Broadway, New York NY 10023 USA. 139 reels, 35 mm, $6,950 or individual reels at $50. per reel. With additional reels published from time to time as the signals are made public by the Public Record Office in England. 9(4): 298-299.

During WW II, German messages enciphered by the Enigma cipher machine we decrypted by the British Government's Code and Cypher School at Bletchley Park. Known as Ultra – their special security classification – these deciphered messages were sent to the intelligence staffs of operational forces.

Copies of the decrypts were eventually deposited at the Public Record Office (PRO) in England, in the Defe 3 section. Their very existence was a secret until 1974, when the files first began to be declassified. Although many books and documents have been written on the importance of Ultra to the history WW II, few individuals have had access to the actual messages. In 1979, Clearwater began microfilming the military signals which now 139 comprise reels. Each reel usually contains about 500 messages.

The firm is now starting to microfilm the naval signals at the rate of 10 reels per month for the next seven years. These were decrypted, translated, and sent from the German Naval Section of the Admiralty's Naval Intelligence Division, at Bletchley Park, to the Division's Operational Intelligence Centre in the Admiralty.

The films are produced by the PRO from carbon copies of the original translated decrypts distributed to Allied field commanders during the war. The messages contain information regarding the addressee of the British telex, identity of the sender, the frequency on which the signal was transmitted, time of origin of the German signal, the German originator, the German addressee, and the German priority assigned to the message. Most important for assessing the value of this intelligence information is the time of origin the telex from Bletchley Park to the Operational Intelligence Centre. In some cases, the decrypted and translated messages left Bletchley within hours of the original transmission; in others the delay was as great as 10 days. Defe 3 files are bound in order of the German time of origin – in some cases upwards from the bottom of the file – regardless of the time and date decrypting. A reel index which indicates the PRO Reference number, serial numbers and dates of the documents on each reel, is supplied with the microfilms.

These films are an invaluable resource for WW II historians, researchers, and scholars seeking to determine the role of Ultra in a particular situation or its influence in certain command decisions. All libraries should be made aware of the availability of this important collection.

REF. CX/MSS/ETPGM/47248 VL 1117 LM SB

ZZZZ

FIRST BATTLE GROUP WAS TO LEAVE (FAIR INDICATIONS PIOMBINO PIOMBINO) ONE SIX THREE NOUGHT HOURS THIRD FOR QUOTE

SWEPT WAY PATROL UNQUOTE SOUTHWARD AS FAR AS PUNTA DEI RIPARTI PUNTA DEI RIPARTI CONTINUING THENCE ON A COURSE TWO SEVEN NOUGHT DEGREES AS FAR SOUTHWESTERN CORNER OF ELBA ELBA. BOATS ((VL1117 1117 LM 45 45 SB 26 26)) TO STAND OFF AND ON ALONG PATROL LINE FOUR MILES TO WESTWARD RETURNING TO PIOMBINO PIOMBINO NOUGHT NOUGHT THREE NOUGHT HOURS FOURTH SOUTH OF ELBA ELBA. TARE ABLE TWO FOUR AND THREE ROGER BOATS ON TASK (COMMENT COMPARE ORDERS FOR POROUS POROUS IN VL VL ONE NOUGHT FIVE THREE) FROM TWO TWO HOURS TO TWO THREE THREE NOUGHT HOURS EIGHT MILES NORTHWEST OF ELBA ELBA

032230Z/12/43

RRT/HDD/NBL

Sample Intercept. (British Crown Copyright 1979.)

ENIGMA AND THE POLISH CONTRIBUTION

Ralph Erskine

Wladyslaw Kozaczuk, *Enigma: How the German Machine Cipher Was Broken, and How It Was Read by the Allies in World War Two*. ed. and trans. Christopher Kasparek. xiv + 348 pp. University Publications of America, Inc., 44 Market Street, Frederick MD 21701 USA. 1984. $24. Arms and Armour Press. 2-6 Hampstead High Street, London NW3 1QQ UK, £15.95. 9(4): 316-323.

Dr. Wladyslaw Kozaczuk was the first author to make public, in 1967, the fact that the Poles had successfully attacked the military version of the German Enigma cipher machine [1]. Unfortunately, no information about his revelations was published in English for a long time, which led various writers to publish nonsense about the Polish success having been due to stolen rotors or Polish workmen in the factory making Enigma machines [2]. The present book is a translation, with minor revisions and added editorial notes, of *W Kregu Enigmy*, which appeared in 1979. Following his 1967 book, the record was largely put straight in English publications by Marian Rejewski (who first reconstructed Enigma's wiring and worked out a method for finding its keys) and others. So Kozaczuk has no cryptanalytical surprises to spring on us. What he does, and does well, using a wide range of sources, is to tell the story of the Polish work on Enigma with a considerable amount of new detail.

Thus he deals fully with the work of AVA, the firm which produced the Enigma duplicates for the Poles, and with the evacuation of the Polish cryptanalytical team to France through Rumania in 1939. He also covers, although not so comprehensively, the Franco-Polish-British collaboration in 1939-40. But we even learn the size of the holes (one-third of an inch square) in the British version of the perforated sheets which had been invented by Henryk Zygalski, a Polish cryptanalyst [3].

Rejewski brings the text alive when he recalls a discussion between Rejewski and Turing about the flower, meadow saffron, which is a powerful poison, during a meal in a restaurant near Paris [4]. Rejewski's excellent memory – which seems to be a common feature among great cryptanalysts [5] – comes out.

One of his earliest cryptanalytical tasks, with Zygalski and Jerzy Różycki, was to reconstruct a German naval code. Almost 50 years later, he could still recall groups from the code (YOPY was "when", BAUG "and" and so on).

Kozaczuk gives the fullest description yet of work at Cadix (the Chateau des Fouzes, just outside Uzes, near Avignon), which was selected – and protected by Major Gustave Bertrand of French military intelligence [6]. Known as Unit 300, 15 of the Poles, including Rejewski, Zygalski and Różycki, worked at Cadix, which was then in the unoccupied zone of southern France, from October 1940 until November 1942. A lot of information emerges about Cadix, including the fact that its radio transmitter was provided by Commander Wilfred (Bill) Dunderdale of the British secret service [7]. It was at Cadix in July 1941, that Rejewski and Różycki broke the Polish LCD rotor cipher machine in a few hours, causing consternation in Polish signal circles!

What did the authorities at the British Government Code and Cypher School (GC&CS) think about Cadix's activities [8]? We do not know, but the Allied penetration of Enigma must have been at risk, if only because some of the Poles who know about it were liable to fall into the hands of the Germans [9]. However, it was not until September 1942, that a radio-detection team with a dozen vehicles arrived at Montpellier, 45 miles away, for the purpose of tracking down transmitters such as that at Cadix. As graphically told here in English for the first time, a car and radio-detection van arrived at the very gates of Cadix in an alarming incident on November 6, 1942 [10]. Astonishingly, Vichy police in the car did not enter Cadix, but instead truncheoned the unfortunate occupants of an adjoining farm.

Following the German invasion of the southern zone on November 11, 1942, Rejewski and Zygalski managed to escape to England [11], after enduring many vicissitudes, including a spell in two Spanish prisons, one of which was very grim. Other members of Unit 300 were not so fortunate: five were captured by the Germans and sent to concentration camps, where two died. Although he was a wanted man, and known to the Germans, Bertrand was ordered to go underground so as to prepare for the invasion of Europe. He was betrayed and arrested, providentially by the *Abwehr* and not the Gestapo, in January 1944. He escaped by a subterfuge and remained in France, on the run, until June 1944 [12]. *Enigma* is worth reading for these chapters alone.

Two chapters entitled "Enigma abroad" and "Enigma at sea" relate to the use of Ultra (Enigma decrypts for present purposes) by the British. They are partly based on books published before the British files on Enigma were released to the Public Record Office, which leads to some errors and omissions. Two examples will suffice. Enigma decrypts did not, pace Winterbotham [13], go to the Admiralty in the original German, although the actual messages were sent in translation, and not summaries as usually happened with army and air force traffic. The brief discussion of the sinking of the German battleship *Bismarck*, refers only to Winterbotham's and Beesly's books [14], both of which contain errors on that incident. Those chapters should, at the minimum, have been accompanied by a note mentioning the generally authoritative British official history [15] and stating that Winterbotham, in particular, is not always accurate on Ultra, since he did not have access to the archives. However, this weakness does not detract significantly from the book, as its real strength lies elsewhere.

The editor and Richard Woytak compare the Polish and British work on Enigma in Appendix F. They quote Welchman's remark "We were lucky" [16]. Part of their next sentence then reads "we can see *clearly* ... that the Allies were *simply* lucky" (my emphasis), which is a *non sequitur* with a vengeance. They conclude that "virtually all the major cryptologic techniques" used by the British including the bombes, had been used by the Poles earlier and that "the chief British contribution was an expansion in scale of operations." Those views are simply without foundation as respects the British bombes and the period after they became operational.

Before May 1940, GC&CS did indeed rely substantially on the invaluable Polish manual methods, such as the perforated sheets, for finding keys [17]. After May 1, 1940, when the Germans stopped doubly enciphering the message key on Red, an air force net [18], GC&CS could not read the Red traffic until May 22 [19]. It then managed to break into Red again with the aid of such devices as the sillies and the Herivel tip [20]. But although the Polish and the British manual methods were invaluable, before and after May 1940, in maintaining continuity with the traffic and for other reasons [21], they were largely stopgaps until the first really useful British bombes came into service around August 1940 [22]. Non-machine methods could not compete with the bombes when time was of the essence.

The Polish bombe had embodied a somewhat primitive approach, testing all the positions in turn; it had already lost much of its usefulness on January 1, 1939, when the number of connections on Enigma's plugboard was increased to ten [23]. Their bombe, and the perforated sheets, depended on the encipherment of the message key [24]; they both therefore became useless after May 1940 [25].

The bombe invented by Turing and Welchman was almost completely different from the Polish model [26]. It had internal logic and so could eliminate many different Enigma plugboard possibilities at a stroke. Most important of all it was not dependent on a doubly-enciphered message key.

Welchman makes it clear that he was writing only about Hut 6 (army and air force Enigma). Air force Enigma was generally the easiest to break and was first broken in January 1940. Army and naval Enigma were cracked from mid1941 onwards, with naval traffic being read earlier, mainly with the help of captured keys [27]. GC&CS broke the army and naval Enigma keys, including the extremely difficult four-rotor U-boat key, Triton (Shark to GC&CS), without any direct help from the Poles [28].

In no sense is this to decry the magnificent Polish contribution to the work done by GC&CS, which was indispensable to the latter's later successes [29]. It is most regrettable that the British official history, by making invalid assumptions and ignoring some factors [30], undervalues that contribution, without which "Hut 6 Ultra would never have gotten off the ground" [31]. But the Polish cause is not advanced by downgrading the innovative cryptanalytical achievements of GC&CS. Rejewski recognized that machines were essential to break Enigma messages quickly and that the Poles had neither the time nor the resources necessary to produce the improved bombes essential after May 1940 [32].

Kozaczak tells us what happened to some of the principals after the war. Happily, Rejewski held a fairly senior position as a bureaucrat before his retirement in Poland in 1967. However, it is almost ineffably sad to read the fate of some of the other members of the Polish cipher bureau, to which we owe so much, Its deputy head, Major Maksymilian Ciezcki, whose striking photograph appears in this book, died on the poverty line in England in 1951, aged 52. Like his chief, Langer [33], his life was almost certainly shortened by two years in concentration camps. Langer himself felt that he had been betrayed by the French and died in England, feeling bitter and disappointed, in 1948.

Christopher Kasparek has done much useful work, both as editor and translator. The translation reads very smoothly, which is no mean feat in such a technical field. He is due a special tribute, since without his efforts it must be very doubtful whether *Enigma* would have been published in English. The book gains considerably from the inclusion of Rejewski's own papers as appendices.

While the two most important have appeared in *Cryptologia* [34] and *Annals of the History of Computing*, it is entirely appropriate that they should be made available to a wider readership. There is an excellent several page bibliography, which must be the most comprehensive yet to be published on Enigma.

This book is definitely to be welcomed as a valuable addition to the literature on Enigma Kozaczuk has rightly done his countrymen proud.

NOTES AND REFERENCES

1. *Bitwa o Tajemnice: Sluzby Wywisdowcze Polski i Rzesy Niemieckiej, 1922-1939* (Battle in Darkness: The Intelligence Services of Poland and the German Reich, 1922-1939). Warsaw: Ksiazka i Wiedza, 1967.

2. Such beliefs were not confined to authors. Around October 1939, Commander Edward Travis (later knighted), then deputy director of the British Government Code and Cypher School, told Dr. Reginald Jones, of Air Ministry scientific intelligence, that the Poles had stolen rotors. There is no reason for him to have invented the alleged theft as a cover story: R. V. Jones, *Most Secret War* (published in America as *The Wizard War*. London: Hamish Hamilton, 1978 at 63).

3. p. 97.

4. Turing was the co-inventor, with Gordon Welchman, of the British bombes. These helped to find the keys used by individual Enigma nets, when suitably programmed with words that occurred in the text of the messages, see Gordon Welchman, *The Hut Six Story: Breaking the Enigma Codes*. New York: McGraw-Hill, 1982 at 80, 98, 42. Peter Calvocoressi, *Top Secret Ultra*. London: Cassell, 1979 at 50-52.

5. See David Kahn, *Kahn on Codes*. New York: Macmillan, 1983 at 3-17.

6. Bertrand had had close links with the Poles since 1931. By supplying them with key lists for Enigma, which he had obtained from the German agent "Asche", he played a critical role in Rejewski's reconstruction of Enigma's wiring. On the importance of the key lists, see Kahn: 306, note 60 and Rejewski as quoted by Jean Stengers in "Enigma, the French, the Poles and the British 1931-1940" in *The Missing Dimension*, Christopher Andrew and David Dilks (eds.), London: Macmillan, 1984 at 271, note 37.

7. Dunderdale had been the British secret service's resident (permanent representative) in Paris before the war: Josef Garlinski, *Intercept: the Enigma War*. London: Dent, 1979 at 40; see also Gustave Bertrand, *Enigma ou la plus Grande Enigme de la Guerre 1939-1945*, Paris: Plon, 1973 at 215, plate 42.

8. GC&CS almost certainly knew about the Polish presence at Cadix. Unit

300 had apparently requested GC&CS to send it the daily keys that GC&CS had found, as at Bruno (the Poles' 1939-40 headquarters outside Paris). Understandably, GC&CS refused to do so.

9. There can be no criticism of the individuals at Cadix, who were under orders. It should never be forgotten that those who fell into the hands of the Gestapo must have displayed considerable courage, since nothing can have been revealed by them about the Polish success against Enigma.

10. Kozaczuk's account includes a translation of part of Bertrand 137, 138.

11. Louis Kruh found it odd that Rejewski and Zygalski were not invited to visit GC&CS: *Cryptologia*, 8(1984) 366. The reason was the basic security principle of "need to know." They did not have to know anything about GC&CS in order to help them with their work at Boxnoor. Secrets shared unnecessarily cease to be secrets.

12. Bertrand, 202-204.

13. F. W. Winterbotham, *The Ultra Story*. London: Weidenfeld and Nicolson, 1974 at 23.

14. Patrick Beesly, *Very Special Intelligence*. London: Hamish Hamilton, 1977.

15. F. H. Hinsley, with F. E. Thomas, C. F. G. Ransom and R. C. Knight. *British Intelligence in the Second World War: Its Influence on Strategy and Operations*. London: Her Majesty's Stationery Office, 1979-84, volumes 1, 2 and 3(1).

16. Welchman, 169.

17. On the perforated sheets, see Marian Rejewski, "Mathematical Solution of the Enigma Cipher," *Cryptologia*. 6 (1982), 15-17. Hinsley states that the British versions were "much less laborious" than the Polish sheets (1:494). Rejewski flatly contradicted this, saying that the sheets differed only in relation to trivia such as the colour of the paper: Marian Rejewski, "Remarks on Appendix 1 to *British Intelligence in the Second World War* by F. H. Hinsley" *Cryptologia*, 6(1982) 82 (henceforth, Rejewski, "Remarks"). There is every reason to accept that Rejewski was right. The two accounts can be completely reconciled if one reads something such as "to prepare" after "laborious" in Hinsley, since there is no doubt that GC&CS carried out its huge task (60 sets, each of 26 sheets, had to be tested and made) very quickly and more efficiently than the Polesone example being that the latter had to cut the 1,000 holes in each sheet using razor blades (Rejewski, "Remarks," 82).

18. On the message key, see Welchman, 46 (described by him as the indicator) Red was one of the two principal keys then being broken by GC&CS. The other key was Yellow, which ceased to be used in July 1940. The Germans stopped

double encipherment on the other nets by about the third week in May.

19. Hinsley, 1:109; cf Calvocoressi, 50. The new keying method was sent out in amendments (operative on May 1) to the Enigma regulations of January 13, 1940 (Army No. 14, Navy No. 168 and *Luftwaffe* No. 14). (I am indebted to Mr. Gilbert Bloch for a copy of the amendments.) However, the amendments had to be distributed widely (which must have presented considerable organizational problems) to the users of anything up to 40,000 machines before they could take effect, Various erroneous dates have been put forward for the change in procedure for Red: see e. g., Stengers (who gives May 15, 1940, but does not refer to Hinsley in this particular context) 135; also Welchman, 96 (May 10, citing an earlier essay by Stengers). Stengers relies on Colonel Gwido Langer, the head of the pre-war Polish cipher bureau and of Unit 300, but Langer's, like most of the Polish accounts, did not name the individual nets. The dates become substantially consistent if the Poles were, until May 10, 1940 (when the German offensive opened), concentrating on the Yellow net, which used in the Norwegian campaign: cf Bertrand, 79. That is highly probable, since Norway was then the only place where fighting was taking place – and there were only three Polish cryptanalysts, who would not time to study traffic on inactive fronts, such as France, where it was still a "phoney war" or "*sitzkrieg*." Cf Rejewski, "Remarks," 82.

20. On the sillies and the Herivel tip, see Welchman, 99-110. An editorial note in Kozaczuk mentions another method which involved coded and enciphered meteorological reports.

21. See Welchman, 164, 165.

22. Cf Welchman, 101. An earlier, and less advanced, bombe is said to have come into service in May 1940 (Hinsley 1:494). If it did, it is most unlikely to have included the diagonal board invented by Welchman, which greatly increased the bombe's power. In that event, it may not of much assistance to GC&CS, as it would have been difficult to program (requiring three closed loops and longer "cribs"); see Welchman, 80, 306

23. Marian Rejewski, "How the Polish Mathematicians Broke Enigma." in Kozaczuk, at 268

24. Rejewski, in Kozaczuk, at 266, 267.

25. The Polish bombe was used only by the Poles, and only while they were still in Poland.

26. Professor Jack Good, who worked at GC&CS, has said that the British and Polish bombes had something in common: Jack Good, *Review of The Hut Six Story*, *New Scientist* (October 7, 1982), 42. Cf Welchman 16. From the published accounts it is not easy to see what the common factor was, other than

the elementary – one that both used Enigma's wiring.

27. On the break into army Enigma, see Hinsley, 2:294, 295; on the captures of naval key settings, see *ibid* 1:337.

28. By accelerating the introduction of the British bombes, the Poles had made a major indirect contribution. The bombes, which were essential to the cracking of army Enigma in 1941 and three and four-rotor naval Enigma, were in service much sooner than would otherwise have happened.

29. Welchman, 164, 165.

30. *Ibid.*

31. Welchman, 289.

32. Rejewski, in Kozaczuk, at 270.

33. On Langer, see note 19.

34. See note 17.

MACHINE SECRETS:
Frode Weierud

Machine Cryptography and Modern Cryptanalysis. Cipher A. Deavours and Louis Kruh. Artech House, Inc., 610 Washington Street, Dedham MA 02026 USA. 1985. 259 + xiv pp. $56.00. Artech Book Company Ltd., London, £56. ISBN: 0-89006-161-0. 10(1): 34-37.

Modern Cryptography and Modern Cryptanalysis is a fascinating text. Here for the first time we get a clear view of the more modern form of cryptography, ciphers based on machines.

In Chapter 1, *A la Recherche du Temps Perdu*, the reader is brought into contact with the first tentative attempts of various inventors to design the ultimately secure cipher machine. Arvid Damm, Edward Hebern, Hugo Koch, Arthur Scherbius, Willi Korn and Alexander von Kryha are a few of the inventors who played an important part in these historical developments.

At the end of WW I, stories about the inadequacy of existing code and hand-cipher systems started to appear in books and newspapers. This undoubtedly was a stimulation for inventors and businessmen to look more closely at cryptography.

The development of the wired rotor, an idea that appears to have come to Damm, Hebern and Koch almost simultaneously, is clearly the most important event following the end of WW I. It is therefore impossible to name any one person as the real father of the rotor principle, but it is perhaps true to say that Edward Hebern was a few horse lengths ahead of the others. While the other rotors were wired in a purely random fashion, Hebern's rotor was wired using the interval method thus insuring a flat, polyalphabetic frequency distribution.

Even if the rotor undoubtedly was the most important development during this epoch, the mechanical genius, Boris Hagelin, who developed purely mechanical machines, does get the credit he deserves. The authors have chosen to limit their text to rotor and pinwheel cipher machines, but they briefly mention several other historic machines such as the German teleprinter machines of Geheimschreiber series.

Chapter 2, Billy Friedman and the Electric Super Code Machine, is of historical interest. It is shown clearly, what has long been suspected, that Edward Hugh Hebern's inventions and machines played a very important role in the later development of US cipher machines.

Apart from putting US cryptologists on the right track for future designs, gave people like William Friedman, Frank Rowlett, Abraham Sinkov and Solomon Kullback the chance to become fully acquainted with rotor machines and their cryptanalysis.

The text goes on to describe rotor machines and the underlying theory, then introduces the possible cryptanalytic techniques. Here Friedman's Index of Coincidence (I.C.) statistics play an important part.

Mood Indigo: The Enigma Variations is the title of Chapter 3. This is another chapter full of new information. The authors clearly point out that Enigma is not one single machine, but is rather a family of rotor machines built on one principle, that went through a long sequence of modifications extensions. The Germans' use of the machine is explained in detail include their fatal choice of message indicators, which were of enormous help to Poles in their initial attack on the machine.

Several extensions to the basic Enigma are treated, among them the Enigma-*Uhr* and the plugable reflecting rotor D. The Enigma-*Uhr* had a 40-position dial and not 60 as indicated in the text and it is not at all clear how and where this device was used

The chapter gives a very good picture of the Enigma and its history.

2 Hours, 41 Minutes, the title of Chapter 4, is apparently the time Friedman, Kullback, Rowlett and Sinkov, the four greats, took to solve a challenge cryptogram enciphered on the Kryha machine.

This happened on February 23, 1933, but it did not prevent the *Internationale Kryha Maschinen Gesellschaft* from stating the following in their 1951 brochure:

> The most astute deciphering experts throughout the world are unable to decipher codes prepared with the Kryha Ciphering and Deciphering Machine. The use of Hollerith machines and electronic brains also can never assist in unauthorized deciphering.

This is something for prospective buyers of cryptographic equipment to keep in mind as similar statements are also made today, a fact the authors mention in their epilogue, The Summing Up.

Chapter 5, The Rags, is the story of a commercial success – the success of Boris Hagelin and his machines. These machines were mainly mechanical machines based on the use of pinwheels and a rotating cage equipped with fixed or removable lugs.

Here, as well as in the other chapters, we find a fine balance between the detailed description of the machines and the cryptanalytic techniques that can be applied.

Rainbow Rhapsody: Orange, Red, Green, Purple, Jade, and Coral is the title of the last chapter which treats the Japanese machines. Apart from explaining the design of these machines and their complete reconstruction by the Americans based on cryptanalytic techniques alone, the chapter shows the total failure of the Japanese in securing their communications.

This might come as a surprise to many, but history shows that the Japanese have had very little contact with the use of codes and ciphers during their long history. This is to some extent related to their language which in its written form does not easily adapt to cryptographic techniques.

In contradiction to what has been claimed by earlier authors dealing with this subject we learn that William Friedman was not the man who single-handedly broke the Japanese ciphers. The actual breakthrough on the RED machine was made by Kullback and Rowlett, while Leo Rosen supplied the missing link in the reconstruction of the PURPLE machine.

The book contains a total of 69 photos of various machines and cryptographic equipment of which several are published for the first time. Among these are the KL-7 rotor machine, the Lorentz *Geheimschreiber Schlüsselzusatz* SZ42, the ECM Mark II and several of the Japanese machines like Purple and Jade.

Machine Cryptography and Modern Cryptanalysis can be warmly recommended to anybody with an interest in cryptography. It is a very well written text overall and the authors should be congratulated for their clear presentation of several rather difficult cryptanalytic techniques. On the other hand, diagrams and simple sketches are missing. It is this reviewer's opinion that a few diagrams might have helped to clarify and complement the text even further.

Unfortunately the book is badly marred by an unreasonably high number of typographical errors and misspellings. On his first reading of the text, the reviewer found 27 pages with one or more typographical errors. Many of these errors occur in tables of ciphertext, message indicators, etc., directly interfering with the authors explanations.

It is a rather expensive book, especially so in Europe, and in this reviewer's opinion the present printing cannot be considered a quality product. Let us hope the publisher will rectify this in future printings.

WHO USED ULTRA INFORMATION FOR THE AMERICANS?
Louis Kruh

Deutsch, H. "Clients of Ultra: American Captains." *Parameters*. Vol. XV, No. 2. Summer. 1985. 55-62. 10(1): 44.

The author, a Professor of Military History at the US Army War College, reviews the manner in which Allied commanders treated Ultra and Magic information which was provided to them. This ranged from General Mark Clark's lack of enthusiasm to Eisenhower's respect for the intelligence. Deutsch also discusses the strategic uses of Ultra and Magic intelligence concluding that as more information is declassified the "reputation" of specific Allied generals, and occasionally of Allied leadership generally may be eroded.

ULTRA AND ITS IMPACT – A RETROSPECT1VE VIEW
Louis Kruh

Murray, W. "Ultra: Some Thoughts on its Impact in The Second World War." *Air University Review*. Vol. XXXV, No. 5, July-Aug. 1984, 52-64. 10(1): 44.

Dr. Murray reviews three instances which resulted in Allied losses, in which Ultra information was available but misused or unused. He emphasizes these were exceptions rather than the rule, and highlights the major role played by Ultra in the land, sea and air war.

Finally, Murray examines the German attitude on the possibility of their ciphers being compromised and their carelessness in the area of security discipline. He concludes properly that the lesson to be learned is never underestimate the capabilities and intelligence of an opponent.

ORIGINS OF ULTRA IN POLAND
Louis Kruh

Woytak, R. L. "The Origins of the Ultra-Secret Code in Poland, 1937-1938," in *The Polish Review*. Vol. XXIII, No. 3. 1978. 79-85. 10(1): 44-45.

The reason why military intelligence was of major interest to Poland is explained from a historical perspective. The author then reviews Poland's involvement with the Enigma machine, and how the Polish General Staff researched the problem and developed an organization which eventually broke the Enigma cipher. He also describes the meetings held with their British and French counterparts and the Enigma material given to them.

ULTRA AND MAGIC DECRYPT APPLICATIONS IN WORLD WAR II

Louis Kruh

Revue d'Histoire de la Deuxième Guerre Mondiale, Jan. 1984, No. 133. Presses Universitaires de France, 108 Blvd. St. Germain, 75279 Paris, France. $8.00. 10(2): 111-112.

A special issue of this French publication is devoted to articles by American military historians on how American commanders used intelligence gained from ULTRA and MAGIC decrypts.

The articles are, "The American Command: ULTRA's Customers," "MacArthur, ULTRA and the War in the Pacific, 1942-1944," "Admiral Nimitz and His Use of Secret Intelligence in the Pacific," "ULTRA in the European Theater," "ULTRA Intelligence in the 6th Army Group," and "ULTRA and the 7th American Army." Two related articles in this issue are, "Success and Failures of the German Cipher Service During WW II," and "Bibliographic Note on the Books and Documents in English on Espionage and Secret Operations."

All articles, which are in French, provide interesting perspectives on the use of decrypted enemy messages.

ENIGMA SOURCE?

Louis Kruh

Paillole, P. *Notre Edition Chez Hitler*. Editions Robert Laffont, 6 Place Street-Sulpice, 75279 Paris, FRANCE. 1985. 285 pp. $11.00. 10(2): 113.

A detailed story in French of the German spy, Hans-Thilo-Schmidt, codenamed H. E. or Asche. For ten years, starting in 1931, H. E. gave France secret information on Germany's plans to conquer Europe and, in particular, detail of their Enigma Cipher Machine. This latter information was passed on to Polish intelligence and eventually to the British which enabled the Allies to decrypt Germany's top secret messages enciphered on the Enigma machine.

The author, a retired Colonel, who vas in charge of the French Counterintelligence Section from the mid-1930's to 1944, has assembled a great deal of information on H. E. and relates the incredible story in novel-like fashion.

U. S. ROLE IN BREAKING THE NAZI CODES
Louis Kruh

Parrish, T. *The Ultra Americans: The U.S. Role in Breaking the Nazi Codes*. Stein and Day, Scarborough House, Briarcliff Manor NY 10510 USA. 1986. 338 pp. $19.95. 10(3): 190-191.

Since 1974, when Group Captain F. W. Winterbotham's book, *The Ultra Secret*, revealed the secret held for over 30 years – that the Allies had broken the German Enigma Cipher Machine – scores of books and papers have been written on the subject. But, until this volume was published, none had told of the crucial role Americans played in the top secret operations at Bletchley Park nor any details of their work as Special Security Officers handling Ultra material.

Based primarily on personal interviews and correspondence with U. S. signal intelligence officers assigned to work with their British counterparts, Parrish has created a thrilling story which includes luminaries such as Friedman, Rowlett, Sinkov, William Bundy, Telford Taylor, Supreme Court Justice Lewis F. Powell and others.

The text abounds with never-before-told tales of Americans at Bletchley Park and of their experiences in Special Liaison Units assigned to American Generals. A particularly fascinating story is of a TICOM mission to Germany as the war was ending to find out that they could about German signal intelligence and to gather German crypto equipment. Truckloads of material were located including Enigmas and *Geheimschreiber*s, but the most valuable find was German equipment that received and decrypted top secret Soviet signals which were the equivalent of German Fish (*Geheimschreiber*) traffic. The Russians split the message into nine elements, transmitting it on nine different channels, and this German equipment would reintegrate it and then it was decrypted. Many previously unpublished photographs taken at Bletchley Park plus others such as the Russian Fish equipment add extra interest to the book.

FRENCH CONTRIBUTION TO ENIGMA DECIPHERMENT
Louis Kruh

Bloch, G. *La contribution francaise a la reconstitution et au decryptement de l'Enigma militaire allemande en 1931-1932*. *Revue Historique Des Armes*. No. 161. Dec. 1985. pp. 17-25. Chateau de Vincennes, 94304 Vincennes, FRANCE. 50 francs (about $7.00). 11(1): 59.

A well researched, illustrated French article, with extensive notes and bibliography, which assesses the role of the French in the breaking of the German Enigma cipher machine by Polish mathematicians.

Bloch describes the genesis of the Enigma, how it operated, its analysis by Polish cryptologists, and the documents delivered by a German spy to French intelligence and given, in turn, to Polish intelligence.

The author concludes that, without detracting in the slightest from the accomplishments of Polish mathematicians, the material supplied by the French was fundamental to their success.

WELCHMAN'S LAST PAPER

Ralph Erskine

Welchman, G. From Polish Bomba to British Bombe: The Birth of Ultra. *Intelligence and National Security*. Vol. 1, No. 1, Jan. 1986. pp. 71-110 (other details as above). 11(4): 251.

Relying heavily in its early sections on papers by Marian Rejewski, the late Gordon Welchman links the pioneer work by Rejewski and other Polish cryptanalysts in solving Enigma before 1939 to BP's attack on Enigma in 1940. Its most interesting new feature is perhaps a table listing the daily keys broken by the Poles and BP between 17 January and mid-June 1940.

WORLD WAR II CRYPTOLOGY ON TAPE

Louis Kruh

Flowers, T. H. *et al.* "The Code-Breaking Computers of 1944," Hinsley, H., "Colossus and the German High-Grade Cyphers," lectures, March 26, 1987. IEE Publications, Station House, Nightingale Road, Hitchin, Hertfordshire SG5 1RJ ENGLAND. Four 90 minute cassette tape recordings of lectures and discussion $20.00. 12(1): 43.

An informative program arranged by the British Institution of Electrical Engineers (IEE) featured key people involved in the development of Colossus, the world's first computer, which was used to break high-level German teleprinter ciphers. Speakers included Dr. T. H. Flowers, "Colossus – Origin and Principles;" Dr. A. C. Lynch, "Colossus – the Photo-electric Cells;" Dr. A. W. M. Coombs, "The Design and Construction of Colossus;" and Professor Sir Harry Hinsley, "Colossus and the German High-Grade Cyphers." Other speakers and the subsequent discussion and questions from the audience provided additional new information.

NAVAL ENIGMA'S SECURITY
Ralph Erskine

Mulligan, T. P. "The German Navy Evaluates Its Cryptographic Security, October 1941," *Military Affairs*. Vol. 49, No. 2, April 1985. pp. 75-79. Eisenhower Hall, Manhattan KS 66506-7186 USA. Annual subscription (quarterly) $20.00 for two years for new subscribers. Single issues, $8.00. 12(1): 44-45.

Mulligan's excellent article deals with two reviews of naval Enigma's security by the head of the German Navy's Communications Service in October 1941. These followed the surrender of U-570 to the British on 27 August 1941, and an attack by the British SM *Clyde* on U-boats re-fuelling in the Cape Verde Islands on 28 September. Mulligan regards the contribution made by the capture of U-570 to Bletchley Park's breaking of naval Enigma as an open question, since a mass of documents was taken from U-570. In fact, no cipher material of any significance was recovered: in the many hours available before a ship with a boarding party arrived (U-570 had surrendered to an aircraft), U-570's admittedly green crew destroyed all the cipher documents and codebooks, save for one list of settings that was apparently of little assistance to Bletchley Park.

This article is based mainly on microfilm copies of German naval documents in the American National Archives. It does not seem to be generally known that the American Archives hold such documents for the period 1850-1945 on 4,383 rolls of microfilm (RG 242/T1022: about 2,000 rolls deal with the years from 1930 on). Although only two printed finding aids are so far available (for U-boat war diaries in WW I and II), these records are a treasure trove for naval historians, who have much reason to be grateful to the originator of the microfilming, Commander Dudley Knox of the Office of Naval Intelligence. The ambitious project, and some of the records, are described by Ernest M. Eller in "United States Navy Microfilm of the German Naval Archives," in Robert Wolfe (ed.), *Captured German and Related Records* (1974).

ULTRA TAKES TO THE AIR
Louis Kruh

Putney, D. T. *ULTRA and the Army Air Force in World War II*. Office of Air Force History, U. S. Air Force. 1987. 197 pp. USGPO, Washington DC 20402 USA. GPO Stock # 008-070-00600-6. $8.00. 12(3): 187-188.

Recently retired U. S. Supreme Court Justice Lewis F. Powell, Jr., was an Army Air Force Intelligence Officer in WW II before being recruited into the

Special Branch, Military Intelligence Service (MIS). (The Special Branch supervised the signals intelligence operations of the War Department and managed the handling and dissemination of special intelligence material.) Powell was sent to Bletchley Park, where he received intensive ULTRA briefings on the German Air Force and later became Special Security Representative to HQ, U. S. Strategic Air Forces in Europe. The first part of this most informative work is an oral history interview with Powell concerning his involvement with ULTRA. He tells how ULTRA information was received and transmitted, and how it shaped the character of Air Force strategy and operations. He recounts special uses of ULTRA in various campaigns and the results achieved. This is a rare, fascinating memoir, complete with illustrations, worth careful reading.

The second half of the book is an essay by Putney, "The U. S. Military Intelligence Service: The ULTRA Mission." In essence, this is a brief, but rather detailed, history of the Special Branch and its relations with their British counterparts. In interesting fashion, also illustrated, it describes their work with ULTRA in Europe and their involvement with Magic in the Pacific. The role of both ULTRA and Magic is outlined, differences in the handling of each are described; also covered is how security was maintained with some details of security lapses. This is an important volume which belongs in your personal library.

TEAMWORK SOLVED NAVAL ENIGMA KEYS
Louis Kruh

Erskine, Ralph "Naval Enigma: The Breaking of Heimisch and Triton." *Intelligence and National Security*. Vol. 3. No. 1. Jan. 1988. pp. 162-183. 13(1): 94.

Erskine provides a trenchant analysis of the problems involved in solving the Atlantic U-boat Enigma signals. He tells how cribs contributed by Huts 4 and 10 at Bletchley led to the breaking of the Heimisch Naval Enigma net. Then he gives a thorough description of the cooperation between Hut 8 and Hut 10 which, combined with the retrieval of codebooks from U-559, resulted in a successful attack on the Triton cipher net.

NAVAL ULTRA
Louis Kruh

Winton, John. *Ultra At Sea*. Leo Cooper Ltd., 190 Shaftesbury Ave., London WC2H 8JL ENGLAND. 1988. 212 pp. $24.00. 13(1): 94.

Success against the German Naval Enigma was not achieved until March and April 1941, and then only sporadically. But success led to more success and in May a German weather-reporting ship was captured along with the "Home Waters" Enigma key for June 1941. Two days later, U-110 was sunk but not before a British boarding party seized its Enigma machine, special code settings for high security traffic, and current code books. After that introduction and other background information, the author describes the vital role of Ultra in determining Allied naval strategy in a variety of sea battles and in the protection of convoys.

Winton relates the near disastrous effect of the Germans adding a fourth rotor to the Enigma. Also, the serious problems which arose when German cryptanalysts broke the Royal Navy's main cipher, Naval Cipher No. 2, and again when they succeeded against Naval Cipher No. 3, a reserve U. S. Navy cipher introduced in June 1941, for use by British, U. S. and Canadian Navies.

In the Mediterranean, the Italians, whose naval ciphers had been secure, yielded to pressure from the Germans to change their ciphers. The Germans claimed that the Italian ciphers were vulnerable. In the fall of 1941, the Italians then began to use the C 38m, a Swedish cipher machine, which GC&CS had broken earlier that year. Information from Italian C 38m messages, sometimes supplemented by Ultra decrypts, enabled the Allies to deploy their limited resources in the most effective fashion against Axis naval and air forces.

An interesting chapter relates many mistakes, carelessness and even gross breaches of security by the British in the way they handled Ultra information, which should have alerted Germans to the insecurity of Enigma ciphers. Instead the Germans attributed Allied successes to either possible treachery, careless talk, French resistance, S.O.E., messages captured by the Allies, external observations or to just about anything else except the possibility that the Enigma had been broken.

Although the book has a useful glossary and detailed index, it suffers from a lack of citations and sources. Still, it is an excellent detailed examination of the practical application of Ultra intelligence in the war at sea.

FINAL HINSLEY VOLUME

Louis Kruh

Hinsley, F. H. *et al. British Intelligence in the Second World War, Vol. III, Part 2*. HMSO, London ENGLAND. 1988. 1,038 pp. U. S. exclusive distributor, UNIPUB, 4611-F Assembly Drive, Lanham MD 20706-4391 USA. Order No. QBOIC. $69.00. 13(1): 95.

The fourth and final volume of the official British history of intelligence in WW II has finally arrived and it was worth waiting for. It is a giant book of over 1,000 pages describing events and associated intelligence gathered during the period from the planning of Overlord, the invasion of Normandy, to the German surrender. The authors assess the intelligence that was available before and during Overlord, the Allied breakout from Normandy, the fighting on the Russian fronts and in Yugoslavia, the war in the Mediterranean, U-boat warfare, the war in the air and the V-weapons offensive.

The influence of intelligence derived from Enigma and Fish decrypts and from other ciphers on strategic and operational decisions is discussed on nearly every page and in almost every battle on land, sea and in the air. It is an amazingly detailed work with over a dozen maps, source notes on virtually every page, a comprehensive index, a bibliography for all four volumes in the series and 30 very informative appendices.

The cryptologic scope of this book is perhaps best demonstrated by a sampling of appendix titles: Appendix 1, The Intelligence Branch at COSSAC and SHAEF; Appendix 6, Sigint Preparations for D-day (i) Arrangements made for the Production of Sigint (ii) Arrangements made for the Dissemination of Sigint to the Commands; Appendix 7, Decrypts of Signals reporting the Tour of the Military Defences of Northern France by the Japanese Naval Attaché in Berlin, 4 and 5 May 1944; Appendix 15, The Sources of High-grade Sigint after D-day (i) The Western Front (ii) The Italian Front (iii) The Soviet Fronts and the Balkans (iv) Naval Sigint (v) Enigma Keys Attacked by GC&CS between June 1944 and May 1945; Appendix 17, The Capture of Cherbourg; the Sigint Evidence; Appendix 19, Decrypts covering the Escape of XXI Mountain Corps; Appendix 30, The Polish, French and British Contributions to the Breaking of the Enigma; a Revised Account.

This massive volume and the equally worthy previous volumes in this series provide an inestimable contribution to the cryptologic and intelligence history of WW II.

SIGINT SECRETS
Louis Kruh

West, Nigel. *The SIGINT Secrets: The Signals Intelligence War, 1900 To Today Including the Persecution of Gordon Welchman.* William Morrow & Co., 105 Madison Ave., New York NY 10016 USA. 1988. 347 pp. $22.95. 13(3): 231-232.

This book was published in Great Britain under the title, *GCHQ: The Secret Wireless War 1900-1986* (see review; *Cryptologia*, 11(1) 62). It is similar to the British edition except for an enlarged Introduction and an appendix of correspondence between NSA and Gordon Welchman pertaining to severe restrictions placed on him after publication of his book, *The Hut Six Story*.

West traces the history of British signals intelligence and the development of electronic intelligence gathering in the west, including the evolution and activities of NSA. He casts new light on some of the important intelligence operations and espionage cases of our time. He asserts that Britain's Ultra operation never actually broke the Enigma cipher but instead made "maximum use of every crib, error, slip and plain-language indiscretion." The real lesson of Ultra, West says, is that any communications system, no matter how perfectly conceived, can be compromised by human error and betrayal.

A well researched book with new information and previously unpublished photographs.

SECRET WAR CONTINUES
Louis Kruh

The Secret War, Volume 3, Deadly Waves & Still Secret. British Regalia Imports, P. O. Box 50473, Nashville TN 37205 USA. Videotape (VHS only), 102 minutes, $39.95 (a $4.00 shipping & handling charge is being omitted for our readers). 13(3): 234.

The highly acclaimed three volume BBC series made in cooperation with the Imperial War Museum recounts the deadly wizard and espionage war waged between Great Britain and Germany in World War II. Volume 3 provides a highly dramatic account of the British effort to neutralize Germany's destructive magnetic mines which caused havoc among convoys delivering vitally needed supplies early in the war.

The second part of the tape presents a visual history of the German Enigma cipher machine and the successful efforts to decrypt its messages. It includes the role of Polish cryptanalysts, French intelligence officer Gustave Bertrand and his German agent, Asche, and the work of the British at Bletchley Park. Although much of the information has been in print, there is no comparison with seeing the actual machines in operation with appropriate commentary. There is a demonstration on how an Enigma's keys are set, how a Bombe is used to recover keys and one part follows a message from its interception to its decryption. There are also interviews with people who worked at Bletchley such as Gordon Welchman, Peter Calvocoressi, Jack Good, Max Newman, who worked on decipherment of *Geheimschreiber* messages, and others.

Newman describes the principles of the *Geheimschreiber*, also shown in use, and he explains how the Heath Robinson machine, predecessor to Colossus, was used to break its messages. T. H. Flowers, who developed Colossus, describes what it did and there is a demonstration on how it operated.

The tape includes WW II footage and the entire production is excellent with much of it shot in the actual secret wartime locations.

ULTRA AT SEA
Louis Kruh

Winton, John. *ULTRA at Sea.* William Morrow & Co., 105 Madison Ave., New York NY 10016 USA. 1989. 207 pp. $18.95. 13(4): 361.

This fascinating account of the use of Ultra intelligence in the Atlantic, the English Channel and other waters, which was published in England last year (see my review, *Cryptologia*, 13: 94-95), has now been issued in the United States.

After the German Naval Enigma was broken in the spring of 1941 it helped the Allies enormously, and by January 1942 there were only 6 German U-boats left in the Atlantic. But, when the German added a fourth rotor to the Enigma in early 1942, Allied cryptanalysts were stymied and eight months later there were 100 U-boats in the Atlantic destroying Allied convoys. It took another six months before the four-rotor Enigma was solved.

Winton describes the many ways Ultra was used such as the search that led to the sinking of the *Tirpitz* and the *Scharnhorst* in the North Sea. He also shows how carefully Ultra was used in order not to arouse Nazi suspicions that the Enigma cipher had been broken.

While the book suffers from a lack of bibliographical references, it is an excellent detailed work on the practical application of Ultra intelligence in the war at sea.

ULTRA IN THE MEDITERRANEAN
Louis Kruh

Bennett, Ralph. *Ultra and Mediterranean Strategy.* William Morrow & Co., 105 Madison Ave., New York NY 10016 USA. 1989. 496 pp. $25.00. 13(4): 363.

Bennett was assigned to Hut 3 at Bletchley Park in February 1941 and remained there until the end of the war. After Hut 6 decrypted an Enigma message it was sent to Hut 3 for translation and evaluation of its significance. And, if deemed important it was sent to the appropriate commanders in the field. Bennett writes with the authority and knowledge of one who was directly involved in handling the decrypted Enigma messages.

The book shows how the first airborne invasion of Crete was really a victory for the Allies that prevented the invasion of Malta; how Rome's supply lines were cut; the secret behind Montgomery's victory at Aliment; how American losses could have been cut at the Passerine Pass; how Ultra led the way for successful Allied invasions of Sicily and Italy; the real story of what happened to American forces on the Anzio beachhead; and how Ultra helped win the war in Italy and Greece. There is also dramatic new information on how Tito was able to seize control of Yugoslavia for the Communists.

Bennett discusses the content of Ultra messages and shows how they influenced vital military decisions made by Allied commanders. A series of 14 appendices provides additional information about interesting battles and events including one on how the Enigma was broken.

CODEBREAKING AND SIGNALS INTELLIGENCE
Louis Kruh

Andrew, Christopher, ed. *Codebreaking and Signals Intelligence*. Frank Cass, c/o Rowan & Littlefield Publishers, Inc., 8705 Bellman Place, Savage MD 20763 USA. 1986. 137 pp. $18.50. 14(3): 235.

This hard-covered slim volume, in an attractive dust jacket with a close-up photograph of an Enigma cipher machine, contains an important collection of articles which first appeared in the inaugural issue of the British journal, *Intelligence and National Security*.

The six articles are "Tsarist Codebreakers and British Codes" which sheds new light on penetration of British ciphers by the Russians in the early 1900s; "No Final Solution: A Survey of the Cryptanalytical Capabilities of German Military Agencies, 1926-35" reviews Germany's military codebreaking and describes its deciphering organization, signals intelligence network, and main targets; "The Government Code and Cypher School Between the Wars" by its operational head, A. G. Denniston, provides a general assessment of the organization and the achievements of British cryptanalysts between the wars; "From Polish Bomba to British Bombe: The Birth of Ultra" by Gordon Welchman, who played a key role, details how the German Enigma was vanquished by Polish and British cryptanalysts with French assistance; "Ultra's Poor Relations" by Christopher Morris, who worked at Bletchley Park, is a reminder of other valuable efforts at BP, namely the deciphering of numerous German hand ciphers; and "Surveillance and Intelligence under the Vichy Regime: The *Service du Controle Technique*, 1939-45" which shows the continuing importance of older and simpler methods of message interception such as letter-opening.

WINTERBOTHAM AUTOBIOGRAPHY

Louis Kruh

Winterbotham, F. W. *The Ultra Spy: An Autobiography.* Macmillan London Ltd., 4 Little Essex St., London WC2R 3LF, ENGLAND. 1989. 258 pp. $21.69. 14(3): 236-237.

Best known for his book, *The Ultra Secret*, which revealed to the world that the Allies had broken Germany's secret Enigma cipher in World War II, Winterbotham now tells the exciting story of his adventurous life. He traveled around the world at age 16 and in World War I ended up in the Royal Flying Corps where he was shot down and captured by the Germans.

In 193O, he rejoined the Air Staff as an intelligence officer and his mission soon was to determine what was happening in Germany in a period of political unrest and a resurgence of militarism. He was enormously successful, making a number of trips to Germany where he met Hitler and many of his top aides. He provides many vignettes of important figures of the time as well as eyewitness accounts of historic events.

An important section of his book tells how early in 1940 he proposed a plan for the translation, distribution and complete security of Ultra decrypts, with his messages were deciphered. He relates the problems of inter-service rivalry resulting in the Navy going its own way, and how the plan for keeping commanders in the field informed as fully as possible was carried out. He explains how Ultra was used in the Battles of France and Britain, its invaluable help in determining whether the Allies' deception plans for D-Day were successful, how Ultra helped the eventual victory, and later, how he came to write *The Ultra Secret*. It is an interesting account of an intriguing life.

ENIGMA BUST – AUF DEUTSCH

Louis Kruh

Kozaczuk, Wladyslaw. *Secret Operation WICHER: Polish Mathematicians Crack the German Radio Cipher Enigma.* Bernard Graefe Verlag, Postfach 2060, D-5400 Koblenz WEST GERMANY. 1989. 365 pp. $35.00. 14(4): 365.

This book is an updated edition, in German, of Kozaczuk's *Enigma: How the German Machine Cipher Was Broken and How it Was Read by the Allies in World War Two*, which was published in the United States in 1984.

Written from the Polish perspective – it was published originally in Warsaw – it is a well researched, authoritative account of the breaking of the Enigma cipher by three Polish mathematician-cryptologists with diagrams and details describing how it was accomplished.

In 1939, just before the outbreak of World War II, the Polish General Staff convened a meeting at which they disclosed to British and French cipher experts, who were baffled by the Enigma ciphers, details of their success. Each country was also given a reconstructed Enigma cipher machine.

After Poland was captured by the Germans, all personnel and material of Operation Wicher, the designation for the entire project in Poland, were transported to Rumania, finally reaching France and later Great Britain where many Polish cryptologists continued their work. It is perhaps ironic that Poland, which was the first country overrun by the Germans, in only 18 days, provided a major contribution to the eventual Allied victory.

New material in this revised and updated edition includes details on the breaking of non-machine ciphers by Polish cryptanalysts, a description of the Polish cipher machine, L. C. D. or Lacida, and other interesting information on Poland's key role in solving the German Enigma cipher.

UNLOCKING ENIGMA'S SECRETS
Vicki Moeser

Information Age: People, Information, and Technology. Exhibit at Smithsonian Institution, Washington DC 20560 USA. 14(4): 366-369.

For more than 40 years, Veronica Mackey Hulick adhered to an oath she had taken in 1945, promising not to tell anyone about her duties as a World War II Wave. But several years ago, she learned that the role she and several hundred other Waves played during the war had been declassified, and she was able to tell her family, friends and others about her contribution to the Allied victory.

Hulick was a Bombe operator during the war. The Bombe – a high-speed electromechanical decrypting machine – enabled the Allies to break the Nazis' secret communications.

A native of Wilmington, Delaware, Hulick joined the Navy early in 1943 and was assigned to the Naval Communications Station in Washington, D. C. From there, she and a contingent of Waves were sent to Dayton, Ohio, where they attended Sugar Camp.

Sugar Camp (named for a grove of maple trees tapped for sap) had been established in 1894 by the National Cash Register Corp. as a training school for salesmen; it was opened to the Navy in 1943.

"At Sugar Camp, they sat us down with a graph and a rotor (a 6- to 7-inch wheel essential to the Bombe's operation) and had us solder wires according to the instructions," Hulick says. "I didn't have the foggiest idea of what I was doing."

Several months later, she was back in Washington. During an orientation lecture, Hulick and other Waves were informed that they should never discuss their work with others. "The commanding officer told us that just because we were women, we shouldn't expect special attention," she says. "He went on to say that if we talked about our duties, we'd be shot."

There were 120 Bombes – complete with the rotors assembled by Hulick and the other Waves – at the U. S. Naval Security Group Command in Washington, D. C. A number of Bombes were also located in London. After the war, the machines were demolished with crowbars and sledgehammers. The only Bombe known to have remained intact is on public display for the first time in a new Smithsonian exhibition, "Information Age: People, Information & Technology," at the National Museum of American History in Washington.

"The ENIGMA machine was used by the German armed forces to encipher messages covering almost all phases of strategic and tactical planning and operations, including messages to and from Adolf Hitler," says Donald Kloster, a curator in the Division of Armed Forces at the museum. "Germany's complete confidence in the invulnerability of the system became a major advantage to Allies after the Allied forces learned to read the enciphered messages."

Although the Waves operated the Bombes, they did not directly decipher messages. The Bombes determined the keys by rapidly evaluating thousands of possibilities for ENIGMA settings and identifying those that were highly probable. Hulick describes the job of a Bombe operator this way: "We were given a chart depicting likely keys for that day and told how to set the switches and rotors on the machine. The machines were noisy and created quite a racket.

"When the machine would stop running, a probable key setting would print out. We called this a strike," she says. "We'd take the sheet of paper down the hall and knock on a door. A hand would come out; we'd turn over the printout and go back and start all over again." Cryptanalysts used the strikes to transform the intercepted communications into their original messages.

Hulick, who now lives in Ft. Pierce, Florida, describes the work as "sometimes dull," but she and the other Bombe operators were highly devoted to their jobs. They were mostly single and away from home for the first time. Joining the Navy and coming to the nation's capital to help win the war seemed very exciting. But the hours were long, the shifts ran around the clock and the pay was low. "I started out making $50 a month," Hulick says, "and by the end of the war I earned $90 a month."

The ENIGMA cipher machine was invented by a Dutchman in 1919 to protect business secrets. Impressed by its security, which was based on statistical analysis, the German government acquired all rights to the machine and adapted it to the needs of its new, modern military forces.

Similar in appearance to a typewriter, ENIGMA had three or four rotors. Each depression of a key on the keyboard would mechanically advance the first rotor one position. After 26 such advances, the next rotor in sequence would advance one step, and so on. A three-rotor ENIGMA had the capability of enciphering 17,576 characters before returning to its original position. Rearranging the rotors or adding additional rotors increased the number of permutations.

From the late 1920s to the late '30s, Polish cryptanalysts deciphered some of ENIGMA's transmissions through mathematical analysis. The French also had penetrated ENIGMA, with the help of a German traitor. But it was the British and the Americans who cracked the ciphers mechanically, by developing the Bombes.

British mathematician Alan Turing, a pioneer in computer theory, was one of the creators of the Bombe. His prototype machine was developed in 1940. Turing shared many of the secrets concerning the Bombe and ENIGMA with U. S. Naval intelligence officers during a trip to the United States in 1942. By the summer of 1943, Americans began producing the machines, which measured about 6 feet tall, 10 feet wide and 3 feet deep, and weighed about 5,000 pounds. Hulick says, at the time she did not realize the magnitude of her duties as a Bombe operator, but remembers that one of her supervisors once told her, "We're breaking the back of the U-boat operations."

Indeed, the Battle of the Atlantic was heating up. The Allies were losing cargo ships and tankers faster than they were being built. In 1942, German U-boats sank more than 1,660 ships in the Atlantic. Hundreds of tons of equipment – tanks, guns, ammunition – ended up on the ocean floor. It is estimated that perhaps one Allied seaman in five died at the hands of U-boat operators.

"The German armed forces, especially its submarine fleet, depended on open radio communication for coordination," David Allison, chief curator of the "Information Age" exhibition, says. "By setting the rotors in various positions on the ENIGMA machines, operators could generate more than a trillion different cipher combinations. Because the settings were changed regularly, the Germans believed it impossible for the Allies to break the ciphers in time to be useful." (Occasionally, the Germans suspected that the Allies had access to their secret information, but they believed spies were to blame, not that ENIGMA had been penetrated.)

Since all German submarine operations were coordinated from shore, messages covered a multitude of topics, from target assessments to fuel and ammunition supplies to crew morale. "Breaking the ENIGMA ciphers was even more valuable when correlated with other forms of electronic intelligence gathering, such as radio direction-finding and sonar," Allison adds.

By the summer of 1943, the Battle of the Atlantic turned in the Allies' favor. The Bombe operators in Washington – along with improved air cover and radar – are credited with pinpointing U-boat positions, resulting in the crippling of their operations. The outcome: An unknown number of lives and ships were saved. Historians say that the Allies' ability to unlock ENIGMA's secrets may also have shortened the length of the war.

The "Information Age" exhibition sums up 150 years of technology. The Bombe is just one of the objects on display in the Smithsonian's new exhibition "Information Age: People, Information & Technology."

"The exhibition is about people and how the technological innovations of the past 150 years have changed our lives and become part of our culture." David Allison, chief curator of "Information Age," says. "We try to make the point that we don't live just in a media age or a computer age we live in the Information Age and depend on a wide range of technologies."

"Information Age" is an ambitious project and a technological achievement in itself. Located in the National Museum of American History, it is among the largest exhibitions ever assembled by the Smithsonian and the most interactive. Some 700 artifacts, 700 graphics, more than 40 computer-driven stations, two films and a number of audio and video programs are tucked within the exhibition's 14,000 square feet. Ten miles of cable link the computers into the exhibition's central network.

The "Information Age" exhibition draws on the Smithsonian's unparalleled collection of computation and communications artifacts, including: Samuel Morse's original telegraph transmitter; components of Alexander Graham Bell's original telephone; the Hollerith tabulating system, used to compile results of the 1890 census; an atomic bomb casing, identical to the one dropped on Nagasaki in 1945; Telstar, the first commercial communications satellite; computers, from UNIVAC I to present-day technology; and robots, including R2-D2 and C-3PO of "Star Wars" fame.

SEIZING THE ENIGMA
Louis Kruh and Paul Edelen

David Kahn, *Seizing the Enigma: The Race to Break the German U-Boat Codes, 1939-1943*. Houghton Mifflin Co., 2 Park Street, Boston MA 02108 USA. 1991. 336 pp. $24.95. 15(3): 237-240.

[Ed. Note: It is unusual to present two reviews of one book, especially when both reviewers agree on the excellent merits of the book under review. But we believe David Kahn's effort merits extra attention as Dr. Kahn gives extra attention, indeed, extraordinary attention, to both small details and large themes.]

Another David Kahn classic – in the tradition of The Codebreakers, and Hitler's Spies – the complete story of British and American cryptanalytic struggles to break German Enigma U-boat ciphers.

The German navy's Enigma system was more complicated than the Enigma used by other German military forces and solved by Polish, British and American cryptanalysts. The Allies inability to break the navy Enigma resulted in devastating convoy losses, which outpaced new ship construction in 1941, and threatened the U. S. lifeline to Great Britain. The Battle of the Atlantic was fast becoming a major factor in the outcome of World War II.

British codebreakers at Bletchley Park were able to eke out sporadic decryptments of the German navy's Enigma messages. They were frustrated, however, by the frequently changing rotor settings and key lists, which kept them from reading the encrypted messages on a timely and regular basis.

A young Bletchley Park intelligence analyst, Harry Hinsley, who was reading German weather ship intercepts, knew the weather messages were enciphered with the Enigma machine. Suddenly, he realized that if weather ships are out at sea for long periods they had to carry Enigma keys for several months. Therefore, Hinsley proposed that the British navy capture Enigma documents from the relatively unprotected, isolated, and lightly armed German weather trawlers. Subsequently, successful attacks on weather ships plus the fortuitous capture of several U-boats yielded the vital information which enabled British cryptanalysts to read Enigma messages almost as fast as their legitimate recipients. With this crucial intelligence on the location of convoy- seeking U-boats, the British Admiralty was able to route ships to safe waters and protect the desperately needed supplies until they reached England.

This fascinating story is told in gripping fashion with the naval battles reading almost like a novel. Of course, the work of Alan Turing, Gordon Welchman and others at Bletchley Park is no less exciting. In addition, with characteristic thoroughness, Kahn delves into the background and the many equally interesting sidelights to these events. These include:

- The complete story of the analogue to the seizure of Enigma documents from German weather ships, which was the capture of a German codebook from the cruiser *Magdeburg* in WW I, its delivery to British codebreakers, and the dire consequences for the Germans;

- the history of the Enigma from its invention by Arthur Scherbius to its adoption and use by the German navy;
- the growth of the Polish Cipher Bureau and its work on Enigma ciphers;
- the German spy who sold Enigma documents to French intelligence agent, Gustave Bertrand, who gave the information to the Polish cryptanalysts;
- a study of British codebreaking from Room 40 to the Government Code & Cypher School;
- life at Bletchley Park; the development and use of the bombe;
- the use of the German navy's Dockyard Cipher, a non-Enigma system, to develop cribs for Enigma cryptograms by matching identical Dockyard and Enigma ciphers, called kisses;
- the addition of a fourth rotor to the Enigma and how it was solved;
- German success with British naval ciphers;
- the role of Americans at Bletchley Park;
- German suspicions and investigations of Enigma's security;
- an incisive analysis of the relationship between the Allied triumph over Enigma and the length and outcome of WW II; and much more.

Kahn's extensive research with original documents, new material he uncovered, and his tracking down and speaking to surviving eyewitnesses on both sides, who were never previously interviewed, provides a powerful action-packed narrative which virtually makes the reader an onlooker to the unfolding events. [LK]

The movie *In Which We Serve* ends with Noel Coward intoning that the British are not only an island people, but also dependent on the mercy of the seas. Nowhere was this made more poignantly clear than in the Battle of the Atlantic during the Second World War, and nowhere is the role intelligence played, both signals and human, more authoritatively and dramatically told than in David Kahn's new book, *Seizing the Enigma: The Race to Break the German U-boat Codes, 1939-1943*. If it were not for the heroism and pluck of the sailors of the Royal Navy, who seized the *Kriegsmarine* Enigma and cryptologic documents, and the intelligence and perseverance of the men and won of Bletchley Park, the war might have been lost or, at the very least, prolonged.

Yes, it was the Allies' ability to solve and read the enciphered messages of the *Kriegsmarine* and in particular Admiral Donitz's U-boat Command that helped considerably in achieving victory; however, their ultimate success, largely unknown to the general public, was due in no small measure to the pioneering work of Marian Rejewski, a Polish mathematician; the disgruntled nature of Hans-Thilo Schmidt, a German cipher clerk; and the spy handling craft of Gustave Bertrand, a French cryptologist. It is the work of the Poles and in particular Rejewski that not only fundamentally changed cryptography from its longstanding linguistic orientation to one based on mathematics, but also demonstrated that the Enigma could, in fact, be solved. Their work laid the solid foundation upon which the British built. But in both the Polish and British solutions to the Enigma and the Kriegsmarine Enigma respectively, a good deal of their work relied on what is called in contemporary intelligence parlance-target exploitation intelligence gathered through means other than mechanical or electronic.

The capture of U-110 and the Santayanaian presence of mind of her captor, Commander A. J. Baker-Cresswell, in remembering the *Magdeburg* incident of the First World War opened the door for the Bletchley Parkers. From that date, May 9, 1941, to the end of the war, the British actively sought to replicate that intelligence coup of World War I by capturing several U-Boats and weather ships. Their precious cryptologic caches were of immeasurable value to the B. P.ers. Yet, even these actions came at a price, as witnessed by the deaths of First Lieutenant Antony Fasson and Seamen Colin Grazier after the capture of U-559.

The heroism and sacrifice of these men would have been in vain if it had not been for the foresight of Alastair Denniston, head of the Government Codes & Cypher School and the incredible accumulation of talent he brought together at Bletchley Park. Like the Poles before him, Denniston realized toward the end of the 1930s that the nature of cryptology was changing and that this change required mathematicians to become cryptanalysts. He also went one step further by realizing that communications intelligence (comint) required not only the talents of linguists and mathematicians, but also generalists. His efforts were the foundation of modern comint.

Drawing on his academic training as a historian and his talent as a writer, David Kahn weaves a spellbinding tale as his narrative describes naval combat, intelligence coups, cryptologic solutions, and the personalities involved on both sides of the conflict. Kahn's work provides a valuable lesson: in the course of human endeavors it is judicious never to say, "Impossible." *Seizing the Enigma* represents, for both the devotee and layman, a singularly outstanding synthesis of history and cryptology as only David Kahn can. [PE]

ENIGMA PERIODICAL
Louis Kruh

Kapera, Zdzislaw Jan, editor. *The Enigma Bulletin*. ul. Borsucza 3/58 30-408 Krakow POLAND. Annual subscription $15.00, add $5.00 for airmail; three year subscription, 1990-1992, $38.00, add $12.00 for airmail. Checks or international money orders in U. S. dollars should be used for payment and made payable to Zdzislaw Jan Kapera. 15(4): 331.

A new journal, *The Enigma Bulletin*, devoted to the German Enigma Cipher Machine and related topics, is being published in Poland. The first issue, dated December 1990, contains 72 pages with articles in English and German.

English articles include The French Contribution to the Breaking of Enigma; Polish Radio Intelligence in the Battle of Monte Cassino; The Polish Cipher Machine Lacida; a profile of Jerry Rózycki, member of the Polish team that solved the Enigma cipher; and reviews. There are two articles in German: a report on the work on the Enigma cipher in 1940, and the personal experiences of George Glunder, former radio operator and communication mechanic with the German army 1941-1945, who worked with the Enigma and the Geheimschreiber.

The Enigma Bulletin was planned as an annual publication, but as soon as there are 250 subscribers, it will be published semiannually for the same subscription price.

TADEUSZ LISICKI DIES
Louis Kruh

Tadeusz Lisicki Obituary, *London Daily Telegram*, 24 August 1991. 16(1): 13.

The following obituary appeared in the *London Daily Telegram*, 24 August 1991.

Lieutenant-Colonel Tadeusz Lisicki, who has died aged 81, was an associate of the brilliant team of young Polish crypto-analysts who broke the secret of the German Enigma coding machine.

The original Enigma machine had been invented by a Dutchman in 1919 but as he did not have the knowledge or facilities to make a working model it was not until 1923 that a German firm manufactured some Enigmas and put them on the market.

In 1926 they were adopted by the German Navy for their encoding and two years later the German Army proceeded to make the machine more sophisticated.

Resembling a complicated typewriter, the Enigma machine had an ingenious system of wheels and jacks which could raise the possible permutations of a message to 150 trillion.

A team of Polish mathematicians then acquired a commercial version of the machine in 1932 and set about deducting the ways in which it had been modified. From 1934 a Pole working in an Enigma factory in Germany had passed out information which enabled the making of the poles' own German-style Enigma machine; the crux was deducing the way the wheels were wired and used.

Just before the outbreak of the Second World War in 1939 the Poles gave two sets and vital information to the British and French intelligence. Some of these Polish pioneers managed to continue working in Britain, others were caught, tortured and executed by the Gestapo. The code- breaking was eventually carried out by the 'Ultra team" at Bletchley Park and its secrets kept until 1974.

The Polish contribution by Lisicki and his friends was one of the most important factors in securing the Allied victory in the Second World War. Although the "Ultra" operation did not break all the German (and Japanese) codes it obtained sufficient vital intelligence to understand and then mislead enemy intelligence.

Tadeusz Lisicki was born in Warsaw on June 29, 1910 and educated at Inoweoclaw. He attended the Officer Cadet Training Centre for Engineers in Warsaw and was commissioned in 1932 as a signals officer.

His outstanding qualities were soon recognized and he was sent to the Institute of Technology in Warsaw and obtained his diploma in 1937. The next year he constructed a prototype of a mine detector which, after some modifications, was used during the Second World War by the British.

Lisicki took part in the September campaign of 1939 against the Germans, crossed the Hungarian frontiers and was interned in the camp at Hidasnemethy.

After escaping from this camp he went to France, took part in the campaign as a commander of a signal unit in the 1st Polish Infantry Division and after the collapse of this made his way, via Gibraltar, to Britain.

Lisicki was seconded to the 6th Bureau of the Polish General Staff in London and in 1943 he went to America to buy parachute equipment for the secret drops to Poland.

Between 1943 and 1945 Lisicki was commander of the Signal Battalion at Stanmore. Two Polish cryptoanalysts, Marian Rejewski and Henryk Zygalski, who had broken the Enigma Secret in 1932, escaped from France and joined the battalion.

Lisicki was in constant touch with the top secret Government Code and Cipher School at Bletchley. They helped to read the current Enigma ciphers.

After the war Lisicki settled in London and was on the staff of the Polish

Resettlement Corps.

A qualified electrical engineer, he set up two businesses, Leron Electronics and Leron Construction. In 1970 he obtained a PhD at the Polish University in Exile in London.

A man of charm and modesty, Lisicki was a well-liked and respected figure in Britain's Polish community and worked for many charitable causes. He was appointed OBE.

POLISH MILITARY INTELLIGENCE AND ENIGMA
Louis Kruh

Woytak, Richard. 1991. Polish Military Intelligence and Enigma. *East European Quarterly*. XXV(1) (March): 49-57. University of Colorado, Boulder CO 80309 USA. $2.50. 16(4): 339.

Polish intelligence monitoring of German military communications in the late 1920s alerted them to the introduction of the Enigma cipher machine. At the same time Polish intelligence was recruiting talented mathematics students at Poznan University who were also proficient in German to work on German codes, and ciphers.

In this concise article, Woytak describes the success of the Polish Cipher Bureau's mathematicians, the assistance of French intelligence who obtained Enigma manuals and other information from a German spy, and the important July 24-26 meeting where the Polish team, knowing they would be overwhelmed in the impending war with Germany, revealed all they knew about Enigma an Anglo-French delegation and gave each a working Enigma.

Fifty years later, almost to the day, July 11, 1989, when U. S. President George Bush toured Gdansk, he praised Poland for giving Enigma to the Allies which, he said, ultimately "played a major role in winning the Second World War."

ROMMEL AND SECRET INTELLIGENCE
Louis Kruh

Piekalkiewicz, Janusz. *Rommel and the Secret War in North Africa, 1941-1943: Secret Intelligence in the North African Campaign*. Schiffer Publishing Ltd., 1469 Morstein Road, West Chester PA 19380 USA. 1992. 239 pp. $29.95. 17(1): 98-99.

The author, a respected military historian, reveals in detail how Ultra affected the outcome of the campaign in North Africa. At the campaign's beginning in

1940, Churchill knew, from Ultra, that Hitler had abandoned the idea of a landing in England. "This news allowed him to throw parts of the British forces spared by the fall of France into the balance in North Africa at the right moment." And when Rommel came to Africa, "Ultra followed him like a shadow."

In a lengthy prologue, the author reviews the history of the German Enigma cipher machine from its invention in 1919, adoption by the German Navy and the Wehrmacht, improvements to it over the years, the role of Polish intelligence, Bletchley Park's involvement, and other developments up to early 1941 in North Africa.

The next five chapters detail the campaign in roughly six month segments up to early 1943 when Rommel was defeated by General Bernard Montgomery. The outcome of the final battle resulted from Enigma decrypts on February 28, 1943, that revealed Rommel's plan to attack with three Panzer divisions. Further Ultra intelligence supplied Rommel's movements, size of force, date and time of attack. Montgomery was able to rush extra troops, tanks and anti-tank guns to match and exceed the forces gathered against him. And, when Rommel launched his attack, Montgomery was ready.

From the beginning to the end of the campaign, virtually every page in this superb book tells of information obtained on an almost daily basis from Army and *Luftwaffe* Enigma messages, its significance, how it was used, and the consequences. The Italian naval code C 38m was also solved and supplied important convoy and cargo information.

Rommel also had his sources of intelligence as the Germans had been solving British codes. He relied greatly on the German Intelligence and Radio Reconnaissance Company led by Lieutenant, later Captain, Alfred Seebohm, one of the best officers in this specialty. Every enemy message of importance was decoded and given to Rommel, after which it was noted on a radio situation chart. Seebohm was also assigned a decoding unit led by a code specialist. He did not hesitate to position his unit far forward and did his job so well that on July 10, 1942, his unit was the target of a successful attack by Australian troops. Seebohm was severely wounded and died a few days later and his unit was annihilated. Equipment, documentation, captured British radio codes, encoded lists of names and other intelligence material fell into British hands. The loss of Seebohm and his unit was a turning point in the North African campaign and possibly decided the coming battle of El Alamein.

In addition to explaining how Ultra was used on a daily basis, this beautifully produced oversized volume on heavy glossy paper contains more than 220 vivid photographs, maps and documents.

ENIGMA WEAKNESS

Louis Kruh

Skillen, Hugh. *Enigma and its Achilles Heel.* Hugh Skillen, 56 St Thomas Drive, Pinner, Middlesex HA5 4SS ENGLAND. 1992. 225 pp. $29.00 postpaid. 17(1): 99-100.

This book was written as a souvenir of the international Enigma Reunion held in England, October 25, 1992.

Skillen recognized that many participants had worked in aspects of the Y Service at Bletchley Park and other locations, in Special Wireless Sections in the field, and in Special Communications Units. Therefore, they probably did not have a clear understanding of the Enigma machine, its history or the problems involved in solving its messages. Accordingly, he provides photographs, a history of the machine and explains, almost step-by-step, how the Enigma was made impregnable by German cryptographic specialists. He also demonstrates how Polish cryptologists unravelled the complexities of its rotor wiring circuits.

A separate chapter on Bletchley Park describes the important advances made there on solving Enigma keys and their work on *Geheimschreiber*s.

The critical role of Captain Gustave Bertrand, Chief of the Cipher Section, French Intelligence Division, who purchased Enigma manuals, key lists and other vital material from a German traitor and gave them to Polish Intelligence is told in detail. Bertrand tells in his own words of his betrayal, capture and interrogation by the Germans in Paris. They wanted details of the Normandy invasion that was just months ahead. Threatened with torture, he promised to cooperate in return for the lives of his wife and himself. Then, in thrilling fashion, he tells of their escape to England.

Skillen also provides details and photographs of Germany's many most secret communications machine, the *Geheimschreiber*. Two *Geheimschreiber*s were captured by the Eighth Army and sent to Bletchley Park. A new electronic machine, Colossus, forerunner of the computer, was built to help solve *Geheimschreiber* messages.

An especially interesting chapter, "Straight From the Horse's Mouth" is written by a German Enigma and *Geheimschreiber* operator, 1941-1945. He describes his experience, methods and rules he followed and gives valuable insights only available from an "insider." In an ironic sidelight he tells of his capture by Americans but despite seeing his pay roll book which mentions "Unit with G-Zusaetze," he was not interrogated when American specialists searched feverishly for cryptographic intelligence.

The final chapter, "The Impact of Ultra on the Conduct of the War" highlights the accomplishments of the Y Service and Special Wireless Groups and describes the battles where Ultra played a decisive role.

Skillen provides an enormous amount of information on the Enigma and *Geheimschreiber* machines and German Enigma manuals are reproduced in an appendix. It is an informative account of their history and the techniques which ultimately solved their ciphers and helped the Allies to victory.

HITLER'S JAPANESE CONNECTION AND MAGIC
Louis Kruh

Boyd, Carl. *Hitler's Japanese Confidant: General Ōshima Hiroshi and Magic Intelligence, 1941-1945*. University Press of Kansas, 2501 W. 15th Street, Lawrence KS 66049-3904 USA. 1993. 271 pp. $25.00. 17(3): 253-254.

In August, 1940, the U.S. Army's Signal Intelligence Service broke the Japanese diplomatic code known as Purple. Thereafter, the Japanese ambassador to Berlin became the main source of information regarding Adolf Hitler's intentions in Europe.

The ambassador, Ōshima Hiroshi, had excellent relations with Hitler and direct access to Joachim von Ribbentrop, Germany's foreign minister and other high ranking Nazis. As a result, he was a key player in the Axis coalition and he communicated everything he learned from Hitler, Ribbentrop and their staffs to Tokyo using his Purple cipher machine. From detailed plans to attack the Soviet Union to the Wehrmacht's coastal defense in France, which was a great assistance to D-Day planners, Ōshima provided American cryptanalysts with an invaluable source of raw intercept data that continued until V-E Day. He even furnished advance warning of the Battle of the Bulge, which, Boyd suggests, Allied cryptanalysts failed to evaluate accurately. The significance of Ōshima's information was perhaps best expressed by Military Intelligence officers who said that one message regarding the production of munitions in Germany that Ōshima sent to Tokyo in August, 1944, was "worth all the expenses of maintaining the SSA [Signal Security Agency]."

From a cryptologic perspective Boyd provides many details of American cryptanalytic efforts and cryptologic cooperation with England. He also offers an analytic appreciation of the high-grade intelligence gained from decrypts of Ōshima's messages and how the Allies used it in their European Theatre campaigns.

After the war was over, General Dwight D. Eisenhower, Supreme Allied Commander, visited Arlington Hall Station, headquarters for the Army's signal intelligence activities, to tour the facility and to meet and thank the people who solved Japanese codes and ciphers. They included William F. Friedman and Frank B. Rowlett, who acted as Eisenhower's guide. Boyd describes Rowlett as being especially responsible for the solution of Purple. Throughout the book, Rowlett offers cryptanalytic insights and sidelights that add a unique flavor to this fascinating history.

THEY WORKED AT BLETCHLEY PARK

Louis Kruh

Skillen, Hugh, ed. *The Enigma Symposium 1992*. H. Skillen, 56 St. Thomas Drive, Pinner HA5 4SS ENGLAND. 1992. 60 pp. $14.00. 17(3): 257-258.

At the first Enigma reunion of persons stationed at Bletchley Park or otherwise involved with Enigma related activities, fourteen speakers related their personal experiences.

The presentations described procedures and work at Bletchley Park, including Huts 2, 3 and 6. One speaker recounted the meticulous recording of details from decrypts on 5" × 9" cards – the military index alone consisted of a half-million cards. Another told of decoding messages sent by the German Military police who used the double Playfair system. First hand accounts described the role of Ultra signals in the Battle of Crete; working with Colonel John H. T. Tiltman; the purpose of Bombes, their construction, and how they were used; and a member of the Colossus team explained how it was developed and how it worked. A member of the Experimental Station at Abbrassia, a small inter-Allied unit concerned with the investigation and modification of enemy apparatus, described various experiments involving cipher machines. On one project, he worked with a knowledgeable Pole who he met again at a conference about 20 years later and learned that his name was Henryk Zygalski. But it was still later when he found out that Zygalski had been one of the three young Polish mathematicians that had solved the Enigma cipher in 1932.

This large size book (8 1/2" × 11 3/4") includes the text of all talks, which provide much new information and details about the interception and decryption of Enigma ciphers by the people who actually did the work. It also contains numerous photographs and diagrams.

BRITISH INTELLIGENCE IN WWII

Louis Kruh

Hinsley, Francis H. *British Intelligence in the Second World War*. Abridged Edition. Cambridge University Press, 40 W. 20 Street, New York NY 10011 USA. 1993. 628 pp. $39.95. 18(1): 2-3.

Originally published in five volumes totaling nearly 4,000 pages, this abridged version is a "mere" 620 pages. But, it is a worthy alternative with much of the important intelligence and cryptologic aspects of the originals included.

The volume's 38 chapters are divided into five chronological sections comprising major segments of the war. In the first chapter, "Before the War," the early history of Britain's Government Code and Cypher School (GC & CS) is traced from its development in 1919 "with remnants of the separate cryptanalytical sections that served the Admiralty (Room 40) and the War Office (MIlb) in the first world war." It survived the usual interservice rivalries, moved to Bletchley Park in 1938, and was struggling to master the German Enigma cipher machine as war loomed. In 1939, Polish authorities divulged their methods and results to French and British delegations and GC & CS began solving wartime Enigma messages.

GC & CS eventually identified nearly 200 keys (each German service had different keys for the machine); at some stages of the war there were as many as 50 different keys in use concurrently. At the beginning of 1943, a more impressive feat was accomplished when British cryptanalysts broke ciphers recently introduced by the Germans for non-Morse transmissions between army commands. The traffic, named Fish at GC & CS, presented intellectual and technological problems much more difficult than those of Enigma. The task would have been impossible without the development of an electronic machine named Colossus which, "unlike the electro-mechanical Bombe with (*sic*) defeated the Enigma, was the first working approximation to the modern computer."

The outstanding contribution of cryptanalysis in virtually every battle, whether on land, sea or in the air, is evident from references on almost every page to the use of Enigma decrypts, often citing specific keys, and other cryptanalytic sources.

This important book, based on unrestricted access to government intelligence archives, is essential for a full understanding of the role of British intelligence in the war and its influence on strategy and operations. A set of the unabridged volumes, 1-6, is also available for $206.

ULTRA IN WAR TIME
Louis Kruh

McKee, Alexander. *El Alamein: Ultra and the Three Battles*. Souvenir Press Ltd., 43 Great Russell Street, London CW1B 3PA ENGLAND. 1991. 192 pp. $24.00. 18(1): 9-11.

This exciting account of one of the most famous campaigns of World War

II, the Desert War, highlights the importance of Ultra, which provided advance information about General Erwin Rommel's supply ships and troop movements. It also gives credit to the air and submarine forces in contributing to the success of the eventual victory.

The breaking of the German Enigma cipher machine is described with appropriate recognition of French, Polish and British roles in solving its encrypted messages.

Throughout the campaign Ultra's successes and failures are examined. On at least one occasion its failure was due to Winston Churchill urging immediate aggressive action "based on undigested decrypts."

Ultra was successful in April, 1941, when the Germans launched an airborne assault and decrypts provided dates, troops involved and the target – Crete. Unfortunately, due in part to efforts to preserve the security of Ultra by not strengthening airfield defenses, Crete fell into German hands.

In a dramatic, fast moving story, which identifies the role of Ultra, McKee recounts the early setbacks in the desert and the gradual reversal of fortunes as General Montgomery moved from a defensive to an offensive position and advanced to victory at El Alemain.

In August, 1942 the prime value of Ultra was to expose the main Axis weaknesses and enable the British to destroy the particular shipments that would inflict the most damage to the enemy. Ultra decodes frequently revealed port of loading, cargo, and date of sailing. Malta based submarines were especially successful against Axis shipping, assisted by Ultra.

Rommel had his intelligence sources too. The American military attaché in Cairo, Colonel Bonner Frank Fellers, used the broken Black Code to transmit to Washington the substance of British briefings at the highest levels, keeping Rommel fully informed of enemy capabilities and intentions. This went on for about a year until the fall of Tobrak in mid-1942. Then on June 29, after decrypts of *Luftwaffe* and Panzer Army Enigma messages alerted the British that the Germans were intercepting and reading Fellers' reports on the British defeat, his circuit fell silent.

Rommel suffered another intelligence setback when his crack 621 W/T Intercept Company, the German equivalent of the British Service, commanded by the very competent Captain Alfred Seerbohm, was overrun by Australian infantry. Most of the company were killed or captured, Seerbohm was fatally wounded, and his irreplaceable files were seized by the Australians, letting the British know how much information they had been giving away.

A gripping feature is the eye-witness accounts of pilots, submarine commanders, army officers and enlisted men who carried out missions and came face to face with the enemy. And, it is fascinating to examine the styles, personalities, and abilities of Rommel, Montgomery, and other leaders. Maps clarify the key elements of the campaign and about 50 photographs from personal collections many previously unpublished, add an extra touch of realism.

CHINA-BURMA-INDIA MAGIC AND ULTRA
Louis Kruh

Fitzgerald, Colonel Stephen K. *Magic and Ultra in the China-Burma-India Theater*. U.S. Army War College Studies Program Paper. 1991. 76 pp. Available as Report No. AD-A249 227/0/XAB from: National Technical Information Service, U.S. Dept. of Commerce, Springfield VA 22161 USA. Microfiche. $9.00 plus $3.00 handling; Paper, $19.50 plus $3.00 handling. 18(1): 9.

The purpose of this study is to determine how the breaking of Japanese codes and ciphers affected the planning and conduct of Allied campaigns in Burma, especially the Second Burma and North Burma campaigns. The author makes use of the official U.S. history of the theater, intelligence histories, the daily "Magic Summaries," and Ultra material to examine the operational use of Magic and Ultra. The former is intelligence derived from "reading" diplomatic ciphers encrypted with the Japanese "Purple" machine while the latter is intelligence obtained from decrypts of Japanese Army high grade codes and ciphers.

The campaigns and individual battles are described from the perspective of Magic and Ultra and the success and failure of each is noted. Magic was more helpful in the strategic area than in operations though it failed to provide either strategic or operational warning of the Japanese invasion of Burma. Although, in time, Ultra became more valuable in exposing Japanese operational intentions, it was most valuable when used with traffic analysis supported by other intelligence. In fact, the study concludes that neither Ultra nor Magic were able to consistently determine Japanese intentions in Burma and that their ultimate importance was to confirm intelligence obtained from other sources.

The paper is well documented with 274 footnotes and a comprehensive bibliography which provides opportunities for further reading or research.

BLETCHLEY PARK – THE INSIDE STORY
Louis Kruh

Hinsley, F. H. and Alan Stripp, eds. *Codebreakers: The Inside Story of Bletchley Park*. Oxford University Press, 200 Madison Ave., New York NY 10016 USA. 1993. 321 pp. $25.90. 18(1): 11-12.

Written by men and women who had participated in the codebreaking effort at Bletchley Park (BP) or one of its outstations during World War II, this splendid book, which is divided into four sections, tells of one of the most amazing feats in cryptologic history.

Part I discusses the production of Ultra intelligence and the people in Hut 3 where "raw" Enigma decrypts from Hut 6 were evaluated and their intelligence put into a form suitable for dispatch to military commanders. It also describes Hut 4 where the Z Watch translated German Naval Enigma decrypts from Hut 8 and processed them for the Admiralty.

Part II is devoted to Enigma and how it was mastered. The work of the cryptanalytical sections, Hut 6 for Army Enigma and Hut 8 for Naval Enigma is described with explanations of the methods and techniques devised by Alan Turing, Gordon Welchman and others. Also covered is the Enigma used by the *Abwehr*, the secret intelligence service of the German High Command. It differs from Army and Navy Enigmas in several ways including an *Umkehrwalze* that rotates during encipherment.

Part III examines Fish, the high-level non-Morse traffic enciphered on a *Schüsselzusatz (SZ)* or *Geheimschreiber*, named "Tunny" and "Sturgeon" respectively at BP. These on-line machines provided simultaneous encipherment and transmission and simultaneous reception and decipherment of messages based on the impulses of the international five-unit teleprinter code. Problems in solving their ciphers were more formidable than those presented by Enigma. The SZ had two sets of five rotors, "each of which was used to modify the five signal element of transmitted teleprinter characters, plus two extra rotors which controlled the movement of the second set of enciphering rotors." Its operation is fully discussed, and though its ciphers were initially solved by hand-methods, development of Colossus, probably the world's first programmable electronic digital computer, was necessary as Fish traffic increased dramatically and security of the machines was upgraded.

Part IV concentrates on the important, but less glamorous, field ciphers and tactical codes, and British cryptanalytic work on Japanese codes and ciphers, both at BP and in Southeast Asia. These subjects, often overlooked, are presented in fascinating detail.

This is a remarkable book, undoubtedly the definitive work on Bletchley Park, with lively anecdotes and detailed stories giving a colorful account of BP's daily life and work, which made a major contribution to shortening the war, as Hinsley demonstrates in an astute analysis.

THOSE BRILLIANT BRITS

C. A. Deavours

Hinsley, F. H. and Alan Stripp, eds. *Codebreakers: The Inside Story of Bletchley Park*. Oxford University Press, 200 Madison Ave., New York NY 10016 USA. 1993. ISBN 0-19-820327-6. 321 pp. $25.00. 18(1): 22-24.

Everyone interested in cryptology or history in general, will want to own a copy of this book. F. H. Hinsley and Alan Stripp are known to most of us. Both of the authors are themselves veterans of Bletchley Park. The former is the author of the four-volume British Intelligence in the Second World War while the latter is director of Cambridge University Summer Schools on British Secret Services. The book is a compilation of short articles, written by people who worked at Bletchley Park during WWII. All of the articles are quite well written and fit together in a nearly seamless fashion. This flowing characteristic of the book is, rightly, a tribute to the book's editors who have done an outstanding job.

Codebreakers does not contain a tremendous amount of new material – that was not the intention of the editors. Rather, the stories contained in the book breathe life into one of the most fascinating aspects of the Second World War. There is material in this book covering just about every phase of cryptanalytic work at Bletchley Park. The scope of the book includes material on the Enigma and its variations, the German telecipher machines as well as the complicated hand ciphers of the German and Japanese military. Even the less glamorous, but usually difficult, work of the intercept translators has not been neglected. Most readers will recognize the names of many of the contributors to this work. One problem I encountered in reading the book was the obvious removal of technical material without which some accomplishments of the cryptanalysts seem like absolute miracles. The reason for these omissions is not due to the editors or writers themselves, but to largely unneeded security concerns on the part of the powers that be.

The story unfolded in this book reiterates concerns often expressed by the late Gordon Welchman about the double edged sword presented by the "need to know" doctrine. Situations are encountered in the text where cryptanalysts are stymied by the lack of information possessed by those working in the next room. It would seem that the compartmentalization of effort at Bletchley Park may often have exceeded what was really necessary.

Many of the machines and ciphers discussed are like old friends to me and I often found myself chuckling at having experienced the same difficulties that beset these multi-talented individuals. (Since I was born in 1941, I missed all of the fun, but, I have spent time working on many of the systems described.) The methods of attacking some of systems are discussed in the book. In particular, the reader will find Noel Currer-Briggs' account of the German "double Playfair" (better known as the "double casket" system) both clearly written and informative.

Peter Twinn's article on the *Abwehr* Enigma and Dillwyn Knox's work on its solution is fascinating. Twinn, one of the very best of that select group of British cryptanalysts, adds much to what is known about the *Abwehr*'s interesting Enigma variation, although I have to disagree with some of his speculation about the origin of that machine. Basically, the *Abwehr* Enigma was a plugboardless reflecting rotor machine whose main security ingredient was the fast stepping of the rotors. Instead of a single stepping position for each 26 letters, the *Abwehr* rotors had 11, 15, or 19 such positions. Twinn's account makes it clear that the group working on that machine considered it has a simple but ingenious variant of the Army machine, possessing, in addition, a reflecting rotor that also moved during encipherment. The physical construction of the machine was different in some essential ways, however, from the Army machine. (Something the cryptographers could not have known since, presumably, they had never seen the actual device.) According to sources who examined the machine, the *Abwehr*'s Enigma had rotors that were incompatible with the usual Enigma rotors. The rotor movement was gear driven, unlike the other Enigma models. I think that we must conclude from these facts that this machine was a separate design based on earlier Enigma models.

Although Twinn explains clearly how Knox used the crab and lobster rotor movement peculiarities of the machine in order to deduce its entrance wiring as well as many operational principles of the device, he does not indicate just how Knox knew to look for such a property. It is not totally out of the question to attribute this feat to Knox's genius, but, I suspect there is more to this story than is indicated. Since Knox's secretive nature was so pronounced, we may never know how he was actually led to look for this feature of the machine.

I must thank the authors for correcting an error that appeared in the book *Machine Cryptography and Modern Cryptanalysis* by Louis Kruh and myself.

ULTRA IN THE PACIFIC
Louis Kruh

Winton, John. *Ultra in the Pacific: How Breaking Japanese Codes and Cyphers Affected Naval Operations Against Japan, 1941-1945*. United States Naval Institute, Annapolis MD 21402 USA. 1993. 247 pp. $22.95. 18(3): 282-283.

Based on an extensive review of Ultra records, official histories and related documents in the National Archives, plus British sources such as Admiralty operational records and interviews, Winton gives an exciting account of the role played by Ultra in the naval war in the Pacific. In a well written, chronological format he relates how information derived from breaking Japanese secret communications affected major battles and campaigns.

After reviewing the Pearl Harbor and Singapore disasters, chapters on The Battle of the Coral Sea, Midway, Guadalcanal, The Yamamoto Ambush, Forward in the Solomons, The Submarine War – Breaking the Maru Code, The Atoll War, The Great Marianas Turkey Shoot, The Submarine War to the End, Kamikazes off Okinawa, and The Surrender of Japan, provide a detailed examination of the practical application of Ultra intelligence. For each battle, Winton highlights the personalities involved, both Allies and Japanese, where pertinent, and the role played by Ultra, often identifying specific codes or ciphers used to position the fleet and/or submarines to help defeat the forces of Japan.

Winton tells how Lieutenant Commander Joseph Rochefort, head of Station HYPO, the U. S. Navy's Combat Intelligence Center based at Pearl Harbor, predicted – in the face of Washington's insistence the attack would occur elsewhere – where and when Japanese carriers would launch their attack on Midway. After the battle, Admiral Chester Nimitz, Commander-in-Chief, Pacific Fleet, invited Rochefort to a staff meeting where he told the group, "This officer deserves a major share of the credit for the victory at Midway." An important side benefit, Winton points out, was that this intelligence feat removed forever any lingering doubts in some quarters of the Navy establishment that Communications Intelligence, all this electronic spying, was a waste of time and effort. In other words, "Who needs all that Comint crap? Much good it did us at Pearl Harbor."

Although many Allied cryptanalysts found that decrypting Japanese communications more tedious than difficult, the task was not easy. Unlike the Germans who used versions of the Enigma machine for enciphering almost all signal traffic, Winton lists more than 20 different crypto systems used by the Japanese.

Cryptanalytic work on JN-25, the Japanese Naval code used to transmit most operational signals about the attack on Pearl Harbor, is reviewed by the author. Combined Bureau (FECB), the British equivalent of Station HYPO at Singapore had made some progress in breaking into JN-25 by September 1939. The British Government's Code & Cypher School "had also broken into JN-25, much of which was thus being read at Singapore by the end of 1939. By March, 1941, FECB was, able to pass their recoveries in JN-25 to the U. S. Asiatic Fleet, delivering their keys to the code to [Station] CAST [Navy intelligence unit in the Philippines] a Cavite on the 5th .... The knowledge, imperfect though it was, both OP-20-G and FECB had of JN-25, and the cryptographic cooperation and exchange of information between the two, makes the surprise the Japanese achieved all the "more remarkable – and reprehensible."

Winton's gratuitous comment is basically a rehash of what James Rusbridge and Eric Nave trumpeted in their book, *Betrayal at Pearl Harbor*, which was refuted by American authorities. But what makes Winton's remarks on page 19 particularly distasteful is that only forty-eight pages later, on page 67, he reveals that on May 26, 1942 "it was estimated that 60 percent of Imperial Navy traffic was being intercepted [by the U. S. Navy] and 40 per cent read although *the content recovered from the typical message averaged only about 10 15 per cent*" (emphasis added). Thus his assessment of the Navy's progress with JN-25, almost six months after the attack on Pearl Harbor, impugns his earlier statement.

Overall, this is a fine work that shouldn't be marred by a rash comment because Winton's detailed story on what the Allies learned from Japan's secret communications in the Pacific War and how they put that knowledge to us deserves your attention.

VANNEVAR BUSH, ULTRA AND THE OTHER MEMEX
Louis Kruh

Burke, Colin. *Information and Secrecy: Vannevar Bush, Ultra, and the other Memex*. Scarecrow Press, 52 Liberty Street, P. O. Box 4167, Metuchen NJ 08840 USA. 1994. 466 pp. $49.50. 18(3): 284-285.

Using hundreds of primary and secret documents, Colin Burke provides a detailed and revealing history of intertwined attempts by Vannevar Bush to use new technologies to develop an automated library information retrieval system and to build a high speed machine to automate the work of cryptanalysts, in the 1930s. Unfortunately, the lack of coherent American science and intelligence policies, combined with bureaucratic infighting and unexpected technical problems, resulted in years of delay.

Bush, a brilliant engineer at MIT, was developing his information machine, the Rapid Selector, while Admiral Stanford C. Hooper, Director of Naval Communications, was seeking advice on ways to automate the process of cryptanalysis to offset the increasing use of machines such as Enigma to create complex ciphers. In 1935, Hooper's search led him and his protegé, Joseph Wenger, who headed the Navy's cryptanalytic unit, OP-20-G, in World War II, to Bush. Hooper described the techniques used by OP-20-G's cryptanalysts, the problems they faced and his goal of automating the cryptanalytic process. After some study Bush came up with the Comparator, a tapebased cryptanalytic machine. The two machines are called "the direct historical link between the birth of the information age and the age of secrecy in the United States."

Burke traces the history of MIT, Carnegie and Rockefeller Foundations, Bell Laboratories, Eastman Kodak, National Cash Register (NCR) and other organizations whose resources helped America and its intelligence agencies to prepare for WW II. He recounts the history of OP-20-G, its methods, accomplishments and people and their aversion to Hooper's goals. There is a lengthy comprehensive section devoted to Enigma, which discusses the contribution of Polish cryptanalysts, how Britain's Government Code & Cypher School (GC&CS) solved Enigma ciphers, how GC&CS developed its Bombe, America's attempts to develop its own Enigma solving abilities and its decision to build an improved Bombe. NCR was chosen to assist OP-20-G with the Bombe (the Army's Signal Intelligence Service worked with Bell Laboratories to build its own version, which was known as Madame X or 003) and Burke describes the enormous technological problems designers and engineers had to overcome before achieving success in 1943. Called "one of the most complex machines in the world," the Bombe could run either three or four wheel tests 200 times faster than the Polish Bomba, at least twenty times faster than the Turing Bombe and 30% faster than Britain's 1943 four wheel Bombe. It cut the time needed to break a U-boat message from 600 hours to 18 hours.

Burke also covers postwar plans for a full electronic Super Bombe, cryptanalytic computers, and other projects. But during the Cold War priorities shifted as "needs arose for more special purpose electronic cryptanalytic machines, ones to solve immediate cryptanalytic and intelligence problems." He also describes Engineering Research Associates, from founding in early 1946 as a private, for profit firm organized by former navy engineers with OP-20-G support to work on a range of navy communication problems including cryptanalysis, to its demise in 1950 when it was purchased by Remington-Rand Corporation.

This highly original work contains previously unpublished information on many subjects, particularly American World War II Rapid Analytical Machines (RAM) for cryptanalytic purposes. These include: Freak – an electromechanical cryptanalytic machine; Copperhead – OP-20-G advanced versions of tape based electronic cryptanalytic machines; Hypo – analog optical cryptanalytic machine built by Eastman-Kodak; IC (Index of Coincidence) Machine – Film plate machines MIT-Eastman made for OP-20-G; Mathew – OP-20-G electromechanical cryptanalytic machine; Mike – U. S. electromechanical cryptanalytic machine; Rattler – U. S. Navy electronic machine to attack Japanese automatic encryption systems; Tessie Optical cryptanalytic machine built by Eastman Kodak, the tetragraph tester; and Goldberg – OP-20-G postwar advanced version of Comparator.

There are more than twenty photographs of mainly cryptanalytic machines and 73 pages of densely packed notes, which attest to the huge research effort involved in writing this innovative book.

ENIGMA SYMPOSIUM
Louis Kruh

Skillen, Hugh. *The Enigma Symposium 1994*. H. Skillen, 56 St. Thomas Drive, Pinner, Middlesex HA5 4SS ENGLAND. 1994. 120 pp. $13 plus $2.50 postage. 19(3): 300.

The second Enigma reunion at Bedford, England, September 30-October 2, 1994, attracted 400 veterans from Australia, Canada, the United States and, of course, England. Aside from a trip to the new museum at Bletchley Park, the program featured presentations by the men and women who participated in the intercept and decryption procedures during World War II, or who built and installed the Bombes and the Colossus machines.

Talks described the variety of Ultra related activities at Bletchley Park and other locations. These included the work of intercept operators; Radio Security Service; building various machines such as Cobra, the modified Bombe used on the 4-rotor Enigma, Heath Robinson to decrypt "Fish" traffic, an all electromechanical machine called the Analyser and known as the Mighty Wurlitzer, and Colossus; Hut 6 and the Machine Room; Naval Enigma; a tribute to Alastair Denniston; a civilian's work in Hut 6; a Wren's work with the Bombe; and Sigint in the Far East.

These first hand experiences are fascinating to read and provide many valuable insights to the Ultra story. Although, as one speaker noted, there was more information he could not mention, almost all presentations contained interesting details not available elsewhere.

A lengthy appendix includes the notebook of a Special Operator of Japanese messages, the notebook of an ATS Special Operator on German wireless procedures and Enigma, a selection of German diplomatic papers released by the Public Record Office in 1994, intercepts sent to the Military Mission, Moscow in November 1942, and other historical material.

The volume also contains many old photographs including the members of Hut 6 on May 3, 1945 and a schematic diagram of Hut 6 in 1943. It is a remarkable book with unique information that is necessary for anyone interested in the personal experiences of some people responsible for the Ultra victory.

BLETCHLEY PARK – ULTRA
Louis Kruh

Enever, Ted. *Britain's Best Secret: Ultra's Base at Bletchley Park*. Alan Sutton Publishing Ltd., Phoenix Mill, Far Throup. Stroud, Gloucestershire GL5 2BU ENGLAND. 1994. 90 pp. £6.99 ($12). In the U. S. Alan Sutton Pub. Inc., 83 Washington Street, Dover NH 03820 USA. 20(1): 17.

In 1938, the British Government's Code and Cypher School (GC&CS) moved to Bletchley Park (BP) in the village of Milton Keynes, England. There it developed the organization that would have a vital role in the coming Second World War.

From a staff of fewer than 200 in 1939, GC&CS grew to almost 7,000 by mid-1944 and BP eventually gained world-wide renown as the source of Ultra intelligence from the German Enigma cipher machine. It was also the location of the world's first electronic computer, Colossus, which was used to break high grade ciphers from the German *Geheimschreiber* and Lorenz machines.

Enever traces BP's history from shortly after the Romans left Britain about AD 400. He tells how BP was recently saved from demolition and is currently the site of budding museums of cryptology and the history of computing. Using separate chapters, devoted to BP's mansion, huts and other structures, Enever takes readers on a walking tour of the complex, interspersed with an account of the activities in each building, machines and equipment, and many of the people who worked there. It is a fascinating "tour" accompanied by more than 65 photographs, maps, and diagrams including some rare contemporary photographs.

VIDEO ON POLISH ENIGMA EFFORTS
Louis Kruh

Sekret Enigmy. (*The Enigma Secret*). Videotape (with English subtitles). POLart, 4583 Clark Road, Suite "B", Sarasota FL 34233-3423 USA. 1979. 158 minutes. $29.95 plus $6.00 UPS shipping charge. 20(2): 185.

Produced in Poland, this realistic movie is based on the breaking of German Enigma messages by three Polish cryptanalysts, Marian Rejewski, Jerzy Rózycki, and Henryk Zygalski.

Other personalities depicted in the film include: Major G. Bertrand, Director of France's Radio Intelligence Service; M. Ciezki, Director of the German Section, Polish Cipher Bureau (PCB); Colonel G. Langer, Director, PCB; E. Fokczynski, cipher machine specialist and co-founder, AVA Radio Mfg. Co.; A. Palluth, engineer and co-founder, AVA (AVA built copies of the Enigma for PCB); Commander A. Denniston, Director of Bletchley Park, Winston Churchill, and Adolf Hitler.

The movie describes operational details of the Enigma, success of the Polish cryptanalysts, use of perforated sheets and the Polish bombe, conference with French and British officials including Denniston, evacuation of PCB from Warsaw to Pyry, then to Paris and later to Vichy France, and eventually a circuitous route to England. Along the way, it becomes a thrilling adventure story with spies, pursuit by German troops and the capture of Langer and others, who are brutally tortured by the Gestapo.

There are amusing touches when scenes of the cryptanalysts' success are followed by Hitler being assured by his signal officers that Enigma is totally secure.

It is a lengthy but interesting film (more than 2 1/2 hours) based on the 1978 book, Seket Enigma, by S. S. Wojtkiewicz, who was co-author of the movie script.

HUNTERS IN THE U-BOAT WAR
Louis Kruh

Blair, Clay. *Hitler's U-Boat War: The Hunters, 1939-1942*. Random House, 201 E. 50th St., New York NY 10022 USA. 1996. 809 pp. $40.00. 21(3): 218.

This hefty book is the result of nine years of research and writing with much of the time spent in naval archives in Washington, London and Berlin. It is the first of two volumes in which Blair attempts to do for World War II German submarine actions in the Atlantic what he did for the United States Pacific submarine effort in Silent Victory (1975).

The book is divided into two parts: "The U-Boat War Against the British Empire" and "The U-Boat War Against the Americas."

Blair chronicles virtually all major and many minor U-boat attacks and antisubmarine counterattacks and does it vividly and dramatically. He also makes sure that a number of previously unknown but distinguished officers on both sides are appropriately recognized.

Radio intelligence played a major role in the war and, similar to the *Wehrmacht* and *Luftwaffe*, the *Kriegsmarine* had also adopted the Enigma cipher machine. But the German Naval Enigma was more complicated than other Enigma models and *Kriegsmarine* signals security was tighter and its traffic lighter. Blair gives the history of Enigma and describes it in detail. He tells how Polish cryptanalysts solved the Enigma and the subsequent work of Alan Turing, John Jeffreys and Gordon Welchman at Bletchley Park, the use of the Turing-Welchman bombes, and the British seizure of Enigma key tables, and ring and plugboard settings when their commandos attacked the Lofoten Islands.

Blair praises the work of Navy Lt. Howard Engstrom, who he says has been largely overlooked by codebreaking historians despite having played "the key role in the American attack on naval Enigma" and "his codebreaking achievements ...produced results on a par with those of the British mathematicians Alan Turing and Gordon Welchman."

Among many other highlights is Blair's dramatic description of the British capture of U-110 with its Enigma, keys and other code material. His detailed account of the tracking and sinking of the German super battleship Bismarck, is exceptional.

Most historians agree that German submarines nearly won the war for Hitler and point to the sinking of thousands of Allied merchant ships and almost 150 naval vessels totaling more than 13 million tons, and the loss of thousands of sailors. But Blair argues that the U-boat threat has been exaggerated. His extensive research reveals that only 5% of all Allied shipping was sunk by German submarines and the vast majority of ships arrived safely.

The U-boat attacks off the coast of the United States were devastating and some critics excoriated the Navy commander of the Atlantic Fleet "for failing to respond more promptly and aggressively." Other critics faulted the Navy for not taking advantage of Britain's 1942 antisubmarine warfare experience. Blair maintains that the United States Navy was well aware of the British experience, but it was a matter of priorities. And the Navy had to leave American coastal shipping unprotected to concentrate scarce resources on escorting troop convoys.

This monumental work is the most thorough study of the U-boat war in the Atlantic and includes 18 appendices that detail virtually any statistic wanted on the activities of the submarines that were involved.

CHASING ENIGMA
Louis Kruh

Berends, A. A. *Chasing Enigma: Procurement of German Army ENIGMA Messages in the North West Europe Campaign 1944-45*. Ancestral Publications, P. O. Box 463, Yarra Glen, Victoria 3775 AUSTRALIA. 1995. 28 pp. $10.00. 21(3): 222-223.

Berends, who was a captain in Australia's 30 Wireless Group Intelligence

Section (WGIS), sets the stage for his monograph with quotations from two books on Ultra: "Everything begins with the intercept" from *Ultra Goes to War* by Ronald Lewin, and "At the basis of the whole Ultra achievement was interception ... Without interception, nothing" from *Top Secret Ultra*, by Peter Calvocoressi.

Since 1979, when Berends read a detailed analysis on the volume of decrypted Enigma messages sent to Allied commanders in the field, he felt that the work involved in intercepting enemy messages should be told. In this small volume he describes the composition of his unit, how they received instructions on where to position the unit, which frequencies to monitor, and how messages were sent to Bletchley Park. After D-Day, wireless activity increased and by using Traffic Analysis and D/F techniques, plus locations of the known front-line, "the enemy network was successfully correlated with the order of battle."

In July 1944, the Mobile Section of 1 Special Wireless Group (SWG) began moving to Normandy where it was the only unit assigned to intercept Enigma signals. Berends recounts the movements and activities of Mobsec, as it was called. When the American troops broke out west and south from the invasion area, interception "became more difficult as enemy transmitters receded out of range of the U. K." Additional segments of WGIS were moved from England to Normandy and the experienced Mobsec went south to operate on the American front. Due to a shortage of resources, a Playfair collecting section was converted to Enigma collection.

Berends relates many interesting details of his unit's operations. One ironic incident stems from the strict security surrounding Britain's success in reading Enigma messages. Intercept operators working on Playfair traffic knew their intercepts were being solved and used to good advantage, which made them feel proud of their contribution to the war effort. In contrast, in units working on Enigma traffic, only the commanding officer and perhaps another senior officer knew the Ultra secret. Others working on Enigma signals, who asked if the encrypted messages were being broken, could only be told that Bletchley Park was working hard and hoped to succeed. As a result, according to Berends, when intercept operators had to switch from collecting Playfair traffic to copy Enigma signals, many could not understand why, and though they did their best, he says in probably understated fashion, "an experienced Enigma unit could probably have procured more traffic."

The paper is especially interesting because it provides an insider's view with details only available from someone on the scene.

HOW ULTRA CHANGED HISTORY

Louis Kruh

Bennett, Ralph. *Intelligence Investigations: How Ultra Changed History.* Frank Cass c/o ISBS, 5804 N. E. Hassalo St., Portland OR 97213-3644 USA. 1996. 203 pp. $39.50. 21(4): 348.

The author, a professional historian, worked at Bletchley Park for four years as a senior producer of Ultra. This collection of ten of his reprinted essays illustrates some of the steps by which he and others developed the new type of information and in the process provides a candid glimpse of the workings of British intelligence.

Bennett notes that the papers fall into two groups. He describes the first five as building blocks from which a new style of history was being constructed. He points out that it had not been previously possible "to document intelligence history so fully and so reliably: operational orders and reports intercepted currently and decrypted without much delay gave it a precision it had hitherto always lacked."

He says the second group of essays provide a "markedly different approach" and are better suited to the term "Intelligence Investigations." Each paper explores a situation where valuable Ultra information was not properly exploited.

Papers include: Ultra and Some Command Decisions. An interesting point made by Bennett is that Ultra played no part in the greatest command decision in the war – where and when to invade Europe; The 'Vienna Alternative', 1944: Reality or Illusion. Planning and execution of policy consistent with intelligence on an enemy's situation and intentions is appropriate but this paper explores a case where policy and intelligence pointed in different directions; FORTITUDE, Ultra and the 'Need to Know'. FORTITUDE was the successful deception effort to mislead Hitler and his generals into believing that the D-Day invasion would take place around Calais rather than in Normandy. The paper describes the successful techniques employed, such as "turned" enemy agents, and how intelligence was used in developing FORTITUDE strategies.

Other essays are: Army Ultra in the Mediterranean Theatre: Darkness and Light; World War II Intelligence: The Last Ten Years' Work Reviewed; Intelligence and Strategy in World War II; Intelligence and Strategy: Some Observations on War in the Mediterranean 1941-45; Knight's Move at Drvar: Ultra and the Attempt on Tito's Life, 25 May 1944; Ultra and the Gothic Line; and Ultra and Crete.

ENIGMA SYMPOSIUM SUMMARY
Louis Kruh

Skillen, Hugh. *The Enigma Symposium 1997.* Hugh Skillen, 56 St. Thomas Drive, Pinner, Middlesex HA5 4SS ENGLAND. 1997. 194 pp. $16.00 plus $2.50 postage (U. S. checks not acceptable due to excessive charges for processing) 22(2): 169.

Skillen's report on the fourth reunion of Bletchley Park (BP) veterans provides a variety of additional in-depth accounts of work at BP and related cryptologic events elsewhere.

The papers in this volume, many with illustrations, include "The Y Sections in the Field," a comprehensive 25-page description of a Canadian Wireless Intelligence unit from its inception in Canada, to the end of its service in Germany on VE-Day, with a wealth of detail in-between; "Teaching the Royal Indian Air Force Japanese Kata Kana"; "German Naval Intercepts – Submarine Warfare in the Atlantic and Far East"; "Swiss Enigmas," a fascinating account of Enigmas sold to Switzerland by Germany during World War II, and subsequent production of an improved machine in 1945, known as NEMA (NEue MAschine) Model 45; "Colossus Revealed at Last" by Harry Fensome, who joined the section at BP headed by Max Newman, to assist in the development of the machine to break the Lorenz cipher; "Huts 11 and 11 A" describe the huts containing the Bombes and the people operating them; "German Diplomatic Papers"; "The Ultra Americans"; "Special Communications Units (SCUs) and Special Liaison Units (SLUs)"; "The Testery"; "Account of the retrieval of German Coding Documents from a U-Boat in October 1942," a first-hand report by Roy Crang, a member of the crew of the destroyer *HMS Petard*; plus many other fascinating papers.

The value and importance of Skillen's reports on these periodic reunions is demonstrated by the continued interest in his account of the first reunion, The Enigma Symposium 1992, which went out-of-print some years ago. Due to persistent requests, Skillen has reprinted additional copies.

BLETCHLEY PARK REPORT SERIES
Louis Kruh

The Bletchley Park (BP) Trust was established in 1992 to save BP as a memorial to the World War II codebreaking that took place there. Since then it has established a Museum in the Park that includes a "rebuild of Colossus, the world's first large electronic valve computer which helped to break the important

German Lorenz cipher." The Trust is also publishing reports on codebreaking techniques and related events. Some reports are transcripts of talks given at a BP Lecture Series. Eight reports are available and more are planned. Descriptions and prices follow.

Carter, Frank. *Codebreaking with the Colossus Computer*. Report No. 1 (6" × 8 1/4"). Nov. 1996. 20 pp. $4.15 plus postage. 22(2): 170.

Includes details of the German Lorenz machine and its five pairs of wheels. The first wheel in each pair is called a "K-wheel" and the other, an "S-wheel" and each moves differently. Techniques developed to solve these complex ciphers are detailed with their mathematical basis. A Top Secret report sent to the US War Department in 1944 by a US Signal Corps cryptanalyst assigned to BP said, "Daily solutions to Fish [Code name for messages enciphered by the Lorenz machine] messages at GC&CS reflect a background of British mathematical genius, superb engineering ability, and solid common sense."

Jarvis, Peter. *The German Battleships*. Report No. 2 (6" × 8 1/2"). Jan. 1997. 18 pp. $3.30 plus postage. 22(2): 170.

Describes German Naval Policy, German warship design, Naval Enigma cipher machines and their role in battles involving the Bismarck, Norway and the Arctic Convoys, Tirpitz, and others.

Carter, Frank. *Codebreaking with the Colossus Computer: An Account of the Methods used for finding the K-wheel settings, including an illustrated example*. Report No. 3 (8 1/2" × ll 1/2"). May 1997. 12 pp. $4.15 plus postage. 22(2): 171.

Purpose of this report is to provide a more detailed account of the technique of "wheel setting" than previously given in Report No. 1 and Carter assumes readers are familiar with that report.

Carter, Frank. *Codebreaking with The Colossus Computer: Finding the K-wheel Patterns. An account of some of the techniques used, with a full illustrative example*. Report No. 4 (8 1/2" × 11 1/2"). June 1997. 37 pp. $9.90 plus postage. 22(2): 171.

Carter's purpose in this report "is to provide detailed information about the process for finding the K-wheel difference patterns for the Lorenz machine, from a coded message. [He seeks] to achieve this by providing a practical example of 'wheel breaking' based on a genuine message originally decoded at Bletchley in

1944. A full set of the resulting documentary material is given (appendices A to Z), together with a set of explanatory notes." Readers should be familiar with Report No. 1.

Wescombe, Peter & John Gallehawk. *Getting back into "Shark": HMS Petard and the George Cross*. Report No. 5 (6" × 8 1/4"). June 1997. 20 pp. $3.30 plus postage. 22(2): 171.

The introduction of a four-rotor Enigma for U-boats, combined with the new 1942 German Meteorological Code and their breaking of the Royal Navy's Code No. 3 was a catastrophe for the Allies. If a four-rotor Enigma's daily key setting sheet could not be acquired, a copy of the new Meteorological Code was urgently needed by Allied cryptanalysts. The authors describe *HMS Petard*'s attack on U-559, which was forced to the surface and abandoned by its crew. Three members of *Petard*'s crew boarded the U-boat to search for secret papers. After several trips that retrieved documents they were ordered to leave the submarine but two members went down with U-559. The papers included the new Weather Code which led to cribs for messages enciphered by U-boats on the four-rotor Enigma. Later, solutions to the four-rotor Enigma U-boat key, codenamed SHARK in BP started to emerge.

Gallehawk, John. *Convoys and the U-boats*. Report No. 7 (6" × 8 1/4"). Aug. 1997.48 pp. $4.15 plus postage. 22(2): 172.

An account of critical events in the Battle of the Atlantic in March 1943. Gallehawk describes three convoys and their involvement with U-boats with an exciting novel-like story of convoy/U-boat battles. Many helpful charts included.

Wescombe, John. *Bletchley Park and the Luftwaffe: The Fall of France, the Battle of Britain and the defence of Crete*. Report No. 8 (6" × 8 1/4"). Oct. 1997. 28 pp. $4.15 plus postage. 22(2): 171.

The German Air Force from the end of World War I to the beginning of World War II from the German perspective and the British perspective. Describes the Battle of Britain and British intelligence. Includes decrypted text of 20 German messages related to the defence of Crete.

Send orders/checks for these reports to: Bletchley Park Company Ltd., Bletchley Park, Bletchley MK3 6EF ENGLAND.

BREAKING ENIGMA CODES

Louis Kruh

Welchman, Gordon. *The Hut Six Story: Breaking the Enigma Codes*. M & M Baldwin, 24 High Street, Cleobury Mortimer, KIDDERMINSTER DY14 8BY ENGLAND. 1997. 263 pp. £8-50 plus £1-25 postage. Orders in North America may be directed to Classic Crypto Books, P. O. Box 1013, Londonderry NH 03053-1013 USA, $16.95 (ACA members $14.95) plus $3.95 postage; CANADA $5.95. 22(2): 178.

This book was originally published in 1982 and has been out-of-print for many years. Many other books on Enigma, Bletchley Park and Ultra have been published since then, but Welchman's first-hand account is still the most thorough and authoritative report of the way codebreakers actually worked, problems they faced, and the variety of ingenious methods they created to solve them.

Welchman describes how he and his colleagues devised various techniques which helped "to break a cipher machine that should have been unbreakable if properly used." These methods included: Welchman's "diagonal board" which could test 200 trillion plugboard combinations used by the Germans in less than a thousandth of a second and aided the design of the bombe; Jeffrey's perforated sheets, which would reduce the possible assumptions of wheel order and ring settings to a manageable number; Herivel tips that enabled them to guess the ring setting of each wheel to within two or three letters; and Sillies/Cillis, which often allowed them to guess text settings. Welchman provides full explanations of these methods with illustrative diagrams.

The publication brought down the wrath of GCHQ and NSA on Welchman. Having moved to the United States in 1948 and becoming an American citizen, he was presumably immune from British penalties. But NSA warned him that U. S. laws protecting classified cryptologic sources and methods limited what he could say in any discussions or interviews about his book. He was given a list of topics "You may discuss" and a list of subjects "You may not discuss." But, according to Nigel West in "The SIGINT Secrets: The Signals Intelligence War, 1900 To Today, "in spite of Welchman's compliance with the prohibition, his security clearance was rescinded" and he could no longer work, even as a consultant, for the U. S. defense contractor he had been associated with for 20 years.

For this edition, the publisher has omitted the section on security in the 1980s and improved the book by substituting Welchman's last account of his wartime work, an extensive article published in 1986 in Intelligence and National Security, "From Polish Bomba to British Bombe: The Birth of Ultra." In this paper, Welchman attempts to set the record straight about the chronology of Bletchley's successes and the role played by Polish cryptanalysts. It also comments on what Welchman believed were misleading passages in Harry Hinsley's official history of British intelligence. Sir Peter Marychurch, Director of GCHQ, was so incensed by the paper that he wrote a letter to Welchman in Massachusetts, which was publicly criticized by Dr. Christopher Andrew as demonstrating "a nasty attitude towards distinguished old intelligence officers who want to set the record straight without causing any damage to national security." Sir Stuart Milner-Barry, one of Welchman's oldest friends and colleagues from Hut Six, wrote, "To suggest that the first head of this organization (and a man who of all the remarkable group assembled at Bletchley Park made possibly the biggest contribution to the success of the whole operation) could be guilty of doing anything to endanger national security does indeed, as Dr. Andrew has said, reveal a nasty attitude." This book is essential for a full understanding of how the secrets of the German Enigma cipher machine were unraveled and the brilliant scholars who were responsible. It stands alone in describing what actually happened in Hut Six, where the bulk of the breaking of German army and air force Enigma ciphers were carried out.

ENIGMA BULLETIN
Louis Kruh

Kapera, Zdzislaw Jan, ed. *The Enigma Bulletin*, No. 3, May 1998. The Enigma Press, ul. Borsucza 3/58, 30-408 Krakow POLAND. 125 pp. $20.00 per issue (add $5.00 for air mail). Previous issues published 12/90 and 5/97 still available. 23(1): 45.

This third issue contains a tribute by Alan Stripp, "A British Cryptanalyst Salutes the Polish Cryptanalysts." The Bulletin cover, under the heading, "Sixty Five Years Ago The Enigma Was Broken" features photographs from a private collection of the three Polish mathematicians who broke the German Enigma cipher machine.

A lengthy article by Carl Boyd deseribes "The Role of Cryptologic Intelligence in the Pacific War, 1941-1943." Another paper contains the full text of an interview by German historian, Michael Foedrowitz, with Heinrich Hamann, Head of the Gestapo Posts in Poland. The article is in German but Kapera published it because "very few Abwehr or SD officers working in Poland during World War II and now living in Germany have even said a word about their activities."

Kapera contributes a report, with photographs of participants, of a symposium held in Strausberg on "Origins of Intelligence Organizations." He also continues his descriptive list of articles on intelligence history, which have appeared in recent Polish publications. Other articles include an excellent review of *Signals Intelligence in World War II: A Research Guide* by Donald J. Sexton (Westport, CT: Greenwood Press, 1996) and an illustrated paper by Jan Heitmann, "The Shots that Opened the Second World War."

GERMAN U-BOAT DEFEAT
Louis Kruh

Gannon, Michael. *Black May: The Epic Story of the Allies' Defeat of the German U-Boats in May 1943*. HarperCollins, 10 E. 53 Street, New York NY 10022 USA. 1998. 492 pp. $30.00. 23(1): 52.

A thrilling and comprehensive account of the turning point of the Battle of the Atlantic in May 1943. The book's focal point is the story of Convoy ONS 5, which was sailing to Halifax with 43 merchantmen and six escorts. In his typical style, Gannon infuses readers with the technicalities and trivia of submarines, convoys, escorts and air coverage, including strengths, weaknesses, weapons, armament, crews, and other details. From the decks of merchantmen to the bridges of destroyers, to the conning towers of submarines and into the cockpits of British and U. S. aircraft, you are part of the action. And the actions involving ON 5 and other Allied sea and air forces in May resulted in a dramatic and vital victory over the largest and most powerful submarine force ever sent to sea, with 41 U-boats sunk and 37 others damaged. By the end of May the Germans were forced to acknowledge defeat and recall almost all remaining U-boats from major traffic lanes of the North Atlantic. Contributing to Allied success was an increase in the minimum speed limit for independently routed ships and improved evasive routing of convoys when Bletchley Park (BP) began to read German Naval Enigma ciphers. Another reason was that U-boat captains were similar to fighter pilots in that a relatively small number were responsible for a disproportionate number of "kills." By May 1943, many of the original "aces" were dead and replacements were less aggressive against improved defensive techniques.

Another factor in the Allies' supremacy stemmed from British success with encrypted radio traffic between Admiral Karl Donitz, head of the German navy, and his boats. From the Polish mathematicians to the Royal Navy capture of German cryptographic material, and Hut 8 cryptanalysts at BP and the use of the decrypts in the Submarine Tracking Room of the Operational Intelligence Centre of the British Admiralty, all played a significant role. Gannon also examines German success with British Naval codes and ciphers, particularly British Naval Cipher No. 3, used for Allied convoys.

Gannon's enormous research has produced the most thoroughly documented study of these battles and their participants, and it belongs in your library along side of his *Operation Drumbeat: The Dramatic True Story of Germany's First U-Boat Attacks Along the American Coast in World War II* (see review *Cryptologia*, 15(1): 72-73).

ENIGMA REUNION
Louis Kruh

Skillen, Hugh. *The Enigma Reunion 1998*. H. Skillen, 56 St. Thomas Drive, Pinner, Middlesex, HA5 4SS ENGLAND. 1998. 206 pp. $21.00 surface mail, $24.00 air mail. (No checks please, as cost of cashing is exorbitant. Use cash which will be acknowledged by return air mail.) 23(2): 172.

This report on the 1998 Enigma Reunion is the largest to date with interesting wartime remembrances of work at Bletchley Park (BP) and secret operations elsewhere, with many photographs and other illustrations.

Fascinating articles describe: The Watch – Hut 3 (Army and Air Force), Hut 4 (Naval Section), WOP/MSRs (Wireless Operators/Morse Slip Readers) at BP, Logging Away (Log Readers at BP), The Birth of Colossus, The U-Boat Index, A Wren's Memoir of the Newmanry, The Testery at BP, The "Y" Group at Kranji, Singapore, up to the Surrender to the Japanese, The Intelligence Corps, plus many more worthwhile accounts of personal experiences. Also included are several historical documents and related information including The Zimmermann Telegram with comments by Cdr. Alastair Denniston in 1958, and a description of the Top Secret plans for the contemplated United States invasion of Japan in 1945.

For anyone interested in first-hand accounts of men and women who were stationed at BP and other secret sites, Skillen has provided another remarkable collection.

ANGLO-AMERICAN NAVAL INTELLIGENCE
Louis Kruh

Bath, Alan Harris. *Tracking the Axis Enemy: The Triumph of Anglo American Naval Intelligence*. University Press of Kansas, 2501 W. 15th St., Lawrence KS 66049 USA. 1998. 308 pp. $34.95. 23(2): 183-184.

In World War II, Naval Intelligence, or the lack of it, was a major factor for both the Allies and the Axis in determining strategy during the key battles of the Atlantic, and throughout the war in the Pacific. But, in intelligence literature, its role is often obscured by concentration on one of its components: the Allied breaking of German or Japanese codes, Ultra and Purple. In addition to examining the work of the code breakers, this excellent study attempts to put in perspective the total contribution of Allied Naval intelligence to victory in WW II.

Bath unfolds his findings in four parts. In Part I, The Road To Cooperation, he traces relationships between American and British navies from WW I, where formal intelligence cooperation operated with suppressed rivalries on both sides and limited efforts. In the late 1930's, possible cooperation was discussed openly but only reluctantly in Washington. As potential hostilities drew closer, the British decrypted German Enigma messages and the Americans broke Japan's diplomatic cipher. Bath describes the navy personalities on both sides, from each country's naval attaches to their respective fleet commanders and naval intelligence directors. The British had concerns about American security practices but wanted information on Japanese ciphers. American navy cryptanalysts, who felt they were ahead of their British counterparts, argued against the release of information. Meanwhile, the British had recognized the importance of a single control point for intelligence analysis and organized accordingly while the Unites States allowed each service to provide its own intelligence.

In 1941, personnel changes occurred including a new U. S. ambassador to England. Soon, both countries softened their stance. In April 1941, two army officers and two navy officers went to Bletchley Park to deliver two copies of the Purple machine and to learn about British cryptologic achievements. By late fall, all major Anglo-American agreements on naval intelligence sharing had been implemented.

When America entered the war after the Japanese attack on Pearl Harbor, other problems surfaced for the U. S. Navy. In the first six months of 1942, German U-boats sank approximately 2 million tons of Allied merchant shipping in the Western Atlantic. There was a need to muster sufficient air and surface escorts to institute a convoy system along the East coast, which took several months. There was also a need to develop a unified command structure to control all aspects of antisubmarine warfare.

Also, in early 1942, the German Navy added a 4th rotor to its Enigma, which caused almost a year-long blackout of Bletchley Park's ability to decrypt this vital traffic. Near the end of 1942, German cryptanalysts were able to read almost 80% of intercepts of British messages sent in Naval Cypher No. 3, introduced in June 1941 and used extensively in the Allied North Atlantic convoy system.

To convince the U. S. Navy of the importance of a centralifed intelligence organization, Captain Humphrey Sandwith, head of the Admiralty's Joint Intelligence/Signals Section in the Operational Intelligence Centre (OIC), made a detailed presentation on the British organization for radio intelligence at the U. S.-British-Canadian Conference in Washington. As a result, U. S. Navy officials rearranged their command structure and set up a plotting center, which subsequently became the nucleus of a U-boat tracking room or OIC. The impetus for this last move came after Commander Roger Winn, head of the British tracking room, spent a week in Washington, first convincing fleet operational intelligence officer, Commander George Dyer, and then Dyer's superior, Admiral Richard S. Edwards, deputy chief of staff, of the need for an OIC.

In Part II, Culmination and Turning Point, Bath points out that at the end of 1943, the naval intelligence structure was functioning smoothly and the "tide had turned." This was apparent in the battle against German U-boats in the Atlantic, "in which the efforts of the mutually supportive submarine tracking rooms in London, Washington, and Ottawa marked the culmination of Anglo-American cooperation in naval intelligence." But, as the war progressed, a combination of personnel changes on the British side, a feeling by American intelligence "that the British were attempting to perpetuate a teacher-pupil relationship" and the growing realization "that the Allies would eventually win caused Anglo-American relationships to become colored by the idea of national postwar advantage."

In Part III, The Pacific, Bath notes that Anglo-American naval intelligence cooperation during 1943-1944 in the Pacific "essentially did not exist." In part, this was due to the British view that "attempts were being made to absorb British intelligence into the American organization and to use the information for purposes other than the prosecution of the war." Also, infighting between the U. S. Navy staffs in Washington and Pearl Harbor "for preeminence in Pacific intelligence analysis and reporting did its share to hamper" cooperation.

In Part IV, Denouement of Wartime Alliances, Bath concludes that Anglo-American intelligence did not completely disappear at the end of the war. There was a sharp retrenchment but in response to the potential threat to both countries from the spread of communism, intelligence cooperation increased again but not as close or as effective in 1942-1943, in the battle against German U-boats in the Atlantic.

Bath has written an essential guide to the Anglo-American intelligence labyrinth in WW II and the role of code breaking. The book is especially interesting because of his insights to the people, personalities and motivations in both the United States and Britain.

BLETCHLEY PARK CODEBREAKERS

Louis Kruh

Smith, Michael. *Station X: The Codebreakers of Bletchley Park*. Channel 4 Books/Macmillan Publications Ltd., 2.5 Eccleston Place, London SW1W 9NF, ENGLAND. 1998. 184 pp. $24.00. 23(3): 283.

The story of Station X, from the summer of 1939, when workmen were up grading roads, telephone lines, water mains and other services for the impending arrival of the Government Code and Cypher School (GC&CS), to June 1946, when the renamed GC&CS, Government Communications Headquarters, left Bletchley Park (BP).

Smith provides an engaging history of the critical codebreaking triumphs that played a vital role in World War II and shortened the war by at least two years.

Smith describes, almost step-by-step, the British codebreakers' first break into Enigma, the techniques they used/developed, and other significant accomplishments. The techniques included the use of cillis, cribs, "kisses," Banburismus, Herivel Tip, and machines such as Colossus and bombes. Smith also relates the successful efforts to solve the more complicated teleprinter transmissions codenamed "Fish." These were enciphered with the Lorenz SZ40 cipher machine. Initially solved by hand, with many messages taking weeks to decipher, Colossus, forerunner of the post-war digital computer, was developed to accelerate the process. A few of the codebreakers who had key roles at BP included Alan Turing, Gordon Welchman, John Herival, Colonel John Tiltman, and Hugh Alexander.

Smith discusses American participation in BP and how mutual distrust was replaced by mutual respect. Americans highlighted include Joe Eachus, Bill Bundy, Art Levenson, and Selmer Norland.

The amazing story of BP has been told before but Smith's work is distinguished by his widespread use of "first hand" comments, descriptions, reports, and personal stories from the people who were there. They range from codebreakers to clerks on subjects from ciphers to social life and there is an average of about one per page. One story describes the search for recruits for BP. A prize was offered to anyone who could solve a Daily Telegraph crossword puzzle in less than twelve minutes. Subsequently, winners were interviewed for positions at BP. Smith includes the puzzle with the answers on another page.

THE U-BOAT WAR

Louis Kruh

Blair, Clay. *Hitler's U-Boat War: The Hunted, 1942-1945*. Random House, 201 E. 50th Street, New York NY 10022 USA. 1998. 909 pp. $45.00. 24(1): 83.

The first volume of Blair's highly praised history of the German submarine war against Allied shipping in World War II, *The Hunters, 1939-1942*, (see review, *Cryptologia* 21(3): 218-219) described the Battle of the Atlantic waged first against the British Empire and then against the Americas. This second and concluding volume covers the period when the fortunes of the German Navy were completely reversed, and it suffered perhaps the most devastating defeat of any of the German forces.

In enormous detail and drawing on sources never used before, Blair continues the dramatic and authoritative story of the failures and fortunes of the German U-boat campaign against the United States and Great Britain. All major patrols and sorties made by the Germans are described in detail and with considerable human interest; the Paleus and Laconia affairs; the capture at sea of U-505; the crisis of German command; the futile operations against the Americans, and the mounting and devastating losses that, in effect, entirely destroyed the German submarine service.

Blair does not neglect the scientific developments of the U-boat war. These include radar and radar detectors, active and passive sonar, high-frequency direction finding (Huff-Duff), Hedgehogs, depth charges, sophisticated U-boat torpedoes, Axis enciphering machines and the remarkable Allied decrypting machines.

He describes cryptologic events on both sides including: German addition of a fourth rotor to the naval Enigma and its consequences; U. S. Navy's decision to develop its own bombe when the British kept delaying delivery of a bombe to copy; assignment of two U. S. Navy officers, Joseph Eachus and Robert Ely, in July 1942, to Hut 8, the Navy cryptanalytic section at Bletchley Park; Alan Turing's visit to the United States and the sites where bombes were being built; recovery of codebooks, rotors and cipher machines from U-boats; Allied codebreakers discover that the Germans were reading the Allied Atlantic Convoy codes; investigation by the Germans to determine if the Allies had broken their naval Enigma; U. S. builds 121 4-rotor bombes at a cost of $6 million; Britain was unsuccessful in developing a suitable bombe for a 4-rotor enigma and similarly the United States was not very successful with the Rapid Analytical Calculator (RAC) or bombe for the 3-rotor Enigma; and, of course, how decrypted German messages enabled Allied ships and planes to locate and destroy German U-boats.

In addition to numerous photographs and maps there are 20 appendices that provide almost any statistic needed on the U-boat war. Similar to what was written in the review of volume I, this monumental work is the most thorough study of the U-boat war.

COMMANDERS WINN AND KNOWLES
Louis Kruh

Kohnen, David. Commanders Winn and Knowles: Winning the U-Boat War with Intelligence, 1939-1945. *The Enigma Bulletin*, No. 4, Special Issue. ul. Borsucza 3/58, 30-408 95. POLAND 168 pp. 1999. $25.00. Available in U. S. from Classical Crypto Books: P. O. Box 1013, Londonderry NH 03058 USA. 24(1): 90.

Based on intensive research and recently available documents, Kohnen describes the development of British-American cooperation in cryptologic and operational intelligence during World War II. At the outset, British naval leaders were "shocked to discover the extent of the inefficiency and irrelevance" prevailing throughout the American naval intelligence organization. In contrast, the British Admiralty was centralized with an Operational Intelligence Center (OIC) that was responsible for dissemination of codebreaking and other intelligence to consumers in the British government and military forces.

In a meeting of British-American military leaders in Washington, the British described the benefits they gained from a centralized OIC. Subsequently, the Americans chose Lt. Commander Kenneth Knowles to visit the Admiralty OIC and work with Commander Roger Winn to learn how the British used intelligence. Knowles would later command the American OIC and with Winn, they would ultimately infiuence the most pivotal decisions and operations in the Atlantic, Indian Ocean and other naval theatres. They fostered an atmosphere of Anglo-American cooperation that was described by Patrick Beasley, in his book, Very Special Intelligence, as "probably closer than between any other British and American organization in any service and in any theatre."

Kohnen has written an excellent account of British-American naval strategies relations between their leaders, and he includes many cryptologic details and information about the codebreakers involved.

BATTLE OF THE ATLANTIC – SIGNALS INTELLIGENCE
Louis Kruh

Syrett, David, ed. *The Battle of the Atlantic and Signals Intelligence: U-Boat Situations and Trends, 1941-1945*. A publication of the Navy Records Society, volume 139. Ashgate Publishing Co., Old Post Road, Brookfield VT 05036-9704 USA. 1998. 668 pp. $131.95. 24(2): 175-176.

England's Navy Records Society (NRS) was established in 1893 for the purpose of printing unpublished manuscripts and rare works of naval interest. In

107 years NRS has published 139 volumes, a likely sign of selectivity and this book is a worthy choice.

The hefty volume contains the U-Boat Situations and U-Boat Trends written during World War II by Rear Admiral J. W. Clayton, RN, head of the Admiralty's Operational Intelligence Centre, and by Commander Roger Winn, RNVR, head of the Submarine Tracking Room. Based largely on the latest available information, usually communications intelligence or Z information, these reports were designed to inform a small number of senior commanders and high-ranking officials of the current state and progress of the war against the U-boats. The weekly U-Boat Situation series showed the worldwide deployment of German U-boats and gave a general account of their activities and those of the Allied anti-U-boat forces. The U-Boat Trends bulletins were designed to keep readers abreast of the latest technological developments and strategic and tactical trends in the war against the U-boats and were issued on an irregular basis, as the situation required. Both documents, based on decryption and other intelligence, written by the two men who were at the center of the Allied intelligence effort against the German U-boats, are of significant importance in understanding the Battle of the Atlantic. They provide an insider's history of the battle and show very clearly the extent of Allied knowledge of U-boat activities at any given time.

In his 29-page introduction, Syrett reviews highlights of the supersecret intelligence war waged by forerunners of organizations such as the National Security Agency and Government Communications Headquarters. Communications intelligence was the most important source of information on the activities of German U-boats and the Allies monitored, intercepted and decrypted thousands of German enciphered radio messages to and from U-boats. The U. S. Navy alone deciphered 49,000 such transmissions. The Allies exploited German U-boat radio communications in four main ways: locating the source of the radio transmission by direction finding (D/F), reading enciphered radio messages by decryption, collecting information on individual U-boats by identifying a radio operator's Morse code transmissions and the electronic characteristics of individual radio sets, and from traffic analysis of radio transmissions.

The British first broke the codes used by the German Navy in 1941 and by August 4, 1941 they were regularly reading enciphered U-boat traffic. They called the system Dolphin and intelligence gained from decryption of Dolphin messages was apparently used to reroute convoys to evade contact with U-boats. One historian estimated that in the latter part of 1941, the British avoided shipping losses that could have reached 1.5 to 2 million tons. But when the Germans introduced a new cipher system, called Shark by the British, on February 1, 1942, which used a fourth rotor in the Enigma, the British were stymied for almost a year before they were able to break these messages.

Syrett reviews key moves including: establishment of the British Submarine Tracking Room, investigation of the time lag between the time of intercepting a radio message and the time of its decoding, how the Allies mastered the special Room, directed by Commander Kenneth A. Knowles, where U-boat decrypts were integrated with other intelligence and sent to the American Submarine Tracking Room. Decrypted U-boat messages revealed almost nothing to the Allies on the development of new weapons and technology. The best source of this information came from decrypting messages sent to Tokyo by the Japanese naval attache in Berlin. It included development of new torpedoes, the *schnorchel*, and new submarines. Other new developments came from prisoner-of-war interrogations. But deployment of new technology often came from decrypted radio messages.

Syrett provides a tightly written and very informative description of signals intelligence by the Allies. He concludes that "Communications intelligence did not win the Battle of the Atlantic by itself, but it greatly increased the effectiveness of Allied naval and air forces, shortening the conflict by months, if not years."

ALLIED AND AXIS SIGNALS INTELLIGENCE
Louis Kruh

Alvarez, David, ed. *Allied and Axis Signals Intelligence in World War II*. Frank Cass Publishers, ISBS, 5804 N. E. Hassalo St., Portland OR 97213-3644 USA. 229 pp. 1999. $24.50 paper, $57.50 cloth. 24(2): 178.

Since 1974, when F. W. Winterbotham divulged *The Ultra Secret*, the significance of cryptanalysis and signals intelligence, particularly in wartime, has become increasingly evident. But most revelations of codebreaking highlight the success of the United States with the Japanese Purple machine and Great Britain with the German Enigma.

The ten studies in this informative collection not only describe British and American cryptanalytic efforts but also the work of codebreakers in Australia, China, France, Hungary, Finland, Italy, and Japan. These articles depict the efforts to apply technology to the problems of radio intercept and cryptanalysis. They also recount the reactions of German and Japanese signal authorities to evidence that their encrypted messages had been penetrated and demonstrate that for the Allies as well as the Axis, success in the crypto war often depended on close collaboration among partners.

Articles include: Signals Intelligence in Australia during the Pacific War by F. Cain; New Evidence on Breaking the Japanese Army Codes by E. J. Drea and J. E. Richard; Axis Sigint Collaboration: A Limited Partnership by D. Alvarez; Chinese Codebreakers, 1927–45 by Maochun Yu; Searching for Security: The German Investigation into Enigma's Security by R. A. Ratcliff; Signals Intelligence and Vichy France, 1940-44: Intelligence in Defeat by M. Thomas; The 'Usual Source': Signals Intelligence and Planning for the Eighth Army 'Crusader' Offensive, 1941 by J. Ferris; Automating American Cryptanalysis 1930-45: Marvelous Machines, a Bit Too Late by C. Bark; Cautious Collaborators: The Struggle for Anglo-American Cryptanalytic Co-operation, 1940-43 by L. E. Gladwin; and New Intelligence Releases: A British Side to the Story by B. F. Smith.

In a cogent foreword, David Kahn concludes "... this fine collection advances cryptologic historiography in many ways ..."

THE ENIGMA SYMPOSIUM 1999 REPORTS
Louis Kruh

Skillen, Hugh. *The Enigma Symposium 1999*. H. Skillen, 56 St. Thomas Drive, Pinner HA5 4SS, ENGLAND. 1999. 210 pp. $24.00 surface mail, $28.00 air mail. (Checks not accepted due to excessive bank charges.) 24(2): 183.

This is the biggest and possibly the best of the always excellent Enigma Symposium reports. The volume contains an eclectic mixture of 30 articles by participants in the signals intelligence war in Europe, the Far East and Australia.

Papers include: BRUSA – The Special Relationship, which describes exchange visits by cryptologic experts of both countries, starting with the Sinkov-Rosen-Weeks-Currier mission to England in February 1941, and provides information on other visits throughout the war. It includes personalities, correspondence, information and cipher material made available plus other types of cooperation.; Bletchley Park and Berkeley Street; The Enigma Family of Machines; The British Hellschreiber; Crosswords and the Y Service, which includes the crossword puzzle that candidates for Bletchley Park had to solve in less than 12 minutes; The Polish Cipher Machine "Lacida"; VENONA – The Secret Ciphers of the KGB and GRU; SLU 9. MacArthur's HQ in Brisbane; US Marines' Radio Intelligence Platoons in the Pacific; US Field Units in Normandy; 3rd Radio Mobile Squadron (US); Katakana; My Experience with Katakana Morse in WW II; Cracking Japanese Codes; Japanese section, Hut 7, Bletchley Park; Black Propaganda by Radio Broadcasting; The Secret World at War: Film by Documedia;

The Special Operations Executive; The Enigma Story; and ten other engaging articles.

These papers have special interest because they are written, for the most part, by participants in the events being described and offer information or views that may be new. There are at least 100 photographs, maps and other illustrations of people, machines, and documents. It is an excellent and informative volume that belongs in your personal library.

DECODING NAZI SECRETS
Louis Kruh

Decoding Nazi Secrets. Two-hour NOVA Special. Videotape available, 1-800-255-9424. $19.95 plus $4.95 shipping and handling. 24(2): 186.

In a converted Victorian mansion in Bletchley Park, 50 miles north of London, an assorted group of mathematicians, champion chess players, crossword experts, Egyptologists, paleontologists and other talented individuals had been assembled from both sides of the Atlantic. Known as Station X, their mission was to break the Enigma, the impregnable cipher machine that protected German radio signals. This outstanding film uses declassified information and vivid interviews with many of the brilliant code breakers including Donald Michie, Peter Calvocoressi, Ralph Bennett, John Herivel, Peter Hilton, Tommy Flowers, plus Andrew Hodges, Alan Turing's biographer, and Americans Art Levenson and William Bundy. The dramatic story uses wartime footage of exciting naval battles in the Atlantic, armored warfare in North Africa and Churchill, Hitler and some of their generals. The film also features meticulous period reenactments shot inside the original buildings at Station X, including recreations of the world's first computing devices that aided code breakers.

The setting of the Enigma rotors, the letter/number rotor rings, and plugboard are described. Also the double encipherment of the message keys which were exploited by cryptanalysts to solve encrypted messages. The addition of a fourth Enigma rotor stymied code breakers for ten months before it finally yielded. The development of the Bombe is also described and how it cut the time it took to solve Enigma ciphers.

The Germans also used a Lorenz SZ 40 machine for high level communications between Hitler and his generals. This was a teleprinter enciphering system for the Baudot Code and used 12 rotors. Decipherment was a lengthy and tedious process. Ultimately, Tommy Flowers, a telephone engineer, and others built a machine with more than 1,000 valves. Called Colossus, it was the first programmable computer, and it performed in minutes what previously took a month.

The film contains much more information but there is a major omission. Gordon Welchman played a crucial role in breaking the Enigma and deserves more than a mere reference, if indeed there was one. (This reviewer does not recall any.) Presumably this is due to the official condemnation for publishing his book, *The Hut Six Story*. He was accused by GCHQ of "direct damage to security' and threatened with prosecution and imprisonment." (Station X by Michael Smith, p. 179.) Nevertheless, this is one of the best television programs produced on code breaking and reminiscent of Hollywood war movies. Check the NOVA web site `www.pbs.org/wgbh/nova/decoding` for other interesting information.

THE BATTLE OF THE ATLANTIC AND ULTRA
Louis Kruh

Gardner, W. J. R. *Decoding History: The Battle the Atlantic and Ultra*. Naval Institute Press, 291 Wood Ave., Annapolis MD 21402 USA. 1999. 263 pp. $34.95. 24(3): 280.

In World War II, a major part of the Allies' strategy was shipping. The Germans understood the vulnerability of this and their attacks on convoys and other vessels, largely by submarines, became known as the Battle of the Atlantic. Shipping was essential for our European allies who desperately needed the military equipment and personnel they carried. At times, the outcome of the battle seemed precarious and German attacks were overcome with some difficulty, by various means. One, which remained virtually unknown until 1974, was the decryption of German ciphers, known as Ultra. Subsequent histories often attributed the winning of the Battle of the Atlantic largely to the Allies' cryptanalytic prowess because there was no hard analysis of all factors involved.

In this important work, Gardner combines rigorous analysis with a full understanding of all causes of the outcome to produce a thorough and rounded assessment of all factors and the relative role of Ultra in the victory.

In his attempt to provide an indication of the true significance of Ultra in the Battle of the Atlantic, Gardner first presents the Battle as a whole together with Ultra in a number of different perspectives or contexts: chronology and time, economics, a German view, convoys, technology and finally, signals intelligence. These are used to provide two case studies, first on the calendar year 1941 and the second covering from the summer of 1942 to May 1943. Then the findings of all analyses are brought together to produce a more realistic view of the overall significance of Ultra. The final assessment seems to suggest that while Ultra was helpful on some occasions, it was not sufficiently critical overall and "many of the claims made for the significance of Ultra over the last quarter of a century are overdrawn at best and specious at worst."

But it also implies that more useful work might be done to reveal how Ultra was used specifically at strategic levels as well as operational and tactical levels.

This intensive analysis by a 30-year veteran of the Royal Navy, where he was a specialist in anti-submarine warfare, is an important contribution to naval history and in particular to the relative importance of Ultra in the Battle of the Atlantic. His chapter on "Signals Intelligence and the Battle of the Atlantic" is especially useful.

SEIZURE OF GERMAN NAVAL CODE – AN ACCOUNT

Louis Kruh

Harper, Stephen. *Capturing Enigma: How HMS Petard Seized the German Naval Codes*. Sutton Publishing Co., 260 Fifth Ave., New York NY 10001 USA. 1999. 180 pp. $24.95. 24(3): 284.

An attack by the British destroyer, *HMS Petard*, on a German U-boat in the Eastern Mediterranean in October 1942 altered the course of the entire war. It resulted in the capture of secret German Enigma coding material from U-559, at the cost of the lives of two of *Petard*'s crew and enabled Bletchley Park code breakers to successfully attack the new U-boat cipher. Ten months earlier the Germans had added a fourth rotor to their Enigma cipher machine for use by U-boats. This added complication had stymied Bletchley Park cryptanalysts and blacked out essential intelligence about U-boat operations previously available. Within six weeks of receiving material captured by *Petard*, British code breakers were again reading the vital messages between U-boats and Admiral Karl Doenitz. It was the crucial factor in defeating Hitler's Atlantic U-boat wolf packs when they were on the brink of success in the winter of 1942-43.

Had it been possible to release the facts of her triumph at the time, the name of *HMS Petard* might have ranked alongside that of Nelson's victory in the annals of British history. The reality was an extended intelligence blackout lasting nearly 40 years that insured *Petard*'s achievement remained unknown and her fame unrecognized.

Harper, who served in the Royal Navy during World War II as a coder on *HMS Petard* on her second commission, from 1945 to 1946, tells the dramatic story of how *Petard* attacked and captured U-559 in the darkness of a Mediterranean night. Using vivid eyewitness accounts he describes how members of her crew swam across to the slowly sinking abandoned U-boat, followed by a boarding party in a whaler, and captured the precious coding material. When, without warning the U-boat sank, two of the *Petard* crew were trapped in the conning tower while passing Enigma key material to their shipmates, and went to the bottom with her. Both men were later recommended for posthumous awards of the Victoria Cross but the Admiralty, concerned this might draw unwanted attention from German intelligence, instead ordered awards of the George Cross, the highest civilian award for bravery. It is an incredible story of a crucial turning point in World War II.

Harper devotes an extensive chapter to the work at Bletchley Park and he describes the use of Enigma decrypts by *Petard* and other ships in the Battle of the Atlantic and in the Mediterranean. He also provides an appendix on The Polish Contribution to Breaking the Enigma and another to Allied Breaking of Naval Enigma.

Corderman was swayed and announced that the problem would be the first priority of the German section and subsequently the system, which became known as "GEE," was solved.

Drawing on military and intelligence archives, interviews with retired and active cryptanalysts, and over a million pages of cryptologic documents declassified in 1996, Alvarez, who is a former scholar-in-residence at the National Security Agency's Center for Cryptologic History, has written an excellent book you will enjoy reading and having in your personal library for future reference.

BLETCHLEY PARK REPORTS

Louis Kruh

The Bletchley Park (BP) Trust established and operates the BP Museum. It also publishes reports on codebreaking and related topics. Some reports are transcripts of talks given at a BP lecture series. Reports 1-8 were reviewed in (*Cryptologia* 22(2): 170-172. Descriptions of reports 9-12, and 15 follow. Checks should be made out to: Bletchley Park Company Ltd. and sent to: Bletchley Park Trust, The Mansion, Bletchley Park, Wilton Avenue, Bletchley MK3 6EF ENGLAND.

> Carter, Frank and John Gallehawk. *The Enigma Machine and the Bombe: The Story of the breaking of the Enigma Cipher over the period 1932-1945*. Report No. 9, revised edition. July 1999. 20 pp. $4.00.

The authors explain the workings of the Enigma, the contribution of the Polish Cipher Bureau, early Enigma operating procedures, elements involved in breaking the Enigma cipher, the rationale of the Bombe, its basic function and the added benefit of Welchman's diagonal board. They also provide an outline description of the Bombe and historical notes.

Carter, Frank. *The First Breaking of Enigma: Some of the pioneering techniques developed by the Polish Cipher Bureau*. Report No. 10. July 1999. 36 pp. $4.00.

An account of three remarkable methods developed by the Polish Cipher Bureau from 1932-1938, to decrypt intercepted German Enigma messages. These were: 1) A search procedure using a catalogue that had been constructed with the assistance of a device known as the "Cyclometer." 2) Another searching process using a small electro-mechanical machine called the "Bomba." (Not to be confused with the British "Bombe," which was developed later using different principles.) Also includes "Supplementary Notes on the Mathematics" 3) A procedure involving a set of pre-perforated sheets of cards referred to as the "Zygalski Sheets." Appendices contain Some illustrative permutation cycles, The theoretical probability of a "female," and illustrative examples of Zygalski sheets.

Gallehawk, John. *How the Enigma Secret was nearly revealed*. Report No. 11. October 1998. 28 pp. $4.00.

The author describes three examples of how the secrecy of Ultra information was potentially compromised but fortunately the Germans never recognized the opportunity that was before them. One example took place in early 1942 in the U-boat war in the Atlantic, which was thoroughly investigated by Admiral Kurt Fricke, chief of the Naval War Command. He examined every possible security measure involving cryptomaterial and found there was "no palpable, unequivocal" cause but favored "coincidence." The second instance occurred in the invasion of Crete and the third was discovered during research through some documents at the Public Records Office at Kew. It requires too much background information to describe it here but it is worth reading and you will be surprised at what the Germans missed.

Pether, John. *The Post Office at War and Ferry Stratford Repeater Station*. Report No. 12. December 1998. 36 pp. $4.00.

Most people today are probably unaware that throughout World War II, every gun battery, Observer Corps Post, Radio Location Station, Air raid siren, Home Guard HQ and a variety of other units depended on the Post Office for their telecommunications. Also, RAF bombers, Fighter and Coastal Commands, and many other military and government departments such as the Foreign Office required circuits, networks and other vital services. Most people are already aware of the Post Office research facilities involvement in the development of Colossus and the secure scrambling equipment installed for telephone calls between Churchill and Roosevelt. This report is a transcript of two lectures given at BP in 1966 and 1967.

Gallehawk, John. *Some Polish Contributions in the Second World War*. Report No. 15. July 1998. 24 pp. $4.00.

This report recounts the pre-war breaking of the German Enigma cipher system and the famous meeting in July 1939, when this work was revealed to the British and French Intelligence Services. Also, three incidents of heroic Polish activity during the war are described; one from the Army, one for the Navy and one from the Air Force. 1) In the fierce and famous battle for Monte Cassino, Polish troops finally captured the stronghold in May 1944; 2) The escape and voyage of the Polish submarine, Orzel, was cited as "an epic of determination, seamanship and endurance, which will be long remembered in the annals of the British Submarine Service" 3) Some 17,000 Poles passed through the ranks of the Polish Air Force while it was on British soil and their contributions extended beyond the crucial role in the Battle of Britain. Examples of their bravery, sacrifice and success are described, for which they were received 342 British gallantry awards, including 9 DSO's and 191 DFC's.

SECRETS OF WAR – HISTORY CHANNEL SERIES

Louis Kruh

Sworn to Secrecy: Secrets of War. The History Channel, 235 E. 45th Street, New York NY 10017 USA. `www.secretsofwar.com`. 1-800-708-1776. 24(4): 375.

Secrets of War is a 52 hour television documentary event airing on The History Channel. This comprehensive series tells the complete story, from all sides, of the hidden wars of spies, stratagems, cryptology, deceptions and other previously classified secrets. The first 52 episodes have been airing in the United States every Sunday at 9pm ET/10pm PT, with repeats on the following Saturday. Twenty-six new one-hour episodes were completed in spring 2000. The web site (address above) contains a descriptive list of all episodes plus other information including transcripts of on-camera interviews with historical experts, authors and veterans of these events, plus many other features. The toll free telephone number provides information for ordering tapes of the episodes.

The Ultra Enigma. This documentary tells the story of the German Enigma cipher machine from its invention by Arthur Scherbius, to its use by Germany in

World War II, efforts by Polish cryptanalysts to decrypt its ciphers and how they shared their success with England, work at Bletchley Park, United States cooperation with British codebreakers and how these efforts helped to shorten the war. In addition to using historic World War II films of Alan Turing, Gordon Welchman, Marian Rejewski, Hans-Thilo Schmidt and others, there are interviews with Harry Hinsley and Peter Hilton who were stationed at Bletchley Park, historians and authors including David Kahn, Josef Garlinski, and Anthony Cave Brown. It is a first-class documentary motion picture, which highlights the workings of the Enigma and how it was broken.

Battle of the Atlantic. The most important battle in World War II was fought in the Atlantic. England, being an island nation, depended on the delivery of vital supplies from the United States to maintain its war against Germany and U. S. convoys became its lifeline. The strategy of Admiral Donitz, commander of the U-boats and later commander of the entire German Navy, was to strangle England by stopping supplies from reaching it and to do it most effectively with concerted attacks by submarines. This meant the action must be coordinated from headquarters and required secure communications between Donitz and his submarine commanders. They relied on the Enigma cipher machine and, after a fourth rotor was introduced, it almost succeeded. The thrilling story of how it failed is told with historic films of sea battles, work at Bletchley Park, and interviews with historians and participants.

CODE WAR MACHINES
Louis Kruh

Budiansky, Stephen. "The Code War: The code-breaking machines of World War II took data-processing technology to its very limits in the era before computers." *American Heritage of Invention and Technology*. Summer 2000. 16(1): 36-43. Published quarterly, annual subscription $15.00, single issue $4.00. 24(4): 379.

The author describes the development and use of WW II cryptanalytic machines that used data-processing technology before the advent of computers. Officially the devices were known as Rapid Analytical Machinery or RAM, which disclosed virtually nothing about their use. Unofficially they had various nick names such as Copperhead, Gypsy, Icky, Mike, and Tessie, which revealed even less. Within a few years these machines became obsolete by the electronic digital computer.

Budiansky explains how advances in enciphering techniques, such as multiple shifting alphabets, codes, machines or other methods, had made traditional paper and pencil techniques extinct. He cites the German Enigma as an example. He also discusses the difficulty of finding overlaps in enemy codes and the initial steps to automate the process with the use of IBM punch-card machines by William F. Friedman and Navy officers, Lt. Joseph Wenger and Lt. Thomas Dyer. Another early machine was the Comparator built by Vannevar Bush of MIT, which made digital comparisons using light or electronic devices to count the number of matches between one message and another. Also described is the early success with efforts to read Russian messages enciphered with the one-time pad system.

It is a fascinating illustrated article with much more information, which will be amplified in Budiansky's new book, *Battle of Wits: The Complete Story of Codebreaking in World War II*, scheduled for release in October 2000.

REGULAR ENIGMA NEWS
Louis Kruh

M. Kapera and J. Zdzislaw, ed. *The Enigma Bulletin No. 5*. June 2000. The Enigma Press, ul. Borsucza 3/58, 30-408 Krakow POLAND. 96 pp. $20.00 (add $5.00 for airmail). Available in U. S. from Classical Crypto Books, P. O. Box 1013, Londonderry NH 03053 USA. 25(1): 68.

With a glossy cover featuring an Enigma cipher machine in color, this attractive issue includes articles by: Carl Boyd, "Imperial Japanese Ambassador Toshima Hiroshi: An Extraordinary Source of Allied Intelligence in the Second World War;" Robert J. Hanyok, "Before Enigma: Jan Kowalewski and the Early Days of the Polish Cipher Bureau, 1919-1922;" Wladyslaw Kozaczak, "German Clandestine Intelligence in the 1920s;" Donald J. Sexton, "Thoughts on the Poles, Ultra and Communications Intelligence in World War II;"

Two papers on Enigma include: A brief piece by Rudolf J. Ritter, "Notes on the Early Use of Machine Cipher in Switzerland" and a lengthy illustrated article by Heinz Ulbricht, "The Enigma Uhr." Dr. Z. J. Kapera provides a summary of the distinguished career of "Mieczyslaw Zygfryd Slowikowski (1896-1989)," a professional soldier and Polish intelligence officer. His exploits earned him many awards including England's Order of the British Empire and the Legion of Merit from the United States.

Two book reviews conclude another fine issue. N. B. All previous issues are still available.

ENIGMA SYMPOSIUM 2000
Louis Kruh

Skillen, Hugh. *The Enigma Symposium 2000*. H. Skillen, 56 St. Thomas Drive, Pinner HA5 4SS, ENGLAND. 2000. 185 pp. $24.00 surface mail, $28.00 air mail. (Checks not accepted due to excessive bank charges.) 25(1): 69.

Skillen's report on Enigma Symposium 2000 is a potpourri of fascinating talks, memoirs, and personal reminiscences of Enigma related experiences plus other significant World War II events.

The report's 21 papers include descriptions of wartime experiences such as: The Hut 3 Liaison Section; Constructing Menus for the Bombes; Reminiscences of Hut 6; Station X 1940/41; The Vital Polish Contribution to the Conquest of Enigma; Station X India Command, which mentions a visit by William F. Friedman that included a tour of some of their units; Enigma by E. W. Humphreys, who reviews "The historical writings of Ultra [which] appear to have been conceived in three major stages;" and many other fine papers including three important articles on the Enigma cipher machine which had appeared in *Cryptologia*.

Many of these papers are especially valuable because they are based on personal experiences at Bletchley Park.

WORLD WAR II INTELLIGENCE
Louis Kruh

Steury, Donald P. *World War II Chronicles: The Intelligence Wars*. MetroBooks, 15 W. 26th Street, New York NY 10010 USA. 2000. 128 pp. $14.98. 25(1): 70-71.

"According to one estimate, 80% of important intelligence events in World War II had to do with signals intelligence" writes Steury. He believes that estimate accurately reflects the important role of signals intelligence and the breaking of Axis codes was perhaps the greatest intelligence coup of WW II. The Germans believed the technology of the Enigma machine made their ciphers impenetrable. But Steury describes how the brilliant cryptanalysts of Bletchley Park proved them wrong. In 1941, convinced that Enigma was secure, the Germans forced their Italian allies to adopt a version of Enigma. As a result, Italian communications, largely unbroken then, became readable by Allied cryptanalysts. Similarly, the Japanese Purple machine, which frustrated William F. Friedman and his Signal Intelligence Agency colleagues, was eventually solved and played a significant role in Japan's defeat.

From signals intelligence and codebreaking to daring exploits of agents in the field, Steury vividly describes the covert activities that comprised the secret war from 1939 through 1945. The book is illustrated with full color maps and almost 150 photographs of battles, bombings, naval, air, and ground warfare, secret agents, spies, the German Enigma cipher machine, Britain's bombe, and scores of other eye-catching photographs. Interesting but oddly out-of-place in a book on WW II, is a photograph of Friedman, in 1930, explaining the workings of a Kryha cipher machine to Louise Newkirk, a new employee.

The book's eight chapters include: Blitzkrieg; The Greatest Secret; Agents and Double Agents; Intelligence in the Pacific War; The War in the Mediterranean; Signals Intelligence and the Battle of the Atlantic; Intelligence and the Victory in Europe; and Ultra and the Invasion of Japan. Throughout the book are lengthy sidebars with informative text crammed with details on a variety of subjects including: Operation Barbarossa; Operation Freshman; The Good Source: Colonel Bonner Frank Fellers; Ultra and the Hecatomb of Tankers; Signals Intelligence and the Sinking of the Atlantis; and more.

Steury appears familiar with cryptanalytic history but two of his claims, highlighted below in italics, are doubtful.

1. "Friedman had great success in breaking Japanese codes and ciphers, *including their Enigma machine ciphers*." Several individuals familiar with Friedman's work, including one of his colleagues, were queried and all were unaware of his work or "great success" with the Japanese Enigma machine.

2. "The Americans were reading ... the main Japanese naval cipher, JN-25 ... but lost that source ... when the Imperial Navy shifted to the *Enigma-based JN-25B*." Through a third party, I turned to a U. S. Naval officer who had worked on Japanese ciphers. His reply was: "I worked on JN-25B and I can assure him it was not based on Enigma." It was a manual code system enciphered with additives.

BATTLE OF WITS
Louis Kruh

Budiansky, Stephen. *Battle of Wits: The Complete Story of Codebreaking in World War II*. The Free Press 1230 Ave. of the Americas, New York NY 10020 USA. 2000. 436 pp. $27.50. 25(1): 72-73.

Using the more than a million pages of new World War II (WWII) codebreaking records released by the U.S. Army, Navy and British government in the last five years plus interviews of cryptanalysts stationed at Arlington Hall, OP-20-G, and Bletchley Park, Budiansky has written the best account to date on WWII codebreaking. It is the story of how some 25,000 Allied codebreakers, despite impossible odds, used providence, persistence and extraordinary intellect to break nearly every one of the enemy's high level military, naval and diplomatic codes. These accomplishments, achieved with the aid of early IBM punch card sorters, mechanical calculators and early precursors of the first electronic computers, were instrumental in the Allied victory. It is a detailed account that includes rarely mentioned machines such as the Navy's Mike and Copperhead, Hypo, I. C. Machine, Comparator, eleven different types of Bombes, and more.

Budiansky's revelations also include how Britain tried to manipulate the American codebreakers and monopolize German Enigma code communications, how American codebreaking machines worked to crack the Japanese, German, and even Russian diplomatic codes. He describes how U. S.-British cooperation on the German diplomatic code that GC&CS called "Floradora" and SIS called "Keyword" was successful due to the American penchant for IBM equipment. But, despite the importance of their work, Allied codebreakers had to struggle against barriers of official indifference and even contempt for their work from within the military bureaucracy. Budiansky also offers an incisive analysis of the differences in the Army, Navy, and Bletchley Park codebreaking organizations.

Budiansky, a Harvard trained mathematician, is able to clearly explain step-by-step how the codes were broken. In addition to the regular text, he includes two appendices, "Naval Enigma: Its Indicating System and the Method of 'Banburismus' " and "Cryptanalysis of the Purple Machine." He uses five pages for each machine to explain in detail with diagrams how the system worked and how it was solved. In addition to his mathematical abilities, Budiansky is also a polished journalist and his compelling narrative moves along almost like a novel, which you can't wait to finish.

THE REAL ENIGMA STORY
Louis Kruh

Sebag-Montefiore, Hugh. *Enigma: The Battle for the Code.* Weidenfeld & Nicolson, Orion House, 5 Upper Martin's Lane, London WC2H 9EA ENGLAND. 2000. 403 pp. $29.00. 25(1): 78-79.

Using new material from British and American archives, research in Warsaw, Berlin and Paris, and interviews with some of the last remaining witnesses to the Enigma saga, Sebag-Montefiore has written one of the most detailed accounts of how the Enigma cipher was broken. His book contains some fascinating revelations and tells, for the first time, the whole story, including:

The tragic tale of Hans Hilo Schmidt, the "Enigma spy," who gave the key to the cipher to the French secret service as early as 1931; The breaking of the Naval Enigma cipher, based on the recently declassified account of how Alan Turing and his fellow codebreakers managed to read the German Navy's most secret messages; How the U-boat U-110 was captured along with its Enigma codebooks, as told by the German seaman who escaped and survived; What happened when the Germans were told that Enigma was being read by the British; How Gustave Bertrand, Schmidt's French spymaster, responsible for giving Schmidt's codebooks to Polish and British codebreakers, was furious when the British suspected him of betraying the Enigma secret after he had been arrested and released by the Germans; plus much more.

In an Epilogue: Where did they go? Sebag-Montefiore describes significant events in the lives of principal characters after their last mention in his book. These include the wife and brother of Schmidt, Polish codebreakers, Dilly Knox, Alan Turing, Gordon Welchman, Harry Hinsley, and subsequent happenings with Naval Enigma. He also provides a detailed, 10-page Chronology of events from November 8, 1931 to June 6, 1944; and a series of six appendices which describe: Polish Codebreaking techniques, The Bombe, Naval Enigma, Cillis, Rodding, and Naval Enigma Offizier – How it was Broken. There are also more then 50 photographs of key people, submarines, Enigma machines and more.

One possible shortcoming is omission of any reference to Arthur Scherbius, inventor of the Enigma. Had it appeared at the beginning, the title could have been: Enigma: From Cradle to the Grave. Nevertheless, Sebag-Montefiore's research is superb and he has written a remarkable book that belongs in your personal library.

THE KNOX BROTHERS
Louis Kruh

Fitzgerald, Penelope. *The Knox Brothers*. Counterpoint, P. O. 65793, Washington DC 20034-5793 USA. 288 pp. $26.00. 25(2): 144-145.

Originally written in 1977, Fitzgerald offers a revised and updated biography of her father and his three brothers. Her father was Edmund Knox, first son of the Bishop of Manchester. Edmund became editor of Punch and its editor from 1932-1947. His next younger brother was Dillwyn, who played a major role as a British codebreaker in WW I and WW II. The next brother was Wilfred, an Anglo-Catholic author and social worker. The youngest brother was Msgr. Ronald

Knox, who converted to Catholicism and single-handedly translated the New Testament from original sources. The book has been widely praised for its lively account of two generations of a remarkable English family who, despite their many differences, seemed to share one heart and soul.

From a cryptologic viewpoint, Dillwyn "Dilly" Knox, a Cambridge Greek scholar, co-opted from his lifelong passion into an almost lifelong assignment as a codebreaker in Room 40 in WW I, at Bletchley Park (BP) in WW II and, in between, at the Foreign Office "as a peacetime cryptographer, continuing to read the secret traffic of the nation's rivals and ill-wishers and, occasionally, of its friends," certainly deserves our attention.

In 1917, one of his major accomplishments in Room 40 was the breaking of the German three-letter flag-code, which prevented the sinking of many convoys. In 1926, after a sensitive Russian document was decrypted, Dilly was promoted but no connection between these two events was ever made. An extensive chapter, The Uses of Intelligence: 1939-1945, covers work at BP. Fitzgerald notes that his section was working full tine on Enigma and she explains how the codebreakers approached the problem and includes a photograph of an Enigma. In July 1938, Dilly accompanied Commander A. G. Denniston to a conference in Poland with Major Gustave Bertrand and Polish codebreakers. In 1939 he moved to BP and Fitzgerald describes the "Park" and the password procedures for entry and exit, which Dilly could never remember or where they were kept. His particular responsibility was the Spy Enigma Variation used by German Embassies in neutral countries and occupied zones. It was a crucial problem because its traffic contained enemy plans. After many frustrations he got an idea that became the first significant "way in" and after some additional work, deciphered text began to appear.

Fitzgerald, who died in April 2000, provides a fascinating biography of an unusual English family from an era that sadly, no longer exists.

SCIENCE IN WWII
Louis Kruh

Hartcup, Guy. *The Effect of Science on the Second World War*. St. Martin's Press, Scholarly and Reference Division, New York NY 10010 USA. 2000. 214 pp. $59.95. 25(2): 150.

Although scientists were involved on a limited basis in World War I, advances made in science and technology between the wars made them indispensable from 1939 to 1945. The Allies recognized this but not the Germans or their partners, who had neglected scientific innovations, hoping to exploit their enemies' unpreparedness by a "blitzkrieg." Consequently, the Allies with superior radar, radio, anti-submarine weapons, computerized cryptanalysis, operational research to improve the quality of equipment and ability to invent an atomic bomb, put them ahead of the Germans.

Hartcup notes that a deluge of books reviewing strategy, campaigns and commanders celebrated the 50th anniversary of the end of World War II. But the effect of science on the war was largely ignored. National security has delayed publication of books on science and war because, even though dated, information might be valuable to a potential enemy. Release of information on the British Ultra secret, for example, first took place in the mid-1970s. With this book, Hartcup intends to bring the story of science and war up-to-date by comparing the Allied scientific effort with that of the enemy. He shows how the intervention of scientists or their developments has an effect on various operations including the use of science in cryptography and cryptanalysis.

In his chapter, "The acquisition of Signals Intelligence," Hartcup describes the birth of modern signals intelligence in the British Admiralty's Room 40, the value of cipher machines was perceived by Arthur Scherbius, a German electrical engineer, who invented a mechanical encryption system and in 1918 notified the German Navy. It was rejected but in 1925, after learning of the success of Room 40, the Navy changed its mind and adopted the machine called Enigma. Next is the Polish success with Enigma and development of the Bombe by Alan Turing and Gordon Welchman, the breaking of Shark, the 4-rotor Enigma used by the German Navy and the American-built Bomb that was "more serviceable than the British machines." The breaking of the Lorenz SZ40/SZ/42 by Maxwell Newman and Thomas Flowers, development of Heath Robinson and Colossus, which was "the first application of logic controlled by an alterable programme." On the American side, they had broken the Japanese Red machine in 1936 and later, the Purple machine in 1940. U. S. Navy cryptanalysts broke Japan's JN25 in time to influence the Battle of Midway in 1942. Hartcup concludes that Magic "undoubtedly contributed to the defeat of Japan" while Ultra was decisive in the U-boat war in conjunction with airborne and seaborne radar, HF DF and very long-range aircraft.

Other chapters are: Organization of Science for War; Radar: Defense and Offence; Diverse Applications of Radio and Radar; Acoustic and Underwater Warfare; Birth of a New Science: Operational Research; The Transformation of Military Medicine; Unacceptable Weapons: Gas and Bacteria; Premature Weapons: the Rocket and the Jet; and The Ultimate Weapon: the Atomic Bomb.

Hartcup has written an essential book on a rarely addressed topic that will contribute to a better understanding of an important subject.

UNRAVELLING ENIGMA
Louis Kruh

Freedman, Maurice. *Unravelling Enigma: Winning the Code War at Station X*. Pen & Sword Books Ltd., 47 Church Street, Barnsley, South Yorkshire S70 2AS UNTED KINGDOM. 2000. 190 pp. $28.95. 25(2): 150-151.

At the outset, Freedman makes two points: 1. He offers a readable account of the breaking of Enigma without causing readers to become discouraged by mathematics and technology; 2. Without Gordon Welchman, who was never recognized for his contribution (ed.note: Undoubtedly due to writing *The Hut Six Story* without submitting it for clearance), "Bletchley Park, as we knew it, would not have existed."

This concise and readable account describes how Bletchley Park rapidly expanded from a small select group to an establishment of about 7,000 men and women processing vast quantities of Top Secret material. It also catalogues the extraordinary series of German blunders that provided vital clues for codebreakers to exploit and also shows how Ultra material played a key role at decisive moments. These included the Battle of the Atlantic, the struggle in North Africa and the invasion of Europe, on which so much was staked. It reveals how Allied commanders used this invaluable information and the deception measures taken to ensure that the enemy did not discover their "unbreakable" codes were broken.

While the Enigma cipher machine is widely known, the German Army's Lorenz SZ 40/42, which Bletchley Park code-named Tunny, is barely recognized by the public. Enigma was used by the three services for operational traffic but Tunny was only used for top level communications between commanders or Hitler and his generals. A mistake by a German cipher clerk led to the breaking of Tunny aided by development of a new machine, Colossus I and subsequently Colossus Mark II, the world's first electronic computer, according to Freedman.

Five appendices provide additional information on: The Codewheel. Operating the Enigma Machine (Military and Air Force) from 13 September 1938 until May 1940, Setting up the Enigma Machine, Bletchley in Danger, and Enigma and SZ 40/42 (Tunny).

ENIGMA U-BOATS CODES
Louis Kruh

Showell, Jak P. Mallman. *Enigma U-Boats: Breaking the Code –The True Story*. Naval Institute Press, 291 Wood Road, Annapolis MD 21402-5034 USA. 2000. 192 pp. $36.95. 25(4): 314-315.

Despite its title, this book is not about breaking the German Enigma cipher machine. Its main purpose is to examine in detail, all U-boats and Weather Ships that had been boarded by the Allies during the war, from which Enigma machines could have been captured. In essence, it is about the British (Americans later) efforts to track down German U-boats to obtain a fully functioning Enigma machine, operation manuals, and key lists to better understand its operation. The search was successful but in early 1942 the German Navy introduced its 4-rotor Enigma. This new development caused a blackout at Bletchley Park, and German U-boats again wreaked havoc on convoy lifelines to the British Isles. It took almost ten months before the blackout ended with the capture of a submarine with a 4-rotor Enigma.

Showell's opening chapter, "Enigma – The Impenetrable Puzzle," describes the development of the Enigma, its use by Germany and especially on U-boats. To increase message security the German Navy introduced a number of code settings, each with a difference name. "Examples of a Few Common Codes Used During the War" included nineteen names such as Hydra, Triton and Hermes.

Some key chapters are: The First Naval Enigma Wheels – The Sinking of U-33; Weather Ships for Bletchley Park; The Secret Capture; The Surrender of U-570; Shark – The Four-wheel Enigma Code; The Capture of U-505; Other Secret Captures?; The Sinking and Raising of U-250; U-1024 – The Last Capture. Each thrilling battle details the actions of the British and the defenses mounted by the submarine's crew under attack. The bravery on both sides is evident.

Other informative chapters are The German Radio System; Bletchley Park and the British Side; The Enigma Machine, and five appendices, particularly Grabbing the Enigma, Occasions Where Allied Forces Boarded German Vessels; Captured U-boats; and The Ireland Letter Code designed by the *Kriegsmarine* for its captured officers to use to send useful information when writing from prison camp.

While the 8" × 10" book has a misleading title, is poorly organized, e. g. two chapters on the Enigma machine, egregious errors, e. g. a photograph of the Lorenz SZ 40/42 is described as a version of the Enigma and a photograph of a *Geheimschreiber* is called "A 10-wheel Enigma type of machine," they are offset by an outstanding collection of an amazing 295 decent-sized photographs plus other illustrations. The photographs include U-boats under attack, sailors being rescued, U-boats on patrols, crewmen at work, U-boat commanders, captured boats, close-ups of the Enigma machine, personalities such as Karl Donitz, Telex operators, the radio receiving room for the U-boat Command's Operation Room, many photos of Bletchley Park, and much more.

STUDY OF THE BIG MACHINES
Louis Kruh

Kelley, Stephen J. *Big Machines: Study of the Cryptographic Security of the German ENIGMA, Japanese PURPLE, and US SIGABA/ECM Cipher Machines*. Aegean Park Press, P. O. Box 2837, Laguna Hills CA 92654 USA. 2001. 242 pp. $38.00. 26(2): 141-143.

It has taken 57 years after the end of World War II for an author to provide a detailed description and comparative analysis of the three most important cipher machines: the German Enigma, the Japanese PURPLE and the American SIGABA/ECM.

Kelley's objective is to explore why Enigma and PURPLE ciphers were solved and SIGABA/ECM messages were not. Were the Allies' successes against Enigma and PURPLE due to inherent weaknesses in the machines, to poor communications security procedures, to physical compromise, or other factors? Was failure to break SIGABA/ECM due to the inherent strength of the machine, superior communications security, or incompetent enemy cryptanalysts? Kelley is obviously familiar with the machines and has reviewed declassified reports and other documents on each one. In successive chapters he reviews the beginnings of each machine.

Kelley describes Arthur Scherbius' invention of Enigma in 1918, his commercial version and the significantly different military model. He reviews the successful attack by Polish cryptanalysts, work at Bletchley Park, the naval Enigma, and other Enigma variations. The breaking of Enigma remained a secret until publication of F. W. Winterbotham's book, *The Ultra Secret* in 1973.

The section on MAGIC reviews the origin of Japanese machine cryptography, RED and ORANGE and, after futile attempts to improve its security, a new system, PURPLE, was introduced. Kelly reviews the lengthy and difficult task undertaken by Frank Rowlett and his team to crack the cipher that, similar to the RED machine, divided the Roman alphabet into two groups of 6 and 20 letters respectively. But its cryptographic principle was much more difficult and it took 18 months before PURPLE was cracked. Success came when LT. Leo Rosen, a recently arrived MIT electrical engineer suggested the use of "a standard telephone stepping switch of 25 positions, capable of handling 6 separate circuits."

For SIGABA/ECM, Kelley reviews, in a terrific chapter, the history of army and navy cryptography between the wars and how the army and navy went their separate ways until 1940 when they agreed on one system that used the best of each of their similar machines.

In reviewing the cryptographic security of the three machines, Kelley evaluates their theoretical security and their practical security. For Enigma he demonstrates that while it had a high degree of theoretical security, from a practical viewpoint there were many negatives, e. g., availability of commercial models to enemy codebreakers, poor operating practices, design flaws, gifted Allied cryptanalysts, the spy, Hans-Thilo Schmidt, and more.

For Purple, Kelley provides an extensive review of the machine and concludes its "theoretical cryptographic security was significantly greater" than Enigma and almost equal to the 4-rotor Enigma. But he points to the decision to use a telephone stepping switch to divide the Roman alphabet into 6 and 20 letter subsets "the most glaring error." He also cites other design flaws but notes "the PURPLE machine remained a powerful cryptographic device."

It is no surprise to find SIGABA\ECM vastly superior to Enigma and PURPLE, from both a theoretical and practical matter. This stems from the use of more rotors in each machine, increased number of possible rotor arrangements, routine issuance of new sets of rotors to all users, stringent operating procedures, each operator selected rotor settings, special physical security for all machines, message length limited, and more.

Big Machines is an excellent book with much new information on an intriguing subject and includes a bibliography. The book belongs in your personal library so it can be enjoyed leisurely. We congratulate Stephen Kelley on his important contribution to the literature of machine cryptography.

MACHINE CRYPTOGRAPHY AND MODERN CRYPTANALYSIS

Louis Kruh

Erskine, Ralph and Michael Smith, eds. *Action This Day: Bletchley Park from the Breaking of the Enigma Code to the Birth of the Modern Computer*. Bantam Press, 61-63 Uxbridge Road, London W5 5SA UK. 2001. 543 pp. £25.00/$36.00. 26(2): 146-149.

Absolutely, the best book ever written about codebreaking at Bletchley Park (BP). Editors are Michael Smith, former Cold War codebreaker and author and

Ralph Erskine, a leading historian of wartime codebreaking and an Enigma expert.

Featuring chapters by some of Britain's outstanding historians, former codebreakers and academics (plus two Americans), they trace the legacy of BP from the innovative work that led to the breaking of Enigma and other wartime codes, to the invention of modern computing and its influence on Cold War codebreaking.

Chapters include:

- "Reminiscences on Enigma" by Hugh Foss, BP codebreaker, describes early British work on the commercial "C model" Enigma and initial contacts with their French and Polish counterparts.
- "Breaking Air Force and Army Enigma" by Ralph Erskine, describes the methods used by Hut 6 to break *Heer* and *Luftwaffe* Enigma, the introduction of British Bombes – the basic design concept was Alan. Turing's – and how Hut 6 evolved into a well-managed and highly adaptable unit.
- "Hut 6 From the Inside" by Derek Taunt, BP codebreaker, offers an insider's view of working in Hut 6. Gordon Welchman was its head with Stuart Milner-Barry second-in-command. Taunt describes the work involved in breaking Enigma messages, cribs, cillies, the Herivel tip, help from Bombes and more. He mentions the arrival of US Army's 6813th Signal Security Detachment commanded by Captain Bill Bundy. Milner-Barry initially viewed their arrival with consternation but based on their work he later said their arrival was "one of the luckiest things that happened to Hut 6." The chapter notes that in 1982, in a talk Bundy gave at the annual convention of the American Cryptogram Association, he said: "I think the level of performance in Hut 6 was as near perfect as anything I have ever been or ever expect to be associated with ..." [This reviewer had organized the 1982 ACA convention and at the urging of David Kahn, invited Bundy. Another guest was Gordon Welchman. Kahn introduced Bundy and we later arranged to have Bundy's fascinating talk published in *Cryptologia* 11(2): 65-76. It is worth your effort to find a copy.]
- "Breaking Italian Naval Enigma" by Mavis Batey, BR codebreaker, describes her working with the legendary Dillwyn "Dilly" Knox, a brilliant cryptanalyst from WW I who attended the 1939 Warsaw meeting with Polish cryptanalysts.
- "A Biographical Fragment: 1942-5" by John Chadwick, BP codebreaker and author of "The Decipherment of Linear B" relates his experiences in breaking Italian naval codes without any formal cryptanalytic training and no knowledge of Italian, just Latin.

- "An Undervalued Effort: How the British Broke Japan's Codes" by Michael Smith, says John Tiltman, Chief Cryptographer, made the first break into the super-enciphered codes adopted by the Japanese in the 1930s and broke Japan's main naval code, JN-25, within weeks of its appearance. The exchange of codebreaking information with the visit of American army and navy codebreakers in January 1941 is described. Difficulties in establishing cooperation with U. S. Navy units are noted.
- "Most Helpful and Co-operative: GC&CS and the Development of American Diplomatic Cryptanalysis, 1941-2" by David Alvarez, Professor, tells how GC&CS helped the US Army's Signal Intelligence Service (SIS) to significantly improve its diplomatic cryptanalytic capability during the war.
- "Breaking German Naval Enigma on Both Sides of the Atlantic" by Ralph Erskine, describes how Hut 8 and its U. S. Navy counterpart broke naval Enigma. A key problem was the lack of sufficient bombes for Hut 8. But excellent cable communications with OP-20-G enabled British use of US Navy bombes go crack naval Enigma.
- "Hut 8 from the Inside by Rolf Noskwith, BP Codebreaker, details an insiders view of breaking naval Enigma.
- "Bletchley Park and the Birth of the Very Special Relationship by Stephen Budiansky, author of Battle of Wits, tells how, despite the problems with individual services, both British and American, refusing to share its secrets with a close ally, there is still an enduring "special relationship." Budiansky credits three "men of vision," William Friedman, Telford Taylor and John Tiltman.
- "Traffic Analysis: A log Reader's Tale" by James W. Thirsk, BP Log Reader, describes how intelligence is obtained from traffic analysis without reading the messages.
- "How Dilly Knox and his Girls Broke the Abwehr Enigma" by Keith Batey, BP Codebreaker, describes the process.
- "Breaking Tunny and the Birth of Colossus" by Shaun Wylie, BP Codebreaker, tells how Lorenz SZ 40/42 was solved, "a far greater achievement" than the breaking of Enigma.
- "Colossus and the Dawning of the Computer Age" by B. Jack Copeland, Professor, recounts how "two extraordinarily gifted men," a telephone engineer, Tommy Flowers who built Colossus based on specifications by Max Newman, a Cambridge mathematician created the world's first electronic digital computer.

Chapters not mentioned above include:

- "Bletchley in Pre-War Perspective" by Christopher Andrew;
- "The Government Code and Cypher School and the First Cold War" by Michael Smith;
- "Mihailovic or Tito? How the Codebreakers Helped Churchill Choose by John Cripps;
- "Bletchley Park, Double Cross and D-Day" by Michael Smith;
- "Enigma's Security: What the Germans Really Knew" by Ralph Erskine;
- "From Amateurs to Professionals: GC&CS and Institution-Building in Sigint" by Philip H. J. Davies;
- "Cold War Codebreaking and Beyond: The Legacy of Bletchley Park" by Richard J. Aldrich; and
- "Bletchley Park in Postwar Perspective" by Christopher Andrew.

There are 4 appendices.

- I. The very simple cipher which 'Snow', the first Double Cross agent, was given by his German controllers.
- II. *Wehrmacht* Enigma Indicating Systems, except the *Kriegsmarine*'s *Kenngruppenbuch* System.
- III. The Naval Enigma *Kenngruppenbuch* Indicator System – used with the main wartime ciphers.
- IV. Cillies.

The book includes Notes and References, Glossary and Abbreviations, Notes on Contributors, and Index.

This volume is one of the best books available on the most important codebreaking that took place in World War II (except for Purple).

HISTORY OF THE CRYPTANALYTIC BOMBE
Louis Kruh

Solving the Enigma: History of the Cryptanalytic Bombe. Center for Cryptologic History, National Security Agency, 9800 Savage Road, Fort Meade MD 20795-6886 USA. 52 pp. Free. 26(4): 310.

Starting with a brief history of the Enigma cipher machine, the author describes how Polish cryptanalysts solved its ciphers. Subsequently, faced with the threat of the German invasion, they shared their secrets with the British. British mathematicians, Alan Turing and Gordon Welchman, sought quicker ways to solve German messages. Ultimately this led to development of the Bombe, which is described in some detail. The addition of a fourth rotor by the German Navy was catastrophic because British Bombes could not find settings for four rotors and German U-boats were sinking convoys loaded with much needed supplies destined for Britain.

At this point the United States began efforts to develop its own Bombes. And most of this publication is devoted to that work. The U. S. Navy contracted with the National Cash Register Company (NCR) in Dayton, Ohio to work on the development and construction of specialized machines and established the Navy Computing Machine Laboratory (NCML). NCR engineer, Joseph Desch, became NCML's research director and was the designer of the U. S. Navy Bombe. His work was cloaked in extreme secrecy and it was decades after the war before his family learned of his work. Waves and sailors were sent to Dayton to construct the Bombes, e. g. over 6,000 rotors had to be wired. An 8-page appendix describes Cribs, Menus and Bombe Set-up. Another appendix compares Army and Navy Bombes. A terrific publication and its FREE.

WITHOUT ENIGMA
Louis Kruh

Macksey, Kenneth. *Without Enigma: The Ultra and Fellgiebel Riddles.* Ian Allan Publishing, Riverdene Business Park, Molesey Road, Hersham, Surrey KT12 4RG UK. 2000. 160 pp. $29.22. 26(4): 314-315.

It was only in the 1970s that the British authorities acknowledged that during World War II they had broken the German Enigma cipher. Since then much of the analysis of the struggle against Nazi Germany has assumed that the British and their allies gained a vital advantage through their knowledge of German plans and often had advance warning of German activities.

For years perceptive researchers have felt that a counter-argument needed to be made, that perhaps undue emphasis had been placed on Allied code-breaking successes.

Macksey, one of Britain's foremost military historians, seeks to explore in depth the impact of Enigma on both sides during the course of the war. Based upon detailed analysis of the records along with well informed interpretation, the author describes a scenario in which the Germans became fully aware of the British breaking of the codes and reconstructs how the Germans would have responded. In part it included greater reliance on codebooks and the Geheimschreiber The story is also interwoven with the grossly underrated role of General Erich Fellgiebel, the German's head of *Wehrmacht* and Army Signal Services, in both the countermeasures and also the plot to assassinate Hitler.

Drawing upon his detailed knowledge of the period and interlacing it with carefully argued speculation, the author's narrative is a compelling counter-argument to the prevailing myth of the importance of Enigma. Each chapter's footnotes, however, are listed in two segments: Deviations from History and Confirmatory footnotes. Macksey provides a realistic and logical scenario of what might have been, along with insights on Hitler's generals and the failed assassination attempt. It is an excellent, imaginative book you will enjoy reading.

ENIGMA SYMPOSIUM 2002
Louis Kruh

Skillen, Hugh, Editor. *The Enigma Symposium 2002*. H. Skillen, 56 St. Thomas Drive, Pinner, Middlesex HA5 4SS ENGLAND. 2002, 82 pp. (12"×8"). $22.00 plus $3.45 postage. 27(1): 62-63.

This is an excellent report on the Ninth Annual Enigma Reunion.

Commander Ellingworth age 15 in 1904, learned about the navy the hard way, as ship's boy. Within ten years he had been selected to study "the new science of wireless telegraphy." In World War 1, he was one of the Navy's youngest Chief Petty Officer Telegraphists, in charge of the radio service of a flotilla of 16 destroyers. Col. Ellingworth retired with the rank of Lieut.-Commander in 1934 and soon, began his civilian duties as OC at Fort Bridgewoods experimental radio work. Then, spanning two world wars, it culminated in his appointment as OC at Beaumanor.

"The E T A Workshop 1943-1951" is described by Michael Gilbert.

"Recollections of Bletchley" by Florence Victoria Lewis describes how she came to Bletchley, her work on cumbersome decoding machines, a temporary assignment encoding messages on a one-time pad, transferring to Berkeley Street, London, to learn other decoding work, which she describes.

"A Light-Hearted Look at One Woman's War - Afterwards" by Kay Stadden.

"The Enigma Years 1941-1945" by Marie Bennett is a lengthy and fascinating account of her work as a log-reader, which helped in the breaking of Enigma messages.

"The Potsdam Conference" by Wilf B. Dent provides the inside story of problems with Russians, dealing with dignitaries including Churchill, Eden, Truman and others. It is an interesting story of an eyewitness to a historic conference.

A lengthy 6-part article, "British and Allied Involvement in Buchenwald Concentration Camp" by Sqd. Ldr. Booker. His quest over a lengthy period of years was to seek justice for the British and other Allied prisoners who died at Buchenwald. First, he had to overcome government attempts to deny that captured British and other allied soldiers were sent to Buchenwald and many died there. It is a frustrating tale that you will not easily forget.

"Traitors at GCHQ" by Hugh Skillen mentions John Cairncross, who confessed to being the "fourth" man (after Filby, Burgess and McLean) in a posthumous book published by his wife. But the most successful traitor, over the longest period was Geoffrey Arthur Prime. He was a Russian linguist at GCHQ in Cheltenham. For more than 20 years he carried out large quantities of documents destined for the Russians. Skillen provides many details of how he operated.

In "Sweeps and Directors of Intelligence," H. W. Everett explains why "The two great events of my stay at No 6 Intelligence School were the visits of the local chimney sweep and the Director of Military Intelligence, though in the latter case it would, perhaps, be more accurate to speak of a visitation."

In another narrative, Everett, who spent his time in the army with a number of Y units, describes the actions of "The Seasoned Campaigners of '110' Section."

These vignettes are especially valuable because they mostly represent the first-hand experiences of the narrators.

LOVE, WAR, AND BLETCHLEY PARK
Louis Kruh

Young, Irene. *Enigma Variations: Love, War & Bletchley Park*. Mainstream Publishing Co., 7 Albany Street, Edinburgh EH1 3UG UNITED KINGDOM. 2000. 191 pp. $11.65. 26(4): 316.

This interesting book is the author's moving testament of life and love during the Second World War. Originally published in 1990, it was one of the first books to describe wartime life at Bletchley Park, Britain's top-secret intelligence headquarters. Ten years later, it remains one of the most enchanting and fascinating books on the little-known aspects of the intelligence community.

Enigma Variations describes the grim, yet at times, hilarious, conditions endured by the rank and file who were essential supporters of the brilliant cryptanalysts at Bletchley. It is a portrait of humor and tragedy culminating in a harrowing mystery when Irene Young's husband vanished while on active service with the SAS in France.

The title takes its name from the Enigma enciphering machine at Bletchley, but it also refers to the character of Irene's husband, and his disappearance.

These variations on the theme of enigma are linked together in a beautifully written social document about destiny and fate - now undated with a new postscript. It is an informative and moving story that readers will not soon forget.

GUIDE TO BLETCHLEY PARK
Louis Kruh

Butters, Lindsey. *Bletchley Park: Home of Station X*. Pitkin Guides, Healey House, Dene Road, Andover, Hampshire SP10 2AA UNITED KINGDOM. (`www.guides@pitkin-unichrome.com`) 16 pp. £1.99 ($2.95) plus shipping. 27(1): 68-69.

A handsome 16 page color brochure briefly describes the history of Bletchley Park from its purchase in 1883 by Sir Herbert Leon as a home for his family, to its acquisition by MI6 as a codebreaking center in 1938, under the command of Alastair Denniston. There is a brief history of the German Enigma cipher machine and the work of Alan Turing.

A map of Bletchley Park shows the vast extent of the huts built to house an army of codebreakers. There is also an aerial view showing the RAF and Army camps at the back of the Park. Photographs include the mansion's entrance hall, codebreakers masquerading as members of 'Captain Ridley's shooting party' (Ridley was the man in charge of the move) arriving at Bletchley Park in August 1938, a four-rotor Enigma machine, Hut 6 decoding room in 1943, Lorenz 12 rotor machine, Colossus and much more. The role of key codebreakers such as Alan Turing, Gordon Welchman, Colonel John Tiltman, Bill Tutte, Max Newman, Ralph Tester, and Tommy Flowers is noted. There is also a page on The Post-War Years.

This is a small attractive guide packed with a lot of information.

REMARKABLE VIEW OF ENIGMA CODEBREAKING
Louis Kruh

Hoare, Oliver. *ENIGMA: Codebreaking and the Second World War, The true story through contemporary documents*. Public Record Office Publications, Kew, Richmond, Surrey TW9 4DU UNITED KINGDOM. 2002. Document pack (16 documents + 12 page booklet), £14.99, US $19.95. 27(1): 69.

Hoare, a specialist in intelligence and military records in the Public Record Office, points out that despite Churchill's orders at the end of the war that all evidence related to codebreaking be destroyed, a variety of important documents and other fascinating material survived. He has assembled 16 key document facsimiles, which include previously unpublished material ranging from top secret memos and letters to original decrypts. They include: Operation RUTHLESS by Ian Fleming (creator of James Bond), Holocaust intercept, Turing's notes on Enigma, double agent Tate's rotating disc code, a poem from Hut 6 at Bletchley Park, an Ultra decrypt of German situation reports during the Normandy landings, "Be Careful what you say" poster, history of Hut 8, letter from 'C' to Churchill, German Police signals traffic and much more.

A 12-page illustrated booklet by Hoare provides a brief summary of codebreaking and the Second World War, the Enigma machine, the Polish head start, Turing and Bletchley Park, Colossus: the world's first programmable computer, the influence of Ultra, and extensive background information on each item in the document pack.

Published in association with Bletchley Park Trust, each pack includes a six-page illustrated folder on Bletchley Park, plus a free entry ticket to the Park. All material is contained in a roughly 9" × 12" cardboard container with a large photograph of an Enigma machine on its cover. It is an imaginative and fascinating publication that is almost guaranteed to please. It belongs in your personal library.

> [Ed Note: If you have the passion we believe you do for cryptology and wish to pass it along, then this wonderful package assembled by Bletchley Park folks should be a must gift for young people (in our your family or acquaintance) say for school grades, birthday, family get together, whatever(!) to help them understand the history of our civilization and the role cryptology played in preserving it.]

ENIGMA BULLETIN NUMBER 5

Louis Kruh

Kapera, Zdzislaw J., ed. *The Enigma Bulletin*, No. 5, June 2000. The Enigma Press, ul. Borsucza 3/58, 30-408 Krakow POLAND. 96 pp. $20.00 (add $5.00 for airmail). Available in U. S. from Classical Crypto Books, P.O. Box 1013, Londonderry NH 03053 USA. 27(2): 183.

With a glossy cover featuring an Enigma cipher machine in color, this attractive issue includes articles by: Carl Boyd, "Imperial Japanese Ambassador Toshima Hiroshi: An Extraordinary Source of Allied Intelligence in the Second World War;" Robert J. Hanyok, "Before Enigma: Jan Kowalewski and the Early

Days of the Polish Cipher Bureau, 1919-1922;" Wladyslaw Kozaczuk, "German Clandestine Intelligence in the 1920s;" Donald J. Sexton, "Thoughts on the Poles, Ultra and Communications Intelligence in World War II."

Two papers on Enigma include: A brief piece by Rudolf J. Ritter, "Notes on the Early Use of Machine Cipher in Switzerland" and a lengthy illustrated article by Heinz Ulbricht, "The Enigma Uhr." Dr. Z. J. Kapera provides a summary of the distinguished carrier of "Mieczyslaw Zygfryd Slowikowski (1896-1989)," a professional soldier and Polish intelligence officer. His exploits earned him many awards including England's Order of the British Empire and the Legion of Merit from the United States.

Two book reviews conclude another fine issue. N. B. All previous issues are still available.

HISTORY OF POLISH ENIGMA
Louis Kruh

Kapera, Zdzislaw J., Editor/Publisher. *Before Ultra There Was Gale: Some Contributions to the History of the Polish Enigma, 1932-1942*. The Enigma Bulletin No. 6, The Enigma Press, ul. Podedwrze 5, 32-031 Mogilany, POLAND. zjkapera@vela.filg.uj.edu.pl. 96 pp., $20.00 ppd. Order from: Classical Crypto Books, P. O. Box 1013, Londonderry, NH 03053 or M & M Baldwin, 24 High Street, Cleobury Mortimer, Kidderminster DY14 8BY UK. 27(4): 375-376.

Kapera wishes this issue to be a reminder that this year (2002) is the seventieth anniversary of the breaking of the military Enigma by the famous Polish mathematician, Marian Rejewski. It also marks the occasion of the first special conference on "The contribution of Polish intelligence to the Allied victory in the second World War."

The first two chapters feature two leading personalities who usually remained in the background: Col. Gwido Karol Langer, head of the Polish Cipher Bureau in the 1930s and Major Maksymillan Ciezki who supervised the famous BS-4, i.e. Biuro Syzfrów (Cipher Bureau), which broke the military Enigma that gave invaluable help to the allies in World War II.

Langer played a vital role in the Enigma solution when he invited Marian Rejewski, Józef Rózycki and Henryk Zygalski to Warsaw to join the newly organized Bureau of Ciphers and the rest is history. Ciezki also played a crucial role in breaking the Enigma machine and when he and Langer were trapped in occupied France, they were interrogated by a Gestapo officer who knew they were the heads of the Polish Cipher Bureau. Only Langer's post-war report on the German interrogation is available and it reveals how he and Ciezki cleverly handled the interrogation and saved the secret of Polish success with the German Enigma machine.

Chapter three, an important section in this issue, is devoted to the history of Polish SIGINT on the German front in the critical month of September 1939. Many sources are noted including personal reports of people who supervised sigint in September 1939, the collections of the Polish Institute and Sikorski Museum, Col. Langer's 1940 detailed report on achievements of Allied sigint in the French campaign, a report by Col. Stefan Mayer, deputy chief of Branch IIA of Polish Intelligence, detailed reports by Ciezki and reports of civilian cryptanalysts, particularly Rejewski. Other sections cover Radio intelligence, The last week of peace, Evacuation, and Results. The closing chapter discusses the fate of the archives of the Polish General Staff's Second Bureau in 1939 and the archives of the Cipher Bureau.

This edition of The Enigma Bulletin provides interesting reading about the vital role of the Polish Cipher Bureau in the Enigma battle and provides many sources for interested researchers.

HUT 3
Louis Kruh

Jackson, John, Ed. *The Secret War of Hut 3: The First Story of How Intelligence from Enigma Signals Decoded at Bletchley Park Was Used During World War II*. The Military Press, 1 Gallagher Close, Milton Keynes MK8 0lQ UK. 2002. 115 pp. 8 1/2" × 11 3/4". Hardback 25.00/$39.30; Paperback £15.00/$23.60.0 pp. $24.95. 28(1): 65-66.

This volume is the first in a new series of publications about Ultra, the high grade intelligence decrypted from the German Enigma coding machine by Bletchley Park during World War II. It was here that German, Italian and Japanese radio signals were sent to be de-cyphered and then distributed to Allied leaders and field commanders. The series represents a unique body of knowledge about the best-kept secret of the War.

The Foreword in this first volume is by Peter Calvocoressi, Head of Air Section at Bletchley Park during the War. At the end of World War II, those who had actually worked in the Hut wrote a history of the activities of Hut 3. The result was so sensitive that it was immediately given the highest security classification: Top Secret - Ultra. Now declassified and in the Public Record Office, this monograph is based on that publication.

Hut 3 was responsible for the processing of signals once the code in which they had been transmitted had been broken. They translated and annotated them and reported the contents to Government departments and commanders in the field. Churchill received the most important decrypts direct. Hut 3, at its peak of activity, had some 580 men and women working on it, which included 21 Americans. Hut 3 developed into an intelligence organization the like of which had never been seen before. Their index system, the technical expertise and research facilities were unique. This monograph explains how Hut 3 handled the signals they received, and how their processing enhanced the value of the signals.

In theory, Enigma was unbreakable and in practice it was broken because the Germans were over confident and careless. The first ciphers broken were almost entirely German Air Force (GAF) and it was an extraordinary achievement even though the Germans did not strictly observe their own regulations for its use. The invasion of Norway forced Hut 3 into a quick reform of its organization and it was remarkable that changes introduced in April 1940 at such short notice stayed in place till the end of the war.

At the outset, Jackson also provides an Organization of Huts by Section with functions and approximate number of staff in each. Some of his 14-chapters are: Duty Officers, Signal Section, Special Liaison Units, The German Book Room, Liaison Section, General Intelligence, Hitler's Secret Weapons, and Enter the Americans, which describes the Americans at Bletchley Park. Major William (Bill) Bundy was operations officer of the 6813th Signal Security Detachment as the American unit was officially designated. (His article on the Bletchley experience, "Some of my Wartime Experiences", which is highly recommended, appeared in *Cryptologia*, Vol. XI, Number 2, April 1987, pp. 65-76).

This is an excellent book that belongs in your personal library. It is also a great gift idea.

ULTRA IN THE ARCTIC
Louis Kruh

Jackson, John. *Ultra's Arctic War: PQ 17 Convoy Disaster, Sinking of the Scharnhorst, Hunting the Tirpitz*. The Military Press, 1 Gallagher Close, Milton Keynes MK8 01Q UNITED KINGDOM. 2003. 127 pp. (8.5" × 11.75"). Hardback \$59.50/£32.99; Paperback \$27.00/£15.00. 28(3): 248.

The Arctic convoys that took vital supplies at enormous risk to Russia during the Second World War did so within range of Germany's Luftwaffe, surface ships and U-boats. These convoys were watched over by Bletchley Park codebreakers and intelligence officers, through decrypts of the German Enigma coding machine. In particular, these decrypts were closely involved in three of the key actions of the Arctic battles - the sinking of the battle cruiser *Scharnhorst*, the destruction of the battleship Tirpitz and the disastrous PQ 17 convoy. This book examines the Ultra decodes, and for the first time lists the key details in these events in chronological order, detailing the role of the decrypts in a virtual minute-by-minute breakdown of how the signals were used in these key actions.

Five Appendices include: PQ17: Countdown to Disaster, key events with notes, June 1 - July 28, 1942. 3+ pp.

Convoy PQ 17: Merchant Ships and Close Escort - Sailing Plan. 1 page.

PQ 17: Fate of the Merchant Vessels. 1 page.

Sinking of the *Scharnhorst* - December 1943. Key Ultra Decodes. 4 pp.

Tracking the Tirpitz, March 1941 - Nov. 13, 1944. 5 pp.

An excellent book (8.5" × 11.75"), highly recommended, about the war at sea and how intelligence derived from breaking German Enigma messages played a vital role.

ENIGMA - A CD
Louis Kruh

Perera, Tom. *The Story of the Enigma - CD, History, Technology and Deciphering.* Artifax Books, 151 Barton Road, Stow MA 01775 USA. 2004. CD, $15.00 plus $2.00 postage in U.S., $5.00 postage elsewhere. 28(3): 251-252.

Perera is well known in ham radio circles as w1tp and in the educational community as Thomas B. Perera, PhD, Professor Emeritus of Psychology, Montclair State University.

Among his several interests is the German Enigma Cipher machine and he makes many trips to Europe searching for Enigmas and to the National Security Agency's National Cryptologic Museum (NSA/NCM) at Fort Meade, to view, study and photograph their excellent collection. As a result, Perera has probably produced the most comprehensive history of historical and technical Enigma information available in one publication, which includes 1,000 color photographs. The text traces the development of codes, cipher machines, and the Enigma, its civilian, and military models, operation, strategies to decipher its messages, and its mechanical and electrical construction. The CD also has an excellent Enigma simulator program, construction projects, a bibliography, Enigma manuals, an Enigma Museum and an Enigma Simulator Software Program. Also two large archival databases that contain a great deal of material on Enigma, Ultra, and Codes. The NSA/National Cryptologic Museum database is a 58 page listing of all holdings in their library dealing with those subjects. The 3200 item Lou Kruh Collection contains listings of his books from 1563-2004, crypto machines and devices, plus a large variety of other cryptologic items. Both databases may be searched, printed or simply browsed.

Other informative items include: A Brief History of Early Codes and Cipher Machines, How to Make Working Code Wheels, How to Make & Use a Simplified Version of the Enigma, Historic Code Wheels in the National Cryptologic Museum, The History of the Invention of the Enigma Cipher Machine, German Military Enigma Accessories, Military Cipher Machines of Other Countries, American Cipher Machines in the NSA/NCM, The Basic Components of the Enigma, Disassembly of the Enigma Machine Box, Plug board, Keyboard, Rotors, and other parts, Enigma Operating Book (English), Enigma Coding Instructions (English), Enigma Operating Book (German), and much, much more.

Perera has created a fabulous illustrated resource for Enigma information at a very affordable price. It belongs in your personal library and also makes an excellent gift.

Recent Titles in the Artech House Computer Security Series

Rolf Oppliger, Series Editor

Bluetooth Security, Christian Gehrmann, Joakim Persson and Ben Smeets

Computer Forensics and Privacy, Michael A. Caloyannides

Computer and Intrusion Forensics, George Mohay, et al.

Defense and Detection Strategies against Internet Worms, Jose Nazario

Demystifying the IPsec Puzzle, Sheila Frankel

Developing Secure Distributed Systems with CORBA, Ulrich Lang and Rudolf Schreiner

Electric Payment Systems for E-Commerce, Second Edition, Donal O'Mahony, Michael Peirce, and Hitesh Tewari

Evaluating Agile Software Development: Methods for Your Organization, Alan S. Koch

The German Enigma Ciper Machine: Beginnings, Success, and Ultimate Failure, Brian J. Winkel, Cipher A. Deavours, David Kahn, and Louis Kruh

Implementing Electronic Card Payment Systems, Cristian Radu

Implementing Security for ATM Networks, Thomas Tarman and Edward Witzke

Information Hiding Techniques for Steganography and Digital Watermarking, Stefan Katzenbeisser and Fabien A. P. Petitcolas, editors

Internet and Intranet Security, Second Edition, Rolf Oppliger

Java Card for E-Payment Applications, Vesna Hassler, Martin Manninger, Mikail Gordeev, and Christoph Müller

Multicast and Group Security, Thomas Hardjono and Lakshminath R. Dondeti

Non-repudiation in Electronic Commerce, Jianying Zhou

Outsourcing Information Security, C. Warren Axelrod

Privacy Protection and Computer Forensics, Second Edition, Michael A. Caloyannides

Role-Based Access Controls, David F. Ferraiolo, D. Richard Kuhn, and Ramaswamy Chandramouli

Secure Messaging with PGP and S/MIME, Rolf Oppliger

Security Fundamentals for E-Commerce, Vesna Hassler

Security Technologies for the World Wide Web, Second Edition, Rolf Oppliger

Techniques and Applications of Digital Watermarking and Content Protection, Michael Arnold, Martin Schmucker, and Stephen D. Wolthusen

User's Guide to Cryptography and Standards, Alexander W. Dent and Chris J. Mitchell

For further information on these and other Artech House titles, including previously considered out-of-print books now available through our In-Print-Forever® (IPF®) program, contact:

Artech House
685 Canton Street
Norwood, MA 02062
Phone: 781-769-9750
Fax: 781-769-6334
e-mail: artech@artechhouse.com

Artech House
46 Gillingham Street
London SW1V 1AH UK
Phone: +44 (0)20 7596-8750
Fax: +44 (0)20 7630-0166
e-mail: artech-uk@artechhouse.com

Find us on the World Wide Web at:
www.artechhouse.com

www.ingramcontent.com/pod-product-compliance
Lightning Source LLC
LaVergne TN
LVHW062109200926
848484LV00007B/1622